Early Praise for *Programming Ruby 3.3: The Pragmatic Programmers' Guide*

The book has such breadth and depth, making it a useful long-term companion. I'd say this is a big win for the Ruby community.

➤ **Stefan Magnuson**
Software Developer

Programming Ruby 3.3: The Pragmatic Programmers' Guide is a valuable resource to anyone looking to get started with developing software tools and systems in Ruby. Thanks to thorough technical explanations accompanied by demonstrative code examples, this book will equip you with a mastery of all the building blocks of Ruby and help you unlock its full power.

➤ **Nishant Roy**
Engineering Manager

I'm ecstatic to see the book that inspired an entire generation of Rubyists revived. I'm excited to see—and use—what the next generation of readers builds thanks to this.

➤ **Kevin Murphy**
Software Developer

Programming Ruby 3.3

The Pragmatic Programmers' Guide

Noel Rappin
with Dave Thomas

The Pragmatic Bookshelf

Dallas, Texas

Many of the designations used by manufacturers and sellers to distinguish their products are claimed as trademarks. Where those designations appear in this book, and The Pragmatic Programmers, LLC was aware of a trademark claim, the designations have been printed in initial capital letters or in all capitals. The Pragmatic Starter Kit, The Pragmatic Programmer, Pragmatic Programming, Pragmatic Bookshelf, PragProg and the linking *g* device are trademarks of The Pragmatic Programmers, LLC.

Every precaution was taken in the preparation of this book. However, the publisher assumes no responsibility for errors or omissions, or for damages that may result from the use of information (including program listings) contained herein.

Our Pragmatic courses, workshops, and other products can help you and your team create better software and have more fun. For more information, as well as the latest Pragmatic titles, please visit us at *http://pragprog.com*.

For our complete catalog of hands-on, practical, and Pragmatic content for software developers, please visit *https://pragprog.com*.

The team that produced this book includes:

Publisher:	Dave Thomas
COO:	Janet Furlow
Managing Editor:	Tammy Coron
Development Editor:	Katharine Dvorak
Copy Editor:	Corina Lebegioara
Indexing:	Potomac Indexing, LLC
Layout:	Gilson Graphics

For sales, volume licensing, and support, please contact *support@pragprog.com*.

For international rights, please contact *rights@pragprog.com*.

ISBN-13: 978-1-68050-982-3
Book version: P1.0—January 2024

Contents

Preface xiii

Acknowledgments xvii

Part I — Facets of Ruby

1. **Getting Started** 3
   Installing Ruby   3
   Installing Ruby for Windows   7
   Running Ruby   11
   Creating Ruby Programs   12
   Getting More Information about Ruby   14
   What's Next   15

2. **Ruby.new** 17
   Ruby Is an Object-Oriented Language   17
   Some Basic Ruby   19
   Arrays and Hashes   22
   Symbols   24
   Control Structures   25
   Regular Expressions   26
   Blocks   28
   Reading and 'Riting   30
   Command-Line Arguments   30
   Commenting Ruby   31
   What's Next   31

3. **Classes, Objects, and Variables** 33
   Defining Classes   33
   Objects and Attributes   36
   Classes Working with Other Classes   42
   Specifying Access Control   45
   Variables   48
   Reopening Classes   49
   What's Next   51

4. **Collections, Blocks, and Iterators** **53**
   Arrays   53
   Hashes   56
   Digging   58
   Word Frequency: Using Hashes and Arrays   58
   Blocks and Enumeration   62
   What's Next   83

5. **More about Methods** **85**
   Defining a Method   85
   Calling a Method   93
   What's Next   99

6. **Sharing Functionality: Inheritance, Modules, and Mixins** **101**
   Inheritance and Messages   101
   Modules   105
   Inheritance, Mixins, and Design   115
   What's Next   116

7. **Basic Types: Numbers, Strings, and Ranges** **117**
   Numbers   117
   Strings   120
   Ranges   125
   What's Next   127

8. **Regular Expressions** **129**
   What Regular Expressions Let You Do   129
   Creating and Using Regular Expressions   129
   Regular Expression Patterns   132
   Regular Expression Syntax   134
   What's Next   142

9. **Expressions** **143**
   Operator Expressions   143
   Command Expressions   146
   Assignment   146
   Conditional Execution   150
   Loops and Iterators   157
   Pattern Matching   163
   What's Next   170

10. **Exceptions** **171**
    The Exception Class   171
    Handling Exceptions   172
    Raising Exceptions   175
    Using Catch and Throw   177
    What's Next   178

11. **Basic Input and Output** **179**
    What Is an I/O Object?   179

Opening and Closing Files 179
Reading and Writing Files 180
Talking to Networks 185
What's Next 186

12. **Threads, Fibers, and Ractors** **187**
Multithreading with Threads 188
Running Multiple External Processes 196
Creating Fibers 200
Understanding Ractors 202
What's Next 206

13. **Testing Ruby Code** **207**
Why Unit Test? 207
Testing with Minitest 208
Structuring Tests 212
Creating Mock Objects in Minitest 215
Organizing and Running Tests 217
Testing with RSpec 219
What's Next 228

Part II — Ruby in Its Setting

14. **Ruby from the Command Line** **231**
Calling the Ruby Command 231
Ruby Command-Line Options 233
Making Your Code an Executable Program 237
Processing Command-Line Arguments to Your Code 237
Accessing Environment Variables 242
Where Ruby Finds Its Libraries 244
Using the Rake Build Tool 245
The Build Environment 249
What's Next 249

15. **Ruby Gems** **251**
Installing and Managing Gems 251
Using Bundler to Manage Groups of Gems 254
Writing and Packaging Your Own Code into Gems 261
Organizing Your Source Code 266
Distributing and Installing Your Code 272
What's Next 275

16. **Interactive Ruby** **277**
Using irb 278
Navigating irb 280
Configuring irb 283
What's Next 288

17.	**Debugging Ruby**	**289**
	Printing Things	289
	The Ruby Debugger	290
	Pry	293
	Debugging Performance Issues with Benchmark	296
	What's Next	297

18.	**Typed Ruby**	**299**
	What's a Type?	299
	Official Ruby Typing with RBS	301
	Ruby Typing with Sorbet	307
	What's Next	311

19.	**Documenting Ruby**	**313**
	Documenting with RDoc	313
	Adding RDoc to Ruby Code	316
	Running RDoc	320
	Documenting with YARD	321
	What's Next	324

Part III — Ruby Crystallized

20.	**Ruby and the Web**	**327**
	Ruby's Web Utilities	327
	Templating with ERB	329
	Serving Ruby Code to the Web	332
	Ruby in the Browser with Web Assembly	340
	What's Next	342

21.	**Ruby Style**	**343**
	Written Ruby Style	343
	Using RuboCop	348
	Using Standard	353
	Ruby Style in the Large	354
	Duck Typing	356
	What's Next	369

22.	**The Ruby Object Model and Metaprogramming**	**371**
	Understanding Objects and Classes	371
	Defining Singleton Methods	374
	Inheritance and Visibility	380
	Modules and Mixins	381
	Metaprogramming Class-Level Macros	387
	Using instance_eval and class_eval	396
	Using Hook Methods	399
	A Metaprogramming Example	405
	Top-Level Execution Environment	407
	What's Next	408

23. Reflection and Object Space **409**
Looking at Objects   409
Looking at Classes   411
Calling Methods Dynamically   413
System Hooks   415
Tracing Your Program's Execution   417
Behind the Curtain: The Ruby VM   419
Marshaling and Distributed Ruby   420
What's Next   425

Part IV — Ruby Language Reference

24. Language Reference: Literal Types and Expressions **429**
Source Layout   429
Ruby Literals   432
Regular Expressions   440
Names   445
Values, Variables, and Constants   447
Expressions, Conditionals, and Loops   453

25. Language Reference: Objects and Classes **465**
Method Definition   465
Invoking a Method   470
Aliasing   475
Defining Classes   476
Defining Modules   478
Access Control   480
Blocks, Closures, and Proc Objects   480
Exceptions   484
Catch and Throw   486
Typed Ruby   487

Part V — Ruby Library Reference

26. Library Reference: Core Data Types **495**
Dates and Times   495
Math   502
Numbers   503
Random and SecureRandom   510
Regexp   511
Strings   523
Symbols   534

27. Library Reference: Ruby's Object Model **537**
BasicObject   537
Class   540
Comparable   540
Kernel   541

Method 551
Module 552
Object 557

28. Library Reference: Enumerators and Containers **561**
Array 561
Enumerable 568
Enumerator 577
Hash 579
Set 584

29. Library Reference: Input, Output, Files, and Formats **587**
CSV 587
Dir 590
File 593
FileUtils 597
IO 600
JSON 609
Pathname 611
StringIO 612
Tempfile 613
URI 614
YAML 616

30. Library Reference: Ruby on Ruby **619**
Benchmark 619
Data 621
Delegator and SimpleDelegator 622
Logger 623
ObjectSpace 624
Observable 625
OpenStruct 627
PP 627
Prism 628
Ripper 630
Singleton 632
Struct 632
Unbound Method 634

Part VI — Appendixes

A1. Troubleshooting Ruby **637**
Common Issues 637
Debugging Tips 640

A2. I Can't Look It Up! **641**
A3. Command-Line Basics **645**
The Command Prompt 645
Folders, Directories, and Navigation 645

A4. Ruby Runtimes **649**
Just-in-Time Compilers   649
TruffleRuby   651
JRuby   652
mRuby   653
Other Runtimes   654

A5. Ruby Changes **655**
Version 2.0   655
Version 2.1   655
Version 2.2   656
Version 2.3   656
Version 2.4   656
Version 2.5   656
Version 2.6   656
Version 2.7   656
Version 3.0   657
Version 3.1   657
Version 3.2   657
Version 3.3   657

Index **659**

Preface

This is the fifth edition of *Programming Ruby*, which many Ruby developers call "The Pickaxe Book." It covers Ruby up to and including Ruby 3.3.

Since the previous edition of this book, Ruby has continued to grow and evolve. New syntax has been added; old syntax has been refined. Major new features, such as pattern matching and type signatures, are now part of the language. Tools that didn't exist or were in their early stages of development then are now in constant use by Ruby developers around the world. The entire ecosystem is thriving.

The Pickaxe Book continues to be your guide to learning Ruby the language and understanding how Ruby's parts work together and how you can use the most popular and important Ruby tools.

Why Ruby?

When Dave Thomas and Andy Hunt wrote the first edition, they explained the appeal of Ruby. Among other things, they wrote, "When we discovered Ruby, we realized that we'd found what we'd been looking for. More than any other language with which we have worked, Ruby *stays out of your way*. You can concentrate on solving the problem at hand, instead of struggling with compiler and language issues. That's how it can help you become a better programmer: by giving you the chance to spend your time creating solutions for your users, not for the compiler."

That belief is even stronger today. More than thirty years after Ruby's first release on February 24, 1993, Ruby still enables developers to focus on their solutions—from the smallest utility script to the services of companies with billions of dollars in revenue. Ruby can support it all.

A Word about Ruby Versions

This edition of The Pickaxe Book documents Ruby up to and including Ruby 3.3. New Ruby version releases come out annually on December 25. The book's code was developed against Ruby 3.3, preview 2, but we don't expect substantial changes in the released version of Ruby 3.3.

In this book, we don't typically note what version of Ruby introduced a new feature, but you can find a brief list of the largest changes in Appendix 5, Ruby Changes, on page 655. We recommend referring to the Ruby Evolution page by Victor Shepelev at https://rubyreferences.github.io/rubychanges/evolution.html for a full listing of the changes implemented since Ruby 2.0.

Exactly what version of Ruby did we use to write this book? Let's ask Ruby:

```
$ ruby -v
ruby 3.3.0dev (2023-11-01T17:47:26Z master 909afcb4fc) [arm64-darwin23]
```

This illustrates an important point. Most of the code samples you see in this book are executed each time we format the book. When you see output from a program, that output was produced by running the code and inserting the results into the book.

Notation Conventions

Literal code examples are shown using a sans-serif font:

```
class SampleCode
  def run
    #...
  end
end
```

In this book, a class name followed by a hash followed by a method name, as in Fred#do_something, is a reference to an instance method (in this case, the method do_something of class Fred). Class methods are written with a dot as in Fred.new, and Fred.EOF is a class constant. In other Ruby documentation, you may see class methods written as Fred::new. This is perfectly valid Ruby syntax; we just happen to think that Fred.new is less distracting to read and is much more common to see in practice.

The decision to use a hash character to indicate instance methods was a tough one. It isn't valid Ruby syntax, but we thought that it was important to differentiate between the instance and class methods of a particular class. When you see us use File.read, you know we're talking about the class method read. When, instead, we use File#read, we're referring to the instance method read. This convention is standard in most Ruby discussions and documentation.

When discussing various commands or Ruby snippets, we'll refer to variable parts of the commands by including them in angle brackets. So, if we say rbenv global <VERSION>, that means the section in the brackets is not a literal part of the command, and you'd replace it with the actual value you wanted to use, for example, rbenv global 3.3.0.

This book contains many snippets of Ruby code. Where possible, we've tried to show what happens when they run. In some cases, we show the value of expressions on the same line as the expression. Here's an example:

```
a = 1
b = 2
a + b      # => 3
```

Here, you can see that the result of evaluating a + b is the value 3, shown in a comment at the end of the line, # => 3. If you typed this fragment of code into a file and executed it using Ruby, you wouldn't see the value 3 output—you'd need to use a method such as puts to have the values written to the program's output.

```
a = 1      # => 1
a + 2      # => 3
```

If the program produces more complex output, we show it after the program code:

```
3.times { puts "Hello!" }
```

produces:

```
Hello!
Hello!
Hello!
```

In some of the library documentation, we wanted to show where spaces appear in the output. You'll see these spaces as ␣ characters.

Unless we're trying to make a point or highlight a specific language feature, Ruby code examples have been formatted to match the rules of the Standard gem[1].

Command-line invocations are shown with literal text in a regular font, and the parameters you supply are shown in an *italic* font. Optional elements are shown in brackets.

ruby ‹*flags*›* *progname* ‹*arguments*›*

In keeping with the style of previous editions of the book, we use the word *we* when referring to the authors collectively in the body of the book. Many of the words come from the first four editions, and I (Noel) don't want to claim any credit for Dave Thomas's, Andy Hunt's, and Chad Fowler's previous work. That said, opinions on recent Ruby features, even when prefaced by "we," are just my (Noel's) opinions and are not an attempt to put words in the mouths of the previous authors.

Road Map

The main text of this book is divided into five parts, each with its own personality and each addressing different aspects of the Ruby language.

Part I, Facets of Ruby, is a Ruby tutorial. It starts with notes on getting Ruby running on your system followed by a short chapter on the terminology and concepts that are unique to Ruby. The initial chapter also includes enough basic syntax so that the other chapters will make sense. The rest of the tutorial is a top-down look at Ruby. There we talk about classes and objects, types, expressions, and all the other things that make up the language. We end with a chapter on unit testing.

Part II, Ruby in Its Setting, investigates one of the great things about Ruby, which is how well it integrates with its environment. Here you'll find practical information on using Ruby: using the interpreter options, working with irb, documenting your Ruby code, type checking, and packaging your Ruby gems so that others can enjoy them.

Part III, Ruby Crystallized, contains more advanced material. Here you'll find all the details about using Ruby for the web, Ruby style, the concept of *duck typing*, the object model, metaprogramming, reflection, and object space. You could probably speed-read this the first time through, but we think you'll come back to it as you start to use Ruby in earnest.

Part IV, Ruby Language Reference, includes more complete notes on syntax and fuller documentation of language features discussed in the first three parts.

Part V, Ruby Library Reference, isn't a complete reference of the entire Ruby library—that's much more readily available at https://docs.ruby-lang.org/en—but it's a map to the most commonly used and most useful features of the library.

1.　https://github.com/testdouble/standard

How should you read this book? Well, depending on your level of expertise with programming in general and object-oriented programming in particular, you may initially want to read just a few portions of the book. Here are our recommendations.

If you're a beginner, you may want to start with the tutorial material in Part I. Keep the library reference close at hand as you start to write programs. Get familiar with the basic classes such as Array, Hash, and String. As you become more comfortable in the environment, you may want to investigate some of the more advanced topics in Part III.

If you're already comfortable with JavaScript, Python, or Java, then we suggest reading Chapter 1, Getting Started, on page 3, which talks about installing and running Ruby, followed by the introduction in Chapter 2, Ruby.new, on page 17. From there, you may want to take the slower approach and keep going with the tutorial that follows, or you can skip ahead to the details starting in Part III, followed by the language reference in Part IV and the library reference in Part V.

Experts, gurus, and "I-don't-need-no-stinking-tutorial" types can dive straight into the language reference in Chapter 24, Language Reference: Literal Types and Expressions, on page 429, skim through the library reference, and then use the book as a (rather attractive) coffee coaster.

Of course, nothing is wrong with starting at the beginning and working your way through page by page.

And don't forget: if you run into a problem that you can't figure out, help is available. For more information, see Appendix 1, Troubleshooting Ruby, on page 637.

Resources

Visit the Ruby website at http://www.ruby-lang.org to see what's new. You can find a list of community resources, including the official mailing list and Discord server, at https://www.ruby-lang.org/en/community.

And we'd certainly appreciate hearing from you. Comments, suggestions, errors in the text, and problems in the examples are all welcome. Email us at rubybook@pragprog.com.

If you find errors in the book, you can add them to the errata page at https://devtalk.com/books/programming-ruby-3-2-5th-edition/errata. If you're reading the PDF version of the book, you can also report an erratum by clicking the link in the page footers.

You'll find links to the source code for almost all of the book's code examples at https://www.pragprog.com/titles/ruby5.

With all that out of the way, let's start learning about Ruby.

Acknowledgments

In January 2001, I bought myself a programming book as a birthday present. It had a pickaxe on the cover, and it was written by the two people who wrote *The Pragmatic Programmer*. It was about this new programming language from Japan that I had heard about on the Extreme Programming mailing list, and which sounded very interesting.

I can't thank Dave Thomas and Andy Hunt enough. It's hard to even begin to list what I've gained from purchasing that initial book and from my association with The Pragmatic Bookshelf. Thanks also to Chad Fowler for his work on subsequent versions of the book. I inherited a great book from the three of you, and I hope this version will continue to bring people into the Ruby language and the Ruby community.

The path from buying a book on a whim to being the person updating that book more than 20 years later doesn't happen without a lot of help.

As much as I love Ruby the language, I also love Ruby the community and the many, many people who I've come to know through Ruby. The risk of starting to list people is that I'm sure I will inadvertently leave somebody out, but I want to particularly thank Gregg Pollack, Jason Seifer, Avdi Grimm, James Edward Gray II, Betsy Haibel, Justin Searls, Marty Haught, Kerri Miller, Brian Hogan, Ray Hightower, Fable Tales, Matt Polito, Even Light, Allison McMillan, and Jim Remsik. There are many more I could list—thank you to all of you.

Mark Guzdial was my graduate advisor and the person who encouraged me to write about programming and teach programming.

This is somehow the seventh title I've worked on with Katharine Dvorak as the editor. As always, she makes working on the book easier and helps structure the book into its most coherent form. Dave Rankin at The Pragmatic Bookshelf was the person who agreed to let me work on this book. Thanks so much for the opportunity and the vote of confidence.

The following people reviewed all or part of the book, and their feedback and knowledge have made this a better and more accurate book: Jean Boussier, Avdi Grimm, Chris Houhoulis, Gabi Jack, Bernard Kaiflin, Brian Lesperance, Stefan Magnuson, Kevin Murphy, Ryan Prinz, Nishant Roy, Victor Shepelev, and Brandon Weaver.

Everything in my life is better because of my family. Thanks to my children, Amit and Elliot, who have enriched my life in so many ways. And something beyond thanks to my wife Erin, these small sentences can't express how much I love you and how much your love and support mean to me.

Part I

Facets of Ruby

Welcome to Ruby! Part I is a tutorial covering all the Ruby you'll need to be able to understand a good-sized Ruby application. We'll explore the most important parts of the syntax and the standard library, and go beyond the basics in a couple of places where Ruby has a particularly interesting or powerful tool at hand.

## CHAPTER 1

Getting Started

We're going to spend a lot of time in this book talking about the Ruby language. Before we do, we want to make sure you can get Ruby installed and running on your computer. That way, you can try the sample code and experiment on your own as you read along. If you want to learn Ruby you should get into the habit of writing code as you're reading.

If you aren't comfortable with using a command line, we can help. Please turn to Appendix 3, Command-Line Basics, on page 645, and we'll give you all the information you need to get started.

Installing Ruby

There is a good chance your operating system already has Ruby installed. Try typing ruby --version at a command prompt—you may be pleasantly surprised. But you're likely to find that the Ruby version is out of date. For example, at the time of this writing, MacOS ships with Ruby 2.6.10, which is multiple versions behind the current Ruby.

The examples in this book are written against Ruby 3.3. While most of the code will work in older versions of Ruby, for performance and security reasons you should try to get on the most current version. Refer to Appendix 5, Ruby Changes, on page 655, for a listing of the features added and changes made to Ruby at each iteration.

You can install Ruby in a variety of different ways, so providing general installation instructions becomes a little bit of a choose-your-own-adventure story. Most of the examples in this book assume you're using a Linux- or Unix-style system that responds to Linux-style commands. This includes all Linux distributions, macOS, Windows systems running Windows Subsystem for Linux (WSL),[1] and most Docker[2] containers as well as cloud-based development environments such as Replit.[3]

That said, Ruby does run on Windows. The process for managing a Ruby installation on Windows is different, and we'll cover it in full detail later in this chapter.

Please note that the tooling for Ruby's installation does change frequently, and some of the specific instructions might be out of date or replaced by newer tools.

---

1. https://docs.microsoft.com/en-us/windows/wsl/install
2. https://www.docker.com
3. https://replit.com

Opting Out of Installation

If you don't want to install anything on your computer for some reason, you can take advantage of cloud-based development environments such as Replit or GitHub Codespaces. These environments enable you to write your code in a browser and run it against a cloud-based virtual machine.

Installing Ruby with the rbenv Version Manager

To facilitate our installation of Ruby, we'll use a *version manager,* which is a tool that allows you to install and switch between multiple Ruby versions on the same machine. There are many reasons to use a version manager to handle your Ruby installation. Being able to easily switch between multiple versions of Ruby gives you the flexibility to work with multiple projects that might have been written at different times. In addition, the version managers have been created for easy installation, so installing multiple Ruby versions with a version manager is easier than installing a single version by itself. More powerful and easier to use is a hard combination to beat. If you're interested in downloading only one version of Ruby, you can find system-by-system instructions at https://www.ruby-lang.org/en/documentation/installation.

The tool we'll use in this book is called rbenv.[4] Rbenv isn't the only Ruby version manager, but it's probably the most commonly used these days. Other commonly used version managers are RVM[5] and chruby.[6] (And yes, having competing tools named "RVM" and "rbenv" is confusing.) If you're using version management for multiple languages, you might want to look at a project called asdf, which unifies different languages' version managers,[7] and is rapidly becoming more popular within Ruby.

We'll install rbenv through the conveniently provided rbenv-installer program. If executing somebody else's shell script makes you nervous, you can inspect the script at https://github.com/rbenv/rbenv-installer/blob/main/bin/rbenv-installer before you run it.

From a command terminal, enter this command all on one line (the line is split here for page-width reasons):

```
$ curl -fsSL
    https://github.com/rbenv/rbenv-installer/raw/HEAD/bin/rbenv-installer | bash
```

Curl is a command-line tool for accessing URLs and doing something useful with the return value—in this case, retrieving a shell script from the rbenv GitHub repo and passing it along to a bash shell to be executed.

This script will install rbenv using the appropriate package manager for your system, and will also install a helper program called ruby-build that will manage the download and installation of different Ruby versions.

The installation command might produce a lot of output—especially if you're on a MacOS system that uses the Homebrew package manager. On a Mac, it should end with the following (a Windows user under WSL might see something different):

---

4.   https://github.com/rbenv/rbenv
5.   https://rvm.io
6.   https://github.com/postmodern/chruby
7.   https://asdf-vm.com

All done! Note that this installer does NOT edit your shell configuration files: 1. Run `rbenv init` to view instructions on how to configure rbenv for your shell. 2. Launch a new terminal window after editing shell configuration files.

Following instructions, run rbenv init. This is the output on a Mac running zshell (your instructions may be different):

```
$ rbenv init
# Load rbenv automatically by appending
# the following to ~/.zshrc:

eval "$(rbenv init - zsh)"
```

No matter what your setup is, what you should get in this instruction is:

- The file that contains the shell configuration you need to update
- The text you need to put at the end of the file

You need to put the suggested line of text at the end of your configuration file and open a new terminal window. The change only takes effect when a window is loaded, so the easiest way to get rbenv started is to open a new terminal window. If you have any questions about how to use the terminal, see Appendix 3, Command-Line Basics, on page 645.

Now, let's install a specific Ruby version.

Installing Rubies with rbenv

Rbenv allows you to see a list of the Ruby versions you'll most likely want to install with the command rbenv install -l. Here's the current list (as I write this, 3.3.0 is not fully released):

```
$ rbenv install -l
2.7.8
3.0.6
3.1.4
3.2.2
jruby-9.4.2.0
mruby-3.2.0
picoruby-3.0.0
truffleruby-22.3.1
truffleruby+graalvm-22.3.1
```

```
Only latest stable releases for each Ruby implementation are shown.
Use 'rbenv install --list-all / -L' to show all local versions.
```

This list has the most up-to-date patch versions of various Ruby implementations. You can see the current minor versions for the major Ruby versions 2.7, 3.0, 3.1, 3.2, and 3.3. (When talking about different Ruby implementations, the main one is sometimes called CRuby and other times called MRI, for "Matz's Ruby Interpreter.") There are also other versions we're not going to talk about much here. JRuby[8] is a Ruby version that runs on the Java Virtual Machine. Mruby is a special limited build of Ruby for running on embedded hardware. TruffleRuby[9] is an implementation of the language that is focused on high performance.

Our interest right now is Ruby 3.3.0, which we can install with the command rbenv install 3.3.0. (If Ruby 3.3.0 isn't out as you read this, you can use 3.2.2 or 3.3.0-dev.) If you don't see

---

8.   https://www.jruby.org
9.   https://github.com/oracle/truffleruby

the most current version of Ruby on the list, and you've installed rbenv previously, you may get instructions on how to update ruby-build to get newer Ruby versions in your list. Note that none of the rbenv commands require us to have superuser access or to use sudo. One of the joys of the Ruby version managers, including rbenv, is that they do everything inside your home directory—you don't have any special system privileges to install or use new Ruby versions.

```
$ rbenv install 3.3.0
To follow progress, use
'tail -f <REDACTED>'
or pass --verbose
Installing openssl-3.1.0...
Installed openssl-3.1.0 to /Users/noel/.rbenv/versions/3.3.0

Installing ruby-3.3.0...
ruby-build: using readline from homebrew
ruby-build: using gmp from homebrew
Installed ruby-3.3.0 to /Users/noel/.rbenv/versions/3.3.0
```

Your output may be slightly different, depending on the exact version number and whether you're re-installing the Ruby version.

We can verify that the Ruby version has been installed with rbenv versions, for example:

```
$ rbenv versions
* system
  3.3.0
```

The system here is the pre-defined Ruby for the operating system if such a thing exists, and the asterisk shows which version is currently active.

Right now, the system Ruby is still active. Let's change that.

Switching Rubies with rbenv

This is where we start to see the payoff. Once different Ruby versions are installed, rbenv allows us multiple ways to switch the Ruby version we're using.

The command rbenv local <version> changes the Ruby version for the directory you're in:

```
$ ruby --version
ruby 2.6.10p210 (2022-04-12 revision 67958) [universal.arm64e-darwin22]
```

```
$ rbenv local 3.3.0
```

```
$ ruby --version
ruby 3.3.0 (2023-11-02T22:34:58Z master ac8ec004e5) [arm64-darwin23]
```

If the new Ruby you think you've installed doesn't seem to be available, you may need to run the command rbenv rehash. This command produces no output, but it does enable rbenv to use the newly installed Ruby.

This setting for the directory persists even if you leave the directory and come back. (If you don't want the change to persist beyond the current session, you can use rbenv shell <VERSION> instead of rbenv local.)

```
$ cd ..
$ cd test
$ ruby --version
ruby 3.3.0 (2023-11-02T22:34:58Z master ac8ec004e5) [arm64-darwin23]
```

Rbenv accomplishes this by putting a file in the directory called .ruby-version, which only contains the version number of the Ruby you've set for that directory.

```
% cat .ruby-version
3.3.0
```

This file also works in reverse. If you have rbenv installed and you change to a directory that contains a .ruby-version file, one of two things will happen. Rbenv will either automatically change to that Ruby version if it's installed or warn you that the directory expects an uninstalled Ruby if it isn't. Many Ruby projects use a .ruby-version file to specify their Ruby version, and it's respected by all the Ruby version managers.

If you want to set a default Ruby version for directories that don't specify their own, you can do so with rbenv global <version>.

This may be more work than you were expecting to install Ruby. If all you ever wanted to do was use a single version of Ruby, we'd agree. But what you've done here is give yourself an incredible amount of flexibility. Maybe in the future, a project comes along that uses Ruby 2.7.5, per its .ruby-version file. That's not a problem—use rbenv install 2.7.5, and rbenv will automatically pick up the version from the .ruby-version file.

What Is rbenv Actually Doing?

Rbenv attempts to provide its dynamic behavior with as little change to your regular terminal environment as possible.

A Unix terminal uses a global environment variable called PATH to determine what directories it looks in for executable programs when you type a command. If you look in your configuration file for your terminal, you'll likely see the PATH variable being modified.

When the rbenv init command is executed as part of your terminal setup, it inserts a directory at the front of your PATH, so that your operating system will look in the rbenv directory before looking anyplace else. That directory has a set of what rbenv calls *shims*—small programs that match all the executable commands in all your Ruby versions. (The reason why you may need to run rbenv rehash after installing a new Ruby is to refresh this directory.) When you call a Ruby command like ruby or (as you'll see in a minute) irb, the rbenv shim is encountered first, and it dynamically chooses which Ruby is active, usually based on the presence of a .ruby-version file. Then the command is handed off to the actual executable program in that current version. You can see these actual versions, they live in your home directory at ~/.rbenv/versions.

Installing Ruby for Windows

Ruby isn't available as a default option in Windows the way it's in Unix distributions or MacOS, but it can be installed and used and can interact with the underlying environment to automate Windows-specific resources.

We're going to focus on two ways to install Ruby on Windows: using the Windows Subsystem for Linux (WSL)[10], which allows you to run a Linux command-line terminal in your Windows system, and using RubyInstaller[11] to install a Windows application that lets you execute Ruby programs.

The two different kinds of Ruby can both be installed on the same machine and have different purposes. Using WSL gives you a command shell that's effectively a Linux distribution, allowing you to seamlessly use any of the other Ruby tooling in this book. Using RubyInstaller gives you access to Ruby from within a regular Windows PowerShell prompt, allowing you to execute Ruby programs from File Explorer, and giving you access to Windows-specific libraries.

No matter which way you want to run Ruby, you should also install Windows Terminal so that you have a fully-featured terminal program available. You can download Windows Terminal at https://docs.microsoft.com/en-us/windows/terminal/install, where you'll also find instructions on how to make it your default terminal program. From Windows Terminal, you can set up new command-line sessions using either Microsoft's PowerShell or the WSL shell. (You can also use Visual Studio Code's terminal to run either kind of command line.)

Also, if you need a brief tutorial on how Unix command lines work, see Appendix 3, Command-Line Basics, on page 645.

Using Windows Subsystem for Linux

Windows Subsystem for Linux (WSL) allows you to run a Linux distribution binary inside your Windows setup without incurring the performance penalty of using a virtual machine or Docker container. WSL defines the wiring between the Linux OS commands and the Windows OS, allowing you to run your favorite Linux distribution from a command line transparently without having to deal with the Windows part at all. You can also have editing tools like Visual Studio Code or RubyMine interact with WSL as they run your Ruby code.

We're going to cover the basics of how to use WSL here, but if you need more information, the official documentation is available from Microsoft.[12]

Installing WSL

The first step in using Ruby with WSL is installing WSL itself. According to the WSL website, you need to be running Windows 10 version 2004 and higher (Build 19041 and higher) or Windows 11 for this to work. We're installing WSL version 2 here.

You need to open an administrator Windows command terminal—it doesn't matter whether it's PowerShell or the regular terminal, but it does have to be an administrator shell. In Windows 11, the easiest way to get an admin shell is to right-click on the start menu and select the "Windows Terminal (Administrator)" option, which will open Windows Terminal in an admin shell. Depending on your Windows version, you may get prompted to say whether you'll allow the program to make changes to your system. Say yes.

From the admin shell, type the command wsl --install. This will give us the default Linux installation, which is Ubuntu. The session looks like this when it's through, but it may take a little time to get through the download and installation process.

---

10. https://docs.microsoft.com/en-us/windows/wsl
11. https://rubyinstaller.org
12. https://docs.microsoft.com/en-us/windows/wsl

```
PS C: \Users\noelr> wsl --install
Installing: Virtual Machine Platform
Virtual Machine Platform has been installed.
Installing: Windows Subsystem for Linux
Windows Subsystem for Linux has been installed.
Downloading: WSL Kernel
Installing: WSL Kernel
WSL Kernel has been installed.
Downloading: GUI App Support
Installing: GUI App Support
GUI App Support has been installed.
Downloading: Ubuntu
The requested operation is successful.
Changes will not be effective until the system is rebooted
```

Reboot the system. This may take some time.

When the system comes back up, open Windows Terminal. The pull-down menu in the tab bar should now give you the option of an Ubuntu prompt. You may get prompted to do a sudo apt-get update to update programs in the Ubuntu distribution.

You'll then get prompted to create a Unix account for WSL:

```
Installing, this may take a few minutes.
Please create a default UNIX user account.
The username does not need to match your Windows username
For more information visit: httos://aka.ms/wslusers
Enter new UNIX username:
```

The username isn't in any way connected to your Windows account—it's a brand-new account for the Linux distribution you've installed using WSL. After you enter the username, you'll be prompted for the password. You won't get challenged for the password every time you open a WSL terminal, but you should write it down just in case because someday you may want to sudo something, and you'll get asked for your password before getting superuser rights. (Ask us how we know.) That said, don't depend on this password being super-secure by default; the root WSL user has no password.

At this point, you can use Windows Terminal to open a WSL terminal by clicking the downward arrow next to the + in the tab bar and selecting Ubuntu from the menu.

Installing Ruby under WSL

We're partway there, but the default Ubuntu installation doesn't include Ruby or a version manager. These instructions are adapted from https://gorails.com/setup/windows/10#linux-subsystem.

The Ubuntu distribution uses a package manager called apt-get to distribute its applications. We need to install some dependencies:

```
$ sudo apt-get update
$ sudo apt-get install git-core curl
$ sudo apt-get install zlib1g-dev build-essential libssl-dev
$ sudo apt-get install libreadline-dev libyaml-dev libsqlite3-dev sqlite3
$ sudo apt-get install libxml2-dev libxslt1-dev libcurl4-openssl-dev
$ sudo apt-get install software-properties-common libffi-dev
```

The first line updates apt-get itself so you can get the most current version of everything, and the following lines install the packages that Ruby will need. Note that you can do all those installs on a single line (we're splitting it up here for page-width purposes).

At this point, you should be able to install the rbenv version manager using the instructions in Installing Ruby with the rbenv Version Manager, on page 4. The GoRails site mentioned before has slightly different rbenv instructions, they should both work.

Using WSL and Ruby

You should be good to go, as you can confirm by opening up a new WSL terminal and typing irb. Within WSL, you can use any of the Unix tools that we've described elsewhere in this book.

Ruby programs can be invoked using ruby from the WSL command line as we'll discuss in Chapter 14, Ruby from the Command Line, on page 231. Where it gets a little bit tricky is in sharing files. WSL sets up what is, in effect, its own file system. For performance reasons, you're encouraged to keep all the files you use in WSL code in the WSL file system (as apparently file read and write between the two systems is expensive).

That said, it is possible to share files. Windows files are set up in WSL under the mnt directory (short for "mount point"). Your C: drive is /mnt/c. You can access Windows files using that path as a prefix. Other drives, like network drives, can also be connected to a mount point, but it doesn't happen by default.

From the Windows side, WSL files show up in File Explorer under their own "Linux" heading. You can right-click those files and open them in a Windows editor, but you can't directly invoke them in WSL from the Windows file system. (You could, in theory, create a shortcut that invokes a terminal and a single bash command to run a WSL file.)

Visual Studio Code has a WSL extension that you can install that allows you to load a WSL directory from the regular Windows version of Visual Studio Code. Run that directory using the WSL ruby, and use the WSL terminal as a prompt. Similarly, RubyMine allows you to connect to WSL as a remote interpreter, open a WSL project, and run it using the WSL Ruby.

Using RubyInstaller

Although WSL is nice, and it's great to be able to seamlessly integrate with existing Ruby tooling, from the point of view of a Windows user, it does have some drawbacks. WSL has some performance overhead, including taking up a lot of memory. It also doesn't integrate with the Windows system directly, meaning that you can't do Windows-specific things.

A native Ruby installation is available for Windows, and it's simply called RubyInstaller.[13] RubyInstaller is a regular Windows installer that gives you a regular Windows executable Ruby interpreter that you can use to run Ruby code.

Installing Ruby with RubyInstaller

You can download RubyInstaller from https://rubyinstaller.org, where you can find versions corresponding to each Ruby patch version for both x64 and x86 machines. There are versions both with and without Devkit, which is an add-on that allows Ruby gems that

---

13.   https://rubyinstaller.org

have native C-language extensions to be compiled. A couple of prominent Ruby gems have extensions, so we recommend the Devkit version.

Once the installer has downloaded, run it and you'll get a standard Windows installer. You'll have options to "Add Ruby executables to your PATH" and "Associate .rb and .rbw files with this Ruby installation," both of which we recommend. You'll then have the option to install "Ruby RI and HTML documentation" and the "MSYS2 development toolchain," which again, we recommend. At the end, you'll be asked to run "ridk install" to set up the development toolchain. Doing so will give you a pop-up window that will ask you which MSYS2 components to install and to confirm the defaults are what you want (which they are, so keep them). Press ENTER to start the MSYS2 installation. After the installation finishes that phase, it'll prompt you again. If the brackets in the prompt are empty, pressing ENTER will finish the installation.

Using Ruby with RubyInstaller

At this point, from a regular Windows terminal, you can run ruby and irb with the same options as we'll discuss in Chapter 14, Ruby from the Command Line, on page 231, and Chapter 16, Interactive Ruby, on page 277.

You'll find two versions of the Ruby interpreter in the RubyInstaller distribution. The ruby version is meant to be used at a command prompt (DOS shell or PowerShell), as in the Unix version. For applications that read and write to the standard input and output, this is fine. This means that any time you run ruby, you'll get a DOS shell even if you don't want one—Windows will create a new command prompt window and display it while Ruby is running.

This may not be appropriate behavior if, for example, you double-click a Ruby script that uses a graphical interface or if you're running a Ruby script as a background task or from inside another program. In these cases, you'll want to use rubyw. This is the same as ruby except that it doesn't provide standard in, standard out, or standard error and doesn't launch a DOS shell when run.

On Windows 11, you can also run Ruby code by right-clicking Ruby files in File Explorer.

Running Ruby

Now that Ruby is installed, you'd probably like to run some programs. Unlike compiled languages, you have two ways to run Ruby: you can type in code interactively, or you can create program files and run them. Typing in code interactively is a great way to experiment with the language, but for code that's more complex or code that you'll want to run more than once, you'll need to create program files and run them. But, before we go any further, let's test to see whether Ruby is installed. Bring up a fresh command prompt, and type this:

```
$ ruby --version
ruby 3.3.0dev (2023-11-01T17:47:26Z master 909afcb4fc) [arm64-darwin23]
```

Technically, you can run Ruby interactively by typing ruby at the shell prompt. You'll get a blank line in response, and you can type your Ruby code there.

```
$ ruby
puts "Hello, world!"
^D
Hello, world!
```

In this example, we typed in a single line of Ruby. That line consists of two parts. The first part, puts, is the name of a *method*. A method is a pre-defined chunk of code. In this case, the puts method is one of several methods defined for us by Ruby. The second part, "Hello, world!", is text surrounded by double quotes, which is called a *string*. Combining the two, the Ruby code puts "Hello, world!" calls the method puts with the argument "Hello, world!". The puts method then outputs that argument back to the terminal—puts is short for "outPUT String".

On the next line, we typed an end-of-file character (Ctrl+D on our system), which exited the program and caused what we typed to be evaluated. Using Ruby like this works, but it only shows responses if you explicitly print them out. Also, it's painful if you make a typo, and you can't see what's going on as you type.

Happily, there's a better way to interact with Ruby.

Interactive Ruby, or *irb*, is the tool of choice for executing Ruby interactively. Irb is a complete Ruby shell, with command-line history, line-editing capabilities, and job control. (In fact, it has its own chapter in this book: Chapter 16, Interactive Ruby, on page 277.) You run irb from the command line. Once it starts, type in Ruby code. It will show you the value of each expression as it evaluates it. Exit an irb session by typing exit or Ctrl+D.

Here's a sample session:

```
$ irb
irb(main):001:1* def sum(n1, n2)
irb(main):002:1*   n1 + n2
irb(main):003:0> end
=> :sum
irb(main):004:0> sum(3, 4)
=> 7
irb(main):005:0> sum("cat", "dog")
=> "catdog"
irb(main):006:0> exit
```

In the first three lines of this session, we're defining a method called sum. The act of defining that method returns a value called :sum, which is a Ruby *symbol* matching the name of the method. We'll talk more about symbols and method names later. In line 4 of the input, we're calling the method, first with arguments 3 and 4, returning 7, then in line 5 with arguments "cat" and "dog". In Ruby, adding strings concatenates them, so the line returns the string "catdog". Then we exit on line 6.

If you try this in Ruby 3.1 or higher, you'll notice that irb attempts to offer autocompletion of variable names or commands, and also color codes, neither of which is easy to show in a book.

We recommend that you get familiar with irb—it's a great way to explore Ruby concepts and debug your code, and it'll make your experience with Ruby more fun.

Creating Ruby Programs

The most common way to write Ruby programs is to put the Ruby code in one or more text files. You'll use a text editor or an Integrated Development Environment (IDE) to create and maintain these files—many popular editors, including Visual Studio Code, vim, Sublime Text, and RubyMine, feature Ruby support. You'll then run the files either from within the

> ## What about Docker?
>
> If you're using Ruby on a larger project or with a larger team, there's a good chance that Docker is part of your development environment. Docker is a tool that allows you to define and run *containers*. A container is a way to package all the dependencies needed to run code—it's a virtual operating system inside your computer. Using Docker, you can simulate a Linux environment no matter what operating system you're running.
>
> A full description of Docker is out of this book's scope. But, if you're already familiar with Docker in general, it's worth mentioning that Docker maintains images with different Ruby versions pre-installed. You can always get to the latest released version with ruby:latest, and you can go straight to a Dockerized irb prompt with docker run -it ruby irb. Running external Ruby files in the Docker container is doable as well but requires a little more Docker knowledge.

editor or from the command line. Both techniques are useful. You might run single-file programs from within the editor and more complex programs from the command line.

Let's create a short Ruby program and run it. Open a terminal window and create an empty directory somewhere, perhaps you could call it pickaxe.

Then, using your editor of choice, create the file myprog.rb, containing the following text:

pickaxe/myprog.rb
```
puts "Hello, Ruby Programmer"
puts "It is now #{Time.now}"
```

Note that the second string contains the text Time.now between curly braces, not parentheses.

You can run a Ruby program from a file as you would any other shell script or program in another scripting language like Python. Run the Ruby interpreter, giving it the script name as an argument:

```
$ ruby myprog.rb
Hello, Ruby Programmer
It is now 2023-11-02 17:15:44 -0500
```

On Unix systems, you can use the "shebang" notation as the first line of the program file. If your system supports it, you can avoid hard-coding the path to Ruby in the "shebang" line by using #!/usr/bin/env ruby, which will search your path for ruby and then execute it.

```
#!/usr/bin/env ruby
puts "Hello, Ruby Programmer"
puts "It is now #{Time.now}"
```

If you make this source file executable (using, for instance, chmod +x myprog.rb), Unix lets you run the file as a program:

```
$ ./myprog.rb
Hello, Ruby Programmer
It is now 2023-11-02 17:15:44 -0500
```

You can do something similar under Microsoft Windows using file associations, and you can run Ruby GUI applications by double-clicking their names in Windows Explorer.

Getting More Information about Ruby

As the volume of the Ruby libraries has grown, it has become impossible to document them all in one book; the standard library that comes with Ruby now contains more than 9,000 methods. The official Ruby documentation is at https://docs.ruby-lang.org, with official pages for the different versions of the core and standard library located there. irb will also give you documentation of standard method names as you type.

Much of this documentation is generated from comments in the source code using a tool called RubyDoc, which we'll look at in Chapter 19, Documenting Ruby, on page 313. The RubyDoc site at https://www.rubydoc.info contains documentation for Ruby projects that use RubyDoc. Third-party libraries in the Ruby world are called *gems*, and the official listing of Ruby gems is at https://rubygems.org. We'll talk lots more about gems in Chapter 15, Ruby Gems, on page 251.

There is also a command-line tool for the Ruby core documentation called ri. To find the documentation for a class, type ri <classname>. For example, the following is the beginning of the summary information for the String class. If you type ri with no arguments, you get a prompt asking you for a class.

```
= String < Object

------------------------------------------------------------------------
= Includes:
Comparable (from ruby core)

(from ruby core)
------------------------------------------------------------------------

A String object has an arbitrary sequence of bytes, typically
representing text or binary data. A String object may be created using
String::new or as literals.

String objects differ from Symbol objects in that Symbol objects are
designed to be used as identifiers, instead of text or data.
```

It goes on to list all the methods of String.

You can also try a method name:

```
$ ri strip
```

```
= .strip

(from ruby core)
=== Implementation from String
------------------------------------------------------------------------
  str.strip    -> new_str

------------------------------------------------------------------------

Returns a copy of the receiver with leading and trailing whitespace
removed.
```

Whitespace is defined as any of the following characters: null, horizontal tab, line feed, vertical tab, form feed, carriage return, space.

```
"    hello    ".strip   #=> "hello"
"\tgoodbye\r\n".strip   #=> "goodbye"
"\x00\t\n\v\f\r ".strip #=> ""
"hello".strip           #=> "hello"
```

You can then exit the listing by typing q.

What's Next

Now that you're up and running, it's time to learn how Ruby works. First, we'll do a quick overview of the main features of the language.

## CHAPTER 2

Ruby.new

Many books on programming languages look about the same. They start with chapters on basic types: integers, strings, and so on. Then they look at expressions like 2 + 3 before moving on to if and while statements and loops. Then, perhaps around Chapter 7 or 8, they'll start mentioning classes. We find that somewhat tedious.

Instead, when we designed this book, we had a grand plan. We wanted to document the language from the top down, starting with classes and objects and ending with the nitty-gritty syntax details. It seemed like a good idea at the time. After all, most everything in Ruby is an object, so it made sense to talk about objects first.

Or so we thought.

Unfortunately, it turns out to be difficult to describe a language top-down. If you haven't covered strings, if statements, assignments, and other details, it's difficult to write examples of classes. Throughout our top-down description, we kept coming across low-level details we needed to cover so that the example code would make sense.

So we came up with another grand plan (they don't call us pragmatic for nothing). We'd still describe Ruby starting at the top. But before we did that, we'd add a short chapter that described all the common language features used in the examples along with the special vocabulary used in Ruby—a mini-tutorial to bootstrap us into the rest of the book. And that mini-tutorial is this chapter.

Ruby Is an Object-Oriented Language

Let's say it again. Ruby is an object-oriented language. In programming terms, an *object* is a thing that combines data with the logic that manipulates that data, and a language is "object-oriented" if it provides language constructs that make it easy to create objects. Typically, object-oriented languages allow their objects to define what their data is, define their functionality, and provide a common syntax to allow other objects to access that functionality.

Many languages claim to be object-oriented, and those languages often have a different interpretation of what object-oriented means and a different terminology for the concepts they employ. Unlike other object-oriented languages such as Java, JavaScript, and Python, all Ruby types are objects, and there are no non-object basic types that behave differently.

Before we get too far into the details, let's briefly look at the terms and notations that we'll be using to talk about Ruby.

When you write object-oriented programs, you're looking to model concepts from the outside world or from your logical domain. During this modeling process, you'll discover categories of related data and behavior that need to be represented in code. In a system representing a jukebox, the concept of a "song" could be such a category. A song might combine state (for example, the name of the song) and methods that use that state (perhaps a method to play the song). In Ruby, you'd define a *class* called Song to represent the general case of what songs do.

Once you have these classes, you'll typically want to create a number of separate *instances* of each. For the jukebox system containing a class called Song, you'd have separate instances for popular hits with different names such as "Ruby Tuesday," "Enveloped in Python," "String of Pearls," "Small Talk," and so on. Each of these instances has its own state but shares the common behavior of the class. The word *object* is often used interchangeably with *instance*.

In Ruby, instances are created by calling a *constructor*, which is a special method associated with a class. The standard constructor is called new. As we'll see later in Chapter 3, Classes, Objects, and Variables, on page 33, the new method is defined for you by Ruby, and you don't need to define it on your own. You might create instances like this:

```
song1 = Song.new("Ruby Tuesday")
song2 = Song.new("Enveloped in Python")
# and so on
```

These instances are both derived from the same class, but they each have unique characteristics. Every object has a unique *object identifier* (abbreviated as *object id*), accessible via the property object_id. In this example, if you were to check song1.object_id and song2.object_id, you'd find they have different values.

For each instance, you can define *instance variables*, variables with values that are unique to that instance. These instance variables hold an object's state. Each of our songs, for example, will have an instance variable that holds that song's title.

Within each class, you can define *instance methods*. Each method is a chunk of functionality that may be called in the context of the class and usually from outside the class, although you can set constraints on what methods can be used externally. These instance methods have access to the object's instance variables and hence to the object's state. A Song class, for example, might define an instance method called play. If a variable referenced a particular Song instance, you'd be able to call that instance's play method and play that song.

Syntactically, a method is invoked using dot syntax, here are some examples:

```
intro/puts_examples.rb
"gin joint".length    # => 9
"Rick".index("c")     # => 2
42.even?              # => true
sam.play(song)        # => "duh dum, da dum de dum ..."
```

Each line shows a method being called. The item before the dot is called the *receiver* of the method, and what comes after the period is the name of the method to be invoked. The first example asks the string "gin joint" for its length. The second asks a different string to find the index within it of the letter c. The third line asks the number 42 if it's even (the question mark is part of the method name even?). Finally, we ask an object called sam to play us a song (assuming there's an existing variable called sam that references an appropriate object which we've defined elsewhere).

When we talk about methods being sent, we often say that we send a *message* to the object. The message contains the method's name along with any arguments the method may expect. The object responds to the message by invoking the method with that name. This idea of expressing method calls in the form of messages to objects comes from the programming language Smalltalk. When an object receives a message, it looks into its own class for a corresponding method. If found, that method is executed. If the method *isn't* found, Ruby goes off to look for it—we'll get to that in Method Lookup, on page 113.

It's worth noting here a major difference between Ruby and other object-oriented languages. In Java, for example, you'd find the absolute value of some number by calling a separate function and passing in that number. You could write this:

```
num = Math.abs(num);     // Java code
```

In Ruby, the ability to determine an absolute value is built into the numbers class which takes care of the details internally. You send the message abs to a number object and let it do the work:

```
num = -1234         # => -1234
positive = num.abs # => 1234
```

The same applies to all Ruby objects. In Python, you'd write len(name), but in Ruby, it would be name.length, and so on. This consistency of behavior is what we mean when we say that Ruby is a pure object-oriented language with no basic types.

Some Basic Ruby

Not everybody likes to read heaps of boring syntax rules when they're picking up a new language, so we're going to cheat. In this section, we'll hit the highlights—the stuff you'll *need* to know if you're going to write Ruby programs. Later, in Part IV, Ruby Language Reference, on page 427, we'll go into all the gory details.

Let's start with a short Ruby program. We'll write a method that returns a personalized greeting. We'll then invoke that method a couple of times:

intro/hello1.rb
```
def say_hello_goodbye(name)
  result = "I don't know why you say goodbye, " + name + ", I say hello"
  return result
end

# call the method
puts say_hello_goodbye("John")
puts say_hello_goodbye("Paul")
```
produces:
```
I don't know why you say goodbye, John, I say hello
I don't know why you say goodbye, Paul, I say hello
```

As the example shows, Ruby syntax is uncluttered. You don't need semicolons at the ends of statements as long as you put each statement on a separate line. Ruby comments start with a # character and run to the end of the line. Code layout is up to you; indentation isn't significant. That said, two-character indentation—spaces, not tabs—is the overwhelming choice of the Ruby community.

Methods are defined with the keyword def, followed by the method name—in this case, the name is say_hello_goodbye—and then the method's parameters between parentheses. (In fact, the parentheses are optional, but we recommend you use them.) Ruby doesn't use braces to delimit the bodies of compound statements and definitions. Instead, you finish the body with the keyword end. Our method's body is pretty short. The first line concatenates the literal string "I don't know why you say goodbye, " and the parameter name and the literal string ", I say hello" and assigns the result to the local variable result. The next line returns that result to the caller. Note that we didn't have to declare the variable result; it sprang into existence when we assigned a value to it.

Having defined the method, we invoke it twice. In both cases, we pass the result to the method puts, which simply outputs its argument followed by a newline (moving on to the next line of output):

```
I don't know why you say goodbye, John, I say hello
I don't know why you say goodbye, Paul, I say hello
```

The line puts say_hello_goodbye("John") actually contains two method calls: one to the method say_hello_goodbye with the argument "John" and the other to the method puts whose argument is the result of the call to say_hello_goodbye . Why does one call have its arguments in parentheses while the other doesn't? In this case, it's purely a matter of taste—the puts method is available to all objects and is often written without parentheses around its argument. Ruby doesn't require parentheses unless they are directly needed for the interpreter to parse the statement the way you want. The following lines are equivalent:

```
puts say_hello_goodbye("John")
puts(say_hello_goodbye("John"))
```

Life isn't always simple, and precedence rules can make it difficult to know which argument goes with which method invocation. So, we recommend using parentheses in all but the simplest cases. You'll see that Ruby programs often omit the parentheses when the method doesn't have an explicit receiver and only has one argument.

This example also shows Ruby string objects. Ruby has many ways to create a string object, but the most common is to use *string literals*, which are sequences of characters between single or double quotation marks. The two forms differ in the amount of processing Ruby does on the string while constructing the literal. In the single-quoted case, Ruby does very little. With a few exceptions, what you enter in the string literal becomes the string's value.

In the double-quoted case, Ruby does more work. First, it looks for substitution sequences that start with a backslash character and replaces them with some binary value. The most common of these substitutions is \n, which is replaced with a newline character. When a string containing a newline is output, that newline becomes a line break:

```
puts "Hello and goodbye to you, \nGeorge"
```

produces:

```
Hello and goodbye to you,
George
```

The second thing that Ruby does with double-quoted strings is expression interpolation. Within the string, the sequence #{EXPRESSION} is replaced by the value of EXPRESSION. We could use this to rewrite our previous method:

```ruby
def say_hello_goodbye(name)
  result = "I don't know why you say goodbye, #{name}, I say hello"
  return result
end
puts say_hello_goodbye("Ringo")
```

produces:

```
I don't know why you say goodbye, Ringo, I say hello
```

When Ruby constructs this string object, it looks at the current value of name and substitutes it into the string. Arbitrarily complex expressions are allowed in the #{...} construct. In the following example, we invoke the capitalize method, defined for all strings, to output our parameter with a leading uppercase letter:

```ruby
def say_hello_goodbye(name)
  result = "I don't know why you say goodbye,  #{name.capitalize}, I say hello"
  return result
end
puts say_hello_goodbye("john")
```

produces:

```
I don't know why you say goodbye,  John, I say hello
```

For more information on strings and the other Ruby standard types, see Chapter 7, Basic Types: Numbers, Strings, and Ranges, on page 117.

We could simplify our say_hello_goodbye method some more. In the absence of an explicit return statement, the value returned by a Ruby method is the value of the last expression evaluated, so we can get rid of the temporary variable and the return statement altogether.

```ruby
def say_hello_goodbye(name)
  "I don't know why you say goodbye, #{name}, I say hello"
end
puts say_hello_goodbye("Paul")
```

produces:

```
I don't know why you say goodbye, Paul, I say hello
```

This version is considered more *idiomatic,* by which we mean that it's more in line with how expert Ruby programmers have chosen to write Ruby programs. Idiomatic Ruby tends to lean into Ruby's shortcuts and specific syntax. A good clearinghouse for the guidelines for idiomatic Ruby style can be found in the documentation for the Standard gem at https://github.com/testdouble/standard, which has been used for the code in this book (except where we deliberately break its rules to make a point).

We promised that this section would be brief. We have one more topic to cover: Ruby names. For brevity, we'll be using some terms (such as *class variable*) that we aren't going to define here. But, by talking about the rules now, you'll be ahead of the game when we actually come to discuss class variables and the like later.

Ruby uses a convention that may seem strange at first: the first characters of a name indicate how broadly the variable is visible. Local variables, method parameters, and method names should all start with a lowercase letter or an underscore (Ruby itself has a couple of methods that start with a capital letter, but in general this isn't something to do in your own code).

Global variables are prefixed with a dollar sign, $, and instance variables begin with an "at" sign, @. Class variables start with two "at" signs, @@. Although we talk about global and class variables here for completeness, you'll find they are rarely used in Ruby programs. There's a lot of evidence that global variables make programs harder to maintain. Class variables aren't as dangerous as global variables, but they are still tricky to use safely—people tend not to use them much because they often use easier ways to get similar functionality. Finally, class names, module names, and other constants must start with an uppercase letter. Samples of different names are given in Table 1, Example variable, class, and constant names, on page 23.

Following this initial character, a name can contain any combination of letters, digits, and underscores, with the exception that the character following an @ sign may not be a digit. But, by convention, multiword instance variables are written with underscores between the words, like first_name or zip_code, and multiword class names are written in MixedCase (sometimes called CamelCase) with each word capitalized, like FirstName or ZipCode. Constant names are written in all caps, with words separated by underscores, like FIRST_NAME or ZIP_CODE. Method names may end with the characters ?, !, and =.

Arrays and Hashes

Ruby provides a few different ways to combine objects into collections. Most of the time, you'll use two of them: Arrays and Hashes. An Array is a linear list of objects, you retrieve them via their index, which is the number of their place in the array, starting at zero for the first slot. A Hash is an association, meaning it's a key/value store where each value has an arbitrary key, and you retrieve the value via that key. Both arrays and hashes grow as needed to hold new elements. Any particular array or hash can hold objects of differing types; you can have an array containing an integer, then a string, then a floating-point number, as we'll see in a minute.

You can create and initialize a new array object using an *array literal*—a set of elements between square brackets. Given an array object, you can access individual elements by supplying an index between square brackets, as the next example shows. Note that Ruby array indices start at zero.

```ruby
a = [1, 'cat', 3.14]   # array with three elements
puts "The first element is #{a[0]}"
 # set the third element
a[2] = nil
puts "The array is now #{a.inspect}"
```

produces:

```
The first element is 1
The array is now [1, "cat", nil]
```

You may have noticed that we used the special value nil in this example. In many languages, the concept of *nil* (or *null*) means "no object." In Ruby, that's not the case; nil is an object, just like any other. It's an object that represents the concept of nothing. Anyway, let's get back to arrays and hashes.

Local Variable:	name fish_and_chips x_axis thx1138 _x _26
Instance Variable:	@name @point_1 @X @_ @plan9
Class Variable:	@@total @@symtab @@N @@x_pos @@SINGLE
Global Variable:	$debug $CUSTOMER $_ $plan9 $Global
Class Name:	String ActiveRecord MyClass
Constant Name:	FEET_PER_MILE DEBUG

Table 1—Example variable, class, and constant names

Ruby hash syntax is similar to array syntax. A hash literal uses braces rather than square brackets. The literal must supply two objects for every entry: one for the key and the other for the value. Most generically, the key and value are separated by =>, but we'll see that a shortcut syntax is commonly used.

For example, you could use a hash to map musical instruments to their orchestral sections.

```ruby
instrument_section = {
  "cello" => "string",
  "clarinet" => "woodwind",
  "drum" => "percussion",
  "oboe" => "woodwind",
  "trumpet" => "brass",
  "violin" => "string"
}
```

The thing to the left of the => is the key, and the thing to the right is the corresponding value. Keys in a particular hash must be unique; you can't have two entries for "drum." The keys and values in a hash can be arbitrary objects. You can have hashes where the values are arrays, other hashes, and so on. The order of the keys in the hash is stable and will always match the order in which the keys were added to the hash. If you assign a new value to a key, the old value is erased.

Hashes are indexed using the same square bracket notation as arrays.

```ruby
instrument_section["oboe"]     # => "woodwind"
instrument_section["cello"]    # => "string"
instrument_section["bassoon"]  # => nil
```

The default behavior of a hash when indexed by a key it doesn't contain is to return nil, representing the absence of a value.

Sometimes you'll want to change this default behavior. For example, if you're using a hash to count the number of times each different word occurs in a file, it's convenient to have the default value be zero. Then you can use the word as the key and increment the corresponding hash value without worrying about whether you've seen that word before. This can be done by specifying a default value when you create a new, empty hash:

```ruby
histogram = Hash.new(0)   # The default value is zero
histogram["ruby"] # => 0
histogram["ruby"] = histogram["ruby"] + 1
histogram["ruby"] # => 1
```

Symbols

Often, when programming, you need to use the same string over and over. Perhaps the string is a key in a Hash, or maybe the string is the name of a method. In that case, you'd probably want the access to that string to be immutable so its value can't change, and you'd also want accessing the string to be as fast and use as little memory as possible.

This brings us to Ruby's *symbols*. Symbols aren't exactly optimized strings, but for most purposes, you can think of them as special strings that are immutable, are only created once, and are fast to look up. Symbols are meant to be used as keys and identifiers, while strings are meant to be used for data.

A symbol literal starts with a colon and is followed by some kind of name:

```
walk(:north)
look(:east)
```

In this example, we're using the symbols :north and :east to represent constant values in the code. We don't need to declare the symbols or assign them a value—Ruby takes care of that for you. The value of a symbol is equivalent to its name.

Ruby also guarantees that no matter where they appear in your program, symbols with the same name will have the same value—indeed, they'll be the same internal object. As a result, you can safely write the following:

```
def walk(direction)
  if direction == :north
    # ...
  end
end
```

Because their values don't change, symbols are frequently used as keys in hashes. We could write our previous hash example using symbols as keys:

```
intro/hash_with_symbol_keys.rb
instrument_section = {
  :cello => "string",
  :clarinet => "woodwind",
  :drum => "percussion",
  :oboe => "woodwind",
  :trumpet => "brass",
  :violin => "string"
}
instrument_section[:oboe]    # => "woodwind"
instrument_section[:cello]   # => "string"
# Note that strings aren"t the same as symbols...
instrument_section["cello"]  # => nil
```

Note from the last line that a symbol key is different from a string key, and access via one won't result in a value associated with the other.

Symbols are so frequently used as hash keys that Ruby has a shortcut syntax. You can use name: value pairs to create a hash instead of name => value if the key is a symbol:

```
intro/hash_with_symbol_keys_19.rb
instrument_section = {
  cello: "string",
  clarinet: "woodwind",
  drum: "percussion",
  oboe: "woodwind",
  trumpet: "brass",
  violin: "string"
}
puts "An oboe is a #{instrument_section[:oboe]} instrument"
```

produces:

```
An oboe is a woodwind instrument
```

This syntax was added, in part, for programmers familiar with JavaScript and Python, both of which use a colon as a separator in key/value pairs.

Control Structures

Ruby has all the usual control structures, such as if statements and while loops. Java or Java-Script programmers may be surprised by the lack of braces around the bodies of these statements. Instead, Ruby uses the keyword end to signify the end of a body of a control structure:

```
intro/weekdays.rb
today = Time.now

if today.saturday?
  puts "Do chores around the house"
elsif today.sunday?
  puts "Relax"
else
  puts "Go to work"
end
```

produces:

```
Go to work
```

One thing you might find unusual is that in the second clause Ruby uses the keyword elsif—one word, missing an "e"—to indicate "else if". Breaking that keyword up into else if would be a syntax error.

Similarly, while statements are terminated with end and loop as long as the condition on the line with the while is true:

```
num_pallets = 0
weight = 0
while weight < 100 && num_pallets <= 5
  pallet = next_pallet()
  weight += pallet.weight
  num_pallets += 1
end
```

Most lines that look like statements in Ruby are actually expressions that return a value, which means you can use those expressions as conditions. For example, the Kernel method gets returns the next line from the standard input stream or nil when the end of the file is reached. Because Ruby treats nil as a false value in conditions, you could write the following to process the lines in a file:

```
while (line = gets)
  puts line.downcase
end
```

The assignment statement sets the variable line to the result of calling gets, which will either be the next line of text or nil. Then the while statement tests the value returned by the assignment statement, which is the value assigned. When the value is nil, that means the output has no further lines and the while loop terminates.

Ruby *statement modifiers* are a useful shortcut if the body of an if or while statement is a single expression. Write the expression, followed by if or while and the condition. For example, here's a single-line if statement:

```
if radiation > 3000
  puts "Danger, Will Robinson"
end
```

Here it is again, rewritten using a statement modifier:

```
puts "Danger, Will Robinson" if radiation > 3000
```

Similarly, this while loop:

```
square = 4
while square < 1000
  square = square * square
end
```

becomes this more concise version:

```
square = 4
square = square * square while square < 1000
```

The if version of these modifiers is perhaps most commonly used as a guard clause at the beginning of a method, as in return nil if user.nil?. The while version is much less commonly used.

Regular Expressions

Most of Ruby's built-in types will be familiar to all programmers. A majority of languages have strings, integers, floats, arrays, and so on. But not all languages have built-in support for regular expressions the way that Ruby or JavaScript do. This is a shame because regular expressions, although cryptic, are a powerful tool for working with text. And having them built in rather than tacked on through a library interface, makes a big difference.

Entire books have been written about regular expressions (for example, *Mastering Regular Expressions* by Jeffrey Friedl), so we won't try to cover everything in this short section. Instead, we'll look at a few examples of regular expressions in action. You'll find more coverage of regular expressions in Chapter 8, Regular Expressions, on page 129.

A regular expression is a way of specifying a pattern of characters to be matched in a string. In Ruby, you typically create a regular expression by writing a pattern between slash characters (/*pattern*/). And, Ruby being Ruby, regular expressions are objects and can be manipulated as such.

For example, you could write a pattern that matches a string containing the text *Ruby* or the text *Rust* using the following regular expression:

```
/Ruby|Rust/
```

The forward slashes delimit the pattern, which consists of the two things we're matching, separated by a pipe character (|). In regular expressions, the pipe character means "either the thing on the right or the thing on the left," in this case either *Ruby* or *Rust*. You can use parentheses within patterns, just as you can in arithmetic expressions, so this pattern matches the same set of strings:

```
/Ru(by|st)/
```

You can also specify *repetition* within patterns. /ab+c/ matches a string containing an *a* followed by one or more *b*_s, *followed by a* _c. Change the plus to an asterisk, and /ab*c/ creates a regular expression that matches one *a*, zero or more *b*_s, *and one* _c.

You can also match one of a group of characters within a pattern. Some common examples are *character classes* such as \s, which matches a whitespace character (space, tab, newline, and so on); \d, which matches any digit; and \w, which matches any character that may appear in a typical word. A dot (.) matches (almost) any character. A table of these character classes appears in Table 2, Character class abbreviations, on page 137.

We can put all this together to produce some useful regular expressions:

```
/\d\d:\d\d:\d\d/      # a time such as 12:34:56
/Ruby.*Rust/          # Ruby, zero or more other chars, then Rust
/Ruby Rust/           # Ruby, exactly one space, and Rust
/Ruby *Rust/          # Ruby, zero or more spaces, and Rust
/Ruby +Rust/          # Ruby, one or more spaces, and Rust
/Ruby\s+Rust/         # Ruby, one or more whitespace characters, then Rust
/Java (Ruby|Rust)/    # Java, a space, and either Ruby or Rust
```

Once you've created a pattern, it seems a shame not to use it. The match operator =~ can be used to match a string against a regular expression. If the pattern is found in the string, =~ returns its starting position; otherwise, it returns nil. This means you can use regular expressions as conditions in if and while statements. For example, the following code fragment writes a message if a string contains the text *Ruby* or *Rust*:

```
line = gets
if line =~ /Ruby|Rust/
  puts "Programming language mentioned: #{line}"
end
```

Both strings and regular expressions have a match? method which is synonymous with the =~ operator:

```
line = gets
if line.match?(/Ruby|Rust/)
  puts "Scripting language mentioned: #{line}"
end
```

The match? form is probably more common in modern Ruby.

The part of a string matched by a regular expression can be replaced with different text using one of Ruby's substitution methods:

```
line = gets
newline = line.sub(/Python/, 'Ruby')      # replace first 'Python' with 'Ruby'
newerline = line.gsub(/Python/, 'Ruby') # replace every 'Python' with 'Ruby'
```

You can replace every occurrence of *JavaScript* and *Python* with *Ruby* using this:

```
line = gets
newline = line.gsub(/JavaScript|Python/, 'Ruby')
```

We'll have a lot more to say about regular expressions as we go through the book.

Blocks

This section briefly describes one of Ruby's particular strengths—*blocks*. A code block is a chunk of code you can pass to a method, as if the block were another parameter. This is an incredibly powerful feature, allowing Ruby methods to be extremely flexible. One of this book's early reviewers commented at this point: "This is pretty interesting and important, so if you weren't paying attention before, you should probably start now." We still agree.

Syntactically, code blocks are chunks of code that can be delimited one of two ways: between braces or between do and end. This is a code block at the end of a message call:

```
foo.each { puts "Hello" }
```

This is also a code block at the end of a message call:

```
foo.each do
  club.enroll(person)
  person.socialize
end
```

The two kinds of block delimiters have different precedence: the braces bind more tightly than the do/end pairs, a fact that will almost never make a difference in your code. In practice, the standard you'll most often see is braces used for single-line blocks and do/end used for multiline blocks.

You can pass a block as an argument to any method call even if the method doesn't do anything with the block. You do this by starting the block at the end of the method call, after any other parameters. For example, in the following code, the block containing puts "Hi" is associated with the call to the method greet (which we don't show here):

```
greet { puts "Hi" }
```

If the method has parameters, they appear before the block, and you can only pass one block per method call. In Blocks and Enumeration, on page 62, we'll see other ways to manage blocks and arbitrary chunks of code.

```
verbose_greet("Dave", "loyal customer") { puts "Hi" }
```

A method can then invoke an associated block one or more times using the Ruby yield statement. The yield statement invokes the block that was passed to the method, passing control to the code inside the block.

The following example shows a block call in action. We define a method that calls yield twice. We then call this method, putting a block on the same line after the call, and after any arguments to the method. You can think of the association of a block with a method as a kind of argument passing. This works on one level, but it isn't really the whole story. The block is effectively an entire other method that can be invoked or passed forward as an argument to another method. For example:

intro/block_example.rb
```
def call_block
  puts "Start of method"
  yield
  yield
  puts "End of method"
end

call_block { puts "In the block" }
```

produces:
```
Start of method
In the block
In the block
End of method
```

In this example, the code in the block (puts "In the block") is executed twice, once for each call to yield passing control to the block.

You can provide arguments to yield, and they'll be passed to the block. Within the block, you list the names of the parameters to receive these arguments between vertical bars (|params...|). The following example shows a method calling its associated block twice, passing the block two arguments each time:

intro/block_example2.rb
```
def who_says_what
  yield("Dave", "hello")
  yield("Andy", "goodbye")
end

who_says_what { |person, phrase| puts "#{person} says #{phrase}" }
```

produces:
```
Dave says hello
Andy says goodbye
```

You can use code blocks to package code to implement a later callback. Code blocks can be used to pass around chunks of code. They are used throughout the Ruby standard library to allow methods to perform an action on successive elements from a collection such as an array. The act of doing something similar to all objects in a collection is called *enumeration* in Ruby; other languages call this *iteration*.

```
animals = ["ant", "bee", "cat", "dog"]    # create an array
animals.each { |animal| puts animal }   # iterate over the contents
```

produces:
```
ant
bee
cat
dog
```

Many of the looping constructs that are built into languages such as Java and JavaScript are method calls in Ruby, with the methods invoking an associated block zero or more times:

```
["cat", "dog", "horse"].each { |name| print name, " " }
5.times { print "*" }
3.upto(6) { |i| print i }
("a".."e").each { |char| print char }
("a".."e").each { print _1 }
```

produces:

```
cat dog horse *****3456abcdeabcde
```

In the first line, we ask an array to call the block once for each of its elements. Next, the object 5 calls a block five times, printing * each time. Rather than use for loops, the third example shows that in Ruby we can ask the number 3 to call a block, passing in successive values until it reaches 6. Finally, we use Ruby's literal syntax for ranges of values to have the range of characters from *a* to *e* invoke a block using the method each. We show that example twice: once using Ruby's normal block parameter syntax and once using Ruby's shortcut for block parameters, which we'll see in Blocks, on page 65.

Reading and 'Riting

Ruby comes with a comprehensive library to manage input and output (I/O). But, in most of the examples in this book, we'll stick to a few simple methods. We've already come across methods that write output: puts writes its arguments with a newline after each; p also writes its arguments but will produce more debuggable output. Both can be used to write to any I/O object, but, by default, they write to the standard output stream.

You can read input into your program in many ways. Probably the most traditional one is to use the method gets—short for "get string"—which returns the next line from your program's standard input stream:

```
line = gets
print line
```

Because gets returns nil when it reaches the end of input, you can use its return value in a loop condition. Notice that in the following code the condition to the while is an assignment. We store whatever gets returns into the variable line and then test to see whether that returned value was nil or false before continuing:

```
while (line = gets)
  print line
end
```

In Chapter 11, Basic Input and Output, on page 179, we'll talk more about how to read and write from a file or other data source.

Command-Line Arguments

When you run a Ruby program from the command line, you can pass in arguments. These are accessible from your Ruby code in two different ways.

First, the global array ARGV contains each of the arguments passed to the running program. Create a file called cmd_line.rb that contains the following:

```
puts "You gave #{ARGV.size} arguments"
p ARGV
```

When we run it with arguments, we can see that they get passed in:

```
$ ruby cmd_line.rb ant bee cat dog
You gave 4 arguments
["ant", "bee", "cat", "dog"]
```

Often, the arguments to a program are the names of files that you want to process. In this case, you can use a second technique: the variable ARGF is a special kind of I/O object that acts like all the contents of all the files whose names are passed on the command line (or standard input if you don't pass any filenames). We'll look at that some more in ARGF, on page 238.

Commenting Ruby

Ruby has two ways of adding comments to source code, one of which you'll use, and the other you'll almost certainly not use. The common one is the # symbol—anything after that symbol until the end of the line is a comment and is ignored by the interpreter. If the next line continues the comment, it needs its own # symbol.

Ruby also has a rarely used multiline comment, where the first line starts with =begin and everything is a comment until the code reaches =end. Both the =begin and =end must be at the very beginning of the line, they cannot be indented.

While we did just say that Ruby ignores comments, Ruby uses a small number of "magic comments" for configuration options on a per-file basis. These comments have the form of # directive: value and must appear in the file before the first line of the actual Ruby code.

The most commonly used magic comment is # frozen_string_literal: true. If this directive is true, then every string literal that doesn't have an interpolation inside it'll automatically be frozen, as though freeze was called on it.

You might also see an # encoding: VALUE directive, which specifies the encoding for string and regular expression literals inside that particular file. Ruby also has a # warn_indent: BOOLEAN flag that will throw code warnings if a file's indentation is mismatched. There's an experimental directive called # sharable_constant_value: which affects how values are shared using the Ractor multithreading tools.

What's Next

We finished our lightning-fast tour of some of the basic features of Ruby. We took a look at objects, methods, strings, containers, and regular expressions. We saw some simple control structures and looked at some rather nifty iterators. We hope this chapter has given you enough ammunition to be able to attack the rest of this book.

It's time to move on and move up—up to a higher level. Next, we'll be looking at classes and objects, things that are at the same time both the highest-level constructs in Ruby and the essential underpinnings of the entire language.

## CHAPTER 3

Classes, Objects, and Variables

From the examples we've shown so far, you may be wondering about our earlier assertion that Ruby is an object-oriented language. Well, here is where we justify that claim. We're going to be looking at how you create classes and objects in Ruby and at some of the ways that Ruby is more flexible than other object-oriented languages.

In Ruby Is an Object-Oriented Language, on page 17, we state that everything we manipulate in Ruby is an object. And every object in Ruby was instantiated either directly or indirectly from a class. In this chapter, we'll look in more depth at creating and manipulating those classes.

Defining Classes

Let's give ourselves a simple problem to solve. Suppose we're running a secondhand bookstore. Every week, we do stock control. A gang of clerks uses portable bar-code scanners to record every book on our shelves. Each scanner generates a comma-separated value (CSV) file containing one row for each book scanned. The row contains (among other things) the book's ISBN and price. An extract from one of these files looks something like this:

```
tut_classes/stock_stats/data.csv
"Date","ISBN","Price"
"2013-04-12","978-1-9343561-0-4",39.45
"2013-04-13","978-1-9343561-6-6",45.67
"2013-04-14","978-1-9343560-7-4",36.95
```

Our job is to take all the CSV files and work out how many of each title we have, as well as the total list price of the books in stock.

Whenever you're designing an Object-Oriented system, a good first step is to identify the *domain concepts* you're dealing with. Typically the domain concepts—which could represent a physical object, a process, or some other kind of entity—become classes in your final program, and then individual examples of those concepts are instances of these classes.

It seems pretty clear that we'll need something to represent each data reading captured by the scanners. Each instance of this class will represent a particular row of data, and the collection of all of these objects will represent all the data we've captured.

Let's call this class BookInStock. (Remember, class names start with an uppercase letter, and method names normally start with a lowercase letter.) Here's how we declare that class in Ruby using the keyword class:

```
class BookInStock
end
```

As we saw in the previous chapter, we can create new instances of this class using the method 'new':

```
a_book = BookInStock.new
another_book = BookInStock.new
```

After this code runs, we'd have two distinct objects, both instances of class BookInStock. But there's nothing to distinguish one instance from the other, aside from the fact that they have different internal object IDs. Worse, these objects don't yet hold any of the information we need them to hold.

The best way to fix this is to provide the class with an initialize method. This method lets us set the state of each object as it's constructed. We store this state in *instance variables* inside the object. (Remember instance variables? They're the ones that start with an @ sign.) Because each object in Ruby has its own distinct set of instance variables, each object can have its own unique state.

Here's our updated class definition:

```
class BookInStock
  def initialize(isbn, price)
    @isbn = isbn
    @price = Float(price)
  end
end
```

The initialize method is special in Ruby programs. When you call BookInStock.new to create a new object, Ruby allocates some memory to hold an uninitialized object and then calls that object's initialize method, passing through all arguments that were passed to new. This gives you a chance to write code that sets up your object's state.

For class BookInStock, the initialize method takes two parameters. These parameters act like local variables within the method, so they follow the local variable naming convention of starting with a lowercase letter. But, as local variables, they'd just evaporate once the initialize method returns, so we need to transfer them into instance variables. This is common behavior in an initialize method—the intent is to have our object set up and usable by the time initialize returns.

This method also illustrates something that often trips up newcomers to Ruby. Notice how we say @isbn = isbn. It's easy to imagine that the two variables here, @isbn and isbn, are somehow related. It looks like they have the same name, but they don't. The former is an instance variable, and the "at" sign is actually part of its name.

Finally, this code illustrates a basic piece of validation. The Float method takes its argument and converts it to a floating-point number, terminating the program with an error if that conversion fails. Later in the book, we'll see other, more resilient, ways to handle these exceptional situations. (We know that we shouldn't be holding prices in inexact old floats.

Ruby has classes that hold fixed-point values exactly, but we want to look at classes, not arithmetic, in this section.)

What we're doing here is saying that we want to accept any object for the price parameter as long as that parameter can be converted to a float. We can pass in a float, an integer, or even a string containing the representation of a float, and it'll work. Let's try this now. We'll create three objects, each with a different initial state. The p method prints out an internal representation of an object. Using it, we can see that in each case our parameters got transferred into the object's state, ending up as instance variables:

tut_classes/stock_stats/book_in_stock_1.rb
```
class BookInStock
  def initialize(isbn, price)
    @isbn = isbn
    @price = Float(price)
  end
end

b1 = BookInStock.new("isbn1", 3)
p b1

b2 = BookInStock.new("isbn2", 3.14)
p b2

b3 = BookInStock.new("isbn3", "5.67")
p b3
```

produces:
```
#<BookInStock:0x0000000102f99720 @isbn="isbn1", @price=3.0>
#<BookInStock:0x0000000102f99180 @isbn="isbn2", @price=3.14>
#<BookInStock:0x0000000102f98fa0 @isbn="isbn3", @price=5.67>
```

Why did we use the p method to write out our objects, rather than puts? Well, let's repeat the code using puts:

tut_classes/stock_stats/book_in_stock_1a.rb
```
class BookInStock
  def initialize(isbn, price)
    @isbn = isbn
    @price = Float(price)
  end
end

b1 = BookInStock.new("isbn1", 3)
puts b1

b2 = BookInStock.new("isbn2", 3.14)
puts b2

b3 = BookInStock.new("isbn3", "5.67")
puts b3
```

produces:
```
#<BookInStock:0x0000000104739628>
#<BookInStock:0x0000000104739150>
#<BookInStock:0x0000000104738fe8>
```

Remember, puts writes strings to your program's standard output. When you pass it an object based on a class you wrote, it doesn't know what to do with the object yet, so it uses a simple expedient: it writes the name of the object's class, followed by a colon and the object's unique object identifier, which is a hexadecimal number. It puts the whole lot inside #<...>.

Our experience tells us that during development we'll be printing out the contents of a BookInStock object many times, and the default formatting leaves something to be desired. Fortunately, Ruby has a standard message, to_s, that it sends to any object it wants to render as a string. The default behavior of to_s, defined in the Object class, is the ClassName, then the colon, and then the object ID behavior we just described. So, when we pass one of our BookInStock objects to puts, the puts method calls to_s in that object to get its string representation.

If we want a different behavior, we can override the default implementation of to_s to give us a better rendering of our objects (we'll talk more about how this works in Chapter 6, Sharing Functionality: Inheritance, Modules, and Mixins, on page 101):

tut_classes/stock_stats/book_in_stock_2.rb

```ruby
class BookInStock
  def initialize(isbn, price)
    @isbn  = isbn
    @price = Float(price)
  end

  def to_s
    "ISBN: #{@isbn}, price: #{@price}"
  end
end
b1 = BookInStock.new("isbn1", 3)
puts b1
b2 = BookInStock.new("isbn2", 3.14)
puts b2
b3 = BookInStock.new("isbn3", "5.67")
puts b3
```

produces:

```
ISBN: isbn1, price: 3.0
ISBN: isbn2, price: 3.14
ISBN: isbn3, price: 5.67
```

The p method actually has a different method it calls on objects, and that method is named inspect. The difference is that inspect is designed to produce a representation that's useful to a developer when debugging, and to_s is supposed to produce a human-readable one for more general output.

Something's going on here that's both trivial and profound. See how the values we set into the instance variables @isbn and @price in the initialize method are subsequently available in the to_s method? That shows how instance variables work—they're stored with each object and available to all the instance methods of those objects.

Objects and Attributes

The BookInStock objects we've created so far have an internal state (the ISBN and price). That state is private to those objects—no other object can access an object's instance variables. In general, this is a Good Thing. It means that the object is solely responsible for maintaining its own consistency. (We feel obligated to note here that there's no such thing as perfect privacy in Ruby, and you shouldn't depend on Ruby's language privacy for security purposes.)

A totally secretive object is pretty useless—you can create it, but then you can't do anything with it. You'll normally define methods that let you access and manipulate the state of an object, allowing the outside world to interact with the object. These externally visible facets of an object are called its *attributes*.

For our BookInStock objects, the first thing we may need is the ability to find out the ISBN and price (so we can count each distinct book and perform price calculations). One way of doing that is to write *accessor methods*:

tut_classes/stock_stats/book_in_stock_3.rb
```ruby
class BookInStock
  def initialize(isbn, price)
    @isbn = isbn
    @price = Float(price)
  end

  def isbn
    @isbn
  end

  def price
    @price
  end
  # ..
end
book = BookInStock.new("isbn1", 12.34)
puts "ISBN  = #{book.isbn}"
puts "Price = #{book.price}"
```

produces:
```
ISBN  = isbn1
Price = 12.34
```

Here we've defined two accessor methods to return the values of the two instance variables. The method isbn, for example, returns the value of the instance variable @isbn because the last (and only) thing executed in the method is the expression that evaluates the @isbn variable. Later, in Method Bodies, on page 86, we'll look at a shorter syntax for declaring one-line methods.

As far as other objects are concerned, there's no difference between calling these attribute accessor methods or calling any other method. This is great because it means that the internal implementation of the object can change without the other objects needing to be aware of the change.

Because writing accessor methods is such a common idiom, Ruby provides convenient shortcuts.

The method attr_reader creates these attribute reader methods for you:

tut_classes/stock_stats/book_in_stock_4.rb
```ruby
class BookInStock
  attr_reader :isbn, :price

  def initialize(isbn, price)
```

```
    @isbn = isbn
    @price = Float(price)
  end

  # ..
end

book = BookInStock.new("isbn1", 12.34)
puts "ISBN  = #{book.isbn}"
puts "Price = #{book.price}"
```

produces:

```
ISBN  = isbn1
Price = 12.34
```

This is the first time we've used *symbols* in this chapter. As we discussed in Symbols, on page 24, symbols are a convenient way of referencing a name. In this code, you can think of :isbn as meaning the *name* isbn and of plain isbn as meaning the *value* of the variable. In this example, we named the accessor methods isbn and price. The corresponding instance variables are @isbn and @price. These accessor methods are identical to the ones we wrote by hand earlier—they'll return the value of the instance variable whose name matches the name of the accessor method. These methods only allow you to read the attribute, but not to change it.

There's a common misconception that the attr_reader declaration actually declares instance variables. It doesn't. It creates the accessor methods, but the variables themselves don't need to be declared. An instance variable pops into existence when you assign a value to it, and any instance value that hasn't been assigned a value returns nil when accessed. Ruby completely decouples instance variables and accessor methods, as we'll see in Attributes Are Just Methods without Arguments, on page 40.

Writing to Attributes

Sometimes you need to be able to set an attribute from outside the object. For example, let's assume that we have to discount the price of some titles after reading in the raw scan data.

In other languages like C# and Java that restrict access to instance variables, you'd do this with *setter functions*:

```
// Java code
class JavaBookInStock {
    private double _price;
    public double getPrice() {
        return _price;
    }
    public void setPrice(double newPrice) {
        _price = newPrice;
    }
}
b = new JavaBookInStock(....);
b.setPrice(calculate_discount(b.getPrice()));
```

In Ruby, the attributes of an object can be accessed via the getter method, and that access looks the same as any other method. We saw this earlier with phrases such as book.isbn. So, it seems natural that setting an attribute's value looks like a normal variable assignment such as book.isbn = "new isbn". You enable that assignment by creating a Ruby method whose name ends with an equals sign. A method so named can be used as the target of assignments:

tut_classes/stock_stats/book_in_stock_5.rb
```ruby
class BookInStock
  attr_reader :isbn, :price

  def initialize(isbn, price)
    @isbn = isbn
    @price = Float(price)
  end

  def price=(new_price)
    @price = new_price
  end

  # ...
end

book = BookInStock.new("isbn1", 33.80)
puts "ISBN     = #{book.isbn}"
puts "Price    = #{book.price}"
book.price = book.price * 0.75        # discount price
puts "New price = #{book.price}"
```

produces:
```
ISBN     = isbn1
Price    = 33.8
New price = 25.349999999999998
```

The assignment book.price = book.price * 0.75 invokes the method price= in the book object, passing it the discounted price as an argument. If you create a method whose name ends with an equals sign, that name can appear on the left side of an assignment. (The Ruby parser will ignore whitespace between the end of the name and the equals sign, which is how book.price = gets parsed to the method named price=.) You can even treat the setter method like a regular method invocation if you want—book.price = 1.50 is identical to the somewhat odder-looking book.price=(1.50).

Again, Ruby provides a shortcut for creating these simple attribute-setting methods. If you want a write-only accessor, you can use the form attr_writer, but that's fairly rare. You're far more likely to want both a reader and a writer for a given attribute, so you'll use the handy-dandy attr_accessor method:

tut_classes/stock_stats/book_in_stock_6.rb
```ruby
class BookInStock
  attr_reader :isbn
  attr_accessor :price

  def initialize(isbn, price)
    @isbn = isbn
    @price = Float(price)
  end
  # ...
end

book = BookInStock.new("isbn1", 33.80)
puts "ISBN     = #{book.isbn}"
puts "Price    = #{book.price}"
```

```
book.price = book.price * 0.75        # discount price
puts "New price = #{book.price}"
```

produces:

```
ISBN      = isbn1
Price     = 33.8
New price = 25.349999999999998
```

In this example, the line attr_accessor :price creates both the getter method that allows you to write puts book.price and the setter method that allows you to write book.price = book.price * 0.75

Attributes Are Just Methods without Arguments

These attribute-accessing methods don't have to be just mere wrappers around an object's instance variables. For example, you may want to access the price as an exact number of cents rather than as a floating-point number of dollars.

tut_classes/stock_stats/book_in_stock_7.rb
```
class BookInStock
  attr_reader :isbn
  attr_accessor :price

  def initialize(isbn, price)
    @isbn = isbn
    @price = Float(price)
  end

  def price_in_cents
    (price * 100).round
  end
  # ...
end

book = BookInStock.new("isbn1", 33.80)
puts "Price          = #{book.price}"
puts "Price in cents = #{book.price_in_cents}"
```

produces:

```
Price          = 33.8
Price in cents = 3380
```

We multiply the floating-point price by 100 to get the price in cents and then use the round method to convert it to an integer. Why? Because floating-point numbers don't always have an exact internal representation. When we multiply 33.8 by 100, we get 3379.9999999999954525265. The Integer method would truncate this to 3379. Calling round ensures we get the best integer representation. This is a good example of why you want to use BigDecimal, not Float, in financial calculations. See Chapter 26, Library Reference: Core Data Types, on page 495, for more on BigDecimal.

We can take this even further and create a writing method parallel to the reader method, mapping the value to the instance variable internally:

tut_classes/stock_stats/book_in_stock_8.rb
```
class BookInStock
  attr_reader :isbn
  attr_accessor :price
```

```ruby
  def initialize(isbn, price)
    @isbn = isbn
    @price = Float(price)
  end

  def price_in_cents
    (price * 100).round
  end

  def price_in_cents=(cents)
    @price = cents / 100.0
  end
  # ...
end
book = BookInStock.new("isbn1", 33.80)
puts "Price           = #{book.price}"
puts "Price in cents = #{book.price_in_cents}"
book.price_in_cents = 1234
puts "Price           = #{book.price}"
puts "Price in cents = #{book.price_in_cents}"
```

produces:

```
Price          = 33.8
Price in cents = 3380
Price          = 12.34
Price in cents = 1234
```

Here we've used attribute methods to create a virtual instance variable. To the outside world, price_in_cents seems to be an attribute like any other. Internally, though, it has no corresponding instance variable.

This is more than a curiosity. In his landmark book, *Object-Oriented Software Construction*, Bertrand Meyer calls this the *Uniform Access Principle*. By hiding the difference between instance variables and calculated values, you're shielding the rest of the world from the implementation of your class. You're free to change how things work in the future without impacting the millions of lines of code that use your class—for example, you could switch from a float to a BigDecimal and the users of this class would never need to know. This is a big win.

Attributes, Instance Variables, and Methods

The previous section's description of attributes may leave you thinking that they're nothing more than methods—why'd we need to invent a fancy name for them? In a way, that's absolutely right. An attribute *is* just a method. Sometimes an attribute simply returns the value of an instance variable. Sometimes an attribute returns the result of a calculation. And sometimes those funky methods with equals signs at the end of their names are used to update the state of an object. So, the question is, where do attributes stop and regular methods begin? What makes something an attribute and not just a plain old method? Ultimately, that's one of those "how many angels can fit on the head of a pin" questions. Here's a personal take.

When you design a class, you decide what internal state it has and also how that state is to appear on the outside to users of your class. The internal state is held in instance variables. The external state is exposed through methods we're calling *attributes*. And the other actions your class can perform are just regular methods. It isn't a crucially important distinction, but by calling the external state of an object its attributes, you're helping clue people in on how they should view the class you've written.

Classes Working with Other Classes

Our original challenge was to read in data from multiple CSV files and produce various simple reports. So far, all we have is BookInStock, a class that represents the data for one book.

During object-oriented design, you identify external things and make them classes in your code. But there's another source of classes in your designs—the classes that correspond to things inside your code itself. For example, we know that the program we're writing will need to consolidate and summarize CSV data feeds. But that's a passive statement. Let's turn it into a design by asking ourselves *what* does the summarizing and consolidating. And the answer (in our case) is a *CSV reader*. Let's make it into a class as follows:

```ruby
class CsvReader
  def initialize
    # ...
  end

  def read_in_csv_data(csv_file_name)
    # ...
  end

  def total_value_in_stock
    # ...
  end

  def number_of_each_isbn
    # ...
  end
end
```

We'd call it using something like this:

```ruby
reader = CsvReader.new
reader.read_in_csv_data("file1.csv")
reader.read_in_csv_data("file2.csv")
    :          :          :
puts "Total value in stock = #{reader.total_value_in_stock}"
```

We need to be able to handle multiple CSV files, so our reader object needs to accumulate the values from each CSV file it is fed. We'll do that by keeping an array of values in an instance variable. And how shall we represent each book's data? Well, we just finished writing the BookInStock class, so that problem is solved. The only other question is how we parse data in a CSV file. Fortunately, Ruby comes with a good CSV library, which we'll cover in detail in Chapter 29, Library Reference: Input, Output, Files, and Formats, on page 587. Given a CSV file with a header line, we can iterate over the remaining rows and extract values by name:

```ruby
tut_classes/stock_stats/csv_reader.rb
class CsvReader
  def initialize
    @books_in_stock = []
  end
```

```
    def read_in_csv_data(csv_file_name)
      CSV.foreach(csv_file_name, headers: true) do |row|
        @books_in_stock << BookInStock.new(row["ISBN"], row["Price"])
      end
    end
end
```

Because you're probably wondering what's going on, let's dissect that read_in_csv_data method. On the first line, we tell the CSV library to open the file with the given name. The headers: true option tells the library to do two things. One is to parse the first line of the file as the names of the columns. The other is to parse each row into a hash with the column names as the keys and the row values as the values.

The library then reads the rest of the file, passing each row in turn to the block (the code between do and end). Inside the block, we extract the data from the ISBN and Price columns and use that data to create a new BookInStock object. We then append that object to an instance variable called @books_in_stock (the << operator does different things in Ruby, in this case, it means "append to an array"). And where does that variable come from? It's an array that we created in the initialize method.

Again, this is the pattern you want to aim for. Your initialize method sets up an environment for your object, leaving it in a usable state. Other methods then use that state.

If you encounter an error along the lines of "'Float': can't convert nil into Float (TypeError)" when you run this code, you likely have extra spaces at the end of the header line in your CSV data file. The CSV library is pretty strict about the formats it accepts.

Let's turn this from a code fragment into a working program. We're going to organize our source into three files. The first, book_in_stock.rb, will contain the definition of the class BookInStock. The second, csv_reader.rb, is the source for the CsvReader class. Finally, a third file, stock_stats.rb, is the main driver program. We'll start with book_in_stock.rb:

tut_classes/stock_stats/book_in_stock.rb

```
class BookInStock
  attr_reader :isbn, :price

  def initialize(isbn, price)
    @isbn = isbn
    @price = Float(price)
  end

  def price_in_cents
    (price * 100).round
  end
end
```

We're keeping the price_in_cents method so we can do money arithmetic without accumulating floating-point errors.

Here's the csv_reader.rb file. The CsvReader class has two external dependencies, which are the standard CSV library and the BookInStock class that's in the file book_in_stock.rb. Ruby has a couple of helper methods that let us load external files.

tut_classes/stock_stats/csv_reader.rb

```
require "csv"
require_relative "book_in_stock"
```

```ruby
class CsvReader
  def initialize
    @books_in_stock = []
  end

  def read_in_csv_data(csv_file_name)
    CSV.foreach(csv_file_name, headers: true) do |row|
      @books_in_stock << BookInStock.new(row["ISBN"], row["Price"])
    end
  end

  def total_value_in_stock
    # later we'll see easier ways to sum a collection
    sum = 0.0
    @books_in_stock.each { |book| sum += book.price_in_cents }
    sum / 100.0
  end

  def number_of_each_isbn
    # ...
  end
end
```

In this file, we use the require method to load in the Ruby CSV library from the Ruby standard library. We also use require_relative to load in the book_in_stock file we wrote. We use require_relative for this because the location of the file we're loading is easiest to define relative to the file we're loading it from—they're both in the same directory.

We're using price_in_cents to compute the total value.

And finally, here's our main program, in the file stock_stats.rb:

tut_classes/stock_stats/stock_stats.rb
```ruby
require_relative "csv_reader"

reader = CsvReader.new

ARGV.each do |csv_file_name|
  $stderr.puts "Processing #{csv_file_name}"
  reader.read_in_csv_data(csv_file_name)
end

puts "Total value = #{reader.total_value_in_stock}"
```

Again, this file uses require_relative to bring in the library it needs (in this case, the csv_reader.rb file). It uses the ARGV variable to access the program's command-line arguments, loading CSV data for each file specified on the command line.

We can run this program using the CSV data that we used in the code on page 33:

```
$ ruby stock_stats.rb data.csv
Processing data.csv
Total value = 122.07
```

Do we need three source files for this? Not necessarily. But as your programs grow (and almost all programs grow over time), you'll find that large files start to get cumbersome. You'll also find it harder to write automated tests against the code if it's in a monolithic chunk. Finally, you won't be able to reuse classes if they're all bundled into the final program. As a result, it's fairly common to only have one Ruby class per individual file.

Let's get back to our discussion of classes.

Specifying Access Control

When designing the interface for a class, it's important to consider how much of your class you'll expose to the outside world. Allow too much access into your class, and you risk increasing the amount that different classes depend on each other's internal implementation, which is called *coupling*. Users of your class will be tempted to rely on details of your class's implementation rather than on its logical interface. The good news is that the only easy way to change an object's state in Ruby is by calling one of its methods. If you control access to the methods, you control access to the object. A good rule of thumb is never to expose methods that could leave an object in an invalid state.

Ruby gives you three levels of access control:

- *Public methods* can be called by anyone—no access control is enforced. Methods are public by default (except for initialize, which is always private).

- *Protected methods* can be invoked only by objects of the defining class and its subclasses. Access is kept within the family. We'll talk more about subclasses in Chapter 6, Sharing Functionality: Inheritance, Modules, and Mixins, on page 101.

- *Private methods* cannot be called with an explicit receiver—the receiver is always the current object, also known as self. This means that private methods can be called only in the context of the current object, and with self as the explicit receiver or with the implicit receiver. You can't invoke another object's private methods with normal dot syntax. (But there are ways around this using metaprogramming tools that we'll discuss in Chapter 22, The Ruby Object Model and Metaprogramming, on page 371)

The difference between "protected" and "private" is fairly subtle and is different in Ruby than in other common object-oriented languages. If a method is protected, it may be called by *any* instance of the defining class or its subclasses. If a method is private, it may be called only within the context of the calling object—it's never possible to access another object's private methods directly, even if the object is of the same class as the caller. In practice, it's somewhat rare to see "protected" in use.

Access control in Ruby is determined dynamically, as the program runs, not statically when the program is compiled or interpreted. You'll get an access violation only when the code attempts to execute the restricted method.

You specify access levels to methods within the class or module definitions using one or more of the three access methods: public, protected, and private. You can use each function in three different ways.

If called with no arguments, the three functions set the default access control of subsequently defined methods. This is probably familiar behavior if you're a C# or Java programmer, where you'd use keywords such as public to achieve the same effect. Although this usage looks like a keyword, in Ruby, the access control is actually a method.

```ruby
class MyClass
  # default is "public"
  def method1
    # This method is public
  end
```

```ruby
  protected
  # subsequent methods will be "protected"
  def method2
    # This method is protected
  end

  private
  # subsequent methods will be private"
  def method3
    # This method is private
  end

  public
  # subsequent methods will be "public"
  def method4
    # this method is public
  end
end
```

Since the default access for methods is public, it's rare to use public explicitly to denote access control.

As a matter of style, the methods after the call to an access method like public are typically not indented—you aren't defining a block, only the access status of subsequent methods.

Alternatively, you can set access levels of named methods by listing them as arguments to the access control functions:

```ruby
class MyClass
  def method1
  end

  def method2
  end
  # ... and so on

  public :method1, :method4
  protected :method2
  private :method3
end
```

This mechanism is somewhat rare in practice, but it does enable the third way to declare access in Ruby.

We've mentioned that most statements in Ruby return a value. In particular, defining a method with def returns a value—the name of the new method as a symbol. As a result, you can declare access directly preceding a method definition.

```ruby
class MyClass
  def method1
    # This method is public
  end

  protected def method2
    # This method is protected
  end
```

```
private def method3
  # This method is private
end

public def method4
  # This method is public
end
end
```

What's happening here is that the def method2 statement is returning the value :method2, which is immediately passed as an argument to protected, resulting in protected :method2, and making that method, and only that method, protected. Access declared this way doesn't propagate down the file, it only applies to the method that the access modifier directly precedes.

We prefer this last form because it's much more explicit about the access level of each method. That said, the first form is older, and currently more common in code you're likely to see.

It's time for some examples. Perhaps we're modeling an accounting system where every debit has a corresponding credit. Because we want to ensure that no one can break this rule, we'll make the methods that do the debits and credits private, and we'll define our external interface in terms of transactions.

```
class Account
  attr_accessor :balance

  def initialize(balance)
    @balance = balance
  end
end

class Transaction
  def initialize(account_a, account_b)
    @account_a = account_a
    @account_b = account_b
  end

  def transfer(amount)
    debit(@account_a, amount)
    credit(@account_b, amount)
  end

  private def debit(account, amount)
    account.balance -= amount
  end

  private def credit(account, amount)
    account.balance += amount
  end
end

savings = Account.new(100)
checking = Account.new(200)

transaction = Transaction.new(checking, savings)
transaction.transfer(50)
```

Protected access is used when objects need to access the internal state of other objects of the same class. For example, we may want to allow two individual Account objects to compare their balances directly but to hide those balances from the rest of the world (perhaps because we present them in a different form):

```
class Account
  protected attr_reader :balance  # accessor method 'balance' but make it protected

  def greater_balance_than?(other)
    @balance > other.balance
  end
end
```

Because balance is protected, it's available only within Account objects.

Variables

Now that we've gone through the trouble of creating all these objects, let's make sure we don't lose them. Variables are used to keep track of objects; each variable holds a reference to an object. Let's confirm this with some code:

```
person = "Tim"
puts "The object in 'person' is a #{person.class}"
puts "The object has an id of #{person.object_id}"
puts "and a value of '#{person}'"
```

produces:

```
The object in 'person' is a String
The object has an id of 60
and a value of 'Tim'
```

On the first line, Ruby creates a new string object with the value Tim. A reference to this object is placed in the local variable person. A quick check shows that the variable has indeed taken on the personality of a string, with a class, an object ID, and a value.

So, is a variable an object? In Ruby, the answer is "no." A variable is simply a reference to an object. Objects float around in a big pool somewhere (the operating system's heap, most of the time) and are pointed to by variables. Let's make the example slightly more complicated:

```
person1 = "Tim"
person2 = person1
person1[0] = 'J'

puts "person1 is #{person1}"
puts "person2 is #{person2}"
```

produces:

```
person1 is Jim
person2 is Jim
```

What happened here? We changed the first character of person1 (Ruby strings are mutable, unlike Java's), but both person1 and person2 changed from Tim to Jim.

It all comes back to the fact that variables hold references to objects, not the objects themselves. Assigning person1 to person2 doesn't create any new objects; it simply copies person1's object reference to person2 so that both person1 and person2 refer to the same object, as shown in the illustration on page 49.

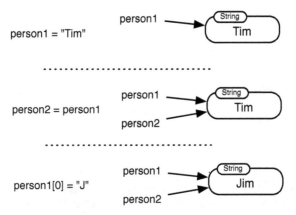

Assignment *aliases* objects, potentially giving you multiple variables that reference the same object.

Can't this cause problems in your code? It can, but not as often as you'd think (objects in Java, for example, work exactly the same way). In the previous example, for instance, you could avoid aliasing by using the dup method of String, which creates a new string object with identical contents:

```
person1 = "Tim"
person2 = person1.dup
person1[0] = "J"
puts "person1 is #{person1}"
puts "person2 is #{person2}"
```

produces:

```
person1 is Jim
person2 is Tim
```

You can also prevent anyone from changing a particular object by freezing it. Attempt to alter a frozen object, and Ruby will raise a RuntimeError exception:

```
person1 = "Tim"
person2 = person1
person1.freeze          # prevent modifications to the object
person2[0] = "J"
```

produces:

```
        from prog.rb:4:in `<main>'
prog.rb:4:in `[]=': can't modify frozen String: "Tim" (FrozenError)
```

Numbers and symbols are always frozen in Ruby, so those values are always immutable.

Reopening Classes

While we're talking about classes in Ruby, we feel like we should at least mention one of the most unique features of Ruby's class structure: the ability to reopen a class definition and add new methods or variables to it at any time, even classes that are part of the third-party tools or the standard library.

In other words, if you have something like this in Ruby:

```
class Book
  attr_accessor :title

  # and a bunch of other stuff
end
```

Later, you can do this:

```
class Book
  def uppercase_title
    title.upcase
  end
end
```

If you declare class Book and a Book class already exists, Ruby won't give an error, and the new definitions in the second declaration will be added to the existing class. This is true even if the existing class is part of Ruby itself. This process of reopening classes to add or change methods is colloquially known as *monkey-patching*.

Typically, you'd only extend a class like this if the original class isn't part of your code, but it's reasonably common in Ruby to use this method to add utility functions to core classes or the standard library. Ruby on Rails, for example, does this a lot.

To give an example, Ruby on Rails defines a method called squish, which clears excessive whitespace in a string, so if you have this:

```
"This        string     has       whitespace"
```

It becomes "This string has whitespace." By monkey-patching, Rails can define the method like this:

```
class String
  def squish
    # implementation
  end
end
```

And then call it using str.squish like any other method.

The alternative, which many other languages use, is to define a utility class or classes and define a class method on them, which looks like this:

```
class StringUtilities
  def self.squish(str)
    # implementation
  end
end
```

Which you would then call with StringUtilities.squish(str).

This example shows the advantage of allowing classes to reopen—the ability to add and easily use utility methods is convenient. It's nice to not have to know which methods are defined by Rails and which of the many possible utility classes a method might be in.

That said, this is something to be done with caution—many teams don't allow it in their own code without a clear reason. And you should be wary of using monkey-patching to change the behavior of existing methods, rather than adding new methods as we did here.

Monkey-patching can make the behavior of code unpredictable. It can be hard to tell where behavior is defined, and these changes are global, meaning that if two files define the same method, the last defined one will win, leading to potentially hard-to-find bugs.

Later in Chapter 22, The Ruby Object Model and Metaprogramming, on page 371, we'll talk about *refinements*, a Ruby feature that gives you the benefit of reopening classes, but also limits the scope of your changes.

What's Next

There's more to say about classes and objects in Ruby. We still have to look at class methods and concepts such as mixins and inheritance. We'll do that in Chapter 6, Sharing Functionality: Inheritance, Modules, and Mixins, on page 101. But, for now, know that everything you manipulate in Ruby is an object and that objects start their lives as instances of classes. And one of the most common things we do with objects is to create collections of them. But that's the subject of our next chapter.

## CHAPTER 4

Collections, Blocks, and Iterators

Most real programs have to manage collections of data: the people in a course, the songs in your playlist, the books in the store, and so on. Ruby comes with two classes that are commonly used to handle these collections: *arrays* and *hashes*. A Ruby array is an ordered collection of data. A Ruby hash is a key/value pair, equivalent to a Python dictionary, a Java Map, or a JavaScript object. Mastery of these two classes, and their large interfaces, is an important part of being an effective Ruby programmer.

But it isn't only these two classes that give Ruby its power when dealing with collections. Ruby also has a block syntax that lets you encapsulate chunks of code. When paired with collections, these blocks can build powerful iterator constructs. In this chapter, we'll look at the two collection classes as well as the blocks and iterators.

Arrays

The class Array holds a collection of object references. Each object reference occupies a position in the array, identified by an integer index. You can create arrays by using literals or by explicitly creating an Array object. A literal array is a comma-delimited list of objects between square brackets:

```ruby
a = [3.14159, "pie", 99]
a.class     # => Array
a.length    # => 3
a[0]        # => 3.14159
a[1]        # => "pie"
a[2]        # => 99
a[3]        # => nil
```

You can create an empty array with either [] or by directly calling Array.new:

```ruby
b = Array.new
b.class     # => Array
b.length    # => 0
b[0] = "second"
b[1] = "array"
b           # => ["second", "array"]
```

As the example shows, array indices start at zero. Index an array with a non-negative integer, and it returns the object at that position, or it returns nil if nothing is there. Index an array with a negative integer, and it counts from the end, with -1 being the last element of the array.

```
a = [1, 3, 5, 7, 9]
a[-1]      # => 9
a[-2]      # => 7
a[-99]     # => nil
```

The following diagram shows array access in a different way:

positive →	0	1	2	3	4	5	6
negative →	-7	-6	-5	-4	-3	-2	-1

```
           a =   [ "ant",   "bat",   "cat",   "dog",   "elk",   "fly",   "gnu" ]

      a[2] →                         "cat"
     a[-3] →                                           "elk"
    a[1..3] →           [ "bat",   "cat",   "dog" ]
    a[1...3] →          [ "bat",   "cat" ]
    a[-3..-1] →                                        [ "elk",   "fly",   "gnu" ]
    a[4..-2] →                                         [ "elk",   "fly" ]
```

Arrays are accessed using the [] operator. As with most Ruby operators, this operator is implemented as a method, specifically, an instance method of class Array. The last two lines of this example are equivalent:

```
a = [3.14159, "pie", 99]
a[0]       # => 3.14159
a.[](0)    # => 3.14159
```

The last line of code treats [] as a normal method. In practice, you wouldn't write code like the last line, we just wanted to show how flexible Ruby is.

You can index arrays with a pair of numbers, [start, count]. This returns a new array consisting of references to count the number of objects starting at position start:

```
a = [1, 3, 5, 7, 9]
a[1, 3]    # => [3, 5, 7]
a[3, 1]    # => [7]
a[-3, 2]   # => [5, 7]
```

You can also index arrays using ranges, in which the start and end positions are separated by two or three dots. The two-dot form includes the end position; the three-dot form doesn't. We'll talk more about ranges in Chapter 7, Basic Types: Numbers, Strings, and Ranges, on page 117.

```
a = [1, 3, 5, 7, 9]
a[1..3]    # => [3, 5, 7]
a[1...3]   # => [3, 5]
a[3..3]    # => [7]
a[-3..-1]  # => [5, 7, 9]
```

The [] operator has a corresponding []= operator, which lets you set elements in the array. If used with a single integer index, the element at that position is replaced by whatever is on the right side of the assignment. Any gaps that result will be filled with nil:

```ruby
a = [1, 3, 5, 7, 9]      #=> [1, 3, 5, 7, 9]
a[1] = 'bat'             #=> [1, "bat", 5, 7, 9]
a[-3] = 'cat'            #=> [1, "bat", "cat", 7, 9]
a[3] = [9, 8]            #=> [1, "bat", "cat", [9, 8], 9]
a[6] = 99                #=> [1, "bat", "cat", [9, 8], 9, nil, 99]
```

Again, []= is a regular method, and you could write it as a.[]=(index, new_value).

If the index to []= is two numbers (a start and a length) or a range, then those elements in the original array are replaced by whatever is on the right side of the assignment. If the length of the selected elements on the left is zero, the right side is inserted into the array before the start position; no elements are removed. If the right side is itself an array, its elements are used in the replacement. The array size is automatically adjusted if the index selects a different number of elements than are available on the right side of the assignment.

```ruby
a = [1, 3, 5, 7, 9]      #=> [1, 3, 5, 7, 9]
a[2, 2] = "cat"          #=> [1, 3, "cat", 9]
a[2, 0] = "dog"          #=> [1, 3, "dog", "cat", 9]
a[1, 1] = [9, 8, 7]      #=> [1, 9, 8, 7, "dog", "cat", 9]
a[0..3] = []             #=> ["dog", "cat", 9]
a[5..6] = 99, 98         #=> ["dog", "cat", 9, nil, nil, 99, 98]
```

In the line a[2, 2] = "cat", the subarray starting at index 2 and of length 2, which is [5, 7], is replaced by cat. In the next line, the subarray [2, 0] is of length 0, so dog is inserted at index 2. Then the subarray represented by [1, 1], which is [3], is replaced by [9, 8, 7] being inserted in the array. Notice that the entire right-side array isn't inserted as one element, rather each element in the right-hand side is inserted individually. The last two lines are similar, but they use ranges instead of a start and a length.

It's common to create arrays of short words, but that can be a pain, what with all the quotes and commas. Fortunately, Ruby has a shortcut, %w, which does just what we want:

Instead of this:

```ruby
a = ["ant", "bee", "cat", "dog", "elk"]
a[0]        # => "ant"
a[3]        # => "dog"
```

You can use %w followed by a delimiter and then by space-separated individual words.

```ruby
a = %w[ant bee cat dog elk]
a[0]        # => "ant"
a[3]        # => "dog"
```

You can use any character after %w as the delimiter. If it's something with a pair, like a bracket or parenthesis, then the array will continue until the other side of the pair. If you don't use a pair, the array will continue until it reaches the same character again.

If you want an array of symbols instead of strings, Ruby has a similar %i shortcut:

```
a = %i[ant bee cat dog elk]
a[0]       # => :ant
a[3]       # => :dog
```

Arrays have a large number of other useful methods. Using them, you can treat arrays as stacks, sets, queues, dequeues, and first-in-first-out (FIFO) queues. (Ruby also has a dedicated Set class, which we'll cover in Chapter 28, Library Reference: Enumerators and Containers, on page 561.)

For example, push and pop add and remove elements from the end of an array, so you can use the array as a stack:

```
stack = []
stack.push "red"
stack.push "green"
stack.push "blue"
stack       # => ["red", "green", "blue"]

stack.pop # => "blue"
stack.pop # => "green"
stack.pop # => "red"
stack       # => []
```

Similarly, unshift and shift add and remove elements from the beginning of an array. Combine shift and push, and you have a first-in-first-out (FIFO) queue.

```
queue = []
queue.push "red"
queue.push "green"
queue.shift # => "red"
queue.shift # => "green"
```

The first and last methods return (but don't remove) the *n* entries at the head or end of an array. If you don't pass an argument, the default number is one.

```
array = [1, 2, 3, 4, 5, 6, 7]
array.first    # => 1
array.first(4) # => [1, 2, 3, 4]
array.last     # => 7
array.last(4)  # => [4, 5, 6, 7]
```

We'll look at more array methods later on in Array, on page 561.

Hashes

Hashes (sometimes known as *associative arrays*, *maps*, or *dictionaries*) are similar to arrays in that they are indexed collections of object references. But, while you index arrays with integers, you index a hash with objects of any type, most often symbols and strings but also regular expressions or anything else in Ruby. When you store a value in a hash, you actually supply two objects: the index, which is called the *key*, and the *value*, or entry, to be stored with that key. You can subsequently retrieve the entry by indexing the hash with the same key value that you used to store it.

Why Are They Called Hashes?

The data structure that Ruby calls a Hash—where an arbitrary key is an index to an arbitrary value—has different names in different programming languages. The most generic term is probably *key-value store*. You'll also see them called *dictionaries* (because the values are looked up based on the keys), *maps* (because the individual keys are mapped to individual values), or *associative arrays* (because they associate keys with values).

The name "Hash" (or the related Java term "HashMap") is named after an implementation detail. The keys are stored in memory based on a function that returns a (hopefully) unique value for each object. Because the location of each key can be found without referring to the entire object, lookup is fast. The function that returns the unique value is called a *hashing function* and so the data structure is called a Hash.

The example that follows uses hash literals (a list of *key/value* pairs between braces), and then it uses square bracket syntax to access the value at each key for both retrieving and setting the value:

```
h = {"dog" => "canine", "cat" => "feline", "bear" => "ursine"}

h.length   # => 3
h["dog"]   # => "canine"
h["cow"] = "bovine"
h[12] = "dodecine"
h["cat"] = 99
h          # => {"dog"=>"canine", "cat"=>99, "bear"=>"ursine", "cow"=>"bovine",
           # .. 12=>"dodecine"}
```

In the previous example, the hash keys were strings, and the hash literal used => to separate the keys from the values. (The => is sometimes called a *hashrocket*.) If the keys are *symbols*, then you can use a shortcut. You can still use => to separate symbol keys from values:

```
h = {:dog => "canine", :cat => "feline", :bear => "ursine"}
```

You can also write the literal by moving the colon to the end of the symbol and dropping the =>.

```
h = { dog: "canine", cat: "feline", bear: "ursine"}
```

Because the value of a symbol doesn't change, symbols are often used as hash keys, and so this shortcut is very common.

You can use an even shorter shortcut. Often when creating a new hash, you're using existing data stored in variables that share the same name as the key that the variable will be indexed under in the hash. Something like this:

```
firstname = "Fred"
lastname = "Flintstone"
user = {firstname: firstname, lastname: lastname}
puts user
```

produces:

```
{:firstname=>"Fred", :lastname=>"Flintstone"}
```

You don't need to duplicate the key and the value if they have the same name:

```
firstname = "Fred"
lastname = "Flintstone"
user = {firstname:, lastname:}
puts user
```

produces:

```
{:firstname=>"Fred", :lastname=>"Flintstone"}
```

Ruby will infer that the value should come from a variable with the same name as the key. If you try to use a key shortcut and no such local variable exists, Ruby will throw an error.

Compared with arrays, hashes have one significant advantage: they can use any object as an index. And you'll find something that might be surprising: Ruby remembers the order in which you add items to a hash. When you subsequently iterate over the entries, Ruby will return them in that order.

You'll find that hashes are one of the most commonly used data structures in Ruby. Later, Chapter 5, More about Methods, on page 85, lists more of the methods implemented by class Hash.

Digging

Often data isn't simply a single hash or array but comes in a complex package that combines hashes and arrays. Accessing data in a complicated structure can be a pain, but Ruby provides a shortcut with the dig method.

The dig method, which is defined for Array, Hash, and Struct, allows you to "dig" through a complicated data structure in a single command.

```
data = {
  mcu: [
    {name: "Iron Man", year: 2010, actors: ["Robert Downey Jr.", "Gwyneth Paltrow"]}
  ],
  starwars: [
    {name: "A New Hope", year: 1977, actors: ["Mark Hamill", "Carrie Fisher"]}
  ]
}
data[:mcu][0][:actors][1]       # => "Gwyneth Paltrow"
data.dig(:mcu, 0, :actors, 1) # => "Gwyneth Paltrow"
```

The biggest advantage of using dig is that if an element isn't in the data structure, the method returns nil and doesn't raise an exception.

Word Frequency: Using Hashes and Arrays

Let's round out this discussion of hashes and arrays with a program that calculates the number of times each word occurs in some text. (So, for example, in this sentence, the word *the* occurs two times.)

The problem breaks down into two parts. First, given some text as a string, return a list of words. That sounds like an array. Then, build a count for each distinct word. That sounds like a use for a hash—we can index it with the word and use the corresponding entry to keep a count.

Let's start with the method that splits a string into words:

tut_containers/word_freq/words_from_string.rb
```ruby
def words_from_string(string)
  string.downcase.scan(/[\w']+/)
end
```

This method uses two useful string methods: downcase, which returns a lowercase version of a string, and scan, which returns an array of substrings that match a given pattern. In this case, the pattern is [\w']+, which matches sequences containing "word characters" and single quotes.

We can play with this method. Notice how the result is an array, and notice that the words are in lowercase and the punctuation is gone:

```ruby
p words_from_string("I like Ruby, it is (usually) optimized for programmer happiness")
```

produces:

```ruby
["i", "like", "ruby", "it", "is", "usually", "optimized", "for", "programmer",
"happiness"]
```

Our next task is to calculate word frequencies. To do this, we'll create a hash object indexed by the words in our list. Each entry in this hash stores the number of times that word occurred. Let's say we've already read part of the list, and we've seen the word *the* already. Then we'd have a hash that contained this data:

```ruby
{..., "the" => 1, ...}
```

If the variable next_word contains the word *the*, then incrementing the count is as simple as setting the hash to increment the value at that key:

```ruby
counts[next_word] += 1
```

We'd then end up with a hash containing the following:

```ruby
{..., "the" => 2, ...}
```

Our only problem is what to do when we encounter a word for the first time. If we try to increment the entry for that word, there won't be one, so our program will fail. This problem has several solutions. One is to check whether the entry exists before doing the increment:

```ruby
if counts.key?(next_word)
  counts[next_word] += 1
else
  counts[next_word] = 1
end
```

But there's a tidier way. If we create a hash object using Hash.new(0), the parameter, 0 in this case, will be used as the hash's default value—it'll be the value returned if you look up a key that isn't yet in the hash. Using that, we can write our count_frequency method:

tut_containers/word_freq/count_frequency.rb
```ruby
def count_frequency(word_list)
  counts = Hash.new(0)
  word_list.each do |word|
    counts[word] += 1
  end
  counts
end
```

```
p count_frequency(["sparky", "the", "cat", "sat", "on", "the", "mat"])
```

produces:

```
{"sparky"=>1, "the"=>2, "cat"=>1, "sat"=>1, "on"=>1, "mat"=>1}
```

We haven't talked about loops or blocks yet, but each takes a block argument and executes the code inside the block once for each element in the array, in this case, checking the hash for each word and incrementing the count associated with that word.

We have one little job left. The hash containing the word frequencies is ordered based on the first time it sees each word. It would be better to display the results based on the frequencies of the words. We can do that using the hash's sort_by method. When you use sort_by, you give it a block that tells the sort what to use when making comparisons. In our case, we'll use the count. The result of the sort is an array containing a set of two-element arrays, with each subarray corresponding to a key/entry pair in the original hash. This makes our whole program look like this:

```
tut_containers/word_freq/ugly_word_count.rb
require_relative "words_from_string"
require_relative "count_frequency"

raw_text = "The problem breaks down into two parts. First, given some text
as a string, return a list of words. That sounds like an array. Then, build
a count for each distinct word. That sounds like a use for a hash---we can
index it with the word and use the corresponding entry to keep a count."

word_list = words_from_string(raw_text)
counts = count_frequency(word_list)
sorted = counts.sort_by { |word, count| count }
top_five = sorted.last(5)

top_five.reverse_each do |word, count|
  puts "#{word}:  #{count}"
end
```

produces:

```
a:   6
the:  3
that:  2
sounds:  2
like:  2
```

Note that the sorted array is low to high, so we use last to take the last five elements of the array, meaning the one with the highest count, and then we use reverse_each to iterate them highest to lowest.

At this point, a quick test may be in order to validate our code. These tests are going to be valuable in a moment because we're going to change that code into a more commonly used Ruby and we want to make sure the behavior doesn't change.

To do this, we're going to use a testing framework called Minitest that comes with the standard Ruby distributions. We won't describe it fully yet (we'll do that in Chapter 13, Testing Ruby Code, on page 207). For now, we'll say that the class MiniTest::Test brings in testing functionality, including the method assert_equal, which checks that its two parameters are equal and complains bitterly if they aren't. We'll use assertions to test our two methods, one method at a time. (That's one reason why we wrote them as separate methods—it makes them testable in isolation.)

Here are some tests for the word_from_string method:

tut_containers/word_freq/test_words_from_string.rb
```ruby
require_relative "words_from_string"
require "minitest/autorun"

class TestWordsFromString < Minitest::Test
  def test_empty_string
    assert_equal([], words_from_string(""))
    assert_equal([], words_from_string("     "))
  end

  def test_single_word
    assert_equal(["cat"], words_from_string("cat"))
    assert_equal(["cat"], words_from_string("  cat   "))
  end

  def test_many_words
    assert_equal(
      ["the", "cat", "sat", "on", "the", "mat"],
      words_from_string("the cat sat on the mat")
    )
  end

  def test_ignores_punctuation
    assert_equal(
      ["the", "cat's", "mat"],
      words_from_string("<the!> cat's, -mat-")
    )
  end
end
```

produces:
```
Run options: --seed 39197
# Running:

....

Finished in 0.000420s, 9523.8109 runs/s, 14285.7164 assertions/s.

4 runs, 6 assertions, 0 failures, 0 errors, 0 skips
```

The test starts by requiring the source file containing our words_from_string method, along with the unit test framework itself. It then defines a test class. Within that class, any methods whose names start with test are automatically run by the testing framework. The results show that four test methods ran, successfully executing six assertions.

We can also test that our count of word frequency works:

tut_containers/word_freq/test_count_frequency.rb
```ruby
require_relative "count_frequency"
require "minitest/autorun"

class TestCountFrequency < Minitest::Test
  def test_empty_list
    assert_equal({}, count_frequency([]))
  end
```

```ruby
  def test_single_word
    assert_equal({"cat" => 1}, count_frequency(["cat"]))
  end

  def test_two_different_words
    assert_equal({"cat" => 1, "sat" => 1}, count_frequency(["cat", "sat"]))
  end

  def test_two_words_with_adjacent_repeat
    assert_equal({"cat" => 2, "sat" => 1}, count_frequency(["cat", "cat", "sat"]))
  end

  def test_two_words_with_non_adjacent_repeat
    assert_equal({"cat" => 2, "sat" => 1}, count_frequency(["cat", "sat", "cat"]))
  end
end
```

produces:

```
Run options: --seed 56174
# Running:

.....
Finished in 0.000503s, 9940.3581 runs/s, 9940.3581 assertions/s.

5 runs, 5 assertions, 0 failures, 0 errors, 0 skips
```

In previous editions of the book, we stopped here. But, since then, the Ruby Standard Library has evolved, and the Array class now has a tally method that does exactly what our count_frequency method does. We can use tally instead:

tut_containers/word_freq/better_word_count.rb
```ruby
require_relative "words_from_string"

raw_text = "The problem breaks down into two parts. First, given some text
as a string, return a list of words. That sounds like an array. Then, build
a count for each distinct word. That sounds like a use for a hash---we can
index it with the word and use the corresponding entry to keep a count."

word_list = words_from_string(raw_text)
counts = word_list.tally
sorted = counts.sort_by { |word, count| count }
top_five = sorted.last(5)

top_five.reverse_each do |word, count|
  puts "#{word}:  #{count}"
end
```

produces:

```
a:   6
the:  3
that:  2
sounds:  2
like:  2
```

And we get the same answer.

Blocks and Enumeration

In our program that wrote out the results of our word frequency analysis, we had the following loop:

```
top_five.reverse_each do |word, count|
  puts "#{word}:  #{count}"
end
```

The method reverse_each is an example of an *iterator*—a general term for a method that invokes a block of code repeatedly. Ruby also uses the term *enumerator* for such a method.

The most general iterator in Ruby is each, which takes a block and invokes the block once for each element in the collection. In this case, we're using reverse_each, a shortcut method that invokes the block once for each element of the list, but in reverse order.

Enumerator methods can have different behaviors beyond just executing the block of code. A Ruby programmer might use a different enumerator method called map to write the code more compactly. For example:

```
puts top_five.reverse.map { |word, count| "#{word}:  #{count}" }
```

The map applies its block to each element of the array in turn, returning a new array made up of the result of each invocation of the block.

Now the whole example looks like this:

tut_containers/word_freq/best_word_count.rb
```
require_relative "words_from_string"

raw_text = "The problem breaks down into two parts. First, given some text
as a string, return a list of words. That sounds like an array. Then, build
a count for each distinct word. That sounds like a use for a hash---we can
index it with the word and use the corresponding entry to keep a count."

word_list = words_from_string(raw_text)
counts = word_list.tally
sorted = counts.sort_by { |word, count| count }
top_five = sorted.last(5)
puts top_five.reverse.map { |word, count| "#{word}:  #{count}" }
```

produces:
```
a:   6
the:  3
that:  2
sounds:  2
like:  2
```

The map method is now taking each element of our top_five array and converting it to a new array made of the strings that come as the result of executing the block.

Because each local variable is only used as the receiver of the next message, you could chain all the values together and get something like this:

tut_containers/word_freq/bester_word_count.rb
```
require_relative "words_from_string"

raw_text = "The problem breaks down into two parts. First, given some text
as a string, return a list of words. That sounds like an array. Then, build
a count for each distinct word. That sounds like a use for a hash---we can
index it with the word and use the corresponding entry to keep a count."

puts words_from_string(raw_text)
  .tally
```

```
  .sort_by { |word, count| count }
  .last(5)
  .reverse
  .map { |word, count| "#{word}:  #{count}" }
```

produces:

```
a:   6
the:   3
that:   2
sounds:   2
like:   2
```

In this example, each message returns a new collection of data that's processed by the next message until we finally return the list of strings that's sent to puts.

You may wonder how to debug that long chain of methods if something isn't working and you want to determine what each individual step is. Ruby provides a method called tap that's designed to allow you to "tap into" this kind of method pipeline. All tap does is take a block, pass the receiver into the block, and then return the original receiver of the method. (From the perspective of the method pipeline, this does nothing—the receiver calls tap, and then the same object is returned to receive the next method in the chain.) So tap is a no-op, except that it does invoke a block.

That block could have a side effect, such as printing a value to the console for debugging purposes:

tut_containers/word_freq/bester_word_count_with_tap.rb
```
require_relative "words_from_string"

raw_text = "The problem breaks down into two parts. First, given some text
as a string, return a list of words. That sounds like an array. Then, build
a count for each distinct word. That sounds like a use for a hash---we can
index it with the word and use the corresponding entry to keep a count."

puts words_from_string(raw_text)
  .tally
  .sort_by { |word, count| count }
  .tap { |result| puts "sorted tally: #{result}\n\n" }
  .last(5)
  .tap { |result| puts "only the last five: #{result}\n\n" }
  .reverse
  .tap { |result| puts "reversed: #{result}\n\n" }
  .map { |word, count| "#{word}:  #{count}" }
```

produces:

```
sorted tally: [["words", 1], ["an", 1], ["array", 1], ["then", 1], ["build", 1],
["each", 1], ["distinct", 1], ["hash", 1], ["we", 1], ["can", 1], ["index", 1],
["it", 1], ["with", 1], ["and", 1], ["corresponding", 1], ["entry", 1], ["to",
1], ["keep", 1], ["problem", 1], ["breaks", 1], ["down", 1], ["of", 1], ["list",
1], ["return", 1], ["string", 1], ["into", 1], ["two", 1], ["parts", 1], ["as",
1], ["first", 1], ["given", 1], ["text", 1], ["some", 1], ["use", 2], ["word",
2], ["for", 2], ["count", 2], ["like", 2], ["sounds", 2], ["that", 2], ["the",
3], ["a", 6]]

only the last five: [["like", 2], ["sounds", 2], ["that", 2], ["the", 3], ["a",
6]]

reversed: [["a", 6], ["the", 3], ["that", 2], ["sounds", 2], ["like", 2]]
```

```
a:      6
the:    3
that:   2
sounds: 2
like:   2
```

It's worth briefly mentioning that Ruby does have traditional for loops, and you could start the code with something like for i in 0...5. But the for loop is too knowledgeable about the array; it magically knows that we're iterating over five elements, and it retrieves values in turn from the array. To do this, it has to know that the structure it's working with is an array of two-element subarrays. All that knowledge makes the code brittle—subject to breaking if the underlying data changes. The enumeration construction is more robust and flexible.

However you use them, enumeration and code blocks are among the more interesting features of Ruby, so let's spend a while looking into them.

Blocks

A *block* is a chunk of code enclosed either between braces or between the keywords do and end. The two forms are identical except for precedence, which is rarely an issue in practice. Ruby style favors using braces for blocks that fit on one line and do/end when a block spans multiple lines. Ruby style also has spaces between the brace and the code to distinguish a block from a Hash literal.

```
some_array.each { |value| puts value * 3 }

sum = 0
other_array.each do |value|
  sum += value
  puts value / sum
end
```

You can think of a block as being somewhat like the body of an anonymous method. Like a method, the block can take parameters (but, unlike a method, those parameters appear at the start of the block between vertical bars). Both blocks in the preceding example take a single parameter, value. And, like a method, the body of a block isn't executed when Ruby first sees it. Instead, the block is saved away to be called later.

Blocks can appear in Ruby source code only immediately after the *invocation* of a method. If the method takes parameters, the block appears after these parameters. You can think of the block as being an extra parameter passed to that method. Let's look at an example that sums the squares of the numbers in an array:

```
sum = 0
[1, 2, 3, 4].each do |value|
  square = value * value
  sum += square
end
puts sum
```

produces:

```
30
```

The block is called by the each method once for each element in the array, with each element passed to the block as the value parameter in turn. But there's something else going on. Take a look at the sum variable. It's declared outside the block, updated inside the block, and then passed to puts after the each method returns.

This example illustrates an important rule: the block has access to the variable scope outside the block, and doesn't, by default, create new variables with existing names. There's only one variable sum in the preceding program. (You can override this behavior, as we'll see later.)

If a variable appears only inside a block, then that variable is local to the block. In the preceding program, we couldn't have written the value of square in the puts statement at the end of the code because square is no longer defined at that point. It's defined only inside the block itself.

This scoping behavior can lead to unexpected problems. For example, say our program was dealing with drawing different shapes. We might have this:

```ruby
# assume Shape is defined elsewhere
square = Shape.new(sides: 4)
# .. lots of code
sum = 0

[1, 2, 3, 4].each do |value|
  square = value * value
  sum += square
end
puts sum

square.draw    # Error! Square is a number now...
```

This code will fail because the variable square, which originally held a Shape object, will have been overwritten inside the block and will hold a number by the time the each method returns. This problem doesn't happen often, but when it does, it can be confusing.

Fortunately, Ruby has a couple of answers.

Parameters to a block are *always* local to that block, even if they have the same name as variables in the surrounding scope. (You'll get a warning message when you do this if you run Ruby with the -w option.)

In this example, declaring thing as a parameter of the block means that the block gets its own version of thing and the value outside the block is undisturbed by the rest of the block:

```ruby
thing = "some shape"
[1, 2].each { |thing| puts thing }
puts thing
```

produces:

```
1
2
some shape
```

Second, you can define block-local variables by putting them after a semicolon in the block's parameter list. So, in our sum-of-squares example, we should have indicated that the square variable was block-local by writing it as follows:

```
square = "some shape"

sum = 0
[1, 2, 3, 4].each do |value; square|
  square = value * value   # this is a different variable
  sum += square
end
puts sum
puts square
```

produces:

```
30
some shape
```

To be fair, this syntax is pretty rare in actual Ruby code.

By making square block-local, values assigned inside the block won't affect the value of the variable with the same name in the outer scope.

Ruby also offers a shortcut way to access the arguments to a block based on their numerical position. Before we wrote our block like this:

```
[1, 2].each { |thing| puts thing }
```

You can instead use the special variable _1 to indicate the first positional argument to the block, meaning you can write this as:

```
[1, 2].each { puts _1 }
```

If the block had more arguments, you could reference them as _2, _3, and so on. We think that if this goes past _1, you're probably better off giving the block variables their own names.

This version is shorter but can be harder to read if the name of the argument was conveying important information. Later, we'll see another common shortcut for simple block invocations.

Iterators

A method that can invoke a block of code repeatedly for one or more elements is sometimes called an *iterator* or an *enumerator*. We said earlier that a block may appear only in the source adjacent to a method call and that the code in the block isn't executed at the time it's encountered. Instead, Ruby remembers the context in which the block appears (the local variables, the current object, and so on—Ruby refers to all of this information as a *binding*) and then enters the method that was called. This is where the magic starts.

Within the method, the block may be invoked, almost as if it were a method itself, using the yield statement. Whenever a yield is executed, it invokes the code in the block passed to the method. If there is no block, Ruby throws an error. When the block exits, control picks back up immediately after the yield. Let's start with a trivial example:

Why "yield"?

 Programming-language buffs will be pleased to know that the keyword yield was chosen to echo the yield function in Liskov's language CLU, a language that's more than forty years old and yet contains features that still haven't been widely exploited by the CLU-less.

```
def two_times
  yield
  yield
end
two_times { puts "Hello" }
```

produces:

```
Hello
Hello
```

The block (the code between the braces) is part of the call to the two_times method. Within this method, yield is called two times. Each time, it invokes the code in the block, and a cheery greeting is printed.

What makes blocks interesting is that you can pass parameters to them and receive values from them. For example, we could write a simple function that calculates members of the Fibonacci series up to a certain value. (The basic Fibonacci series is a sequence of integers, starting with two 1s, in which each subsequent term is the sum of the two preceding terms. The series is sometimes used in sorting algorithms and in analyzing natural phenomena.)

Continuing the example, let's say we want the method to be able to do something arbitrary with each new Fibonacci number. We can allow that by passing a block to the method and then yielding to the block each time we identify a new Fibonacci number.

tut_containers/fibonacci_up_to.rb
```
def fibonacci_up_to(max)
  # parallel assignment (i1 = 1 and i2 = 1)
  i1, i2 = 1, 1
  while i1 <= max
    yield i1
    i1, i2 = i2, i1 + i2
  end
end

fibonacci_up_to(1000) { |f| print f, " " }
puts
```

produces:

```
1 1 2 3 5 8 13 21 34 55 89 144 233 377 610 987
```

In this example, the yield statement has an argument. This value is passed to the associated block, which tells the method what to do with each successive element.

In the definition of the block, the parameter list appears between vertical bars. In this instance, the variable f receives the value passed to yield in the statement yield i1 and then passed from the yield statement to the block, so the block prints successive members of the series. (This example also shows parallel assignment in action. We'll come back to this later in Parallel Assignment, on page 148.) Using the shortcut syntax we saw earlier, this block could also have been written as { print _1, " " }.

Although it's common to pass only one value to a block, this isn't a requirement; a block may have any number of arguments. Blocks can use any of the argument patterns that methods use, including keyword arguments, * and ** splats, and & arguments. These patterns are discussed further in Chapter 5, More about Methods, on page 85.

Ruby provides many iterators that are available to all Ruby collections. Let's look at three: each, find, and map.

The each method is probably the simplest iterator—all it does is yield successive elements of its collection:

```
[1, 3, 5, 7, 9].each { |i| puts i }
```

produces:

```
1
3
5
7
9
```

The each iterator has a special place in Ruby. We'll describe how it's used as the basis of the language's for loop in for ... in, on page 160, and we'll see how all the other enumerable methods are defined in terms of each in Iterators and the Enumerable Module, on page 110. Just defining an each method can add a whole lot more functionality to your classes.

A block returns a value to the method that yields to it. The value of the last expression evaluated in the block is passed back to the method as the value of the yield expression. This is how the find method used by class Array works. (The find method is actually defined in module Enumerable, which is mixed into class Array.) Its implementation would look something like the following:

```ruby
class Array
  def find
    each do |value|
      return value if yield(value)
    end
    nil
  end
end

[1, 3, 5, 7, 9].find { |number| number * number > 30 } # => 7
```

Let's break this down. The find method is defined here as an instance method of Array. The last line of code creates a literal array, [1, 3, 5, 7, 9], and sends it the find method.

The find method uses each to pass successive elements of the array to the associated block. You can assume that the each method here is being called as if on the same array instance (as if it was [1, 3, 5, 7, 9].each). We'll talk about why that's so in Method Receiver, on page 87.

So, each takes its own block and passes values to that block in succession. On the first iteration, that'll be the first element of the array, or 1. We then get to the line return value if yield(value). The first part evaluated is yield(value), which passes control of the block argument to find, namely { |number| number * number > 30 }. With 1 as the argument, that's 1 * 1 > 30, which is false. Because the if clause value is false, the return value part of that line isn't evaluated, and the each method goes on to the next value in the array, which in this case is 3.

If the block returns true (that is, a value other than nil or false), the method exits, returning the corresponding element, which is the return value part. In this case, that return will happen when the block gets to the element 7. If the method goes through the entire array and no element matches, the method goes to the expression after the each and returns nil—methods and blocks both return the value of their last expression.

There's a not-so-obvious piece of control flow here: when you return from inside a block, the return also acts as a return on the associated method. So when the return value finally does execute inside the each block, that value is also returned from the entire find method.

The example shows the benefit of Ruby's approach to iterators. The Array class does what it does best, accessing array elements, and leaves the application code to concentrate on its particular requirement (in this case, finding an entry that meets some criteria).

Another common iterator is map (also sometimes known as collect), which takes each element from the collection and passes it to the block. The results returned by the block are used to construct a new array. The following example uses the String#succ method, which increments a string value:

```
["H", "A", "L"].map { |x| x.succ } # => ["I", "B", "M"]
```

The implementation of map looks something like this:

```
class Array
  def map
    result = []
    each do |value|
      result << yield(value)
    end
    result
  end
end
```

We start off with an empty result array. For each element in the array, yield is invoked on the block, and the resulting value is appended to the array. At the end of the method, the result, now containing all the individual values that have been returned by blocks, is itself returned.

Iterators aren't limited to accessing existing data in arrays and hashes. As we saw in the Fibonacci example, an iterator can return derived values. This capability is used by Ruby's input and output classes, which implement an iterator interface that returns successive lines (or bytes) in an I/O stream. In other words, they implement an each method that invokes its block once for each line in the file, so you can iterate through a file like so:

```
f = File.open("testfile")
f.each do |line|
  puts "The line is: #{line}"
end
f.close
```

produces:

```
The line is: This is line one
The line is: This is line two
The line is: This is line three
The line is: And so on...
```

Sometimes you want to keep track of how many times you've been through the block. The with_index method is your friend. You can use with_index as a method call after an iterator, it adds a sequence number to each value returned by that iterator. The original value and that sequence number are then passed to the block:

```
f = File.open("testfile")
f.each.with_index do |line, index|
  puts "Line #{index} is: #{line}"
end
f.close
```

produces:

```
Line 0 is: This is line one
Line 1 is: This is line two
Line 2 is: This is line three
Line 3 is: And so on...
```

The cool thing about with_index is that if the receiving object properly defines each, then with_index can be chained to any iterator method, you can do map.with_index or find.with_index or whatever.

Let's look at one more useful iterator. The reduce method (which can also be referred to as inject for historical reasons) lets you accumulate a value across the members of a collection. It lets you reduce an array to a single scalar value. For example, you can sum all the elements in an array or find their product using code such as this:

```
[1,3,5,7].reduce(0) { |sum, element| sum + element }        # => 16
[1,3,5,7].reduce(1) { |product, element| product * element } # => 105
```

Here's how reduce works: the first time the associated block is called, the first argument to the block is set to the first argument passed to reduce and the second argument to the block is set to the first element in the collection. In this case, for sum, the first time through the block, sum is 0 (the argument) and element is 1 (from the collection). The block performs sum + element, returning 1.

The second and subsequent times the block is called, the first block argument is set to the value returned by the block on the previous call, while the second argument continues to be passed successive items from the collection. So, the next time through the block, sum is 1 and the element is 3, so the block returns 4. The next time, sum is 4 and the element is 5, which returns 9, and the next time, 9 and 7 returns 16. The final value of reduce is the value returned by the block the last time it was called.

If reduce is called with no parameter, it uses the first element of the collection as the initial value and starts the iteration with the second value. This means that we could've written the previous examples like this:

```
[1,3,5,7].reduce { |sum, element| sum + element }        # => 16
[1,3,5,7].reduce { |product, element| product * element } # => 105
```

To make things shorter, instead of a block, you can pass it the name of the method you want to apply to successive elements of the collection. These examples work because, in Ruby, addition and multiplication are simply methods defined on the classes that represent numbers, and :+ is the symbol corresponding to the method +:

```
[1,3,5,7].reduce(:+) # => 16
[1,3,5,7].reduce(:*) # => 105
```

But for one of these examples, there's a shortcut:

```
[1,3,5,7].sum # => 16
```

(Array#product is also a method, but it does something different, it returns the cross-product of two arrays...)

```
[1,3,5,7].product([2, 4, 6]) # => [[1, 2], [1, 4], [1, 6], [3, 2], [3, 4], [3,
                             # .. 6], [5, 2], [5, 4], [5, 6], [7, 2], [7, 4], [7,
                             # .. 6]]
```

Using Blocks for Transactions

Although blocks are often used as the target of an iterator, they have other uses. Let's look at a few.

You can use blocks to define a chunk of code that must be run as part of some kind of transaction. For example, you'll often open a file, do something with its contents, and then need to ensure that the file is closed when you finish. Opening and closing the file is a transaction that you want to happen together regardless of what you do with the contents. Although you can manage a transaction using conventional linear code, a version using blocks is simpler and turns out to be less error-prone. A naive implementation (ignoring error handling) could look something like the following:

```
class File
  def self.open_and_process(*args)
    f = File.open(*args)
    yield f
    f.close()
  end
end

File.open_and_process("testfile", "r") do |file|
  while line = file.gets
    puts line
  end
end
```

produces:

```
This is line one
This is line two
This is line three
And so on...
```

The method open_and_process is a *class method*—its receiver is the class itself, and it may be called independently of any particular file object. We'll discuss class methods more in Chapter 5, More about Methods, on page 85. We want open_and_process to take the same arguments as the conventional File.open method, but we want to pass them through no matter what the arguments are. So, we've specified the parameter list as *args meaning "collect the positional parameters passed to the method into an array named args". We then call File.open, passing it *args as an argument. This expands the array back into individual parameters. The net result is that open_and_process transparently passes its non-block arguments to File.open.

Once the file has been opened, open_and_process calls yield, passing the open file object to the block. When the block returns, the file is closed. In this way, the responsibility for closing an open file has been shifted from the users of file objects to the file objects themselves.

The technique of having files manage their own life cycle is so useful that the class File supplied with Ruby supports it directly. If File.open has an associated block, then that block will be invoked with a file object, and the file will be closed when the block terminates. This is interesting because it means that File.open has two different behaviors. When called with a block, it executes the block and closes the file. When called without a block, it just returns the file object. This is made possible by the method block_given?, which returns true if a block is associated with the current method. Using this method, you could implement something similar to the standard File.open (again, ignoring error handling) using the following:

```ruby
class File
  def self.my_open(*args)
    file = File.new(*args)
    return file unless block_given?
    result = yield file
    file.close
    result
  end
end
```

In this version, we use the guard clause return file unless block_given? to exit the method early if block_given? is false. Otherwise, we proceed with the same yield and then close as in our previous code.

This code has one last missing piece: in the previous examples of using blocks to control resources, we didn't address error handling. If we wanted to implement these methods properly, we'd need to ensure that we closed a file even if the code processing that file somehow aborted. We do this using exception handling, which we'll talk about later in Chapter 10, Exceptions, on page 171.

Using Blocks as Objects

Blocks are like anonymous methods, but there's more to them than that. You can also store a block in a variable, pass it as an argument to a function, and then invoke its code later.

Remember we said that you can think of blocks as an extra implicit argument that's passed to a method? Well, you can make that argument explicit. If the last parameter in a method definition is prefixed with an ampersand (such as &action), Ruby looks for a code block whenever that method is called. That code block is converted to an object of class Proc and assigned to the parameter. You can then treat the parameter as any other variable.

Here's an example where we create a Proc object in one instance method and store it in an instance variable. We then invoke the proc from a second instance method.

```ruby
class ProcExample
  def pass_in_block(&action)
    @stored_proc = action
  end

  def use_proc(parameter)
    @stored_proc.call(parameter)
  end
end

eg = ProcExample.new
eg.pass_in_block { |param| puts "The parameter is #{param}" }
eg.use_proc(99)
```

produces:

```
The parameter is 99
```

Do you see how the call method on a proc object invokes the code in the original block?

Many Ruby programs store and later call blocks in this way—it's a great way of implementing callbacks, dispatch tables, and so on. But you can go one step further. If a block can be turned into an object by adding an ampersand parameter to a method, what happens if that method then returns the Proc object to the caller? What can you do with that Proc object?

Well, you can call it, for one thing…

```ruby
def create_block_object(&block)
  block
end

bo = create_block_object { |param| puts "You called me with #{param}" }

bo.call(99)
bo.call("cat")
```

produces:

```
You called me with 99
You called me with cat
```

The create_block_object method converts its block argument to the variable named block and then returns it. The returned value is a Proc object and can be called with the call method.

Creating a variable with a block value is so useful that Ruby provides multiple ways to do so. The one you might see the most in newer code is the "stabby lambda" syntax, where the -> operator declares that a block is coming:

```ruby
bo = ->(param) { puts "You called me with #{param}" }
bo.call(99)
bo.call("cat")
```

produces:

```
You called me with 99
You called me with cat
```

The stabby lambda is a shortcut for the Ruby Kernel method lambda:

```ruby
bo = lambda { |param| puts "You called me with #{param}" }
bo.call 99
bo.call "cat"
```

produces:

```
You called me with 99
You called me with cat
```

There's a related Kernel method called proc:

```ruby
bo = proc { |param| puts "You called me with #{param}" }
bo.call 99
bo.call "cat"
```

produces:

```
You called me with 99
You called me with cat
```

Both proc and lambda invoke the new method of the Proc class, although the current style prefers using one of the previous mechanisms to using Proc.new directly:

```
bo = Proc.new { |param| puts "You called me with #{param}" }
bo.call 99
bo.call "cat"
```

produces:

```
You called me with 99
You called me with cat
```

There are slight differences between the behavior of the resulting object based on the lambda calls versus the proc calls. Specifically, the lambda values return an error if called with the wrong number of arguments, while proc will allow the call, and either truncate extra arguments or assign nil to unspecified arguments. Also, using return inside a proc will return from the method the proc is inside, whereas using return inside a lambda will not.

Blocks Are Closures

We said earlier that a block can use local variables from the surrounding scope. Let's look at a slightly different example of a block doing simply that:

```
def n_times(thing)
  ->(n) { thing * n }
end

p1 = n_times(23)
p1.call(3) # => 69
p1.call(4) # => 92
p2 = n_times("Hello ")
p2.call(3) # => "Hello Hello Hello "
```

The method n_times uses stabby lambda syntax to return a Proc object that references the method's parameter, thing. Even though that parameter is out of scope by the time the block is called outside the method, the parameter remains accessible to the block. This is called a *closure*—variables in the surrounding scope that are referenced in a block remain accessible for the life of that block and the life of any Proc object created from that block.

Here's another example—a method that returns a Proc object that returns successive powers of 2 when called:

```
def power_proc_generator
  value = 1
  -> { value += value }
end

power_proc = power_proc_generator

puts power_proc.call
puts power_proc.call
puts power_proc.call
```

produces:

```
2
4
8
```

Stabby Lambdas

Let's look at that lambda syntax a little more. You can write the following:

```
-> (params) { ... }
```

As a shortcut to:

```
lambda { |params| ... }
```

Why ->?

Let's start by getting something out of the way. Why ->? For compatibility across all the different source file encodings, Matz is restricted to using pure 7-bit ASCII for Ruby operators, and the choice of available characters is severely limited by the ambiguities inherent in the Ruby syntax. He felt that -> was (kind of) reminiscent of a Greek lambda character λ.

The parentheses around the parameters are optional. Here are some examples:

```
proc1 = -> arg { puts "In proc1 with #{arg}" }
proc2 = -> arg1, arg2 { puts "In proc2 with #{arg1} and #{arg2}" }
proc3 = ->(arg1, arg2) { puts "In proc3 with #{arg1} and #{arg2}" }

proc1.call "ant"
proc2.call "bee", "cat"
proc3.call "dog", "elk"
```

produces:

```
In proc1 with ant
In proc2 with bee and cat
In proc3 with dog and elk
```

The -> form is more compact than using lambda and is especially useful when you want to pass one or more Proc objects to a method:

```
def my_if(condition, then_clause, else_clause)
  if condition
    then_clause.call
  else
    else_clause.call
  end
end

5.times do |val|
  my_if(
    val < 2,
    -> { puts "#{val} is small" },
    -> { puts "#{val} is big" }
  )
end
```

produces:

```
0 is small
1 is small
2 is big
3 is big
4 is big
```

One good reason to pass blocks to methods is that you can reevaluate the code in those blocks at any time.

Here's an example of reimplementing a while loop using a method. Because the condition is passed as a block, it can be evaluated each time around the loop:

```ruby
def my_while(cond, &body)
  while cond.call
    body.call
  end
end

a = 0
my_while(-> { a < 3 }) do
  puts a
  a += 1
end
```

produces:

```
0
1
2
```

Block Parameter Lists

When you're using the -> syntax, you declare the parameters in a separate list before the block body, similar to a method definition. Blocks written using the other syntax forms declare their parameter lists between vertical bars. In both cases, the parameter list looks like the list you can give to methods. It can take default values, splat arguments (described later in Variable-Length Parameter Lists, on page 89), keyword arguments, and its own block parameter (a trailing argument starting with an ampersand). You can write blocks that are as versatile as methods. Actually, they are more versatile because these blocks are also closures, while methods are not. Here's a block using the lambda notation:

```ruby
proc1 = lambda do |a, *b, &block|
  puts "a = #{a.inspect}"
  puts "b = #{b.inspect}"
  block.call
end

proc1.call(1, 2, 3, 4) { puts "in block1" }
```

produces:

```
a = 1
b = [2, 3, 4]
in block1
```

And here's one using the -> notation:

```ruby
proc2 = -> (a, *b, &block) do
  puts "a = #{a.inspect}"
  puts "b = #{b.inspect}"
  block.call
end

proc2.call(1, 2, 3, 4) { puts "in block2" }
```

produces:

```
a = 1
b = [2, 3, 4]
in block2
```

Enumerators

As powerful and flexible as the Ruby enumeration methods are, the ones we've seen all have the same structure. A block is passed to an object, and that object controls how it interacts with the block and traverses the collection.

As useful as that structure is, it doesn't cover all the cases where iteration is useful. Sometimes, you want an external object or method to control how the collection is traversed. You may need a more complicated kind of access to the block methods. For example, you might want to iterate over two collections in parallel, which is difficult using Ruby's internal iterator scheme.

Fortunately, Ruby comes with a built-in Enumerator class, which implements external iterators in Ruby for just such occasions. An *external* iterator is an iterator where you control the iteration behavior outside the iterator itself, meaning we have a specific way of explicitly triggering when the iterator should move to the next element in its collection.

The Enumerator class is not to be confused with the Enumerable module, which we'll discuss in Chapter 6, Sharing Functionality: Inheritance, Modules, and Mixins, on page 101. The Enumerable module is a mixin that provides functionality to a variety of classes. The Enumerator class is a class that allows for external iterators.

You can create an Enumerator object by calling the to_enum method (or its synonym, enum_for) on a collection such as an array or a hash. Once you have an Enumerator, you can access the next element in the collection with the method next:

```
a = [1, 3, "cat"]
enum_a = a.to_enum
enum_a.next # => 1
enum_a.next # => 3

h = {dog: "canine", fox: "vulpine"}
enum_h = h.to_enum
enum_h.next # => [:dog, "canine"]
enum_h.next # => [:fox, "vulpine"]
```

By default, the new enumerator uses the each method as the way it walks through the underlying enumeration, but you can use any method that successively yields values to a block:

```
a = [1, 3, "cat"]
enum_a = a.to_enum(:reverse_each)
enum_a.next # => "cat"
enum_a.next # => 3
```

Most of Ruby's internal iterator methods—the ones that normally yield successive values to a block—will return an Enumerator object if called without a block:

```
a = [1, 3, "cat"]

enum_a = a.each
```

```
enum_a.next # => 1
enum_a.next # => 3
```

Ruby's Kernel module has a method called loop that does nothing but repeatedly invoke its block. Typically, your code in the block will look for an ending condition and break out of the loop when that condition occurs. But loop is also smart when you use an Enumerator—when an enumerator object runs out of values inside a loop, the loop will terminate cleanly.

The following example shows this in action—the loop iterates both arrays in parallel and ends when the three-element enumerator runs out of values. You can also handle this in your own iterator methods by rescuing the StopIteration exception, but, because we haven't talked about exceptions yet, we won't go into details here.

```
short_enum = [1, 2, 3].to_enum
long_enum  = ('a'..'z').to_enum

loop do
  puts "#{short_enum.next} - #{long_enum.next}"
end
```

produces:

```
1 - a
2 - b
3 - c
```

Enumerators Are Objects

Enumerators take something that's normally executable code (the act of iterating—by default, calling each) and turn it into an object. This means you can do things programmatically with enumerators that aren't easily done with regular loops.

For example, the Enumerable module defines the method each_with_index. This invokes its host class's each method, returning successive values along with an index:

```
result = []
['a', 'b', 'c'].each_with_index { |item, index| result << [item, index] }
result    # => [["a", 0], ["b", 1], ["c", 2]]
```

What if you wanted to iterate and receive an index but use a different method than each to control that iteration? For example, you might want to iterate over the characters in a string. There's no method called each_char_with_index built into the String class.

Enumerators to the rescue. The each_char method of strings will return an enumerator if you don't give it a block, and you can then call each_with_index on that enumerator:

```
result = []
"cat".each_char.each_with_index { |item, index| result << [item,  index] }
result    # => [["c", 0], ["a", 1], ["t", 2]]
```

In fact, this is such a common use of enumerators that Matz has given us with_index, which makes the code read better:

```
result = []
"cat".each_char.with_index { |item, index| result << [item,  index] }
result    # => [["c", 0], ["a", 1], ["t", 2]]
```

By separating the with_index from the each_char, we can even chain in a map call and simplify the code even further:

```
"cat".each_char.with_index.map { |item, index| [item,  index] }
```

You can also create the Enumerator object explicitly—in this case, we'll create one that calls our string's each_char method. We can call to_a on that enumerator to iterate over it:

```
enum = "cat".each_char
enum.to_a # => ["c", "a", "t"]
```

If the method we're using as the basis of our enumerator takes parameters, we can pass them to enum_for:

```
enum_in_threes = (1..10).enum_for(:each_slice, 3)
enum_in_threes.to_a # => [[1, 2, 3], [4, 5, 6], [7, 8, 9], [10]]
```

Enumerators Used as Generators and Filters

In addition to creating enumerators from existing collections, you can create an enumerator explicitly with Enumerator.new, passing it a block that takes a single argument. The code in the block will be used when next is called on the enumerator object, and it needs to supply a fresh value to your program. But the block isn't simply executed from top to bottom. When first called, execution starts at the top of the block and pauses when the block calls yield on its argument, which yields a value to the calling code. When next is called again, execution resumes at the statement following the yield.

Among other things, this lets you write enumerators that generate infinite sequences:

```
triangular_numbers = Enumerator.new do |yielder|
  number = 0
  count = 1
  loop do
    number += count
    count += 1
    yielder.yield(number)
  end
end

5.times { print triangular_numbers.next, " " }
puts
```

produces:

```
1 3 6 10 15
```

We start by creating an iterator using Enumerator.new and assigning that value to the variable triangular_numbers. After that, we loop 5.times, each time calling triangular_numbers.next. The first time next is called, we start at the top of the block, setting number and count before entering the loop. In the loop, number is set to 1, count is incremented to 2, and then yielder.yield is called, passing number back to the caller.

The following time that next is called, we continue at the point of yield meaning that we stay in the loop rather than start at the beginning again. The code updates number to 3, increments count to three, and yields. And so on…

That syntax for infinite sequences is confusing, though. So, a simpler mechanism was added for creating infinite sequences. The produce method takes an initial value and a block. Every time the block is invoked via next, the resulting value is stored and used as the input to the next call. This means all you need to do is define the succession function, and you don't need to worry about managing yielders and whatnot:

```
triangular_numbers = Enumerator.produce([1, 2]) do |number, count|
  [number + count, count + 1]
end

5.times { print triangular_numbers.next.first, " " }
puts
```

produces:

```
1 3 6 10 15
```

Note that we're returning a two-element array to keep both values, so we need to call first on the result to get the actual number. We'll see a workaround in a second.

Enumerator objects are also enumerable (that is to say, the methods available to enumerable objects are also available to them). So we can use Enumerable's methods (such as first) on them:

```
triangular_numbers = Enumerator.produce([1, 2]) do |number, count|
  [number + count, count + 1]
end

p triangular_numbers.first(5).map { _1.first }
```

produces:

```
[1, 3, 6, 10, 15]
```

You have to be careful with enumerators that can generate infinite sequences. Some of the regular Enumerable methods, such as count and select, will happily try to read the whole enumeration before returning a result. If you want a version of select that works with infinite sequences, you need to use the lazy method of Enumerable.

If you call lazy on any Ruby enumerable, you get back an instance of class Enumerator::Lazy. This enumerator acts like the original, but it reimplements methods such as select and map so that they can work with infinite sequences. Putting it another way, none of the lazy versions of the methods actually consume any data from the collection until that data is requested, and then they only consume enough to satisfy that request. In other words, they are "lazy".

To work this magic, the lazy versions of the various methods don't return arrays of data. Instead, each returns a new enumerator that includes its own special processing—the select method returns an enumerator that knows how to apply the select logic to its input collection, the map enumerator knows how to handle the map logic, and so on. The result is that if you chain a bunch of lazy enumerator methods, what you end up with is a chain of enumerators—the last one in the chain takes values from the one before it, and so on.

Let's play with this a little. To start, let's create a class that generates a stream of integers...

```
class InfiniteStream
  def all
    Enumerator.produce(0) do |number|
      number += 1
    end.lazy
  end
end

p InfiniteStream.new.all.first(10)
```

produces:

```
[0, 1, 2, 3, 4, 5, 6, 7, 8, 9]
```

See how we convert the basic generator into a lazy enumerator with the call to lazy after the end of the block.

Calling the first method on this with the argument 10 returns the numbers 1 through 10, but this doesn't exercise the method's lazy characteristics. Let's instead get the first 10 multiples of three.

```
p InfiniteStream.new.all
    .select { (_1 % 3).zero? }
    .first(10)
```

produces:

```
[0, 3, 6, 9, 12, 15, 18, 21, 24, 27]
```

Without the lazy enumerator, the call to select would effectively never return, as select would try to read all the values from the generator. But the lazy version of select only consumes values on demand, and in this case the subsequent call to first only asks for 10 values.

Let's make this a little more complex—how about multiples of 3 whose string representations are palindromes?

```
def palindrome?(n)
  n = n.to_s
  n == n.reverse
end
```

```
p InfiniteStream.new.all
    .select { (_1 % 3).zero? }
    .select { palindrome?(_1) }
    .first(10)
```

produces:

```
[0, 3, 6, 9, 33, 66, 99, 111, 141, 171]
```

Remember that our lazy filter methods simply return new Enumerator objects? That means we can split up the previous code:

```
multiple_of_three = InfiniteStream.new.all.select { (_1 % 3).zero? }

p multiple_of_three.first(10)

m3_palindrome = multiple_of_three.select { palindrome?(_1) }

p m3_palindrome.first(10)
```

produces:

```
[0, 3, 6, 9, 12, 15, 18, 21, 24, 27]
[0, 3, 6, 9, 33, 66, 99, 111, 141, 171]
```

You could also code up the various predicates as free-standing procs if you feel it aids readability or reusability.

```
multiple_of_three = -> n { (n % 3).zero? }
palindrome = -> n { n = n.to_s; n == n.reverse }
```

```
p InfiniteStream.new
  .all
  .select(&multiple_of_three)
  .select(&palindrome)
  .first(10)
```

produces:

```
[0, 3, 6, 9, 33, 66, 99, 111, 141, 171]
```

This also gives us a way to fix our definition of triangular numbers so that the user of that method doesn't have to know about the two-element array, we use lazy and map to return only the number we care about:

```
triangular_numbers = Enumerator.produce([1, 2]) do |number, count|
  [number + count, count + 1]
end.lazy.map { _1.first }

p triangular_numbers.first(5)
```

produces:

```
[1, 3, 6, 10, 15]
```

What's Next

Collections, blocks, and iterators are core concepts in Ruby. The more you write in Ruby, the more you'll find yourself moving away from conventional looping constructs. Instead, you'll write classes that support iteration over their contents. And you'll find that this code is compact, easy to read, and a joy to maintain. If this all seems too weird, don't worry. After a while, it'll start to come naturally. And you'll have plenty of time to practice as you use Ruby libraries and frameworks. Now, let's talk more about how Ruby lets you define and call methods.

## CHAPTER 5

More about Methods

So far in this book, we've been defining and using methods without much thought. Now it's time to get into the details.

Defining a Method

As we've seen, a method is defined using the keyword def.

The keyword def creates a method and returns the name of the method as a symbol, which, as we saw in Specifying Access Control, on page 45, allows us to put decorator methods like private before the declaration.

The body of a method contains normal Ruby expressions. The return value of a method is the value of the last expression executed or the argument of an explicit return expression.

An important fact about def is that if you define a method a second time, Ruby won't raise an error, it'll print a warning, and then it'll redefine the method using the second definition:

```ruby
class Batman
  def who_is_robin
    puts "Dick Grayson"
  end

  def who_is_robin
    puts "Damian Wayne"
  end
end

Batman.new.who_is_robin
```

produces:

```
Damian Wayne
```

When combined with the ability to reopen classes that we saw in Reopening Classes, on page 49, the ability to redefine methods is an important, but potentially dangerous, feature of how classes work.

Method Bodies

In a "regular" method definition, the method body starts on the line after the method decla-ration and continues until a matching end. Ruby doesn't require the method body to be indented, but standard code style does indent method bodies by two characters:

```
def a_method_name(arg)
  puts arg
end
```

Starting in Ruby 3.0, you can create one-line methods with a different syntax, sometimes called an "endless method," because you don't need the end statement.

It's the method name, any arguments, an optional space, an =, and the method body:

```
def a_method_name(arg) = puts arg
```

The right side of the equal sign is a single expression. If the method takes arguments, the argument list must be surrounded by parentheses (which are optional in a regular definition). There must be either a parenthesis or a space between the method name and the equals sign, or else the parser will consider the equals sign to be part of the method name.

Sometimes you'll want to define a method with no body, often because it's a method that will be fully defined by subclasses. While you can do that in two lines, you'll sometimes see this idiom:

```
def a_method_name; end
```

The semicolon, which is rare in Ruby code, is used here as a separator between multiple expressions on the same line. If the method is called, it returns nil.

Method Names

Method names should begin with a lowercase letter or underscore followed by a combination of letters, digits, and underscores. You won't get an error if you start a method name with an uppercase letter, but when Ruby sees you calling the method, it might guess that's a constant, not a method invocation, and, as a result, it may parse the call incorrectly. By con-vention, method names starting with an uppercase letter are in the Kernel module and are used for type conversion. The Integer method, for example, converts its parameter to an integer.

In addition to letters, digits, and underscores, a method name may end with ?, !, or =.

Methods that return a boolean result (so-called predicate methods) are often named with a trailing ?:

```
1.even?               # => false
2.even?               # => true
1.instance_of?(Integer) # => true
```

Methods that are "dangerous" or that modify their receiver, may be named with a trailing exclamation point, !. These are sometimes called *bang methods* and are often paired with a "safe" version that doesn't end in an exclamation point. For instance, class String provides both chop and chop! methods. The first returns a modified string; the second modifies the receiver in place.

```
sample = "this is my code"
sample.chop  # => "this is my cod"
sample       # => "this is my code"

sample.chop! # => "this is my cod"
sample       # => "this is my cod"
```

Methods that can appear on the left side of an assignment (a feature we discussed back in Writing to Attributes, on page 38) end with an equal sign (=).

?, !, and = are the only weird characters allowed as method name suffixes. These characters are only allowed at the end of a method name.

In addition, you can override a limited set of operators by defining them as methods. For example:

```
class Matrix
  attr_reader :x, :y

  def initialize(x, y)
    @x = x
    @y = y
  end

  def to_s = "(#{x}, #{y})"

  def +(other)
    Matrix.new(x + other.x, y + other.y)
  end
end

first = Matrix.new(1, 2)
second = Matrix.new(3, 4)
puts first + second
```

produces:

```
(4, 6)
```

Here we're defining the + operator to implement a matrix addition and return a new matrix object. Even though the + is defined as a method, it's still written as a binary operator. You can find the full list of operator names that you can define as methods in Chapter 25, Language Reference: Objects and Classes, on page 465.

Method Receiver

An instance method definition, like the ones we just saw, adds the method to the class it's defined within and makes the method available to instances of that class. (In Chapter 25, Language Reference: Objects and Classes, on page 465, we'll talk about what Ruby does for method definitions that aren't inside a class.)

Ruby also allows you to define a method for one specific object rather than the current class. The most common use of this feature is to assign methods to the class itself rather than to instances of the class.

The syntax is to put the object name, followed by a dot, before the method name:

```
class Computer
  def self.function
```

```
    "I'm afraid I can't do that"
  end
end
```

```
puts Computer.function
```

produces:

```
I'm afraid I can't do that
```

In this example, the object name is self, and at the point of the method declaration, self means "The class this method is being declared inside," in this case Computer, so the method is accessible as Computer.function. (You could actually define the method as def Computer.function, and you might see older Ruby code that uses that syntax.) We'll talk more about self in Chapter 22, The Ruby Object Model and Metaprogramming, on page 371.

Although class methods are the most common use of this feature, methods can be attached to any object:

```
class Computer
end
```

```
mac = Computer.new
pc = Computer.new
```

```
def mac.introduction = "I'm a Mac"
```

```
def pc.introduction = "I'm a PC"
```

```
puts mac.introduction
puts pc.introduction
```

produces:

```
I'm a Mac
I'm a PC
```

In this case, we've attached separate methods to each of the two instances, so calling introduction on each instance behaves differently.

You'll see this syntax for class methods frequently, and the individual object version of it quite rarely. We'll talk more in Chapter 25, Language Reference: Objects and Classes, on page 465, about why this works and how class methods behave in Ruby.

Method Parameters

Now that we've defined our new method, we may need to declare some parameters to the method. Parameters are defined using a list of local variable names. Using parentheses around a method's parameters in the definition is optional. The standard convention is to use them when a method has parameters and omit them when it doesn't. Note that if the method is defined using the "endless method" syntax, the parameter list must be surrounded by parentheses, but you don't need to include empty parentheses.

```
def my_new_method(arg1, arg2, arg3)      # 3 parameters
  # Code for the method would go here
end
```

```
def my_other_new_method                  # No parameters
  # Code for the method would go here
end
```

Ruby lets you specify default values for a method's parameters—values that will be used if the caller doesn't pass them explicitly. You do this using an equal sign (=) followed by a Ruby expression. That expression can include references to previous parameters in the list:

```ruby
def cool_dude(arg1="Miles", arg2="Coltrane", arg3="Roach")
  "#{arg1}, #{arg2}, #{arg3}."
end
```

```ruby
cool_dude                           # => "Miles, Coltrane, Roach."
cool_dude("Bart")                   # => "Bart, Coltrane, Roach."
cool_dude("Bart", "Elwood")         # => "Bart, Elwood, Roach."
cool_dude("Bart", "Elwood", "Linus") # => "Bart, Elwood, Linus."
```

Here's an example where the default parameter references a previous parameter:

```ruby
def surround(word, pad_width=word.length/2)
  "[" * pad_width  + word +  "]" * pad_width
end
```

```ruby
surround("elephant") # => "[[[[elephant]]]]"
surround("fox")      # => "[fox]"
surround("fox", 10)  # => "[[[[[[[[[[fox]]]]]]]]]]"
```

The default parameter value is re-evaluated every time the method is called, and any variable that would be visible inside the method itself is available for the default value expression.

Variable-Length Parameter Lists

But what if you want to pass in a variable number of parameters or want to capture multiple arguments into a single parameter? Placing an asterisk before the name of the parameter lets you do just that. This is sometimes called a *splat* (presumably because the asterisk looks somewhat like a bug after hitting the windscreen of a fast-moving car).

```ruby
def variable_args(arg1, *rest)
  "arg1=#{arg1} -- rest=#{rest.inspect}"
end
```

```ruby
variable_args("one")                 # => arg1=one -- rest=[]
variable_args("one", "two")          # => arg1=one -- rest=["two"]
variable_args("one", "two", "three") # => arg1=one -- rest=["two", "three"]
```

In this example, the first argument is assigned to the first method parameter as usual. But the next parameter is prefixed with an asterisk, so all the remaining arguments are bundled into a new Array, which is then assigned to that parameter.

Folks sometimes use a splat to specify parameters that aren't used by the method but that are perhaps used by the corresponding method in a superclass. (Note that in this example we call super with no parameters. This is a special case that means "invoke this method in the superclass, passing it all the parameters that were given to the original method." More about this is found in Super Lookup, on page 114.)

```ruby
class Child < Parent
  def do_something(*not_used)
    # our processing
    super
  end
end
```

If the parameter isn't used, you can also leave off the name of the parameter and just write an asterisk:

```
class Child < Parent
  def do_something(*)
    # our processing
    super
  end
end
```

And you can pass the anonymous splat parameter to another method without giving it a name.

```
class Example
  def method_1(*)
    method_2(*)
  end

  def method_2(*array_args)
    puts array_args.join(", ")
  end
end

puts Example.new.method_1("a", "b", "c")
```

produces:

```
a, b, c
```

You do have to give the splat a name if you want to use it, though, so you can't write *.join or something like that.

You can put the splat parameter anywhere in a method's parameter list, allowing you to write this:

```
def split_apart(first, *splat, last)
  puts "First: #{first.inspect}, splat: #{splat.inspect}, " +
    "last: #{last.inspect}"
end

split_apart(1,2)
split_apart(1,2,3)
split_apart(1,2,3,4)
```

produces:

```
First: 1, splat: [], last: 2
First: 1, splat: [2], last: 3
First: 1, splat: [2, 3], last: 4
```

In practice, many developers will find this confusing.

If you cared only about the first and last parameters, you could define this method using the bare asterisk syntax:

```
def split_apart(first, *, last)
```

You can have only one array splat parameter in a method—if you had two, parameter assignment would be ambiguous. You also can't put parameters with default values after the splat parameter. In all cases the splat argument receives any values left over after the positional variables have been assigned.

Hash and Keyword Parameters

Ruby allows you to define parameters to methods using keywords, with the requirement that the arguments will also be passed using the same keyword. In Calling a Method, on page 93, we'll talk more about how those arguments are passed.

The difference between a positional and keyword parameter in the method definition is that a keyword parameter name is followed by a colon:

```
def method_with_keywords(city:, state:, zip:)
end

method_with_keywords(city: "Chicago", state: "IL", zip: "60606")
```

As with positional parameters, you can specify a default value for a keyword parameter that's not called. For keyword parameters, this involves placing the default value after the colon. Keyword parameters with default values don't need to be included in each call:

```
def method_with_keywords(city:, state: "IL", zip:)
end

method_with_keywords(city: "Chicago", zip: "60606")
```

When a method with keywords is called, each keyword parameter must either be part of the call or have a default value, otherwise Ruby raises an ArgumentError.

If a method has both positional and keyword parameters, the keyword parameters must come after the positional parameters.

You can collect arbitrary keyword arguments into a Hash with the double-splat, or **:

```
def varargs(arg1, **rest)
  "arg1=#{arg1}.  rest=#{rest.inspect}"
end

varargs("one")                           # => arg1=one.  rest={}
varargs("one", color: "red")             # => arg1=one.  rest={:color=>"red"}
varargs "one", color: "red", size: "xl"  # => arg1=one.  rest={:color=>"red",
                                         # .. :size=>"xl"}
```

As with the single splat, you can use the bare double splat (**) to ignore keyword parameters or to pass the entire hash on to another method. A bare single splat will catch positional arguments, a bare double splat will catch keyword arguments.

```
class Child < Parent
  def do_something(**)
    do_something_else(**)
  end
end
```

Ruby also allows you to use **nil to explicitly indicate that the method doesn't accept any keyword arguments. Otherwise, a method definition that uses a single splat will pull in keyword arguments as a hash. If you don't want that behavior, **nil will raise an exception.

> ### Ruby Keywords Pre 3.0
>
> We don't normally mention deprecated or removed Ruby features in this book, but this is a pattern you're extremely likely to see in older Ruby code.
>
> Before Ruby had true keyword parameters, it had a syntax that simulated them. Any arbitrary key/value pair passed after the positional parameters to a method were automatically rolled up and converted to a Hash. In other words, you could do this:
>
> ```ruby
> class SongList
>   def search(field, options = {})
>     # implementation
>   end
> end
>
> Songlist.new.search(:titles, genre: "jazz", duration_less_than: 270)
> ```
>
> Here, the genre and duration_less_than parameters would be rolled together and placed in the last parameter of the method. In this case, options (the default empty hash is there in case no extra parameters are passed). It was then the responsibility of the method to determine if the list of key/value pairs in the hash were valid.
>
> Ruby added true keyword parameters in version 2.0, and the true keyword parameters and hash parameters lived awkwardly together until Ruby 3.0, which removed the arbitrary hash parameters, fully replacing them with keyword arguments and the double splat.

Methods and Block Parameters

As we discussed in Blocks and Enumeration, on page 62, when a method is called, it may be associated with a block. Normally, you call the block from within the method using yield:

```ruby
def double(p1)
  yield(p1 * 2)
end

double(3) { |val| "I got #{val}" }          # => "I got 6"
double("tom") { |val| "Then I got #{val}" } # => "Then I got tomtom"
```

But, if the last parameter in a method definition list is prefixed with an ampersand, any associated block is converted to a Proc object, and that object is assigned to the parameter. This allows you to store the block for use later.

```ruby
tut_methods/tax_calculator.rb
class TaxCalculator
  def initialize(name, &block)
    @name, @block = name, block
  end

  def get_tax(amount)
    "#{@name} on #{amount} = #{@block.call(amount)}"
  end
end

tc = TaxCalculator.new("Sales tax") { |amt| amt * 0.075 }

tc.get_tax(100)  # => "Sales tax on 100 = 7.5"
tc.get_tax(250)  # => "Sales tax on 250 = 18.75"
```

You don't have to give the block parameter a name if you're only going to pass it along, you can just use a bare & character.

```
class Child < Parent
  def do_something(&)
    do_something_else(&)
  end
end
```

Combining all these mechanisms, if you want to roll all the arguments of a method along to a different method, then def(*args, **kwargs, &block) is an awkward way to gather all the arguments. Ruby has a simpler way:

```
class Thing
  def do_something(...)
    do_something_else(...)
  end
end
```

The triple dot syntax is an anonymous way to pass all arguments to one method onward to a different method.

Calling a Method

You call a method by optionally specifying a receiver, giving the name of the method, and optionally passing some arguments and an optional block. Here's a code fragment that shows us calling a method with a receiver, a positional argument, a keyword argument, and a block:

```
connection.download_mp3("jitterbug", speed: :slow) { |p| show_progress(p) }
```

In this example, the object connection is the receiver, download_mp3 is the name of the method, the string "jitterbug" is the positional parameter, the key/value pair speed: :slow is a keyword parameter, and the code between the braces is the associated block argument. When the method is called, Ruby invokes the method in that object, and inside that method, self is set to that receiver object. For class and module methods, the receiver will be the class or module object.

```
File.size("testfile") # => 66
Math.sin(Math::PI/4)  # => 0.7071067811865475
```

Ruby allows you to omit the receiver, in which case the default receiver is self, the current object. In this example, all the methods in write_on are called with the current object as the implicit receiver.

```
class InvoiceWriter
  def initialize(order)
    @order = order
  end

  def write_on(output)
    # called on current object, as there is no receiver
    write_header_on(output)
    write_body_on(output)
    write_totals_on(output)
  end
```

```
    def write_header_on(output)
      # ...
    end

    def write_body_on(output)
      # ...
    end

    def write_totals_on(output)
      # ...
    end
end
```

This defaulting mechanism is how Ruby handles private methods. Private methods may *not* be called with a receiver other than self, so they must be methods available in the current object. In the previous example, we might want to make the helper methods private because they shouldn't be called from outside the InvoiceWriter class:

```
class InvoiceWriter
  def initialize(order)
    @order = order
  end

  def write_on(output)
    write_header_on(output)
    write_body_on(output)
    write_totals_on(output)
  end

  private def write_header_on(output)
    # ...
  end

  private def write_body_on(output)
    # ...
  end

  private def write_totals_on(output)
    # ...
  end
end
```

If the method name ends in =, and only if the method name ends in =, Ruby allows you to call the method as the left side of an assignment statement. Ruby allows you to place whitespace between the rest of the method name and the closing =. The last two lines of this example are equivalent:

```
class Person
  def name=(new_name)
    @name = new_name
  end
end

p = Person.new
p.name = "Brandi Carlile"
p.name=("Elton John")
```

This use of methods on the left side of an assignment leads to a potential ambiguity between a local variable assignment and a method call:

```ruby
class Person
  def name=(new_name)
    @name = new_name
  end

  def change_things(new_name, address)
    name = new_name
  end
end
```

In this example, it's potentially ambiguous whether the line name = new_name creates a local variable called name and assigns new_name to it or whether it uses the implicit receiver syntax to call the method self.name= with new_name as an argument.

Ruby handles this potential issue consistently and is always in favor of creating the local variable. When calling a method on the left side of an assignment, you must specify the receiver explicitly. In this case, the highlighted line must be changed to self.name = new_name. Not doing so can lead to some hard-to-track-down bugs. (Ask us how we know.)

Passing Arguments to a Method

Any arguments follow the method name. If no ambiguity exists, you can omit the parentheses around the argument list when calling a method. Ruby documentation sometimes describes method calls without parentheses as *commands*. As you've seen, method calls that look like commands or macros, such as puts, are often written without parentheses. A lot of Ruby tools, like RSpec, skip parentheses to make their domain-specific languages flow more naturally.

But, except in the simplest cases, we don't recommend skipping parentheses—some subtle problems can trip you up. In particular, you *must* use parentheses on a method call that is itself an argument to another method call (unless it's the last parameter). Our rule is simple: if you have any doubt, use parentheses.

```ruby
# for some suitable value in obj:
a = obj.hash      # Same as
a = obj.hash()    # this.

obj.some_method "Arg1", arg2, arg3    # Same thing as
obj.some_method("Arg1", arg2, arg3)   # with parentheses.
```

Positional arguments are passed to the method based on their position, but keyword arguments are passed based on the keyword and can be listed in any order:

```ruby
def method_with_keywords(city:, state:, zip:)
  "I live in #{city}, #{state} #{zip}"
end

puts method_with_keywords(city: "Chicago", state: "IL", zip: "60606")
puts method_with_keywords(zip: "02134", city: "Boston", state: "MA")
```

produces:

```
I live in Chicago, IL 60606
I live in Boston, MA 02134
```

Method Return Values

Every method you call returns a value (although no rule says that you have to use that value). The value of a method is the value of the last expression executed by the method:

```
def method_one
  "one"
end

method_one     # => "one"

def method_two(arg)
  case
  when arg > 0 then "positive"
  when arg < 0 then "negative"
  else
    "zero"
  end
end
method_two(23) # => "positive"
method_two(0)  # => "zero"
```

Ruby has a return statement, which exits from the currently executing method. The value of a return is the value of its argument(s). An idiomatic Ruby practice is to omit the return in the last expression of a method since it's redundant, as shown by the previous two examples.

This next example uses return to exit from a loop inside the method:

```
def method_three
  100.times do |num|
    square = num * num
    return num, square if square > 1000
  end
end
method_three # => [32, 1024]
```

As this case illustrates, if you give return multiple parameters, the method returns them in an array. You can use parallel assignment to collect this return value:

```
num, square = method_three
num       # => 32
square    # => 1024
```

Splat! Expanding Collections in Method Calls

We've seen that if you prefix the name of a method argument with an asterisk, multiple arguments in the call to the method will be passed as an array. Well, the same thing works in reverse.

When you call a method, you can convert any collection, enumerable object, or object that implements to_a into its constituent elements and pass those elements as individual arguments to the method. Do this by prefixing array arguments with an asterisk:

```
def five(a, b, c, d, e)
  "I was passed #{a} #{b} #{c} #{d} #{e}"
end
```

```
five(1, 2, 3, 4, 5 )        # => "I was passed 1 2 3 4 5"
five(1, 2, 3, *['a', 'b'])  # => "I was passed 1 2 3 a b"
five(*['a', 'b'], 1, 2, 3)  # => "I was passed a b 1 2 3"
five(*(10..14))             # => "I was passed 10 11 12 13 14"
five(*[1,2], 3, *(4..5))    # => "I was passed 1 2 3 4 5"
```

Splat arguments can appear anywhere in the argument list, and you can intermix splat and regular arguments.

Similarly, you can expand hashes, or anything that implements to_h, into keyword arguments by prefixing the argument with a double-splat:

```
def method_with_keywords(city:, state:, zip:)
  "I live in #{city}, #{state} #{zip}"
end

data = {city: "Chicago", state: "IL", zip: "60606"}
puts method_with_keywords(**data)
```

produces:

```
I live in Chicago, IL 60606
```

You can also use the shortcut access syntax if the name of the keyword and the name of the variable in the local context are the same, similar to the hash shortcut we saw in Hashes, on page 56.

```
def method_with_keywords(city:, state:, zip:)
  "I live in #{city}, #{state} #{zip}"
end

city = "Chicago"
state = "IL"
zip = "60606"
puts method_with_keywords(city:, state:, zip:)
```

produces:

```
I live in Chicago, IL 60606
```

Passing Block Arguments

Earlier we saw how an & in a parameter list converted a block argument to a Proc object. You can also do this in reverse by passing a Proc object, or anything that implements the method to_proc, and prefixing it with an & to convert it to a block argument.

A common example of the use of objects that implement to_proc is Symbol. The following two lines of code behave identically:

```
["a", "b", "c"].map { |s| s.upcase } # => ["A", "B", "C"]
["a", "b", "c"].map(&:upcase)        # => ["A", "B", "C"]
```

The reason why this works is that the class Symbol implements the to_proc method, returning a Proc object that says "take the argument to this proc, and call the method whose name matches this symbol". The returned Proc object gets used as the block argument and behaves the same as the explicit block in the first line. You'll frequently see this syntax as a shortcut for methods that take simple blocks like map or sort_by.

We've already seen how to associate a block with a method call:

```
collection.each do |member|
  # ...
end
```

Usually, this is perfectly good enough—you associate a fixed block of code with a method in the same way you'd have a chunk of code after an if or while statement.

But sometimes you'd like to be more flexible. In this example, we're teaching math skills. The student could ask for an *n*-plus table or an *n*-times table. If the student asked for a 2-times table, we'd output 2, 4, 6, 8, and so on. (This code doesn't check its inputs for errors.)

```
print "(t)imes or (p)lus: "
operator = gets
print "number: "
number = Integer(gets)

if operator.start_with?("t")
  puts((1..10).collect { |n| n*number }.join(", "))
else
  puts((1..10).collect { |n| n+number }.join(", "))
end
```

produces:

```
(t)imes or (p)lus: t
number: 2
2, 4, 6, 8, 10, 12, 14, 16, 18, 20
```

This works, but it's ugly, with virtually identical code on each branch of the if statement. It would be nice if we could factor out the block that does the calculation:

```
print "(t)imes or (p)lus: "
operator = gets
print "number: "
number = Integer(gets)
if operator.start_with?("t")
  calc = -> (n) { n * number }
else
  calc = -> (n) { n + number }
end
➤ puts((1..10).map(&calc).join(", "))
```

produces:

```
(t)imes or (p)lus: t
number: 2
2, 4, 6, 8, 10, 12, 14, 16, 18, 20
```

In this version, we assign the correct block to a variable named calc, and then in the highlighted line, we pass calc to the standard method map, prefixing it with an &, (&calc).

If the last argument to a method is preceded by an ampersand, Ruby calls to_proc on the object. It removes it from the argument list, converts the Proc object into a block, and associates it with the method. In this case, the object is already a Proc, so that means that map is called with the lambda as its block argument and uses that block to convert the elements of the method receiver.

There's a shorter way to write this code. Ruby objects have a method named method, which takes a symbol and returns the object's method of the same name. We can use the same to_proc feature that symbols have:

```
print "(t)imes or (p)lus: "
operator = gets
print "number: "
number = Integer(gets)
method = number.method(operator.start_with?("t") ? :* : :+)
➤ puts((1..10).map(&method).join(", "))
```

produces:

```
(t)imes or (p)lus: t
number: 2
2, 4, 6, 8, 10, 12, 14, 16, 18, 20
```

In this case, we're using method to grab the method named :+ or :* based on the input and using the ampersand's to_proc powers to create a proc that calls that method.

What's Next

A well-written Ruby program will typically contain many methods, each quite small, so it's worth getting familiar with the options available when defining and using them. At some point, you'll probably want to read Chapter 25, Language Reference: Objects and Classes, on page 465, to see exactly how arguments in a method call get mapped to the method's formal parameters when you have combinations of default parameters and splat parameters.

Now that we have methods, we need to talk about how different classes can share functionality defined by their methods, so it's time to talk about inheritance and modules.

Sharing Functionality: Inheritance, Modules, and Mixins

One of the principles of good software design is the elimination of unnecessary duplication. We work hard to make sure that each concept in our application is expressed only once in our code. Why? Because the world changes. And when you adapt your application to each change, you want to know that you've changed exactly the code you need to change. If each real-world concept is implemented at a single point in the code, this becomes vastly easier.

We've already seen how classes help reduce duplication. All the methods in a class are automatically accessible to instances of that class. But we want to do other, more general types of sharing. Maybe we're dealing with an application that ships goods. Many forms of shipping are available, but all forms share some basic functionality, perhaps weight calculation. We don't want to duplicate the code that implements this functionality across the implementation of each shipping type.

Or maybe we have a more generic capability that we want to inject into a number of different classes. For example, an online store may need the ability to calculate sales tax for carts, orders, quotes, and so on. Again, we don't want to duplicate the sales tax code in each of these places.

In this chapter, we'll look at two different but related mechanisms for this kind of sharing in Ruby. The first, *class-level inheritance*, is common in object-oriented languages. We'll then look at *mixins*, a technique that's often preferable to inheritance. We'll wind up with a discussion of when to use each.

Inheritance and Messages

In a previous chapter, we saw that when the puts method needs to convert an object to a string, it calls that object's to_s method. But we've also written our own classes that don't explicitly implement to_s. Despite this, instances of these classes respond successfully when we call to_s on them. How this works has to do with inheritance and how Ruby uses it to determine what method to run when you send a message to an object.

Inheritance allows you to create a class that's a specialization of another class. This specialized class is called a *subclass* of the original, and the original is a *superclass* of the subclass. People also refer to this relationship as *child* and *parent* classes.

The basic mechanism of subclassing is that the child inherits all of the capabilities of its parent class. All the parent's instance methods are available to instances of the child.

Let's look at a minimal example and then later build on it. Here's a definition of a parent class and a child class that inherits from it:

```ruby
class Parent
  def say_hello
    puts "Hello from #{self}"
  end
end

p = Parent.new
p.say_hello

class Child < Parent
end

c = Child.new
c.say_hello
```

produces:

```
Hello from #<Parent:0x0000000100937780>
Hello from #<Child:0x0000000100936f60>
```

The parent class defines a single instance method, say_hello. We call that method by creating a new instance of the class, storing a reference to that instance in the variable p, and then using dot syntax, p.say_hello.

We then create a subclass using class Child < Parent. The < notation means we're creating a subclass of the thing on the right. The fact that we use the less-than sign is meant to signal that the child class is supposed to be a specialization of the parent.

Note that the child class defines no methods, but when we create an instance of it, we can call say_hello. That's because the child inherits all the methods of its parent. Also note that when we output the value of self—the current object—it shows that we're in an instance of class Child, even though the method we're running is defined in the parent.

The superclass method returns the parent of a particular class:

```ruby
class Parent
end

class Child < Parent
end

Child.superclass # => Parent
```

But what's the superclass of Parent?

```ruby
class Parent
end
Parent.superclass # => Object
```

If you don't define an explicit superclass when defining a class, Ruby automatically uses the built-in class Object as the class's parent. Let's go further:

```ruby
Object.superclass # => BasicObject
```

Class BasicObject is a very, very minimal object that's used in certain kinds of metaprogramming, acting as a blank canvas. What's its parent?

```ruby
BasicObject.superclass # => nil
```

So, we've finally reached the end. BasicObject is the root class of our hierarchy of classes. Given any class in any Ruby application, you can ask for its superclass, then the superclass of that class, and so on, and you'll eventually get back to BasicObject.

We've seen that if you call a method in an instance of class Child and that method isn't in Child's class definition, Ruby will look in the parent class. It goes deeper than that because if the method isn't defined in the parent class, Ruby continues looking in the parent's parent, the parent's parent's parent, and so on, through the ancestors until it runs out of classes. Method lookup in Ruby is actually a little bit more complex, we'll talk more about it in Method Lookup, on page 113.

And this explains our original question about to_s. We can work out why to_s is available in just about every Ruby object. to_s, it turns out, is defined in class Object. Because Object is an ancestor of every Ruby class except BasicObject, instances of every Ruby class have a to_s method defined:

```ruby
class Person
  def initialize(name)
    @name = name
  end
end

p = Person.new("Michael")
puts p
```

produces:

```
#<Person:0x0000000100e781b8>
```

We saw in the previous chapter that we can override the to_s method:

```ruby
class Person
  def initialize(name)
    @name = name
  end

  def to_s
    "Person named #{@name}"
  end
end

p = Person.new("Michael")
puts p
```

produces:

```
Person named Michael
```

Armed with our knowledge of subclassing, we now know there's nothing special about this code. The puts method calls to_s on its arguments. In this case, the argument is a Person object. Because class Person defines a to_s method, that method is called. If it doesn't define a to_s method, then Ruby looks for (and finds) to_s in Person's parent class, Object.

It's common to use subclassing to add application-specific behavior to a standard library or framework class. If you've used Ruby on Rails,[1] you'll have subclassed ActionController::Base when writing your own controller classes. Your controllers get all the behavior of the base controller and add their own specific handlers to individual user actions.

Let's look at an example where inheritance can spare us a significant amount of duplication. Imagine you're working on a task-tracker application. A task might be in one of several states—it might be done, it might be started but incomplete, or it might be defined but not started. There may be other statuses, but just those three are probably enough to make the point.

If you're writing code that interacts with the tasks in this system, you'll likely have to take a task's status into account in your code. In other words, you'll likely be forever writing code like this:

```ruby
def chatty_string(task)
  case task.status
  when "done" then "I'm done"
  when "started" then "I'm not done"
  when "unstarted" then "I haven't even started"
  end
end
```

You'll be continually switching on the status of a task. This is a form of duplication. If the list of statuses changes, every one of these if statements or case statements would need to be updated. So it seems worth trying to reduce the number of times we use that switching logic.

We can use inheritance to create a hierarchy of status classes, and then only do our switching logic once:

tut_modules/status.rb
```ruby
class Status
  def self.for(status_string)
    case status_string
    when "done" then DoneStatus.new
    when "started" then StartedStatus.new
    when "defined" then DefinedStatus.new
    end
  end

  def done? = false

  def chatty_string = raise NotImplementedError
end

class DoneStatus < Status
  def to_s = "done"

  def done? = true

  def chatty_string = "I'm done"
end
```

---

1.   http://www.rubyonrails.org

```
class StartedStatus < Status
  def to_s = "started"

  def chatty_string = "I'm not done"
end

class DefinedStatus < Status
  def to_s = "defined"

  def chatty_string = "I'm not even started"
end
```

Now, if we want to get at that particular chatty string, rather than having to do the case expression explicitly, we can write something like this:

```
Status.for(task.status).chatty_string
```

The case logic is now behind the scenes, in our Status.for method. Once we call it, we know what kind of status we have, and each kind of status knows its own behavior, so we can now call chatty_string directly on the status. More to the point, once we call Status.for, we don't need to have that case logic again; we've removed the potential duplication.

The done? method is defined in the parent class as being false, which is fine for the StartedStatus and DefinedStatus classes, but incorrect for the DoneStatus class, which therefore overrides done? to the correct value—true—for that class. There is no default for the chatty_string method though, so the parent class throws an exception if it's somehow called. This is a signal that all the subclasses must define this method.

This is a common idiom when using subclassing. A parent class assumes that it'll be subclassed and calls a method that it expects its children to implement. The parent takes on the brunt of the processing but also invokes what are effectively hook methods in subclasses to add application-level functionality. As we'll see at the end of this chapter, just because this idiom is common doesn't always make it a good design.

Instead, let's look at *mixins*, a different way of sharing functionality in Ruby code. But, before we look at mixins, we'll need to get familiar with Ruby *modules*.

In Ruby, a module can do everything that a class can do, except create instances. It turns out, that even without creating instances, it still can be useful to group related methods and data together. Let's explore how.

Modules

Modules are a way of grouping together methods, classes, and constants. Modules give you two major benefits:

* Modules provide a namespace and prevent name clashes.
* Modules can be included in other classes, a facility known as a *mixin*.

Namespaces

As you start to write bigger Ruby programs, you'll find yourself producing chunks of reusable code—libraries of related routines that are applicable in many different contexts. You'll want to break this code into separate files so the contents can be shared among different Ruby programs.

Often this code will be organized into classes, so you'll probably stick a class into each file. But sometimes you want to group things together that don't naturally form a class—for example, the methods that you want to group together may be utility methods that don't manage their own state.

An initial approach may be to put all these things into a file and simply load that file into any program that needs it. This is the way the C language works. But this approach has a potential problem—name collisions. To give an admittedly contrived example, say you write a set of trigonometry functions, sin, cos, and so on. You stuff them all into a file, trig.rb, for future generations to enjoy. Meanwhile, another developer is working on a role-playing game where characters might choose to be good or evil and codes a set of her own useful routines, including be_good and sin, and sticks them into a file called morality.rb. Now you want to add some physics calculations to this game and so you need to load both trig.rb and morality.rb into your program. But both define a method called sin. Bad news.

The answer is the module mechanism. Modules define a *namespace*, a sandbox in which your methods and constants can play without having to worry about being stepped on by other methods and constants. The trig functions can go into one module:

```
tut_modules/trig.rb
module Trig
  PI = 3.141592654
  def self.sin(x)
   # ..
  end

  def self.cos(x)
   # ..
  end
end
```

and the good and bad "moral" methods can go into another:

```
tut_modules/morals.rb
module Morals
  VERY_BAD = 0
  BAD = 1
  def self.sin(badness)
   # ...
  end
end
```

Module names are like class names, both are global constants with an initial uppercase letter. Their method definitions look similar too: module methods are defined like class methods, using the def self.method_name syntax.

If a third program wants to use these modules, it can simply load the two files (using the Ruby require or require_relative method). To reference the name sin unambiguously, our code can then qualify the name using the name of the module containing the implementation we want:

```
tut_modules/pin_head.rb
require_relative "trig"
require_relative "morals"
y = Trig.sin(Trig::PI / 4)
wrongdoing = Morals.sin(Morals::VERY_BAD)
```

As with class methods, you call a module method by preceding its name with the module's name and a period. As a result, one method is now accessible as Trig.sin, the other is Moral.sin, and the names no longer conflict. Module constants are referenced using the module name followed by two colons, which is called the *scope resolution* operator, so in this example, Trig::PI and Moral::VERY_BAD.

Mixins

Modules have another wonderful use. They can provide an alternative to inheritance as a way of extending classes. This facility is sometimes called a *mixin*. Mixins enable something very much like multiple inheritance in other languages.

In the previous section's examples, we defined module methods, methods whose names were prefixed with self. If this made you think of class methods, your next thought may well be "What happens if I define instance methods within a module?" Good question. A module can't have instances because a module isn't a class. But you can *include* a module within a class definition. When this happens, all the module's instance methods are suddenly available as instance methods in the class as well. They get *mixed in*. In fact, for method lookup, mixed-in modules effectively behave as superclasses.

```
tut_modules/who_am_i.rb
module Debug
  def who_am_i?
    "#{self.class.name} (id: #{self.object_id}): #{self.name}"
  end
end

class Phonograph
  include Debug

  attr_reader :name

  def initialize(name)
    @name = name
  end
  # ...
end

class EightTrack
  include Debug

  attr_reader :name

  def initialize(name)
    @name = name
  end
  # ...
end

phonograph = Phonograph.new("West End Blues")
eight_track = EightTrack.new("Surrealistic Pillow")

phonograph.who_am_i?   # => "Phonograph (id: 60): West End Blues"
eight_track.who_am_i?  # => "EightTrack (id: 80): Surrealistic Pillow"
```

By including the Debug module, both the Phonograph and EightTrack classes gain access to the who_am_i? instance method.

We'll make a couple of points about the include statement before we go on.

First, although include looks like a statement, it's actually a method of the Module class. The include method has nothing to do with files. The Ruby include method simply makes a reference to a module. If that module is in a separate file, you must use require or require_relative to drag that file in before using include. The require call is at the file level, and loads the module into the Ruby application as a whole. The include call is at the class level and adds the module's behavior to the class in which it's included.

Second, a Ruby include doesn't copy and paste the module's instance methods into the class. Instead, it makes a reference from the class to the included module. If multiple classes include that module, they'll all point to the same thing. If you change the definition of a method within a module, even while your program is running, all classes that include that module will exhibit the new behavior. Of course, we're speaking only of methods here. Instance variables are always different per object.

Mixins give you a wonderfully controlled way of adding functionality to classes. But their true power comes out when the code in the mixin can make assumptions about the code in the class that uses it and then can interact with that code.

Ruby uses mixin behavior in the standard library extensively. Many of the behaviors we've seen that are available to all objects are actually defined in a module called Kernel which is included into Object and therefore in all objects. Methods like puts, p, lambda, proc, and many more are added to objects using mixin behavior.

The standard Ruby module Comparable is another great example of a mixin, but one that makes an assumption about the classes that use it. Including Comparable as a mixin adds the comparison operators (<, <=, ==, >=, and >) as well as the method between? to a class. For these methods to work, Comparable assumes that any class that uses it defines the method <=>, also known as the "spaceship operator". The spaceship operator compares two values and returns -1, 0, or +1 depending on whether the first is less than, equal to, or greater than the second, respectively. As a class writer, you can define one method, <=>; include Comparable; and get six comparison functions for free.

Let's take a Person class. We'll make people comparable based on their names:

```ruby
tut_modules/comparable.rb
class Person
  include Comparable
  attr_reader :name

  def initialize(name)
    @name = name
  end

  def to_s
    @name.to_s
  end

  def <=>(other)
    name <=> other.name
  end
end
```

```
p1 = Person.new("Matz")
p2 = Person.new("Guido")
p3 = Person.new("Larry")

if p1 > p2
  puts "#{p1.name}'s name > #{p2.name}'s name"
end

puts "Sorted list:"
puts [p1, p2, p3].sort
```

produces:

```
Matz's name > Guido's name
Sorted list:
Guido
Larry
Matz
```

We included Comparable in our Person class and then defined a <=> method. We were then able to perform comparisons (such as p1 > p2) and even sort an array of Person objects.

Inheritance and Mixins

Some object-oriented languages (such as C++ or Python) support multiple inheritance, where a class can have more than one immediate parent, inheriting functionality from each. Although powerful, this technique can be dangerous because the inheritance hierarchy can become ambiguous.

Other languages, such as Java, JavaScript, and C#, support single inheritance. Here, a class can have only one immediate parent. Although cleaner (and easier to implement), single inheritance also has drawbacks—in the real world, objects often inherit attributes from multiple sources (a ball is both a *bouncing thing* and a *spherical thing*, for example).

Ruby offers an interesting and powerful compromise, giving you the simplicity of single inheritance and the power of multiple inheritance. A Ruby class has only one direct parent, so Ruby is a single-inheritance language. But Ruby classes can include the functionality of any number of *mixins* (a mixin is like a partial class definition). This provides a controlled multiple-inheritance-like capability with an unambiguous inheritance hierarchy and method lookup path.

Ruby provides two mechanisms for mixing in module behavior which are related to include but combine the module and the class differently. The behavior of include is to add the module's methods as instance methods to the class in which the module is being included, and to have those module methods be looked up after the class itself is checked for a method.

Ruby also provides the method extend. The behavior of extend is to add the methods directly to the receiver of extend rather than as instance methods of a class. As most commonly used, the effect of extend is to add the module methods as class methods:

tut_modules/extend.rb
```
module ExtendedNew
  def new_from_string(string, delimiter = ",")
    new(*string.split(delimiter))
  end
end

class Person
  extend ExtendedNew
```

```ruby
  def initialize(first_name, last_name)
    @first_name = first_name
    @last_name = last_name
  end

  def full_name = "#{@first_name} #{@last_name}"
end
superman = Person.new_from_string("Clark,Kent")
batman = Person.new_from_string("Bruce|Wayne", "|")
puts superman.full_name
puts batman.full_name
```

produces:

```
Clark Kent
Bruce Wayne
```

In this example, the ExtendedNew module is extended into the Person class, and so Person.new_from_string is available.

Ruby also provides prepend. The behavior of prepend is the same as that of include except that a method in a prepended module is executed before a method of the same name in the class. Typically, the method in the prepended module calls super so that the method in the class is also called. Prepending is often used to add logging or other logistical information to classes.

Iterators and the Enumerable Module

The Ruby collection classes (Array, Hash, and so on) support a large number of operations that do various things with the collection: traverse it, sort it, and so on. You may be thinking, "Gee, it'd sure be nice if *my* class could support all these neat-o features too!"

Well, your classes *can* support all these neat-o features, thanks to the magic of mixins and the Enumerable module. All you have to do is write an iterator called each, which returns the elements of your collection in turn. Mix in Enumerable, and suddenly your class supports methods such as map, include?, and find_all?. If the objects in your collection implement meaningful ordering semantics using the spaceship operator <=> method, you'll also get methods such as min, max, and sort.

Composing Modules

Enumerable is a mixin in the Ruby standard library, implementing a bunch of methods in terms of the host class's each method. One of the methods defined by Enumerable is reduce, which we saw previously in on page 71. This method applies a function or operation to the first two elements in the collection and then applies the operation to the result of this computation and to the third element, and so on until all elements in the collection have been used.

Because reduce is made available by Enumerable, we can use it in any class that includes the Enumerable module and defines the method each. Many built-in classes do this.

```ruby
[1, 2, 3, 4, 5].reduce(:+) # => 15
("a".."m").reduce(:+)      # => "abcdefghijklm"
```

We could also define our own class that mixes in Enumerable and hence gets reduce support:

tut_modules/vowel_finder.rb

```ruby
class VowelFinder
  include Enumerable

  def initialize(string)
    @string = string
  end

  def each
    @string.scan(/[aeiou]/) do |vowel|
      yield vowel
    end
  end
end
```

tut_modules/vowel_finder_eg.rb

```ruby
require_relative "vowel_finder"
vf = VowelFinder.new("the quick brown fox jumped")
puts vf.reduce(:+)
```

produces:

```
euiooue
```

Note that we used the same pattern in the call to reduce in these examples—we're using it to perform a summation. When applied to numbers, it returns the arithmetic sum; when applied to strings, it concatenates them. We can use a module to encapsulate this functionality too:

tut_modules/vowel_finder_sum.rb

```ruby
require_relative "vowel_finder"

module Summable
  def sum
    reduce(:+)
  end
end

class Array
  include Summable
end

class Range
  include Summable
end

class VowelFinder
  include Summable
end

puts [1, 2, 3, 4, 5].sum
puts ("a".."m").sum

vf = VowelFinder.new("the quick brown fox jumped")
puts vf.sum
```

produces:

```
15
abcdefghijklm
euiooue
```

Note that you don't need to define this particular example in Ruby since sum is already defined as part of the Enumerable module.

Instance Variables in Mixins

People learning Ruby often ask, "What happens to instance variables in a module that's used as a mixin?"

Remember how instance variables work in Ruby: the first mention of an @-prefixed variable creates the instance variable *in the current object*, self.

For a mixin, this means the module you mix into your client class may create instance variables in the client object and may use attr_reader and friends to define accessors for these instance variables. For instance, the Observable module in the following example adds an instance variable @observer_list to any class that includes it:

tut_modules/observer_impl.rb
```ruby
module Observable
  def observers
    @observer_list ||= []
  end

  def add_observer(obj)
    observers << obj
  end

  def notify_observers
    observers.each { |o| o.update }
  end
end
```

But this behavior exposes us to a risk. A mixin's instance variables can clash with those of the host class or with those of other mixins. The example that follows shows a class that uses our Observable module but that unluckily also uses an instance variable called @observer_list. At runtime, this program will go wrong in some hard-to-diagnose ways:

tut_modules/observer_impl_eg.rb
```ruby
require_relative "observer_impl"

class TelescopeScheduler
  # other classes can register to get notifications
  # when the schedule changes
  include Observable

  def initialize
    @observer_list = []   # folks with telescope time
  end

  def add_viewer(viewer)
    @observer_list << viewer
  end

  # ...
end
```

For the most part, mixin modules don't use instance variables directly—they use accessors to retrieve data from the client object. But if you need to create a mixin that has to have its own state, ensure that the instance variables have unique names to distinguish them from any other mixins in the system (perhaps by using the module's name as part of the variable name). Alternatively, the module could use a module-level hash, indexed by the current object ID, to store instance-specific data without using Ruby instance variables:

```
tut_modules/state_eg.rb
module Test
  def self.states
    @states ||= {}
  end

  def state=(value)
    Test.states[object_id] = value
  end

  def state
    Test.states[object_id]
  end
end

class Client
  include Test
end

c1 = Client.new
c2 = Client.new
c1.state = "cat"
c2.state = "dog"
c1.state   # => "cat"
c2.state   # => "dog"
```

A downside of this approach is that the data associated with a particular object won't get automatically deleted if the object is deleted. In general, a mixin that requires its own state isn't a mixin—it should be written as a class.

Method Lookup

Because of modules being mixed in, Ruby's story for method lookup becomes more complicated. In particular, what happens if methods with the same name are defined in a class, in that class's parent class, and in a module included into the class?

When a method is called, Ruby looks for a definition of the method. Typically, this search starts in the receiver's class. If the method is found there, great! Ruby executes that method. If not, Ruby continues up the search tree to included modules and superclasses.

The exact order of places that Ruby searches for an instance method is the following:

1. Methods that have specifically been added to that instance using the def foo.bar that we've seen or the class << foo syntax that we haven't talked about yet.

2. Any module that has been added to the receiver's class using prepend, the last module so added is checked first.

3. Methods that are actually defined in the receiver's class.

4. Any module that's added to the receiver's class using include, the last module so added is checked first.

5. If the method hasn't yet been found at this point, the entire loop is started over with the superclass of the receiver's class.

This continues until either a match is found or the top of the inheritance structure is reached and no match is found.

The entire list of classes and modules in this lookup path can be accessed by calling the method ancestors, as in String.ancestors. Modules that have been prepended will show up before the receiver, and superclasses and appended modules will show up after.

If no match is found, the entire loop is tried again from the receiver's class, this time for looking for a special method called method_missing. If no method_missing is found to handle the message, a NameError is thrown.

Class or module methods have a slightly different path:

*   Methods added directly to the class or module via the def self.foo or class << self syntax
*   Methods in modules that are added to the receiving class or module via extend

And so on upward via superclasses.

Super Lookup

When executing a method, if Ruby encounters the keyword super, it acts as though a method of the same name as the method being executed had been called, but starts the search later. Specifically, the method lookup for super starts one step after the point where the method being executed is located. If the method being executed is defined inside the class as a normal instance method (step 3 in the method lookup steps described in Method Lookup, on page 113), then Ruby starts looking in step 4, with included modules, and then goes looking to the superclass. If, instead, the method is defined in a prepended module (step 1 in the steps described in Method Lookup, on page 113) then Ruby starts looking in steps 2 and 3 for regular instance methods.

If super has no argument list, the same method arguments from the original method call are passed forward, if any argument list (even an empty one with empty parentheses) is specified, those arguments are passed through.

Short examples of method lookup are kind of contrived, but let's try one anyway:

```
tut_modules/lookup.rb
module Log
  def execute
    puts "logging"
    super
  end
end

module Caller
  def execute
    puts "calling"
    super
  end
end

class Parent
  def execute
```

```
      puts "parenting"
  end
end

class Child < Parent
  prepend Log
  include Caller

  def execute
    puts "childing"
    super
  end
end

puts Child.new.execute
```

produces:

```
logging
childing
calling
parenting
```

When the execute method is called, Ruby looks first at the prepended module, Log, and executes there. That method calls super, which continues the lookup chain upward, to the actual Child class. The super in that method moves up the lookup chain to the included module Caller, and the super in that method moves up the chain to Parent.

Inheritance, Mixins, and Design

Inheritance and mixed-in modules both allow you to write code in one place and use that code in multiple classes. So, when do you use each?

As with most questions of design, the answer is, well…it depends. But over the years, developers have come up with some general guidelines to help us decide.

First, let's look at subclassing. Classes in Ruby are related to the idea of types. It would be natural to say that "cat" is a string and [1, 2] is an array. And that's another way of saying that the class of "cat" is String and the class of [1, 2] is Array. When we create our own classes, you can think of it as adding new types to the language. And when we subclass either a built-in class or our own class, we're creating a *subtype*.

Now, a lot of research has been done on type theories. One of the more useful concepts is the *Liskov Substitution Principle*. The Liskov Substitution Principle states that you should be able to substitute an object of a child class wherever you use an object of the parent class—the child should honor the parent's contract. There's another way of looking at this relationship: we should be able to say that the child object *is a* kind of the parent. We're used to saying this in English: a car *is a* vehicle, a cat *is an* animal, and so on. This means that a cat should, at the very least, be capable of doing everything we say that a generic animal can do.

So, when you're looking for subclassing relationships while designing your application, be on the lookout for these *is-a* relationships.

But here's the bad news. In the real world, there aren't that many true *is a* relationships. Instead, it's far more common to have *has a* or *uses a* relationships between things. The real world is built using composition, not strict hierarchies.

In the past, we've tended to gloss over that fact when programming. When inheritance is the only scheme available for sharing code, it's easy to say things like "My Person class is a subclass of my DatabaseWrapper class." (Indeed, the Ruby on Rails framework makes this design choice.) But a person object *is not* a kind of database wrapper object. A person object *uses* a database wrapper to provide persistence services.

Is this just a theoretical issue? No! Inheritance represents an incredibly tight coupling of two components. Change a parent class, and you risk breaking the child class. But, even worse, if code that uses objects of the child class relies on those objects also having methods defined in the parent, then all that code will break too. The parent class's implementation leaks through the child classes and out into the rest of the code. With a decent-sized program, this becomes a serious inhibitor to change.

And that's why we tend to move away from inheritance in our designs. Instead, we need to be using *composition* wherever we see a case of A *uses a* B, or A *has a* B. Our persisted Person object won't subclass DataWrapper. Instead, it'll construct a reference to a database wrapper object and use that object reference to save and restore itself.

But that can also make code messy. And that's where a combination of mixins comes to the rescue, because we can say this:

```ruby
class Person
  include Persistable
  # ...
end
```

instead of this:

```ruby
class Person < DataWrapper
  # ...
end
```

If you're new to object-oriented programming, this discussion may feel remote and abstract. But as you start to code larger and larger programs, we urge you to think about the issues discussed here. Try to reserve inheritance for the times when it's justified. And try to explore all the cool ways that mixins let you write decoupled, flexible code.

What's Next

In this chapter, we looked at using Ruby modules to encapsulate code into namespaces and to share code by using the include method to mix modules into classes. We also talked about how module inclusion affects method lookup and when to use mixins versus inheritance.

Now that we've learned some of Ruby's class and object structure, let's look at some of the classes that Ruby uses for standard types.

## CHAPTER 7

Basic Types: Numbers, Strings, and Ranges

We've been having fun implementing programs using arrays, hashes, and procs, but we haven't yet covered the most basic types in Ruby: numbers, strings, and ranges. Let's spend a few pages on these basic building blocks now.

Numbers

Ruby supports integers, floating-point, rational, and complex numbers. Integers can be of any length (up to a maximum determined by the amount of free memory on your system) and are of type Integer.

Integers are assumed to be decimal base 10, but, you can write integers using a leading sign as an optional base indicator—0 for octal, 0x for hex, or 0b for binary (and 0d for decimal)—followed by a string of digits in the appropriate base.

Underscore characters are ignored in the digit string, you'll see them used in place of commas in larger numbers.

```
123456                    => 123456    # base 10
0d123456                  => 123456    # base 10
123_456                   => 123456    # underscore ignored
-543                      => -543      # negative number
0xaabb                    => 43707     # hexadecimal
0377                      => 255       # octal
-0b10_1010                => -42       # binary (negated)
123_456_789_123_456_789   => 123456789123456789
```

A numeric literal with a decimal point and/or an exponent is turned into a Float corresponding to double-width floating-point numbers in the underlying system. You must both precede and follow the decimal point with a digit—if you write 1.0e3 as 1.e3, Ruby will try to invoke the method e3 on the object 1.

The standard Ruby library contains the BigDecimal class, which is Ruby's high-precision decimal class. When you require BigDecimal, in addition to the class itself, the Kernel module gets a BigDecimal method for converting strings or numbers to BigDecimal instances.

```
require "bigdecimal"
x = BigDecimal("3.14")
y = BigDecimal("4.13")
x + y     # => 0.727e1
```

Ruby includes support for rational and complex numbers. Rational numbers are the ratio of two integers—they are fractions—and hence have an exact representation (unlike floats). Complex numbers represent points on the complex plane. They have two components, the real and imaginary parts.

Ruby has a literal syntax for both Rational and Complex numbers, but it might not be what you expect. Rationals first. If you try to directly represent a fraction like 3/4, Ruby will interpret that as integer division and return 0. To make the fraction into a Ruby Rational instance, you need to add the letter r, as in 3/4r. You can also convert decimals into rationals with this syntax, for example, 0.75r will also convert into three-fourths (but note that .75r is still a syntax error because decimal numbers need to have digits on both sides of the decimal point). Strings can be converted to rationals with the to_r method. Finally, Ruby offers a conversion method, Rational, which takes either a string or two arguments and creates a Rational instance.

```
3/4             # => 0
3/4r            # => (3/4)
0.75r           # => (3/4)
"3/4".to_r      # => (3/4)
Rational(3, 4)  # => (3/4)
Rational("3/4") # => (3/4)
```

The literal syntax for Complex numbers uses i as a suffix. Alternatively, you can convert strings via the to_c method. There is also a Complex conversion method.

```
1+2i            # => (1+2i)
"1+2i".to_c     # => (1+2i)
Complex(1, 2)   # => (1+2i)
Complex("1+2i") # => (1+2i)
```

If you were wondering, a number can be both rational and imaginary, as in 5.7ri, but the r needs to come before the i otherwise you get a syntax error.

All numbers are objects and respond to a variety of messages. Unlike Python, for example, you find the absolute value of a number by writing num.abs, not abs(num).

Finally, we'll offer a warning for users of other languages. Strings that contain only digits are *not* automatically converted into numbers when used in expressions. This tends to bite when reading numbers from a file or when trying to use the parameters from a web request.

For example, we may want to find the sum of the two numbers on each line for a file such as the following:

```
3 4
5 6
7 8
```

The following code doesn't work:

```
some_file.each do |line|
  v1, v2 = line.split    # split line on spaces
  print v1 + v2, " "
end
```

produces:

```
34 56 78
```

The problem is that the input was read as strings, not numbers. The plus operator for strings concatenates them, and that's what we see in the output. To fix this, use the Integer method to convert the strings to integers:

```
some_file.each do |line|
  v1, v2 = line.split
  print Integer(v1) + Integer(v2), " "
end
```

produces:

```
7 11 15
```

How Numbers Interact

Most of the time, numbers work the way you'd expect. If you perform some operation between two numbers of the same class, the answer will typically be a number of that same class. If the two numbers are of different classes, the result will have the class of the more general one. If you mix integers and floats, the result will be a float; if you mix floats and complex numbers, the result will be complex.

```
1 + 2      # => 3
1 + 2.0    # => 3.0
1.0 + 2    # => 3.0
1.0 + 1+2i # => (2.0+2i)
1 + 2/3r   # => (5/3)
1.0 + 2/3r # => 1.6666666666666665
```

The return-type rule still applies when it comes to division. But this often confuses folks because division between two integers yields an integer result. If you want integer division to yield a float, you can either convert one side of the division with the to_f method or multiply one side by 1.0, which is the same thing, or you can use the fdiv method.

```
1.0 / 2     # => 0.5
1 / 2.0     # => 0.5
1 / 2       # => 0
1.to_f / 2  # => 0.5
1 * 1.0 / 2 # => 0.5
1.fdiv(2)   # => 0.5
```

Looping Using Numbers

Integers support several iterators. We've seen one already: 5.times. Others include upto and downto for iterating up and down between two integers. Class Numeric also provides the more general method step, which is more like a traditional for loop.

```
3.times { print "X " }
1.upto(5) { |i| print i, " " }
99.downto(95) { |i| print i, " " }
50.step(80, 5) { |i| print i, " " }
```

produces:

```
X X X 1 2 3 4 5 99 98 97 96 95 50 55 60 65 70 75 80
```

As with other iterators, if you leave the block off, the call returns an Enumerator.

```
10.downto(7).with_index { |num, index| puts "#{index}: #{num}" }
```

produces:

```
0: 10
1: 9
2: 8
3: 7
```

Strings

Ruby strings are sequences of characters. They normally hold printable characters, but that isn't a requirement; a string can also hold binary data. Strings are instances of class String and are often created using string literals—sequences of characters between delimiters.

Ruby has a lot of different ways to create string literals, which differ in how much processing is done on the characters in the string. One kind of processing is an *escape sequence*. An escape sequence allows you to represent data that is otherwise impossible to represent in the string. Escape sequences in Ruby start with a backslash (\).

The simplest literal in Ruby is the single-quoted string. Inside a single-quoted string, only two escape sequences are recognized. Two consecutive backslashes (\\) are replaced by a single backslash, and a backslash followed by a single quote (\') becomes a single quote. In these cases, the escape sequence allows you to represent a character that would otherwise cause problems because the character has meaning to the Ruby parser.

```
'escape using "\\"'    # => escape using "\"
'That\'s right'        # => That's right
```

Note that the double quote inside the top string is handled normally.

Double-quoted strings support a boatload of escape sequences. The most common is probably \n, the newline character. For a complete list, see Table 11, Substitutions in double-quoted strings, on page 434.

Double-quoted strings also support *string interpolation*. With string interpolation, you can substitute the value of any Ruby code into a string using the sequence #{ *expr* }. If the expression being evaluated is a global variable, a class variable, or an instance variable, you can omit the braces, as in #@foo, #@@foo, or #$foo.

```
"Seconds/day: #{24 * 60 * 60}"       # => Seconds/day: 86400
"#{'Ho! ' * 3}Merry Christmas!"      # => Ho! Ho! Ho! Merry Christmas!
"The input file name is #$FILENAME"  # => The input file name is -
```

The interpolated code can be one or more statements, not just an expression—we don't recommend this, but here's an example:

```
puts  "now is #{
  def the(a)
    'the ' + a
  end
  the('time')
} for all bad coders..."
```

produces:

```
now is the time for all bad coders...
```

Some style guides prefer single quotes if interpolation isn't used because they are faster. As far as we've been able to tell, there's no significant speed difference between the two, so you'll need a different justification if you want to prefer that style quirk.

Ruby will concatenate string literals that are next to each other if no operator is between them:

```
"This" "is" "just" "one" "string" # => "Thisisjustonestring"
```

Ruby provides an alternative to single- and double-quote delimiters, which comes in handy sometimes when the string you want to quote contains the delimiter you need. The syntax is %q or %Q followed by a delimiter character. The %q delimiter is equivalent to single quote, and %Q is equivalent to double quote. In fact, the Q is optional, a % followed by the delimiter is equivalent to double quote:

```
%q/general single-quoted string/    # => general single-quoted string
%Q!general double-quoted string!    # => general double-quoted string
%Q{Seconds/day: #{24*60*60}}        # => Seconds/day: 86400
%!general double-quoted string!     # => general double-quoted string
%{Seconds/day: #{24*60*60}}         # => Seconds/day: 86400
```

Notice that the delimiter changes from line to line. Whatever character follows the initial *q* or *Q* is the delimiter—this also goes for other variants on the flexible delimiter syntax we'll see. If the character is an opening bracket [, a brace {, a parenthesis (, or a less-than sign <, the string is read until the matching closing symbol is found. Otherwise, the string is read until the next occurrence of the same delimiter. The delimiter can be any nonalphanumeric or nonmultibyte character. Current code style guidelines will often suggest that you stick to parentheses as the string delimiters, %q().

Finally, you can construct a string using a *here document,* or *heredoc.* A heredoc allows you to build a multiline string.

```
string = <<END_OF_STRING
  The body of the string is the input lines up to
  one starting with the same text that followed the '<<'
END_OF_STRING
```

A here document consists of lines in the source up to but not including the terminating string that you specify after the << characters. Normally, this terminator must start in column one. But, if you put a minus sign after the << characters, you can indent the terminator:

```
string = <<-END_OF_STRING
The body of the string is the input lines up to
one starting with the same text that followed the '<<'
  END_OF_STRING
```

And if you put a tilde after the << characters you can indent the text. Well, you can always indent the text, but if you use a ~, then Ruby will remove the indentation spaces from the beginning of each line, making it easier to lay out a long string:

```
def a_long_string
  <<~END_OF_STRING
    Faster than a speeding bullet, more powerful than
    a locomotive, able to leap tall buildings in a single
    bound—look, up there in the sky, it's a bird, it's a
    plane, it's Superman!
```

```
    END_OF_STRING
end
puts a_long_string
```

produces:

```
Faster than a speeding bullet, more powerful than
a locomotive, able to leap tall buildings in a single
bound—look, up there in the sky, it's a bird, it's a
plane, it's Superman!
```

You can also have multiple here documents on a single line. Each acts as a separate string. The bodies of the here documents are fetched sequentially from the source lines that follow:

```
print <<-STRING1, <<-STRING2
  Concat
        STRING1
  enate
  STRING2
```

produces:

```
Concat
enate
```

This is generally considered super confusing.

Note that Ruby doesn't strip leading spaces off the contents of the strings in these cases. If you want to do so, you can call a method on the initial delimiter, x = <<EOL.strip

Strings and Encodings

An *encoding* is a mechanism for translating bits into characters. For many years, most developers who used English used ASCII, a 7-bit encoding of English characters, such as binary 101 to capital A—it used to be extremely common for programming books to include a table of ASCII values as an appendix. Somewhat later, an 8-bit representation called Latin-1 that included most characters in European languages became common.

All of these were eventually superseded by Unicode,[1] a global standard for all text characters used in all languages. A Unicode character is two bytes long, which makes a Unicode string twice as long internally as a Latin-1 string. As a result, the overwhelming majority of web pages use an encoding called UTF-8, which represents any Unicode character but uses fewer bytes for ASCII or Latin-1 characters. UTF-8 isn't the only encoding you'll encounter but is the default for Ruby and the one you'll likely encounter most often.

Every string in Ruby has an associated encoding. The default encoding of a string literal depends on the encoding of the source file that contains it. With no explicit encoding specified, a source file (and its strings) is encoded using UTF-8:

```
plain_string = "dog"
puts "Encoding of #{plain_string.inspect} is #{plain_string.encoding}"
```

produces:

```
Encoding of "dog" is UTF-8
```

---

1.   https://home.unicode.org

If you want to use your own encoding for some reason (and honestly, it's hard to think of a good reason), you can use a magic comment at the top of the file to change the encoding for that file. If you override the encoding, you'll do that for all strings in the file:

```
#encoding: utf-8
plain_string = "dog"
puts "Encoding of #{plain_string.inspect} is #{plain_string.encoding}"
utf_string = "δog"
puts "Encoding of #{utf_string.inspect} is #{utf_string.encoding}"
```

produces:

```
Encoding of "dog" is UTF-8
Encoding of "δog" is UTF-8
```

If there's a shebang line, the encoding comment must be after the shebang but before any actual Ruby code:

```
#! /usr/local/rubybook/bin/ruby
# encoding: utf-16
```

The special constant _ENCODING_ returns the encoding of the current source file.

Working with Strings

String is probably the largest built-in Ruby class, with more than one hundred standard methods. We won't go through them all here; the online API documentation has a complete list. Instead, we'll look at some common string idioms—things that are likely to pop up during day-to-day programming.

Maybe we've been given a file containing information on a song playlist. For historical reasons (are there any other kind?), the list of songs is stored as lines in the file. Each line holds the name of the file containing the song, the song's duration, the artist, and the title, all in vertical bar–separated fields. A typical file may start like this:

```
tut_stdtypes/songdata
/jazz/j00132.mp3 | 3:45 | Fats     Waller      | Ain't Misbehavin'
/jazz/j00319.mp3 | 2:58 | Louis    Armstrong   | Wonderful World
/bgrass/bg0732.mp3| 4:09 | Strength in Numbers | Texas Red
```

Looking at the data, it's clear that we'll be using some of class String's many methods to extract and clean up the fields before we use them. At a minimum, we'll need to do the following:

- Break each line into fields
- Convert the running times from mm:ss to seconds
- Remove those extra spaces from the artists' names

Our first task is to split each line into fields, and String#split will do the job nicely. In this case, we'll pass split a regular expression, /\s*\|\s*/, that splits the line into tokens wherever split finds a vertical bar, optionally surrounded by spaces (more about regular expressions in Chapter 8, Regular Expressions, on page 129). And, because the line read from the file has a trailing newline, we'll use chomp to strip it off each line as we read it.

We'll store details of each song in a Struct that contains an attribute for each of the three fields. (A Struct is simply a data structure that contains a given set of attributes—which in this case is the title, name, and length. It's a shortcut for declaring a class that only has instance variables but little to no logic. For more on this subject, see Struct, on page 632.)

tut_stdtypes/read_songdata_1.rb
```
Song = Struct.new(:title, :name, :length)

songs = File.readlines("code/tut_stdtypes/songdata", chomp: true).map do |line|
  _file, length, name, title = line.chomp.split(/\s*\|\s*/)
  Song.new(title, name, length)
end
puts songs[1]
```

produces:
```
#<struct Song title="Wonderful World", name="Louis    Armstrong", length="2:58">
```

We're using readlines and map here to convert each line of the input file into its own Song.

Unfortunately, whoever created the original file entered the artists' names in columns, so some of them contain extra spaces that we'd better remove before we go much further. We have many ways of doing this, but probably the simplest is String#squeeze, which trims runs of repeated characters.

tut_stdtypes/read_songdata_2.rb
```
Song = Struct.new(:title, :name, :length)

songs = File.readlines("code/tut_stdtypes/songdata", chomp: true).map do |line|
  _file, length, name, title = line.chomp.split(/\s*\|\s*/)
  Song.new(title, name.squeeze(" "), length)
end
puts songs[1]
```

produces:
```
#<struct Song title="Wonderful World", name="Louis Armstrong", length="2:58">
```

Finally, we have the minor matter of the time format. The file says 2:58, but we want it to say the number of seconds, 178. We could use split again, this time splitting the time field around the colon character:

```
"2:58".split(":") # => ["2", "58"]
```

Instead, we'll use a related method. String#scan is similar to split in that it breaks a string into chunks based on a pattern. But, unlike split, with scan you specify the pattern that you want the chunks to match. In this case, we want to match one or more digits for both the minutes and seconds components. The pattern for one or more digits is /\d+/. Then we convert the resulting minutes and seconds to the length in seconds.

tut_stdtypes/read_songdata_3.rb
```
Song = Struct.new(:title, :name, :length)

songs = File.readlines("code/tut_stdtypes/songdata", chomp: true).map do |line|
  _file, length, name, title = line.chomp.split(/\s*\|\s*/)
  minutes, secs = length.scan(/\d+/)
  Song.new(title, name.squeeze(" "), minutes.to_i * 60 + secs.to_i)
end
puts songs[1]
```

produces:
```
#<struct Song title="Wonderful World", name="Louis Armstrong", length=178>
```

We could spend the next fifty pages looking at all the methods in class String (see Strings, on page 523 for a fuller list). For now, let's move on instead to look at a simpler data type: the range.

Ranges

Ranges occur everywhere: January to December, 0 to 9, rare to well done, lines 50 through 67, and so on. If Ruby is to help us model reality, it seems natural for it to support these ranges. In fact, Ruby goes one better: it uses ranges to implement sequences and intervals.

Ranges as Sequences

The first and perhaps most natural use of ranges is to express a sequence of values. Sequences have a start point, an end point, and a way to produce successive values in the sequence. In Ruby, these sequences are created using the .. and ... range operators. The two-dot form creates an inclusive range, and the three-dot form creates a range that excludes the specified high value:

```
1..10
"a".."z"
0...3
```

If you're looking for a way to remember which is which, you can imagine the third dot as replacing the high-end value. The two-dot form is more common in actual code, and we recommend not switching between the two—it's a subtle distinction and hard to read.

You can convert a range to an array using the to_a method and convert it to an Enumerator using to_enum.

```
(1..10).to_a        # => [1, 2, 3, 4, 5, 6, 7, 8, 9, 10]
('bar'..'bat').to_a # => ["bar", "bas", "bat"]
enum = ('bar'..'bat').to_enum
enum.next           # => "bar"
enum.next           # => "bas"
```

Sometimes people worry that ranges take a lot of memory. That's not an issue: the range 1..100000 is held as a Range object containing references to two Fixnum objects. But, convert a range into an array, and all that memory will get used.

Ruby also allows you to specify ranges that have no beginning or no end. While this can be useful for generating infinite sequences, it's also pretty useful to define a subrange for an array or string. A range starting with [..x] goes from the beginning of the sequence to index x, while [x..] goes from x to the end of the sequence:

```
arr = [1, 2, 3, 4, 5, 6]
arr[..2]  # => [1, 2, 3]
arr[2..]  # => [3, 4, 5, 6]
```

Ranges have methods that let you iterate over them and test their contents in a variety of ways:

```
digits = 0..9
digits.include?(5)          # => true
digits.max                  # => 9
digits.reject { |i| i < 5 } # => [5, 6, 7, 8, 9]
digits.reduce(:+)           # => 45
```

So far, we've shown ranges of numbers and strings. But, as you'd expect from an object-oriented language, Ruby ranges can be based on objects that you define. The only constraints are that the objects must respond to succ by returning the next object in sequence and they must be comparable using <=> (as described in Mixins, on page 107).

In reality, this isn't something you do often, so examples tend to be a bit contrived. Here's one—a class that presents numbers that are powers of 2. Because it defines <=> and succ, we can use objects of this class in ranges:

```ruby
class PowerOfTwo
  attr_reader :value
  def initialize(value)
    @value = value
  end

  def <=>(other)
    @value <=> other.value
  end

  def succ
    PowerOfTwo.new(@value + @value)
  end

  def to_s
    @value.to_s
  end
end

p1 = PowerOfTwo.new(4)
p2 = PowerOfTwo.new(32)

puts (p1..p2).to_a
```

produces:

```
4
8
16
32
```

Ranges as Intervals

A final use of the versatile range is as an interval test: seeing whether some value falls within the interval represented by the range. We do this using ===, the case equality operator, which is equivalent to the include? methods for boolean testing. Ranges also provide the cover? method, which is identical to include? for numbers, but for nonnumeric sequences the method behaves differently. The cover? method includes any item between the start and end of the range even if the item isn't in the range itself.

```ruby
(1..10) === 5               # => true
(1..10) === 15              # => false
(1..10) === 3.14159         # => true
('a'..'j') === 'c'          # => true
('a'..'j') === 'z'          # => false
('a'..'j').include?('c')    # => true
('a'..'j').include?('bb')   # => false
('a'..'j').cover?('bb')     # => true
```

Since case statements use triple-equals for comparisons, ranges are often used as a convenient shortcut for branch conditions.

```
tut_stdtypes/range_case.rb
car_age = gets.to_f # let's assume it's 9.5
case car_age
when 0...1
  puts "Mmm.. new car smell"
when 1...3
  puts "Nice and new"
when 3...10
  puts "Reliable but slightly dinged"
when 10...30
  puts "Clunker"
else
  puts "Vintage gem"
end
```

produces:

```
Reliable but slightly dinged
```

Note the use of exclusive ranges in the previous example. These are usually the correct choice in **case** statements. If instead we had written the following, we'd get the wrong answer because 9.5 doesn't fall within any of the ranges, so the else clause triggers:

```
tut_stdtypes/range_case_2.rb
car_age = gets.to_f # let's assume it's 9.5
case car_age
when 0..0
  puts "Mmm.. new car smell"
when 1..2
  puts "Nice and new"
when 3..9
  puts "Reliable but slightly dinged"
when 10..29
  puts "Clunker"
else
  puts "Vintage gem"
end
```

produces:

```
Vintage gem
```

What's Next

In this chapter, we covered some of Ruby's most commonly used types: numbers, strings, and ranges. We showed how to create literals and how to use the functionality of these types. Now let's look at one of Ruby's most powerful standard types—regular expressions.

## CHAPTER 8

Regular Expressions

We spend much of our time in Ruby working with strings, so it seems reasonable for Ruby to have great tools for working with those strings. As we've seen, the String class itself is no slouch—it has more than 100 methods. But it still can't do everything on its own. For example, we might want to see whether a string contains two or more repeated characters, or we might want to replace every word longer than fifteen characters with its first five characters and an ellipsis. This is when we turn to the power of regular expressions.

Regular expressions are powerful and are used in many languages besides Ruby. In this chapter, we'll cover the basics of what regular expressions can do in Ruby; later, in Regular Expressions, on page 440, we'll show you all the details and more complex techniques.

What Regular Expressions Let You Do

A regular expression is a pattern that can be matched against a string. It can be a simple pattern, such as *the string must contain the sequence of letters "cat,"* or the pattern can be complex, such as *the string must start with a protocol identifier, followed by two literal forward slashes, followed by...,* and so on. This is cool in theory. But what makes regular expressions so powerful is what you can do with them in practice:

- You can test a string to see whether it matches a pattern.
- You can extract from a string the sections that match all or part of a pattern.
- You can change the string, replacing the parts that match a pattern.

Ruby provides built-in support that makes pattern matching, extraction, and substitution convenient and concise. In this first section, we'll work through the basics of regular expression patterns and see how Ruby supports matching and replacing based on those patterns. In the sections that follow, we'll dig deeper into both the patterns and Ruby's support for them.

Creating and Using Regular Expressions

Ruby has many ways of creating a regular expression pattern. By far, the most common is to write the pattern between forward slashes. Thus, the pattern /cat/ is a regular expression literal in the same way that "cat" is a string literal.

/cat/ is an example of a simple pattern. It matches any string that contains the substring cat. In fact, inside a regular expression pattern, all characters except ., |, (,), [,], {, }, +, \, ^, $, *, and ? match themselves. So, at the risk of creating something that sounds like a logic puzzle, here are some patterns and examples of strings they match and don't match:

/cat/	Matches "dog and cat" and "catch" but not "Cat" or "c.a.t."
/123/	Matches "86512312" and "abc123" but not "1.23"
/t a b/	Matches "hit a ball" but not "table"

If you want to match one of the special characters literally in a pattern, precede it with a backslash, so /*/ is a pattern that matches a single asterisk, and /\// is a pattern that matches a forward slash. Those backslashes can be confusing, so Ruby provides a %r delimiter for regular expressions, similar to %q for strings. The recommended delimiter is the curly brace, so you can write regular expression literals as %r{cat} or %r{\/}.

Regular expression literals are processed like double-quoted strings. In particular, you can use #{...} expression interpolations in the pattern.

Matching Strings with Patterns

The Ruby operator =~ matches a string against a pattern. It returns the character offset of the string at which the beginning of the match occurred:

```
/cat/ =~ "dog and cat" # => 8
/cat/ =~ "catch"       # => 0
/cat/ =~ "Cat"         # => nil
```

If you only want the boolean true or false result of whether the match occurred and don't need the character offset, you can use the match? method. The use of match? is more common than the operator in current Ruby style.

```
/cat/.match?("dog and cat") # => true
/cat/.match?("catch")       # => true
/cat/.match?("Cat")         # => false
```

You can put the string on the left-hand side of either the =~ operator or the match? method if you prefer.

```
"dog and cat" =~ /cat/ # => 8
"catch" =~ /cat/       # => 0
"catch".match?(/cat/)  # => true
"Cat" =~ /cat/         # => nil
```

Because pattern matching returns nil when it fails and because nil is equivalent to false in a boolean context, you can use the result of a pattern match as a condition in statements such as if and while.

```
str = "cat and dog"

if str.match?(/cat/)
  puts "There's a cat here somewhere"
end
```

produces:

```
There's a cat here somewhere
```

The following code prints the lines in testfile that have the string on in them:

```
File.foreach("testfile").with_index do |line, index|
  puts "#{index}: #{line}" if line.match?(/on/)
end
```

produces:

```
0: This is line one
3: And so on...
```

You can test to see whether a pattern doesn't match a string using the negative match operator !~:

```
File.foreach("testfile").with_index do |line, index|
  puts "#{index}: #{line}" if line !~ /on/
end
```

produces:

```
1: This is line two
2: This is line three
```

Changing Strings with Patterns

The String method sub takes a pattern and some replacement text. (Actually, it does more than that, but we won't get to that for a while.) If it finds a match for the pattern in the string, it replaces the matched substring with the replacement text.

```
str = "Dog and Cat"
new_str = str.sub(/Cat/, "Gerbil")
puts "Let's go to the #{new_str} for a pint."
```

produces:

```
Let's go to the Dog and Gerbil for a pint.
```

The sub method changes only the first match it finds. To replace all matches, use gsub. (The *g* stands for global.)

```
str = "Dog and Cat"
new_str1 = str.sub(/a/, "*")
new_str2 = str.gsub(/a/, "*")
puts "Using sub: #{new_str1}"
puts "Using gsub: #{new_str2}"
```

produces:

```
Using sub: Dog *nd Cat
Using gsub: Dog *nd C*t
```

Both sub and gsub return a new string. (If no substitutions are made, that new string will just be a copy of the original.)

If you want to modify the original string, use the sub! and gsub! forms—often in the Ruby library, the use of ! at the end of a method name means the method modifies the receiver in place rather than duplicating it.

```
str = "now is the time"
str.sub!(/i/, "*")
str.gsub!(/t/, "T")
puts str
```

produces:

```
now *s The Time
```

Unlike sub and gsub, sub! and gsub! return the string only if the pattern was matched. If no match for the pattern is found in the string, they return nil instead. This means it can make sense (depending on your need) to use the ! forms in conditions.

Regular Expression Patterns

Like most things in Ruby, regular expressions are just objects—they are instances of the class Regexp. This means you can assign them to variables, pass them to methods, and so on:

```
str = "dog and cat"
pattern = /nd/
pattern.match?(str) # => true
str.match?(pattern) # => true
```

You can also create regular expression objects by calling the Regexp class's new method or by using the arbitrary delimiter %r{...} syntax. The %r syntax is particularly useful when creating patterns that contain forward slashes:

```
/mm\/dd/              # => /mm\/dd/
Regexp.new("mm/dd")   # => /mm\/dd/
%r{mm/dd}             # => /mm\/dd/
```

> ## Playing with Regular Expressions
>
> If you're like us, you'll sometimes get confused by regular expressions. You create something that *should* work, but it doesn't seem to match. That's when we fall back to irb. We'll cut and paste the regular expression into irb and then try to match it against strings. We'll slowly remove portions until we get it to match the target string and add stuff back until it fails. At that point, we'll know what we were doing wrong.
>
> Another option is to use the website Rubular, at https://rubular.com. Rubular allows you to enter a regular expression and a test string and shows what the match result is. The site also allows you to create a permalink for your particular regular expression and a test string which is excellent for using as a comment where the regular expression is defined in your code.

Regular Expression Options

A regular expression may include one or more options that modify the way the pattern matches strings. If you're using literals to create the Regexp object, then the options are one or more characters placed immediately after the terminator. If you're using Regexp.new, the options are constants used as the second parameter of the constructor.

i	*Case insensitive.*	The pattern match will ignore the case of letters in the pattern and string.
o	*Substitute once.*	Any #{...} substitutions in a particular regular expression literal will be performed just once, the first time it's evaluated. Otherwise, the substitutions will be performed every time the literal generates a Regexp object.

m	*Multiline mode.*	Normally, "." matches any regexp option character except a newline. With the /m option, "." matches any character.
x	*Extended mode.*	Complex regular expressions can be difficult to read. The x option allows you to insert spaces and newlines in the pattern to make it more readable. You can also use # to introduce comments.

It's worth taking a second to explore extended mode, which allows you to add whitespace and comments into the regular expression definition. If there's actually whitespace in the pattern, you need to explicitly use character classes to denote the whitespace. This can make the regular expression more readable. We'll see what all this syntax means in a moment:

```
city_state_zip = %r{
  (\w.*),          # city name followed by a comma
  \s               # a space
  ([A-Z][A-Z])     # a two character state abbreviation
  \s               # a space
  (\d{5})          # 5 digits for the US simple zip code
}x

"Chicago, IL 60601".match?(city_state_zip) # => true
```

Another set of options allows you to set the language encoding of the regular expression. If none of these options is specified, the regular expression will have US-ASCII encoding if it contains only 7-bit characters. Otherwise, it'll use the default encoding of the source file containing the literal. The options are:

- n: no encoding (ASCII)
- e: EUC
- s: SJIS
- u: UTF-8

Matching against Patterns

Once you have a regular expression object, you can match it against a string using the Regexp#match method, the boolean match? method, or the match operators =~ (positive match) and !~ (negative match). The methods and match operators are defined for both String and Regexp objects. One operand of the match operator must be a regular expression.

```
name = "Fats Waller"
name =~ /a/                        # => 1
name =~ /z/                        # => nil
/a/ =~ name                        # => 1
/a/.match(name)                    # => #<MatchData "a">
Regexp.new("all").match(name) # => #<MatchData "all">
```

The different versions return different results:

Method or operator	Return on match	Return on no match
=~	index of beginning of first match in string	nil
!~	false	true
match	MatchData object	nil
match?	true	false

After a successful match using either =~ or match, but *not* using match?, Ruby sets a whole bunch of magic global variables with data:

- The global variable $~ receives the entire MatchData object.
- The same MatchData object is also accessible as Regexp.last_match.
- $& receives the complete matched text.
- $` receives the part of the string that preceded the match.
- $' receives the string after the match.
- $1 receives the first capture group, $2 the second, and so on. More on that in Grouping, on page 138.

But these particular variables are considered to be fairly ugly, so most Ruby programmers use the MatchData object returned from the match method instead, because it encapsulates all the information Ruby knows about the match. Given a MatchData object, you can call pre_match to return the part of the string before the match, post_match for the string after the match, and index using [0] to get the matched portion.

```ruby
"Faster than a speeding bullet" =~ /speed/ # => 14
$~                                          # => #<MatchData "speed">
$&                                          # => "speed"
$`                                          # => "Faster than a "
$'                                          # => "ing bullet"

match_data = "Faster than a speeding bullet".match(/speed/)
match_data                                  # => #<MatchData "speed">
match_data[0]                               # => "speed"
match_data.pre_match                        # => "Faster than a "
match_data.post_match                       # => "ing bullet"
```

We can use these to write show_regexp, a method that shows where a pattern matches:

tut_regexp/show_match.rb
```ruby
def show_regexp(string, pattern)
  match = pattern.match(string)
  if match
    "#{match.pre_match}->#{match[0]}<-#{match.post_match}"
  else
    "no match"
  end
end
```

We could use this method like this:

```ruby
show_regexp('very interesting', /t/) # => very in->t<-eresting
show_regexp('Fats Waller', /lle/)    # => Fats Wa->lle<-r
show_regexp('Fats Waller', /z/)      # => no match
```

Regular Expression Syntax

We said earlier that, within a pattern, all characters match themselves except for . | ( ) [ ] { } + \ ^ $ * and ?. Those characters all have special meanings in regular expression patterns. First, always remember that you need to escape any of these characters with a backslash if you want them to be treated as regular characters to match:

```
show_regexp('yes | no', /\|/)        # => yes ->|<- no
show_regexp('yes (no)', /\(no\)/)    # => yes ->(no)<-
show_regexp('are you sure?', /e\?/)  # => are you sur->e?<-
```

Now let's see what some of these characters mean if you use them without escaping them.

Anchors

By default, a regular expression will try to find the first match for the pattern in a string. Match /iss/ against the string "Mississippi," and it'll find the substring "iss" starting at position 1 (the second character in the string). But what if you want to force a pattern to match only at the start or end of a string?

The patterns ^ and $ match the beginning and end of a line, respectively. These are often used to *anchor* a pattern match; for example, /^option/ matches the word *option* only if it appears at the start of a line. Similarly, the sequence \A matches the beginning of a string, and only at the beginning of a string, whereas ^ would match the first character after a newline even if it isn't the beginning of the string. Similarly, you have \z and \Z which match the end of the entire string rather than the end of a line. The difference is that \Z matches the end of a string *unless* the string ends with \n, in which case it matches just before the \n.

```
str = "this is\nthe time"
show_regexp(str, /^the/)    # => this is\n->the<- time
show_regexp(str, /is$/)     # => this ->is<-\nthe time
show_regexp(str, /\Athis/)  # => ->this<- is\nthe time
show_regexp(str, /\Athe/)   # => no match
```

The pattern \b is an anchor that matches a *word boundary*. A word boundary is the separation between a word character—an ASCII letter, a number, or an underscore—and something that isn't a word character. The string "six o'clock" has six word boundaries:

- Before the s—the beginning of the string is considered a non-word character
- After the x—between the ASCII letter x and the space
- Before the o—between the space and the letter o
- Before and after the '—because apostrophes aren't word characters
- After the k—the end of the string is also considered a nonword character

You can see where word boundaries occur by replacing every instance of a word boundary with an * using gsub:

```
"six o'clock".gsub(/\b/, "*") # => "*six* *o*'*clock*"
```

The \B pattern is the inverse, it matches the boundary between any two characters that's not a word boundary. The string "six o'clock" also has six of those.

```
"six o'clock".gsub(/\B/, "*") # => "s*i*x o'c*l*o*c*k"
```

You use these anchors to limit a match to the beginning or end of a word (\b) or prevent a match from happening at the beginning or end of a word (\B).

```
show_regexp("this is\nthe time", /\bis/) # => this ->is<-\nthe time
show_regexp("this is\nthe time", /\Bis/) # => th->is<- is\nthe time
```

Character Classes

A *character class* is a set of characters between brackets: [*characters*]. The character class pattern matches any individual character between the brackets, with no delimiter separating them, so [aeiou] matches any of the five vowels, [,.:;!?] matches some punctuation, and so on. The significance of the special regular expression characters—.|()\{+^$*?—is turned off inside the brackets. But normal string substitution still occurs. So, for example, \b represents a backspace character, and \n represents a new line.

```
show_regexp('Price $ 12.', /[aeiou]/)       # => Pr->i<-ce $ 12.
show_regexp('Price $ 12.', /[0123456789]/) # => Price $ ->1<-2.
show_regexp('Price $ 12.', /[$.]/)          # => Price ->$<- 12.
```

Within the brackets, a sequence such as c_1-c_2 represents all the characters from c_1 to c_2 in the current string encoding:

```
a = 'see [The PickAxe-page 123]'
show_regexp(a, /[A-F]/)       # => see [The Pick->A<-xe-page 123]
show_regexp(a, /[A-Fa-f]/)    # => s->e<-e [The PickAxe-page 123]
show_regexp(a, /[0-9]/)       # => see [The PickAxe-page ->1<-23]
show_regexp(a, /[0-9][0-9]/) # => see [The PickAxe-page ->12<-3]
```

It's common to see [a-zA-Z] to represent all the English letters or [0-9] to represent all the digits.

You can negate a character class by putting an up arrow (^, sometimes called a *caret*) immediately after the opening bracket:

```
show_regexp('Price $12.', /[^A-Z]/)       # => P->r<-ice $12.
show_regexp('Price $12.', /[^\w]/)        # => Price-> <-$12.
show_regexp('Price $12.', /[a-z][^a-z]/) # => Pric->e <-$12.
```

> Some character classes are used so frequently that Ruby provides abbreviations for them. These abbreviations are listed in Table 2, Character class abbreviations, on page 137. They may be used both within brackets and in the body of a pattern.

```
show_regexp('It costs $12.', /\s/) # => It-> <-costs $12.
show_regexp('It costs $12.', /\d/) # => It costs $->1<-2.
```

If you want to include the literal characters] and - in a character class, escape them with a backslash:

```
a = 'see [The PickAxe-page 123]'
show_regexp(a, /[\]]/)      # => see [The PickAxe-page 123->]<-
show_regexp(a, /[0-9\]]/) # => see [The PickAxe-page ->1<-23]
show_regexp(a, /[\d\-]/)   # => see [The PickAxe->-<-page 123]
```

Finally, a period (.) appearing outside the brackets represents any character except a newline (though in multiline mode it matches a newline, too):

```
a = 'It costs $12.'
show_regexp(a, /c.s/) # => It ->cos<-ts $12.
show_regexp(a, /./)   # => ->I<-t costs $12.
show_regexp(a, /\./)  # => It costs $12->.<-
```

Sequence	Logical intent	Characters matched
\d	Decimal digit	(?a), (?d) → [0-9] (?u) → *Decimal_Number*
\D	Any character except a decimal digit	All characters not matched by \d
\h	Hexadecimal digit character	[0-9a-fA-F]
\H	Any character except a hex digit	All characters not matched by \h
\R	A generic linebreak sequence	Matches any ASCII or Unicode linebreak may also match the two characters \r\n
\s	Whitespace	(?a), (?d) → [␣\t\r\n\f\v] (?u) → [\t\n\r\x{000B}\x{000C}\x{0085}] plus *Line_Separator, Paragraph_Separator, Space _Separator*
\S	Any character except whitespace	Any character not matched by \s
\w	A "word" character (really, a programming language identifier)	(?a), (?d) → [a-zA-Z0-9_] (?u) → *Letter, Mark, Number ,Connector_ Punctuation*
\W	Any character except a word character	Any character not matched by \w
\X	An extended Unicode grapheme (two or more characters that combine to form a single visual character)	

Table 2—Character class abbreviations

For some of these classes, the meaning depends on the character set mode selected for the pattern. In these cases, the different options are shown like this:

(?a), (?d) → [a-zA-Z0-9_]
(?u) → *Letter, Mark, Number, Connector_Punctuation*

In this case, the first line applies to ASCII and default modes, and the second to Unicode. In the second part of each line, the [...] is a conventional character class. Words in italic are Unicode character classes.

Repetition

Back in Working with Strings, on page 123, we specified the pattern that split the song list line, /\s*\|\s*/, and we said we wanted to match a vertical bar surrounded by an arbitrary amount of whitespace. We now know that the \s sequences match a single whitespace character and \| means a literal vertical bar, so it seems likely that the asterisks somehow mean "an arbitrary amount." In fact, the asterisk is one of a number of modifiers that allow you to match multiple occurrences of a pattern.

If *r* stands for the immediately preceding regular expression within a pattern, then:

*r**	Matches zero or more occurrences of *r*
r+	Matches one or more occurrences of *r*
r?	Matches zero or one occurrence of *r*
r{m,n}	Matches at least m and at most n occurrences of *r*
r{m,}	Matches at least m occurrences of *r*
r{,n}	Matches at most n occurrences of *r*
r{m}	Matches exactly m occurrences of *r*

These repetition constructs have a high precedence—they bind only to the immediately preceding matching construct in the pattern. /ab+/ matches an "a" followed by one or more "b"s, not a sequence of "ab"s. If you want a sequence of "ab"s, you need to group the pattern, /(ab)+/.

These patterns are called *greedy* because by default they'll match as much of the string as they can. You can alter this behavior and have them match the minimum by adding a question mark suffix. The repetition is then called *lazy*—it stops once it has done the minimum amount of work required.

```
a = "The moon is made of cheese"
show_regexp(a, /\w+/)          # => ->The<- moon is made of cheese
show_regexp(a, /\s.*\s/)       # => The-> moon is made of <-cheese
show_regexp(a, /\s.*?\s/)      # => The-> moon <-is made of cheese
show_regexp(a, /[aeiou]{2,99}/) # => The m->oo<-n is made of cheese
show_regexp(a, /mo?o/)         # => The ->moo<-n is made of cheese
show_regexp(a, /mo??o/)        # => The ->mo<-on is made of cheese
```

The lazy versions on lines three and six behave differently than their matching greedy versions on lines two and five.

Be careful when using the * modifier. It matches zero or more occurrences. We often forget about the zero part. In particular, a pattern that contains only a * repetition will always match, whatever string you pass it. For example, the pattern /a*/ will always match because every string contains zero or more "a"s.

Both of these examples match an empty substring at the start of the string:

```
a = "The moon is made of cheese"
show_regexp(a, /m*/) # => -><-The moon is made of cheese
show_regexp(a, /Z*/) # => -><-The moon is made of cheese
```

Alternation

We know that the vertical bar is special because our line-splitting pattern had to escape it with a backslash. That's because an unescaped vertical bar, as in |, matches either the construct that precedes it or the construct that follows it:

```
a = "red ball blue sky"
show_regexp(a, /d|e/)                  # => r->e<-d ball blue sky
show_regexp(a, /al|lu/)                # => red b->al<-l blue sky
show_regexp(a, /red ball|angry sky/) # => ->red ball<- blue sky
```

There's a trap for the unwary here because | has a very low precedence. The last example in the previous lines matches *red ball* or *angry sky*, not *red ball sky* or *red angry sky*. To match *red ball sky* or *red angry sky*, you'd need to override the default precedence using grouping, /red (ball|angry) sky/.

Grouping

You can use parentheses to group terms within a regular expression. Everything within the group is treated as a single regular expression.

The first example here, without a group, matches an 'a' followed by one or more 'n's. The second, using a group, matches the sequence 'an' one or more times.

```
show_regexp('banana', /an+/)    # => b->an<-ana
show_regexp('banana', /(an)+/) # => b->anan<-a

a = 'red ball blue sky'
show_regexp(a, /blue|red/)             # => ->red<- ball blue sky
show_regexp(a, /(blue|red) \w+/)       # => ->red ball<- blue sky
show_regexp(a, /(red|blue) \w+/)       # => ->red ball<- blue sky
show_regexp(a, /red|blue \w+/)         # => ->red<- ball blue sky
show_regexp(a, /red (ball|angry) sky/) # => no match
a = 'the red angry sky'
show_regexp(a, /red (ball|angry) sky/) # => the ->red angry sky<-
```

Parentheses do double duty in regular expressions. They also collect the results of pattern matching. Ruby counts opening parentheses and stores the result of the partial match between each opening parenthesis and the corresponding closing parenthesis. You can use this partial match both within the rest of the pattern and in your Ruby program. Within the pattern, the sequence \1 refers to the match of the first group, \2 refers to the second group, and so on. Outside the pattern, the special global variables $1, $2, and so on, serve the same purpose and are reset on every regular expression match, just like $~.

```
/(\d\d):(\d\d)(..)/ =~ "12:50am"    # => 0
"Hour is #$1, minute #$2"           # => "Hour is 12, minute 50"
/((\d\d):(\d\d))(..)/ =~ "12:50am" # => 0
"Time is #$1"                       # => "Time is 12:50"
"Hour is #$2, minute #$3"           # => "Hour is 12, minute 50"
"AM/PM is #$4"                      # => "AM/PM is am"
```

If you're using the MatchData object returned by the match method, you can index into it to get the corresponding subpatterns. This is much more common than using the global magic variables.

```
md = /(\d\d):(\d\d)(..)/.match("12:50am")
"Hour is #{md[1]}, minute #{md[2]}" # => "Hour is 12, minute 50"
md = /((\d\d):(\d\d))(..)/.match("12:50am")
"Time is #{md[1]}"                  # => "Time is 12:50"
"Hour is #{md[2]}, minute #{md[3]}" # => "Hour is 12, minute 50"
"AM/PM is #{md[4]}"                 # => "AM/PM is am"
```

The ability to use part of the current match later in that match allows you to look for various forms of repetition:

```
  # match duplicated letter
show_regexp('He said "Hello"', /(\w)\1/) # => He said "He->ll<-o"
  # match duplicated substrings
show_regexp('Mississippi', /(\w+)\1/)     # => M->ississ<-ippi
```

Rather than use numbers, you can use names to refer to previously matched content. You give a group a name by placing ?<_name_> immediately after the opening parenthesis. You can subsequently refer to this named group using \k<_name_> (or \k'_name_').

```
tut_regexp/named_regex_groups_1.rb
  # match duplicated letter
str = 'He said "Hello"'
show_regexp(str, /(?<char>\w)\k<char>/)  # => He said "He->ll<-o"
```

```
 # match duplicated adjacent substrings
str = "Mississippi"
show_regexp(str, /(?<seq>\w+)\k<seq>/)    # => M->ississ<-ippi
```

The named matches in a regular expression are also available as local variables, but only if you use a literal regexp and that literal appears on the left-hand side of the =~ operator. (So you can't assign a regular expression object to a variable, match the contents of that variable against a string, and expect the local variables to be set.)

tut_regexp/named_regex_groups_2.rb
```
/(?<hour>\d\d):(?<min>\d\d)(..)/ =~ "12:50am"   # => 0
"Hour is #{hour}, minute #{min}"                # => "Hour is 12, minute 50"

# You can mix named and position-based references
"Hour is #{hour}, minute #{$2}"                 # => "Hour is 12, minute 50"
```

Finally, the named matches also can be used as indexes into a MatchData instance.

tut_regexp/named_regex_groups_3.rb
```
md = /(?<hour>\d\d):(?<min>\d\d)(..)/.match("12:50am")
"Hour is #{md[:hour]}, minute #{md[:min]}" # => "Hour is 12, minute 50"
```

As you can see in these examples, named groups are a mixed bag. They can make the actual regular expressions look more complicated, but they can also make expressions using the result of the match clearer.

Pattern-Based Substitution

We've already seen how sub and gsub replace the matched part of a string with other text. In those previous examples, the pattern was always fixed text, but the substitution methods work equally well if the pattern contains repetition, alternation, and grouping.

```
a = "quick brown fox"
a.sub(/[aeiou]/,  "*") # => "q*ick brown fox"
a.gsub(/[aeiou]/, "*") # => "q**ck br*wn f*x"
a.sub(/\s\S+/,  "")    # => "quick fox"
a.gsub(/\s\S+/, "")    # => "quick"
```

The substitution methods can take a string or a block. If a block is used, the block is passed each matching substring, and the block's return value is substituted into the original string.

```
a = "quick brown fox"
a.sub(/^./) { |match| match.upcase }       # => "Quick brown fox"
a.gsub(/[aeiou]/) { |vowel| vowel.upcase } # => "qUIck brOwn fOx"
```

Maybe we want to normalize city names entered by users into a web application even if the city name is multiple words. They may enter NEW YORK, new york, or nEw yORk, and we'd like to store it as New York. The following method is a simple first iteration. The pattern that matches the first character of a word is \b\w—look for a word boundary followed by a word character. Combine this with gsub, and we can hack the names:

```
def mixed_case(name)
  name.downcase.gsub(/\b\w/) { |first| first.upcase }
end
mixed_case("NEW YORK") # => "New York"
mixed_case("new york") # => "New York"
mixed_case("nEw yORk") # => "New York"
```

As we saw previously, that substitution block could also be written as either { _1.upcase } or &:upcase as a second argument written.

```ruby
def mixed_case(name)
  name.downcase.gsub(/\b\w/, &:upcase)
end

mixed_case("nEw yORk") # => "New York"
```

You can also give sub and gsub a hash as the replacement parameter, in which case they'll look up matched groups and use the corresponding values as replacement text:

```ruby
replacement = { "cat" => "feline", "dog" => "canine" }
replacement.default = "unknown"

"cat and dog".gsub(/\w+/, replacement) # => "feline unknown canine"
```

Backslash Sequences in the Substitution

Earlier we noted that the sequences \1, \2, and so on, are available in the pattern, standing for the _n_th group matched so far. The same sequences can be used in the second argument of sub and gsub.

```ruby
puts "fred:smith".sub(/(\w+):(\w+)/, '\2, \1')
puts "nercpyitno".gsub(/(.)(.)/, '\2\1')
```

produces:

```
smith, fred
encryption
```

You can also reference named groups:

```ruby
tut_regexp/named_regex_groups_4.rb
puts "fred:smith".sub(/(?<first>\w+):(?<last>\w+)/, '\k<last>, \k<first>')
puts "nercpyitno".gsub(/(?<c1>.)(?<c2>.)/, '\k<c2>\k<c1>')
```

produces:

```
smith, fred
encryption
```

Additional backslash sequences work in substitution strings: \& (last match), \+ (last matched group), \` (string prior to match), ' (string after match), and \' (a literal backslash).

It gets confusing if you want to include a literal backslash in a substitution. Your first attempt might be str.gsub(/\\/, '\\\\').

Clearly, this code is trying to replace each backslash in str with two. The programmer doubled up the backslashes in the replacement text, knowing that they'd be converted to \\ in syntax analysis. But when the substitution occurs, the regular expression engine performs another pass through the string, converting \\ to \, so the net effect is to replace each single backslash with another single backslash. You need to write gsub(/\\/, '\\\\\\\\')!

```ruby
str = 'a\b\c'                # => "a\b\c"
str.gsub(/\\/, '\\\\\\\\') # => "a\\b\\c"
```

But, using the fact that \& is replaced by the matched string, you could also write this:

```ruby
str = 'a\b\c'              # => "a\b\c"
str.gsub(/\\/, '\&\&') # => "a\\b\\c"
```

If you use the block form of gsub, the string for substitution is analyzed only once (during the syntax pass), and the result is what you intended:

```
str = 'a\b\c'              # => "a\b\c"
str.gsub(/\\/) { '\\\\' } # => "a\\b\\c"
```

What's Next

So that's it! If you've made it this far, consider yourself a regular expression ninja. Get out there and match some strings. Now we'll take a more general look at Ruby expressions.

## CHAPTER 9

Expressions

So far, we've been fairly cavalier in our use of expressions in Ruby. After all, a = b + c is pretty standard stuff. That said, Ruby expressions are different than what you might see in JavaScript, Python, or Java, and there's a lot of power and flexibility there. You could write a whole lot of Ruby code without reading any of this chapter, but it wouldn't be as much fun.

One of the first differences in Ruby is that anything that can reasonably return a value does: just about everything is an expression. What does this mean in practice?

Well, for one thing, we have the ability to chain statements together:

```ruby
a = b = c = 0
[3, 1, 7, 0].sort.reverse # => [7, 3, 1, 0]
```

Code structures that are statements in languages like JavaScript or Java are expressions in Ruby. For example, the if and case statements both return the value of the last expression executed:

```ruby
song_type = if song.mp3_type == MP3::Jazz
              if song.written < Date.new(1935, 1, 1)
                Song::TradJazz
              else
                Song::Jazz
              end
            else
              Song::Other
            end

rating = case votes_cast
         when 0...10 then Rating::SkipThisOne
         when 10...50 then Rating::CouldDoBetter
         else
           Rating::Rave
         end
```

We'll talk more about if and case later in if and unless Expressions, on page 153.

Operator Expressions

Ruby has the basic set of operators (+, -, *, /, and so on) as well as a few surprises. A complete list of the operators, and their precedences, is given in Table 19, Ruby operators (high to low precedence), on page 454.

In Ruby, many binary operators are implemented as method calls. For example, when you write a * b + c, you're actually asking the object referenced by a to execute the method *, passing in the parameter b. You then ask the object that results from that calculation to execute the + method, passing c as a parameter. This is the same as writing the following (perfectly valid) Ruby:

```
a, b, c = 1, 2, 3
a * b + c      # => 5
(a.*(b)).+(c) # => 5
```

Because everything is an object and because you can redefine instance methods, you can always redefine basic arithmetic if you don't like the answers you're getting:

```
class Integer
  alias old_plus +

  # Redefine addition of Integers. This is a BAD IDEA!
  def +(other)
    old_plus(other).succ
  end
end

1 + 2      # => 4
a = 3
a += 4     # => 8
a + a + a # => 26
```

What's going on here? First off, we're reopening the Integer class to allow new definitions inside it, a feature of the Ruby object model that we talked about in Reopening Classes, on page 49. Inside the class, the keyword alias allows you to give a new name to an existing method; here we rename the + method to old_plus. The syntax here might seem odd because there's only a space between the new name and the old name. Typically, you'd use alias because you're planning on overwriting the existing method but you want that new method to still be able to access the original, as in this case, we've rewritten + to use old_plus but added 1.

More useful is that classes you write can participate in operator expressions just as if they were built-in objects. For example, the left shift operator, <<, is often used to mean *append to receiver*.

Arrays support this:

```
a = [1, 2, 3]
a << 4     # => [1, 2, 3, 4]
```

You can add similar support to your classes:

```
class ScoreKeeper
  def initialize
    @total_score = @count = 0
  end

  def <<(score)
    @total_score += score
    @count += 1
    self
  end
```

```ruby
  def average
    fail "No scores" if @count.zero?
    Float(@total_score) / @count
  end
end

scores = ScoreKeeper.new
scores << 10 << 20 << 40
puts "Average = #{scores.average}"
```

produces:

```
Average = 23.333333333333332
```

Note that there's a subtlety in this code—the << method explicitly returns self. It does this to allow the method chaining in the line scores << 10 << 20 << 40. Because each call to << returns the scores object, you can then call << again, passing in a new score. (Arrays also implement << the same way, and for the same reason.)

In addition to operators such as +, *, and <<, indexing using square brackets is also implemented as a method call:

```ruby
some_obj[1, 2, 3]
```

Here you're actually calling a method named [] on some_obj, passing it three parameters, equivalent to some_obj.[](1, 2, 3). You'd define this method using this:

```ruby
class SomeClass
  def [](p1, p2, p3)
    # ...
  end
end
```

Similarly, assignment to an element is implemented using the []= method. This method receives each object passed as an index as its first *n* parameters and the value of the assignment as its last parameter:

```ruby
class SomeClass
  def []=(*params)
    value = params.pop
    puts "Indexed with #{params.join(', ')}"
    puts "value = #{value.inspect}"
  end
end

s = SomeClass.new
s[1] = 2
s['cat', 'dog'] = 'enemies'
```

produces:

```
Indexed with 1
value = 2
Indexed with cat, dog
value = "enemies"
```

Command Expressions

If you enclose a string in backquotes (sometimes called *backticks*) or use the delimited form %x{...}, the string will (by default) be executed as a command by your underlying operating system. The value returned is the standard output of that command. Newlines will not be stripped, so the value you get back will likely have a trailing return or linefeed character.

```
`date`                  # => "Thu Nov  2 17:16:02 CDT 2023\n"
`ls`.split[34]          # => "irb.md"
%x{echo "hello there"}  # => "hello there\n"
```

You can use expression expansion and all the usual escape sequences in the command string:

```
0..3.each do |i|
  status = `dbmanager status id=#{i}`
  # ...
end
```

The exit status of the command is available in the global variable $?, also aliased as Process.last_status.

In the description of the command expression, we said that the string in backquotes would "by default" be executed as a command. In fact, the string is passed to the Kernel method called ` (a single backquote). If you want, you can override this method. This example uses Process.last_status, which contains the status of the last external process run:

```
alias old_backquote `

def `(cmd)
  result = old_backquote(cmd)
  unless Process.last_status.success?
    puts "*** Command #{cmd} failed: status = #{Process.last_status.exitstatus}"
  end
  result
end

print `ls -l /etc/passwd`
print `ls -l /etc/wibble`
```

produces:

```
-rw-r--r-- 1 root  wheel  8460 Oct 20 02:35 /etc/passwd
ls: /etc/wibble: No such file or directory
*** Command ls -l /etc/wibble failed: status = 1
```

Assignment

Almost every example we've given so far in this book has featured assignment. It's about time we said something about it.

An assignment statement sets the variable or attribute on its left side (the *lvalue*) to refer to the value on the right (the *rvalue*). It then returns that rvalue as the result of the assignment expression. This means you can chain assignments, and you can perform assignments in some unexpected places:

```
a = b = 1 + 2 + 3
a           # => 6
```

```
b              # => 6
a = (b = 1 + 2) + 3
a              # => 6
b              # => 3
```

```
File.open(name = gets.chomp)
```

Ruby has two basic forms of assignment. The first assigns an object reference to a variable or constant. This form of assignment is hardwired into the language:

```
instrument = "piano"
MIDDLE_A = 440
```

The second form of assignment involves having an object attribute or element reference on the left side. These forms are special because they are implemented by calling methods in the lvalues, which means you can override them.

We've already seen how to define a writable object attribute. Simply define a method name ending in an equals sign. This method receives as its parameter the assignment's rvalue. We've also seen that you can define [] as a method:

tut_expressions/assignment.rb
```
class ProjectList
  def initialize
    @projects = []
  end

  def projects=(list)
    @projects = list.map(&:upcase) # store list of names in uppercase
  end

  def [](offset)
    @projects[offset]
  end
end

list = ProjectList.new
list.projects = %w[strip sand prime sand paint sand paint rub paint]
list[3]    # => "SAND"
list[4]    # => "PAINT"
```

As this example shows, these attribute-setting methods don't have to correspond with internal instance variables, and you don't need an attribute reader for every attribute writer (or vice versa).

The value of the assignment is *always* the value of the parameter; the return value of the method is discarded. In the code that follows, result will be set to 2, even though the attribute setter actually returns 99.

tut_expressions/assignment_setter.rb
```
class Test
  def val=(val)
    @val = val
    return 99
  end
end
```

```
t = Test.new
result = (t.val = 2)
result    # => 2
```

You can also flip the order of assignments in Ruby using the => operator, which is sometimes called "rightward assignment" and is a special case of Ruby's general Pattern Matching, on page 163.

```
2 => x
puts x
```

produces:

2

Note that the return value of the rightward assignment itself is nil, not the value of the assignment.

Parallel Assignment

You may have had to write code to swap the values in two variables and have done so by creating a temporary variable:

```
# C, or Java, or ...
int a = 1;
int b = 2;
int temp;

temp = a;
a = b;
b = temp;
```

You can do this swap much more cleanly in Ruby with parallel assignment:

```
a, b = 1, 2    # a=1, b=2
a, b = b, a    # b=2, a=1
```

Ruby lets you have a comma-separated list of rvalues (the things on the right of the assignment). Once Ruby sees more than one rvalue in an assignment, the rules of parallel assignment come into play. What follows is a description at the logical level: what happens inside the interpreter is somewhat hairier.

When Ruby interprets a parallel assignment, the values on the left are evaluated before the values on the right.

Then all the rvalues are evaluated, left to right, and collected into an array (unless they are already an array). This array will be the eventual value returned by the overall assignment.

Next, the left side result is inspected. If it contains a single element, the array is assigned to that element.

```
a = 1, 2, 3, 4    # a=[1, 2, 3, 4]
b = [1, 2, 3, 4]  # b=[1, 2, 3, 4]
```

If the left side contains a comma, Ruby matches values on the right side against successive elements on the left side. Excess elements are discarded.

```
a, b = 1, 2, 3, 4    # a=1, b=2
c, = 1, 2, 3, 4      # c=1
```

Splats and Assignment

If Ruby sees any splats on the right side of an assignment (that is, rvalues preceded by an asterisk), each will be expanded inline into its constituent values during the evaluation of the rvalues and before the assignment to lvalues starts:

```
a, b, c, d, e = *(1..2), 3, *[4, 5]    # a=1, b=2, c=3, d=4, e=5
```

Exactly one lvalue may be a splat. This makes it greedy—it'll end up being an array, and that array will contain as many of the corresponding rvalues as possible. So, if the splat is the last lvalue, it'll soak up any rvalues that are left after assigning rvalues to previous lvalues:

```
a, *b = 1, 2, 3    # a=1, b=[2, 3]
a, *b = 1          # a=1, b=[]
```

If the splat isn't the last lvalue, then Ruby ensures that the lvalues that follow it will all receive values from rvalues at the end of the right side of the assignment. The splat lvalue will soak up only enough rvalues to leave one for each of the remaining lvalues.

```
*a, b = 1, 2, 3, 4          # a=[1, 2, 3], b=4
c, *d, e = 1, 2, 3, 4       # c=1, d=[2, 3], e=4
f, *g, h, i, j = 1, 2, 3, 4 # f=1, g=[], h=2, i=3, j=4
```

As with method parameters, you can use a raw asterisk to ignore some rvalues:

```
first, *, last = 1,2,3,4,5,6    # first=1, last=6
```

Nested Assignments

The left side of an assignment may contain a parenthesized list of terms. Ruby treats these terms as if they were a nested assignment statement. It extracts the corresponding rvalue, assigning it to the parenthesized terms, before continuing with the higher-level assignment.

```
a, (b, c), d = 1,2,3,4         # a=1, b=2, c=nil, d=3
a, (b, c), d = [1,2,3,4]       # a=1, b=2, c=nil, d=3
a, (b, c), d = 1,[2,3],4       # a=1, b=2, c=3, d=4
a, (b, c), d = 1,[2,3,4],5     # a=1, b=2, c=3, d=5
a, (b,*c), d = 1,[2,3,4],5     # a=1, b=2, c=[3, 4], d=5
```

Operator Plus Assignment

Ruby has a syntactic shortcut for applying an operation to a value and immediately assigning that value the new result: a = a + 2 may be written as a += 2. The second form is converted internally to the first. This means that the operators you've defined as methods in your own classes work as you'd expect:

```
class List
  def initialize(*values)
```

```
    @list = values
  end

  def +(other)
    @list.push(other)
  end

end

a = List.new(1, 2)      # => [1, 2]
a += 3                  # => [1, 2, 3]
```

Ruby doesn't have the autoincrement (++) and autodecrement (–) operators that C, Java, and JavaScript have. Use the += and -= forms instead.

Conditional Execution

Ruby has several different mechanisms for the conditional execution of code; they should feel similar to other programming languages, but many have some neat twists. Before we get into them, we need to spend a short time looking at boolean expressions.

Boolean Expressions

Ruby has a simple definition of truth. Any value that isn't nil or the constant false is true—"cat", 99, 0, and :a_song—are all considered true. An empty string "", an empty array [], and an empty hash {} are all true in Ruby. (You'll sometimes see Rubyists refer to the set of all false values as "falsey" and the set of all true values as "truthy".)

In this book, when we want to talk about a general true or false value, we use regular Roman type: true and false. When we want to refer to the actual constants, we write true and false.

The fact that nil is considered to be false is convenient. For example, gets, which returns the next line from a file, returns nil at the end of the file, enabling you to write loops such as this:

```
while (line = gets)
 # process line
end
```

And, Or, and Not

Ruby supports all the standard boolean operators. Both the keyword and and the operator && (logical and) return their first argument if it's falsey. Otherwise, they evaluate and return their second argument (this is sometimes known as *short circuit* evaluation).

```
nil && 99    # => nil
false && 99 # => false
"cat" && 99 # => 99
```

The only difference in the two forms is precedence—the && operator has higher precedence than and, meaning that where there's a choice of operators to evaluate, && will be evaluated first but and will be evaluated last.

```
result = "a" && "b"
result     # => "b"

result = "a" and "b"
result     # => "a"
```

In the first line, the operator && has higher precedence than the assignment, so it's evaluated first, returning "b", and the result is set to "b", as if the line was written result = ("a" && "b").

In the second line, the assignment has higher precedence than and, so the result is set to "a" first, and then the and is evaluated, as if it was written (result = "a") and "b". The entire sequence still returns "b", but in the second line, the result is set to "a". We strongly recommend that you use parentheses when the order of execution might be ambiguous or confusing.

The && and and operators return a true value only if both of their arguments are true.

Similarly, both or and || return their first argument unless it's falsey, in which case they evaluate and return their second argument.

```
nil   || 99   # => 99
false || 99 # => 99
"cat" || 99 # => "cat"
```

As with and, the only difference between or and || is their precedence. To make life interesting, and and or have the same precedence, but && has a higher precedence than ||.

The spelled-out versions of and and or are useful as a kind of control flow. EXPRESSION or exit will perform the expression, no matter how complex it is, and return that value if it's truthy, exiting only if the entire expression is false.

A common idiom is to use ||= to assign a value to a variable only if that variable isn't already set:

```
var ||= "default value"
```

This is almost, but not quite, the same as var = var || "default value". It differs in that no assignment is made at all if the variable is already set. In pseudocode, this might be written as var = "default value" unless var or as var || var = "default value".

not and ! (logical not) return the opposite of their operand (false if the operand is any true value and true if the operand is any false value). And, yes, not and ! differ only in precedence. You'll sometimes see a !! used as an implicit conversion to boolean, since the first ! converts any value to either true or false and the second ! reverses the value to match the boolean status of the original value. Teams will have different opinions about whether !! is good style, so keep an eye out for that.

All these precedence rules are summarized in Table 19, Ruby operators (high to low precedence), on page 454.

The defined? Keyword

The defined? keyword returns nil if its argument (which can be an arbitrary expression) isn't defined in the current scope; otherwise, it returns a description of that argument. If the argument is yield, defined? returns the string "yield" if a code block is associated with the current context.

```
defined? 1         # => "expression"
defined? dummy     # => nil
defined? printf    # => "method"
defined? String    # => "constant"
defined? $_        # => "global-variable"
defined? Math::PI # => "constant"
```

```
defined? a = 1      # => "assignment"
defined? 42.abs     # => "method"
defined? nil        # => "nil"
```

Comparing Objects

In addition to the boolean operators, Ruby objects support comparison using the methods ==, ===, <=>, =~, eql?, and equal? (see Table 3, Common comparison operators, on page 153). All but <=> are defined in class Object but are often overridden by descendants to provide appropriate semantics. For example, class Array redefines == so that two array objects are equal if they have the same number of elements and the corresponding elements are equal.

It's relatively rare to see eql? or equal? in Ruby code. Also, if you're familiar with JavaScript, please note that triple equal, ===, means something very different in Ruby than in JavaScript.

Both == and =~ have negated forms, != and !~. When evaluating the negated versions, Ruby first looks for methods called != or !~, calling them if found. If not, it'll then invoke either == or =~, negating the result.

In the following example, Ruby calls the == method to perform both comparisons:

tut_expressions/equality.rb
```ruby
class Type
  def ==(other)
    puts "Comparing self == #{other}"
    other == "value"
  end
end

t = Type.new
p(t == "value")
p(t != "value")
```

produces:
```
Comparing self == value
true
Comparing self == value
false
```

If instead we explicitly define !=, Ruby calls it:

tut_expressions/negated_equality.rb
```ruby
class Type
  def ==(other)
    puts "Comparing self == #{other}"
    other == "value"
  end

  def !=(other)
    puts "Comparing self != #{other}"
    other != "value"
  end
end

t = Type.new
p(t == "value")
p(t != "value")
```

produces:
```
Comparing self == value
true
Comparing self != value
false
```

You can use a Ruby range as a boolean expression. A range such as exp1..exp2 will evaluate as false until exp1 becomes true. The range will then evaluate as true until exp2 becomes true.

Once this happens, the range resets, ready to fire again.

Operator	Meaning
==	Test for equal value.
===	Test for "matching" as defined by the type of the operand. Used most often to compare each of the items with the target in the when clause of a case statement.
<=>	General comparison operator. Returns -1, 0, or +1, depending on whether its receiver is less than, equal to, or greater than its argument.
<, <=, >=, >	Comparison operators for less than, less than or equal, greater than or equal, and greater than.
=~	Regular expression pattern match.
eql?	True if the receiver and argument have both the same type and equal values. 1 == 1.0 returns true, but 1.eql?(1.0) is false.
equal?	True if the receiver and argument have the same object ID.

Table 3—Common comparison operators

if and unless Expressions

An if expression in Ruby is pretty similar to if statements in other languages:

```
if artist == "Gillespie" then
  handle = "Dizzy"
elsif artist == "Parker" then
  handle = "Bird"
else
  handle = "unknown"
end
```

The then keyword is optional if you lay out your statements on multiple lines:

```
if artist == "Gillespie"
  handle = "Dizzy"
elsif artist == "Parker"
  handle = "Bird"
else
  handle = "unknown"
end
```

But, if you want to lay out your code more tightly, you must separate the boolean expression from the following statements with the then keyword:

```
if artist == "Gillespie" then handle = "Dizzy"
elsif artist == "Parker" then handle = "Bird"
```

```
else handle = "unknown"
end
```

You can have zero or more elsif clauses and an optional else clause. And notice that there's no e in the middle of elsif.

As we've said before, an if statement is an expression—it returns a value. You don't have to use the value of an if statement, but it can come in handy:

```
handle = if artist == "Gillespie"
           "Dizzy"
         elsif artist == "Parker"
           "Bird"
         else
           "unknown"
         end
```

Ruby also has a negated form of the if statement:

```
unless volume.nil?
  play_the_song
end
```

The unless statement does support else, but it's always clearer to switch to an if statement in these cases.

Finally, Ruby also supports the ternary operator conditional expression, as seen in C, Java-Script, and Java:

```
cost = duration > 180 ? 0.35 : 0.25
```

A ternary expression returns the value of the expression either before or after the colon, depending on whether the boolean expression before the question mark is true or false. In the previous example, if the duration is greater than three minutes, the expression returns 0.35. For shorter durations, it returns 0.25. The result is then assigned to cost.

if and unless Modifiers

Statement modifiers let you tack conditional statements onto the end of a normal statement:

```
mon, day, year = $1, $2, $3 if date =~ /(\d\d)-(\d\d)-(\d\d)/
puts "a = #{a}" if $DEBUG
print total unless total.zero?
```

For an if modifier, the preceding expression will be evaluated only if the condition is true. The unless modifier works the other way around:

```
File.foreach("/etc/passwd") do |line|
  next if line =~ /^#/          # Skip comments
  parse(line) unless line =~ /^$/   # Don't parse empty lines
end
```

case Expressions

The Ruby case expression is a powerful beast: a multiway if on steroids.

A Ruby case expression can be written as basically a series of if statements. It lets you list a series of conditions and execute a statement corresponding to the first one that's true:

```
case
when song.name == "Misty"
  puts "Not again!"
when song.duration > 120
  puts "Too long!"
when Time.now.hour > 21
  puts "It's too late"
else
  song.play
end
```

The else clause at the end is optional and is evaluated if none of the earlier expressions are true.

Note that standard Ruby style has the when statements at the same level as the parent case, not indented.

More commonly, you can specify a target at the top of the case statement, and each when clause lists one or more comparisons to be tested against that target:

```
case command
when "debug"
  dump_debug_info
  dump_symbols
when /p\s+(\w+)/
  dump_variable($1)
when "quit", "exit"
  exit
else
  print "Illegal command: #{command}"
end
```

The first comparison to match the target is evaluated. Again, the else clause is optional and evaluates if none of the other clauses do.

Unlike JavaScript, you don't need to explicitly break out of each when clause, Ruby will only evaluate the expression of the first clause to match.

As with if, case returns the value of the last expression executed, and you can use a then keyword to place the expression on the same line as the condition:

```
kind = case year
  when 1850..1889 then "Blues"
  when 1890..1909 then "Ragtime"
  when 1910..1929 then "New Orleans Jazz"
  when 1930..1939 then "Swing"
  else "Jazz"
end
```

A case expression operates by comparing the target (the expression after the keyword case) with each of the comparison expressions after the when keywords. This test is a little unusual in that it uses an operator that's unique to Ruby, the === operator. Please note that Ruby's === is different than JavaScript's. Ruby's means "matches, as defined by the type of the left operand," which is different from JavaScript's "equal and of the same type" operator.

What does _comparison_ === _target_ mean? It depends on how the class defines it. Different classes define different meaningful semantics for ===.

For example, regular expressions define === as a pattern match:

```
case line
when /title=(.*)/
  puts "Title is #$1"
when /track=(.*)/
  puts "Track is #$1"
end
```

Ruby classes are instances of class Class. (Try saying that three times quickly.) The === operator is defined in Class to test whether the argument is an instance of the receiver or one of its superclasses. So (abandoning the benefits of polymorphism and bringing the gods of refactoring down around your ears), you can test the class of objects:

```
case shape
when Square, Rectangle
  # ...
when Circle
  # ...
when Triangle
  # ...
else
  # ...
end
```

This example shows another syntactic feature of Ruby's case statement, which is that if you have multiple comparisons for the same result, you can put them in the same when statement and separate them with a comma, as this example does with Square, Rectangle.

There are a couple of other interesting uses of ===. For a Range, === means the target is inside the range. A Set is === if the target is in the set. A Proc checks for === by calling the proc with the target as an argument and using the truth value of whatever the proc returns.

Safe Navigation

It's common to have a chain of method calls on a series of objects. For example, you might want to retrieve a string from a hash and perform other processing on it:

```
data[:name].upcase
```

There's only one problem: you might have no way of knowing if data[:name] returns a value or returns nil. If a value is returned, great! The line of code works as intended. If nil is returned, there's a problem because nil.upcase isn't defined and will raise an exception.

As a result, checking for nil is a common pattern:

```
name = data[:name]
if name then name.upcase else nil end
```

This is often written with the && as a shortcut:

```
data[:name] && data[:name].upcase
```

But this version is a little awkward, and it requires the fetch to be executed twice.

To make this pattern a little nicer, Ruby offers the *safe navigation* operator, &. (ampersand followed by a dot). You'll sometimes see this called the lonely operator because Matz thought that the ampersand dot combination looked like a person sitting alone staring off into space. It works like this:

```
data[:name]&.upcase
```

The way the &. operator works is that if the receiver of the message on the left side (in this case data[:name]) is nil, then the message isn't sent and the nil value is returned without raising an exception. If the receiver isn't nil, then the message is processed normally.

This is what we want—the code works as desired for both nil and non-nil values for the data[:name].

The safe navigation operator's powers only last for the one message. If you want to continue with more downstream messages, you need more safe navigation operators.

```
data[:name]&.upcase&.strip&.split
```

The safe navigation operator is a great shortcut, but it's not a substitute for software design. If you have a lot of values and you don't know whether or not they are nil, it's worth thinking about whether there's a better way to structure the code.

Loops and Iterators

We discussed Ruby blocks and iterators back in Chapter 4, Collections, Blocks, and Iterators, on page 53. In this section, we'll talk about all of Ruby's looping constructs in more depth.

Loops

Ruby has primitive built-in looping constructs, separate from the iterator constructs we've already seen.

The most basic loop of all that Ruby provides is a built-in iterator method called loop:

```
loop do
  # block ...
end
```

The loop iterator calls the associated block forever (or at least until you break out of the loop, but you'll have to read ahead to find out how to do that).

The while loop executes its body zero or more times as long as its condition is true. For example, this idiom reads until the input is exhausted, assigning each line to the local variable line:

```
while (line = gets)
  # ...
end
```

The until loop is the opposite; it executes the body *until* the condition becomes true:

```
until play_list.duration > 60
  play_list.add(song_list.pop)
end
```

As with if and unless, you can use both of the loops as statement modifiers:

```
a = 1
a *= 2  while a < 100
a               # => 128
a -= 10 until a < 100
a               # => 98
```

Earlier, we said that a range can be used as a kind of flip-flop, returning true when some event happens and then staying true until a second event occurs. This facility is normally used within loops. In the example that follows, we read a text file containing the first ten ordinal numbers ("first," "second," and so on) but print only the lines starting with the one that matches "third" and ending with the one that matches "fifth":

```
file = File.open("ordinal")
while line = file.gets
  puts(line)  if line =~ /third/ .. line =~ /fifth/
end
```

produces:

```
third
fourth
fifth
```

The start and end of a range used in a boolean expression can themselves be expressions. These are evaluated each time the overall boolean expression is evaluated. For example, the following code uses the fact that the variable $. contains the current input line number to display the first three lines as well as those lines between a match of /eig/ and /nin/:

```
File.foreach("ordinal") do |line|
  if (($. == 1) || line =~ /eig/) .. (($. == 3) || line =~ /nin/)
    print line
  end
end
```

produces:

```
first
second
third
eighth
ninth
```

You'll come across a wrinkle when you use while and until as statement modifiers. If the statement they are modifying is a begin…end block, the code in the block will always execute at least one time, regardless of the value of the boolean expression:

```
print "Hello\n" while false
begin
  print "Goodbye\n"
end while false
```

produces:

```
Goodbye
```

Iterators

If you read the beginning of the previous section, you may have been discouraged. "Ruby has primitive built-in looping constructs," it said. Don't despair, gentle reader, for we have good news. Ruby doesn't need sophisticated built-in loops because all the fun stuff is implemented using Ruby's iterators.

As we'll see, even Ruby's for loop is defined in terms of Ruby iterators.

Ruby uses methods defined in various built-in classes to provide equivalent, but less error-prone functionality to other languages' primitive for loops.

Let's look at some examples:

```ruby
3.times do
  print "Ho! "
end
```

produces:

```
Ho! Ho! Ho!
```

It's easy to avoid fence-post and off-by-one errors; this loop will execute three times, period. In addition to times, integers can loop over specific ranges by calling downto and upto, and all numbers can loop using step. For instance, a simple "for" loop that runs from 0 to 9 (something that you'd write in JavaScript as for(let i = 0; i < 10; i++)) is written as follows:

```ruby
0.upto(9) do |x|
  print x, " "
end
```

produces:

```
0 1 2 3 4 5 6 7 8 9
```

A loop from 0 to 12 by 3 can be written as follows:

```ruby
0.step(12, 3) { |x| print x, " " }
```

produces:

```
0 3 6 9 12
```

Similarly, iterating over arrays and other containers is easy if you use their each method:

```ruby
[ 1, 1, 2, 3, 5 ].each { |val| print val, " " }
```

produces:

```
1 1 2 3 5
```

And once a class supports each, it can also include Enumerable, and the additional methods in the Enumerable module become available. (We talked about this back in Chapter 6, Sharing Functionality: Inheritance, Modules, and Mixins, on page 101.) For example, the File class provides an each method, which returns each line of a file in turn. Using the grep method in Enumerable, we could iterate over only those lines that end with a d:

```ruby
File.open("ordinal").grep(/d$/) do |line|
  puts line
end
```

produces:

```
second
third
```

for ... in

Earlier we said that the only built-in Ruby looping primitives were while and until. Technically, that's not true, Ruby does have a for keyword. What's this for thing, then? Well, for is a different way to write an each loop.

When you write this:

```ruby
for song in playlist
  song.play
end
```

Ruby translates it into something like this:

```ruby
playlist.each do |song|
  song.play
end
```

The only difference between the for loop and the each form is the scope of local variables that are defined in the body.

You can use for to iterate over any object that responds to the method each, such as an Array or a Range:

```ruby
for i in ['fee', 'fi', 'fo', 'fum']
  print i, " "
end

for i in 1..3
  print i, " "
end

for i in File.open("ordinal").find_all { |line| line =~ /d$/ }
  print i.chomp, " "
end
```

produces:

```
fee fi fo fum 1 2 3 second third
```

As long as your class defines a sensible each method, you can use a for loop to traverse its objects:

```ruby
class Periods
  def each
    yield "Classical"
    yield "Jazz"
    yield "Rock"
  end
end

periods = Periods.new
for genre in periods
  print genre, " "
end
```

produces:

```
Classical Jazz Rock
```

break, redo, and next

The loop control constructs break, redo, and next let you alter the normal flow through a loop or iterator.

break terminates the immediately enclosing loop; control resumes at the statement following the block. redo repeats the current iteration of the loop from the start but without reevaluating the condition or fetching the next element in an iterator. next skips to the end of the loop, effectively starting the next iteration:

```
while (line = gets)
  next  if line.matches?(/^\s*#/)  # skip comments
  break if line.matches?(/^END/)   # stop at end

  # substitute stuff in backticks and try again
  redo if line.gsub!(/`(.*?)`/) { eval($1) }

  # process line ...
end
```

These keywords can also be used within blocks. Although you can use them with any block, they make the most sense when the block is being used for iteration:

```
i=0
loop do
  i += 1
  next if i < 3
  print i
  break if i > 4
end
```

produces:

```
345
```

A value may be passed to break or next. A value passed to break is returned as the value of the loop when the break is triggered. A value passed to next is effectively lost, while you can pass a value to next, there's no reason to do so. If a conventional loop doesn't execute a break, its value is nil.

Here's a contrived example:

```
result = while (line = gets)
  break(line) if line =~ /answer/
end

process_answer(result) if result
```

Variable Scope, Loops, and Blocks

The while, until, and for loops are built into the language and don't introduce new scope. Previously existing locals can be used in the loop, and any new locals created will be available afterward. Depending on what languages you might be used to, this will either seem normal (Python), very weird (Java), or actually a model of relative clarity (JavaScript).

The scoping rules for blocks (such as those used by loop and each) are different. Normally, the local variables created in these blocks aren't accessible outside the block:

```
[1, 2, 3].each do |x|
  y = x + 1
end
[x, y]
```

produces:

```
[x, y]
 ^
prog.rb:4:in `<main>': undefined local variable or method `x' for main
(NameError)
```

But, if at the time the block executes a local variable already exists with the same name as that of a variable in the block, the existing local variable will be used in the block. So its value will be available after the block finishes. As the following example shows, this applies to normal variables in the block but not to the block's parameters:

```
x = "initial value"
y = "another value"
[1, 2, 3].each do |x|
  y = x + 1
end
[x, y]    # => ["initial value", 4]
```

Note that the assignment to the outer variable doesn't have to be executed. The Ruby interpreter just needs to see that the variable exists on the left side of an assignment:

```
a = "never used" if false
[99].each do |i|
  a = i
end
a          # => 99
```

The a = i statement in the block sets the outer value of a even though a = "never used" isn't executed.

You can list *block-local variables* in the block's parameter list, preceded by a semicolon. This code doesn't use block-locals:

```
square = "yes"
total = 0

[1, 2, 3].each do |val|
  square = val * val
  total += square
end

puts "Total = #{total}, square = #{square}"
```

produces:

```
Total = 14, square = 9
```

In contrast, the following code, which uses a block-local variable, square in the outer scope isn't affected by a variable of the same name within the block:

```
square = "yes"
total = 0

[1, 2, 3].each do |val; square|
```

```
    square = val * val
    total += square
end
puts "Total = #{total}, square = #{square}"
```

produces:

```
Total = 14, square = yes
```

If you're concerned about the scoping of variables with blocks, turn on Ruby warnings, and declare your block-local variables explicitly.

Pattern Matching

When you're dealing with a complicated data structure, but you only need to use part of the structure, it can be awkward to access the structure through regular [] methods, with something like movies[:mcu][1][:actors][1][:first_name]. Not only is the access complicated but validating that the data has the shape you're looking for can also be difficult.

In Ruby, *pattern matching* is designed to make both these tasks easier by allowing you to specify the structure of the data as a pattern, and assign values to the parts of the data that match. Please note that many programming languages have features they call "pattern matching," but Ruby's implementation is somewhat different from many of these. The most similar seems to be in Python.

Pattern matching in Ruby compares a *target*, which can be any Ruby object, to a *pattern*. A pattern is also a Ruby object, but the pattern can also contain the names of not-yet-defined local variables. If the target matches the pattern, the target is deconstructed into the pattern, setting the value of those variables.

Single-Line Pattern Matching

Ruby uses the keyword in to match a target to a pattern. When used this way, the expression returns true if the target matches and false if it doesn't.

The simplest pattern match is that values match themselves:

```
"banana" in "banana" # => true
"banana" in "apple"  # => false
3 in 3               # => true
3 in 5               # => false
2i in 2i             # => true
```

Behind the scenes, the pattern match for values uses the same === triple-equal operator that case statements do. This means that classes that implement === can do more general matches. As we saw earlier, a class is === to instances of that class, regular expressions are === to strings that match the expression, and ranges are === to elements covered by the range.

So we can write the following patterns:

```
"banana" in String  # => true
"banana" in Integer # => false
"banana" in /b(an+)/ # => true
3 in 1..10           # => true
```

That's starting to look a little more interesting.

The next step is that you can match not only scalar values but also arrays and hashes. Each subelement of the array or hash can be a pattern that matches the associated element in the target. For an array, every element in the array must match the associated pattern element. For a hash, only keys in the pattern must match. The existence of other keys in the target doesn't fail the match. If you want to have an exact hash match, you need to include **nil in the pattern.

```
[1, 2, 3] in [Integer, Integer, Integer]              # => true
[3, "banana", "apple"] in [1..10, String, /p{2}/] # => true
{name: "Fred", city: "Bedrock"} in {city: String} # => true
{name: "Fred", city: "Bedrock"} in {}                 # => false
```

That last line shows that the empty hash is treated differently—an empty hash only matches another empty hash.

You can use * at the end of an array pattern to indicate rest, and you can use one at the front to indicate a "find pattern", where you're looking for an element in the middle.

```
[1, "potato", 2, "potato"] in [Integer, "potato", Integer, "potato"] # => true
[1, "potato", 2, "potato"] in [Integer, "potato", *]                  # => true
[1, "potato", 2, "potato"] in [*, "potato", 2, *]                     # => true
```

You can nest the data:

```
{likes: [3, 5], dislikes: [2, 4]} in {likes: [3, *], dislikes: [2, *]} # => true
```

And you can provide multiple patterns using "or" logic:

```
[1, 2, 3] in [Integer, Integer, Integer] | [String, String, String]
# => true

["a", "b", "c"] in [Integer, Integer, Integer] | [String, String, String]
# => true

["a", "b", 3] in [Integer, Integer, Integer] | [String, String, String]
# => false
```

The last example is false because the left side of the expression does not match either of the patterns completely.

Variable Binding

Where pattern matching starts to get really powerful is that you can also assign values in the target to variables in the pattern and then use those values. You can include a bare variable in the pattern by adding a hashrocket => and a local variable name to any part of a pattern:

```
"value" in String => a
puts a
```

produces:

```
value
```

Note that the in expression still returns true, and the variable assignment is a side effect.

If you only want the variable assignment and don't care about the truth value, you can replace the in operator with =>, which we've already seen can be used for rightward assignment:

```
"value" => String => a
puts a
```

produces:

```
value
```

There's a shortcut if the part of the pattern being assigned doesn't have any other pattern-matching syntax. You can leave off the hashrocket and just put in the local name:

```
"value" in a
puts a

"Another value" => b
puts b
```

produces:

```
value
Another value
```

The second form here is the rightward assignment we've already seen. This can be used in more complex patterns:

```
[1, "potato", 2, "potato"] => [first, String, second, String]

puts "the numbers are #{first} and #{second}"
```

produces:

```
the numbers are 1 and 2
```

There's a shorter shortcut for hash patterns where you're only asserting that the key exists, including the name of the key assigned a local variable with that name.

```
{rank: "Ace", suit: "Hearts"} => {rank:, suit:}

puts "Your card is the #{rank} of #{suit}."
```

produces:

```
Your card is the Ace of Hearts.
```

If the pattern doesn't match, the variable assignment behavior is technically "undefined" to allow for potential performance improvements in the future. It looks like variables are assigned up to the point of the first mismatch, but we wouldn't recommend depending on that. This pattern assigns first but not second:

```
[1, "potato", 2, "potato"] in [Integer => first, Integer, Integer => second, String]

puts "the numbers are #{first} and #{second}"
```

produces:

```
the numbers are 1 and
```

If you use => instead of in here, the behavior is much more clearly defined: you get a NoMatchingPatternError error, and neither variable is assigned.

There are two limitations on assigning variables in pattern matching. First, you can only assign a value to a local variable. Specifically, you cannot assign a value to an @ instance variable inside a pattern match. This seems to be related to performance and thread-safety concerns (it's actually related to the undefined performance of failed matches mentioned earlier), and there's a decent chance this will change in the future.

Second, you cannot do a variable assignment inside a pattern that uses the | to provide alternative patterns because you'll get a syntax error. We're honestly not 100% sure why this is, but we suspect it's related to performance concerns. (Technically, you can do this if the variable names start with an _, but the official docs suggest not relying on this behavior, since the underscore is supposed to indicate a variable that's being discarded.)

Case Pattern Matching

Having mentioned that pattern matching uses the Ruby === operator and that it compares a target value against another value, this might remind you of Ruby's case statement in case Expressions, on page 154, which also uses the === operator and compares a target value.

And in fact, Ruby does support a case/in statement that pattern matches the target against one or more successive patterns:

```
tut_expressions/pick_a_card_1.rb
def pick_a_card(cards)
  case cards
  in [*, {rank: "Ace", suit: String => s}, *]
    "You have an Ace! Its suit is #{s}."
  in [*, {rank: r, suit: "Diamonds"}, *]
    "You have a Diamond! Its rank is #{r}."
  in [*, {rank: "Queen", suit:}, *]
    "You have a Queen! Its suit is #{suit}."
  else
    "You have no interesting cards,"
  end
end

puts pick_a_card([
  {rank: "Ace", suit: "Hearts"},
  {rank: "King", suit: "Diamonds"},
  {rank: "Queen", suit: "Clubs"}
])
```

produces:

```
You have an Ace! Its suit is Hearts.
```

The case/in statement works like a successive set of pattern matchings the way we've already seen pattern matches work. The target variable, in this case, our list of card hashes that's passed to cards, is matched against the first pattern. The first pattern is a find pattern, matching against the first hash with key rank and value Ace. The rest of the pattern assigns the variable in the suit key to s, and then that variable is local to all the code within that pattern.

If that pattern doesn't match, the next one is tried. In this case, the second pattern looks for a suit of Diamonds, and we're not expecting anything in particular for the matching rank, so we can just bind it to r. If that doesn't match, the third line shows another shortcut for variable assignment, in this one the hash key shortcut is used to assign suit to the suit of the card that matches rank: "queen".

Eventually, we run out of patterns. If there's an else clause, then the else clause is executed. If not, the statement raises a NoMatchingPatternError. The expectation is that the case statement will be complete and always have a clause to execute, even if that clause is the else clause.

A case statement either has in clauses or when clauses; you can't mix the two in a single statement.

Pinning Values

Pattern matching is a great way to combine validating data with variable assignment, but we're still missing an important piece of the puzzle. In our earlier card example, the pick_a_card example hard codes the ranks of cards it's looking for. But what if you wanted to use an existing value, for example, if you wanted to pass a value to look for?

tut_expressions/pick_a_card_2.rb
```
def pick_a_card(rank_to_look_for, suit_to_look_for, cards)
  case cards
  in [*, {rank: ^rank_to_look_for, suit:}, *]
    "You have a #{rank_to_look_for}! Its suit is #{suit}."
  in [*, {rank:, suit: ^suit_to_look_for}, *]
    "You have a {rank}! Its suit is #{suit_to_look_for}."
  else
    "You have no interesting cards,"
  end
end

puts pick_a_card("King", "Clubs", [
  {rank: "Ace", suit: "Hearts"},
  {rank: "King", suit: "Diamonds"},
  {rank: "Queen", suit: "Clubs"}
])
```

produces:

```
You have a King! Its suit is Diamonds.
```

The new syntax in that example is the ^ operator, which is called the *pin operator* because it "pins" a value to part of the pattern. Without the ^ operator, Ruby would interpret the use of rank_to_look_for and suit_to_look_for as variables to be bound by the pattern match. With the ^ operator, Ruby interprets them as existing values that are part of the pattern.

Unlike a variable assignment, you can pin any value, including an instance variable ^@foo, or a global variable ^$global.

You can even pin a local variable assigned earlier in the pattern match, which makes pattern matching much more powerful:

tut_expressions/pick_a_card_3.rb
```
def pick_a_card(cards)
  case cards
  in [*, {rank: }, {rank: ^rank}, *]
    "You have a pair of #{rank}s."
  else
    "You have no interesting cards,"
  end
end

puts pick_a_card([
  {rank: "Ace", suit: "Hearts"},
  {rank: "Ace", suit: "Diamonds"},
  {rank: "Queen", suit: "Clubs"}
])
```

produces:

```
You have a pair of Aces.
```

In this example, the pattern [*, {rank: }, {rank: ^rank}, *] looks for a match where the first matching object sets the rank local variable using the hash shortcut syntax, and the second matching object matches if its rank is equal to the existing rank by pinning the value using ^rank.

You can also pin an expression rather than a mere value, allowing for something like this (we converted the rank attribute to an integer to make this a little easier to write, and we're also sorting the cards by rank up front):

tut_expressions/pick_a_card_4.rb
```ruby
def pick_a_card(cards)
  cards = cards.sort_by { _1[:rank] }
  case cards
  in [{rank:}, {rank: ^(rank + 1)}, {rank: ^(rank + 2)}]
    "You have three consecutive cards"
  else
    "You have no interesting cards,"
  end
end

puts pick_a_card([
  {rank: 7, suit: "Hearts"},
  {rank: 8, suit: "Diamonds"},
  {rank: 9, suit: "Clubs"}
])
```

produces:
```
You have three consecutive cards
```

In this example, the pattern matches if the first card has a rank, the second card has a rank that's rank + 1, and the third card has rank + 2.

Pinning also works on single-line patterns, it's not limited to patterns within case statements.

Guard Clauses

There's one other thing that you can do with patterns. You can use a boolean statement to add a guard clause at the end of the pattern, the pattern only matches if the clause is true.

tut_expressions/pick_a_card_5.rb
```ruby
def pick_a_card(cards)
  cards = cards.sort_by { _1[:rank] }
  case cards
  in [{rank:}, {rank: ^(rank + 1)}, {rank: ^(rank+ 2)}] if rank > 6
    "You have three consecutive high cards"
  else
    "You have no interesting cards,"
  end
end

puts pick_a_card([
  {rank: 7, suit: "Hearts"},
  {rank: 8, suit: "Diamonds"},
  {rank: 9, suit: "Clubs"}
])
```

produces:
```
You have three consecutive high cards
```

In the previous example, the clause if rank > 6 limits the pattern to match only cases where the lowest rank of the three cards is greater than 6. As you can see, variables assigned as part of the pattern can be used in the clause. You can use unless instead of if here, in which case the pattern matches when the unless clause is false.

Custom Pattern Matching

Our "pick a card" examples so far have had our card data stored in a Ruby hash, but it's not unlikely that we'd rather have them stored in their own class.

At this point, we can no longer pattern match against our card class because a hash match no longer works:

```
tut_expressions/pick_a_card_6.rb
class Card
  attr_accessor :rank, :suit

  def initialize(rank, suit)
    @rank = rank
    @suit = suit
  end
end

def pick_a_card(cards)
  cards = cards.sort_by(&:rank)
  case cards
  in [{rank:}, {rank: ^(rank + 1)}, {rank: ^(rank+ 2)}] if rank > 6
    "You have three consecutive high cards"
  else
    "You have no interesting cards,"
  end
end

puts pick_a_card([
  Card.new(7, "Hearts"),
  Card.new(8, "Diamonds"),
  Card.new(9, "Clubs")
])
```

produces:

```
You have no interesting cards,
```

The problem is that {rank:} no longer matches anything because Card isn't a hash.

Happily, Ruby provides a way for this to work, the Card class can implement a method called deconstruct_keys that returns a Hash version of the class suitable for pattern matching.

Here we use the hash shortcut to define our deconstruct_keys method:

```
tut_expressions/pick_a_card_7.rb
class Card
  attr_accessor :rank, :suit

  def initialize(rank, suit)
    @rank = rank
    @suit = suit
  end

  def deconstruct_keys(keys)
```

```ruby
    {rank:, suit:}
  end
end

def pick_a_card(cards)
  cards = cards.sort_by(&:rank)
  case cards
  in [{rank:}, {rank: ^(rank + 1)}, {rank: ^(rank+ 2)}] if rank > 6
    "You have three consecutive high cards"
  else
    "You have no interesting cards,"
  end
end

puts pick_a_card([
  Card.new(7, "Hearts"),
  Card.new(8, "Diamonds"),
  Card.new(9, "Clubs")
])
```

produces:

```
You have three consecutive high cards
```

This works because now the pattern match runs against the hash returned by deconstruct_keys.

The deconstruct_keys method takes an argument that in many cases you can ignore. The value of that argument is the set of keys that the pattern is actually inquiring about, and the purpose of that information is to allow you to send back a subset of your object for performance reasons. For simple cases, the subset operation is probably more expensive than creating the hash. If the argument is nil, then the pattern has used ** to request the entire hash. The return value of deconstruct_keys is arbitrary, but typically it's a hash representation of the data in the object.

An analogous method called deconstruct allows your class to match against array patterns. It takes no arguments, and the expectation is that you return an array that's a representation of your instance. We suspect that fewer classes will use deconstruct than deconstruct_keys because many classes don't seem to have an array representation with a clear order. But if you do have a class where the data has a clearly ordered representation, like a date or a cartesian point, then deconstruct would be useful. A class can implement both deconstruct_keys and deconstruct if both a useful array and a hash representation exist.

What's Next

In this chapter, we went through a lot of different Ruby expressions, from assignment to math to logic to loops to patterns. Next, we'll look at Ruby's exception handling and see what to do when things go wrong.

## CHAPTER 10

Exceptions

So far, we've been developing code in Pleasantville, a wonderful place where nothing ever, ever goes wrong. Every library call succeeds, users never enter incorrect data, and resources are plentiful and cheap. Well, that's about to change.

In the real world, errors happen. Good programs (and programmers) anticipate them and arrange to handle them gracefully. This isn't always as easy as it may sound. Often the code that detects an error doesn't have the context to know what to do about it. For example, attempting to open a file that doesn't exist is acceptable in some circumstances and is a fatal error at other times. What's your file-handling module to do?

One approach is to use return codes to signal errors (for example, the Go language uses this pattern). In this approach, Ruby's File.open method could return some specific value to say it failed. This value is then propagated back through the layers of calling routines until someone wants to take responsibility for it.

The problem with this approach is that managing all these error codes can be a pain. If a function calls open, then read, and finally close and if each can return an error indication, how can the function distinguish these error codes in the value it returns to its caller?

Ruby uses *exceptions* to help solve the problem of responding to errors. Exceptions let you package information about an error into an object. That exception object is then propagated back up the calling stack automatically until the runtime system finds code that explicitly declares that it knows how to handle that type of exception.

The Exception Class

Information about an exception is encapsulated in an object of class Exception or in one of class Exception's children. Ruby predefines a tidy hierarchy of exceptions, see https://docs.ruby-lang.org/en/master/Exception.html for the full list. As we'll see later, this hierarchy makes handling exceptions considerably easier.

The most important subclass of Exception is StandardError. The StandardError exception and its subclasses represent the exceptional conditions that you're going to want to capture in your code. Other subclasses of Exception are raised by Ruby internals or system-level problems. Almost all of the time, if you want to capture exceptions, you capture StandardError or one of its children.

When you need to raise an exception, you can use one of the built-in Exception classes, or you can create one of your own. Your own exception classes should be subclasses of StandardError or one of its children, for the same reason we just gave. Making your exceptions children of StandardError ensures that regular Ruby processes will capture them appropriately.

Often, the only new piece of data associated with a custom exception is that it's a custom exception, so you can declare it in one line:

```
class MissingUserError < StandardError; end
```

Semicolons, which are rare in Ruby, are used to separate expressions when you put more than one on a line. This syntax is often used to indicate a class with no particular new data other than its parent class. By convention, custom exception class names end with Error.

Every Exception has associated with it a message string and a stack backtrace. If you define your own exceptions, you can add extra information, see Adding Information to Exceptions, on page 176.

Handling Exceptions

Here's some simple code that uses the open-uri library to download the contents of a web page and write it to a file, line by line:

```
tut_exceptions/fetch_web_page/fetch1.rb
require "open-uri"
URI.open("https://pragprog.com/news/index.html") do |web_page|
  output = File.open("index.html", "w")
  while (line = web_page.gets)
    output.puts line
  end
  output.close
end
```

What happens if we get a fatal error halfway through? We certainly don't want to store an incomplete page to the output file.

Let's add some exception-handling code and see how it helps. To start exception handling, we enclose the code that could raise an exception in a begin/end block and use one or more rescue clauses to tell Ruby the types of exceptions we want to handle. If our code was already inside a method or an existing Ruby block, we wouldn't need a separate begin/end block to trigger exception handling—the method or block is considered to be a begin/end block on its own. This code isn't in a method, so we need to create an explicit begin/ end block.

```
tut_exceptions/fetch_web_page/fetch2.rb
require "open-uri"

file_name = "index.html"
URI.open("https://pragprog.com/news/#{file_name}") do |web_page|
  output = File.open(file_name, "w")
  begin
    while (line = web_page.gets)
      output.puts line
    end
    output.close
```

```
  rescue StandardError
    $stderr.warn "Failed to download #{file_name}: #{$!}"
    output.close
    File.delete(file_name)
    raise
  end
end
```

Because we specified StandardError in the rescue line, that clause will handle the exceptions of class StandardError and all of its children, which means that we won't catch Ruby's internal errors, which is fine. In the error-handling block, we report the error, close and delete the output file, and then reraise the exception. It's also worth noting that the close and delete calls could also raise exceptions, and those exceptions aren't caught in this code example. We'll see a partial fix for that in a moment.

As a matter of style, the rescue statement is outdented to the level of the begin/end block.

When an exception is raised, independent of any subsequent exception handling, Ruby places a reference to the associated exception object into the global variable $!. (The exclamation point presumably mirroring our surprise that any of *our* code could cause errors.) In the previous example, we used the $! variable to format our error message.

After closing and deleting the file, we call raise with no parameters, which reraises the exception that's currently stored in $!. This is a useful technique because it allows you to write code that filters exceptions, passing on those you can't handle to higher levels. It's almost like implementing an inheritance hierarchy for error processing.

You can have multiple rescue clauses in a method or begin block, and each rescue clause can specify multiple exceptions to catch. At the end of each rescue clause, you can give Ruby the name of a local variable to receive the matched exception. Most people find this more readable than using $! all over the place:

```
begin
  eval string
rescue SyntaxError, NameError => e
  print "String doesn't compile: " + e
rescue StandardError => e
  print "Error running script: " + e
end
```

How does Ruby decide which rescue clause to execute? It turns out that the processing is similar to that used by the case statement. For each rescue clause in the begin block, Ruby compares the raised exception against each of the parameters in turn. If the raised exception matches a parameter, Ruby executes the body of the rescue and stops looking. The match is made using _parameter_ === $!.

This means that the match will succeed if the exception named in the rescue clause is the same as or a superclass of the type of the currently thrown exception. This comparison happens because exceptions are classes, and classes in turn are kinds of Module. The === method is defined for modules, returning true if the class of the operand is the same as or is a descendant of the receiver. If you write a rescue clause with no parameter list, the parameter defaults to StandardError, so technically our declaration of StandardError in the earlier code is redundant.

If no rescue clause matches or if an exception is raised outside a begin/end block, Ruby moves up the stack and looks for an exception handler in the caller, then in the caller's caller, and so on. If nothing catches the exception, the program typically halts.

Although the parameters to the rescue clause are typically the names of exception classes, they can be arbitrary expressions (including method calls) that return an Exception class.

Tidying Up

Sometimes you need to guarantee that particular processing is done at the end of a block of code, regardless of whether an exception was raised. For example, you may have a file open on entry to the block, and you need to make sure it always gets closed as the block exits.

The ensure clause does just this. An ensure clause goes after the last rescue clause and contains a chunk of code that will always be executed as the block terminates. It doesn't matter if the block exits normally, raises and rescues an exception, or it's terminated by an uncaught exception—the ensure block will get run:

```ruby
f = File.open("testfile")
begin
  # .. process
rescue
  # .. handle error
ensure
  f.close
end
```

You might assume that the File.open call should be inside the begin block. In this case, having the File.open inside this begin block would be a problem because open can itself raise an exception. If the exception happened on open, you wouldn't want to run the code in the ensure block because there'd be no file to close.

In the specific case of File.open, you can pass the call a block argument that uses exception handling techniques to ensure the file is closed at the end of the block, as in the next example. (We talked about this in Using Blocks for Transactions, on page 72.)

```ruby
File.open("testfile") do |f|
  # .. process
end
```

The else clause is a similar, although less useful, construct. If present, it goes after the rescue clauses and before any ensure. The body of an else clause is executed only if no exceptions are raised by the main body of code.

```ruby
f = File.open("testfile")
begin
  # .. process
rescue
  # .. handle error
else
  puts "Congratulations-- no errors!"
ensure
  f.close
end
```

Play It Again

Sometimes you may be able to correct the cause of an exception. In those cases, you can use the retry statement within a rescue clause to repeat the entire begin/end block. Clearly, tremendous scope exists for infinite loops here, so this is a feature to use with caution (and with a finger resting lightly on the interrupt key).

As an example of code that retries on exceptions, take a look at the following simplified code that you might find making a network connection.

```
attempts = 0
begin
  attempts += 1
  @connection = @remote_server.read_data
rescue TimeOutError
  if @remote_server && attempts < 10 then
    sleep(attempts ** 2)
    retry
  else
    raise
  end
end
```

This code tries to read data from remote_server. If the code returns a TimeOutError and if the remote_server exists, the code sleeps for a while and then tries again. It keeps track of the number of attempts, lengthening the time out, until eventually if the number of attempts gets too high, it stops trying to connect and just raises the error.

Raising Exceptions

So far, we've been on the defensive, handling exceptions raised by others. It's time to turn the tables and go on the offensive. It's time to raise some…exceptions.

You can raise exceptions in your code with the raise method (or its judgmental and less commonly used synonym, fail):

```
raise
raise "bad mp3 encoding"
raise InterfaceException, "Keyboard failure"
```

The first form simply reraises the current exception (or raises a RuntimeError if no current exception exists). This is used in exception handlers that intercept an exception before passing it on.

The second form creates a new RuntimeError exception, setting its message to the given string. This exception is then raised up the call stack.

The third form uses the first argument to create an exception and then sets the associated message to the second argument. Typically, the first argument will be either the name of a class in the Exception hierarchy or a reference to an instance of one of these classes. If the argument is a class name, then Ruby will create an instance using a call to new with no arguments. Technically, this argument can be any object that responds to the message exception by returning an object such that object.kind_of?(Exception) is true.

Here are some typical examples of raise in action:

```
raise

raise "Missing name" if name.nil?

if i >= names.size
  raise IndexError, "#{i} >= size (#{names.size})"
end

raise ArgumentError, "Name too big", caller
```

In this example, we show that we can add a stack trace as an optional third argument to the raise method. The effect of this usage is to remove the current routine from the stack backtrace, which is often useful in library modules. We do this using the Kernel#caller method, which returns the current stack trace. The ability to edit the stack trace sent to the exception for more focused information is why you have the optional third argument.

The Kernel#caller method returns an array of strings with information about the call stack. We can take this further by manipulating that array. The following code removes two routines from the backtrace by passing only a subset of the call stack to the new exception:

```
raise ArgumentError, "Name too big", caller[1..]
```

Adding Information to Exceptions

You can define your own exceptions to hold any information that you need to pass out from the site of an error. For example, certain types of network errors may be transient depending on the circumstances. If such an error occurs and the circumstances are right, you could set a flag in the exception to tell the handler that it may be worth retrying the operation.

Here's what part of the remote server from the previous example might look like:

```
tut_exceptions/retry_exception.rb
class RetryException < RuntimeError
  attr_reader :ok_to_retry
  def initialize(ok_to_retry)
    @ok_to_retry = ok_to_retry
  end
end
```

Somewhere down in the depths of the code, a transient error occurs:

```
tut_exceptions/read_data.rb
def read_data(attempt_count)
  data = @socket.read(512)
  if data.nil?
    raise RetryException.new(attempt_count < 10), "transient read error"
  end
  # .. normal processing
end
```

And we might incorporate that in our call:

```
attempts = 0
begin
  attempts += 1
  @connection = @remote_server.read_data(attempts)
```

```
rescue RetryException => e
  retry if e.okay_to_retry
  raise
end
```

Using Catch and Throw

Although the exception mechanism of raise and rescue is great for abandoning execution when things go wrong, it's sometimes nice to be able to jump out of some deeply nested construct during normal processing. This is where the rarely used catch and throw come in handy.

Here's a trivial example. The following code reads a list of words one at a time and adds them to an array. When done, it prints the array in reverse order. But, if any of the lines in the file don't contain a valid word, we want it to abandon the whole process.

```
tut_exceptions/catch_1.rb
word_list = File.open("wordlist")
catch(:done) do
  result = []
  while (line = word_list.gets)
    word = line.chomp
    throw :done unless /^\w+$/.match?(word)
    result << word
  end
  puts result.reverse
end
```

catch defines a block that's labeled with the given name (which may be a Symbol or a String). The block is executed normally until a throw is encountered.

When Ruby encounters a throw, it zips back up the call stack looking for a catch block with a matching symbol. When it finds it, Ruby unwinds the stack to that point and terminates the block. So, in the previous example, if the input doesn't contain correctly formatted lines, the throw will skip to the end of the corresponding catch, not only terminating the while loop but also skipping the code that writes the reversed list. If the throw is called with the optional second parameter, that value is returned as the value of the catch. In the next example, our word list incorrectly contains the line *wow*. Without the second parameter to throw, the corresponding catch returns nil.

```
tut_exceptions/catch_2.rb
word_list = File.open("wordlist")
word_in_error = catch(:done) do
  result = []
  while (line = word_list.gets)
    word = line.chomp
    throw(:done, word) unless /^\w+$/.match?(word)
    result << word
  end
  puts result.reverse
end
if word_in_error
  puts "Failed: '#{word_in_error}' found, but a word was expected"
end
```

produces:

```
Failed: '*wow*' found, but a word was expected
```

The following example uses a throw to terminate interaction with the user if ! is typed in response to any prompt:

```
tut_exceptions/catchthrow.rb
def prompt_and_get(prompt)
  print prompt
  res = readline.chomp
  throw :quit_requested if res == "!"
  res
end

catch :quit_requested do
  name = prompt_and_get("Name: ")
  age  = prompt_and_get("Age:  ")
  sex  = prompt_and_get("Sex:  ")
  # ..
  # process information
end
```

As this example illustrates, the throw doesn't have to appear within the static scope of the catch.

What's Next

In this chapter, we looked at how to make our Ruby code more error-proof by catching and raising exceptions, and you saw how to create your own exception classes that might have their own data. Next up, we're going to talk about a leading cause of exceptions in code: managing input and output.

CHAPTER 11

Basic Input and Output

Ruby provides what looks at first sight like two separate sets of input and output (I/O) routines. The first is the simple interface we've been using a lot so far:

```
print "Enter your name: "
name = gets
```

This whole set of I/O-related methods is implemented in the Kernel module, including gets, open, print, printf, putc, puts, readline, readlines, and test. The I/O methods are available to all objects, and they make it simple and convenient to write straightforward Ruby programs. These methods typically do I/O to standard input and standard output, which makes them useful for writing simple tasks.

The other way to do I/O, which gives you more control, is to use Ruby's dedicated IO classes.

What Is an I/O Object?

Ruby defines a single base class, IO, to handle input and output. This base class is subclassed by classes File and BasicSocket to provide more specialized behavior, but the principles are the same. An IO object is a bidirectional channel between a Ruby program and some external resource.

In this chapter, we'll focus on class IO and its most commonly used subclass, class File.

Opening and Closing Files

You can create a new file object using File.new:

```
file = File.new("testfile", "r")
 # ... process the file
file.close
```

The first parameter to the method is the filename. The second is called the *mode string*, which lets you declare whether you're opening the file for reading, writing, or both. Here we opened testfile for reading with an "r". We could also have used "w" for write or "r+" for read-write. The full list of allowed modes appears in Table 28, Mode values, on page 593.

You can also optionally specify file permissions when creating a file. After opening the file, we can write and/or read data as needed and as specified by the mode string. When we're done, as responsible software citizens, we close the file, ensuring that all buffered data is written and that all related resources are freed.

But Ruby can make life a little bit easier for you. The method File.open also opens a file. In regular use, it behaves like File.new. But, if you associate a block with the call, open behaves differently (see Using Blocks for Transactions, on page 72). Instead of returning a new File object, it invokes the block, passing the newly opened File as a parameter. When the block exits, the file is automatically closed.

```ruby
File.open("testfile", "r") do |file|
  # ... process the file
end    # <- file automatically closed here
```

Using File.open with a block has an added benefit. When using File.new as we did earlier, if an exception is raised while processing the file, the call to File.close may not happen. Once the file variable goes out of scope, then garbage collection will eventually close it, but this may not happen for a while. Meanwhile, resources are being held open.

This doesn't happen with the block form of File.open. If an exception is raised inside the block, the file is closed before the exception is propagated on to the caller. It's as if the File.open method looks like the following:

```ruby
class File
  def self.open(*args)
    f = File.new(*args)
    result = f
    if block_given?
      begin
        result = yield f
      ensure
        f.close
      end
    end
    result
  end
end
```

Reading and Writing Files

The same methods that we've been using for "simple" I/O from standard input and output are available for File objects. So, where Kernel#gets reads a line from standard input (or from any files specified on the command line when the script was invoked), File#gets reads a line from the file object.

For example, we could create a program called copy.rb:

```ruby
tut_io/copy.rb
while (line = gets)
  puts line
end
```

If we run this program with no arguments, it'll read lines from the console and copy them back to the console. Note that each line is echoed once the Return key is pressed. (In this and later examples, we show user input in a bold font.) The ^D is the end-of-file character on Unix systems.

```
$ ruby copy.rb
These are lines
These are lines
that I am typing
that I am typing
^D
```

We can also pass in one or more filenames on the command line. In this case, the filenames are passed to standard input and the Kernel#gets will read from each in turn as if all the files in the command line were concatenated into a single file. From the top directory of the sample code, we get this:

```
$ ruby code/tut_io/copy.rb code/tut_io/testfile
This is line one
This is line two
This is line three
And so on...
```

We have another option. We can explicitly open the file and read from it using File#gets:

```
File.open("testfile") do |file|
  while line = (file.gets)
    puts line
  end
end
```

produces:

```
This is line one
This is line two
This is line three
And so on...
```

In addition to gets, I/O objects define an additional set of access methods, all intended to make our lives easier.

Iterators for Reading

While the usual loops work to allow you to read data from an IO stream, Ruby also defines some task-specific iterators. The method each_byte invokes a block with the next 8-bit byte from an IO object (in this case, an object of type File). The Integer#chr method converts an integer to the corresponding ASCII character:

```
File.open("testfile") do |file|
  file.each_byte.with_index do |ch, index|
    print "#{ch.chr}:#{ch} "
    break if index > 10
  end
end
```

produces:

```
T:84 h:104 i:105 s:115  :32 i:105 s:115  :32 l:108 i:105 n:110 e:101
```

The method IO#each_line calls the block with each line from the file. In the next example, we'll make the original newlines visible using String#dump, which returns the string in double quotes with escape characters, so you can see that we're not cheating:

```
File.open("testfile") do |file|
  file.each_line { |line| puts "Got #{line.dump}" }
end
```

produces:

```
Got "This is line one\n"
Got "This is line two\n"
Got "This is line three\n"
Got "And so on...\n"
```

The each_line method includes the line ending at the end of each line of data. That's why you see the \n characters in the output of the previous example. You don't have to use \n as the separator, though. You can pass each_line an argument, any sequence of characters. The method will use that argument as a line separator, and break up the input accordingly, returning the separator at the end of each line of data. In the next example, we'll use the character e as the line separator:

```
File.open("testfile") do |file|
  file.each_line("e") { |line|  puts "Got #{ line.dump }" }
end
```

produces:

```
Got "This is line"
Got " one"
Got "\nThis is line"
Got " two\nThis is line"
Got " thre"
Got "e"
Got "\nAnd so on...\n"
```

If you combine the idea of an iterator with the autoclosing block feature, you get IO.foreach, or the subclass method File.foreach. This method takes the name of an I/O source, opens it for reading, calls the iterator once for every line in the file, and then closes the file automatically:

```
File.foreach("testfile") { |line| puts line }
```

produces:

```
This is line one
This is line two
This is line three
And so on...
```

Or, if you prefer, you can retrieve an entire file into a string:

```
str = IO.read("testfile")
str.length # => 66
str[0, 30] # => "This is line one\nThis is line "
```

Or into an array of lines:

```
arr = IO.readlines("testfile")
arr.length # => 4
arr[0]     # => "This is line one\n"
```

Don't forget that I/O is never certain in an uncertain world—exceptions will be raised on most errors, and you should be ready to rescue them and take appropriate action.

Writing to Files

So far, we've been merrily calling puts and print, passing in any old object and trusting that Ruby will do the right thing (which, of course, it does). But what exactly *is* it doing?

With a couple of exceptions, every object you pass to puts or print is converted to a string by calling that object's to_s method. If for some reason the to_s method doesn't return a valid string, a string is created containing the object's class name and ID, something like <Class-Name:0x123456>. This example opens a file for writing (note the mode string is "w") and then reads the file in and prints its contents to STDOUT. As with the other Kernel methods, there's an equivalent IO#puts that we can use.

```
File.open("output.txt", "w") do |file|
  file.puts "Hello"
  file.puts "1 + 2 = #{1+2}"
end

puts File.read("output.txt")
```

produces:

```
Hello
1 + 2 = 3
```

There is one slight difference between puts and print. The puts method inserts a newline after the output unless the output already ends in a newline, but print does not.

The "every object calls its to_s method" rule has two exceptions. The nil object will print as the empty string, and an array passed to puts will be written as if each of its elements in turn were passed separately to puts.

More generally, we have File#write, which writes its argument to the file, converting non-strings to strings with to_s. The difference is that write returns the number of bytes written to the file, while puts returns nil.

```
File.open("output.txt", "w") do |file|
  file.write "Hello"
  file.write "1 + 2 = #{1+2}"
end

puts File.read("output.txt")
```

produces:

```
Hello1 + 2 = 3
```

What if you want to write binary data and don't want Ruby messing with it? Well, normally, you can simply use print and pass in a string containing the bytes to be written. You can also get at the low-level I/O routines if you really want them (look at the documentation for sysread and syswrite at https://docs.ruby-lang.org/en/master/IO.html#method-i-sysread).

And how do you get the binary data into a string in the first place? The three common ways are to use a literal, poke it in byte by byte, or use Array#pack, which takes an array of data and packs it into a string.

```
str1 = "\001\002\003" # => "\u0001\u0002\u0003"
str2 = ""
str2 << 1 << 2 << 3    # => "\u0001\u0002\u0003"
[1, 2, 3].pack("c*")   # => "\x01\x02\x03"
```

The first example here is using escape sequences to put raw bytes into the string, the second is using the shovel operator to add the numbers one by one, and the third is using Array#pack. The argument c* says that all the elements of the array should be converted as 8-bit unsigned values.

Finding Files

Ruby has a couple of utility methods that can help you find files. Typically, when you search for a file, the pathname is relative to the directory from where the script was invoked, but in a large code base that's unlikely to be the file you're writing code in.

To help orient yourself, Ruby provides _FILE_, which always has the relative name of the file it's contained in, and _dir_, which has the absolute pathname of that file. File.realpath returns the absolute path to a file, so File.realpath(_FILE_) gives you the absolute path to the current file. This means _dir_ is equivalent to File.dirname(File.realpath(_FILE_)).

You're probably wondering why _FILE_ is capitalized, while _dir_ isn't. Technically, _FILE_ is a reserved word (not quite a constant, but close), while _dir_ is a method of Kernel. That's not much of an explanation, but it's what we've got.

One way you might use realpath is to figure out what Ruby is thinking of as the base path. You might try to do something like File.open("local.txt"), only to have Ruby tell you that local.txt doesn't exist. In that case, putting in a debug statement like puts File.realpath("local.txt") will go a long way toward orienting you as to where Ruby thinks it's looking.

I/O with Streams

> Just as you can append an object to an Array using the << operator, you can also append an object to an output IO stream:

```
endl = "\n"
$stdout << 99 << " red balloons" << endl
```

produces:

```
99 red balloons
```

Again, the << method uses to_s to convert its arguments to strings before printing them.

There are actually some good reasons for using the << operator. Because other classes (such as String and Array) also implement a << operator with similar semantics, you can often write code that appends to something using << without caring whether it's added to an array, a file, or a string. This kind of flexibility also makes unit testing easy. We'll discuss this idea in greater detail in Chapter 21, Ruby Style, on page 343.

Doing I/O with Strings

Sometimes you need to work with code that assumes it's reading from or writing to one or more files. But you have a problem: the data isn't in files. Perhaps it's available instead via a remote network call, or it has been passed to you as command-line parameters. Or maybe you're running unit tests, and you don't want to alter the real file system.

Enter StringIO objects. They behave like other I/O objects, but they read and write strings, not files. If you open a StringIO object for reading, you supply it with a string. All read operations on the StringIO object and then read from this string. Similarly, when you want to write to a StringIO object, you pass it a string to be filled.

```
require "stringio"

ip = StringIO.new("now is\nthe time\nto learn\nRuby!")
op = StringIO.new("", "w")

ip.each_line do |line|
  op.puts line.reverse
end
op.string # => "\nsi won\n\nemit eht\n\nnrael ot\n!ybuR\n"
```

Talking to Networks

Ruby is fluent in most of the Internet's protocols, both low-level and high-level.

For those who enjoy groveling around at the network level, Ruby comes with a set of classes in the socket library (https://docs.ruby-lang.org/en/master/Socket.html). These give you access to TCP, UDP, SOCKS, and Unix domain sockets, as well as any additional socket types supported on your architecture. The library also provides helper classes to make writing servers easier. Here's a simple program that gets information about our user website on a local web server using the HTTP OPTIONS request:

tut_io/socket.rb
```
require "socket"

client = TCPSocket.open("127.0.0.1", "www")
client.send("OPTIONS /~dave/ HTTP/1.0\n\n", 0)     # 0 means standard packet
puts client.readlines
client.close
```

At a higher level, the "lib/net" set of library modules provides handlers for a set of application-level protocols (currently FTP, HTTP, HTTPS, IMAP, POP, and SMTP). For example, the following program lists the images that are displayed on this book's home page. (To save space, we show only the first three.)

tut_io/networking.rb
```
require "net/http"

uri = URI("https://pragprog.com/titles/ruby5/programming-ruby-3-2-5th-edition/")
Net::HTTP.start(
  "pragprog.com",
  Net::HTTP.https_default_port,
  use_ssl: true
) do |http|
  request = Net::HTTP::Get.new(uri)
  response = http.request(request)
  if response.code == "200"
    puts response.body.scan(/<img class=".*?" src="(.*?)"/m).uniq[0, 3]
  end
end
```

produces:
```
/titles/ruby5/programming-ruby-3-2-5th-edition/ruby5-beta-250.jpg
/img/pdf_icon.png
/titles/rails7/agile-web-development-with-rails-7/rails7-125.jpg
```

This example could be improved significantly. In particular, it doesn't do much in the way of error handling. It should report "Not Found" errors (the infamous 404) and should handle redirects (which happen when a web server gives the client an alternative address for the requested page).

We can take this to a higher level still. By bringing the open-uri library into a program, the URI.open method recognizes http:// and ftp:// URLs in the filename. Not just that—it also handles redirects automatically.

tut_Io/networking_2.rb
```
require "open-uri"

url = "https://pragprog.com/titles/ruby5/programming-ruby-3-3-5th-edition/"
URI.open(url) do |f|
  puts f.read.scan(/<img class=".*?" src="(.*?)"/m).uniq[0,3]
end
```

produces:
```
/titles/ruby5/programming-ruby-3-3-5th-edition/ruby5-beta-250.jpg
/img/pdf_icon.png
/titles/rails7/agile-web-development-with-rails-7/rails7-125.jpg
```

What's Next

In this chapter, we've seen both Ruby's simple I/O library, implemented as a series of methods in the Kernel module, and the more complicated I/O methods in the class IO and its children. We've also seen how to read and write data.

A common problem with I/O is that it's slow and blocks programs. A common workaround is to use threading to allow the program to do multiple things at once. Let's take a look at some of Ruby's threading options.

## CHAPTER 12

Threads, Fibers, and Ractors

Being able to do more than one thing at the same time is pretty useful. When a computer program has to wait for one task to finish, like an API call to a slow server, multitasking allows it to turn control over to another task and do other useful work while it waits. When a computer has more than one CPU—which, these days, means a computer—the program can split tasks across multiple CPUs. You can achieve tremendous speed boosts this way.

Being able to multitask is also pretty complicated. When a program multitasks, a task can change the state of the data another task is using, so the other task's understanding of the data may no longer be correct. When a program multitasks, its tasks may fight for access to limited resources, like the filesystem, and might even overwrite each other's changes. People are notoriously bad at predicting the effects of even mildly complicated threading scenarios, so unexpected bug cases are a real problem.

When writing programs that are doing multiple things at once, each "thing" is called a *thread*, and the goal is to have *thread safety*, meaning the code will execute correctly no matter in what order the threads operate. In some cases, the order of operation matters. For example, if two threads are writing to a log file and instead of appending to the log file, the last thread overwrites the first one, the final contents of the log file will depend on which thread executed first. This is called a *race condition* and it is bad because it can lead to hard-to-diagnose bugs.

A key to achieving thread safety is to avoid having data or status information shared between threads, especially if that data is changeable by one thread without the knowledge of the other. But sometimes you must share information such as access to a common database. In that case, you need constructs that limit access to shared resources such that only one thread can access them at a time.

Historically, Ruby programs have a Global Interpreter Lock (GIL), which ensures that only one thread is actually being executed by Ruby at any time. The GIL is one way Ruby protects thread safety. Since only one thread can run at a time, shared global resources within Ruby are automatically protected from being changed behind your thread's back. You still get the advantage of allowing one thread to take over execution if other threads are blocked. But you can't take advantage of, say, multiple parallel CPUs with a single Ruby interpreter (with the exception of the Ractor library). Ruby installations that do want to take advantage of multiple CPUs typically run multiple Ruby interpreters that communicate via an external data source or message system. (There's one relatively new Ruby construct that works around this—called Ractors—which we'll talk about at the end of this chapter.)

In this chapter, we'll look at Ruby's different threading abstractions that allow you to organize your program so that you can run different parts of it apparently "at the same time." The Thread class is the basic unit of multithreaded behavior in Ruby. Ruby also allows you to spawn processes out to the underlying operating system and multithread those processes. *Fibers* are an additional abstraction that lets you suspend the execution of one part of your program and run some other part. Finally, the Ractor library allows you to bypass the GIL and have true multithreading using Ruby.

Let's start with the Thread class, which is the basis for Ruby's multithreaded behavior.

Multithreading with Threads

The lowest-level mechanism in Ruby for doing two things at once is to use the Thread class. Although threads can in theory take advantage of multiple processors or multiple cores in a single processor, there's a major catch. Many Ruby extension libraries aren't thread-safe because they expect to be protected by the GIL. So, Ruby uses native operating system threads but operates only a single thread at a time. Unless you use the Ractor library, you'll never see two threads in the same application running Ruby code truly concurrently. You'll instead see threads that are busy executing Ruby code while another thread waits on an I/O operation.

Creating Ruby Threads

The code that follows is a simple example. It downloads a set of web pages in parallel. For each URL the code is asked to download, it creates a separate thread that handles the HTTP transaction:

tut_threads/fetcher.rb
```
require "net/http"

pages = %w[www.rubycentral.org www.pragprog.com www.google.com]

threads = pages.map do |page_to_fetch|
  Thread.new(page_to_fetch) do |url|
    http = Net::HTTP.new(url, 80)
    print "Fetching: #{url}\n"
    response = http.get("/")
    print "Got #{url}:  #{response.message}\n"
  end
end
threads.each { |thread| thread.join }
print "We're done here!\n"
```

The results look something like this:

```
Fetching: www.rubycentral.org
Fetching: www.pragprog.com
Fetching: www.google.com
Got www.google.com:  OK
Got www.pragprog.com:  Moved Permanently
Got www.rubycentral.org:  OK
We're done here!
```

Let's look at this code in more detail because a few subtle things are happening.

New threads are created with the Thread.new call. The Thread.new call is given a block that contains the code to be run in the new thread. In our case, the block uses the net/http library to fetch the page from the URL that's passed to the thread. Once the thread is created, it's available to be scheduled for execution by the operating system, and, in this code at least, we don't have direct control over when the thread runs.

This code uses a map call to create three new threads from the list of sites to call and stores the threads in an array. Threads, like everything else in Ruby, are objects that can be assigned to variables, returned from blocks or methods, and passed as parameters.

Our output tracing shows that these fetches are going on in parallel because all three "fetch" statements happen before any of the "got" statements do. Broadly, what's happening is that the first thread is created, is scheduled for control, makes its HTTP request, and is blocked while it waits for the answer. Control reverts back to the main program, which immediately creates the second thread, and so on. The thread creation is much faster than the HTTP request, so even with the overhead of making the threads, all three threads will usually be created before any of them return.

Just to be clear, our discussion is using the word "block" in two ways: one meaning "a chunk of Ruby code" and the other meaning "being stalled waiting for a response."

When we create the thread, we pass the required URL as a parameter to the block as url, even though the same value is already available as page_to_fetch outside the block. Why do we do this? The answer relates to thread safety and how threads share values.

A thread shares all global, instance, and local variables that are in existence and available at the time the thread starts. Despite what Mr. Rogers says, sharing isn't always a good thing. In this case, all three threads share the variable page_to_fetch, defined outside the Thread.new block. The first thread gets started, and page_to_fetch is set to "www.rubycentral.org". In the meantime, the loop creating the threads is still running. The second time around, page_to_fetch gets set to "pragprog.com". If the first thread hasn't yet finished using the page_to_fetch variable, it'll suddenly start using this new value. In our case, that would likely manifest as one value being used in the actual http.get command, then the value changing while the thread is blocked, and then a different value being used in the print statement on the next line. This would be, to say the least, confusing. These kinds of bugs are difficult to track down.

However, local variables created within a thread's block are truly local to that thread—each thread will have its own copy of these variables. In our case, the variable url will be set at the time the thread is created, and each thread will have its own copy of the page address. You can pass any number of arguments into the block via Thread.new, the arguments to the method become the arguments to the block.

This code also illustrates a gotcha. Inside the loop, the threads use print to write out the messages, rather than puts. Why? Well, behind the scenes, puts splits its work into two chunks: it writes its argument, and then it writes a newline. Between these two, a thread could get scheduled, and the output would be interleaved. Calling print with a single string that already contains the newline gets around the problem.

Manipulating Threads

Another subtlety occurs in the next to last line of our program, where we call join on each thread.

When a Ruby program terminates, all threads are killed, regardless of their states. Since we don't control the scheduling of any internally created threads, it'd be easy for this program to reach the end while one or more threads are still waiting for responses. The program would terminate, and we'd never get those responses.

You can wait for a particular thread to finish by calling that thread's Thread#join method. The thread in which the join method is called—in our case, that's the original program—will block until the thread receiving the join call has finished. The subthread has been off on its own, but rejoins the parent thread so the parent thread can move forward.

By calling join on each of the requested threads, you can make sure that all three requests have completed before you terminate the main program. We can see this in our code because the "we're done here" print statement will always happen after all three threads complete. Even though the join methods are called one at a time, the order and speed of the subthread execution ultimately don't matter because the main thread will wait on all of them.

The join method normally returns the thread itself. If you don't want to block forever, you can give join a timeout parameter—if the timeout expires before the thread terminates, the join call returns nil. The expiration of the timeout doesn't actually terminate the thread, but it does allow the calling thread to continue, which might mean that the program will end before the thread is complete. Another variant of join, the method Thread#value, returns the value of the last statement executed by the thread. The value method doesn't have a timeout parameter.

In addition to join, a few other handy routines are used to manipulate threads. The current thread is always accessible using Thread.current. You can obtain a list of all threads using Thread.list, which returns a list of all Thread objects that are runnable or stopped. You can stop a thread with Thread#exit which is aliased as kill and terminate.

To determine the status of a particular thread, you can use Thread#status and Thread#alive?. The status method returns "run" if the thread is executing normally, "sleep" if it has been paused or is blocked, "aborting" if it is in the process of being killed. If the thread ended normally it returns false; if the thread terminated exceptionally, it returns nil. The alive? method returns true if the status is "run" or "sleep."

You can adjust the priority of a thread using Thread#priority=. Higher-priority threads will run before lower-priority threads, though the operating system is free to ignore this setting.

Thread Variables

A thread can normally access any variables that are in scope when the thread is created. Variables local to the block containing the thread code are local to the thread and aren't shared. But what if you need per-thread variables that can be accessed by other threads—including the main thread? Class Thread has a facility that allows thread-local variables to be created and accessed by name. You can treat the thread object as if it were a Hash, writing to elements using []= and reading them back using []. A true thread-local variable can be accessed using Thread.thread_variable_get and Thread.thread_variable_set.

In the example that follows, each thread records the current value of the variable count in a thread-local variable with the key mycount. To do this, the code uses the symbol :mycount when indexing thread objects:

```
tut_threads/thread_variables.rb
count = 0
threads = 10.times.map do
  Thread.new do
```

```
      sleep(rand(0.1))
      Thread.current[:mycount] = count
      count += 1
    end
end

threads.each do |t|
  t.join
  print t[:mycount], ", "
end
puts "count = #{count}"
```

produces:

```
7, 0, 8, 6, 5, 4, 1, 9, 3, 2, count = 10
```

The main thread waits for the subthreads to finish and then prints that thread's value of count. Just to make it interesting, we use rand(0.1) to have each thread wait a random amount of time before recording the value so that we can't predict the order in which the threads will finish.

A subtle *race condition* exists in this code. A race condition occurs when two or more pieces of code (or hardware) try to access some shared resource, and the outcome changes depending on the order in which they do so. In the example here, it's possible for one thread to set the value of its mycount variable to count, but before it gets a chance to increment count, the thread gets descheduled and another thread reuses the same value of count. These issues are fixed by synchronizing the access to shared resources such as the count variable (see Synchronization via Mutual Exclusion, on page 193).

Threads and Exceptions

If a thread raises an unhandled exception, what happens next depends on the setting of the Thread.abort_on_exception flag and on the setting of the interpreter's $DEBUG flag.

If abort_on_exception is false and the debug flag isn't enabled (the default condition), an unhandled exception simply kills the current thread—all the rest continue to run. In fact, you don't even hear about the exception until you issue a join on the thread that raised it. In the following example, thread 1 blows up and fails to produce any output. But you can still see the trace from the other threads:

tut_threads/exception_01.rb
```
4.times.map do |number|
  Thread.new(number) do |i|
    raise "Boom!" if i == 1
    print "#{i}\n"
  end
end
puts "Waiting"
sleep 0.1
puts "Done"
```

produces:

```
#<Thread:0x0000000104bb97e8 code/tut_threads/exception_01.rb:2 run> terminated
with exception (report_on_exception is true):
code/tut_threads/exception_01.rb:3:in `block (2 levels) in <main>': Boom!
(RuntimeError)
Waiting
```

```
0
2
3
Done
```

You normally don't sleep waiting for threads to terminate; you'd use join. If you join to a thread that has raised an exception, then that exception will be raised in the thread that does the joining:

tut_threads/exception_02.rb
```ruby
threads = 4.times.map do |number|
  Thread.new(number) do |i|
    raise "Boom!" if i == 1
    print "#{i}\n"
  end
end

puts "Waiting"
threads.each do |t|
  t.join
rescue RuntimeError => e
  puts "Failed: #{e.message}"
end
puts "Done"
```

produces:
```
#<Thread:0x0000000103166d00 code/tut_threads/exception_02.rb:2 run> terminated
with exception (report_on_exception is true):
code/tut_threads/exception_02.rb:3:in `block (2 levels) in <main>': Boom!
(RuntimeError)
Waiting
0
2
3
Failed: Boom!
Done
```

If you set abort_on_exception to true or use -d to turn on the debug flag, if an unhandled exception occurs, it kills the main thread. This is shown in the following code, where the message Done never appears.

tut_threads/exception_03.rb
```ruby
Thread.abort_on_exception = true
threads = 4.times.map do |number|
  Thread.new(number) do |i|
    raise "Boom!" if i == 1
    print "#{i}\n"
  end
end

puts "Waiting"
threads.each { |t| t.join }
puts "Done"
```

produces:
```
#<Thread:0x00000001047c95c0 code/tut_threads/exception_03.rb:3 run> terminated
with exception (report_on_exception is true):
```

```
code/tut_threads/exception_03.rb:4:in `block (2 levels) in <main>': Boom!
(RuntimeError)
code/tut_threads/exception_03.rb:4:in `block (2 levels) in <main>': Boom!
(RuntimeError)
Waiting
0
2
3
```

Controlling the Thread Scheduler

In a well-designed application, you'll normally let threads do their thing. Building timing dependencies into a multithreaded application is generally considered to be bad form because it makes the code far more complex and also prevents the thread scheduler from optimizing the execution of your program.

That said, the Thread class provides a number of methods that control or give hints to the scheduler. Invoking Thread.stop stops the current thread, and invoking Thread#run arranges for a particular thread to be run. The method Thread.pass deschedules the current thread, allowing others to run, and Thread#join and Thread#value block the calling thread until a given thread finishes. These last two are the only low-level thread control methods that the average program should use. In fact, we believe that the low-level thread control methods are too complex and dangerous to be used correctly in programs we write. Fortunately, Ruby has support for higher-level thread synchronization.

Synchronization via Mutual Exclusion

Let's start by looking at a simple example of a race condition—multiple threads updating a shared variable:

tut_threads/race_condition.rb
```ruby
sum = 0
threads = 10.times.map do
  Thread.new do
    100_000.times do
      new_value = sum + 1
      print "#{new_value}    " if new_value % 250_000 == 0
      sum = new_value
    end
  end
end
threads.each(&:join)
puts "\nsum = #{sum}"
```
produces:
```
250000   250000   250000   250000   250000   250000   250000   250000
sum = 349999
```

We create ten threads, and each increments the shared sum variable 100,000 times. But when the threads all finish, the final value in sum is considerably less than 1,000,000. We have a race condition. The reason is the print call that sits between the code that calculates the new value and the code that stores it back into sum. In one thread, the updated value gets calculated. Let's say that the value of sum is 99,999, so new_value will be 100,000. Before storing the new value back into sum, we call print, and that causes another thread to be scheduled (because the first thread blocks waiting for the I/O to complete). So, a second thread also fetches the value of 99,999 and increments it. It stores 100,000 into sum. It then loops around again and stores 100,001, 100,002, and so on. Eventually, the original thread continues running because it finished writing its message. It immediately stores its value of 100,000 into the sum, over-writing (and losing) all the values stored by the other thread(s). We lost data.

Fortunately, that's easy to fix. We use the built-in class Mutex (short for "mutually exclusive") to create synchronized regions—areas of code that only one thread may enter at a time.

Some grade schools coordinate students' hall access during class time using a system of hall passes. The number of passes is limited, and to leave the classroom, you need to take a pass with you. If someone else already has that pass, you have to wait for that person to return. The pass controls access to the shared resource—you have to own the pass to use the resource, and only one person can own it at a time.

A mutex is like that hall pass. You create a mutex to control access to a resource and then lock it when you want to use that resource. If no one else has it locked, your thread continues to run. If someone else has already locked that particular mutex, your thread suspends until they unlock it.

Here's a version of our counting code that uses a mutex to ensure that only one thread updates the count at a time:

tut_threads/mutex_1.rb
```
sum = 0
mutex = Thread::Mutex.new
threads = 10.times.map do
  Thread.new do
    100_000.times do
      # one at a time, please
      mutex.lock
      new_value = sum + 1
      print "#{new_value}  " if new_value % 250_000 == 0
      sum = new_value
      mutex.unlock
    end
  end
end
threads.each(&:join)
puts "\nsum = #{sum}"
```

produces:
```
250000   500000   750000   1000000
sum = 1000000
```

This pattern—lock a mutex, do something, and then unlock—is so common that the Mutex class provides Mutex#synchronize, which locks the mutex, runs the code in a block, and then unlocks the mutex. This also ensures that the mutex will get unlocked even if an exception is thrown while it's locked. Otherwise, an exception might cause the mutex to never unlock and permanently prevent other threads from gaining access to the shared resource.

tut_threads/mutex_2.rb
```
sum = 0
mutex = Thread::Mutex.new
threads = 10.times.map do
```

```
    Thread.new do
      100_000.times do
        mutex.synchronize do
          new_value = sum + 1
          print "#{new_value}  " if new_value % 250_000 == 0
          sum = new_value
        end
      end
    end
end

threads.each(&:join)
puts "\nsum = #{sum}"
```

produces:

```
250000  500000  750000  1000000
sum = 1000000
```

Sometimes you want to claim a lock if a mutex is currently unlocked, but you don't want to suspend the current thread if the mutex is locked. The Mutex#try_lock method takes the lock if it can, but returns false if the lock is already taken. The following code illustrates a hypothetical currency converter. The ExchangeRates class caches rates from an online feed, and a background thread updates that cache once an hour. This update takes a minute or so. In the main thread, we interact with our user. But rather than just go dead if we can't claim the mutex that protects the rate object, we use try_lock and print a status message if the update is in process.

tut_threads/mutex_3.rb
```
rate_mutex = Thread::Mutex.new
exchange_rates = ExchangeRates.new
exchange_rates.update_from_online_feed

Thread.new do
  loop do
    sleep(3600)
    rate_mutex.synchronize do
      exchange_rates.update_from_online_feed
    end
  end
end

loop do
  print "Enter currency code and amount: "
  line = gets
  if rate_mutex.try_lock
    begin
      puts(exchange_rates.convert(line))
    ensure
      puts "Ensuring unlock"
      rate_mutex.unlock
    end
  else
    puts "Sorry, rates being updated. Try again in a minute"
  end
end
```

By using ensure the unlock command is guaranteed to run even if puts raises an exception.

If you're holding the lock on a mutex and you want to temporarily unlock it, allowing others to use it, you can call Mutex#sleep.

We could use this to rewrite the previous example:

```
tut_threads/mutex_4.rb
rate_mutex = Thread::Mutex.new
exchange_rates = ExchangeRates.new
exchange_rates.update_from_online_feed

Thread.new do
  rate_mutex.lock
  loop do
    rate_mutex.sleep(3600)
    exchange_rates.update_from_online_feed
  end
end

loop do
  print "Enter currency code and amount: "
  line = gets
  if rate_mutex.try_lock
    begin
      puts(exchange_rates.convert(line))
    ensure
      puts "Ensuring unlock"
      rate_mutex.unlock
    end
  else
    puts "Sorry, rates being updated. Try again in a minute"
  end
end
```

Running Multiple External Processes

Sometimes you may want to split a task into several process-sized chunks—maybe to take advantage of all those cores in your shiny new processor. Or perhaps you need to run a separate process that was not written in Ruby. Not a problem: Ruby has a number of methods by which you may spawn and manage separate processes.

Spawning New Processes

You have several ways to spawn a separate process. The easiest is to run some command and wait for it to complete. You may find yourself doing this to run a system command or retrieve data from the host system. Ruby lets you spawn a process with the system or by using backquote (or backtick) methods:

```
system("tar xzf test.tgz") # => true
spawn("date")              # => 38483\nThu Nov  2 17:16:10 CDT 2023
`date`                     # => "Thu Nov  2 17:16:10 CDT 2023\n"
```

The method Kernel#system executes the given command in a subprocess; it returns true if the command was found and executed properly. It raises an exception if the command cannot be found. It returns false if the command ran but returned an error. In case of an error, you'll find the subprocess's exit code in the global variable $?. The spawn method is the same as system, except that it returns the process ID of the spawned process and doesn't wait for the process to be finished to move forward.

One problem with system is that the command's output will simply go to the same destination as the program's output, which may not be what you want. To capture the standard output of a subprocess, you can use the backquote characters, as with date in the previous example. Note that you may need to use String#chomp to remove the line-ending characters from the result.

This is fine for simple cases—we can run an external process and get the return status. But many times we need a bit more control than that. We'd like to carry on a conversation with the subprocess, possibly sending it data and possibly getting some back. The method IO.popen does just this. The popen method runs a command as a subprocess and connects that subprocess's standard input and standard output to a Ruby IO object. Write to the IO object, and the subprocess can read it on standard input. Whatever the subprocess writes is available in the Ruby program by reading from the IO object.

For example, on our systems, one of the more useful utilities is pig, a program that reads words from standard input and prints them in pig Latin (or igpay atinlay). We can use this when our Ruby programs need to send us output that our five-year-olds shouldn't be able to understand:

```ruby
pig = IO.popen("local/util/pig", "w+")
pig.puts "ice cream after they go to bed"
pig.close_write
puts pig.gets
```

produces:

```
iceway eamcray afterway eythay ogay otay edbay
```

This example illustrates both the apparent simplicity and the more subtle real-world complexities involved in driving subprocesses through pipes. The code certainly looks simple enough: open the pipe, write a phrase, and read back the response. But it turns out that the pig program doesn't flush the output it writes. Our original attempt at this example, which had a pig.puts followed immediately by a pig.gets, hung forever. The pig program processed our input, but its response was never written to the pipe. We had to insert the pig.close_write line. This sends an end-of-file to pig's standard input, and the output we're looking for gets flushed as pig terminates.

The popen method has one more twist. If the command you pass is a single minus sign (-), popen will fork a new Ruby interpreter. Both this and the original interpreter will continue running by returning from the popen. The original process will receive an IO object back, and the child will receive nil. This works only on operating systems that support the fork call[1] (and for now, this excludes Windows, unless you use WDSL).

```ruby
tut_threads/fork.rb
new_pipe = IO.popen("-","w+")
if new_pipe
  new_pipe.puts "Get a job!"
  $stderr.puts "I'm the parent, the child said to me '#{new_pipe.gets.chomp}'"
else
```

---

1. https://www.freebsd.org/cgi/man.cgi?query=fork

```
  $stderr.puts "I'm the child, the parent said to me '#{gets.chomp}'"
  puts "OK"
end
```

produces:

```
I'm the child, the parent said to me 'Get a job!'
I'm the parent, the child said to me 'OK'
```

Let's walk this one through. The original, soon-to-be parent interpreter calls IO.popen with the minus sign argument. We now have two Ruby interpreters each of which moves forward from this point. The original interpreter gets an IO pipe back as new_pipe, and the new child interpreter gets nil. At this point, the parent can send text to the child using new_pipe.puts and can listen for text from the child using new_pipe.gets. From the child's perspective, new_pipe is nil, but it can communicate with the parent using the regular Kernel methods, gets to listen for input and puts to send output to the parent.

The code splits on the if new_pipe expression. For the child, the pipe is nil, this expression is false, and the child goes down the else branch. For the parent, the pipe exists, the expression is true, and the parent goes down the main branch.

In the parent branch, the parent immediately uses new_pipe.puts to send a string to the child branch, and then it calls $stderr.puts to write something to the global standard error output. That string contains new_pipe.gets, meaning that it will block waiting for something to be sent from the child.

In the child branch, similar things happen. The $stderr.puts call includes a call to gets which is listening for the text coming from the parent process, and then the child puts text to be read by the parent process.

We're using the standard error port here rather than standard out because standard error automatically flushes its text after being called. If we used standard output, we'd likely get the first part of each output statement interleaved while it waits for the text coming from the other process.

In addition to the popen method, some platforms support the methods Kernel#fork, Kernel#exec, and Kernel#pipe. The file naming convention of many IO methods and Kernel#open will also spawn subprocesses if you put a pipe character, |, as the first character of the filename. Note that you *cannot* create pipes using File.new; that method is only for files.

Independent Children

Sometimes we don't need to be so hands-on; we'd like to give the subprocess its assignment and then go on about our business. Later, we'll check to see whether it has finished. For instance, we may want to kick off a long-running external sort:

```
pid = spawn("sort testfile > output.txt")
 # The sort is now running in a child process
 # carry on processing in the main program

 # ... dum di dum ...

 # then wait for the sort to finish
Process.wait(pid)
```

The call to Kernel#spawn here executes a system-level command and returns its process ID. But it does not wait for the command to finish, so Ruby processing continues apace. Later, we issue a Process.wait call with the process ID, which causes the parent process to wait for the child process running the sort to complete and returns the child process ID.

If you'd rather be notified when a child exits (instead of just waiting around), you can set up a signal handler using Kernel#trap. Here we set up a trap on SIGCLD, which is the signal sent on "death of child process":

tut_threads/trap.rb
```
trap("CLD") do
  pid = Process.wait
  puts "Child pid #{pid}: terminated"
end

spawn("sort testfile > output.txt")

# Do other stuff...
```
produces:
```
Child pid 38545: terminated
```

Blocks and Subprocesses

The IO.popen method takes a command as an argument and an optional block. It runs the command and returns an IO object attached to that command. The method then passes the IO object to the block, where you can read from it or (more rarely) write to it.

```
IO.popen("date") { |f| puts "Date is #{f.gets}" }
```
produces:
```
Date is Thu Nov  2 17:16:10 CDT 2023
```

The IO object will be closed automatically when the code block exits, just as it is with IO.open.

If you associate a block with Kernel#fork, the code in the block will be run in a Ruby subprocess, and the parent will continue after the block:

tut_threads/fork_02.rb
```
fork do
  puts "In child, pid = #{$$}"
  exit 99
end
pid = Process.wait
puts "Child terminated, pid = #{pid}, status = #{$?.exitstatus}"
```
produces:
```
In child, pid = 38576
Child terminated, pid = 38576, status = 99
```

The $$ here is a global variable that's the process ID of the running process.

The wait method will, by default, wait for any subprocess to complete, but you can pass it a process ID (pid) as an argument if you want to wait on a specific process.

$? is a global variable that contains information on the termination of a subprocess.

Although Ruby's thread utilities are powerful, they are kind of low-level and have some common usage patterns. Ruby gives us two built-in higher-level patterns to support common usage: fibers and ractors. We'll talk about fibers first.

Creating Fibers

Although the name "fibers" suggests some kind of lightweight thread, Ruby's fibers are a mechanism for denoting a block of code that can be stopped and restarted, which is sometimes called a *coroutine*. Fibers in Ruby are *cooperatively multitasked*, meaning that the responsibility for yielding control rests with the individual fibers and not the operating system. Fibers can explicitly yield control, or be set to automatically yield control when its operations are blocked.

Fibers let you write programs that share control without incurring all of the complexity inherent in low-level threading. Let's look at a simple example. We'd like to analyze a text file, counting the occurrence of each word. We could do this (without using fibers) in a simple loop:

tut_threads/loop_word_count.rb
```
counts = Hash.new(0)
File.foreach("./testfile") do |line|
  line.scan(/\w+/) do |word|
    word = word.downcase
    counts[word] += 1
  end
end
counts.keys.sort.each { |k| print "#{k}:#{counts[k]} " }
```

produces:

```
and:1 is:3 line:3 on:1 one:1 so:1 this:3 three:1 two:1
```

But this code is messy—it mixes word finding with word counting. We could fix this by writing a method that reads the file and yields each successive word. But fibers give us a simpler solution:

tut_threads/fiber_word_count.rb
```
words = Fiber.new do
  File.foreach("./testfile") do |line|
    line.scan(/\w+/) do |word|
      Fiber.yield word.downcase
    end
  end
  nil
end

counts = Hash.new(0)
while (word = words.resume)
  counts[word] += 1
end
counts.keys.sort.each { |k| print "#{k}:#{counts[k]} " }
```

produces:

```
and:1 is:3 line:3 on:1 one:1 so:1 this:3 three:1 two:1
```

The constructor for the Fiber class takes a block and returns a fiber object. Unlike a thread, the code in the block for a Fiber isn't immediately executed.

After the Fiber is created, we can call resume on the fiber object. Calling resume the first time causes the block to start execution. In this case, the file is opened, and the scan method starts extracting individual words and passing each individual word to the block passed to scan.

Inside that block, Fiber.yield is called. Calling Fiber.yield suspends execution of the fiber—the resume method that we called to run the block returns any value passed to Fiber.yield.

Upon receiving the yielded value as the return value of resume, our main program enters the body of the loop and increments the count for the first word returned by the fiber. It then loops back up to the top of the while loop, which again calls words.resume while evaluating the condition. The resume call goes back into the block, continuing where it left off at the line after the Fiber.yield call.

When the fiber runs out of words in the file, the foreach block exits, and the code in the fiber terminates. Just as with a method call, the return value of the fiber will be the value of the last expression evaluated (which this code sets to nil). In this case, nil isn't strictly needed, as foreach will return nil when it terminates. But here nil just makes it explicit. The next time resume is called, it returns this value, nil. You'll get a FiberError if you attempt to call resume again after the fiber has terminated.

Fibers can be used to generate values from infinite sequences on demand. Here's a fiber that returns successive integers divisible by 2 and not divisible by 3:

tut_threads/infinite_fiber.rb
```
twos = Fiber.new do
  num = 2
  loop do
    Fiber.yield(num) unless num % 3 == 0
    num += 2
  end
end
10.times { print twos.resume, " " }
```
produces:
```
2 4 8 10 14 16 20 22 26 28
```

But you can more easily use lazy enumerators to gracefully create infinite lists. These are described in Enumerators Used as Generators and Filters, on page 80.

Because fibers are just objects, you can pass them around, store them in variables, and so on. Fibers can be resumed only in the thread that created them.

Fibers can also use the transfer method to explicitly transfer control between specific fibers. The tricky part here is that the receiver of transfer is the thread to be resumed—in other words, the call is fiber_that_gets_control.transfer(args) and not calling_fiber.transfer(fiber_that_gets_control). The return value of the transfer call is the same as yield—the last expression before the fiber pauses control again.

The yield/resume mechanism for switching control and the transfer method don't work well together. Specifically, if a fiber is started with resume then cedes control, it can only receive control using the same mechanism. If it uses yield, it can only be returned with resume. If it transfers out, it can only be transfered back. If a fiber is started with transfer, it can only return control using transfer, not yield. Using the wrong mechanism will result in an exception.

Fibers can be *non-blocking*, meaning that when a fiber would otherwise block because of I/O or waiting on another process, it automatically cedes control to a fiber scheduler which chooses another fiber to wake up and controls resuming the original fiber when it has whatever it needs to proceed.

To create a non-blocking fiber, you need to do two things:

- Call Fiber.set_scheduler to set a scheduler
- Create the fiber with Fiber.new(blocking: false)

The scheduler is the tricky part because instead of distributing a standard scheduler, Ruby only provides an interface that schedulers are expected to implement. Bruno Sutic's website https://github.com/bruno-/fiber_scheduler_list maintains a list of available schedulers and recommends using FiberScheduler[2] in Ruby 3.1 and up.

Understanding Ractors

Ruby 3.0 introduced *ractors*, a Ruby implementation of the Actor pattern for multithreaded behavior. (Experimental support for the feature was originally developed under the name "Guilds.")

How Ractors Work

Ractors allow true parallelism within a single Ruby interpreter: each ractor maintains its own GIL, allowing for potentially better performance. In order for this to work, ractors have only limited ability to access variables outside their scope and can communicate with each other in only specific, pre-defined ways. (Also, if for some reason you're running multiple threads inside a single ractor—probably you shouldn't do this—those threads are subject to the equivalent of a global lock on the ractor and won't run in parallel.)

We think that showing trivial examples of ractor code tends to obfuscate what's going on, so we're first going to explain conceptually how ractors work and talk about the API and then show some code that can actually do a thing.

You can think of a ractor as a chunk of code that has a single input port and a single output port. Metaphorically, you can think of a room with one door marked "entrance" and one door marked "exit." The entrance door has a potential queue to get in.

You create a ractor with Ractor.new, which always takes a block. The block becomes the inside of our metaphorical room. The new method optionally takes an arbitrary number of positional arguments, and there's an optional keyword argument called name: that you should use to give the ractor a unique name. We find it helps in understanding ractors to realize that in many useful cases, the block will contain a loop of some kind. Once a ractor is created, the pre-existing part of the thread is called the *main* ractor and can be accessed with Ractor.main.

Ractors mostly interact with each other in one of four ways:

- A ractor (including the main thread) can send arguments to a known other ractor. In our metaphorical room, this is asking somebody to stand in line at the entrance door to a different ractor. The entrance lines are infinite, and the sending call is guaranteed not to block (by "guaranteed" we mean "if this goes wrong you have much bigger problems"). The API call is send, and the receiver of the message is the ractor that the message is being sent to, other_ractor.send(my_args). This is similar to the API for fibers.

- A ractor (or the main thread) can take output from an other known ractor. Metaphorically, we're waiting by the exit door for the next value to emerge and grabbing it. The

---

2.   https://github.com/bruno-/fiber_scheduler

API call here is take, as in new_value = other_ractor.take, and the take call will block waiting for a value to be sent by the other ractor.

- Inside the ractor, the ractor can block waiting for an incoming message. Metaphorically, the ractor is waiting for somebody to show up at the entrance door. The API call here is Ractor.receive, and yes, that's a class method of the class Ractor.

- Inside the ractor, the ractor can block waiting for another ractor to ask for a value. Metaphorically, the ractor is waiting for somebody to knock on the exit door, and will then send a value out for them. The API call is Ractor.yield(obj), and the argument is the value that's sent out. The pattern here is that the external calls are messages sent to a ractor and the internal calls are class messages sent to Ractor that know that they take place inside a specific ractor. The API is constrained here to allow for some automatic thread safety to happen as values are passed to a ractor using send or from a ractor using yield or take.

Let's take a closer look at the lifecycle of a ractor.

First, the ractor is created using Ractor.new. The block is immediately started, and any arguments passed to new are passed to the block as though they came from a send message—we'll show what that means in How Ractors Pass Variables, on page 205.

The new ractor is *isolated*. This concept comes from other languages but is a new thing for Ruby that was added just for ractors. Being isolated means that the code inside the block won't be able to access any variables that aren't defined in the block—no globals and no external locals. The only way to have a value be visible to a ractor is via send.

The code block passed to the ractor executes until one of the following happens:

- The code block hits a Ractor.yield call. In this case, it waits for a different ractor to call ractor.take with this ractor as the receiver. When that happens, it passes away the argument to yield and continues operation.

- The code block hits a Ractor.recieve call. In this case, the ractor waits to receive another call to send (the arguments passed to send become the result returned by the recieve call) and then continues operation.

- The code block ends. The last expression value is available for one other ractor to retrieve using take.

Let's take a look at how ractors might be used to do the same word count example we did using fibers:

```
tut_threads/ractor_word_count.rb
reader = Ractor.new(name: "reader") do
  File.foreach("testfile") do |line|
    line.scan(/\w+/) do |word|
      Ractor.yield(word.downcase)
    end
  end
  nil
end

counter = Ractor.new(reader, name: "counter") do |source|
  result = Hash.new(0)
  while(word = source.take)
```

```
    result[word] += 1
  end
  result
end

counts = counter.take
counts.keys.sort.each { |k| print "#{k}:#{counts[k]} " }
```

produces:

```
and:1 is:3 line:3 on:1 one:1 so:1 this:3 three:1 two:1
```

We've maintained the same structure of the code. There's one ractor that's reading the file and another ractor that's actually doing the word count.

Here's more or less how this plays out, with the understanding that because this is parallel code, the exact order may differ slightly.

First, we create the reader ractor. The block starts immediately (or is scheduled to start immediately) and opens the file and scans the first line, at which point it blocks on Ractor.yield with the first word scanned.

Moving down the file, the counter ractor is created, with—and this is important—the reader as an argument. The counter block is now executed with the reader passed in as source. We have to pass the ractor to the block because the ractor is isolated. The block inside the ractor doesn't have access to the local variable reader.

Inside the counter ractor block, we build an empty hash and then a while loop on source.take. Each time we call source.take, we grab the most recent value yielded by the reader, and the reader continues forward until it blocks on the next yield call.

Eventually, the reader runs out of words in the file and hits nil at the end of the block. Subsequently, the last source.take returns nil and ends the while loop, and the counter returns the result.

After these two blocks comes the counter.take call, which will block the main ractor until the counter ractor is ready to return a value. Since the counter ractor doesn't yield anywhere, that call waits until it exits, and then the final value is available to take. It's a good thing we have that take call blocking because, if we didn't block on something in the main ractor, the code would terminate and all the internal ractors would be stopped.

Having pulled that last value, we then print out the results.

And it works. The two ractors run in parallel. But I don't like that the reader is blocked on every word; it seems like you'd rather allow the reader to get as far ahead as it can, and let the counter catch up.

You can do that by reversing the direction of the interaction, like this:

```
tut_threads/ractor_word_count_flipped.rb
counter = Ractor.new(name: "counter") do
  result = Hash.new(0)
  while (word = Ractor.receive)
    result[word] += 1
  end
  result
end
```

```
Ractor.new(counter, name: "reader") do |worker|
  File.foreach("./testfile") do |line|
    line.scan(/\w+/) do |word|
      worker.send(word.downcase)
    end
  end
  worker.send(nil)
end

counts = counter.take
counts.keys.sort.each { |k| print "#{k}:#{counts[k]} " }
```

produces:

```
and:1 is:3 line:3 on:1 one:1 so:1 this:3 three:1 two:1
```

Same logic, same result. This time, though, we start the counter first, it creates its hash and then blocks at Ractor.receive. Then we create the reading ractor, which takes the counter as an argument, again because otherwise the ractor block would be isolated. Inside the block, the reader opens the files and scans as before, but this time it uses send to pass each word back to the counter without blocking. Note that in this case, we need to explicitly also send nil at the end to terminate the loop.

The final two lines are the same, waiting on the counter to be finished, but overall, this version of the code should block less and allow the reader to get ahead of the worker if it can.

How Ractors Pass Variables

We've hinted that variables passed to and from ractors don't behave the same way as regular variable passing does in Ruby. The goal of the ractor implementation is to prevent ractors from changing values that other ractors depend on. One way that's done is by preventing ractors from having access to mutable variables that exist outside the ractor scope.

As we've already mentioned, ractors are isolated from the rest of their binding. Variables that would normally be in scope for the block aren't available inside the ractor.

Additionally, ractors apply special semantics to values that are passed to a ractor using send or yield. The ractor world divides Ruby objects into "shareable" or "unsharable."

Broadly, sharable objects are objects whose value can't be changed—immutable objects and objects that have been frozen. Specifically, the following are all considered shareable:

- The special values true, false, and nil.

- Symbols.

- "Small integers." What's a small integer? If you're familiar with Ruby before 2.4, it's an integer small enough to be represented as a Fixnum. For everybody else, it's an integer small enough to fit in one memory location, so, on a 64-bit machine, that's $2^{62} - 1$. (That's one bit for the sign and one bit to mark it as an integer.)

- Instances of type Float, Complex, Rational, String, or Regexp or larger Integers if they've been frozen.

- Instances of Class or Module – not instances of an individual class, instances of Class itself.

- Individual ractors.

- An instance of an object whose instance variables are all sharable.

Ruby provides the method Ractor.make_sharable(obj) which tries to make an arbitrary object sharable by walking through all its attributes and freezing them all. With the keyword argument copy: true, it makes a copy of the object and returns the copy.

Sharable objects are shared when passed to a ractor, meaning that a reference to them is passed along and both the sender and the receiver are still able to access the object. Unsharable objects are copied, unless you pass move: true to either Ractor.send or Ractor.yield. If you move the unsharable object, then it's available to the new ractor but no longer available to the ractor that sent it, attempting to access that variable after it moves will raise an exception.

Conditional Reception

A ractor can be made to be picky about what it lets in the front door by using the Ractor.receive_if method, which takes a block argument. If another ractor tries to send to a ractor that's waiting on receive_if, the receiving ractor will call the block argument on the objects sent. If the block returns a truthy value, then recieve_if returns the object the same way that plain ordinary recieve does. If the block returns a falsey value, the ractor continues to wait. But the failing object stays at the head of the line, so if the ractor ever does get an object that passes the block, all the failed objects are still in the entrance queue and are able to get picked up by future receive calls in the ractor.

Waiting on Multiple Ractors

If you have multiple ractors you might be waiting on and you want to respond to whichever of them yields a value on the outgoing port first, you can use Ractor.select. The argument to Ractor.select is an arbitrary number of ractors, as in Ractor.select(r1, r2, r3). The value returned is a two-object array; the first object is the ractor that has put the value on the port, and the second is the value itself, so r, val = Ractor.select(r1, r2, r3).

Now, there are a couple of weirdnesses here. First off, one of the ractors in the argument could be the ractor making the call, as in Ractor.select(r1, Ractor.current). If the current ractor is somehow the one that emits the value, then the select call still returns the value, but instead of returning the ractor, it returns :receive.

Also, you can use Ractor.select to deal with multiple other ractors that you expect to take rather than yield. In this case, our call needs to provide the value for the take call, which you do with a yield_value keyword argument: Ractor.select(r1, r2, yield_value: 37). In the yield case, the return values are :yield and nil. It's frankly not clear why those aren't two different methods.

You can slam shut either the entrance or exit door with the close_incoming and close_outgoing methods. Attempts to access a closed port on a ractor return an exception, as do attempts to access the outgoing port of a ractor that has ended and returned its last value.

What's Next

That covers the basics of threading in Ruby. We've talked about basic threads, using system processes, fibers, and ractors. Now let's look at how we can use testing to help ensure that our code does what we expect.

## CHAPTER 13

Testing Ruby Code

Automated testing has long been an important part of how Ruby developers validate their code. Not only does testing ensure that the code behaves as expected, but the process of writing tests can also expose weaknesses in the structure of the code. Ruby provides a core library called *minitest* to make it easy to write automated tests. A more complex and fully-featured library, *RSpec*, is also commonly used. The two tools have different terminologies and a slightly different focus. In this chapter, we'll look at how these tools are used for *unit testing*, which is testing that focuses on small chunks of code, typically individual methods or branches within methods.

Why Unit Test?

It's important to be able to test individual units for many reasons, one of which is that being able to isolate code into testable units is useful for ongoing changes and maintenance. Code in one unit often relies on the correct operation of the code in other units. If one unit turns out to contain bugs, then all the code that depends on that unit is potentially affected. This is a big problem.

When you unit test this code as you write it, two things can happen. First, you're more likely to find the bug while the code was still fresh in your mind. Second, because the unit test was only interacting with the code you just wrote, when a bug does appear, you only have to look through a handful of lines of code to find it, rather than doing archaeology on the rest of the code base.

Unit testing helps developers write better code. It helps before the code is actually written because thinking about testing naturally leads you to create better, more decoupled designs. It helps as you're writing the code because it gives you instant feedback on how accurate your code is. And it helps after you've written code because it both gives you the ability to check that the code still works and helps others understand how to use your code.

Unit testing is a Good Thing.

Unit testing and dynamic languages such as Ruby go hand in hand. The flexibility of Ruby makes writing tests easy, and the tests make it easier to verify that your code is working. Once you get into the swing of it, you'll find yourself writing a little code, writing a test or two, verifying that everything is copacetic, and then writing some more code. You may even find yourself writing the test before you write a little code.

Testing with Minitest

If all that seems a little abstract, let's look at an example of how you use the minitest library to write automated testing. We'll start with a Roman numeral class. Our first pass at the code is pretty simple; it lets us create an object representing a certain number and display that object in Roman numerals:

unittesting/romanbug.rb

```ruby
# This code has bugs
class Roman
  MAX_ROMAN = 4999

  def initialize(value)
    if value <= 0 || value > MAX_ROMAN
      fail "Roman values must be > 0 and <= #{MAX_ROMAN}"
    end
    @value = value
  end

  FACTORS = [
    ["m", 1000], ["cm", 900], ["d", 500], ["cd", 400],
    ["c", 100], ["xc", 90], ["l", 50], ["xl", 40],
    ["x", 10], ["ix", 9], ["v", 5], ["iv", 4],
    ["i", 1]
  ]

  def to_s
    value = @value
    roman = ""
    FACTORS.each do |code, factor|
      count, value = value.divmod(factor)
      roman << code unless count.zero?
    end
    roman
  end
end
```

We could test this without a framework code by writing another plain Ruby script, like this:

unittesting/manual_romanbug.rb

```ruby
require_relative "romanbug"

r = Roman.new(1)
fail "'i' expected" unless r.to_s == "i"

r = Roman.new(9)
fail "'ix' expected" unless r.to_s == "ix"
```

As the number of tests in a project grows, this kind of ad hoc approach can get complicated to manage. The Ruby standard library comes with minitest—a framework originally written by Ryan Davis and the seattle.rb user group, which makes tests easier to write, run, and manage.

The minitest testing framework has three facilities wrapped into a neat package:

- It gives you a way of expressing individual tests.
- It provides a framework for structuring the tests.
- It gives you flexible ways of invoking the tests.

Assertions == Expected Results

Rather than have you write series of individual if or unless statements in your tests, the testing framework allows you to define assertions that achieve the same thing. Although a number of different styles of assertion exist, they all follow the same pattern. Each gives you a way of specifying an expected result and a way of passing in the actual outcome. If the actual value doesn't match the expected value, the assertion outputs a nice message and records the failure.

For example, we could rewrite our previous test of the Roman class using minitest. For now, ignore the scaffolding code at the start and end, and just look at the assert_equal method:

unittesting/test_romanbug1.rb
```ruby
require_relative "romanbug"
require "minitest/autorun"

class TestRoman < Minitest::Test
  def test_simple
    assert_equal("i", Roman.new(1).to_s)
    assert_equal("ix", Roman.new(9).to_s)
  end
end
```

produces:
```
Run options: --seed 38570
# Running:

.

Finished in 0.000223s, 4484.3059 runs/s, 8968.6118 assertions/s.

1 runs, 2 assertions, 0 failures, 0 errors, 0 skips
```

The first assertion says that we're expecting the Roman number string representation of 1 to be "i," and the second test says we expect 9 to be "ix."

We can run the test by running the file as a Ruby file—the minitest/autorun module will automatically load and run our tests (more on that in a bit). Luckily for us, both expectations are met, and the tracing reports that our tests pass. Let's add a few more tests:

unittesting/test_romanbug2.rb
```ruby
require_relative "romanbug"
require "minitest/autorun"

class TestRoman < Minitest::Test
  def test_simple
    assert_equal("i", Roman.new(1).to_s)
    assert_equal("ii", Roman.new(2).to_s)
    assert_equal("iii", Roman.new(3).to_s)
    assert_equal("iv", Roman.new(4).to_s)
    assert_equal("ix", Roman.new(9).to_s)
  end
end
```

produces:
```
Run options: --seed 32554
# Running:

F
Finished in 0.000392s, 2551.0207 runs/s, 5102.0414 assertions/s.
```

```
1) Failure:
TestRoman#test_simple [code/unittesting/test_romanbug2.rb:7]:
Expected: "ii"
  Actual: "i"

1 runs, 2 assertions, 1 failures, 0 errors, 0 skips
```

Uh-oh! The second assertion failed. The error message uses the fact that the assertion knows both the expected and actual values: it expected to get "ii" but instead got "i." Looking at our code, you can see a clear bug in to_s. If the count after dividing by the factor is greater than zero, then we should output that many Roman digits. The existing code outputs only one. The fix is easy, change the line roman << code unless count.zero? to roman << (code * count):

unittesting/roman3.rb
```ruby
def to_s
  value = @value
  roman = ""
  FACTORS.each do |code, factor|
    count, value = value.divmod(factor)
    roman << (code * count)
  end
  roman
end
```

Now let's run our tests again:

unittesting/test_roman3.rb
```ruby
require_relative "roman3"
require "minitest/autorun"
class TestRoman < Minitest::Test
  def test_simple
    assert_equal("i", Roman.new(1).to_s)
    assert_equal("ii", Roman.new(2).to_s)
    assert_equal("iii", Roman.new(3).to_s)
    assert_equal("iv", Roman.new(4).to_s)
    assert_equal("ix", Roman.new(9).to_s)
  end
end
```

produces:
```
Run options: --seed 59738
# Running:

.

Finished in 0.000451s, 2217.2952 runs/s, 11086.4759 assertions/s.

1 runs, 5 assertions, 0 failures, 0 errors, 0 skips
```

It's looking good. You can see there's some duplication in the test, and you might be tempted to address it by running each expected and actual value pair in a loop. We recommend avoiding loops in tests because they are often hard to read and debug if the tests fail. Instead, we recommend making the assertions as clear as possible, so we might re-write the test like this:

unittesting/test_roman4.rb
```ruby
require_relative "roman3"
require "minitest/autorun"
```

```ruby
class TestRoman < Minitest::Test
  def assert_roman_value(roman_numeral, arabic_numeral)
    assert_equal(roman_numeral, Roman.new(arabic_numeral).to_s)
  end

  def test_simple
    assert_roman_value("i", 1)
    assert_roman_value("ii", 2)
    assert_roman_value("iii", 3)
    assert_roman_value("iv", 4)
    assert_roman_value("ix", 9)
  end
end
```

produces:

```
Run options: --seed 44317
# Running:

.

Finished in 0.000279s, 3584.2290 runs/s, 17921.1451 assertions/s.

1 runs, 5 assertions, 0 failures, 0 errors, 0 skips
```

We think this does a good job of separating the boilerplate action of the comparison from the data values we're trying to compare.

What else can we test? Well, the constructor of our Roman class checks that the number we pass in can be represented as a Roman number, throwing an exception if it can't. Let's test the exception:

unittesting/test_roman5.rb
```ruby
require_relative "roman3"
require "minitest/autorun"

class TestRoman < Minitest::Test
  def assert_roman_value(roman_numeral, arabic_numeral)
    assert_equal(roman_numeral, Roman.new(arabic_numeral).to_s)
  end

  def test_simple
    assert_roman_value("i", 1)
    assert_roman_value("ii", 2)
    assert_roman_value("iii", 3)
    assert_roman_value("iv", 4)
    assert_roman_value("ix", 9)
  end

  def test_range
    # no exception for these two...
    Roman.new(1)
    Roman.new(4999)
    # but an exception for these
    assert_raises(RuntimeError) { Roman.new(0) }
    assert_raises(RuntimeError) { Roman.new(5000) }
  end
end
```

produces:

```
Run options: --seed 4358
# Running:

..
Finished in 0.000328s, 6097.5622 runs/s, 21341.4676 assertions/s.

2 runs, 7 assertions, 0 failures, 0 errors, 0 skips
```

We could do more testing on our Roman class, but let's move on. We've only scratched the surface of the set of assertions available inside the testing framework. For example, for every positive assertion (such as assert_equal) there's a negative refutation (such as refute_equal).

The final parameter to every assertion is an optional message that will be output before any failure message. This normally isn't needed because the failure messages are normally pretty reasonable. The one exception is the assertion refute_nil, where the default message "Expected nil to not be nil" doesn't help much. In that case, you may want to add some annotation of your own. (This code assumes the existence of some kind of User class.)

```ruby
require 'minitest/autorun'
class ATestThatFails < Minitest::Test
  def test_user_created
    user = User.find(1)
    refute_nil(user, "User with ID=1 should exist")
  end
end
```

produces:

```
Run options: --seed 16917
# Running:

F
Finished in 0.000252s, 3968.2549 runs/s, 3968.2549 assertions/s.

  1) Failure:
ATestThatFails#test_user_created [prog.rb:11]:
User with ID=1 should exist.
Expected nil to not be nil.

1 runs, 1 assertions, 1 failures, 0 errors, 0 skips
```

Structuring Tests

Earlier we asked you to ignore the scaffolding around our tests. Now it's time to look at it.

You include the testing framework facilities in your unit by including minitest/autorun.

```ruby
require "minitest/autorun"
```

The minitest/autorun module includes minitest itself, which has most of the features we've talked about so far. It also includes an alternate minitest/spec syntax that's more like RSpec and the minitest/mock mock object package. (We're not going to talk about minitest/spec syntax in this book. If you want that style of syntax, we recommend actually using RSpec.) Finally, it calls Minitest.autorun, which starts the test runner. This is why our test files have been executing tests when invoked just as plain Ruby files.

Unit tests are often combined into high-level groupings, called *test cases*. The test cases generally contain all the tests relating to a particular facility or feature—in Ruby, often each application class will have one associated test case. Within the test case, you'll typically want to organize your assertions into separate test methods, where each method contains the assertions for one type of test; one method could check regular number conversions, another could test error handling, and so on. (We'll see later that RSpec allows you to structure tests a little bit differently.)

The classes that represent test cases must be subclasses of Minitest::Test. The methods that hold the assertions must have names that start with test_. This is important: the testing framework dynamically searches the test methods to find tests to run, and only methods whose names start with test_ are eligible.

Quite often you'll find that all the test methods within a test case start by setting up a particular scenario. Each test method then probes some aspect of that scenario. Finally, each method may then tidy up after itself. For example, we could be testing a class that extracts jukebox playlists from a database. (The playlist_builder file contains a DBI class that simulates a database connection for our purposes here.)

unittesting/test_playlist_builder1.rb
```ruby
require "minitest/autorun"
require_relative "playlist_builder"

class TestPlaylistBuilder < Minitest::Test
  def test_empty_playlist
    database = DBI.new("DBI:mysql:playlists")
    playlist_builder = PlaylistBuilder.new(database)
    assert_empty(playlist_builder.playlist)
    playlist_builder.close
  end

  def test_artist_playlist
    database = DBI.new("DBI:mysql:playlists")
    playlist_builder = PlaylistBuilder.new(database)
    playlist_builder.include_artist("krauss")
    refute_empty(playlist_builder.playlist, "Playlist shouldn't be empty")
    playlist_builder.playlist.each do |entry|
      assert_match(/krauss/i, entry.artist)
    end
    playlist_builder.close
  end

  def test_title_playlist
    database = DBI.new("DBI:mysql:playlists")
    playlist_builder = PlaylistBuilder.new(database)
    playlist_builder.include_title("midnight")
    refute_empty(playlist_builder.playlist, "Playlist shouldn't be empty")
    playlist_builder.playlist.each do |entry|
      assert_match(/midnight/i, entry.title)
    end
    playlist_builder.close
  end

  # ...
end
```

produces:

```
Run options: --seed 19023
# Running:

...
Finished in 0.000397s, 7556.6751 runs/s, 115869.0188 assertions/s.

3 runs, 46 assertions, 0 failures, 0 errors, 0 skips
```

Each test starts by connecting to a database and creating a new playlist builder. Each test ends by disconnecting from the database. The idea of using a real database in unit tests is questionable because unit tests are supposed to be fast-running, context-independent, and easy to set up, but it illustrates a point. (And that said, Ruby on Rails makes database calls in its unit tests all the time.)

We can extract all this common code into *setup* and *teardown* methods. Within a Minitest::Test class, if a method called setup exists, it'll be run before each and every test method, and if a method called teardown exists, it'll be run after each test method finishes. The setup and teardown methods bracket each test rather than being run only once for the entire test case. This is shown in the code that follows:

unittesting/test_playlist_builder2.rb
```ruby
require "minitest/autorun"
require_relative "playlist_builder"

class TestPlaylistBuilder < Minitest::Test
  def setup
    @database = DBI.new("DBI:mysql:playlists")
    @playlist_builder = PlaylistBuilder.new(@database)
  end

  def teardown
    @playlist_builder.close
  end

  def test_empty_playlist
    assert_empty(@playlist_builder.playlist)
  end

  def test_artist_playlist
    @playlist_builder.include_artist("krauss")
    refute_empty(@playlist_builder.playlist, "Playlist shouldn't be empty")
    @playlist_builder.playlist.each do |entry|
      assert_match(/krauss/i, entry.artist)
    end
  end

  def test_title_playlist
    @playlist_builder.include_title("midnight")
    refute_empty(@playlist_builder.playlist, "Playlist shouldn't be empty")
    @playlist_builder.playlist.each do |entry|
      assert_match(/midnight/i, entry.title)
    end
  end

  # ...
end
```

produces:

```
Run options: --seed 17223
# Running:

...
Finished in 0.000437s, 6864.9875 runs/s, 105263.1415 assertions/s.

3 runs, 46 assertions, 0 failures, 0 errors, 0 skips
```

Inside the teardown method, you can detect whether the preceding test succeeded with the passed? method.

Creating Mock Objects in Minitest

Minitest allows you to create *mock objects*, which are objects that simulate the API of an existing object in the system, typically providing a canned response instead of a more expensive or fragile real response. A minitest mock object can be *verified*, meaning it'll raise a failure if the methods you expected to be called were not called during the test.

Using these mock object expectations allows for a style of testing where, instead of testing the result of a method by verifying its output, you test the behavior of the method by verifying that it makes expected calls to other methods.

In minitest, a mock object is created like any other Ruby object. Then you add the methods you wish the mock to respond to via the expect method. At the end, you can optionally test that all expected methods were called with verify.

For example, we can re-write our playlist builder test so that we don't need to create a "real" DBI instance. (The word *real* is in scare quotes because, for this contrived example, even the DBI instance in the previous code was faked....) Behind the scenes, our playlist builder calls connect and disconnect on the DBI instance.

We can instead create a mock object:

```
unittesting/test_playlist_builder_mock.rb
require "minitest/autorun"
require_relative "playlist_builder"

class TestPlaylistBuilder < Minitest::Test
  def setup
    @database = Minitest::Mock.new
    @database.expect(:connect, true)
    @database.expect(:disconnect, false)
    @playlist_builder = PlaylistBuilder.new(@database)
  end

  def teardown
    @database.disconnect
    @database.verify
  end

  def test_empty_playlist
    assert_empty(@playlist_builder.playlist)
  end

  def test_artist_playlist
    @playlist_builder.include_artist("krauss")
    refute_empty(@playlist_builder.playlist, "Playlist shouldn't be empty")
```

```
    @playlist_builder.playlist.each do |entry|
      assert_match(/krauss/i, entry.artist)
    end
  end

  def test_title_playlist
    @playlist_builder.include_title("midnight")
    refute_empty(@playlist_builder.playlist, "Playlist shouldn't be empty")
    @playlist_builder.playlist.each do |entry|
      assert_match(/midnight/i, entry.title)
    end
  end

  # ...
end
```

produces:

```
Run options: --seed 61004
# Running:

...
Finished in 0.000585s, 5128.2049 runs/s, 78632.4745 assertions/s.

3 runs, 46 assertions, 0 failures, 0 errors, 0 skips
```

Now, the setup method is creating the @database as a Minitest::Mock and then setting the expectation that the test will call connect and disconnect on the object (which is done behind the scenes by the PlaylistBuilder). The second argument to each method is a value returned when the mocked method is called. At the end of each test, in the teardown method, we verify the mock object, which raises a failure if both expectations aren't met.

Minitest mock objects can get more complicated. A mock object can take an optional third argument, which is an array of arguments, and an optional block argument. If those arguments are used, then the mock object only accepts the method call if the arguments match. If not, it raises a MockExpectationError when called with arguments that don't match. If you want to call the mock object multiple times, you need to have multiple expect calls, which are used in the order defined.

It's common to want to override one method on an existing object rather than create an entire mock object (this isn't necessarily recommended, but it's common). In minitest, you can do this with the stub method, which is added to Object, so it's available to all objects.

The first argument to stub is the name of the method you want to intercept, as a symbol. The second argument is the value you want returned, or you can pass a block argument. The return value of the stub is one of these:

- The value returned by the block if there is a block.

- The result of second_arg.call if the second argument responds to call, usually meaning that it's a Proc or lambda.

- The second argument itself if neither of the first two options is true.

So, we could re-write the setup of that test using stub as follows:

```
def setup
  @database = DBI.new("DBI:mysql:playlists")
  @database.stub(:connect, true)
```

```
  @database.stub(:disconnect, true)
  @playlist_builder = PlaylistBuilder.new(@database)
end
```

This version calls stub to make calls to connect or disconnect be handled by the stubbing functionality to return true rather than making the actual method call.

Stubs don't get verified, so they are most useful for replacing an expensive or flaky method call with a canned value for use as part of some larger logic.

If you want a more complex mock object behavior, the longstanding Ruby library Mocha[1] is the next step up in using mock objects in minitest.

Organizing and Running Tests

The test cases we've seen so far are all runnable Ruby programs. If, for example, the test case for the Roman class was in a file called test_roman.rb, we could run the tests from the command line using this:

```
$ ruby test_roman.rb
Run options: --seed 29842
# Running:
..
Finished in 0.000407s, 4914.0040 runs/s, 17199.0141 assertions/s.
2 runs, 7 assertions, 0 failures, 0 errors, 0 skips
```

Minitest is clever enough to run the tests even though there's no main program. It collects all the test case classes and runs each in turn.

If we want, we can ask it to run a particular set of test methods based on a naming pattern:

```
$ ruby test_roman.rb -n test_range
Run options: -n test_range --seed 26287
# Running:
.
Finished in 0.000276s, 3623.1883 runs/s, 7246.3767 assertions/s.
1 runs, 2 assertions, 0 failures, 0 errors, 0 skips
```

In this case, minitest will run test methods whose names exactly match the text passed to -n. That's pretty restrictive. So, if you want to run more than one test based on a naming pattern and include any regular expression punctuation in the argument, minitest will match the test name against the regular expression:

```
$ ruby test_roman.rb -n /range/
Run options: -n /range/ --seed 52301
# Running:
.
Finished in 0.000321s, 3115.2648 runs/s, 6230.5296 assertions/s.
1 runs, 2 assertions, 0 failures, 0 errors, 0 skips
```

This last capability is a great way of grouping your tests. Use meaningful names, and you'll be able to run (for example) all the shopping cart–related tests by running tests with -n /cart/.

---

1. https://mocha.jamesmead.org

Where to Put Tests

Once you get into unit testing, you may well find yourself generating as much test code as production code. All of those tests have to live somewhere. But if you put them alongside your regular production code source files, your directories start to get bloated, and you end up with two files for every production source file.

A common solution is to have a test/ directory where you place all your test source files. This directory is then placed parallel to the directory containing the code you're developing. For example, for our Roman numeral class, we may have this:

```
roman/
  lib/
    roman.rb
    OTHER FILES

  test/
    test_roman.rb
    OTHER TESTS

  OTHER STUFF
```

This works well as a way of organizing files but leaves you with a small problem: how do you tell Ruby where to find the library files that are being tested? For example, if our TestRoman test code is in a test/ subdirectory, how does Ruby know where to find the roman.rb source file that we're trying to test?

An option that *doesn't* work reliably is to build the path into require statements in the test code and run the tests from the test/ subdirectory:

```
require 'test/unit'
require '../lib/roman'

class TestRoman < Minitest::Test
  # ...
end
```

This doesn't work in general because our roman.rb file may itself require other source files in the library we're writing. The roman.rb file will load them using require (without the leading ../lib/), and, because they aren't in Ruby's $LOAD_PATH, they won't be found. Our test just won't run. A second, less immediate problem is that we won't be able to use these same tests to test our classes once installed on a target system because then they'll be referenced simply using require "roman".

You could do this using require_relative '../lib/roman', which would be more stable and doesn't assume anything about the load path. A better solution is to assume that your Ruby program is packaged according to the conventions we'll be discussing in Chapter 15, Ruby Gems, on page 251. In this arrangement, the top-level lib directory of your application is assumed to be in Ruby's load path by all other components of the application. Your test code would then be as follows:

```
require 'minitest/autorun'
require 'roman'

class TestRoman < Minitest::Test
  # ...
end
```

And you'd run it using this:

```
$ ruby -I path/to/app/lib path/to/app/test/test_roman.rb
```

The normal case, where you're already in the application's directory, would be as follows:

```
$ ruby -I lib test/test_roman.rb
```

This would be a good time to investigate using Rake to automate your testing (see Using the Rake Build Tool, on page 245).

Test Suites

After a while, you'll grow a decent collection of test cases for your application. You may well find that these tend to cluster: one group of cases tests a particular set of functions, and another group tests a different set of functions. If so, you can group those test cases together into *test suites*, letting you run them all as a group.

This is easy to do. You create a Ruby file that requires minitest/autorun and then requires each of the files holding the test cases you want to group. This way, you build a helpful hierarchy of test material.

- You can run individual tests by name.
- You can run all the tests in a file by running that file.
- You can group a number of files into a test suite and run them as a unit.
- You can group test suites into other test suites.

This gives you the ability to run your unit tests at a level of granularity that you can control, testing one method or the entire application.

Most people seem to use test_ as the test-case filename prefix. A sample test suite file might look like this:

```
require 'minitest/autorun'
require_relative 'test_connect'
require_relative 'test_query'
require_relative 'test_update'
require_relative 'test_delete'
```

Now, if you run Ruby on this file, you execute the test cases in the four files you've required.

Testing with RSpec

The minitest framework has a lot going for it. It's simple and compatible in style with frameworks from other languages (such as JUnit for Java and pytest for Python).

RSpec has different things going for it. It's feature-rich (or "complicated," as some would say), and it has a different vocabulary for discussing testing. It also has a different syntax. Even so, that syntax has influenced the design of other testing tools including the Jasmine and Jest JavaScript testing frameworks.

In RSpec, the focus isn't on assertions. Instead, you write *expectations*. RSpec is very much concerned with driving the design side of things. As a result, the vocabulary words of RSpec (expectation and specification) are associated with ways you might reason about your code before you write it. A "spec" is something you'd write before coding; an "assertion" is something you use to describe code that already exists.

To be clear, you can write RSpec after you write your code, just as you can write minitest before you write your code. The design goal of RSpec is to encourage thinking about tests as a way to influence the design of code yet to be written and express those tests in a way that's closer to natural language. Then, as you fill in the code, the specs can continue to act as tests that validate that your code meets your expectations.

Let's start with a simple example of RSpec in action.

Starting to Score Tennis Matches

The scoring system used in lawn tennis originated in the Middle Ages. As players win successive points, their scores are shown as 15, 30, and 40. The next point is a win unless your opponent also has 40. If you're both tied at 40, then different rules apply. The first player with a clear two-point advantage is the winner. Some say the 0, 15, 30, 40 system is a corruption of the fact that scoring used to be done using the quarters of a clock face. We just think those medieval folks enjoyed a good joke.

We want to write a class that handles this scoring system. Let's use RSpec specifications to drive the process. We install RSpec with gem install rspec, or place it in our Gemfile (see Chapter 15, Ruby Gems, on page 251). We'll then create our first specification file:

```
unittesting/bdd/1/ts_spec.rb
RSpec.describe "TennisScorer" do
  describe "basic scoring" do
    it "starts with a score of 0-0"
    it "makes the score 15-0 if the server wins a point"
    it "makes the score 0-15 if the receiver wins a point"
    it "makes the score 15-15 after they both win a point"
  end
end
```

This file contains nothing more than a description of the beginning of how a tennis scoring class that we haven't yet written should behave. Inside the declaration of the class is a grouping (describe "basic scoring") and inside that is a set of four expectations, all of which start with it. We can run this specification using the rspec command.

```
$ rspec ts_spec.rb
****
Pending: (Failures listed here are expected and do not affect your suite's status)
  1) TennisScorer basic scoring starts with a score of 0-0
     # Not yet implemented
     # ./ts_spec.rb:3
  2) TennisScorer basic scoring makes the score 15-0 if the server wins a point
     # Not yet implemented
     # ./ts_spec.rb:4
  3) TennisScorer basic scoring makes the score 0-15 if the receiver wins a point
     # Not yet implemented
     # ./ts_spec.rb:5
  4) TennisScorer basic scoring makes the score 15-15 after they both win a point
     # Not yet implemented
     # ./ts_spec.rb:6
Finished in 0.00191 seconds (files took 0.0777 seconds to load)
4 examples, 0 failures, 4 pending
```

That's pretty cool. Executing the tests echoes our expectations back at us, telling us that each has yet to be implemented. Fixing things is just a few keystrokes away. Let's start by meeting the first expectation—when a game starts, the score should be 0 to 0. We'll start by fleshing out the spec:

unittesting/bdd/2/ts_spec.rb
```ruby
require_relative "tennis_scorer"

RSpec.describe TennisScorer do
  describe "basic scoring" do
    it "starts with a score of 0-0" do
      ts = TennisScorer.new
      expect(ts.score).to eq("0-0")
    end

    it "makes the score 15-0 if the server wins a point"
    it "makes the score 0-15 if the receiver wins a point"
    it "makes the score 15-15 after they both win a point"
  end
end
```

Our tests assume that we have a class TennisScorer, both in the line of code that creates an instance and also in the top line of code RSpec.describe TennisScorer. Inside that, we have a second call to describe that groups our expectations. Our first expectation now has a code block associated with it. Inside that block, we create a TennisScorer and then use RSpec's expectation syntax to validate that the score starts out at "0-0". This particular aspect of RSpec syntax probably generates the most controversy—some people love it, others find it awkward. Either way, expect(ts.score).to eq("0-0") is equivalent to assert_equal("0-0", ts.score).

We can run our tests at this point with the same command, and we'll see the test fail because the TennisScorer class doesn't exist.

Before we create that class and pass the test, let's take a moment to explain what RSpec is doing here. RSpec is an example of a *domain-specific language* (DSL), an alternate syntax built on Ruby with the goal of making it easier to express the intent of the test. Like a lot of Ruby DSLs, RSpec takes advantage of Ruby's flexibility to result in code that doesn't look exactly like regular Ruby.

When trying to understand RSpec, it's helpful to reinstate full parentheses and implicit self message receivers as a guide to what's actually happening. Here's what that looks like for our current spec:

unittesting/bdd/2/ts_spec_paren.rb
```ruby
require_relative "tennis_scorer"

RSpec.describe(TennisScorer) do
  self.describe("basic scoring") do
    self.it("starts with a score of 0-0") do
      ts = TennisScorer.new
      self.expect(ts.score).to(self.eq("0-0"))
    end

    self.it("makes the score 15-0 if the server wins a point")
    self.it("makes the score 0-15 if the receiver wins a point")
    self.it("makes the score 15-15 after they both win a point")
  end
end
```

With all the parentheses, the structure of the code becomes more familiar. The top line shows that describe is a method of an object named RSpec, and that the inner describe and it lines are also methods with block arguments. There's actually an important part of how this fits together that we haven't discussed (it's a method called instance_eval, which is discussed in Chapter 22, The Ruby Object Model and Metaprogramming, on page 371), but the basic idea is that RSpec takes the blocks that are arguments to describe and it, holds on to them, and then invokes them later in order to run the spec.

You can see that the actual expectation is also just a set of method calls. The expect method is called with an object as an argument. The result of that method is passed the to method, which itself takes an argument that's generated by calling eq. The result of the call to eq is a *matcher*, and RSpec defines a series of matchers that interact with the to method (or its sibling method not_to) to determine whether the expectation is fulfilled or not.

We'll set up our TennisScorer class but only enough to let it satisfy this assertion:

unittesting/bdd/2/tennis_scorer.rb
```ruby
class TennisScorer
  def score
    "0-0"
  end
end
```

Now we can run our spec again:

```
$ rspec ts_spec.rb
.***
Pending: (Failures listed here are expected and do not affect your suite's status)
  1) TennisScorer basic scoring makes the score 15-0 if the server wins a point
     # Not yet implemented
     # ./ts_spec.rb:10
  2) TennisScorer basic scoring makes the score 0-15 if the receiver wins a point
     # Not yet implemented
     # ./ts_spec.rb:11
  3) TennisScorer basic scoring makes the score 15-15 after they both win a point
     # Not yet implemented
     # ./ts_spec.rb:12
Finished in 0.0016 seconds (files took 0.04504 seconds to load)
4 examples, 0 failures, 3 pending
```

Now we have only three pending specs; the first one has been satisfied.

Let's write the next couple of specs (I've added a new one for an error case):

unittesting/bdd/3/ts_spec.rb
```ruby
require_relative "tennis_scorer"

RSpec.describe TennisScorer do
  describe "basic scoring" do
    it "starts with a score of 0-0" do
      ts = TennisScorer.new
      expect(ts.score).to eq("0-0")
    end

    it "makes the score 15-0 if the server wins a point" do
      ts = TennisScorer.new
      ts.give_point_to(:server)
```

```
      expect(ts.score).to eq("15-0")
    end

    it "raises an error if it doesn't know the player" do
      ts = TennisScorer.new
      expect { ts.give_point_to(:referee) }.to raise_error(RuntimeError)
    end

    it "makes the score 0-15 if the receiver wins a point"
    it "makes the score 15-15 after they both win a point"
  end
end
```

This won't pass yet because our TennisScorer class doesn't implement a give_point_to method. Let's rectify that. Our code isn't finished, but now the existing specs will pass:

unittesting/bdd/3/tennis_scorer.rb
```
class TennisScorer
  PLAYERS = %i[server receiver]

  def initialize
    @score = {server: 0, receiver: 0}
  end

  def score
    "#{@score[:server] * 15}-#{@score[:receiver] * 15}"
  end

  def give_point_to(player)
    raise "Unknown player #{player}" unless PLAYERS.include?(player)
    @score[player] += 1
  end
end
```

Again, we'll run the file:

```
$ rspec ts_spec.rb
...**
Pending: (Failures listed here are expected and do not affect your suite's status)
  1) TennisScorer basic scoring makes the score 0-15 if the receiver wins a point
     # Not yet implemented
     # ./ts_spec.rb:21
  2) TennisScorer basic scoring makes the score 15-15 after they both win a point
     # Not yet implemented
     # ./ts_spec.rb:22
Finished in 0.0031 seconds (files took 0.04484 seconds to load)
5 examples, 0 failures, 2 pending
```

We're now meeting two of the four initial expectations. But, before we move on, note there's a bit of duplication in the specification: all of our expectations create a new TennisScorer object. We can fix that by using a before method in the specification. This works a bit like the setup method in minitest, allowing us to run code before expectations are executed. Let's use this feature and, at the same time, build out the last two expectations:

unittesting/bdd/4/ts_spec.rb
```
require_relative "tennis_scorer"

RSpec.describe TennisScorer do
  describe "basic scoring" do
```

```ruby
  before(:example) do
    @ts = TennisScorer.new
  end

  it "starts with a score of 0-0" do
    expect(@ts.score).to eq("0-0")
  end

  it "makes the score 15-0 if the server wins a point" do
    @ts.give_point_to(:server)
    expect(@ts.score).to eq("15-0")
  end

  it "raises an error if it doesn't know the player" do
    expect { @ts.give_point_to(:referee) }.to raise_error(RuntimeError)
  end

  it "makes the score 0-15 if the receiver wins a point" do
    @ts.give_point_to(:receiver)
    expect(@ts.score).to eq("0-15")
  end

  it "makes the score 15-15 after they both win a point" do
    @ts.give_point_to(:receiver)
    @ts.give_point_to(:server)
    expect(@ts.score).to eq("15-15")
  end
  end
end
```

Let's run it:

```
$ rspec ts_spec.rb
.....
Finished in 0.00193 seconds (files took 0.04763 seconds to load)
5 examples, 0 failures
```

RSpec gives us an alternative, preferred way of setting up variables that are conditions for our tests. The let method creates what looks like a variable whose value is given by evaluating a block. This lets us write the following:

unittesting/bdd/5/ts_spec.rb
```ruby
require_relative "tennis_scorer"

RSpec.describe TennisScorer do
  describe "basic scoring" do
    let(:ts) { TennisScorer.new }

    it "starts with a score of 0-0" do
      expect(ts.score).to eq("0-0")
    end

    it "makes the score 15-0 if the server wins a point" do
      ts.give_point_to(:server)
      expect(ts.score).to eq("15-0")
    end

    it "raises an error if it doesn't know the player" do
      expect { ts.give_point_to(:referee) }.to raise_error(RuntimeError)
    end
```

```
    it "makes the score 0-15 if the receiver wins a point" do
      ts.give_point_to(:receiver)
      expect(ts.score).to eq("0-15")
    end

    it "makes the score 15-15 after they both win a point" do
      ts.give_point_to(:receiver)
      ts.give_point_to(:server)
      expect(ts.score).to eq("15-15")
    end
  end
end
```

The let block is only evaluated when the associated variable is used, and then the block is evaluated once, and further uses of that variable use the stored value from the first evaluation.

We're going to stop here, but I suggest that you take this code and continue to develop it. Write expectations such as these:

```
it "is 40-0 after the server wins three points"
it "is W-L after the server wins four points"
it "is L-W after the receiver wins four points"
it "is Deuce after each wins three points"
it "is Advantage-server after each wins three points and the server gets one more"
```

RSpec and Matchers

In the previous code, we kind of ran right past RSpec's matchers—lines like expect(@ts.score).to eq("15-0"). RSpec has a rich syntax of matchers to cover the same ground that minitest does with different assertions.

We've already seen eq, but that matcher is a little unusual. Many of RSpec's matchers start with be, as with this set of matchers that cover basic logic:

```
expect(value).to be_truthy
expect(value).to be_falsey
expect(value).to be_an_instance_of(Product)
expect(value.price).to be > 10
expect(value.price).to be_between(5, 15)
```

You can substitute any Ruby comparison operator for the greater than symbol in be >.

RSpec also provides matchers for structured data, such as objects, arrays, hashes, and strings:

```
expect(array).to contain_exactly(:a, :b, :c)
```

```
expect(hash).to include(key: value)
```

```
expect(string).to start_with("abc")
expect(string).to end_with("xyz")
```

```
expect(instance).to have_attributes(color: "blue")
```

```
expect(array_string_or_hash).to include("value")
```

In addition, RSpec has a generic matcher match, which can be applied to arrays, strings, or hashes. Typically, the argument to match is a pattern, and the expectation passes if the expected value fits the pattern. You can use other RSpec matchers to fill part of the pattern.

Some examples:

```
expect(string).to match(/regex/)
expect(array).to match([3, 5])
expect(hash).to match(color: a_string_starting_with("b"))
```

The last example shows that RSpec offers aliases for most of its matchers so they read more like natural language when used internally, so "a_string_starting_with" is an alias for "starts_with". This is where people's opinions about RSpec start to split—some people find this kind of linguistic wordplay elegant and clever, while others find it confusing and overly complicated.

Which is a great lead into RSpec's dynamic matcher syntax.

Often, an object has boolean methods that you want to test. In Ruby, the community standard is to end boolean methods with a ? as in: paperback?.

```
class Book
  def paperback?
    type == :paper
  end
end
```

You can test this method in RSpec using normal RSpec syntax, which would look something like this:

```
expect(book.paperback?).to be_truthy
```

And that's fine, and it works. But if you read it out loud it sounds weird—more like how computers talk and not like how people talk. You might want to be able to write this:

```
expect(book).to be_a_paperback
```

Read that out loud, and it sounds like natural language.

So, to make that work in RSpec, you need to do...nothing. It already works.

When RSpec sees a matcher that starts with be, be_a, or be_an, it does some parsing on the name of the matcher and looks for a method in the object under test. If the matcher has no arguments, it looks for a predicate method that ends in a question mark, so expect(book).to be_a_paperback looks for book.paperback? and failing that, book.paperbacks?. If the matcher has arguments, it looks for a regular method, so expect(book).to be_published_at(Date.today) would look for book.published_at(Date.today). RSpec will do the same thing with have and has. The matcher expect(book).to have_cover will look for book.has_cover?, while expect(book).to have_author("Dave") will look for book.has_author("Dave").

There is also a set of matchers that take a block. The general structure is expect { SOMETHING }.to MATCHER. The most common is probably expect { }.to raise_error(arg), where the argument is usually a Ruby exception class and the matcher passes if the block raises the expected error. The argument could also be a string or regular expression matching the error message.

There are also a series of matchers based on expect { BLOCK 1 }.to change { BLOCK 2 }. Here's how this works: RSpec runs block 2 and stores the value, then it runs block 1, and then it checks block 2 again, and the matcher passes if block 2's value has changed. You can chain additional methods to the end if you want to specify details, as in expect { book.publish! }.to change { book.publication_date }.from(nil).to(Date.today).

There's a lot more to RSpec matchers, including the ability to create your own. For more information, see *Effective Testing with RSpec 3* by Myron Marston and Erin Dees.

RSpec and Mocks

rb In addition to minitest, RSpec also allows you to create mock and stub objects and has a lot of features available by default. Here's an overview of the most common.

In RSpec, the generic term for a fake object is *test double*, an object that stands in for another object, by analogy to "stunt double." The simplest way to create one is by using the method double. You can create the double and assign it a method to respond to using the RSpec method allow:

```
obj = double
allow(obj).to receive(:cost).and_return("cheap")
allow(obj).to receive(:name).and_return("banana")
obj.cost
obj.name
```

If you pass multiple arguments to and_return, you specify responses for multiple times that the method is called. You can limit the arguments under which the double is invoked by chaining in .with, as in allow(obj).to receive(:availability).with("January").and_return(true).

You can define multiple responses at once with the receive_messages method, which takes a hash. Keys become the methods to respond to, and values are the fake values returned:

```
obj = double
allow(obj).to receive_messages(cost: "cheap", name: "banana")
obj.cost
obj.banana
```

Or you can use a shortcut by passing keyword arguments directly to double:

```
obj = double(cost: "cheap", name: "banana")
obj.cost
obj.banana
```

In minitest, we talked about *validating* mock objects by having the test fail if the method being faked isn't called during the test. In RSpec, you manage this with the expect method.

You can call expect on a double before the main action of the spec. In this case, expect is an exact replacement for allow:

```
obj = double
expect(obj).to receive(:cost).and_return("cheap")
expect(obj).to receive(:name).and_return("banana")
obj.cost
obj.banana
```

The expect method behaves the same as allow except that, at the end of the spec, RSpec additionally and automatically validates whether the expected methods have been called. If not, it fails the spec.

A downside of this mechanism is that the expectation happens at the beginning of the spec, but the validation happens at the end, and only implicitly. This can make the spec hard to read. An alternative is to use a slightly different form of expect at the end of the spec:

```
obj = double
allow(obj).to receive(:cost).and_return("cheap")
obj.cost
expect(obj).to have_received(:cost)
```

The allow and expect constructs in RSpec are powerful. You can even use them on objects that aren't test doubles to stub a particular method on an existing object:

```
kermit = Muppet.new
allow(kermit).to receive(:greeting).and_return("Hi ho")
```

A potential problem with test doubles is that the API of the underlying object might change, but the test, with its stubbed method, blissfully continues to pass. RSpec offers some protection from that with the instance_double variation. An instance_double call takes a class as an argument:

```
fake_product = instance_double(Product)
allow(fake_product).to receive(:name).and_return("pretzel")
```

Now, when you call allow or expect with the instance double as an argument, RSpec checks to see if the class in question actually defines the method you're stubbing. (There's a similar RSpec creator, class_double, for class methods rather than instance methods.) If the method doesn't exist, RSpec raises an error at the point of the declaration.

This only scratches the surface of RSpec's mock package.

What's Next

In this chapter, we covered Ruby's two most commonly used test frameworks: minitest and RSpec. Which should you use? Well, if you're working on a project that already uses one of them, we recommend sticking with that one. There's not so much difference between the two that it's worth re-writing all your tests.

If you're starting a new project, consider whether you like RSpec's syntax. RSpec is probably more widely used, but some prominent Ruby projects still use minitest, including Ruby on Rails. RSpec has a higher initial complexity but is also more flexible and has more available functionality out of the box. Ultimately, though, it's a question of which syntax you like better and will get you to write more tests.

We've finished our tutorial of the Ruby language, and now it's time to widen our view and take a look at the larger Ruby tool ecosystem.

Part II

Ruby in Its Setting

Ruby isn't just a programming language. It's an entire ecosystem of tools that enables you to leverage the language and make it valuable for a variety of tasks in a range of different contexts. These tools include the Ruby command-line program itself, the Ruby gems tool for including libraries, and tools for interacting with and debugging Ruby. Ruby also has support for automated documentation, can be used in various editors and different operating systems, and has runtime versions that are optimized for performance in different settings.

## CHAPTER 14

Ruby from the Command Line

If you're using Ruby as a scripting language, you'll be starting it from the command line. In this chapter, we'll look at how to use Ruby as a command-line tool and how to interact with your operating system environment. The two most common ways for a Ruby program to kick off from the command line are with the Ruby interpreter itself and with Rake, a utility that makes it easy to define a series of interrelated tasks. You also might want to create your own command-line programs, and Ruby can help with that as well.

Please note that some of the details of this chapter only apply to Unix-based systems like Linux, MacOS, and WSL.

Calling the Ruby Command

The most direct way to start the Ruby interpreter and run a Ruby program is by calling the ruby command from the command line. Regardless of the system in which Ruby is deployed, you have to start the Ruby interpreter somehow, and doing so gives us the opportunity to pass in command-line arguments both to Ruby itself and to the script being run.

A Ruby command-line call consists of three parts, none of which are required: options for the Ruby interpreter itself, the name of a program to run, and arguments for that program.

ruby ‹options› ‹–› ‹programfile› ‹arguments›*

You only need the double-dash if you're separating options to Ruby itself from options being passed to the program being run. The simplest Ruby command is ruby followed by a filename:

```
$ ruby my_code.rb
```

This command will cause the Ruby interpreter to load the my_code.rb file, parse it, and then execute it.

If the file has a syntax error, Ruby will attempt to locate the error and suggest where the problem is.

Here's an example:

```
rubyworld/syntax_error.rb
class HasAnError
  def this_method_ends
    p "it sure does"
  end
```

```
  def this_doesnt_end
    return "a thing"

  def this_one_is_also_right
    p "fine"
  end
end
```

```
sh: code/rubyworld/syntax_error.rb:12: syntax error, unexpected end-of-input,
    expecting 'end' or dummy end (SyntaxError)
```

Ruby notices the error—a missing end—and attempts to find the actual location of the item missing the end. In this case, it gets it right.

Any options after the command ruby are sent to the Ruby interpreter. The Ruby interpreter options end with the first word on the command line that doesn't start with a hyphen or with the special flag -- (two hyphens).

There are ways to invoke the Ruby interpreter without passing it a filename. One way is to use the -e command-line option, which executes one line of script.

This lets us use Ruby as a powerful command-line calculator. Here's a one-liner that returns the first five square numbers:

```
ruby -e "p (1..5).map { _1 ** 2 }"
[1, 4, 9, 16, 25]
```

When you do this, remember that the command you run needs to be a string and that you have to print it, or you won't see the result.

You can also pipe a file into the command using Unix standard input and then access that file using Kernel#gets:

```
ruby -e 'puts "line: #{gets}"' < testfile
```

That works swimmingly, but it only processes the first line of the file. However, we can use Ruby's while expression clause to loop over the file in a single line:

```
$ ruby -e 'puts "line: #{$_}" while gets' < testfile
line: This is line one
line: This is line two
line: This is line three
line: And so on...
```

In this snippet, we're not only taking advantage of the while clause, we're also using the Ruby global $_, which contains the most recent text read in by a gets call. So, the while gets reads the line and puts it in $_ and the body of the statement prints out the line.

Still, that while at the end seems kind of awkward for something you might do often. If only there were some kind of shortcut:

```
$ ruby -ne 'puts "line: #{$_}"' < testfile
line: This is line one
line: This is line two
line: This is line three
line: And so on...
```

The -n command-line option wraps whatever else is sent to the Ruby interpreter in a while gets; <INPUT>; end loop. This is frequently a single line passed in using -e, but it doesn't have to be. You could have a script file that processes a single line of input and use -n to apply that script to an entire input.

Now, looking at it, that puts statement seems like boilerplate, and it turns out there's a shortcut for that as well...sort of:

```
ruby -pe '"line: #{$_}"' < testfile
This is line one
This is line two
This is line three
And so on...
```

The -p option behaves like n but also prints the line as it is being input, not the line that we're processing, which is sometimes helpful.

There's one more twist to the looping input, which is -a for auto-split mode. With -a set, the incoming gets line is automatically split using String#split, and the result goes into the global $F. The default delimiter is space, but you can set a delimiter with the command-line option -F, as in -F"\n". So this code uses -a to split the line from the input:

```
$ ruby -nae 'puts "line: #{$F}"' < testfile
line: ["This", "is", "line", "one"]
line: ["This", "is", "line", "two"]
line: ["This", "is", "line", "three"]
line: ["And", "so", "on..."]
```

And this code uses -F to also set a custom delimiter:

```
$ ruby -F"i" -nae 'puts "line: #{$F}"' < testfile
line: ["Th", "s ", "s l", "ne one\n"]
line: ["Th", "s ", "s l", "ne two\n"]
line: ["Th", "s ", "s l", "ne three\n"]
line: ["And so on...\n"]
```

And just to clear one thing up—the options can be stacked if they don't have any arguments, so -nae is identical to -n -a -e.

If no filename is present on the command line or if the filename is a single hyphen, Ruby reads the program source from standard input.

Arguments for the program itself follow the program name:

```
$ ruby -w - "Hello World"
```

In this snippet, -w will enable warnings, and then Ruby will read a program from standard input, and pass that program the string "Hello World" as an argument. We'll talk in a moment about how to deal with incoming command-line arguments.

Ruby Command-Line Options

Following is a complete list of Ruby's command-line options roughly organized by functionality.

Options That Determine What Ruby Runs

-0[octal]

The 0 flag (the digit zero) specifies the record separator character (\0, if no digit follows). -00 indicates paragraph mode: records are separated by two successive default record separator characters. 0777 reads the entire file at once (because it's an illegal character). Sets $/.

-a

Autosplit mode when used with -n or -p; equivalent to executing $F = $_.split at the top of each loop iteration.

-c

Checks syntax only; does not execute the program.

--copyright

Prints the copyright notice and exits.

-e 'command'

Executes *command* as one line of Ruby source. Several -es are allowed, and the commands are treated as multiple lines in the same program. If *programfile* is omitted when -e is present, execution stops after the -e commands have been run. Programs that run using -e can use ranges and regular expressions in conditions—ranges of integers compare against the current input line number, and regular expressions match against $_.

-F pattern

Specifies the input field separator ($;) used as the default for split (affects the -a option).

-h, --help

Displays a short help screen.

-l

Enables automatic line-ending processing; sets $\ to the value of $/ and chops every input line automatically.

-n

Assumes a while gets; ...; end loop around your program. For example, a simple grep command could be implemented as follows:

```
$ ruby -n -e "print if /wombat/" *.txt
```

-p

Places your program code within the loop while gets; ...; print; end.

```
$ ruby -p -e "$_.downcase!" *.txt
```

--version

Displays the Ruby version number and exits.

Options That Change the Way the Interpreter Works

--backtrace-limit=num

Sets a limit on the number of lines of backtrace that are sent to standard error when the program sends a backtrace (when the program terminates unexpectedly, for example). The default value is -1, meaning unlimited backtrace.

-C directory

Changes working directory to directory before executing.

-d, --debug

Sets $DEBUG and $VERBOSE to true. This can be used by your programs to enable additional tracing.

--disable={FEATURE}

Disables one of the features described in Features That Can Be Enabled or Disabled, on page 236.

-Eex[:in], --encoding=ex[:in], external-encoding=encoding, internal-encoding=encoding

Specifies the default character encoding for data read from and written to the outside world. This can be used to set both the external encoding (the encoding to be assumed for file contents) and optionally the default internal encoding (the file contents are transcoded to this when read and transcoded from this when written). The format of the single *encoding* parameter is -E external, -E external:internal, or -E :internal.

-I directories

Specifies directories to be prepended to $LOAD_PATH ($:). Multiple -I options may be present. Multiple directories may appear following each -I, separated by a colon on Unix-like systems and by a semicolon on DOS/Windows systems.

-I [extension]

Edits ARGV files in place. For each file named in ARGV, anything you write to standard output will be saved back as the contents of that file. A backup copy of the file will be made if the *extension* is supplied, as in the following code sample:

```
$ ruby -pi.bak -e "gsub(/Perl/, 'Ruby')" *.txt
```

--jit, --rjit, --yjit

Enables one of the two just-in-time compilers available in Ruby. The Rust-based compiler can be enabled with --jit or --yjit, while the experimental Ruby-based version can be enabled with --rjit. Ruby versions prior to 3.3 also had -mjit. The JIT compilers are designed to improve program performance in long-running Ruby applications. Both compilers have several of their own command-line options.

-r library

Requires the named library or gem before executing.

-S

Looks for the program file using the RUBYPATH or PATH environment variable.

-s

Any command-line switches found after the program filename, but before any filename arguments or before a --, are removed from ARGV and set to a global variable named for the switch. In the following example, the effect of this would be to set the variable $opt to "electric":

```
$ ruby -s prog -opt=electric ./mydata
```

-v, --verbose

Sets $VERBOSE to true, which enables verbose mode. Also prints the version number. In verbose mode, compilation warnings are printed. If no program filename appears on the command line, Ruby exits.

-w

Enables warning mode, which is like verbose mode, except it reads the program from standard input if no program files are present on the command line. We recommend running your Ruby programs with -w.

-W level

Sets the level of warnings issued. With a *level* of 2 (or with no level specified), which is the equivalent to -w, additional warnings are given. If *level* is 1, it runs at the standard (default) warning level. With -W0, absolutely no warnings are given (including those issued using Object.warn).

-x [directory]

Strips off text before #!ruby line and changes working directory to *directory* if given.

Other Options

--dump option...

Tells Ruby to dump various items of internal state. options... is a comma or space separated list containing one or more of insns, insns_without_opt, parsetree, parsetree_with_comment, and yydebug. This is intended for Ruby core developers.

Features That Can Be Enabled or Disabled

All of these features can be explicitly enabled or disabled from the command line, using an option such as --enable=gems or --disable=did_you_mean.

did_you_mean

When enabled, a NameError will also show the results of a search of the receiving object for similarly named messages that might have been the intended message. Helpful when you can't remember the name of the message you want. Enabled by default.

error_highlight

When enabled, error messages will have arrows highlighting the exact part of the line where the error was triggered. Useful in tracking down errors in a long line of code that chains multiple method calls. Enabled by default.

frozen-string-literal

When enabled, acts as if the magic comment # frozen_string_literal: true is placed at the front of all Ruby files. This comment causes all string literals to be implicitly frozen without freeze being called on them. Disabled by default.

gems

Stops Ruby from automatically loading RubyGems from require. Enabled by default.

rjit

Enables the rjit compiler. Disabled by default.

rubyopt

Prevents Ruby from examining the RUBYOPT environment variable. You should probably disable this in an environment you want to secure. Enabled by default.

syntax_suggest

Enables the syntax_suggest tool which provides better handling of syntax errors when code is loaded.

yjit
> Enables the yjit compiler. Disabled by default.

Making Your Code an Executable Program

It's a little clunky to have to call ruby my_code.rb when you want to run your code; it'd be easier if you could use my_code.rb. This is more of an operating system tip than a Ruby tip, but on Unix systems, this is doable with just a couple of steps.

First, you need to make the file executable by changing the mode of the file. To oversimplify slightly, the mode of the file is metadata that determines if the current user can read from, write to, or execute a given file. Typically, on a Unix-based system, the command to make a file executable is chmod +x <FILENAME>. The chmod command is Unix-speak for "change the mode of the file," +x means "make it executable," and FILENAME is the filename. For more on the Unix command line, see Appendix 3, Command-Line Basics, on page 645.

Having made the file executable, we also need to tell Unix what it means for the file to be executable. For a Ruby script, what we mean is "run this file through the Ruby runtime". And we tell that to the Unix system through a special comment on the first line of the file that starts with #! and contains the name of an interpreter program that should be used to run the file. (This comment is often referred to as "shebang" because the two characters that make it up are the #, which is a musical sharp, and !, which coders often call "bang".)

In most cases, the shebang command you use to invoke Ruby can look like this:

```
#!/usr/bin/env ruby

# Ruby code goes here
```

The path /usr/bin/env is, for weird Unix reasons, a common cross-platform way to ensure you're running the proper shell and ruby is the Ruby interpreter. (You can use other ways to specify the Ruby interpreter, but this is the most recommended way to have the script run in most common Unix setups.)

Anyway, once you've done both these steps, you can invoke your script directly:

```
$ my_code.rb
```

If for some reason you want to send command-line options to Ruby itself (for example, you might want to run in warning mode), you can do so by setting an environment variable called RUBYOPTS:

```
RUBYOPTS="-w" my_code.rb
```

The Ruby interpreter will, by default, look in that environment variable for options before it starts.

Any arguments after the filename are passed to the Ruby code itself, so this would be a good time to show how to access those arguments…

Processing Command-Line Arguments to Your Code

Just as you can pass arguments to methods in your Ruby code, you can pass arguments from the command line to the Ruby script itself. Ruby provides mechanisms for capturing arguments passed to the script and allowing you to read and parse them as part of your script.

ARGV

Any command-line arguments after the program filename are available to your Ruby program in the global array ARGV. For instance, assume test.rb contains the following program:

```
ARGV.each { |arg| p arg }
```

If you invoke it with the following command line:

```
$ ruby -w test.rb "Hello World" a1 1.6180
```

It'll generate the following output:

```
"Hello World"
"a1"
"1.6180"
```

There's a gotcha here for all you C programmers. In Ruby, ARGV[0] is the first argument to the program, not the program name. The name of the current program is available in the global variable $0, which is aliased to $PROGRAM_NAME. All the values in ARGV are strings.

If your program reads from standard input (or uses the special object ARGF, described in the next section), the arguments in ARGV will be taken to be filenames, and Ruby will read from these files. If your program takes a mixture of arguments and filenames, make sure you empty the nonfilename arguments from the ARGV array before reading from the files.

ARGF

It's common for a command-line program to take a list of zero or more filenames to process. It'll then read through these files in turn, doing whatever it does. Imagine a command that takes a list of log files and processes them line by line, like process.rb log1 log2 log3. It'd be handy to be able to treat all the log file arguments as a single logical file object.

Ruby provides a convenience object, referenced by the name ARGF, that handles access to these files, allowing you to treat the files as a single stream. The data for the ARGF object is taken from the values in ARGV. The assumption is that when you use ARGF all the elements in the ARGV array are filenames. This means that any nonfilename arguments need to be removed from the ARGV array before you start reading from them using ARGF. Conversely, any filenames you add to ARGV in your code will be available to ARGF just as though they were supplied in the command line. We recommend that you do any ARGV manipulation before you start reading from ARGF.

The ARGF object defines most of the same read methods that IO does, including gets, read, and readline. If you read from ARGF, Ruby will open the file whose name is the first element of ARGV and perform the I/O on it. If, as you continue to read, you reach the end of that file, Ruby closes it, shifts it out of the ARGV array, and then opens the next file in the list. At some point, when you've finished reading from the last file, ARGF will return an end-of-file condition (so gets will return nil, for example). If ARGV is initially empty, ARGF will read from standard input.

You can get to the name of the file currently being read from using ARGF.filename, and you can get the current File object as ARGF.file. ARGF keeps track of the total number of lines read in ARGF.lineno—if you need the line number in the current file, use ARGV.file.lineno. Here's a program that uses this information:

```
while (line = gets)
  printf "%d: %10s[%d] %s", ARGF.lineno, ARGF.filename, ARGF.file.lineno, line
end
```

If we run it, passing a couple of filenames, it'll copy the contents of those files.

```
$ ruby copy.rb testfile otherfile
1:   testfile[1] This is line one
2:   testfile[2] This is line two
3:   testfile[3] This is line three
4:   testfile[4] And so on...
5: otherfile[1] ANOTHER LINE ONE
6: otherfile[2] AND ANOTHER LINE TWO
7: otherfile[3] AND FINALLY THE LAST LINE
```

In-Place Editing of ARGF Files

In-place editing is a hack inherited from Perl. It allows you to alter the contents of files passed in on the command line, retaining a backup copy of the original contents.

To turn on in-place editing, give Ruby the file extension to use for the backup file, either with the -i [_ext_] command-line option or by calling ARGF.inplace_mode=_ext_ in your code.

Now, as your code reads through each file given on the command line, Ruby will rename the original file by appending the backup extension. It'll then create a new file with the original name and open it for writing on standard output. For example, you might code a program like this:

```
while (line = gets)
  puts line.chomp.reverse
end
```

You invoke it like this:

```
$ ruby -i.bak reverse.rb testfile otherfile
```

The result is that testfile and otherfile would now have reversed lines and the original files would be available in testfile.bak and otherfile.bak.

For finer control over the I/O to these files, you can use the methods provided by ARGF. They're rarely used, so rather than document them here, we'll refer you to the online documentation.

Option Parsing

It's quite handy that Ruby packages up all the options into the ARGV array. If you have a complex script, and you want your script to use conventional patterns of options, where there's something like -a true --database sqlite, then the ARGV array isn't enough. You'd also like to be able to respond to these options by running code in your script based on them. Ruby provides the conveniently named class OptionParser to allow you to run code based on command-line options or to convert those options into a more convenient data object.

The API here is a little tricky, but, basically, you need to do the following:

- Create a new instance of OptionParser.

- Tell the instance about various options it should respond to and what it should do for each one.

- Tell the instance to parse and also to do something with the options as it parses.

Along the way, the OptionParser instance also does a few things for you, including automatically generating a --help response based on the options. We'll also note here that the OptionParser class has a couple of different ways to do the things we're discussing in this section. We're only going to talk about the main one, but the official API reference has other options.

To create the parser, you can use parser = OptionParser.new. Then you can define options to match with the method on. For option parser purposes, an option is either of these:

- Short: A single dash and a single character, as in -x
- Long: A double dash and more than one character, as in --database

The basic idea is the same either way, the on method is called with the option, an optional string that defines it, and a block that's invoked if the option is in ARGV. You can also define both a short and a long version of the same option.

rubyworld/option_1.rb
```ruby
require "optparse"

parser = OptionParser.new

sort_type = nil
parser.on("-a", "Alphabetical") do
  sort_type = :alphabetical
end

parser.on("--recent", "Most Recent") do
  sort_type = :recency
end

parser.on("-s", "--size", "Size") do
  sort_type = :size
end

parser.parse!

p "we are sorting by #{sort_type}"
```

In this example, each option is setting a sort type local variable. Options created with on are invoked in the order they are defined, so if more than one of these is invoked, the last one defined wins. The parse! at the end is what actually triggers the parsing of the options, and it's also a signal that you're done defining options.

At this point, if you call your script with a --help option (whether you do it via ruby or make it a standalone executable script), you get a useful help message:

```
$ ruby code/rubyworld/option_1.rb --help
Usage: option_1 [options]
    -a                               Alphabetical
        --recent                     Most Recent
    -s, --size                       Size
```

You can use the method banner to add a message to the top of this help listing as in parser.banner = "Usage: option_1.rb [options]".

If you call with one of the various options, the appropriate value is set:

```
$ ruby code/rubyworld/option_1.rb -a
"we are sorting by alphabetical"
```

Often, you want a command-line option to take an argument, as in -xSort or --database postgres. You can specify those arguments using OptionParser as well. Generally, the idea is that you add text in all caps after the option, like SORT. The actual text doesn't matter, only that you put some marker there. If the text marker is surrounded by square brackets, the argument is optional; if not, the option is required. There's one slight bit of weirdness here: which is that a required argument is separated from a long option by a space but can be flush against a short option, so -x THING or -xTHING but only --example THING. Optional arguments are separated by a space in both cases. If you're specifying multiple options in the same on call — for example, both a long and short option — then the argument only needs to be specified once, and it applies to all the options in that call.

In any case, the argument to the option is then passed as an argument to the block:

```
rubyworld/option_2.rb
require "optparse"

parser = OptionParser.new

sort_type = nil

parser.on("-sSORT", "Sort Type") do |value|
  sort_type = value
end

parser.on("-a [DIR]", "Alphabetical") do |value|
  sort_type = :alphabetical
end

parser.on("--recent DATE", "Most Recent") do
  sort_type = :recency
end

parser.on("-h", "--height [METRIC]", "Height") do
  sort_type = :size
end

parser.parse!

p "we are sorting by #{sort_type}"
```

You can do a few more things with options to limit values or coerce types — be sure to check out the official API documentation.

Once you've defined all the options, you need to tell the OptionParser to do something. Again, the OptionParser class provides a few different mechanisms, but most of the time, we think you'll want to call parse!.

Calling parse! triggers a walk through the ARGV array, calling the blocks of any options that it encounters and destructively removing those options and their arguments from ARGV. Removing the options allows you to easily have a command line that mixes options and non-options, so you can do something like my_code.rb -x --database postgres other_file other_thing. Then the parse! removes the option switches, and you end up with ARGV equals ["other_file", "other_thing"].

You can also specify a keyword argument, into:, which takes an existing object (usually a hash) and causes all the parsed options to be placed into that argument. The key is the option itself. The value is the return value of the block, the argument value if there is no block, or true if there is neither a block nor an argument:

rubyworld/option_3.rb
```
require "optparse"

parser = OptionParser.new

parser.on("-x") do
  puts "yep, do the x thing"
  true
end

parser.on("-yTYPE", "--y") do |value|
  puts "There's a y with #{value}"
  value
end

options = {}
parser.parse!(into: options)

p ARGV
p options
```

If you want a more powerful framework for building CLI interfaces, you should check out Thor,[1] which uses a different API to attach subcommands and options to different parts of your code.

Program Termination

The method exit terminates your program, returning a status value to the operating system. However, unlike some languages, exit doesn't terminate the program immediately—exit first raises a SystemExit exception, which you may catch, and then performs a number of cleanup actions, including running any registered at_exit methods and object finalizers.

Accessing Environment Variables

You can access operating system environment variables using the predefined variable ENV. It responds to the same methods as Hash. Technically, ENV isn't actually a hash—it's a separate class—but if you need to, you can convert it into a Hash using ENV#to_h.

```
ENV['SHELL']
ENV['HOME']
ENV['USER']
ENV.keys.size
ENV.keys[0, 4]
```

Standard Environment Variables

The values of some environment variables are read by Ruby when it first starts. These variables modify the behavior of the interpreter. Some of the environment variables used by Ruby are listed in the table shown on page 243.

---

1. http://whatisthor.com

Variable Name	Description
DLN_LIBRARY_PATH	Specifies the search path for dynamically loaded modules.
HOME	Points to the user's home directory. This is used when expanding ~ in file and directory names.
LOGDIR	Specifies the fallback pointer to the user's home directory if $HOME is not set. This is used only by Dir.chdir.
OPENSSL_CONF	Specifies the location of OpenSSL configuration file.
PATH	The Unix list of places to look for files, Ruby uses it when calling Kernel#system.
RUBY_YJIT_ENABLE	Enables the YJIT just-in-time compiler.
RUBYLIB	Specifies an additional search path for Ruby programs ($SAFE must be 0).
RUBYLIB_PREFIX	(Windows only) Mangles the RUBYLIB search path by adding this prefix to each component.
RUBYOPT	Specifies additional command-line options to Ruby; examined after real command-line options are parsed ($SAFE must be 0).
RUBYPATH	With -S option, specifies the search path for Ruby programs (defaults to PATH).
RUBYSHELL	Specifies shell to use when spawning a process under Windows; if not set, will also check SHELL or COMSPEC.

Table 4—Ruby environment variables

Other Ruby tools like Bundler or your Ruby version manager will also add environment variables.

Ruby uses several environment variables to manage its garbage collector during runtime. These variables all start with RUBY_GC, and you can find them in the man page for Ruby by typing man ruby. Similarly, a few variables that start with RUBY_THREAD or RUBY_FIBER control the amount of size allocated for threads and fibers. These variables are generally used to tweak performance for long-running Ruby programs.

Writing to Environment Variables

A Ruby program may write to the ENV object. On most systems, this changes the values of the corresponding environment variables. However, this change is local to the process that makes it and to any subsequently spawned child processes. This inheritance of environment variables is illustrated in the code that follows. A subprocess changes an environment variable, and this change is inherited by a process that it then starts. However, the change isn't visible to the original parent. (This goes to prove that parents never really know what their children are doing.)

```
rubyworld/envvar.rb
puts "In parent, term = #{ENV['TERM']}"
fork do
  puts "Start of child 1, term = #{ENV['TERM']}"
  ENV['TERM'] = "ansi"
  fork do
    puts "Start of child 2, term = #{ENV['TERM']}"
  end
```

```
  Process.wait
  puts "End of child 1, term = #{ENV['TERM']}"
end
Process.wait
puts "Back in parent, term = #{ENV['TERM']}"
```

produces:

```
In parent, term = xterm-256color
Start of child 1, term = xterm-256color
Start of child 2, term = ansi
End of child 1, term = ansi
Back in parent, term = xterm-256color
```

Setting an environment variable's value to nil removes the variable from the environment.

Where Ruby Finds Its Libraries

You use require to bring a library into your Ruby program. Some of these libraries are supplied with Ruby, some may have been packaged as RubyGems, and some you may have written yourself. How does Ruby find them?

Let's start with the basics. When Ruby is built for your particular machine, it predefines a set of standard directories to hold library stuff. Where these are depends on the machine in question. You can determine this from the command line with something like this:

```
$ ruby -e 'puts $LOAD_PATH'
```

On our MacOs box, with rbenv installed, this produces the following list:

```
/opt/homebrew/Cellar/rbenv/1.2.0/rbenv.d/exec/gem-rehash
/Users/noel/.rbenv/versions/3.3.0-dev/lib/ruby/site_ruby/3.3.0+0
/Users/noel/.rbenv/versions/3.3.0-dev/lib/ruby/site_ruby/3.3.0+0/arm64-darwin23
/Users/noel/.rbenv/versions/3.3.0-dev/lib/ruby/site_ruby
/Users/noel/.rbenv/versions/3.3.0-dev/lib/ruby/vendor_ruby/3.3.0+0
/Users/noel/.rbenv/versions/3.3.0-dev/lib/ruby/vendor_ruby/3.3.0+0/arm64-darwin23
/Users/noel/.rbenv/versions/3.3.0-dev/lib/ruby/vendor_ruby
/Users/noel/.rbenv/versions/3.3.0-dev/lib/ruby/3.3.0+0
/Users/noel/.rbenv/versions/3.3.0-dev/lib/ruby/3.3.0+0/arm64-darwin23
```

The site_ruby directories are intended to hold modules and extensions that you've added. The architecture-dependent directories (arm64-darwin21 in this case) hold executables and other things specific to this particular machine. All these directories are automatically included in Ruby's search for libraries.

Sometimes this isn't enough. Perhaps you're working on a large project written in Ruby, and you and your colleagues have built a substantial library of Ruby code. You want everyone on the team to have access to all this code. And, for some reason, you don't want to package it as a Ruby gem, you just want it to be in a known location in the file tree.

You have a couple of options to accomplish this. You can set the environment variable RUBYLIB to a list of one or more directories to be searched. (The separator between entries is a semicolon on Windows; for Unix, it's a colon.) If your program is not setuid, you can use the command-line parameter -I to do the same thing.

The Ruby variable $: is an array of places to search for loaded files. As we've seen, this variable is initialized to the list of standard directories, plus any additional ones you specified using RUBYLIB and -I. You can always add directories to this array from within your running program. Prior to Ruby 1.9, this used to be a common idiom:

```
$: << File.dirname(__FILE__)
require 'other_file'
```

This added the directory of the running file to the search path, so other_file.rb could be found there by the subsequent require. Now we use require_relative instead.

```
require_relative 'other_file'
```

Using the Rake Build Tool

Another way to structure code that can be easily invoked from the command line is with a useful utility program called Rake. Written by Jim Weirich, Rake was initially implemented as a Ruby version of Make, the Unix build utility. However, calling Rake a build utility is to miss its true power. Really, Rake is an automation tool—it's a way of putting all those tasks that you perform in a project into one neat and tidy place.

Rake gives you a convenient way to define small tasks and task dependencies, allowing you to say that a particular task requires a different task to run first. Rake also allows you to automate transitions between files based on file extensions, for example, converting all your .csv files to .json.

Let's start with an example. As you edit files, you might accumulate backup files in your working directories. On Unix systems, these files usually have the same name as the original files, but with a tilde character appended. On Windows boxes, the files usually have a .bak extension.

We could write a Ruby program that deletes these files. For a Unix box, it might look something like this:

```
require "fileutils"
files = Dir["*~"]
FileUtils.rm(files, verbose: true)
```

The FileUtils module defines methods for manipulating files and directories (see the description in the library section on page 597). Our code uses its rm method. We use the Dir class to return a list of filenames in the current directory matching the given pattern and pass that list to rm.

Let's package this code as a Rake *task*—a chunk of code that Rake can execute for us.

By default, Rake searches the current directory (and its parents) for a file called Rakefile. This file contains definitions for the tasks that Rake can run.

So, put the following code into a file called Rakefile:

```
desc "Remove files whose names end with a tilde"
task :delete_unix_backups do
  files = Dir["*~"]
  rm(files, verbose: true) unless files.empty?
end
```

Although it doesn't have an .rb extension, the Rakefile is actually just a file of Ruby code. Rake defines an environment and methods including desc and task and then executes the Rakefile.

The desc method provides a single line of documentation for the task that follows it. The task method defines a Rake task that can be executed from the command line. The parameter is the name of the task (a symbol), and the block that follows is the code to be executed. Here we can just use rm—all the methods in FileUtils are automatically available inside Rake files.

We can invoke this task from the command line:

```
$ rake delete_unix_backups
```

One quick note: if you're using Ruby on Rails, the rails command also searches for available Rake tasks, so within a Rails application, you could execute this as rails delete_unix_backups.

Okay, now let's write a second task in the same Rakefile. This one deletes Windows backup files.

```ruby
desc "Remove files with a .bak extension"
task :delete_windows_backups do
  files = Dir["*.bak"]
  rm(files, verbose: true) unless files.empty?
end
```

We can run this with rake delete_windows_backups.

But let's say that our application could be used on both platforms, and we wanted to let our users delete backup files on either one of them. We *could* write a combined task, but Rake gives us a better way—it lets us *compose* tasks. Here, for example, is a new task:

```ruby
desc "Remove Unix and Windows backup files"
task delete_backups: [:delete_unix_backups, :delete_windows_backups] do
  puts "All backups deleted"
end
```

The task's name is delete_backups, and it depends on the two other tasks. This isn't some special Rake syntax. We're simply passing the task method a Ruby hash containing a single entry whose key is the task name and whose value is the list of antecedent tasks. Rake parses the hash to create the list of task dependencies. In this case, Rake will execute the two platform-specific tasks in the order they are listed before executing the delete_backups task:

```
$ rake delete_backups
rm entry~
rm index.bak list.bak
All backups deleted
```

If those dependent tasks have their own dependent tasks, then those tasks are run first, and as a result, it's possible to build complex trees of task execution while keeping each individual task relatively small.

Our current Rakefile contains some duplication between the Unix and Windows deletion tasks. As it is just Ruby code, we can define a Ruby method to eliminate this:

```ruby
def delete(pattern)
  files = Dir[pattern]
  rm(files, verbose: true) unless files.empty?
end
```

```
desc "Remove files whose names end with a tilde"
task :delete_unix_backups do
  delete("*~")
end

desc "Remove files with a .bak extension"
task :delete_windows_backups do
  delete("*.bak")
end

desc "Remove Unix and Windows backup files"
task delete_backups: [:delete_unix_backups, :delete_windows_backups] do
  puts "All backups deleted"
end
```

All these tasks as written here use the current directory, but you might want to run the task on an arbitrary directory passed via the command line (something like rake delete_unix_backups subdir). But there's a problem:

```
$ rake delete_unix_backups subdir
Don't know how to build task 'subdir'
(See the list of available tasks with `rake --tasks`)
```

Rake interprets a command-line argument as another task to run. (Rake doesn't interpret flag arguments like -d as tasks, but that doesn't help us here.)

If you do want to pass a command-line argument to Rake, you have a couple of options. Rake has a mechanism to allow command-line arguments, but it's a little convoluted.

First, you need to define the arguments in the task, the syntax sets them up as extra arguments in the task definition:

```
def delete(dir, pattern)
  files = Dir["#{dir}/#{pattern}"]
  rm(files, verbose: true) unless files.empty?
end

desc "Remove files with a .bak extension"
task :delete_windows_backups, [:dir] do
  delete(args[:dir], "*.bak")
end

desc "Remove files whose names end with a tilde"
task :delete_unix_backups, [:dir] do |t, args|
  delete(args[:dir], "*~")
end

task :delete_backups, [:dir]: [:delete_unix_backups, :delete_windows_backups]
```

So, the second argument to the task is an array of the names of all the expected command-line arguments. If the task has both dependencies and expected command-line arguments, then the hash is keyed off the command-line arguments, as in task :delete_backups, [:dir]: [:delete_unix_backups, :delete_windows_backups]. The block that defines the task takes a new argument, which this code calls args. That argument is a hash, the keys are the names specified in the task definition, in this case :dir and the values are the passed values from the command line.

The command-line invocation is a little weird:

```
$ rake delete_backups[code]
```

The arguments go inside square brackets, and if multiple arguments exist, they are separated by commas as in $ rake delete_backups[code,verbose]. As an extra syntax gotcha, you can't have spaces before the brackets or on either side of the comma. So this is a little awkward.

Making it more awkward is that if you're using Z shell, this flat-out doesn't work because Z shell uses brackets for its own purposes. You can get around this by defining an alias alias rake="noglob rake", which will turn off Z shell's use of brackets for the command. (If you don't use Z shell or this paragraph doesn't make sense, you can safely ignore it.)

So, while you can pass command-line arguments using Rake, the syntax isn't exactly easy. An alternative to consider is just using OptionParser. With OptionParser, you can pass arguments after a --, and they'll get passed to the task and parsed. It's a little tricky because you want to make sure you don't get the --, so you need to add an OptionParser call to clarify that:

```ruby
def delete(dir, pattern)
  files = Dir["#{dir}/#{pattern}"]
  rm(files, verbose: true) unless files.empty?
end

desc "Remove files whose names end with a tilde"
task :delete_unix_backups do
  dir = "."
  parser = OptionParser.new
  parser.on("-d DIR") { |opt| dir = opt }
  args = parser.order!(ARGV) {}
  parser.parse!(args)
  delete(dir, "*~")
end
```

Then you'd call this with rake delete_unix_backups -- -d code. The parse! command removes the options from ARGV, preventing Rake from considering them as their own tasks.

If a Rake task is named default, it'll be executed if you invoke Rake with no parameters: just $ rake. Most Ruby applications and gems set the default task to run tests. Rake also allows you to set up two special variables called CLEAN and CLOBBER, which initially are an empty list of files that you can add to, as in CLEAN << Dir["*.bak"]. If those lists aren't empty, then Rake automatically defines two tasks named clean and clobber that delete all the files in the respective file list. The terms "clean" and "clobber" are inherited from Make. Typically, "clean" removes intermediate files but allows the end files to stick around, while "clobber" removes intermediate and final files.

You can find a list of the tasks implemented by a Rake file (or, more accurately, the tasks for which there's a description) using this:

```
$ rake -T
(in /Users/dave/BS2/titles/ruby4/Book/code/rake)
rake delete_backups          # Remove Unix and Windows backup files
rake delete_unix_backups     # Remove files whose names end with a tilde
rake delete_windows_backups  # Remove files with a .bak extension
```

This section only touches on the full power of Rake. It can handle dependencies between files (for example, rebuilding an executable file if one of the source files has changed), it knows about running tests and generating documentation, and it can even package gems for you. Martin Fowler has written a good overview of Rake[2] if you're interested in digging deeper.

The Build Environment

When Ruby is compiled for a particular architecture, all the relevant settings used to build it (including the architecture of the machine on which it was compiled, compiler options, source code directory, and so on) are written to the module RbConfig within the library file rbconfig.rb. After installation, any Ruby program can use this module to get details on how Ruby was compiled:

```
require "rbconfig"
include RbConfig
CONFIG["host"]   # => "arm64-apple-darwin23"
CONFIG["libdir"] # => "/Users/noel/.rbenv/versions/3.3.0-dev/lib"
```

Extension libraries use this configuration file to compile and link properly on any given architecture.

What's Next

Now that we've seen how to run our Ruby files from the command line and use command-line and environment options within Ruby, we're ready to look at the entire Ruby gems system for packaging tools, managing dependencies, and organizing code.

---

2.   http://martinfowler.com/articles/rake.html

## CHAPTER 15

Ruby Gems

One of the tremendous benefits of being a Ruby developer is being able to take advantage of the entire ecosystem of other Ruby developers who have written and shared useful tools with the community. These tools are called *gems*, a term that can refer to the individual tools and the library of code that manages packaging the tools and distributing them. Ruby comes standard with RubyGems, a command-line tool for installing and managing Ruby gems, and Bundler, a tool for creating manifests of gem versions so that developers all use the same set of dependencies.

Not only can you use existing gems, but you can also write your own. Even if you don't intend on sharing your gem, the basic structure of a Ruby gem is a good skeleton for your application. And if you do want to share your gem, you can do that via the central repository at http://www.rubygems.org.

Installing and Managing Gems

All the RubyGems tooling comes standard as a part of Ruby, including the command-line application gem, which you can use for many of your RubyGem-related needs. Ruby gems conform to a standardized format that provides metadata about the gems and most importantly about any other gems that this gem might depend on. The gem command-line tool knows to look in the central repository for gems, but you can also point it to look at other sources. Using other sources allows you to maintain a private gem repository, for example, as a place to keep internal tooling that you don't want to be made public.

In this section, we'll talk about managing gems directly from the command line, which is useful, but please keep in mind that on any application that's at all complex, much of the installation and gem management will be handled by Bundler, which we'll look at in Using Bundler to Manage Groups of Gems, on page 254.

Searching for Gems

Let's start by finding a gem to install. So far, the only gem we've discussed is RSpec, which will be a suitable example for our purposes. To download a gem, we need to know the exact name under which the gem is stored in the central gems repository. In this case, which is fairly typical, the internal name of the gem, rspec, is the lowercase version of the colloquial name, RSpec.

Gem naming can be complicated, especially if the gem name is more than one word. You can find out the official name of a gem in a couple of different ways.

If you go to the RubyGems website at rubygems.org, you'll see a very prominently placed search feature. Typing "RSpec" into the search bar gives us a list of search results which tells us that rspec is the gem's official name and that there are a lot of gems whose names start with rspec-. (RSpec is split among several smaller gems, and there are also extensions to RSpec that use the same naming convention.) Clicking on RSpec takes us to the RubyGems page for RSpec.

This page has a lot of useful information including the name of the gem, its self-description ("BDD for Ruby"), the current version (3.12.0, as of this writing), a list of previous versions, and a list of the owners of the gem. The right column includes the number of times the gem has been downloaded, the syntax for including the gem in a Gemfile or for installing it from the command line (we'll get to that in a second), a Homepage link, a Source Code repo link (often the same as the Homepage link), and a few other links that for most gems will all link back to the same GitHub page.

You can get some of this information from the command line:

```
$ gem search rspec -erd
rspec (3.12.0)
    Authors: Steven Baker, David Chelimsky, Myron Marston
    Homepage: http://github.com/rspec

    rspec-3.12.0
```

The gem search command searches the local and remote gem repositories for the text argument. The options used here are -e for "exact", which is searching for an exact match rather than a partial match (a partial match would give us a page or two of gems that contain the word "rspec"), -r for "remote only", and -d for "details" (without this we'd just get the names of the gems).

If we want to list gems locally, the command is gem list. You can find a full description of all the gem command-line commands at https://guides.rubygems.org/command-reference.

Installing a Gem

After identifying the gem, the next step is to install it locally, which you can do with gem install:

```
$ gem install rspec
Successfully installed rspec-3.12.0
Parsing documentation for rspec-3.12.0
Installing ri documentation for rspec-3.12.0
Done installing documentation for rspec after 0 seconds
1 gem installed
```

The resulting text tells us that the most recent version of RSpec has been installed, as well as the documentation for RSpec via the ri tool that we'll talk about in Chapter 19, Documenting Ruby, on page 313. Uninstalled dependent gems, if any, would also be installed at this time. (The machine this is running on already has RSpec's dependencies installed.)

What does it mean to install a gem? First off, the gem tool interacts with your current Ruby runtime to place the gem in a known location.

We can find out where that is:

```
$ gem which rspec
/Users/noel/.rbenv/versions/3.3.0/lib/ruby/gems/3.3.0/gems/rspec-3.12.0/lib/rspec.rb
```

If you're running gem install on a Unix platform and you aren't using a Ruby version manager, you'll need to prefix the command with sudo because by default the local gems are installed into shared system directories.

The exact location will depend on the operating system and the Ruby version manager you're using. In this case, the Ruby version manager maintains a hidden directory in my home directory for all the Ruby versions it is managing (/Users/noel/.rbenv/versions), and a specific subdirectory for the currently running version (/3.3.0). Inside that directory, the rest of the structure is managed by Ruby gems. There is a general set of directories for the version (/lib/ruby/gems/3.3.0/gems), a specific directory for this gem (/rspec-3.12.0), and then the path to the actual main script of the gem, which will typically install everything needed to use the gem (lib/rspec.rb).

Gem Version Numbers

You might wonder why the path to a gem file contains two apparently redundant folder names based on the version, in our case, 3.3.0 and 3.3.0. The two directories are managed by different parts of the system. The outer 3.3.0 is managed by the Ruby version manager, and if you have multiple Ruby versions installed, you'll see that they each have different directories. This means that each version of Ruby gets its own separate copy of each gem. (It also means that you can reclaim some disc space by deleting versions of Ruby you don't use anymore.) The inner 3.3.0 is managed by Ruby itself and is the name of the directory that Ruby is using to look for gems. Each version of Ruby should have only one directory here.

Now the gem is installed, which means that any Ruby program can use require "rspec" and the RSpec library will be usable as if it were part of the Ruby standard library. You'll need to check out the documentation for each gem to see how to use it. Often that documentation is accessible from the gem's home page.

The gem command has a lot of options, but the one you're most likely to use is -v or --version. When we installed RSpec, RubyGems installed the most recent version of the gem. Sometimes, you actually need a different gem version from the most recent, usually for compatibility with a specific version of Ruby. You can specify the version string at the command line with -v "3.0.0" or whatever the actual version you need. You can have multiple versions of the same gem installed locally, but a general require statement will load the one with the highest version number. If you need to use a different version number, we recommend using Bundler.

With the gem installed, you can browse the source code locally with gem open <GEMNAME>, which opens the directory with that gem in your current system editor. You can edit the files in the gem, and because Ruby is an interpreted language, those edits will be available to other code that uses the gem, the interpreter will load your changes. The most common case here is to place logging statements to aid in debugging. If you get too tangled up in your own edits, the command gem pristine <GEMNAME> will reinstall the original gem, and gem uninstall <GEMNAME> will remove the gem.

Using Bundler to Manage Groups of Gems

Gems are pretty great, and any reasonably sized Ruby program will likely depend on many of them, each of which may have its own gem dependencies. This can easily become a management problem in and of itself. How can you have multiple programs on one machine that might use different versions of a gem? Or, because gems change all the time, how can you guarantee that everybody working on the application will be using the same set of gems?

The answer to both of these questions and many more is Bundler.[1] Bundler is itself a Ruby gem, and it manages a manifest file of the gems and versions in use on a project. Bundler allows you to specify the versions in use and limit your Ruby programs to only find the specific version of a gem endorsed by Bundler.

To use Bundler, you first must install it. It's a Ruby gem, so gem install bundler will do it for you. The installation gives you the bundler command-line program, which you then use to manage your gems.

Building a Gemfile

To use Bundler effectively, you create a listing of all the gems in your application in a file called Gemfile. The Gemfile should be in the root directory of your application.

Here's a small sample, which happens to be the Gemfile used for this book's code examples and code management, at least so far (slightly edited):

```
source "https://rubygems.org"

ruby "3.3.0"

gem "debug"
gem "i18n"
gem "nokogiri"
gem "pry"
gem "pry-byebug"
gem "rack"
gem "rackup"
gem "rspec"
gem "solargraph"
gem "standard"
gem "yard"
```

The Gemfile is made up of a series of different statements that describe the set of all the gems being used by the project. The Gemfile is actually Ruby code, which means that each line is actually a Ruby method call (without parentheses) and also that Ruby syntax can be used if the Gemfile gets more complicated.

The first line declares a source, we're using "https://rubygems.org", which is the central repository for RubyGems, but you could also create your own server and use that as a source. Many companies use internal gem servers to distribute common internal code that's not public. You can declare multiple sources, but the recommendation is to have one top-level source and limit the scope of secondary sources. (You'll see how to do that in a moment.)

---

1. http://bundler.io

The next line specifies the Ruby version that this application expects. As we saw in the previous section, Ruby gems are matched to specific versions of Ruby and stored separately for different versions. This line of code specifies an exact version of Ruby—unlike gem declarations, the Ruby version must be exact.

After that, we declare gems. Each gem declaration is the word gem followed by the official name of the gem. The order of the gem listings doesn't matter, but it's considered polite to keep them alphabetical.

That's a pretty basic Gemfile, as you'll see shortly, but they can get more complicated.

Using a Gemfile

Now that we have a Gemfile, we are most likely to do these three important things:

- Install the listed gems.
- Run a program that has visibility to those gems, and only those gems.
- Update the gems when new versions are released.

Bundle Install

To install a set of gems, you use the command bundle install, which performs a gem install on all the gems listed in the Gemfile. If you run the command, you'll see something like the following example. (The exact output depends on what's already installed.)

```
$ bundle install
bundle install
Fetching gem metadata from https://rubygems.org/.........
Fetching ast 2.4.2
Installing ast 2.4.2
... MORE GEMS ...
Bundle complete! 6 Gemfile dependencies, 40 gems now installed.
Use `bundle info [gemname]` to see where a bundled gem is installed.
```

If you compare that output to the Gemfile for this book listed earlier, you'll see that the first gem that Bundler installs is ast, which is interesting because our Gemfile doesn't reference ast.

Bundler is installing not only the gems listed in our Gemfile, but also their dependencies and transitive dependencies all the way down. Bundler downloads those files to exactly the same place that a regular gem install would, meaning it depends on your operating system and Ruby version manager. Unless otherwise specified, Bundler installs the most recent version of the gem.

When you install your Gemfile with Bundler, Bundler creates a new file, Gemfile.lock. The lock file is important because that's where Bundler stores the actual versions of the gems that have been installed.

```
GEM
  remote: https://rubygems.org/
  specs:
    ast (2.4.2)
    backport (1.2.0)
    benchmark (0.2.0)
    concurrent-ruby (1.1.10)
    debug (1.5.0)
```

```
    irb (>= 1.3.6)
    reline (>= 0.2.7)

  ... THERE'S MORE, LOCK FILES CAN GET LONG ...
PLATFORMS
  arm64-darwin-21

DEPENDENCIES
  debug
  i18n
  nokogiri
  rspec
  solargraph
  standardrb

RUBY VERSION
   ruby 3.3.0p0

BUNDLED WITH
   2.4.20
```

This shows the actual version loaded for each gem, and in the case of debug, it shows the dependent gems (irb and reline) and the acceptable version range for each of them. It ends with a list of platforms that the bundle has been built for (this information is used for gems that include native code components, and so they need to be compiled locally by the operating system), the Ruby version, and the version of Bundler.

The lock file is there to be an exact snapshot of the versions of all the gems in use by the application. When bundle install is called again, if there is a Gemfile.lock file, Bundler uses the information in the lock file to determine which version of each gem to install. The lock file, if it exists, is the most trusted source for which version of each gem should be installed.

If, after I install this bundle, there's a new version of RSpec released, my bundle will continue using the older version as listed in the lock file until I explicitly update RSpec's version.

This is great because any developer in the future who'll work on this code base will automatically use Bundler to install the exact same set of gem versions as every other developer. (And of course, "any developer" doesn't just mean other people, it also means you in six months.)

Bundle Exec and Bundle.require

Being able to load a specific set of gem versions is a good start, but you also need to be able to find those specific versions when you run your code. You might have multiple different applications that use different versions of RSpec. RubyGems will store all those different versions for you, but each individual application needs to be matched to the version it expects given its lock file. How can we ensure that when we use require we get the expected gem version?

Bundler provides a command called bundle exec that manages this bookkeeping for us. You use it by prepending bundle exec before whatever command you want to run, as in bundle exec rspec spec/my_spec.rb.

The bundle exec command does some manipulation of your environment. Basically, it modifies RubyGems itself to limit RubyGems to loading the gems in the bundle, and it also manages the command-line environment so that normal command-line things work without surprise. Calling rspec, for example, which is an executable script created by a gem, requires some background environment management to make sure the correct version of RSpec is called.

Alternatively, inside your code, before you use any gems, you can use require "bundler/setup", which will do the same RubyGems manipulation to manage references to gems, and will autoload the gems so you don't have to require them individually. Many frameworks, such as Ruby on Rails, do the Bundler setup as part of their regular boot process. That said, if you bundle exec code that also has a require "bundler/setup" that's fine, the management work will only be done once.

If you get tired of typing bundle exec and you're using gems that don't autoload when you run them (like RSpec), Bundler offers *binstubs*, which are a way for Bundler to create a wrapper program around a specific executable Ruby program defined by your gems that invokes Bundler before it starts.

As you'll see in Writing and Packaging Your Own Code into Gems, on page 261, gems can signal to their users that there are top-level executable commands that are part of the gem. RSpec, the gem, offers rspec the command as its test runner. But if we don't want to keep typing bundle exec rspec, we can ask Bundler to create a binstub for us.

```
$ bundle binstubs rspec
rspec has no executables, but you may want one from a gem it depends on.
  rspec-core has: rspec
```

Oops. Turns out the rspec gem itself has almost no code. It's only a way to get all the dependent pieces of RSpec in one place. Let's try this again:

```
$ bundle binstubs rspec-core
```

There's no output here, but we now have a file at bin/rspec. (If you call bundle binstubs and don't specify a gem, it'll run through all the gems in your bundle and create all their binstubs.)

The generated binary file has some boilerplate to make sure the environment is correct, but the main part is at the end:

```
require "rubygems"
require "bundler/setup"

load Gem.bin_path("rspec-core", "rspec")
```

It requires bundler/setup and then loads the rspec script via RubyGems. As a result, you now have a bin/rspec that behaves the same as bundle exec rspec.

If you don't think that's much better, what you can then do is set up your Unix shell's $PATH variable with something like export PATH="./bin:$PATH", and then you can use $ rspec like before and the version in ./bin will be found first and executed. If this paragraph doesn't make sense, check out Appendix 3, Command-Line Basics, on page 645, for context.

By default, when you engage Bundler via Bundler.require or require "bundler/setup" each gem will be autoloaded under the name of the gem. In other words, gem rspec implies require "rspec". In some cases this behavior isn't helpful. Sometimes the gem actually has a require file that's not the same as the name of the gem (this was much more common in the past, but gems have tended to converge on the convention that makes using Bundler easier).

Sometimes the gem has undesirable behavior when loaded at the top of the program and you only want to require it at a specific point—perhaps it does extra logging or something.

You can control the require behavior by augmenting the line of gem code with a require: keyword option. If the option is false, then the gem isn't auto-required:

```
gem "rspec", require: false
```

If the option is a string, then the gem is auto-required, but using the name of the require option rather than the name of the gem. More rarely, if the gem is an array of strings, each of those names is required when Bundler autoloads.

Bundle Update

Now that we've loaded our gems and made sure we're using the right versions, things are great. For a while. But then, time passes, as it does, and new versions of gems are released. And as great as it is that Bundler is keeping our gems stabilized, we'd like to upgrade.

The command for upgrading is bundle update. If it's called without any arguments, it'll update all gems in the Gemfile to the most recent version (or the most recent version allowed by the version specifier, which we'll look at later) and then will update the entire Gemfile.lock in response. Normally, Bundler will attempt to resolve existing version dependencies before updating. But you can force it to reconsider the entire file with bundle update --all. You can get the same functionality by deleting the Gemfile.lock and re-running bundle install, which is a fact that you might want to keep in your back pocket for a day when Bundler's dependency management seems to be spinning its wheels.

You can update a subset of your Gemfile by listing those gems after the command, as in bundle update rspec. The gems you list can either be gems that are explicitly in the Gemfile itself or any dependency in the lock file. Bundler will update the listed gems to their most recent versions (again bounded by version specifiers) and will also update all dependencies of these gems. There may be some reason why you don't want to update the downstream dependencies, in which case you can attach the option --conservative to the end of the bundle update command.

Gemfile Options

The Gemfile you saw earlier in Building a Gemfile, on page 254, is a minimal file. In particular, each gem listing can have options that specify more information about where to get the gem in question.

Versioning

The most important information to list about the gem is whether to restrict its version. If you don't specify a version, Bundler will load the most recent version. But you may not want Bundler to load the most recent version. If you're depending on a feature that was added to the gem along the way, you may want to specify a minimum version. If you know that a future version of the gem breaks compatibility, you'd want to add a maximum version. Or, you may want to say "don't update this gem without me explicitly saying so."

When you add a gem to a Gemfile, you can add one or more optional version specifiers. (We'll see in Writing and Packaging Your Own Code into Gems, on page 261, that individual gems also use version specifiers to manage their dependency lists.)

The simplest version specifier is just an exact version number:

```
gem rspec, "3.11.0"
```

Specifying an exact version number means that Bundler won't change the version behind your back, but it also means that you lose some flexibility to respond to version changes or requirements. If you want that version to be a minimum, you can use a greater-than or greater-than-or-equal symbol.

```
gem rspec, ">= 3.11.0"
```

Similarly, a < or <= operator sets the version as a maximum. If you're setting a version ceiling, there's often a reason, and we recommend commenting the Gemfile to say what the reason is and what to look for to be able to lift the ceiling. Otherwise, over time, you'll wind up with multiple gems in the Gemfile that you want to upgrade but are afraid of negative side effects. Ask us how we know.

You can use the full set of Ruby operators for version specifiers—this table outlines what they mean in context.

Operator	Description
=	Exact version match. Major, minor, and patch levels must be identical.
!=	Any version that's not the one specified.
>	Any version that's greater (even at the patch level) than the one specified.
<	Any version that's less than the one specified.
>=	Any version greater than or equal to the specified version.
<=	Any version less than or equal to the specified version.
~>	Pessimistic version constraint operator, officially. Sometimes called the "twiddle-wakka" or "squiggle rocket" because the Ruby community contains multitudes. This operator allows updated versions if the new version differs from the current version only in the last digit specified.

Table 5—Version operators

That last operator in the table (~>) could use a little explanation. The idea is to allow for patch updates that are probably bug fixes but not allow larger updates that might have breaking changes. So, you might want to specify gem "rspec", "~> 3.11.0", and when RSpec releases a patch version 3.11.1, you'll get that version with a bundle update, but when they update the minor version to 3.12.0, you won't get that version. The ~> operator is usually used with major, minor, and patch versions specified, but you don't have to do that. You could specify gem "rspec", "~> 3.11", in which case you'd get 3.11.1 and 3.12.0, but not 4.0.0.

There's one other twist here: sometimes you want to use a gem that has been released in a beta version. Gem versioning assumes that a version number is a pre-release version if it contains a letter character. You can get pre-release versions of gems by including letters in your version specifier: gem "rspec", ">= 3.11.0.beta.1".

If you've specified a pre-release version, Bundler will look at all pre-release versions when resolving its install or update, so >= 3.11.0.beta.1 would still receive the updated version when 3.11.0.beta.2 is released because the operator is greater than and beta.2 is higher than beta.1.

The sorting is alphabetical for sections that contain letters and numeric for sections that don't. Sometimes this can be confusing. For example, RubyGems considers 7.0.0.pre.1 to be greater than 7.0.0.beta.1, but Ruby on Rails releases pre before beta, so you can get the wrong version if you aren't careful. (Be sure to check the lock file to see what version you're actually using.)

Sometimes you need to use a gem that's so far into pre-release that it hasn't actually been released as a gem and only exists in a git repo or even in a local directory on your computer. Often you need this to test gems that you're currently developing or to help test other people's work before the official release.

You can get access to unreleased gems via Bundler with different options in the Gemfile. Generically, I can access any remote git server with the git: option:

```
gem "rspec", git: "git@github.com:rspec/rspec-metagem.git"
```

Any of the Git access versions will work here, assuming that you have the appropriate access to the remote Git server.

If the gem is hosted on GitHub, there's a shortcut:

```
gem "rspec", github: "rspec/rspec"
```

And Bundler will use your GitHub access to install the gem. (There's a similar option for BitBucket.) In both cases, you can further specify which part of the repo you want with a branch:, tag:, or ref: option.

When using a git source, you must bundle update to change the git commit that you are pointing to.

If you're working on the gem yourself locally, you can specify a path option that points to the top-level directory of the gem (specifically, the location of the .gemspec file) relative to the location of the Gemfile:

```
gem "rspec", path: "../development/rspec"
```

Unlike a git source, when you use a path, Bundler executes the local source directly each time, so you don't need to bundle update to get the newest version of a gem you're working on locally.

Gemfile Groups

Another way to specify more information about a gem is with the groups feature. A group is a collection of gems within a Gemfile that can be included or not included together when Bundler is used. Commonly, this feature is used to limit what gems are loaded based on environment or context. You may have certain gems that are only useful in production, or only needed when running tests.

You can attach gems to groups in two ways.

You can specify one or more groups for a gem by using the group: option inside the gemfile. The argument is either a single symbol or an array of symbols representing the group or groups that the gem is a part of:

```
gem "rspec", group: [:development, :test]
```

We've assigned RSpec to the :development, and :test groups. The group names are arbitrary, but it's conventional to match them to environment names when possible.

The other way you can attach gems to groups is to use the block form of group. This is shorter in the common case where you have several gems belonging to the same group or groups.

```
group :development do
  gem "standardrb"
  gem "debug"
end

group :development, :test do
  gem "rspec"
end
```

If you have multiple group blocks with the same group name, the group adds the contents of all of the blocks. In this example, the :development group contains Standard, debug, and RSpec, while the :test group contains only RSpec.

To use groups, you modify the Bundle setup instead of using require "bundle/setup". You just use require "bundler" and then explicitly call Bundler.setup with one or more group names.

```
require "bundler"
Bundler.setup(:development, :test)
```

Gems that aren't a part of any group will always be installed, calling setup with arguments additionally adds the gems that are in the specified groups.

If you're using bundle exec to load a program, the default will be to install all gems in all groups, but you can modify this with the environment variables BUNDLE_WITH or BUN-DLE_WITHOUT. BUNDLE_WITH creates a list of groups to include and ignores other groups, and BUNDLE_WITHOUT creates a list of groups to exclude and includes all other groups.

```
$ BUNDLE_WITH=test bundle exec rspec
```

If one of the environment variables is set, then groups will only be loaded if they conform to the logic of the environment variables.

Writing and Packaging Your Own Code into Gems

RubyGems isn't only for downloading gems; you can also write and distribute your own gems. Even if you don't plan to distribute a gem, the default packaging for RubyGems can help you plan the basic structure of your Ruby code. There used to be multiple sources for how to structure a Ruby gem, but Bundler also provides a default template that has become the basic standard.

As your programs grow (and they all seem to grow over time), you'll find that you'll need to start organizing your code. Simply putting everything into a single huge file becomes unworkable and makes it hard to reuse chunks of code in other projects. So, we need to find a way to split our project into multiple files and then knit them together as our program runs.

There are two major aspects to this organization. The first is internal to your code: how do you prevent different things with the same name from clashing? The second area is related: how do you conveniently organize the source files in your project?

Single File Projects

Small, self-contained scripts can be in a single file. But if you do this, you won't easily be able to write automated tests for your program because the test code won't be able to load the file containing your source without the program itself running. So, if you want to write a small program that also has automated tests, split that program into a trivial driver that provides the external interface (the command-line part of the code) and one or more files containing the rest. Your tests can then exercise these separate files without actually running the main body of your program.

Let's try this for real. Here's a simple program that finds anagrams in a dictionary. Feed it one or more words, and it gives you the anagrams of each. Here's an example:

```
$ ruby anagram.rb teaching ruby
Anagrams of teaching: cheating, teaching
Anagrams of ruby: bury, ruby
```

If we were typing in this program for casual use, we might enter it into a single file (perhaps anagram.rb).

gems/anagram.rb
```ruby
#!/usr/bin/env ruby

require 'optparse'

dictionary = "/usr/share/dict/words"

OptionParser.new do |opts|

  opts.banner = "Usage:  anagram [ options ]  word..."

  opts.on("-d", "--dict path", String, "Path to dictionary") do |dict|
    dictionary = dict
  end

  opts.on("-h", "--help", "Show this message") do
    puts opts
    exit
  end

  begin
    ARGV << "-h" if ARGV.empty?
    opts.parse!(ARGV)
  rescue OptionParser::ParseError => e
    STDERR.puts e.message, "\n", opts
    exit(-1)
  end
end

# convert "wombat" into "abmotw". All anagrams share a signature
def signature_of(word)
  word.unpack("c*").sort.pack("c*")
end

signatures = Hash.new
```

```ruby
File.foreach(dictionary) do |line|
  word = line.chomp
  signature = signature_of(word)
  (signatures[signature] ||= []) << word
end

ARGV.each do |word|
  signature = signature_of(word)
  if signatures[signature]
    puts "Anagrams of #{word}: #{signatures[signature].join(', ')}"
  else
    puts "No anagrams of #{word} in #{dictionary}"
  end
end
```

You might be wondering about the line word.unpack("c*").sort.pack("c*"). This uses the function unpack to break a string into an array of characters, which are then sorted and packed back into a string.

Anyway, this is fine as far as it goes. It's a small bit of code that does a small thing. We're somewhat limited because it's awkward to test code in the same file (not impossible, but generally, the Ruby test libraries assume they'll be in their own files). We've put a bunch of variables in the global namespace, which isn't ideal, and generally, this code isn't well-situated to manage complexity.

You might think that because Bundler requires a separate Gemfile, you can't use it with a standalone single-file Ruby script. Actually, you can, through the magic of bundler/inline.

Here's an admittedly contrived example where we want to print the date that we're requesting an Anagram report, and we want to use the date_by_example gem to display the date. By requiring bundler/inline we can then use a method called gemfile that takes a block, like so:

gems/anagram_inline.rb
```ruby
#!/usr/bin/env ruby

require "optparse"

➤ require "bundler/inline"
➤
➤ gemfile do
➤   source "https://rubygems.org"
➤   gem "date_by_example"
➤ end

dictionary = "/usr/share/dict/words"

OptionParser.new do |opts|
  opts.banner = "Usage:  anagram [ options ]  word..."

  opts.on("-d", "--dict path", String, "Path to dictionary") do |dict|
    dictionary = dict
  end

  opts.on("-h", "--help", "Show this message") do
    puts opts
    exit
  end
```

```ruby
  begin
    ARGV << "-h" if ARGV.empty?
    opts.parse!(ARGV)
  rescue OptionParser::ParseError => e
    warn e.message, "\n", opts
    exit(-1)
  end
end

# convert "wombat" into "abmotw". All anagrams share a signature
def signature_of(word)
  word.unpack("c*").sort.pack("c*")
end

signatures = {}

File.foreach(dictionary) do |line|
  word = line.chomp
  signature = signature_of(word)
  (signatures[signature] ||= []) << word
end

puts "Anagram Report for #{Date.today.by_example("Jan 02, 2006")}"

ARGV.each do |word|
  signature = signature_of(word)
  if signatures[signature]
    puts "Anagrams of #{word}: #{signatures[signature].join(", ")}"
  else
    puts "No anagrams of #{word} in #{dictionary}"
  end
end
```

Inside the gemfile block, we can do exactly the same things we can do in a Gemfile, here we list a source and one dependent gem. When we run the file normally, Bundler ensures that the gems are downloaded and automatically requires them so that later in the script we can just use the gems—in this case, the by_example call later on comes from the gem.

The main limitation to using bundle/inline is that because it's meant to work on one file, it doesn't create a lock file. Other than that, it's a great way to add a little depth to a simple script before it becomes a full-fledged app.

Namespaces

One issue with our existing anagram script right now is that it puts variable names in the global scope. We don't declare a class in the script (at least, not yet), but we do create dictionary and signatures, and if we had created a class, that class would be in the global namespace, meaning that any other code in the script could easily collide and overwrite it. This is, to put it mildly, not a good feature for long-term growth. We need to be able to separate out different parts of the code into different areas where they won't interfere with each other.

We've already encountered a way that Ruby helps you manage the names of things in your programs. If you define methods or constants in a class, Ruby ensures that their names can be used only in the context of that class (or its objects, in the case of instance methods):

```ruby
class Triangle
  SIDES = 3
  def area
    # ..
  end
end

class Square
  SIDES = 4
  def initialize(side_length)
    @side_length = side_length
  end

  def area
    @side_length * @side_length
  end
end

puts "A triangle has #{Triangle::SIDES} sides"

sq = Square.new(3)
puts "Area of square = #{sq.area}"
```

produces:

```
A triangle has 3 sides
Area of square = 9
```

Both classes define a constant called SIDES and an instance method area, but these names don't get confused. You access the instance method via objects created from the class, and you access the constant by prefixing it with the name of the class followed by a double colon. The double colon (::) is Ruby's namespace resolution operator. The thing to the left must be a class or module, and the thing to the right is a constant defined in that class or module.

So, putting code inside a module or class is a good way of separating it from other code. Ruby's Math module is a good example—it defines constants such as Math::PI and Math::E and methods such as Math.sin and Math.cos. You can access these constants and methods via the Math module object:

```ruby
Math::E             # => 2.718281828459045
Math.sin(Math::PI/6.0) # => 0.49999999999999994
```

(Modules have another significant use—they implement Ruby's *mixin* functionality, which we discussed in Mixins, on page 107.)

Ruby has an interesting little secret. The names of classes and modules are themselves just constants. Remember that we said that almost everything in Ruby is an object. Well, classes and modules are too. The name that you use for a class, such as String, is actually a Ruby constant containing the object representing that class. And that means that, if you define classes or modules inside other classes and modules, the names of those inner classes are constants that follow the same namespacing rules as other constants:

```ruby
module Formatters
  class Html
    MEDIA_TYPE = "text/html"
    # ...
  end
```

```ruby
  class Pdf
    # ...
  end
end

html_writer = Formatters::Html.new
html_media_type = Formatters::Html::MEDIA_TYPE
```

You can nest classes and modules inside other classes and modules to any depth you want (although it's rare to see them nested more than three deep).

So, now we know that we can use classes and modules to partition the names used by our programs.

Organizing Your Source Code

We have two related problems to solve: how do we split our source code into separate files, and where in the file system do we put those files? Some languages, such as Java, make this easy. They dictate that each outer-level class should be in its own file and that file should be named according to the name of the class. Other languages, such as Ruby, have no rules that relate source files and their content. In Ruby, you're free to organize your code as you like.

That said, you'll find that some kind of consistency helps. It'll make it easier for you to navigate your own projects, and it'll also help when you read (or incorporate) other people's code.

The Ruby community has largely adopted a de facto standard. In many ways, it follows the spirit of the Java model—each file is intended to have one top-level module or class, and the name of that class is based on the name of the file. (If you use Rails, the Zeitwerk[2] auto-loader enforces this pattern. You can also use Zeitwerk to add auto-loading to your own gems.)

Looking at the anagram code, there appear to be three sections. The first twenty-five or so lines do option-parsing, the next ten or so lines read and convert the dictionary, and the last few lines look up each command-line argument and report the result. Let's split our file into four parts:

- An option parser
- A class to hold the lookup table for anagrams
- A class that looks up words given on the command line
- A small command-line interface

The first three of these are effectively library files, used by the fourth. We can turn this into a gem, allowing access to anagram features for any program, and the command-line interface. The standard gem structure is given to us by Bundler, which doesn't go with Bundler's other features but is a standard tool that you're extremely likely to have around.

All we need is to name the gem. As it happens, both "anagrams" and "anagram" are already taken. Let's go with "aaagmnr", which is the "signature" of anagram given the code's implementation of signatures and is somehow not taken in the RubyGems central listing as I write this (there's a note about changing the initial git branch that we elided from the output):

```
$ bundle gem aaagmnr
```

---

2.   https://github.com/fxn/zeitwerk

```
Creating gem 'aaagmnr'...
MIT License enabled in config
Code of conduct enabled in config
Changelog enabled in config
Standard enabled in config
Initializing git repo in /Users/noel/projects/pragmatic/ruby5/Book/code/gems/aaagmnr
        create  aaagmnr/Gemfile
        create  aaagmnr/lib/aaagmnr.rb
        create  aaagmnr/lib/aaagmnr/version.rb
        create  aaagmnr/sig/aaagmnr.rbs
        create  aaagmnr/aaagmnr.gemspec
        create  aaagmnr/Rakefile
        create  aaagmnr/README.md
        create  aaagmnr/bin/console
        create  aaagmnr/bin/setup
        create  aaagmnr/.gitignore
        create  aaagmnr/.rspec
        create  aaagmnr/spec/spec_helper.rb
        create  aaagmnr/spec/aaagmnr_spec.rb
        create  aaagmnr/.github/workflows/main.yml
        create  aaagmnr/LICENSE.txt
        create  aaagmnr/CODE_OF_CONDUCT.md
        create  aaagmnr/CHANGELOG.md
        create  aaagmnr/.standard.yml
Gem 'aaagmnr' was successfully created.
For more information on making a RubyGem visit
https://bundler.io/guides/creating_gem.html
```

The "config" referred to here is the bundle config, which contains some global options for bundler, and which you can update with bundle config set ci github or whatever the config variable and setting you want. Anything in the configuration can also be set using command-line options to the bundle gem command itself.

What has Bundler created for us?

- A aaagmnr.gemspec file. A .gemspec file contains all the metadata that RubyGems uses to manage this gem. We'll talk about that in a second in Distributing and Installing Your Code, on page 272. We've also got a regular Gemfile.

- A series of logistical files. These include an open-source license, a basic change log, a code of conduct file, a readme, and a Rakefile. Some of these are managed by the configuration (such as the type of license and whether to include the code of conduct).

- The lib directory. This is where our code will go.

- The sig directory. This is where Ruby type info would go if we were using Ruby types. See Chapter 7, Basic Types: Numbers, Strings, and Ranges, on page 117.

- A bin directory. This has some useful pre-created setup scripts.

- We've been set up as a Git repo. You can choose other source control repositories in the config.

- We've been set up with a spec directory and RSpec. You can choose a different testing tool in the config.

- A linter file to enforce coding style; we're using the Standard gem.[3] The choice is a configurable option.

That's a lot of work already done for us. Now we can fit our code inside that structure.

Let's look at the lib directory. This is where we put our source code. Right now it has two files in it, aaagmnr.rb, which will be our top-level access to the code, and aaagmnr/version.rb, which contains a VERSION constant. We'll see more of this later.

The intention is that our actual logic will go alongside that version.rb in the lib/aaagnmr directory. Why is that?

We know we're going to be defining (at least) three classes. Right now, these classes will be used only by our command-line program, but it's conceivable that other people might want to include one or more of our libraries in their own code. This means that we should be polite and not pollute the top-level Ruby namespace with the names of all our classes and so on. We'll create one top-level module, Aaagnmr, and then place all our classes inside this module. This means that the full name of our options-parsing class will be Aaagnmr::Options.

This choice informs our decision on where to put the corresponding source files. Because class Options is inside the module Aaagnmr, it makes sense to put the corresponding file, options.rb, inside the lib/aaagnmr/ directory. This helps people who read your code in the future; when they see a name like A::B::C, they know to look for c.rb in the b/ directory in the a/ directory of your library. It also helps autoloaders find the file. When an autoloader sees a reference to Aaagnmr::Options, it knows that the corresponding file is lib/aaagnmr/options.rb.

Let's add the option parser. Its job is to take an array of command-line options and return to us the path to the dictionary file and the list of words to look up as anagrams. The source, in lib/aaagnmr/options.rb, looks like this:

gems/aaagmnr/lib/aaagmnr/options.rb
```ruby
module Aaagmnr
  class Options
    DEFAULT_DICTIONARY = "/usr/share/dict/words"
    attr_reader :dictionary, :words_to_find

    def initialize(argv)
      @dictionary = DEFAULT_DICTIONARY
      parse(argv)
      @words_to_find = argv
    end

    private def parse(argv)
      OptionParser.new do |opts|
        opts.banner = "Usage:  anagram [ options ]  word..."

        opts.on("-d", "--dict path", String, "Path to dictionary") do |dict|
          @dictionary = dict
        end

        opts.on("-h", "--help", "Show this message") do
          puts opts
          exit
        end
```

---

3. https://github.com/testdouble/standard

```
        begin
          argv = ["-h"] if argv.empty?
          opts.parse!(argv)
        rescue OptionParser::ParseError => e
          warn e.message, "\n", opts
          exit(-1)
        end
      end
    end
  end
end
```

Notice how we define the Options class inside a top-level Aaagnmr module.

Let's write some unit tests. This should be fairly easy because options.rb is self-contained — the only dependency is to the standard Ruby OptionParser. (Note that it's not explicitly required in this file because we've moved the require to the top-level aaagnmr.rb, which we'll show in a little bit.)

We're going to use RSpec here because the gem library has already loaded it.

gems/aaagmnr/spec/aaagmnr/options_spec.rb
```
module Aaagmnr
  RSpec.describe Options do
    describe "without specifiying a dictionary" do
      it "returns the default dictionary" do
        opts = Options.new(["someword"])
        expect(opts.dictionary).to eq(Options::DEFAULT_DICTIONARY)
      end

      it "should retain specified words" do
        opts = Options.new(["word1", "word2"])
        expect(opts.words_to_find).to eq(["word1", "word2"])
      end
    end

    describe "when specifying a dictionary" do
      it "should be able to reference the specified dictionary" do
        opts = Options.new(["-d", "mydict", "someword"])
        expect(opts.dictionary).to eq("mydict")
      end

      it "should retain specified words" do
        opts = Options.new(["-d", "mydict", "word1", "word2"])
        expect(opts.words_to_find).to eq(["word1", "word2"])
      end
    end
  end
end
```

You should note a few things to note in this file:

- You won't be able to run this without also updating the .gemspec file (as shown later in Distributing and Installing Your Code, on page 272). The gem system will block you from running an incomplete .gemspec.

- We didn't need to use require to load anything in this file—not our code, and not the option parser gem. That's because the RSpec spec_helper.rb requires our main file at lib/aaagmnr.rb (we'll see this code in a moment), which does all of those things.

- We've put the RSpec file inside our module Aaagmnr, meaning that we can refer to our Options class directly rather than qualifying it as Aaagmnr::Options. Alternatively, we could've started the file with RSpec.describe Aaagmnr::Options, but that has the potential to be flaky, since it depends on the Aaagmnr module to already exist.

These tests pass (after you update the .gemspec file), you can run them from the root directory of the gem:

```
$ rspec spec/aaagmnr/options_spec.rb
Aaagmnr::Options
  without specifiying a dictionary
    returns the default dictionary
    should retain specified words
  when specifying a dictionary
    should be able to reference the specified dictionary
    should retain specified words
Finished in 0.00104 seconds (files took 0.0532 seconds to load)
4 examples, 0 failures
```

The finder code (in lib/aaagmnr/finder.rb) is modified slightly from the original version. To make it easier to test, we'll have the default constructor take a list of words, rather than a filename. We'll then provide an additional factory method, from_file, that takes a filename and constructs a new Finder from that file's contents:

```
gems/aaagmnr/lib/aaagmnr/finder.rb
module Aaagmnr
  class Finder
    def self.from_file(file_name)
      new(File.readlines(file_name))
    end

    def initialize(dictionary_words)
      @signatures = {}
      dictionary_words.each do |line|
        word = line.chomp
        signature = signature_of(word)
        (@signatures[signature] ||= []) << word
      end
    end

    def lookup(word)
      signature = signature_of(word)
      @signatures[signature]
    end

    def signature_of(word)
      word.unpack("c*").sort.pack("c*")
    end
  end
end
```

Again, we embed the Finder class inside the top-level Aaagmnr module. And, again, this code is self-contained, allowing us to write some simple unit tests:

gems/aaagmnr/spec/aaagmnr/finder_spec.rb

```ruby
module Aaagmnr
  RSpec.describe Finder do
    describe "signature" do
      subject(:finder) { Finder.new([]) }

      specify { expect(finder.signature_of("cat")).to eq("act") }
      specify { expect(finder.signature_of("act")).to eq("act") }
      specify { expect(finder.signature_of("wombat")).to eq("abmotw") }
    end

    describe "lookup" do
      subject(:finder) { Finder.new(["cat", "wombat"]) }

      it "returns the word if the word is given" do
        expect(finder.lookup("cat")).to eq(["cat"])
      end

      it "returns the word if an anagram is given" do
        expect(finder.lookup("act")).to eq(["cat"])
        expect(finder.lookup("tca")).to eq(["cat"])
      end

      it "returns nil if no word matches the anagram" do
        expect(finder.lookup("wibble")).to be_nil
      end
    end
  end
end
```

```
$ rspec spec/aaagmnr/finder_spec.rb
Aaagmnr::Finder
  signature
    is expected to eq "act"
    is expected to eq "act"
    is expected to eq "abmotw"
  lookup
    returns the word if the word is given
    returns the word if an anagram is given
    returns nil if no word matches the anagram
Finished in 0.00176 seconds (files took 0.04836 seconds to load)
6 examples, 0 failures
```

We now have all the support code in place. We just need to run it. We'll make the command-line interface (the thing the end user actually executes) really thin. It's in the exe/ directory in a file called aaagmnr, which has no .rb extension because that would be unusual in a command. (If you're on Windows, you might want to wrap the invocation of this in a cmd file.)

gems/aaagmnr/exe/aaagmnr

```ruby
#!/usr/bin/env ruby
require_relative "../lib/aaagmnr"

runner = Aaagmnr::Runner.new(ARGV)
runner.run
```

The code that this script invokes (lib/anagram/runner.rb) knits our other libraries together:

```ruby
gems/aaagmnr/lib/aaagmnr/runner.rb
module Aaagmnr
  class Runner
    def initialize(argv)
      @options = Options.new(argv)
    end

    def run
      finder = Finder.from_file(@options.dictionary)
      @options.words_to_find.each do |word|
        anagrams = finder.lookup(word)
        if anagrams
          puts "Anagrams of #{word}: #{anagrams.join(", ")}"
        else
          puts "No anagrams of #{word} in #{@options.dictionary}"
        end
      end
    end
  end
end
```

With all our classes created, we can finally see the entire top-level file that's required by users of this gem:

```ruby
gems/aaagmnr/lib/aaagmnr.rb
# frozen_string_literal: true

require_relative "aaagmnr/finder"
require_relative "aaagmnr/options"
require_relative "aaagmnr/runner"
require_relative "aaagmnr/version"
require "optparse"

module Aaagmnr
  class Error < StandardError; end
  # Your code goes here...
end
```

It requires all our files, the version, and optparse. The custom error is created by the gem boilerplate; we don't really have any reason to use it yet.

Now that all our files are in place, we can run our program from the command line (use chmod to make the program executable).

```
$ exe/aaagmnr teaching ruby
Anagrams of teaching: cheating, teaching
Anagrams of ruby: bury, ruby
```

Distributing and Installing Your Code

There are a few parts of using RubyGems we haven't discussed. We need to consider the metadata that allows the RubyGems ecosystem to know things about our gem. In particular, we want to see how we can inject executables into code that uses our gem and also how our gem declares its dependencies.

RubyGems needs to know information about your project that isn't contained in the directory structure. Instead, you have to write a short RubyGems specification. Our gem creation tool has already created one with most of the boilerplate at aaagmnr.gemspec. This comes with some lines marked TODO which must be changed before the gem can be used. Here's the completed file, after the TODO lines have been changed:

```
gems/aaagmnr/aaagmnr.gemspec
# frozen_string_literal: true

require_relative "lib/aaagmnr/version"

Gem::Specification.new do |spec|
  spec.name = "aaagmnr"
  spec.version = Aaagmnr::VERSION
  spec.authors = ["Noel Rappin"]
  spec.email = ["noel.rappin@pragprog.com"]

  spec.summary = "A simple anagrams tool"
  spec.homepage = "http://pragprog.com"
  spec.license = "MIT"
  spec.required_ruby_version = ">= 2.6.0"

  spec.metadata["homepage_uri"] = spec.homepage
  spec.metadata["source_code_uri"] = "http://pragprog.com"
  spec.metadata["changelog_uri"] = "http://pragprog.com"

  # Specify which files should be added to the gem when it is released.
  # The `git ls-files -z` loads the files in the RubyGem that have been added
  # into git.
  spec.files = Dir.chdir(File.expand_path(__dir__)) do
    `git ls-files -z`.split("\x0").reject do |f|
      (f == __FILE__) ||
        f.match(%r{\A(?:(?:test|spec|features)/|\.(?:git|travis|circleci)|appveyor)})
    end
  end
  spec.bindir = "exe"
  spec.executables = spec.files.grep(%r{\Aexe/}) { |f| File.basename(f) }
  spec.require_paths = ["lib"]

  spec.add_dependency "date_by_example", '~> 0.1'
end
```

The specification itself happens inside that Gem::Specification.new block, where the spec argument is the specification object and we're setting all kinds of attributes on it. Most of these are basically what they claim to be and are used, among other things, to populate the gem's page on rubygems.org should we submit it there.

The first line of the spec gives our gem a name. This is important because it'll be used as part of the package name and will appear as the name of the gem when installed. The convention is for gem names to be all lowercase, and to use underscores to separate words, as in date_by_example, but use a dash to mark an extension to another gem, as in rspec-mocks. The dash indicates a submodule in the structure of the code, the main file of rspec-mocks would be rspec/mocks.

We pull the version string from the file inside the gem itself. The version string is significant because RubyGems will use it both for package naming and dependency management. The required_ruby_version tells RubyGems what versions of Ruby the gem would be expected to run with.

Eventually, we get to spec.files which lists all the files that we want to be distributed when the gem is downloaded. That boilerplate code basically says "everything in the git repository that isn't a test or part of source control or CI." You can choose to change that if you want; you just need a list of files.

The spec.executables line tells RubyGems where to look for command-line scripts that get exposed to any other code that uses this gem. The default is to include all files in the exe directory (because bin is used for developer scripts).

Finally, we've used add_dependency to include the date_by_example gem. This tells RubyGems that any user of this gem must also install date_by_example. The second argument is a version specifier using the same syntax as we used in Gemfile. If we wanted a dependency that was only used for development, we'd use add_dev_dependency, but in practice, development dependencies are just as often added to the Gemfile.

Speaking of Gemfile, here it is:

```
gems/aaagmnr/Gemfile
# frozen_string_literal: true

source "https://rubygems.org"

# Specify your gem's dependencies in aaagmnr.gemspec
gemspec
gem "rake", "~> 13.0"
gem "rspec", "~> 3.0"
gem "standard", "~> 1.3"
```

The important part here is the gemspec method, which pulls in all the dependencies and development dependencies specified in the .gemspec and adds them as though they were part of the Gemfile.

Packaging Your RubyGem

Once the gem specification is complete, you can create a packaged gem file for distribution. This is as easy as navigating to the top level of your project and typing this:

```
$ gem build aaagmnr.gemspec
  Successfully built RubyGem
  Name: aaagmnr
  Version: 0.1.0
  File: aaagmnr-0.1.0.gem
```

You'll find you now have a file called anagram-0.0.1.gem.

You can install it:

```
$ gem install aaagmnr-0.1.0.gem
Successfully installed aaagmnr-0.1.0
Parsing documentation for aaagmnr-0.1.0
Installing ri documentation for aaagmnr-0.1.0
Done installing documentation for aaagmnr after 0 seconds
1 gem installed
```

You can check to see that it is there:

```
$ gem list aaagmnr -d

*** LOCAL GEMS ***

aaagmnr (0.1.0)
    Author: Noel Rappin
    Homepage: http://pragprog.com
    License: MIT
    Installed at: /Users/noel/.rbenv/versions/3.1.2/lib/ruby/gems/3.1.0

    A simple anagrams tool
```

Now you can send your gem file to friends and colleagues or share it from a server—many corporate environments use gem servers to share code. Or, you could go one better and publish it to the central RubyGems server.

Serving Public RubyGems

RubyGems.org[4] is the main repository for public Ruby libraries and projects. If you create a RubyGems.org account, you can push your gem file to their public servers. We're not actually going to do that here, but the command is gem push.

And, at that point, any Ruby user in the world can use it with gem install aaagmnr.

What's Next

In this chapter, we looked at how to build Ruby programs and package them as gems. Now it's time to dig a little deeper into working with Ruby itself. In the next chapter, we'll talk about interacting with Ruby using irb, the interactive Ruby shell.

---

4.   http://rubygems.org

## CHAPTER 16

Interactive Ruby

If you want to play with Ruby, we recommend Interactive Ruby—irb, for short. irb is a Ruby command-line "shell" similar in concept to an operating system shell (complete with job control). It's sometimes called a REPL (which is an abbreviation for "Read, Evaluate, Print Loop") and provides an environment where you can play around with the language in real time.

You launch irb at the command prompt:

```
$ irb
```

irb displays the value of each expression as you complete it.

```
$ irb
irb(main):001:0* a = 1 +
irb(main):002:0* 2 * 3 /
irb(main):003:0> 4 % 5
=> 2
irb(main):004:0> 2 + 2
=> 4
irb(main):005:0> x = _
=> 4
irb(main):006:0> x
=> 4
irb(main):007:1* def test
irb(main):008:1*   puts "Hello, world!"
irb(main):009:0> end
=> :test
irb(main):010:0> test
Hello, world!
=> nil
irb(main):011:0>
```

You should note a couple of things about this session. If you typed along with it in Ruby 3.1 or higher, you may have noticed that irb tried to autocomplete text as you typed it. You may also have noticed that it color-coded the text as you entered it and even backdented the end line to line up.   Also, irb always stores the result of the last expression in a special variable (_) as you can see in line 5, where we use it in an assignment statement x = _, which can be a useful way to capture data and use it in the future.

irb is a great learning tool. It's very handy if you want to try an idea quickly and see if it works.

Using irb

irb is run with this command:

irb ‹ *irb-options* › ‹ *ruby_script* › ‹ *program arguments* ›

The command-line options for irb are listed in the following table. Typically, you'll run irb with no options, but if you want to run a script and watch the step-by-step description as it runs, you can provide the name of the Ruby script and any options for that script.

Option	Description
--autocomplete, --noautocomplete	Uses or doesn't use the autocomplete feature. The default is --autocomplete.
--back-trace-limit n	Displays backtrace information using the top n and last n entries. The default value is 16.
--colorize, --nocolorize	Uses or doesn't use color syntax highlighting. The default is --colorize.
--context-mode n	Specifies what binding to use for the new workspace. 0 is a proc at the top level, 1 is a loaded file, 2 is per thread binding in a load file, 3 is binding in a top-level function. 4, the default, is the top-level binding.
-d	Sets $DEBUG and $VERBOSE to true (same as ruby -d).
-E enc	Same as Ruby's -E option; sets internal or external encodings with in or ex.
--echo, --noecho	Echoes or doesn't echo the result of each line. The default is --echo.
--echo-on-assignment, --noecho-on-assignment, truncate-echo-on-assignment	Echoes, doesn't echo, or partially echoes the result of an assignment statement. The default is truncated.
--extra-doc-dir	Specifies an extra directory for documentation.
-f	Suppresses reading ~/.irbrc.
-h, --help	Displays usage information.
-I directories	Same as Ruby's -I option. Sets directories on the load path.
--inf-ruby-mode	Sets up irb to run in inf-ruby-mode under Emacs. Same as --prompt inf-ruby --nomultiline.
--inspect, --noinspect	Uses or doesn't use Kernel#inspect to format output (--inspect is the default).
--multiline, --nomultiline	Use or don't use multiline editor mode. The default is multiline. You can also specify modes with --singleline or --nosingleline.
--noprompt	Doesn't display a prompt. Same as --prompt null.
--prompt prompt-mode	Switches prompt. Predefined prompt modes are null, default, classic, simple, xmp, and inf-ruby.
--prompt-mode prompt-mode	Same as --prompt.
-r module	Requires *module*. Same as ruby -r.
--sample-book-mode	Same as --prompt simple.
--single-irb	Nested irb sessions will all share the same context.

Option	Description
--tracer	Displays trace for execution of commands.
-U	Same as Ruby's -U option. Sets encoding to UTF-8.
-v, --version	Prints the version of irb.
--verbose, --noverbose	Shows or doesn't show verbose details. The default is --noverbose.
-W[level]	Sets warning level: 0 is no warnings, 2 is verbose, and 1 is in the middle.
-w	Suppresses warning mode, like Ruby's -w.

Table 6—irb command-line options

Once started, irb displays a prompt and waits for you to type Ruby code. irb understands Ruby, so it knows when statements are incomplete. When this happens, irb will indicate that status as part of the prompt.

```
irb(main):001:0> 1 + 2
=> 3
irb(main):002:0* 3 +
irb(main):003:0> 4
=> 7
```

That * sign on line two happened after the + sign was typed, and indicates that the statement is incomplete. You get the same * if you type an opening parenthesis. The first number between the colons is the line number, and the second number between the colon and the final prompt is the indent level—you'll see that number will increase if you add an opening parenthesis.

You can leave irb by typing exit or quit or by entering an end-of-file character (usually command-d). The latter behavior can be blocked by setting IGNORE_EOF mode. We'll talk about configuration options in the next section.

During an irb session, the work you do is accumulated in irb's workspace. Variables you set, methods you define, and classes you create are all remembered and may be used subsequently in that session.

```
irb(main):001:1* def fib_up_to(n)
irb(main):002:1*   f1, f2 = 1, 1
irb(main):003:2*   while f1 <= n
irb(main):004:2*     puts f1
irb(main):005:2*     f1, f2 = f2, f1 + f2
irb(main):006:1*   end
irb(main):007:0> end
=> :fib_up_to
irb(main):008:0> fib_up_to(4)
1
1
2
3
=> nil
irb(main):009:0>
```

In this session, we defined a method in the irb session and then used it. Note that the irb session handles indent and outdent automatically. Also, the method definition returns the symbol name of the method, but the method call prints items and returns nil.

The internals of this method definition and the arithmetic expression are both split over multiple lines. When in the middle of editing something over multiple lines, pressing the up and down arrows will move you through that expression to allow you to edit across lines until the expression is complete. If you're not in the middle of a multiline expression, pressing the up or down arrows will move you through the command history.

A great use of irb is experimenting with code you've already written. Perhaps you want to track down a bug, or maybe you just want to play. If you load your program into irb, you can then create instances of the classes it defines and invoke its methods. For example, the file code/irb/fibbonacci_sequence.rb contains the following method definition:

irb/fibonacci_sequence.rb

```
def fibonacci_sequence
  Enumerator.new do |generator|
    i1, i2 = 1, 1
    loop do
      generator.yield i1
      i1, i2 = i2, i1 + i2
    end
  end
end
```

We can load this into irb and play with the method:

```
irb(main):001:0> load("code/irb/fibonacci_sequence.rb")
=> true
irb(main):002:0> fibonacci_sequence.first(10)
=> [1, 1, 2, 3, 5, 8, 13, 21, 34, 55]
```

In this example, we use load, rather than require, to include the file in our session. We do this as a matter of practice. Using load allows us to load the same file multiple times, so if we find a bug and edit the file, we can reload it into our irb session.

Navigating irb

From the irb prompt, if you're not in the middle of typing a multiline expression, pressing the up arrow will move you through your command history, showing the previous command, then the one before it and so on. The down arrow will move you forward in the history once you've started backward. The command history is persisted between sessions.

Unlike the way your shell might be set up, the up arrow doesn't act as a partial search. If you type a character and then press the up arrow, your typing will be replaced by the entire previous command regardless of whether the character you typed is the beginning of the previous command. By default, irb stores 1000 commands in its history, but this amount can be configured.

If you're in the middle of an expression, pressing the arrow keys will move you through that expression, allowing you to edit the expression before it's evaluated. This is relatively hard to demonstrate in a static book, but let's give it a try. For example, you might open up irb, type def foo, press return, type 1 + 1, and press return. Then an up arrow will allow you to navigate to change the 1 + 1 expression until you eventually come back to where you started and type end to complete the method expression.

irb has its own native autocompletion functionality. When you press Tab partway through a word, irb will look for possible completions that make sense at that point. If only one completion exists, irb will fill it in automatically and show you the beginning of the documentation for that completion (if any documentation exists).

If multiple completions exist, irb will display them in a list. Pressing Tab again will move you through the list of completions, each one displaying its documentation when selected, and then pressing Return will complete the selected entry.

For example, the following image shows the middle of an irb session:

```
✅😀 irb
irb(main):001:0> a = "cat"
=> "cat"
irb(main):002:0> a.reverse
                a.replace                        Press Alt+d to read the full document
                a.reverse                        String.reverse
                a.reverse!
                a.remove_instance_variable(from ruby core)
                a.respond_to?                    ------------------------------------------
                                                 reverse -> string


                                                 ------------------------------------------

                                                 Returns a new string with the characters
                                                 from self in reverse order.

                                                 'stressed'.reverse # => "desserts"
```

In this session, we assigned a string object to the variable a. Now we want to try the method String#reverse on this object. The screenshot here comes from typing a.re and hitting Tab twice.

You can see that irb lists all the methods supported by the object in a, whose names start with *re*, and that reverse is now selected and irb has filled out our input line with reverse—all we typed was a.re<tab><tab>. The documentation from the method is now also displayed.

irb responds to the Return key by expanding the name as far as it can go, in this case completing the word reverse. If we keyed Tab twice at this point, it would show us the current options, reverse and reverse!. Because reverse is the one we want, we instead hit Return again, and the line of code is executed.

Tab completion isn't limited to built-in names. If we define a class in irb, then tab completion works when we try to invoke one of its methods:

```
✅😀 irb
irb(main):001:1* class Test
irb(main):002:2*   def my_method
irb(main):003:1*   end
irb(main):004:0> end
=> :my_method
irb(main):005:0> t = Test.new
=> #<Test:0x000000001045f86d8>
irb(main):006:0> t.m
                t.my_method
                t.methods
                t.method
```

In this example, my_method is included in the autocomplete for the new object in the defined class.

Subsessions

irb supports multiple concurrent sessions. One is always current, and the others lie dormant until activated. Entering the command irb within irb creates a subsession, entering the jobs command lists all sessions, and entering fg activates a particular dormant session. This example also illustrates the -r command-line option, which loads in the given file before irb starts:

```
$ irb -r ./code/irb/fibonacci_sequence.rb
irb(main):001:0> result = fibonacci_sequence.first(5)
=> [1, 1, 2, 3, 5]
irb(main):002:0> # Creating nested irb session
=> nil
irb(main):003:0> irb
irb#1(main):001:0> result = %w[cat dog elk]
=> ["cat", "dog", "elk"]
irb#1(main):002:0> result.map(&:upcase)
=> ["CAT", "DOG", "ELK"]
irb#1(main):003:0> jobs
=>
#0->irb on main (#<Thread:0x00000001025e4d60 sleep_forever>: stop)
#1->irb#1 on main (#<Thread:0x000000010656caf0
/Users/noel/.rbenv/versions/3.1.2/lib/ruby/3.1.0/irb/ext/multi-irb.rb:192
run>: running)
irb#1(main):004:0> fg 0
=> #<IRB::Irb: @context=#<IRB::Context:0x00000001064ed9d0>,
  @signal_status=:IN_EVAL, @scanner=#<RubyLex:0x000000010659e370>>
irb(main):004:0> result
=> [1, 1, 2, 3, 5]
irb(main):005:0> fg 1
=> #<IRB::Irb: @context=#<IRB::Context:0x000000010656c960>,
  @signal_status=:IN_EVAL, @scanner=#<RubyLex:0x0000000106567258>>
irb#1(main):005:0> result
=> ["cat", "dog", "elk"]
irb#1(main):006:0>
```

In this example, we start a job and set result to the list of the first five Fibonacci numbers, and then we use the irb command internally to start a second job, setting result to something else. Then we switch back and forth to show that the namespaces are independent.

Bindings

If you specify an object when you create a subsession, that object becomes the value of self in that binding. This is a convenient way to experiment with objects. In the following example, we create a subsession with the string "wombat" as the default object. Methods with no receiver will be executed by that object.

```
irb
irb(main):001:0> self
=> main
irb(main):002:0> irb "wombat"
irb#1(wombat):001:0> self
=> "wombat"
```

```
irb#1(wombat):002:0> upcase
=> "WOMBAT"
irb#1(wombat):003:0> size
=> 6
irb#1(wombat):004:0> gsub(/[aeiou]/, '*')
=> "w*mb*t"
irb#1(wombat):005:0> irb_exit
=> #<IRB::Irb: @context=#<IRB::Context:0x0000000108fa9e80>,
    @signal_status=:IN_EVAL, @scanner=#<RubyLex:0x00000001090be8e8>>
irb(main):003:0> self
=> main
irb(main):004:0> upcase
(irb):4:in `<main>': undefined local variable
  or method `upcase' for main:Object (NameError)
Did you mean?  case
  from /[elided]/gems/irb-1.4.1/exe/irb:11:in `<top (required)>'
```

Configuring irb

irb is remarkably configurable. You can set configuration options with command-line options, from within an initialization file, and while you're inside irb itself.

irb uses an initialization file in which you can set commonly used options or execute any required Ruby statements. When irb is run, it'll try to load an initialization file from one of the following sources in order: ~/.irbrc, .irbrc, irb.rc, _irbrc, and $irbrc.

Within the initialization file, you may run any arbitrary Ruby code. For example, you can use require for any gem that you might want included in an irb session (such as irbtools[1] or awesome-print[2]).

You can also set configuration values. The list of configuration variables is given in irb Configuration Options, on page 285. The values that can be used in an initialization file are the symbols (starting with a colon). You use these symbols to set values into the IRB.conf hash. For example, to make SIMPLE the default prompt mode for all your irb sessions, you could have the following in your initialization file:

```
IRB.conf[:PROMPT_MODE] = :SIMPLE
```

For a dynamic twist on configuring irb, you can set IRB.conf[:IRB_RC] to a Proc object. This proc will be invoked whenever the irb context is changed and will receive the configuration for that context as a parameter. You can use this facility to change the configuration dynamically based on the context. For example, the following .irbrc file sets the prompt so that only the main prompt shows the irb level, but the continuation prompts and the result still line up:

```
IRB.conf[:IRB_RC] = lambda do |conf|
  leader = " " * conf.irb_name.length
  conf.prompt_i = "#{conf.irb_name} --> "
  conf.prompt_s = leader + ' |-" '
  conf.prompt_c = leader + ' |-+ '
  conf.return_format  = leader + " ==> %s\n\n"
  puts "Welcome!"
end
```

---

1.   https://irb.tools
2.   https://github.com/awesome-print/awesome_print

An irb session using this .irbrc file looks like the following:

```
irb
Welcome!
irb --> 1 + 2
    ==> 3

    \-+ 2 +
irb --> 6
    ==> 8
```

The static nature of this code listing doesn't quite capture some dynamic behavior that appears where the prompts change while typing.

Extending irb

Because the things you type into irb are interpreted as Ruby code, you can effectively extend irb by defining new top-level methods. For example, you may want to time how long certain things take. You can use the measure method in the Benchmark library to do this, but this is more convenient to use if you wrap it in a helper method.

Add the following to your .irbrc file:

```ruby
def time(&block)
  require 'benchmark'
  result = nil
  timing = Benchmark.measure do
    result = block.()
  end
  puts "It took: #{timing}"
  result
end
```

The next time you start irb, you'll be able to use this method to get timings:

```
irb(main):001:0> time { 1_000_000.times { "cat".upcase } }
It took:    0.106198    0.000795    0.106993 (   0.106986)
=> 1000000
```

Another common thing to do is reopen the Object class and add some diagnostic methods. Here's one that looks up the source location of a method (via https://medium.com/simply-dev/do-more-with-rails-console-by-configuring-irbrc-e5c25284305d).

```ruby
class Object
  def sl(method_name)
    self.method(method_name).source_location rescue "#{method_name} not found"
  end
end
```

We'll see in Chapter 17, Debugging Ruby, on page 289, that the built-in debugger and the Pry tool also provide great support for looking up source locations.

You can configure irb to remember the commands you enter between sessions. Simply add the following to your .irbrc file, where the number indicates the amount of commands you want to save:

```ruby
IRB.conf[:SAVE_HISTORY] = 50
```

Interactive Configuration

Most configuration values are also available while you're running irb. The list in irb Configuration Options, on page 285, shows these values as conf._xxx_. For example, to change your prompt back to SIMPLE, you could use the following:

```
irb(main):001:0* 1 +
irb(main):002:0> 2
=> 3
irb(main):003:0> conf.prompt_mode = :SIMPLE
=> :SIMPLE
?> 1 +
>> 2
=> 3
>>
```

irb Configuration Options

In the descriptions that follow, a label of the form :XXX signifies a key used in the IRB.conf hash in an initialization file, and conf.xxx signifies a value that can be set interactively.

:AUTO_INDENT / auto_indent_mode
> If true, irb will indent nested structures as you type them. Default is true.

:BACK_TRACE_LIMIT / back_trace_limit
> Displays n initial and n final lines of backtrace. Default is 16.

:CONTEXT_MODE
> Specifies what binding to use for the new workspace. 0 is a proc at the top level, 1 is a loaded file, 2 is per thread binding in a load file, 3 is binding in a top-level function. 4, the default, is the top-level binding

:EVAL_HISTORY / save_history
> Stores the result of all ERB commands, you can use _ to retrieve this or _[line_no] to get a specific line's result. Default is nil.

:IGNORE_EOF / ignore_eof
> Specifies the behavior of an end of file received on input. If true, it'll be ignored; otherwise, irb will quit. Default is false.

:IGNORE_SIGINT / ignore_sigint
> If false, ^C (Ctrl+C) will quit irb. If true, ^C during input will cancel input and return to the top level; during execution, ^C will abort the current operation. Default is true.

:INSPECT_MODE / inspect_mode
> Specifies how values will be displayed: true or nil means use inspect, false uses to_s. Default is nil.

:IRB_NAME / irb_name
> The name of an irb session, defaults to irb.

:IRB_RC
> Can be set to a proc object that will be called when an irb session (or subsession) is started. Default is nil.

prompt_c
> The prompt for a continuing statement (for example, immediately after an if).

prompt_i
> The standard, top-level prompt. (The defualt depends on the prompt mode.)

:PROMPT_MODE / prompt_mode
> The style of prompt to display. The default is :DEFAULT.

prompt_s
> The prompt for a continuing string. (The default depends on the prompt mode.)

:PROMPT
> See Configuring the Prompt, on page 287.

:SAVE_HISTORY / save_history
> The number of commands to save between irb sessions. Default is nil.

:USE_AUTOCOMPLETE
> If true or nil use the autocomplete feature. Default is true.

:USE_COLORIZE
> If true or nil colorize irb output. Default is true.

:USE_LOADER / use_loader
> Specifies whether irb's own file reader method is used with load/require. Default is false.

:USE_MULTILINE
> If true or nil use multiline edit mode. Default is nil.

:USE_SINGLELINE
> If true or nil use singleline edit mode. Default is nil.

:USE_TRACER / use_tracer
> If true, traces the execution of statements. Default is false.

Commands

At the irb prompt, you can enter any valid Ruby expression and see the results. You can also use any of the following commands to control the irb session. (For some inexplicable reason, many of these commands have up to nine different aliases. We don't bother to show all of them.)

bindings
> Lists the current bindings.

cb, irb_change_binding ‹obj›
> Creates and enters a new binding (sometimes called a *workspace*) that has its own scope for local variables. If *obj* is given, it'll be used as self in the new binding.

conf, context, irb_context
> Displays current configuration. Modifying the configuration is achieved by invoking methods of conf. The list in irb Configuration Options, on page 285, shows the available conf settings.

> For example, to set the default prompt, you could use this:

```
irb(main):001:0> conf.prompt_i = "Yes, Master? "
=> "Yes, Master? "
Yes, Master? 1 + 2
```

exit, quit, irb_exit, irb_quit
> Quits this irb session or subsession. If you've used cb to change bindings (as detailed under the cb entry in this list), it exits from this binding mode.

fg n, irb_fg n
> Switches into the specified irb subsession. *n* may be any of the following: an irb subsession number, a thread ID, an irb object, or the object that was the value of *self* when a subsession was launched.

help ClassName, string, or symbol
> Displays the ri help for the given thing.

irb ‹ obj ›
> Starts an irb subsession. If *obj* is given, it'll be used as self.

irb_cwws
> Prints the object that's the binding of the current workspace.

jobs, irb_jobs
> Lists irb subsessions.

kill n, irb_kill n
> Kills an irb subsession. *n* may be any of the values as described for irb_fg.

pushb obj, popb
> Pushes and pops the current binding.

source filename
> Loads and executes the given file, displaying the source lines.

Configuring the Prompt

You have a lot of flexibility in configuring the prompts that irb uses. Sets of prompts are stored in the prompt hash, IRB.conf[:PROMPT].

For example, to establish a new prompt mode called MY_PROMPT, you could enter the following (either directly at an irb prompt or in the .irbrc file):

```
IRB.conf[:PROMPT][:MY_PROMPT] = { # name of prompt mode
  :PROMPT_I => '-->',              # normal prompt
  :PROMPT_S => '--"',              # prompt for continuing strings
  :PROMPT_C => '--+',              # prompt for continuing statement
  :RETURN => "    ==>%s\n"         # format to return value
}
```

Once you've defined a prompt, you have to tell irb to use it. From the command line, you can use the --prompt option. (Notice how the name of the prompt on the command line is automatically converted to uppercase, with hyphens changing to underscores.)

```
$ irb --prompt my-prompt
```

If you want to use this prompt in all your future irb sessions, you can set it as a configuration value in your .irbrc file:

```
IRB.conf[:PROMPT_MODE] = :MY_PROMPT
```

The symbols :PROMPT_I, :PROMPT_N, :PROMPT_S, and :PROMPT_C specify the format for each of the prompt strings. In a format string, certain % sequences are expanded, as shown in the following table:

Flag	Description
%N	Current command.
%m	to_s of the main object (self).
%M	inspect of the main object (self).
%l	Delimiter type. In strings that are continued across a line break, %l will display the type of delimiter used to begin the string, so you'll know how to end it. The delimiter will be ", ', /,], or `.
%NNi	Indent level. The optional number *n* is used as a width specification to printf, as printf("%NNd").
%NNn	Current line number (*n* used as with the indent level).
%%	A literal percent sign.

Table 7—irb prompt string substitutions

The default prompt mode is defined as:

```
IRB.conf[:PROMPT][:DEFAULT] = {
  :PROMPT_I => "%N(%m):%03n:%i> ",
  :PROMPT_N => "%N(%m):%03n:%i> ",
  :PROMPT_S => "%N(%m):%03n:%i%l ",
  :PROMPT_C => "%N(%m):%03n:%i* ",
  :RETURN   => "=> %s\n"
}
```

What's Next

In this chapter, we looked at how to use Ruby interactively with irb. Debugging is a common use case for irb. In the next chapter, we'll dive into the official Ruby debugging tools.

## CHAPTER 17

Debugging Ruby

Sometimes code doesn't work as you expect. Ruby provides different ways for you to see what's happening as you execute your code, which better enables you in understanding and debugging it. From humble print statements to elaborate inline debugging tools, you can get the visibility you need into your code.

Printing Things

If you want to debug code and you don't want to use any fancy tools, then printing things out to the console is the way to go. We don't mean to make fun—we extensively use this method. It's quick and lends itself to faster cycle times than using a debugger to step through code.

We've seen a few options for this already, like puts, which uses to_s to convert its argument to a string, and p, which does the same thing but uses inspect. Ruby also provides print and pretty-print via the pp method. Here's a table of what they all look like for nil, a string, a symbol, an array, a hash, and an array with a hash element:

print	p	puts	pp
	nil		nil
test	"test"	test	"test"
test	:test	test	:test
[1, 2, 3]	[1, 2, 3]	1	[1, 2, 3]
		2	
		3	
{:a=>1, :b=>2}	{:a=>1, :b=>2}	{:a=>1, :b=>2}	{:a=>1, :b=>2}
[1, 2, {:a=>1, :b=>2}]	[1, 2, {:a=>1, :b=>2}]	1	[1, 2, {:a=>1, :b=>2}]
		2	
		{:a=>1, :b=>2}	

Table 8—print method

You can see some differences here, but they are subtle. (This is, by the way, exactly the kind of table an author puts in a book when the author can never remember the differences. It's now a convenient place for the author to look them up.)

Ruby has some other print tools that do a better job with more complex structured data. One of these tools is the jj method, which creates pretty-printed JSON. You need to use require "json" to have access to this method. Another tool is y, which comes when you use require "yaml" and produces the argument in YAML syntax. We also recommend the awesome-print gem, which, when loaded and required, gives you ap, a method that produces a clear structure of complex data.

You should find one of these tools useful when writing output. For example, it's often faster to put one of these statements in a test, run the test, and inspect the output than it is to use a step debugger.

You can use Ruby's reflection abilities quite powerfully for printing information to the console. The caller method is part of Kernel and will always show you the current call stack. Aaron Patterson has a lot of helpful output tips at https://tenderlovemaking.com/2016/02/05/i-am-a-puts-debuggerer.html.

The Ruby Debugger

Debuggers can also be quite powerful, and Ruby 3.1 came with a big improvement to Ruby's standard debugger. The new debugger is distributed as a separate Ruby gem rather than part of the standard library:

```
$ gem install debug
```

Note that the gem is named *debug* and not *debugger*. The *debugger* gem is a separate tool that hasn't been maintained since 2015. Similarly, if you're using Bundler, specify a version constraint of ">= 1.0.0" or else you'll get a different, older gem. Global, permanent namespaces are fun!

After you have installed the debugger gem, there are a few different ways to start the debugger.

You can start your script with the command rdbg rather than ruby:

rdbg code/trouble/profileeg.rb

The script will start in debug mode, which we'll talk about in a moment.

If you want to run the debugger on a Ruby process that's invoked via a separate command like rake, then you use rdbg -c --:

rdbg -c -- rake test:load.

More commonly, you'd use the debugger by inserting the line binding.break into your code. (For this to work, you must have done a require "debug" somewhere along the code path.) The debugger is invoked at that line.

Visual Studio Code also has a plugin[1] that allows you to invoke the new Ruby debugger using VS Code's existing debugging interface. (To be clear, many editors support Ruby debugging but may do so via a different tool.)

You can also use the debugger remotely against an application that's not running in your terminal (often because it's running in a Docker container, it's a background process, or it's not using the standard in and out ports). To connect to a remote process, you start with rdbg --open SCRIPT_NAME, which starts your script as a background process. Then in a different terminal, you run rdbg --attach to connect to the running process in a debugger session.

---

1. https://marketplace.visualstudio.com/items?itemName=KoichiSasada.vscode-rdbg

Alternatively, you can use require "debug/open" in the background process, which allows you to skip the rdbg --open step and go straight to the attach step. Doing so stops the program on the first line; if you want the program to run normally, use require "debug/open_nonstop". But don't do that in production—it'll leave the debug socket open waiting for a debugger to attach.

Here's a short sample program that we'll use to demonstrate the Ruby debugger:

```ruby
debugging/debugger_test.rb
require "debug"

class CashRegister
  attr_accessor :tax_rate

  def initialize(tax_rate)
    @tax_rate = tax_rate
    @items = []
  end

  def add_item(item, quantity, price_in_cents)
    @items << {item:, quantity:, price_in_cents:}
  end

  def subtotals
    @items.map {_1[:quantity] * _1[:price_in_cents]}
  end

  def pre_tax_total = subtotals.sum

  def tax = pre_tax_total * tax_rate

  def total = pre_tax_total + tax

  def sale_price(price_in_cents, discount)
    price_in_cents * (1.0 - discount)
  end
end

register = CashRegister.new(0.05)
register.add_item("pen", 3, 499)
binding.break
register.add_item("paper", 2, register.sale_price(799, 25))
p register.total
```

We don't think there's a bug in here, but let's trace through it via the debugger.

When you enter the debugging tool via either rdbg or binding.break, you're taken to the command-line interface for the tool, which looks like this:

```
[27, 34] in code/debugger/debugger_test.rb
    27|   end
    28| end
    29|
    30| register = CashRegister.new(0.05)
    31| register.add_item("pen", 3, 499)
=>  32| binding.break
    33| register.add_item("paper", 2, register.sale_price(799, 25))
    34| p register.total
=>#0    <main> at code/debugger/debugger_test.rb:32
```

The first line shows what file is being executed and what lines are being displayed. You then see about ten lines of code (fewer here because we hit the end of the file), with a pointer to the line currently about to be executed. The final line, <main> at, shows both the current self object at the beginning of the line and the line you're at.

Below that is a prompt at which you can type commands. The full list is at https://github.com/ruby/debug.

Control Flow

Most of what you'll want to do is move through the program. The debugger will helpfully give you comments as to what your commands do, so when I type s at the next prompt, I also see # step command. The most common commands are:

- step or s. The step command moves to the next place the code can stop, even if that's on a different line than what is called from this line. If you put a number after the command as in s 5, the command moves that number of steps before stopping. If I type s at this prompt, I end up at the beginning of the next line. If I type s again, I jump to the sale_price method because that's the next thing invoked.

- next or n. The next command steps over or moves to the next line. It executes the entire line of code and then stops. Again, you can add a number argument if you want to go more than one line at a time. If I type n at this prompt, I end up at the beginning of the next line. If I type n again, I end up at the beginning of the following line; the sale_price method is already complete.

- continue or c. The continue command moves forward until the script ends or you hit a breakpoint or a binding.debug line. If I type c at the prompt, the program runs until the end because no other stopping points exist.

The difference between step and next is worth mentioning. For example, you have a line of code such as this:

```
register.add_item("paper", 2, register.sale_price(799, 25))
```

Typing s will take you to the sale_price method, and you'll be able to walk through that. Typing n will run the entire line of code and take you to the next one.

To exit the debugger, the command is q. Ctrl+D will also work. If you're remote debugging and want to end the remote process without exiting the debugger, the command is kill. Both of those commands prompt for a confirmation. If you want to skip that prompt, you can use q! or kill! to exit directly.

Breakpoints

A breakpoint is a location in the code where the debugger stops execution and gives you control at the debugger prompt to inspect or navigate through the code. As we saw, binding.break creates a breakpoint, but the debugger provides alternate ways to denote breakpoints without adding lines to the code.

You can set a breakpoint from the debugger's command prompt with break n or b n, where n is the line number of the currently displayed file. You have a lot of other options, including break FILENAME:n, which lets you set a breakpoint on a different file, and break CLASS-NAME#METHOD or break EXPRESSION.METHOD, both of which set a breakpoint at the beginning of the given method. All of those options can add an if EXPRESSION such that the breakpoint only stops the code if the expression is true. You also have the suffixes pre: COMMAND and do: COMMAND, which run the command at the breakpoint—the difference being that pre stops the debugger, and do runs the command and keeps going.

Typing b by itself with no other arguments will give you a numbered list of breakpoints, which is useful because del NUM allows you to delete a specific breakpoint and del with no numbers deletes them all.

A reasonable thing to do in a debugger is look for errors, and the Ruby debugger allows you to catch ERROR as in catch ArgumentError, which stops execution when an exception of that type is raised, at which point you can continue to navigate or query the system using the methods in the next section. The catch command also takes the if, pre, and do suffixes just as break does.

You can also cause the debugger to stop when a value is changed—in kind of a limited way. The watch command takes an instance variable name, as in watch @name, and stops execution if that instance variable of the object in the current scope changes. The official docs do point out that this is, and we quote, "super slow." The watch command also takes if, pre, and do suffixes.

Querying the System

When you're stopped via a breakpoint, that's a great time for you to look around and try to find out what the code is doing.

Most generally, you can type eval EXPRESSION and evaluate an arbitrary expression in the context of the current set of active variables. You can even use this to change the value of variables, which means you can easily break things if you want, or you can explicitly set up edge cases that are otherwise hard to create. You can also use p EXPRESSION or pp EXPRESSION to print or pretty-print the result of the expression. And you can type irb, which will take you into an irb session with the current set of variable values.

You can specifically see the current call stack with bt or backtrace. If you put a number after the command, the debugger will only show that number of lines. If you put a regular expression after the command, it'll only show you lines that match the expression. The i command will show you all the values active at the current point, and i i and i l will show instance values and local values, respectively.

The debugger has the concept of a "tracer" where you can get a message from the debugger when running code triggers an event. The command trace call will show you all method calls (and I mean *all* method calls). You can add a regular expression on the end of the command to filter the calls you see. You can use trace exception to see what exceptions get raised, and trace line to track lines of code as the script bounces along.

There's more to the debugger. See a full list of commands at https://github.com/ruby/debug.

Pry

In addition to the official Ruby debugger and the official irb client, there is a third-party alternative called Pry.[2] Pry predates the Ruby 3.1 debugger and contains many overlapping features, but with a slightly different command-line interface.

---

2.   http://pry.github.io

To install Pry, you need the Pry gem. Pry also has a plugin system that allows extensions, and we'll be adding the pry-byebug gem that gives step-by-step debugging control to Pry. You can add them to a Gemfile:

```
gem "pry"
gem "pry-byebug"
```

The main way to use Pry is by adding the method call binding.pry into a code base. If we do that with the same code we used for the debugger earlier, just by replacing require "debug" with require "pry" and the binding.break call with binding.pry we get this:

```
From: /Users/noel/projects/pragmatic/ruby5/Book/code/debugging/pry_test.rb:32 :

    27:    end
    28: end
    29:
    30: register = CashRegister.new(0.05)
    31: register.add_item("pen", 3, 499)
 => 32: binding.pry
    33: register.add_item("paper", 2, register.sale_price(799, 25))
    34: p register.total

[1] pry(main)>
```

That certainly looks familiar. We've got the line of code we're blocked at with a few lines of context surrounding it, and then a command prompt below it.

This command prompt is a full REPL, similar to irb, and you can type in arbitrary Ruby expressions within it, including the creation of new methods or classes. You can also type commands. One important command to start with is exit, which takes you out of the current frame. If you're at the top level, you exit the program. You can also exit the program at any time by typing !!!.

For all Pry output, if the output runs longer than the current screen, it'll act like a paging reader (specifically the Unix less program), which is to say it'll pause output at the bottom of the screen with a : prompt and await navigation. The space bar will move you one screen forward; the letter b will move you one page back. The Enter key or j moves you one line forward, and k moves you one line back. You need to type q to quit and go back to regular input.

Like irb, Pry considers itself to be running inside a particular scope, which is self to anything you type at the command prompt and is the target of other Pry commands. The Pry command structure was based on Unix command shell syntax, so you can change the scope to a different object with cd OBJECT. The object in question must be visible to Pry.

As with Unix, cd .. goes back to the previous scope, cd / takes you back to the original top level scope of the session, and cd - toggles you between the last two scopes.

What does that look like in a session? Let's pick up our Pry session, already in progress:

```
[1] pry(main)> self
=> main
[2] pry(main)> cd register
[3] pry(#<CashRegister>):1> self
=> #<CashRegister:0x000000010277ecc0
 @items=[{:item=>"pen", :quantity=>3, :price_in_cents=>499}],
 @tax_rate=0.05>
```

```
[4] pry(#<CashRegister>):1> cd @items
[5] pry(#<Array>):2> size
=> 1
[6] pry(#<Array>):2> cd first
[7] pry(#<Hash>):3> keys
=> [:item, :quantity, :price_in_cents]
[8] pry(#<Hash>):3> cd ..
[9] pry(#<Array>):2>
```

The session starts out with the scope pointed at main. On line 2, we change to register, a local variable in scope. We can prove this on line 3 by checking the value of self. Note the number after the colon in the prompt, which tells us how many levels deep we are. On line 4, we change scope again, this time to @items, an instance variable that is part of register. Then on line 5, we show that size is sent to the item in scope, effectively @items.size, giving us 1. Then we use cd again, this time changed to first, the first item of that array, and we show that keys is sent to that hash. Then on line 9, we use cd .. to pop back up a level to the array scope.

At any time you can use the command nesting to see a list of the current stack of contexts and the jump-to n command to immediately go back up the stack to a particular point in that stack. Intervening contexts are exited.

Pry gives you some ways to explore the context that it's currently embedded in. The main way is with the ls method. The ls method gives you access to all of the ways Ruby lets you learn things about an item. You can see a list of the instance variables of an object and also the methods available from that object.

If you type ls without an argument, it'll give you that list on the current context, but if you give it an object argument, as in ls items, Pry will display the information for that object. You have a number of options for how to limit the fire hydrant of information (see https://github.com/pry/pry/wiki/State-navigation#Ls for a full list).

Pry also gives you a lot of ways to learn about the code you're looking at. You can type find-method with a method name, and Pry will search the Ruby libraries to show you what classes define methods that include that string in the name. In the following code, we see that String and Symbol both define the method upcase:

```
[2] pry(main)> find-method upcase
String
String#upcase
String#upcase!
Symbol
Symbol#upcase
```

Pry's most distinctive feature is its ability to show you the source code for methods that you might be looking at. The show-source command takes a method or class name, and if that name is defined in the current context, it shows you the source code:

```
> cd register
[2] pry(#<CashRegister>):1> show-source add_item

From: code/debugging/pry_test.rb:11:
Owner: CashRegister
Visibility: public
Signature: add_item(item, quantity, price_in_cents)
Number of lines: 3
```

```ruby
def add_item(item, quantity, price_in_cents)
  @items << {item:, quantity:, price_in_cents:}
end
```

If you type show-source without an argument, it will show the source of the current context's class or, if you are at the top level, the method you were in the middle of when you invoked Pry.

The similar command show-doc will show the documentation of the method or class used as the argument.

Another useful quirk of Pry is that you can easily treat it like a regular Unix command line. Any command you start with a dot (.) is sent to the underlying terminal shell. By using this, you can interact with the operating system directly without using Pry. Pry also overrides the common file reading program cat. You can invoke cat FILENAME without using a ., and Pry will display the output paged and with the syntax highlighted.

Pry is a big program with a plugin-filled ecosystem of its own, and there's more to it that we can cover here. Check out http://pry.github.io for full details.

Debugging Performance Issues with Benchmark

Ruby is an interpreted, high-level language, and as such it may not perform as fast as a lower-level language such as C. In the following sections, we'll list some basic things you can do to inspect its performance.

Typically, slow-running programs have one or two performance graveyards—places where execution time goes to die. Find and improve them, and suddenly your whole program springs back to life. The trick is finding them—developers are notoriously bad at guessing where performance hangups actually are. The Benchmark module can help.

You can use the Benchmark module to time sections of code. For example, we may wonder what the overhead of method invocation is. You can use Benchmark.bm or Benchmark.bmbm to find out.

```ruby
require "benchmark"

LOOP_COUNT = 1_000_000

Benchmark.bmbm(12) do |test|
  test.report("inline:") do
    LOOP_COUNT.times do |x|
      # nothing
    end
  end

  test.report("method:") do
    def method
      # nothing
    end

    LOOP_COUNT.times do |x|
      method
    end
  end
end
```

produces:

```
Rehearsal --------------------------------------------------
inline:        0.019779   0.000008   0.019787 (  0.019800)
method:        0.035100   0.000015   0.035115 (  0.035148)
------------------------------------- total: 0.054902sec

                  user     system      total        real
inline:        0.020352   0.000009   0.020361 (  0.020378)
method:        0.034613   0.000005   0.034618 (  0.034648)
```

The bm or bmbm methods take a block, execute it while calculating the time that the block takes, and report that result in four columns:

- The time in seconds used by the CPU executing the user process.
- The time in seconds used by the CPU in system calls during the block.
- The sum of the first two columns.
- The actual amount of elapsed time during the block, sometimes called "clock time" or "wall time."

Because the resulting value is in seconds, lower values are faster, which we only mention because some timing tools give an "executions per second" measure, and that can be confusing.

The argument to bm or bmbm is the width of the columns of the output.

You may be wondering what the difference is between bm and bmbm. It has to do with trying to make the output of the benchmarking test more consistent.

Ruby programs can run slowly because of the overhead of garbage collection. Because this garbage collection can happen at any time during your program's execution, you may find that benchmarking gives misleading results, showing a section of code running slowly when, in fact, the slowdown was caused because garbage collection happened to trigger while that code was executing. So the bmbm method runs the tests twice—once as a rehearsal and once to actually measure performance—in an attempt to minimize the distortion introduced by garbage collection. In fact, the official docs even say "there's only so much that bmbm can do, and the results are not guaranteed to be isolated from garbage collection and other effects."

The benchmarking process itself is relatively well-mannered—it won't slow down your program much.

What's Next

In this chapter, we talked about different ways to debug Ruby, including printing information to the console, using the official Ruby debugger and the popular third-party program, Pry. We also looked at how to use Ruby's benchmarking tools to identify slow spots in your code.

Type errors are a common source of bugs in Ruby, and there are some attempts to allow developers to add type information to their Ruby code so that tooling can identify type problems before they can become bugs. Let's check this out.

## CHAPTER 18

Typed Ruby

When you see a variable in your code, it's useful to know what values can be assigned to that variable without the code breaking. For example, you might have the following Ruby method:

```ruby
def mystery_method(x)
  x * 3
end
```

You'd likely expect that x should be a number. But it's also completely valid Ruby for x to be a string ("a" * 3 resolves to "aaa") or an array ([:a] * 3 resolves to [:a, :a, :a]).

Let's say that this method is in your code, and over time people call mystery_method with strings, integers, floating-point numbers, and so on, until somebody changes the method and inadvertently changes what variables it'll accept. Here's an example:

```ruby
def mystery_method(x)
  x.abs * 3
end
```

Now all of those string and array uses break because abs isn't defined for strings and arrays. If the original developer had been able to specify that x must be numeric, then the string and array uses would've found some other place to multiply by three and wouldn't have broken when the method changed.

Historically, Ruby has gotten along just fine without requiring or allowing developers to augment code with this kind of information about the expected values of a variable, which is often called the *type* of the variable.

Spurred by the increasing complexity of large Ruby projects and the possibility of improved performance, Ruby 3.0 added RBS, a mechanism for allowing developers to specify type information about classes and methods. In addition, a third-party tool called Sorbet provides a separate mechanism for type control in Ruby. In this chapter, we take a look at both RBS and Sorbet.

What's a Type?

The terminology around types in programming languages can be confusing because each language community uses the terms slightly differently.

Most generally, setting the *type* of a variable, attribute, or method argument limits the set of values that can be assigned to that variable, attribute, or method argument. The type also determines the behavior of the variable within the program. For example, the result of x / y depends on the type of x and y. In many languages, the result will be different if the numbers are integers than if they are floating-point types.

Many programming languages have a set of "basic types" that can be used, often including strings, boolean values, different kinds of numerical values, and so on. Ruby doesn't have basic types. Every variable in Ruby is an instance of a class, and that class determines the behavior of the variable. In Ruby, x / y is equivalent to the method call x./(y), and the behavior depends on what class x is.

In many typed programming languages, you must declare the type of a variable before it's used. This is called *explicit typing*. Some programming languages can infer the type of a variable from its first use, so if I say let x = 3 in TypeScript, TypeScript knows that x is a number. This is called *type inference*.

In either case, there is usually a tool, often part of the compiler, that evaluates every variable interaction to see if type information is followed. If, later in the TypeScript code, I try to say x = "foo", TypeScript will give a compilation error because "foo" is a string. This is called *static typing*.

Without type information, Ruby doesn't do this. In Ruby, the type of a variable is determined while the code is running by the variables that are assigned to it, and Ruby determines if the variable can receive a method only at runtime. This is called *dynamic typing*, and the process of determining the behavior of the method at the last possible moment is called *late binding*.

There's another distinction here that isn't as useful to us. In some languages, the type barriers are more permeable, and if you type 3 + "3", the language will automatically coerce the string to an integer and allow the addition to continue. This is called *weak typing*, and languages that don't do this have *strong typing*. You'll sometimes see "strong typing" incorrectly used as a synonym for "static typing," but these are two different concepts and it's useful to keep them separate.

These are some of the benefits of static typing and a compilation step that validates all assignments:

- If the compiler and runtime know information about what type to expect, they can often optimize internal behavior and improve performance.

- A person reading the code can get more information about the intent and behavior of the code if there is type information.

- A developer tool like an IDE or editor can use type information to provide information to the developer as the code is being written.

These are some of the drawbacks:

- Statically typed code is usually more verbose than dynamic code. Though type inferencing has improved this situation.

- Sometimes a developer has to spend time convincing the type system that the code that has been written is correct.

- Statically typed code is often less flexible than dynamic code and harder to change. (To be fair, lots of people would see this as an advantage.)

The goal of the type systems in Ruby is to allow for as many of the benefits of typed languages as we can get without giving up the flexibility that makes Ruby, Ruby.

Official Ruby Typing with RBS

The official Ruby typing system is called RBS (short for Ruby Signature). With RBS, you create a separate file that contains type signature information for all or part of your code.

Writing RBS

To take a look at how RBS works, we'll use the gem we created in Writing and Packaging Your Own Code into Gems, on page 261, and augment it with RBS typing. If you look at the Aaagmnr gem code, you'll see that it contains a directory named sig that we didn't talk much about. That directory is where you're supposed to put the type information, and right now it contains one file:

gems/aaagmnr/sig/aaagmnr.rbs
```
module Aaagmnr
  VERSION: String
  # See the writing guide of rbs: https://github.com/ruby/rbs#guides
end
```

The only thing this file tells us is that the module Aaagmnr has a VERSION constant, which is a String. True enough, but not useful.

Here's what an RBS file for the entire gem looks like:

typed_ruby/aaagmnr/sig/aaagmnr.rbs
```
module Aaagmnr
  class Finder
    @signatures: Hash[String, Array[String]]
    def self.from_file: (String file_name) -> Finder
    def initialize: (Array[String] dictionary_words) -> void
    def lookup: (String word) -> Array[String]
    def signature_of: (String word) -> String
  end

  class Options
    attr_reader dictionary: Array[String]
    attr_reader words_to_find: Array[String]

    def initialize: (Array[String] argv) -> void
    private def parse: (Array[String] argv) -> void
  end

  class Runner
    @options: Array[String]
    def initialize: (Array[String] argv) -> void
    def run: () -> void
  end

  VERSION: String
end
```

The goal here is to describe the expected types of all the modules, constants, and methods in the gem. The syntax is meant to be similar enough to Ruby to be readable, while still providing for type information.

A full description of the syntax may be found at https://github.com/ruby/rbs/blob/master/docs/syntax.md. We'll talk about the most common usages here.

The .rbs file typically combines one or more entire modules into a single file, but, as with typical Ruby, there's nothing preventing you from splitting the file up as you please.

The basic structure of module and class declarations has the same syntax as regular Ruby and the side effect of allowing those constant names to be used as type names. In other words, the same way we use String as a type name, after declaring class Finder, we could also use Finder as a type in a method argument or return value or wherever.

Inside each class, this gem has two different kinds of declarations.

We declare attributes and constants, including VERSION: String. The Finder class declares @signatures: Hash[String, Array[String]], meaning it expects to have an instance variable called @signatures and the type of that variable is a Hash whose keys are of type String and whose values are of type Array[String]. The general syntax is the name of the instance variable, followed by a colon and then by the type. The square bracket syntax here is called a *generic* (more on this in Advanced RBS Syntax, on page 305), and it allows us to define both the type of a container and the type of objects in the container, so Array[String] is an Array container where each element is a String.

In general, any time you see a type in RBS, you can add a ? to the end of it to indicate that the value can be nil. So, @name: String means the name has to be a string, but @name: String? means the name can be a string or can be nil.

The lines attr_reader dictionary: Array[String] and attr_reader words_to_find: Array[String] are also attribute declarations. Similar to how Ruby code works, attr_reader is both a shortcut for declaring the type of an instance variable and a getter method. The related declaration attr_writer declares the type of the instance variable and the setter method, and attr_accessor declares all three. The syntax is: the kind of declaration, the name of the attribute, a colon, and the type.

The rest of the lines in the file are type signatures of methods. For example, def lookup: (String word) -> Array[String] tells us that the lookup method takes a positional argument named word of type String and returns an array of strings.

The general syntax here is def followed by the name of the method, a colon, the attributes inside parentheses, the -> arrow, and the return type.

The attribute listing has a few variants. As that declaration shows, positional arguments have the type first followed by the variable name—the name is actually optional and isn't checked against the name in the actual code. The keyword arguments are in a different order: name, colon, and then type. So def lookup: (word: String) -> Array[String] would indicate that word is a keyword argument. Keyword arguments are checked against the actual Ruby method signature.

An optional argument is denoted with a ? prefix, so def lookup: (?String) is a method with an optional positional argument, but if the argument is specified, it can't be nil. The two kinds of optional can be combined: def lookup: (?String?) is a method that takes an argument that's both optional and can take a nil value.

Before we talk about more complex RBS syntax, let's take a look at how you can use RBS.

Using RBS

Having taken the effort to create these type annotations, what can we do with them? Well, there are two answers:

- There are some command-line tools that will do static analysis of your Ruby code. For example, based on the RBS files, a tool might find cases where the code doesn't match the type information, indicating a potential bug.

- Depending on the editor or development environment you're using, the tool may be able to use the RBS files to provide hints or real-time error analysis as you type. RubyMine provides significant support for RBS files.

The Ruby interpreter could also use RBS information to optimize code generation, it seems as though more on that line of work is yet to come.

You may need to gem install rbs to get access to the RBS command-line tools.

RBS offers its own command-line tools. These are generally proof-of-concept tools. The rbs list tool gives you a list of classes and modules used by the application. The rbs ancestors and rbs methods tools both take the name of a class and provide what RBS knows about the ancestors or methods of that class:

```
$ rbs ancestors String
::String
::Comparable
::Object
::Kernel
::BasicObject
```

And the rbs method call takes a class and a method name and provides what RBS knows about that method:

```
rbs method String gsub
::String#gsub
  defined_in: ::String
  implementation: ::String
  accessibility: public
  types:
      (::Regexp | ::string pattern, ::string replacement) -> ::String
    | (::Regexp | ::string pattern, ::Hash[::String, ::String] hash) -> ::String
    | (::Regexp | ::string pattern) { (::String match) -> ::_ToS } -> ::String
    | (::Regexp | ::string pattern) -> ::Enumerator[::String, self]
```

There are other RBS commands that aren't documented, and which presumably are either not expected to be in use or are not yet complete.

The entire Ruby standard library has RBS files, so you can get type information about any method in that library.

Ruby also provides a tool called TypeProf, which can help you generate RBS files. To use this tool, first add gem "typeprof" to the gemfile of the application you're working on and then bundle install.

TypeProf takes a Ruby file, which should be the top-level file of your gem or application, and optionally takes an RBS file, and it then spits out an RBS file. Here's what running TypeProf without the existing RBS file looks like for our gem:

```
$ typeprof lib/aaagmnr.rb
# TypeProf 0.21.3

# Classes
module Aaagmnr
  VERSION: String

  class Finder
    @signatures: Hash[String, Array[String]]

    def self.from_file: (untyped file_name) -> Finder
    def initialize: (Array[String] dictionary_words) -> void
    def lookup: (untyped word) -> Array[String]?
    def signature_of: (String word) -> String
  end

  class Options
    DEFAULT_DICTIONARY: String

    attr_reader dictionary: String?
    attr_reader words_to_find: untyped
    def initialize: (untyped argv) -> void

    private
    def parse: (untyped argv) -> bot
  end

  class Runner
    @options: bot

    def initialize: (untyped argv) -> void
    def run: -> untyped
  end

  class Error < StandardError
  end
end
```

This is similar to the RBS file that we created by hand, with a few changes:

- We forgot a couple of constants, like DEFAULT_DICTIONARY and Error.
- In quite a few cases, TypeProf can't determine a type and puts in untyped. We know that Finder#lookup takes a string and returns an array of strings, but TypeProf returns def lookup: (untyped word) -> Array[String]?, meaning that it can't infer a type for the parameter, and it's also assuming that nil is a potential output (which, looking at the code as written, is correct—that method can return nil if the word being looked up isn't in the dictionary).

What you get from TypeProf, then, is a mix of items that we know about the code that TypeProf can't figure out and items that TypeProf can figure out but that we, the developers, didn't necessarily see. This makes TypeProf a useful way to start with RBS, but not necessarily the completed goal.

As an alternative to running TypeProf from the command line, an experimental plugin for Visual Studio Code (https://marketplace.visualstudio.com/items?itemName=mame.ruby-typeprof) will generate method type signatures as you write code.

To generate these type signatures, TypeProf executes your Ruby code…kind of. The phrase the documentation uses is "abstractly executes," which means that it walks through the code paths knowing the types of variables but not their values.

In other words, TypeProf tracks type information through the code, using variable assignments and what it knows about method calls.

As an example, run the following code through TypeProf:

```
def approximate_word_count(sentence)
  sentence.split(/\W+/).size
end

approximate_word_count("This is a sample word count")
```

TypeProf will infer that sentence is a string from the literal assignment, and then it'll walk through the known type signatures in the method. The split method takes a string and returns an array of strings, and the size method takes an array and returns an integer. So TypeProf deduces that approximate_word_count takes a string argument and returns an integer.

TypeProf has some limitations. If there's no call to a method or no assignment in the code, then TypeProf is limited in how much information it has and will only provide limited and probably overly general results. Metaprogramming will often confuse TypeProf, especially if a lot of the data is unknown at load time. For example, TypeProf might be able to manage a define_method over a known array, but using send where the argument is a variable will confound it.

TypeProf continues to be under active development. An up-to-date description of changes can be found at https://github.com/ruby/typeprof/blob/master/doc/doc.md.

Advanced RBS Syntax

RBS syntax, for the most part, uses : CLASS after method names, argument names, and attribute names, and it uses the -> CLASS syntax for the return values of methods. In some cases, that's not enough to capture the complexity of a Ruby program. You need to be aware of some additional syntax. We can't cover all the intricacies here, and also, Ruby syntax may change. So be sure to check out the current documentation at https://github.com/ruby/rbs/blob/master/docs/syntax.md.

In general, the type of an object is its class name, but there are some special cases. You can reflexively refer to the type of the receiver inside a class with self and to the singleton object of the class with singleton. The class itself is accessible with class, and instances of the class are accessible as instance.

Sometimes a proc or method is used as a return value or argument. The syntax is ^(ARGLIST) -> RETURN_TYPE, as in:

```
def apply_a_function: (^(String, Integer) -> String) -> String
```

In this case, the argument to apply_a_function is a function that takes a string and an integer argument and returns a string.

You can use alias to give a new name to an existing name or pattern, so you could simplify the previous code like this:

```
alias func ^(String, Integer) -> String
def apply_a_function: (func) -> String
```

In some cases, you might have a variable that's more than one type. For example, we sometimes write methods that take either an ID pointing to an object in a database or an object itself. RBS lets you create *union types*, which are one type or another, with the | character. So a method that takes an ID or an object might have the signature def name: (Integer | User) -> String.

Any Ruby literal (including nil) can be used as an RBS type, such as in the unusual example where you want to limit a variable to a single value. That's rare, but you can use it to build up union types, such as the built-in type bool, which is defined as true | false. In Ruby, any object has a truth value, not just the boolean literals. In RBS, if you want to mark that you're taking in an arbitrary object to use for its truth value, RBS provides the type boolish, as in def name: (use_full: boolish) -> String.

Because any Ruby object can have a truth value, any Ruby object can be of type boolish, it's more a marker for the developers that the value is only being used for its truth value. RBS has a couple of other defined ways to refer to a value that can be of any type. Generically, if you want to specify that an object is known to have any type, you use top, which is a supertype of all types. If you're allowing any object, but only because you don't know any better about the type system, you should use untyped rather than top. And if you're signaling that a value shouldn't be used, as in a method whose return value is uninteresting, you should use void.

You can specify the type of each element of a fixed-length array using something like array syntax: [String, String]. Similarly, you can specify the type of a hash per key: {name: String, age: Integer}. Note that Ruby doesn't enforce these at runtime; they are currently used only for static analysis and for hints when developing.

For methods, if the return value is overloaded, you can use union syntax to define multiple versions of the method at once:

```
def name: (Integer) -> String
  | (User) -> String
```

Somewhat unusually for Ruby, RBS allows you to define an *interface*, meaning a subset of methods that might be implemented by more than one class. By convention, interface names start with an underscore:

```
interface _Loggable
  def log: (?String) -> String
end
```

You can then use _Loggable as an RBS type, and it'll assume nothing about the underlying object, other than that it defines a log method.

```
class LogManager
  def generate_log: (_Loggable) -> String
end
```

RBS provides the & operator as an intersection operator, so you can define the intersection of, say, multiple interfaces.

If you've used other type systems, like TypeScript or Java, you may be familiar with the concept of a *generic type*. For example, in Ruby, an array works the same whether it's an array of strings, an array of numbers, or an array of arbitrary user objects. For many purposes, which type makes up the array doesn't matter (for example, the size method behaves the same no matter what). But for other purposes, it does matter (the find method behaves the same but the type of the return value is the type of the elements of the array).

We've already seen the syntax for declaring a variable to be of type Array[String], this is the RBS generic syntax, it's a generic array with String elements.

You can declare your own class with a generic parameter:

```
class MyArray[T]
  def first () -> T
end

class Classroom
  attr_attribute students: MyArray[Student]
end
```

The MyArray has a generic type T (by cross-language convention, generic types are single capital letters), and the first method takes no arguments and returns a value with type T, whatever T turns out to be.

Later, we can use that definition to declare that Students is a MyArray[Student], meaning that each element in the array is of type Student.

Ruby Typing with Sorbet

You may have noticed that while RBS is an interesting way to add type hints to your application, the actual usage of it is still a little light. A third-party tool called Sorbet that's managed by a team at Stripe also provides type checking. At the moment Sorbet has more powerful analysis tools.

As with some other third-party tools, we're covering Sorbet here because there's a good chance you'll see it out in the world, but third-party tools often change quickly, so we recommend https://sorbet.org/docs for the full scoop of Sorbet, so to speak.

Sorbet is different from RBS in that the type annotations generally go in the Ruby file, though there is also an external file format. The type annotations are plain Ruby, and the type analysis tools parse them to check the code. Sorbet can do static analysis and it can also do type checking at runtime.

Installing Sorbet

To set up Sorbet, we'll start from a completely fresh copy of our Aaagmnr gem. Step one is to add a few gems to our Gemfile:

```
sorbet/aaagmnr/Gemfile
# frozen_string_literal: true

source "https://rubygems.org"

gemspec
gem "rake", "~> 13.0"
gem "rspec", "~> 3.0"
gem "standard", "~> 1.3"
```

```
gem "sorbet", group: :development
gem "sorbet-runtime"
gem "tapioca", require: false, group: :development
```

We've added the sorbet and sorbet-runtime gems, which manage static and runtime checking, and the tapioca gem, which manages external type information that Sorbet puts in .rbi files. The Sorbet gem gives us a runtime command called srb which we'll do type checking with momentarily.

To initialize Sorbet, we need to run tapioca init. This may take a bit and will generate a lot of output:

$ bundle exec tapioca init

This should generate a folder called sorbet. It contains a top-level sorbet/config file, a subdirectory called rbi that has RBI type definitions for all the gems in the project, and a subdirectory called tapioca that has configurations and settings for the tapioca tool.

The next step is to run static type checking analysis, the command is bundle exec srb tc. In theory, because we've added no type checking this should pass, but in practice, if we've done anything that Sorbet doesn't like, it'll get flagged here. This might include dynamic references to constants or included modules that would make static analysis difficult.

Let's see what we get:

```
bundle exec srb tc
No errors! Great job.
```

That's encouraging, and a testament to the Aaagmnr gem being somewhat simple.

Now let's add the type checks.

Adding Type Checks

Type checks in Sorbet are written in the Ruby file, in—well, it's probably not accurate to say they are written in plain Ruby, but the Sorbet-type checks are written as Ruby method calls in valid Ruby syntax. They do take a little getting used to.

Here's what the Finder class looks like with Sorbet annotations added:

sorbet/aaagmnr/lib/aaagmnr/finder.rb
```
# typed: true

require "sorbet-runtime"

module Aaagmnr
  class Finder
    extend T::Sig

    sig { params(file_name: String).returns(Aaagmnr::Finder) }
    def self.from_file(file_name)
      new(File.readlines(file_name))
    end

    sig { params(dictionary_words: T::Array[String]).void }
    def initialize(dictionary_words)
      @signatures = T.let({}, T::Hash[String, T::Array[String]])
      dictionary_words.each do |line|
```

```
      word = line.chomp
      signature = signature_of(word)
      (@signatures[signature] ||= []) << word
    end
  end

  sig { params(word: String).returns(T.nilable(T::Array[String])) }
  def lookup(word)
    signature = signature_of(word)
    @signatures[signature]
  end

  sig { params(word: String).returns(String) }
  def signature_of(word)
    word.unpack("c*").sort.pack("c*")
  end
  end
end
```

There's a lot to look at here, but it's worth emphasizing that the basic idea is the same as with RBS—we're trying to explicitly denote the types of method arguments, return values, and class attributes.

The file itself starts with two pieces of boilerplate: the magic comment # typed: true, which tells Sorbet to pay attention to this file, and then the Finder class has extend T::Sig, which puts Sorbet's type signature methods in the class.

Each individual method gets its type signature specified by prefacing the method with a call to sig. The sig method is provided by Sorbet, and it takes a block. Inside that block, you can optionally specify the parameters to the method, and you must specify the return value of the method.

The parameters are specified with the params method. The params method takes keyword arguments, the keys of which are the names of each parameter of the actual method, and the values of which are the type of the method.

For example, the from_file method has the sig call sig { params(file_name: String).returns(Aaagm-nr::Finder) }. The params(file_name: String) part says that there is a parameter to the method named file_name and its expected type is String. For Sorbet's purpose, the params method has the same structure—parameter name and type—no matter whether the parameter in the actual method is positional or keyword and whether the argument is required or optional. (Sorbet can infer whether the argument is optional from the Ruby code.)

One gotcha is that splat and double-splat types are annotated with the type of an individual element of the resulting data structure, not the data structure as a whole:

```
sig { params(args: String, kwargs: String) }
def i_have_splats(*args, **kwargs)
end
```

In this snippet args is of type String, not an array of strings, and kwargs is also of type String and not an array with symbol keys and string values. Sorbet can infer the data structure from the code.

The return value of the method is handled by chaining a call to returns. The argument to returns is the type returned by the method. If the method's return value isn't used, call void instead of returns—in the example, the initialize method uses void.

Sorbet can infer the type of local variables from the initial assignment to the valuable. For constants and for cases where the initial assignment isn't enough information, Sorbet would like you to replace the right hand of the initial assignment to the attribute or constant with a call to the Sorbet method T.let. You can see an example in the intialize method: @signatures = T.let({}, T::Hash[String, T::Array[String]]). The T.let method takes two arguments: the first is the actual value being assigned, and the second is the type of the variable going forward. In this case, the assignment to an empty hash is not enough information to tell Sorbet that the hash actually has string keys and arrays of string values.

Sorbet treats attr_reader and attr_writer like any other method, so they need to have sig annotations. For attr_accessor, which defines both a reader and a writer, the sig annotation should be for the reader, and Sorbet will infer the writer.

The type value is usually just the Ruby type name, with a couple of exceptions. As you can see in this file, arrays and hashes are handled specially, through types defined in Sorbet's T module. Arrays are specified as T::Array[TYPE], and hashes are T::Hash[KEY TYPE, VALUE TYPE]. There's also a special T::Boolean for true or false values.

If you want to specify that a value can optionally be nil, as with the return value to lookup, then you wrap the value in a call to T.nilable. A union type is specified with T.any as in T.any(String, Integer).

There's more to the Sorbet-type system; see full documentation at https://sorbet.org/docs.

Using Sorbet

Sorbet allows for static type checking and runtime type checking. The static checking comes from a command line:

```
$ bundle exec srb tc FILES
```

Usually you'll want to run your entire project, which you can do like so:

```
$ srb tc .
No errors! Great job.
```

On the first pass, the T.nilable was missing, and Sorbet definitely noticed. The output included errors like: aaagmnr/lib/aaagmnr/finder.rb:25: Expected T::Array[String] but found T.nilable(T::Array[String]) and aaagmnr/lib/aaagmnr/runner.rb:20: This code is unreachable.

Alternatively, you can list one or more specific paths (.rb or .rbi files after the tc) to limit checking, or you can use the --ignore=PATTERN flag to take specific files out. The --autocorrect option will give you a limited amount of autocorrect. The default sorbet/config file generated with Sorbet includes the option --dir=.

Sorbet will also check code at runtime, which we can verify by going into the gem's console and trying to pass in a non-array of strings to the runner:

```
$ bin/console
irb(main):001:0> Aaagmnr::Runner.new(3)
/Users/noel/.rbenv/versions/3.1.2/lib/ruby/gems/3.1.0/gems/sorbet-runtime-0.5.10346/
lib/types/configuration.rb:296:in `call_validation_error_handler_default': \
```

```
Parameter 'argv':
Expected type T::Array[String], got type Integer with value 3 (TypeError)
```

Here Sorbet is telling us that if we pass the Runner a 3 instead of an array of words, that violates the type signature of the runner. The advantage here, at least in theory, is that the error is detected as soon as possible, even before some message is called that would trigger a different error. Without the type checking, at some point we'd try to do something with the Integer that expects a string. In this case, no harm is done by letting the code go to that point, but in a complex system, there's some advantage in not letting code go any further than necessary. Sorbet's runtime checking can also catch dynamic method calls that would be challenging for the static type checker to analyze.

What's Next

To be honest, we're a little conflicted about types in Ruby. We like the potential performance benefit, and the tooling advantages are promising. There's definitely a communication benefit to being explicit with types. But we worry that some of Ruby's dynamic power and flexibility is being traded for static typing, and for developers who came to Ruby for that flexibility, that can be a hard trade-off.

Some of that communication benefit can also come from documentation. In the next chapter, we'll discuss RDoc, the official Ruby documentation solution, and YARD, a commonly used third-party extension.

## CHAPTER 19

Documenting Ruby

Documentation is a critical part of communicating across teams. Code comments can help share the intent of the developer or can be a way to explain constraints on the code that might not be clear from just reading code. It's not enough to add comments to the code; it's also useful to be able to publish those comments onto the web and to make them consumable by your editor or command-line tools like ri or irb.

Two tools in the Ruby ecosystem are used for converting code comments into external documentation: RDoc and YARD. Ruby comes bundled with RDoc, which is used by Ruby itself to document the built-in Ruby classes and modules. Those who like a more formal, tag-based scheme might want to look at YARD (http://yardoc.org). We'll cover both in this chapter. As YARD is mostly a superset of RDoc, we'll cover RDoc first and then talk about YARD's extensions.

Documenting with RDoc

RDoc does two jobs. Its first job is to analyze source files. Ruby files, of course, but it will also analyze C files and Markdown files. Within those files, RDoc looks for information to document. Its second job is to take this information and convert it into something readable—usually HTML or Ruby's ri documentation format.

Let's look at an example.

```ruby
rdoc/example/counter.rb
class Counter
  attr_reader :counter

  def initialize(initial_value = 0)
    @counter = initial_value
  end

  def inc
    @counter += 1
  end
end
```

Going into that directory and running rdoc will create an entire doc directory with HTML files.

Here's what one of the files looks like:

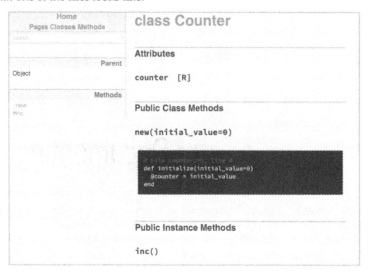

Even though the source contains no internal documentation, RDoc manages to extract interesting information from it. We have three panes at the top of the screen showing the files, classes, and methods for which we have documentation. For class Counter, RDoc shows us the attributes and methods (including the method signatures). If we clicked a method signature, RDoc would pop up a window containing the source code for the corresponding method.

If our source code contains comments, RDoc can use them to spice up the documentation it produces.

Take for example, the following source code:

```
rdoc/example_with_comments/counter.rb
# Implements a simple accumulator, whose
# value is accessed via the attribute
# _counter_. Calling the method Counter#inc
# increments this value.
class Counter
  # The current value of the count
  attr_reader :counter

  # create a new Counter with the given
  # initial value
  def initialize(initial_value = 0)
    @counter = initial_value
  end

  # increment the current value of the count
  def inc
    @counter += 1
  end
end
```

This results in a similar RDoc page.

Notice how the comments before each element now appear in the RDoc output, reformatted into HTML. Less obvious is that RDoc has detected hyperlink opportunities in our comments. In the class-level comment, the reference to Counter#inc is a hyperlink to the method description, and in the comment for the new method, the reference to class Counter hyperlinks back to the class documentation. This is a key feature of RDoc's design. Instead of being intrusive in the Ruby source files, RDoc tries to be clever when producing output.

RDoc can also be used to produce documentation that can be read by the ri command-line utility. For example, if we ask RDoc to document the code in the previous example into ri format (with $ rdoc -r .), we can access the documentation from the command line:

```
$ ri Counter
 = Counter < Object

(from /Users/noel/.local/share/rdoc)
------------------------------------------------------------------------
Implements a simple accumulator, whose value is accessed via the
attribute counter. Calling the method Counter#inc
increments this value.
------------------------------------------------------------------------
= Class methods:

  new

= Instance methods:

  counter, inc

= Attributes:

  attr_reader counter
```

The documentation will even get picked up by irb, as shown in the figure on page 316.

Ruby distributions document the built-in classes and modules this way. It's the documentation you'll see at https://docs.ruby-lang.org/en/master.

```
☑☺ irb
irb(main):001:0> require_relative "./counter"
=> true
irb(main):002:0> Counter.new
                 Counter.newPress Alt+d to read the full document
                        Counter.new

                 (from /Users/noel/.local/share/rdoc)
                 ------------------------------------------
                   new(initial_value=0)

                 ------------------------------------------
                 create a new Counter with the given
                 initial value
```

Adding RDoc to Ruby Code

RDoc parses Ruby source files to extract the major elements (such as classes, modules, methods, attributes, and so on). You can choose to associate additional documentation with these by simply adding a comment block before the element in the file.

One of the design goals of RDoc was to leave the source code looking totally natural. In most cases, you don't need any special markup in your code to get RDoc to produce decent looking documentation. For example, comment blocks can be written fairly naturally:

```
# Calculate the minimal-cost path though the graph using Debrinkski's algorithm,
# with optimized inverse pruning of isolated leaf nodes.
def calculate_path
  . . .
end
```

You can also use Ruby's block-comments by including the documentation in a =begin…=end block. If you use this (which isn't generally done), the =begin line must be flagged with an rdoc tag to distinguish the block from other styles of documentation:

```
=begin rdoc
Calculate the minimal-cost path though the graph using Debrinkski's algorithm,
with optimized inverse pruning of isolated leaf nodes.
=end
def calculate_path
  . . .
end
```

Within a documentation comment, paragraphs are lines that share the left margin. Text indented past this margin is formatted verbatim.

Nonverbatim text can be marked up. To set individual words in italic, bold, or typewriter fonts, you can use _word_, *word*, and +word+, respectively. If you want to do this to multiple words or text containing nonword characters, you can use multiple words, more words, and <tt>yet more words</tt>. Putting a backslash before inline markup stops it from being interpreted.

RDoc stops processing comments if it finds a comment line starting with #--. This can be used to separate external from internal comments or to stop a comment from being associated with a method, class, attribute, or module. Documenting can be turned back on by starting a line with the comment #++:

```
# Extract the age and calculate the
# date of birth.
#--
# FIXME: fails if the birthday falls on February 29th, or if the person
# was born before epoch and the installed Ruby doesn't support negative time_t
#++
# The DOB is returned as a Time object.
#--
# But should probably change to use Date.

def get_dob(person)
  ...
end
```

Hyperlinks

Names of classes, source files, and any method names containing an underscore or preceded by a hash character are automatically hyperlinked from comment text to their description.

In addition, hyperlinks starting with http:, mailto:, ftp:, and www: are recognized. An HTTP URL that references an external image file is converted into an inline img tag. Hyperlinks starting with link: are assumed to refer to local files whose paths are relative to the --op directory, where output files are stored.

Hyperlinks can also be of the form label[url], where the label is used in the displayed text and url is used as the target. If the label contains multiple words, surround it in braces: {two words}[url].

Lists

Lists are typed as indented paragraphs with the following:

- As asterisk (*) or hyphen (-) for bullet lists
- A digit followed by a period for numbered lists
- An uppercase or lowercase letter followed by a period for alpha lists

For example, you could produce something like the previous text with this:

```
#  Lists are typed as indented paragraphs with
#  * a * or - (for bullet lists),
#  * a digit followed by a period for
#    numbered lists,
#  * an uppercase or lowercase letter followed
#    by a period for alpha lists.
```

Note how subsequent lines in a list item are indented to line up with the text in the element's first line.

Labeled lists (sometimes called *description lists*) are typed using square brackets for the label:

```
#  [cat]     Small domestic animal
#  [+cat+]   Command to copy standard input
#            to standard output
```

Labeled lists may also be produced by putting a double colon after the label. This sets the result in tabular form so the descriptions all line up in the output:

```
#  cat::    Small domestic animal
#  +cat+:: Command to copy standard input
#            to standard output
```

For both kinds of labeled lists, if the body text starts on the same line as the label, then the start of that text determines the block indent for the rest of the body. The text may also start on the line following the label, indented from the start of the label. This is often preferable if the label is long. Both of the following are valid labeled list entries:

```
#  <tt>--output</tt> <i>name [, name]</i>::
#      specify the name of one or more output files. If multiple
#      files are present, the first is used as the index.
#
#  <tt>--quiet:</tt>:: do not output the names, sizes, byte counts,
#                      index areas, or bit ratios of units as
#                      they are processed.
```

Headings

Headings are entered on lines starting with equal signs. The more equal signs, the higher the level of heading:

```
#  = Level One Heading
#  == Level Two Heading
#  and so on...
```

Rules (horizontal lines) are entered using three or more hyphens:

```
#  and so it goes...
#  ----
#  The next section...
```

Documentation Modifiers

Method parameter lists are extracted and displayed with the method description. If a method calls yield, then the parameters passed to yield will also be displayed. For example:

```
def fred
  # ...
  yield line, address
```

This will be documented as follows:

```
fred() { |line, address| ... }
```

You can override this using a comment containing :yields: ... on the same line as the method definition:

```
def fred        # :yields: index, position
  # ...
  yield line, address
```

This will be documented as follows:

```
fred() { |index, position| ... }
```

:yields: is an example of a documentation modifier. These appear immediately after the start of the document element they are modifying. Other modifiers include:

:nodoc: ‹ all ›

Don't include this element in the documentation. For classes and modules, the methods, aliases, constants, and attributes directly within the affected class or module will also be omitted from the documentation. But, by default, modules and classes within that class or module will be documented. This is turned off by adding the *all* modifier. For example, in the following code, only class SM::Input will be documented:

```ruby
module SM  #:nodoc:
  class Input
  end
end

module Markup #:nodoc: all
  class Output
  end
end
```

:doc:

This forces a method or attribute to be documented even if it wouldn't otherwise be. This is useful if, for example, you want to include documentation of a particular private method.

:notnew:

This is applicable only to the initialize instance method. Normally, RDoc assumes that the documentation and parameters for #initialize are actually for the corresponding class's new method, so it fakes a new method for the class. The :notnew: modifier stops this. Remember that #initialize is protected, so you won't see the documentation unless you use the -a command-line option.

Other Directives

Comment blocks can contain other directives:

:call-seq: lines...

Text up to the next blank comment line is used as the calling sequence when generating documentation (overriding the parsing of the method parameter list). A line is considered blank even if it starts with #. For this one directive, the leading colon is optional.

:include: filename

This includes the contents of the named file at this point. The file will be searched for in the directories listed by the --include option or in the current directory by default. The contents of the file will be shifted to have the same indentation as the : at the start of the :include: directive.

:title: text

This sets the title for the document. It's equivalent to the --title command-line parameter. (The command-line parameter overrides any :title: directive in the source.)

:main: name

This is equivalent to the --main command-line parameter, setting the initial page displayed for this documentation.

:stopdoc: / :startdoc:

This stops and starts adding new documentation elements to the current container. For example, if a class has a number of constants that you don't want to document, put a :stopdoc: before the first and a :startdoc: after the last. If you don't specify a :startdoc: by the end of the container, this disables documentation for the entire class or module.

:enddoc:

This documents nothing further at the current lexical level.

Running RDoc

RDoc can be run from the command line, like this:

```
$ rdoc OPTIONS FILENAMES
```

Type rdoc --help for an up-to-date option summary.

Files are parsed, and the information they contain is collected before any output is produced. This allows cross-references between all files to be resolved. If a name is that of a directory, it is traversed. If no names are specified, all Ruby files in the current directory (and subdirectories) are processed.

A typical use may be to generate documentation for a package of Ruby source (such as RDoc itself):

```
$ rdoc
```

This command generates HTML documentation for the files in and below the current directory. These will be stored in a documentation tree starting in the subdirectory doc/.

RDoc uses file extensions to determine how to process each file. Filenames with rb and rbw extensions are assumed to be Ruby source. Filenames with c, h, or cpp extension are parsed as C files. Files with md and markdown are parsed as Markdown. A file named ChangeLog will be parsed as a change log. All other files are assumed to contain just markup (with or without leading # comment markers). If directory names are passed to RDoc, they are scanned recursively for source files only. To include non-source files such as READMEs in the documentation process, their names must be given explicitly on the command line.

When writing a Ruby library, you often have some source files that implement the public interface, but the majority are internal and of no interest to the readers of your documentation. In these cases, construct a .document file in each of your project's directories. If RDoc enters a directory containing a .document file, it'll process only the files in that directory whose names match one of the lines in that file. Each line in the file can be a filename, a directory name, or a wildcard (a file system "glob" pattern). For example, to include all Ruby files whose names start with main, along with the file constants.rb, you could use a .document file containing this:

```
main*.rb
constants.rb
```

Some project standards ask for documentation in a top-level README file. You may find it convenient to write this file in RDoc format and then use the :include: directive to incorporate the README into the documentation for the main class.

RDoc has a lot of command-line options for how the output is generated and styled that you'll likely use approximately never, use the command rdoc --help for a full rundown.

Using RDoc to Create Documentation for ri

RDoc is also used to create documentation that will be later displayed using ri or by the irb inline documentation.

When you run ri, it looks by default for documentation in three places:

- The *system* documentation directory, which holds the documentation distributed with Ruby and is created by the Ruby install process

- The *site* directory, which contains sitewide documentation added locally

- The *user* documentation directory, which is stored under the user's own home directory

You can find these three directories using ri --list-doc-dirs.

You can override the directory location using the --op option to RDoc and subsequently using the --doc-dir option with ri.

To add documentation to ri, you need to tell RDoc which output directory to use. For your own use, it's easier to use the --ri option, which installs the documentation into ~/.rdoc:

```
$ rdoc --ri file1.rb file2.rb
```

If you want to install sitewide documentation, use the --ri-site option:

```
$ rdoc --ri-site file1.rb file2.rb
```

The --ri-system option is normally used only to install documentation for Ruby's built-in classes and standard libraries. You can regenerate this documentation from the Ruby source distribution (not from the installed libraries themselves):

```
$ cd ruby source base/lib
$ rdoc --ri-system
```

Documenting with YARD

YARD (http://yardoc.org) is an extension of RDoc that uses tags to allow you to add metadata to your comments. It then uses the metadata to create more interesting documentation.

Yet Another Aside

While YARD claims to be short for "Yay! A Ruby Documentation Tool," it likely was named in reference to the long-standing open-source tradition of starting acronyms with YA for "yet another." We think the first tool to this was the Yacc parser-generator (for "Yet Another Compiler Compiler"), but there's also YAML (originally "Yet Another Markup Language," now styled as "YAML Ain't Markup Language," which is a whole other open-source tradition of recursive acronyms), and some quick internet searching reveals YaST, YAF, YAPM, YAPP, and who knows how many more.

Here's our minimal counterexample with some YARD tags added:

```
rdoc/example_with_yardoc/counter.rb
# Implements a simple accumulator, whose
# value is accessed via the attribute
# _counter_. Calling the method Counter#inc
# increments this value.
# @author Dave Thomas
# @note This is only a minimal example
# @version 1.0
class Counter
  # The current value of the count
  attr_reader :counter

  # create a new Counter with the given
  # initial value
  # @param initial_value [Integer] the initial value of the counter
  def initialize(initial_value = 0)
    @counter = initial_value
  end

  # increment the current value of the count
  # @example Increment the counter
  #   Counter.new.increment #=> counter.value == 1
  # @return [Integer] The new value of the counter
  def inc
    @counter += 1
  end
end
```

The comments are the same, but we've augmented them with tags like @author, @param, and @return.

To use YARD, we need to get gem install yard or have it in our Gemfile. The command to run the current directory is this:

```
$ yard doc .
```

The resulting HTML documentation goes in a doc directory. (YARD also creates a .yardoc directory with its own information.) As you can see, the HTML is more detailed and uses the tags appropriately, as shown in the figure on page 323.

YARD Tags

YARD allows you to augment your documentation with tags (which start with @) and directives (which start with !@). As you can see from the earlier example, some tags have a little bit of syntax structure.

Here are the tags you're likely to use most often:

- @author—The name of the author or authors of the class, method, or module.

- @deprecated—Marks a method as deprecated in the docs. Followed with a description, ideally one that shows how to work around the deprecated item.

- @example—The first line of the example tag is a title for the example. Subsequent lines should be indented further in than the tag and should contain code showing the item in use.

- @note—A note that's placed at the top of the page for an item.

- @param—A parameter to a method. Followed with the name, the expected type in square brackets, and a description.

- @raise—The method may raise an exception. Followed with the name of the exception in square brackets and a description, as in @raise [NoArgumentError] if the user does not exist.

- @since—A version number where the item was first added.

- @version—The version of the item being documented.

- @yield—Describes what the method would yield to a passed-in block. Consists of a list of parameters in square brackets followed by a description string.

You can find a full list of tags and directives at https://rubydoc.info/gems/yard/file/docs/Tags.md.

Using YARD

The YARD executable lets you generate a few different kinds of files.

The command yard doc, which is also aliased as yardoc, generates HTML documentation for the current directory or for a list of given files or directories. It looks for a file named .yardopts for options.

The yard ri command, aliased as yri, displays your documentation in an ri style interface. The yri command doesn't work on the core Ruby classes, only on your own project's YARD documentation.

The command yard graph spits out text in GraphViz format https://graphviz.org, which will generate a class diagram of the documented code.

What's Next

In this chapter, we talked about the two most commonly used tools for documenting Ruby: RDoc and YARD. If you look around the web at documentation for Ruby gems, you'll see both of their distinctive HTML styles in regular use. Now let's take a bit of a turn and talk about Ruby's tools for working with the web itself.

Part III

Ruby Crystallized

Ruby is a sophisticated and flexible object-oriented language, and using it effectively can mean exploring reflection, metaprogramming, and other related ideas.

## CHAPTER 20

Ruby and the Web

There's a good chance that if you're reading this book, you're intending to use Ruby in the context of some kind of Web application. Ruby is used as the language for a lot of web tools, not only for Ruby on Rails,[1] but also for many other web frameworks and third-party tools.

While the Ruby ecosystem is full of web tools, most of those tools are third-party gems and not part of the core Ruby distribution. Core Ruby does provide an implementation of the Common Gateway Interface (CGI), which was the original dynamic web standard, but as we write this, you're unlikely to be writing CGI scripts directly, so we're not going to spend time on CGI scripts in this book. That said, for historical reasons, a lot of Ruby's web-related behavior is in a class called CGI, so we'll be referencing that class throughout.

Many options are available for using Ruby to implement web applications, and a single chapter can't do them all justice. Instead, we'll touch on some of the highlights and point you toward libraries and resources that can help. In particular, we'll focus on the following:

- Ruby's web utilities—a part of the Ruby Standard Library
- ERB—the most common third-party tool for templating
- Rack—a third-party standard for all behavior common to Ruby web frameworks
- Sinatra—perhaps the simplest of the powerful Ruby web frameworks
- Wasm (Web Assembly)—a tool to run Ruby in a browser

Ruby's Web Utilities

The Ruby standard distribution includes some core utilities as part of the CGI class and CGI::Util module.

CGI Encoding

When dealing with URLs and HTML code, you must be careful to quote certain characters. For instance, a slash character (/) has special meaning in a URL, so it must be "escaped" if it's not part of the path name. That is, any / in the query portion of the URL is translated to the string %2F, and then it must be translated back to a / for you to use it. Space and ampersand are also special characters.

---

1.   http://www.rubyonrails.org

To handle this, CGI provides the methods escape and unescape:

```
require "cgi"
puts CGI.escape("Nicholas Payton/Trumpet & Flugel Horn")
```

produces:

```
Nicholas+Payton%2FTrumpet+%26+Flugel+Horn
```

More frequently, you may want to escape HTML special characters:

web/escape_01.rb
```
require "cgi"
puts CGI.escapeHTML("a < 100 && b > 200")
```

produces:

```
a &lt; 100 &amp;&amp; b &gt; 200
```

To get really fancy, you can decide to escape only certain HTML elements within a string:

web/escape_02.rb
```
require "cgi"
puts CGI.escapeElement("<hr><a href='/mp3'>Click Here</a><br>", "A")
```

produces:

```
<hr>&lt;a href=&#39;/mp3&#39;&gt;Click Here&lt;/a&gt;<br>
```

Here, only the <a...> element is escaped; other elements are left alone. Each of these methods has an un- version to restore the original string:

web/escape_03.rb
```
require "cgi"
puts CGI.unescapeHTML("a &lt; 100 &amp;&amp; b &gt; 200")
```

produces:

```
a < 100 && b > 200
```

Using the CGI Class to Handle Cookies

Cookies are a way of letting web applications store their state on the user's machine. Frowned upon by some, cookies are still a convenient (if unreliable) way of remembering session information.

The Ruby CGI class handles the loading and saving of cookies for you, assuming you're working within a web framework that receives cookies. You can access the cookies associated with the current request using the cookies method, and you can set cookies back into the browser by setting the cookie parameter of out to reference either a single cookie or an array of cookies:

web/cookies.rb
```
#!/usr/bin/ruby
require "cgi"

COOKIE_NAME = "chocolate chip"

cgi = CGI.new
values = cgi.cookies[COOKIE_NAME]
```

```
msg = if values.empty?
  "It looks as if you haven't visited recently"
else
  "You last visited #{values[0]}"
end

cookie = CGI::Cookie.new(COOKIE_NAME, Time.now.to_s)
cookie.expires = Time.now + 30 * 24 * 3600 # 30 days
cgi.out("cookie" => cookie) { msg }
```

Using the CGI Class to Generate HTML

CGI contains a huge number of methods that can be used to create HTML—one method per element. To enable these methods, you must create a CGI object by calling new and passing in the required version of HTML. In this example, we'll use html5.

To make element nesting easier, these methods take their content as code blocks. The code blocks should return a String, which will be used as the content for the element.

```
require 'cgi'
cgi = CGI.new("html5")
cgi.out do
  cgi.html do
    cgi.head { cgi.title { "This Is a Test"} } +
    cgi.body do
      cgi.form do
        cgi.hr +
        cgi.h1 { "A Form: " } +
        cgi.textarea("get_text") +
        cgi.br +
        cgi.submit
      end
    end
  end
end
```

Although interesting, this method of generating HTML is fairly laborious and probably isn't used much in practice. Most people write HTML directly and use a templating system or an application framework such as Rails. Unfortunately, we don't have space here to discuss Rails—take a look at the online documentation at http://rubyonrails.org—so let's look at templating.

Templating with ERB

Templating systems let you separate the presentation and logic of your application.

So far, we've looked at using Ruby to create HTML output, but we can turn the problem inside out: we can actually embed Ruby in an HTML document. The embedded Ruby (or ERB) library is included with Ruby's standard distribution.

Embedding Ruby in HTML is a powerful concept—it gives us the equivalent of a scripting tool such as PHP, but with the full power of Ruby.

Using ERB

ERB is a filter. Input text is passed through untouched, with the following exceptions:

Expression	Description
<% *ruby code* %>	This executes the Ruby code between the delimiters. Any resulting value isn't sent to the output.
<%= *ruby expression* %>	This evaluates the Ruby expression and places the resulting value of the expression in the output.
<%# *ruby code* %>	The Ruby code between the delimiters is ignored (useful for testing).
% *line of ruby code*	A line that starts with a percent is assumed to contain just Ruby code.

You can run ERB from the command line:

erb ‹ *options* › ‹ *document* ›

If *document* is omitted, ERB will read from standard input. The command-line options for ERB are listed in the following table:

Option	Description
-d	Sets $DEBUG to true
-E ext[:int]	Sets the default external/internal encodings
-n	Displays resulting Ruby script (with line numbers)
-r library	Loads the named library
-P	Doesn't do erb processing on lines starting %
-S level	Sets the *safe level*
-T mode	Sets the *trim mode*
-U	Sets default encoding to UTF-8
-v	Enables verbose mode
-x	Displays resulting Ruby script

Let's look at some simple examples. We'll run the ERB executable on the following input:

web/f1.erb
```
<% 99.downto(96) do |number| %>
  <%= number %> bottles of beer...
<% end %>
```

The lines starting with the percent sign simply execute the given Ruby. In this case, it's a loop that iterates the line between them. The sequence <%= number %> in the middle line calculates the value of number and inserts the result into the output:

```
$ erb f1.erb
  99 bottles of beer...
  98 bottles of beer...
  97 bottles of beer...
  96 bottles of beer...
```

ERB works by rewriting its input as a Ruby script and then executing that script. You can see the Ruby code ERB generates using the -n or -x option—the output here is slightly edited for spacing:

```
$ erb -x f1.erb
#coding:UTF-8
_erbout = +'';
99.downto(96) do |number| ;
_erbout.<< "\n".freeze;
_erbout.<< " ".freeze;
_erbout.<<(( number ).to_s);
_erbout.<< " bottles of beer...\n".freeze;
end;
_erbout.<< "\n".freeze;
_erbout
```

Notice how ERB builds a string, _erbout, that contains both the static strings from the template and the results of executing expressions (in this case the value of number).

Embedding ERB in Your Code

So far, we've seen ERB running as a command-line filter. But the most common use is as a library in your own code. Many Ruby web frameworks automatically use ERB templates for output.

web/erb.rb
```
require "erb"

source = <<~SOURCE
  <% (min..max).each do |number| %>
    The number is <%= number %>
  <% end %>
SOURCE

erb = ERB.new(source)

min = 4
max = 6
puts erb.result(binding)
```

produces:
```
The number is 4

The number is 5

The number is 6
```

Notice how we can use local variables within the ERB template. This works because we pass the current *binding* to the result method. ERB can use this binding to make it look as if the template is being evaluated in the context of the calling code. Using bindings is sometimes awkward, especially if you want to limit what values are available to the template. ERB also provides result_with_hash, which, true to its name, takes a hash argument, and within the template, variable names are resolved as keys to the hash.

Be aware that in the default version of ERB, you can't use the -%> trick to suppress blank lines. (That's why we have the extra blank lines in the output in the previous example.) You can specify the way ERB handles blanks by passing a trim_mode: keyword argument to ERB.new.

Here are the values that trim_mode can take:

- % — Allows you to have lines starting with % processed as Ruby code.
- > — Lines ending in %> don't have a newline added to the result.
- <> — Same as above, but for lines starting with <% and ending with %>.
- - — Blank lines ending in -%> are omitted. (This is the setting used in Rails.)

ERB comes with excellent documentation.[2]

Sending JSON

It's also quite common for web tools to send responses formatted using JSON. The Ruby JSON library is available with require "json" and provides a JSON.generate(object) that converts a Ruby object into a JSON representation. Many Ruby classes define a to_json method as well. Many third-party libraries are also available to handle more complex JSON serialization patterns.

See JSON, on page 609, for more details on the Ruby library that manages JSON.

Serving Ruby Code to the Web

Ruby is commonly used as the back end of a web application. In this pattern, a request is made to a web server, which executes Ruby code. The Ruby code returns HTML (usually), which is sent back to the web browser as the response.

While you could write all this in plain Ruby yourself, there's no need for you to do all that work. The Ruby ecosystem has multiple web servers, including Puma,[3] Unicorn,[4] Thin,[5] and Falcon.[6] You can also use multiple web frameworks, including Ruby on Rails,[7] Sinatra,[8] Roda,[9] and Hanami.[10]

You might look at that incomplete list of web servers and frameworks and think that compatibility between the two sets might be a nightmare of continually having to adjust the framework code based on what server you're using or vice versa. In fact, it's not a nightmare, and it's even possible for behavior to be written once and shared between multiple web servers. This compatibility is not a problem because of a library called Rack.[11]

Rack and Web Servers

Rack is a minimal interface for the relationship between a web server and a web application framework. Imagine that you are writing a web server that wants to work with an application framework. Certain logistical details of the relationship between the server and the framework exist no matter what the details of either tool's internal structure are.

---

2. https://docs.ruby-lang.org/en/master/ERB.html
3. https://puma.io
4. https://yhbt.net/unicorn
5. https://github.com/macournoyer/thin
6. https://github.com/socketry/falcon
7. https://rubyonrails.org
8. https://sinatrarb.com
9. https://github.com/jeremyevans/roda
10. https://hanamirb.org
11. https://github.com/rack/rack

A user request comes as text, whose structure is defined by the HTTP specification. The web server's job is to convert that text into Ruby objects and pass them to the framework. The framework's job is to take that object, do something with it, and return Ruby objects to the web server, which converts them back to HTTP text or data to send to the browser.

Rack provides the following:

- A standard structure for the environment data coming into the web server via the user request—specifically, a hash with a pre-defined set of keys.

- A standard structure for the response data coming back to the web server from the frameworks. The response is an array with three elements: the return status, the headers, and the body.

- A mechanism for the interface between the two. A rack app is a method or block that takes the environment as input and returns the response as output. Rack provides the method run, which takes rack apps, sends them environments, and returns the result.

Rack also provides a structure for chaining Rack applications together. For example, you might have a series of small rack applications where one does authentication, another sanitizes input, and another cleans up image sizing. Rack makes it easy to create a pipeline of these *middleware* apps so that they can be integrated into any Ruby web framework.

Here's a minimal example of Rack in action (rack-tion?):

```
web/rack_01/config.ru
require "bundler/inline"

gemfile do
  source "https://rubygems.org"
  gem "rack"
  gem "rackup"
end

run do |env|
  [200, {"content-type" => "text/plain"}, ["Welcome to Rack"]]
end
```

This is a configuration file for Rack, often called a "rackup file." This particular rackup file is doing two things.

First, it's using Bundler's inline function (see Single File Projects, on page 262) to ensure that the gems Rack and Rackup are installed. The Rack gem manages most of the Rack functionality. Rackup is the default command-line application for serving applications defined using Rack.

Second, it's creating a Rack app and running it using the Rack command run.

To make this work, in the directory with the code run this:

```
$ bundle install
$ rackup
[2022-09-25 10:04:10] INFO  WEBrick 1.7.0
[2022-09-25 10:04:10] INFO  ruby 3.2.2 (2023-03-30) [arm64-darwin23]
[2022-09-25 10:04:10] INFO  WEBrick::HTTPServer#start: pid=31252 port=9292
```

This has started a web server called WEBrick and it's serving at port 9292, which you can confirm by going into a browser and hitting http://localhost:9292. You'll receive "Welcome to Rack" as the response.

Rack Versions

 If you're familiar with Rack, this example may look a little strange. This example uses Rack 3.0, which is relatively new at the time of this writing. The rackup gem was extracted from Rack 3.0 in part because WEBrick is now a separate project and is no longer part of the standard Ruby distribution. Also, the run method taking a block argument is new in 3.0.

That shows that it works, but what's Rack doing?

The run method is part of Rack. Typically, a Rack application defined in a rackup file will have one run method (though, as we'll see, you can specify multiple run methods if each one is matched to a different URL path). The run method takes as its argument either a block or any Ruby object that can respond to the call method. Because both lambdas and Procs define call, either one of them can be an argument to run.

Here's what our app would look like with a stabby lambda:

```
run -> (env) { [200, {"content-type" => "text/plain"}, ["Welcome to Rack"]] }
```

And here is the app with a custom object:

```
class SmallRackApp
  def call(env)
    [200, {"content-type" => "text/plain"}, ["Welcome to Rack"]]
  end
end

run SmallRackApp.new
```

In all these cases, the callable takes one argument—the *environment*—and returns a three-element array as the response. The structure of both the environment and response are defined by the Rack Specification.[12]

The environment is a regular Ruby hash. Because hash objects are mutable, a Rack app can modify it, often to add new keys. The environment is required to have several specific keys even if sometimes those keys are empty.

Those keys include the URL of the request, which is split into the keys SERVER_NAME, SCRIPT_NAME, PATH_INFO, QUERY_STRING, and SERVER_PORT. The HTTP verb of the request is in the key REQUEST_METHOD. Any HTTP request headers are placed in corresponding keys starting with HTTP_. Rack puts information of whether the request uses HTTP or HTTPS in the key rack.url_scheme and adds a raw input stream at rack.input and an error stream at rack.errors.

The response is a three-element unfrozen array made up of the following:

- The HTTP status, which must be an integer greater than or equal to 100.

- The headers to be sent as part of the response, as an unfrozen hash. Keys in this hash that start with rack. aren't sent back to the client browser.

---

12.   https://github.com/rack/rack/blob/main/SPEC.rdoc

- The body of the response. Most commonly, the body is an array of strings.

The body element of the response can be more complicated. Rather than an array, the body can be any Ruby enumerable that responds to the method each and results in a series of strings.

Less commonly, the body can act as something that's streamed, rather than returned all at once. In this case, the body is Proc or anything that responds to call, and the result of call should be something that behaves like an I/O stream, where reading from the stream returns data.

This gets even more powerful with the ability of these Rack applications to chain together, allowing an application to act on the environment or the response of a different application. This is called Rack middleware. While the middleware uses the same environment and response objects, there's a little bit more structure.

Here's an example:

```ruby
web/rack_02/config.ru
require "bundler/inline"

gemfile do
  source "https://rubygems.org"
  gem "rack"
  gem "rackup"
end

class PrefixingMiddleware
  def initialize(app)
    @app = app
  end

  def call(env)
    status, headers, body = @app.call(env)
    new_body = ["<h2>This is a prefix</h2>"] + body
    [status, headers, new_body]
  end
end

class PostfixingMiddleware
  def initialize(app)
    @app = app
  end

  def call(env)
    status, headers, body = @app.call(env)
    new_body = body + ["<h2>This is a postfix</h2>"]
    [status, headers, new_body]
  end
end

class RackApplication
  def call(env)
    [
      200,
      {"content-type" => "text/html"},
      ["<h1>Welcome to Rack</h1>"]
    ]
  end
end
```

```
use PrefixingMiddleware
use PostfixingMiddleware
run RackApplication.new
```

This Rack application is built from three smaller applications, PrefixingMiddleware, PostfixingMiddleware, and RackApplication. Where our previous example used the run command, this example has the use command once for each of the middleware classes. The use command takes as an argument the name of the middleware class, in contrast to the run method, which takes an instance of a Rack app as its argument.

When you execute this file with rackup, the following things happen:

- Rack takes the instance passed to run as the first application.

- Then starting from the bottommost use call and working up, Rack creates an instance of each middleware class, passing it the previous instance as the argument. In our case, an instance of PostfixingMiddleware is created with the RackApplication instance as the argument, and then an instance of PrefixingMiddleware is created with that previous instance as the argument.

- At this point, we have a chain of Rack apps, each of which knows the identity of the next item in the chain. We trigger the chain by calling the call method on the topmost element in the chain. As part of being a good Rack citizen, each middleware app is expected to invoke the call method on its app argument. In this way, every Rack app is invoked.

Let's trace this through our sample Rack app. We start with run RackApplication.new, giving us an instance of RackApplication. The code then goes up a line to use PostfixingMiddleware, and it creates an instance of PostfixingMiddleware, passing it the already created RackApplication instance. We repeat the process going upward, creating a PrefixingMiddleware instance that has a relationship with the PostfixingMiddlware instance.

Now that we have an entire chain of objects that conform to the Rack standard and respond to call, we invoke call on the object at the end of the chain, so our PrefixingMiddleware instance gets called with the env environment directly from the web request. The first thing that happens in that call method is status, headers, body = @app.call(env)—meaning we immediately call the next app in the chain, which is PostfixingMiddleware. The first thing that happens in the PostfixingMiddleware#call method is the same status, headers, body = @app.call(env), which takes us down to the bottom Rack app, which responds to call and returns the three-element array [200, {"content-type" => "text/html"},["<h1>Welcome to Rack</h1>"]].

At this point, we walk back up the chain. That return value is extracted by the call method in PostfixingMiddleware, which promptly takes the three values, appends some text to the body, and returns a new three-element array with the new body. That return value is, in turn, extracted by PrefixingMiddleware, which takes the values, prefixes some text to the new body, and returns the new three-element array, which is the final result of the call.

And, if you run rackup on this file and then hit http://localhost:9292, you'll see all three lines of text in your browser, correctly formatted as HTML.

Although our Rack middleware classes both do similar things—retrieve the previous call and adjust the body text—Rack middleware can do far more. You have complete freedom to adjust the environment, status, headers, and response body. You can completely ignore the work of other middleware and change the response to ["Never gonna give you up"]. More usefully, you can add API tokens to the environment, perform external services like logging, or filter the response body in some way. There's a lot of power there.

And although we've been using rackup, Rack applications work with a variety of compatible Ruby web servers. To use the popular Puma server, do this:

```
$ gem install puma
$ puma
```

Puma will, by default, look for a config.ru file in the current directory and run it.

Every major Ruby web framework is structured as a Rack application that can be triggered with Rack's run. Not only can your middleware be run with any web server, it can be integrated into any web framework. Any problem that can be solved with a Rack middleware can be applied to any compatible framework.

Sinatra and Web Frameworks

While Rack is powerful, it's also a little low-level and writing more complex web interactions with it is complicated. For more involved web applications, Ruby has many different web frameworks. The most popular is Ruby on Rails, which provides web features along with database connectivity, and a complete grab bag of everything you'd need to build full-featured web applications.

Rails is great, but it's also a lot to learn. In this book, we're going to show a simpler framework called Sinatra[13], which is one of the fastest ways to get a basic web application up and running in Ruby.

Here's a minimal Sinatra file:

web/sinatra_01/sinatra.rb
```ruby
require "bundler/inline"

gemfile do
  source "https://rubygems.org"
  gem "sinatra", require: false
  gem "thin"
end

require "sinatra"

get "/" do
  "<h1>Fly me to the moon!</h1>"
end
```

To start a web server, all you need to do is run this file like an ordinary Ruby program.

```
$ ruby sinatra.rb
== Sinatra (v3.1.0) has taken the stage on 4567
for development with backup from Thin
2022-10-15 08:48:20 -0500 Thin web server (v1.8.2 codename Infinite Smoothie)
2022-10-15 08:48:20 -0500 Maximum connections set to 1024
2022-10-15 08:48:20 -0500 Listening on localhost:4567, CTRL+C to stop
```

---

13. https://sinatrarb.com

From there, pointing a web browser at http://localhost:4567 will result in a web page being served, with "Fly me to the moon," just as specified at the end of the code.

How is this working? Logistically, the first ten lines or so of this example are using bundler/inline to install gems as part of the script, which is a useful trick for simple Sinatra scripts. We're pulling in both Sinatra itself and the Thin web server; when it runs, Sinatra will automatically use Thin if it's available. (You can use other servers, but you need to create a rackup file to do so.) Because of the way Sinatra decides when to run, we need to explicitly use require "sinatra", which means we need Bundler not to require Sinatra, so the line in the gemfile section for Sinatra needs to include require: false.

The actual web serving part is the last three lines. Generically, a Sinatra application is a collection of routes. A route is an HTTP verb followed by a path, some optional options, and then a block. The HTTP verb, path, and options tell Sinatra how to match requests to routes, and the block tells Sinatra how to reply when the request matches the route.

In this case, we've defined one route, the HTTP verb is GET, which matches the root path of /, and there are no other options. The return value of the block is the string "<h1>Fly me to the moon!</h1>". And so, if we hit the root route, we get that response. Hitting any other URL within that server triggers a 404 error page, since Sinatra has no routes matching the URL.

As you might imagine, you can build up considerably more advanced logic from there. A full description is at https://sinatrarb.com/intro.html, but we'll cover some of the most important parts here.

We can start with the return value of the block. In our example, it's a plain string. For more complex output, you'll likely want to use ERB or some other templating language. In Sinatra, you can do that with the erb method:

web/sinatra_01/sinatra_with_erb.rb
```
get "/" do
  erb(:root)
end
```

The first argument to erb is a symbol and matches a filename, which is in a views subdirectory by default. So the previous snippet will render an ERB template in views/root.erb. Less commonly, the first argument can be a string, in which case the string is expected to be an ERB template itself, and is rendered as-is.

After the name of the template, you can pass in key/value pairs to erb as options. By default, the ERB template has access to instance variables set in the route, but if you want local variables to be visible, you can set them with a locals: option. You can also set a layout with a layout: option. The layout is an ERB template that includes a call to <%= yield %> somewhere, at which point the actual template for the route is inserted. A few other options for erb are available in the official docs together with a wide range of other template tools that are supported with their own similar helper methods.

The erb method also returns a string. You can also return an object that responds to each and returns a series of strings, in which case you're streaming output to the browser. You can also return a complete Rack response, meaning the entire three-element array, or you can return an integer, which is assumed to be an HTTP status code over an otherwise-empty response.

The route selectors can be made more flexible and complicated. You can match delete, get, link, options, patch, post, put, and unlink. You cannot by default have multiple HTTP verbs connected to the same route, though there are a couple of workarounds for this including an extension called sinatra/multi_route.

In the route name, you can have parameters or wild cards. Parameters are either available in a hash called params or are passed as arguments to the block associated with the route.

```
web/sinatra_01/sinatra_with_param.rb
get "/user/:username" do |block_un|
  [
    "<p>Hello, #{params["username"]}</p>",
    "<p>#{block_un} has the same value</p>"
  ]
end
```

A request to this route might look like "http://webhost.com/user/noelrap," and the resulting output would be <p>Hello, noelrap</p><p>noelrap has the same value</p>. The block takes all the parameters from the URL in positional order, rather than as a hash—we suspect that using the hash will typically be more readable and flexible. In this example, we're also taking advantage of Sinatra's ability to return an object that responds to each—an array—and its ability to return a series of strings. We like this slightly better than concatenating the strings together in the block.

The parameters are passed to the block in the order they are in the URL, and the block parameters can be named arbitrarily, but the params hash will pick up the name used in the path description. If the parameter name ends in a question mark, like :username?, then the parameter is optional. Sinatra treats trailing slashes as full elements, so user and user/ are different strings, but you can make the trailing slash optional with a question mark, as in user/?.

You can also include a *, which will match an arbitrary number of segments in the path, the unnamed variable will either be a block parameter or be accessible as params["splat"].

If multiple routes match the request, the first one defined and matched is taken. You can use pass which tells Sinatra to move to the next matching route.

Instead of a string, the first argument to the path matcher can be a regular expression, in which case any path string that matches the regular expression triggers the route. If you use parentheses to capture part of the regular expression, then the capture groups are available as arguments to the block or as params["captures"], so our route with the variable example could've been written as:

```
web/sinatra_01/sinatra_with_regex.rb
get %r{/user/(\w+)} do |capture|
  [
    "<p>Hello, #{params["captures"].first}</p>",
    "<p>#{capture} has the same value</p>"
  ]
end
```

Note the use of the %r for the regex literal since the string being matched contains slashes.

After the string or regex, you can also pass some optional keyword parameters to a route definition. These keyword parameters act as a condition that the request must meet to trigger the route. Perhaps the most useful of these is provides:, which compares against the Accept header to match the route based on what media type the browser is expecting.

The Sinatra code we've seen so far is very powerful for being so short, but as you build up more complex Sinatra scripts, you'll probably want to go beyond a top-level script and add some classes or modularity.

Sinatra allows you to import a sinatra/base module which gives you a Sinatra::Application class that you can use the same Sinatra DSL inside, like this:

web/sinatra_01/sinatra_class.rb
```ruby
require "sinatra/base"

class SinatraApp < Sinatra::Application
  get "/" do
    "<h1>Fly me to the moon!</h1>"
  end
end
```

There's also a Sinatra::Base, which sets fewer defaults and allows you to have more control over the Sinatra setup.

Once the Sinatra code is set up as a class, it won't run as a script. You have a few ways to get it to run, one of which is to use Rack. We can run the file in a config.ru rackup file as just another Rack app:

web/sinatra_01/config.ru
```ruby
require_relative "./sinatra_class"
run SinatraApp
```

Now we've got multiple files, we've moved all the gem requirements out of inline and into a Gemfile:

web/sinatra_01/Gemfile
```ruby
source "https://rubygems.org"
gem "rack", "~> 2.2"
gem "puma"
gem "sinatra", "> 3.0"
```

Sinatra doesn't currently support Rack 3.0, so we've used the Gemfile to ensure that we have the most recent 2.2.x version of Rack.

At this point, we can run bundle install, and the Puma gem is installed. Then, running puma from the command line, Puma will find the config.ru file and run the Sinatra app. Pointing the browser at http://localhost:9292 will show that this works.

There's a lot more to Sinatra, so please check out https://sinatrarb.com for additional information. And if Sinatra doesn't meet your needs, many other Ruby web frameworks might.

Ruby in the Browser with Web Assembly

Web Assembly (Wasm) is a virtual machine runtime engine that runs in a web browser, allowing any Wasm-compliant programming language to be used as a scripting language in that browser.

Ruby 3.2 added support for Wasm as a compilation target of Ruby. You can see full instructions for creating your own Wasm build at https://github.com/ruby/ruby/blob/master/wasm/

README.md, but in most cases you'll likely either pull in the Wasm build as a module in Node Package Manager (NPM) or point to a source for the Wasm build in your web page.

So, you can do this in an HTML file:

web/wasm.html

```html
<html>
<script
  src="https://cdn.jsdelivr.net/npm/ruby-head-wasm-wasi@0.5.0/dist/browser.script.iife.js"
></script>
<script type="text/ruby">
  puts "Welcome To Ruby!"
</script>
</html>
```

The first script tag downloads the Wasm-compliant Ruby build from a known CDN location. This will take some time on first download at least, so it's probably not quite production-ready as we write this. The first script tag registers the Ruby build as the interpreter for Ruby scripts, so subsequent text/ruby scripts will be interpreted by Ruby and their output sent to the browser.

In this case, the subsequent script prints "Welcome to Ruby!" to the browser console.

You can do more complex things:

web/wasm_2.html

```html
<html>
<head>
  <script
    src="https://cdn.jsdelivr.net/npm/ruby-head-wasm-wasi@0.5.0/dist/browser.script.iife.js"
  ></script>
  <script type="text/ruby">
    require "js"
    document = JS.global[:document]
    button = document.getElementById("button")
    response = document.getElementById("response")
    guess = document.getElementById("guess")
    button.addEventListener("click") do |e|
      real_number = (1..10).to_a.sample
      result_text = "The number was #{real_number}. "
      if guess[:value].to_i == real_number
        result_text << "You were right!!"
      else
        result_text << "You were incorrect"
      end
      response[:innerText] = result_text
    end
  </script>
</head>
<body>
  <p>Pick a number 1 through 10</p>
  <input id="guess" />
  <button id="button">Am I right?</button>
  <div id="response"></div>
</body>
</html>
```

The HTML at the end of this script has a button, a text field, and a placeholder for a response. In the script, after we require a module called js, we have access to the JavaScript document object as JS.global[:document]. From there, we can use the DOM method getElementById to retrieve DOM elements and access their values as if they were in a hash (not as attributes). We can even call methods on them, as in addEventListener.

It all adds up to a button that causes a random number to be generated and compared to the value in a text field, as shown here:

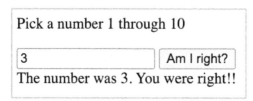

You don't have to do this in the HTML script. You can grab the NPM package directly and evaluate Ruby code, but you have to pass the Ruby code as a string. This is a little clunky right now, but you can see an example at https://github.com/ruby/ruby.wasm/blob/main/packages/npm-packages/ruby-wasm-wasi/example/index.node.js.

This is a very new project, and we look forward to further developments of the coding experience here.

What's Next

We've covered many different ways Ruby interacts with the web. We've seen Ruby's own utilities, the Rack framework for interactions between web servers and application frameworks, and the Sinatra framework for building basic web applications. Next we'll look at Ruby style.

## CHAPTER 21

Ruby Style

As you become familiar with Ruby and the Ruby community, you will see references to "Ruby style" or "idiomatic Ruby." These terms refer to the way in which developers who love Ruby tend to write Ruby code. Ruby provides a broad range of allowed syntax and different ways of performing similar tasks and interacting with existing code. Ruby is such a flexible language that style and community standards of practice go a long way toward keeping Ruby code readable from project to project.

There are two distinct kinds of Ruby style. The first is the kind that's syntax-based, governs how you write individual lines and small blocks of code, and can (to some extent) be evaluated by a linting program. In this chapter, we'll discuss two tools that can check your code to see if it matches style rules: RuboCop and Standard. Often, these tools can automatically reformat your code to align with style guidelines.

The second kind of Ruby style is more nebulous, and it involves larger decisions than individual lines and has to do more with how to use Ruby as a tool. We'll discuss how to lean into Ruby's dynamism and support of dynamic typing (sometimes called "duck typing") as a way to make your code's intent clearer and give you less code to maintain and change in the future.

Before we say anything else about style in this chapter, it's important to remember that style is subjective, and nearly all of these guidelines are dependent on what you and your team find clear and readable. Team style is a case where consistency is more important than perfection—any time spent arguing over where the square brackets go is time lost. You want to avoid "bikeshedding"—spending inordinate time on trivial cosmetic issues like what color to paint the bike shed, rather than the important issues of your project. We'll offer some advice, but our overall recommendation is to pick the tooling to support a common set of practices and then spend your time on larger and more interesting code issues.

Written Ruby Style

The goal of having a written coding style is to make the intent and functionality of the code clear and easy to maintain. When the physical layout of the file matches its logical layout and the constructs are presented consistently, it's easier for a reader of the code to understand what the code is doing.

Programming languages tend to offer flexibility in how the code is actually laid out in the file as written by the developer. Some languages are stricter in arranging the physical layout of their syntax. For example, Python is known for enforcing the use of indentation to denote logical blocks of code. Ruby, for better or worse, isn't like that. Ruby offers the developer tremendous flexibility.

In the face of that flexibility, various common practices have emerged. In some cases, a particular style was found to have genuine clarity or modification benefits. In other cases, the community picked from equally fine choices, but the consistency of going with only one choice has its own benefit.

Currently, the two most commonly used Ruby style guides can be found at https://rubystyle.guide, which is maintained by Bozhidar Batsov and the team that maintains the RuboCop tool, and at https://ruby-style-guide.shopify.dev, which is a slightly different version maintained by the team of Ruby developers at Shopify.

It's not our intention to litigate every element in those guides, but we do want to mention a few of the most important or most widely observed features. (You'll notice the features we highlight have a strong correlation with the ones used by the Standard tool.)

Indentation and Spacing

Ruby code almost without exception uses two spaces for indentation—not tabs and not four spaces:

```ruby
module Game
  class Team
    def initialize
    end
  end
end
```

We could go on about how this is optimal, but honestly, it's largely a question of consistency (and to some extent, a preference for more compact code).

It's important to note that a couple of things aren't indented in Ruby that might be indented in other languages. For example, in a case statement, the when clauses aren't indented relative to the case:

```ruby
case name
when :superman
  "Clark Kent"
when :batman
  "Bruce Wayne"
end
```

Similarly, exception keywords like rescue and ensure aren't indented relative to the blocks they are within:

```ruby
def a_sample_method(name)
  a_dangerous_call
rescue StandardError
  return "Oops"
ensure
  something_else
end
```

The rationale for this spacing is that if you squint hard enough, when and rescue aren't subordinate blocks and shouldn't be indented. In practice, like the two-space indenting, this lack of indentation tends to make Ruby code more compact on the screen than code from other languages.

If you use private as a keyword, typically the methods below it aren't indented, again because private is a method call and doesn't create a logical block:

```ruby
class Sample
  def public_method
  end

  private

  def private_method
  end
end
```

As you've seen in the code samples in the book so far, Ruby code uses the end of a line to end statements, so you don't typically use a semicolon at the end of a line.

Ruby code style uses spaces around operators, around equal signs, and after commas, but it doesn't use spaces inside square brackets or parentheses. For example:

```ruby
def do_some_things(x, y = "default")
  a = x + y
  b = [1, 2, 3]
end
```

Here are a few exceptions:

- Range literals generally don't have spaces, as in 1..10.

- When ! is used as a negation operator it doesn't have spaces, as in !foo.

- The &. safe navigation operator doesn't get spaces so that it visually is just part of a method chain as in user&.name&.first.

- Exponent operators don't have spaces, as in x**2.

- Rational and complex literal markers don't have spaces, as in 3/5r.

Curly braces are a little more complicated. The most common style is to put spaces inside curly braces for block literals, but not for hash literals or string interpolation, because the spacing gives an immediate visual clue as to whether the braces enclose a block or a hash:

```ruby
def sample
  data = {a: 1, b: 2}
  data.each { |key, value| p "#{key}/#{value}" }
end
```

That said, you'll see styles that put spaces inside hash literals as well.

As for block literals, the most common Ruby style is to use curly braces for single-line blocks and do/end for multiline blocks:

```ruby
def another_sample
  [1, 2, 3].map { |x| x**2 }
  [1, 2, 3].map do |x|
```

```
    print "working on #{x}"
    x**2
  end
end
```

There's another convention, associated with Jim Weirich (the creator of Rake), where braces are used for multiline blocks if the return value of the method is immediately used in a method chain like this:

```
def another_sample
  [1, 2, 3].map { |x|
    do_something_with(x)
  }.sort.first
end
```

In this example, the result of the map call is passed directly to sort, so the Weirich convention uses braces because the feeling is that end.sort.first looks odd.

Typically, we put blank lines between method and class definitions, and only rarely inside methods. Ruby methods tend to be short, and needing internal space might be a sign that the method should be split.

Parentheses, especially for method calls, also have a couple of popular styles. The most common style is to use parentheses for all method calls unless the method call is one of these:

- A Kernel method like puts or p that's meant to look like a command.
- A class method being invoked as part of the definition of a class, like include or private.
- Used in a Ruby domain-specific language that doesn't use parentheses, like RSpec's it or describe.

No matter what, method calls with no arguments in Ruby shouldn't get empty parentheses (except in the one case where super() has a different meaning than super).

You may sometimes see references to "Seattle Style" Ruby code, in which parentheses are only included if they are needed to resolve ambiguity.

Naming and Calling

Local variables, symbols, method names, and filenames in Ruby use underscores to separate words, as in a_multi_word_name. Modules and classes that start with capital letters use intercaps to separate words, as in AMultiWordName. Our preference is to lowercase acronyms in inter-capped names—as in HttpReceiver, not HTTPReceiver—on the grounds that it's easier to separate the words, but this is an example where people's opinion definitely varies.

Constants are typically written in all caps and use underscores to separate names, as in A_MULTI_WORD_NAME.

Ruby tends not to prefix getters, setters, and predicate methods. *Getters* are typically the name of the attribute, *setters* are the name of the attribute with an = suffix, and *predicate methods* don't typically start with is or a similar prefix. Instead, predicate methods in Ruby end with ?, such as empty?.

The ! suffix on a method name indicates that the method is "dangerous." In Ruby-speak this means that the method does one of the following:

- Modifies the receiver of the message
- Raises an exception or error

There is typically a "safe" version of the same method that doesn't end in ! and doesn't modify the receiver or raise an exception.

Ruby style tends to avoid explicitly using self as the receiver of a method unless it's required to avoid ambiguity (as in the left side of an assignment). Ruby style also avoids explicitly and redundantly using return on the last line of a method where the return value is already specified. Only explicitly use return when exiting early from a method.

Single-line method calls should only be used when the body of the method is a single expression and has no side effects. Ideally, it also has no arguments. Here's an example:

```
def price_in_dollars = price_in_cents * 1.0 / 100.
```

Also, you should use attr_reader, attr_writer, and attr_accessor when appropriate rather than explicitly defining simple setters and getters.

Ruby allows parallel assignment between multiple left and right arguments. In general, use parallel assignment to do one of the following:

- Swap values: first, second = second, first
- Capture multiple return values from a method: user, count = post.user_with_most_comments

Logical Flow

Ruby has a number of different looping and conditional flow constructs that control the logical flow of the program through the code. Because these flow statements are usually the most complex individual bits of logic, using consistent style for clarity is important in keeping the code readable and maintainable. Following are a few suggestions.

Even though Ruby has a for keyword, it's better to use each for looping over an enumeration—for is defined in terms of each, so you don't gain speed and you lose some clarity by using for.

In if and when statements, only use then where the condition and the result are on the same line. Only use guard clauses at the end of the line like foo if x.nil? if the clause is simple. If the clause is complex, consider breaking it out into its own method with a meaningful name.

It's fine to use unless instead of if !, but please don't use unless followed by else because that tends to be confusing.

The if and case statements return a value, and you should use this fact to make code clearer, like this:

```
result = if a_thing
           x
         else
           y
         end
```

Note the indentation (you can also indent relative to the beginning of the line). Also, note that Ruby style doesn't put parentheses around the boolean condition in an if or while statement.

For single-line conditional assignments, both of these styles are correct: result = if a_thing then x else y end and result = a_thing ? x : y. They each have their fans.

For equality, Ruby has a couple of different versions, though the one you want is almost always ==. It's the version that compares on the value of the object, not the identity of the object.

Finally, avoid using assignment in the conditional, as in if x = gets (even though some examples in this book do this for compactness). If you do, it's probably a good idea to put parentheses around the conditional, like this: if (x = gets), to draw attention to the unusual code.

Data

When creating an array or a hash, it's better to use the literal syntax [] or {} over Array.new or Hash.new. If applicable, use %w for an array of short strings or %i for an array of symbols.

In general, prefer symbols as hash keys or, at the very least, some other immutable object. When using a symbol as a key, you should use the newer {foo: bar} syntax rather than {:foo => :bar}. (This is a declaration against our own tastes; we personally love the way the hash rocket looks, but objectively, more people find the shorter syntax easier.)

Ruby has a handful of pre-existing methods that combine iteration functions, like flat_map and reverse_each. These tend to be faster than chaining the two methods, so you should use these when appropriate.

For strings, use interpolation syntax rather than concatenating strings with bits of stuff, so use "#{last_name}, #{first_name}" instead of last_name + ", " + first_name. We prefer using double-quoted strings in all cases because that's easier to modify if you later add interpolation to the strings. Double-quoted strings aren't appreciably slower than single-quoted strings. If the string itself includes double quotes, use the %Q syntax. For long strings use heredocs, especially the <<~SQUIGGLE syntax that manages indentation.

Similarly, use %r for regular expressions that contain / characters. Consider using x as a modifier for complex regular expressions to allow for more expressive spacing. Use a comment on regular expression literals to point to Rubular or something similar where a reader can try the regular expression.

The Ruby style guides offer a lot of other suggestions; this is only some of what a full-style guide might include.

Using RuboCop

When you write Ruby code, you often don't want to have to think about style. What you want to do is write your code and solve your problem. But what usually happens is that once you have your team review your code, people on your team start to nitpick your minor style choices, sometimes contradicting each other. This is, to say the least, not compatible with great team morale.

Enter RuboCop.[1] RuboCop is a *linter*, which means that it automatically checks your code for style and then either flags discrepancies or optionally autocorrects them. (The name

---

1.   https://rubocop.org

"linter" comes from the first such program, lint, written in 1978 by Stephen C. Johnson for C code and named by analogy to a lint trap as a thing that catches small issues.)

RuboCop is highly customizable. It ships with dozens of individual style rules, which it calls "cops," plus there's a plugin system to add sets of rules and a mechanism for writing your own rules. After adding RuboCop, in theory, you have just one discussion among your team to set RuboCop's preferences, and then you let RuboCop handle the style-checking rather than continually debating it in code review.

RuboCop's documentation[2] is thorough. It includes a description of every individual rule with examples of code that passes and fails each one.

Getting Started with RuboCop

Let's look at how to get started using RuboCop in your code. For demonstration purposes, we're going to go through the process of adding RuboCop to our Aaagmnr gem from Chapter 15, Ruby Gems, on page 251. RuboCop is a Ruby gem, so you first need to add it to the Gemfile as gem "rubocop". (If you're literally following along with a copy of Aaagmnr, note that the previous version had Standard installed. Here, we're replacing it with RuboCop for the sake of demonstration.)

Next, run bundle install to install the RuboCop gem and enable a command-line program called rubocop, which you can run from the command line:

```
$ rubocop
Inspecting 14 files
CCCCCCCCCCCCCC

Offenses:
Gemfile:3:8: C: [Correctable] Style/StringLiterals:
 Prefer single-quoted strings when you don't need
 string interpolation or special symbols.
source "https://rubygems.org"
       ^^^^^^^^^^^^^^^^^^^^^^^
<LOTS OF THOSE>

14 files inspected, 108 offenses detected, 102 offenses auto-correctable

Tip: Based on detected gems, the following RuboCop extension libraries
     might be helpful:
  * rubocop-rake (https://rubygems.org/gems/rubocop-rake)
  * rubocop-rspec (https://rubygems.org/gems/rubocop-rspec)
You can opt out of this message by adding the following to your config
(see https://docs.rubocop.org/rubocop/extensions.html#extension-suggestions
     for more options):
  AllCops:
    SuggestExtensions: false
```

If you're using the sample code that came with this book, you'll only get these results if you remove or rename the configuration files .rubocop.yml and .rubocop_todo.yml described later in this chapter. Also, newer versions of RuboCop may change this output.

---

2.   https://docs.rubocop.org/rubocop/1.38/index.html

Let's parse this. RuboCop first tells us how many Ruby files it found to inspect—14 in this case. Then it gives us a running progress bar. If this was a live video and not a book, you'd see those C's coming in one at a time.

RuboCop and Editors

If you're using an integrated development environment (IDE) or coding editor, there's likely an extension that'll read your RuboCop configuration and display RuboCop issues in your editor as you type. You may even be able to autocorrect from the editor without running the command-line tool. (This goes for Standard as well.)

Each file gets one character. If the file has no issues, it's represented with a dot. Apparently, we have an issue in each file, so we have no dots. If RuboCop does flag something, the file is represented by the most serious issue. Each individual cop specifies its own severity level. Following are RuboCop's severity levels in order of least serious to most serious:

- I is used for "info." It's rare for an "info" failure to be reported. Typically an "info" failure won't be counted as a failure of the entire run as a whole.

- R is used for "refactor," as in "something you might want to refactor."

- C is used for "convention," meaning a style issue that's part of your team's conventions, rather than something that might objectively be a problem for all teams. Cops whose names don't start with Lint default to this severity.

- W is used for "warning," meaning the file is legal Ruby but has something that you might consider an "objective" problem. The indentation is unbalanced, there's some ambiguity, or something like that. Cops whose names start with Lint default to this severity.

- E is used for "error," meaning the file isn't legal Ruby.

- F is used for "fatal," meaning the file has a syntax error that prevents it from being parsed.

After the files comes a listing of all the offenses. The example code has a lot of identical offenses; we've chosen to include the display of only one of them. The layout looks like this:

- The location of the issue, Gemfile:3:8 gives the filename, line number, and character where the issue begins.

- The severity of the issue, which in this case is level C.

- If RuboCop can autocorrect the issue, it says so with [Correctable].

- The name of the cop, which in this case is Style/StringLiterals, and a description of what the cop shows.

- The line of code with the text at issue underlined.

After the list of all the offenses is a summary line: 14 files inspected, 108 offenses detected, 102 offenses auto-correctable. Also, RuboCop helpfully tells us that we could install plugins for rubocop-rake and rubocop-rspec.

That's a lot of offenses. We can get a sense for what's going on by using a different formatter from the command line:

```
rubocop --format offenses
 14/14 files |=====| Time: 00:00:00

90   Style/StringLiterals
6    Style/FrozenStringLiteralComment
4    Style/WordArray
3    Style/Documentation
1    Gemspec/RequiredRubyVersion
1    Metrics/MethodLength
1    Style/AccessModifierDeclarations
1    Style/MutableConstant
1    Style/StringLiteralsInInterpolation
--
108  Total
```

Most of these issues are that RuboCop's default, for some reason, prefers single-quoted strings. Most of the rest of these are other differences of opinion between the gem author and RuboCop's defaults. (To be honest, the RequiredRubyVersion and MutableConstant cops are probably worth fixing.)

Anyway, at this point we have a couple of options for what we can do with RuboCop just from the command line. As with many other command-line programs, we can pass directory names, filenames, or filename patterns to the CLI to limit RuboCop to the listed files (rubocop lib, for example).

We can auto-correct all the correctable cops. This will change all the double-quoted strings to single-quoted strings and various and sundry other things that RuboCop is currently complaining about.

To do that, we'd use the -a option, rubocop -a, and RuboCop would apply auto-correct logic for all the issues it identifies. In this case, it would replace all double-quoted strings with single-quoted strings. We don't want to do that right now, but the autocorrect is a quick way to fix many simple RuboCop issues. RuboCop is generally cautious about what it chooses to autocorrect, and most of the corrections are simple. But "cautious" doesn't mean "perfect," and "most of" doesn't mean "all," so when you do autocorrect, you want to check the result to make sure the new code is functionally equivalent to the old code.

On the other hand, we could decide that the code base is so gnarly that we don't want to fix old issues; we just want to start fresh and not create new issues. RuboCop allows us to create a to-do list of existing issues that are excluded from being flagged by future runs with this:

```
$ rubocop --auto-gen-config
```

This will produce a lot of output, and in the end it'll create a minimal .rubocop.yml configuration file and a .rubocop_todo.yml file. The .rubocop_todo.yml is an extension of the RuboCop configuration. It lists files where existing issues have been found and which we don't want to fix yet. Future runs of RuboCop will ignore these issues. After running the auto-configuration, we get this:

```
$ rubocop
# A LOT OF OUTPUT ABOUT SPECIFIC COPS AND OUR CONFIGURATION BEING TOO MINIMAL

Inspecting 14 files
..............

14 files inspected, no offenses detected
```

To be clear, the offenses are still there, they are just being suppressed by the todo file.

Configuring RuboCop

Almost everything in RuboCop can be configured, and the file in which to make these changes is .rubocop.yml. Here's a sample configuration that configures RuboCop to be more in line with the style of the existing code. It removes most of the issues RuboCop identified in our earlier code example:

```
ruby_style/aaagmnr/.rubocop.yml
#inherit_from: .rubocop_todo.yml

AllCops:
  TargetRubyVersion: 3.3
  NewCops: enable
  SuggestExtensions: false
  Exclude:
    - "bin/**/*"

Metrics/MethodLength:
  Enabled: false

Style/AccessModifierDeclarations:
  EnforcedStyle: inline

Style/Documentation:
  Enabled: false

Style/FrozenStringLiteralComment:
  Enabled: false

Style/StringLiterals:
  EnforcedStyle: double_quotes

Style/StringLiteralsInInterpolation:
  EnforcedStyle: double_quotes

Style/WordArray:
  MinSize: 3
```

At the top, we commented out the line inherit_from: .rubocop_todo.yml. That line was generated in the previous section when we ran the --auto-gen-config command. In general, RuboCop lets you inherit from other configurations so as to modularize the configuration. If we wanted to include separate projects like RuboCop's Rails or RSpec cops, we'd use inherit_from:. The inherit_from mechanism is often used for an organization to specify a common set of standards, and then individual projects use their own configurations to extend or override those standards.

Below that is a section in which we set default values by using the AllCops name. In this case, we're telling RuboCop to treat the code as though it was being written for Ruby 3.3 and to exclude any file in the bin directory. We're also explicitly opting in to new cops and telling RuboCop not to suggest extensions because if we don't, RuboCop complains about both of those things in the output every time we run the command.

The settings for individual cops can be changed directly, as this configuration does. We don't need RuboCop to tell us about method length—we trust our team to only have long methods when necessary—so we set Enabled: false for that cop. Any cop can have its Enabled setting set to true or false. Most cops default to true.

If you look at the .rubocop_todo.yml file, notice that every cop also has an Exclude setting that takes a list of files or file patterns that shouldn't have that cop applied. This is helpful in transitioning a code base to RuboCop because it allows you to be judicious in switching individual files, but in general, you wouldn't use it in your main configuration.

Some cops have their own parameters to set—we set the Style/StringLiterals cop to double_quotes. We still want this cop to work, we just want it to accept double quotes as the ideal and flag single quotes. Similarly, the Style/WordArray cop, which wants us to change all our ["cat", "dog"] tests to the word array syntax of %w[cat dog], has a parameter that sets the minimum size of the array that it cares about. We don't mind the array syntax for two-element arrays, so we set the minimum value to 3.

With this configuration in place (and with the todo shut off), our RuboCop tells us there are four problems:

- It wants us to set a config parameter for rubygems_mfa_required in the .gemspec, which sets multi-factor security on the gem itself.

- The target ruby in RuboCop is different from the Ruby version specified in the .gemspec.

- There's a single-quote string in the .gemspec.

- It wants us to freeze the constant DEFAULT_DICTIONARY = "/usr/share/dict/words".

Most of the problems are in the .gemspec. We can now fix these either by updating the configuration, by running rubocop -a to autocorrect, or running rubocop -A to autocorrect and include some cops that might be unsafe to autocorrect. Using rubocop -A will correct all but the first issue.

You can also disable a cop inline in your file with a magic comment: # rubocop/disable Style/WordArray or whatever the name of the cop you want to disable is. If the comment comes at the end of a line, it merely disables for that line. If it stands on its own, it disables until the end of the file or a matching # rubocop/enable comment, whichever comes first. This is sometimes useful, but again is something you want to use sparingly. Frequent use of disabling RuboCop suggests that the settings you have aren't quite right.

There's more to RuboCop, including a lot of extensions, and you can write your own cops to identify whatever Ruby style options you want. See the RuboCop documentation[3] for more information.

Using Standard

RuboCop is powerful, but also complicated. If we're being honest, we don't like all the defaults. As a result, our typical project winds up with a long configuration file that's a bit unwieldy and continually subject to argument. If only somebody would come up with a more consensus-based Ruby style-checker.

Enter Standard,[4] a default configuration of RuboCop created by Justin Searls that is minimally configurable and conforms to a small, but commonly used, set of rules.

What rules? You can see the entire list in the Standard RuboCop's setup, but the gist is similar to the common rules we set out in the first part of this chapter:

---

3. https://docs.rubocop.org
4. https://github.com/testdouble/standard

- Two-space indentation
- Double-quoted strings
- No hash rockets for symbol hash keys
- Spaces inside curly braces for blocks and not for hashes
- Braces for single line blocks (Standard doesn't specify how you handle multiline blocks)

Installing Standard just requires putting gem "standard" in your gemfile. You don't need a configuration.

To run Standard, just enter standardrb from the command line and you'll get RuboCop output. Using standardrb --fix will autocorrect errors, and using standardrb --generate-todo will create a .standard_todo.yml file just like the todo file RuboCop generates.

You can only do a minimal amount of configuration to a .standard.yml file. These are the available keys:

- default_ignores: Defaults to true. If set to false, Standard will not ignore files that it would normally ignore.

- extend_config: Takes the name of additional RuboCop yaml files that can themselves configure RuboCop. The idea is to allow you to run Standard and RuboCop extensions. The default is an empty list.

- fix: If true, Standard will autocorrect on a regular run, which you can turn off with standard --no-fix. The default is false.

- format: Sets the formatter for output. The default is the standard formatter.

- ignore: Takes a list of file patterns to ignore. The default is an empty list.

- parallel: If true, Standard will run in parallel. The default is false.

- ruby_version: Sets the Ruby version to target; it defaults to the version of Ruby that's running. The default is the value of RUBY_VERSION.

You can use Standard as a base for a RuboCop configuration, which you might want to do if you want to use additional RuboCop extensions like the Rails or RSpec cops. In your .standard.yml:

```
extend_config:
  - test_cops.yml
  - rails_cops.yml
```

Those additional files are regular RuboCop files and can do whatever a RuboCop config can do, but the idea of the feature is that you'd require and configure a RuboCop extension that Standard doesn't cover.

Ruby Style in the Large

Ruby style isn't just a matter of how you code line-by-line, it also manifests in how you approach problems and how you build solutions. The goal of all of these style recommendations is to allow the code to clearly reflect the intent of the programmer. Taking advantage of what Ruby does best and most simply will make it easier to read and modify your code going forward.

Ruby code is often written with shorter methods and smaller classes than more strongly typed languages. Not only do smaller methods give you more chances to give blocks of code meaningful names, but also having small pieces of functionality made into methods makes it easier to build functionality by combining methods using Ruby syntax such as blocks.

For example, let's say we're sending an email to a user to confirm whether the user is eligible for a promotion and that there are a few different facets to eligibility:

```
def send_promotion_email
  if last_active_date <= 1.year.ago ||
    %w[TX AZ FL].includes?(state) ||
    opted_out?
    return false
  end
  send_the_email
end
```

In this example, the intent of the if condition is somewhat obscured by the syntactic clutter of the three boolean choices. Giving the combined boolean its own method with a meaningful name clears that up. And while many programming languages will suggest extracting methods, in Ruby you get the added bonus of making it possible to easily use the guard clause syntax in a separated method:

```
def gets_promotion_email?
  return false if last_active_date <= 1.year.ago
  return false if %w[IL GA MA].includes?(state)
  return false if opted_out?
  true
end

def send_promotion_email
  return false unless gets_promotion_email?
  send_the_email
end
```

You should note a few things about this:

- You could do the gets_promotion_email as a single boolean expression as it was done in the first code snippet. We just find it easier to reason about each cause individually, and breaking them into a method makes that easier to do.

- It's also true that some of those clauses might be clearer with their own method. For example, the middle clause might use a method name to say why those states are blocked.

- The send_promotion_email method is now shorter and the meaning of the initial if clause is now clearer. The use of the end-of-line syntax, enabled by the fact that there's now just one method to call, is a signal that the first line is meant as a guard clause protecting the rest of the method.

Blocks have a similar mechanism. Many commonly used Ruby methods use blocks, and having the body of a block encapsulated in a method can enable you to use one of Ruby's shorter syntaxes, like this:

```
users.map { |user| user.convert_to_json }
users.map { _1.convert_to_json }
users.map(&:convert_to_json)
```

All three of these are equivalent, but they all depend on the body of the conversion being broken out into its own method.

Duck Typing

You may have noticed that in Ruby you don't explicitly declare the types of variables or methods. Whether the particular value of a variable is correct for the messages being passed to it's evaluated at run time when the message is sent.

Folks tend to react to this in one of two ways. Some like this flexibility and feel comfortable writing code with dynamically typed variables and methods. Others get nervous when they think about all those objects floating around unconstrained. If you've come to Ruby from a language such as C#, Java, or TypeScript, where you're used to giving all your variables and methods an explicit type, you may feel that Ruby is just too permissive for writing "real" applications.

It isn't.

We'd like to spend a couple of paragraphs trying to convince you that the lack of static typing isn't a problem when it comes to writing reliable applications. In fact, an important part of Ruby style is trusting Ruby's dynamic typing to help you and not hurt you. We're not trying to criticize other languages here. Instead, we'd just like to contrast approaches.

The reality is that the static type systems in most mainstream languages don't help that much in terms of program correctness. If Java's type system were perfectly reliable, for example, it wouldn't need to implement ClassCastException. But the exception is necessary because there is runtime type uncertainty in Java (as there is in TypeScript, C#, and others). Static typing can be good for optimizing code, can be useful for communicating intent, and can help IDEs do clever things with tooltip help, but we haven't seen much evidence that it promotes more reliable code.

Static typing also has costs. Statically typed languages are typically more verbose than dynamic ones, which can cause the business logic to be obscured by the type declaration clutter. It's not unheard of to spend time convincing the type checking system that the thing you know is right is actually also legal.

On the other hand, once you use Ruby for a while, you realize that dynamically typed variables add to your productivity in many ways. You'll also be surprised to discover that your worst fears about the type chaos were unfounded. Large, long-running Ruby programs run significant applications and just don't throw many type-related errors. Why is this?

Partly it's a question of program structure. In many cases the structure of the program makes type errors unlikely even if the language isn't explicitly checking for them. You put Person objects in, and a few lines later the code sends Person objects out. Add in some reasonably meaningful variable names, and you're already minimizing the possibility of type errors.

Good style techniques limit the possibility of type errors in Ruby. If you use a variable for some purpose, chances are good you'll be using it for the same purpose when you access it again three lines later. Object-oriented design and polymorphism let you take advantage of dynamic typing to limit type errors. The kind of chaos that *could* happen just doesn't happen.

On top of that, folks who code Ruby a lot tend to adopt a certain style of coding. They write lots of short methods and tend to test as they go along. The short methods mean that the scope of most variables is limited; there just isn't that much time for things to go wrong with their type. The testing catches the silly errors when they happen; typos and the like just don't get a chance to propagate through the code. As an added bonus, short, testable methods tend to have other benefits for code quality in addition to limiting the possibility of type errors.

The upshot is that the "safety" in "type safety" is often illusory and that coding in a more dynamic language such as Ruby is both safe and productive. So, if you're nervous about the lack of static typing in Ruby, we suggest you try to put those concerns on the back burner for a little while and give Ruby a try. We think you'll be surprised how rarely you see errors because of type issues and how much more productive you feel once you start to exploit the power of dynamic typing.

Classes Aren't Types

If you've coded in strongly typed languages, you may have been taught that the *type* of an object is the same as its *class*—all objects are instances of some class, and that class is the object's type. The class defines the operations (methods) the object can support, along with the state (instance variables) on which those methods operate. Let's look at some Java code:

```
Customer c;
c = database.findCustomer("dave");    /* Java */
```

This fragment declares the variable c to be of type Customer and sets it to reference the customer object for Dave that we've created from some database record. So, the type of the object in c is Customer, right?

Maybe. However, even in Java, the issue is slightly deeper. Java supports the concept of *interfaces*. An interface is a list of methods that are supported together by classes that implement the interface. A Java class can be declared as implementing multiple interfaces. More to the point, a variable can be declared as being typed to an interface, rather than a class. Using this facility, you may have defined your classes as follows:

```
public interface Customer {
  long  getID();
  Calendar getDateOfLastContact();
  // ...
}

public class Person implements Customer {
  public long getID() { ... }
  public Calendar getDateOfLastContact() { ... }
  // ...
}
```

So, even in an explicitly-typed language, the class isn't always the type—sometimes the type is a subset of the class, and sometimes objects implement multiple types.

In Ruby, the class is never (well, almost never) the type. Instead, the type of an object is defined by what messages it responds to. The idea that typing is implicitly based on messages defined rather than being explicitly declared is called *duck typing*. If an object walks like a duck and quacks like a duck, then the interpreter is happy to treat it as if it were a duck, even if it's just a duck-shaped puppet.

Earlier in the book, we said that a type defined both the values that could be assigned to a variable and the expected behavior of those values. In Ruby (when not using RBS or Sorbet), those values and behavior are both enforced only by the set of messages that are passed to the value when the program runs.

Let's look at an example to see why taking advantage of Ruby's dynamic nature can be helpful. Perhaps we have written a method to write our customer's name to the end of an open file:

ducktyping/add_customer.rb
```ruby
class Customer
  def initialize(first_name, last_name)
    @first_name = first_name
    @last_name = last_name
  end

  def append_name_to_file(file)
    file << @first_name << " " << @last_name
  end
end
```

Being good programmers, we'll write a unit test for this. Be warned, though—it's messy (and we'll improve on it shortly):

ducktyping/test_add_customer_1.rb
```ruby
require "minitest/autorun"
require_relative "add_customer"

class TestAddCustomer < Minitest::Test
  def test_add
    customer = Customer.new("Ima", "Customer")
    File.open("tmpfile", "w") do |f|
      customer.append_name_to_file(f)
    end
    File.open("tmpfile") do |f|
      assert_equal("Ima Customer", f.gets)
    end
  ensure
    File.delete("tmpfile") if File.exist?("tmpfile")
  end
end
```

produces:
```
Run options: --seed 3880
# Running:

.

Finished in 0.000537s, 1862.1973 runs/s, 1862.1973 assertions/s.

1 runs, 1 assertions, 0 failures, 0 errors, 0 skips
```

We have to do all that work in the test to create a file to write to. Then we reopen it and read in the contents to verify the correct string was written. We also have to delete the file when we've finished (but only if it exists).

Because Ruby is dynamic, we don't actually have to do all that work on actual files to make the test run. Instead, we could rely on duck typing. All we need is something that walks like a file and quacks like a file that we can pass in to the method under test. And all that means *in this circumstance* is that we need an object that responds to the << method by appending something. Do we have something that does this? How about a humble String?

```
ducktyping/test_add_customer_2.rb
require "minitest/autorun"
require_relative "add_customer"

class TestAddCustomer < Minitest::Test
  def test_add
    customer = Customer.new("Ima", "Customer")
    fake_file = ""
    customer.append_name_to_file(fake_file)
    assert_equal("Ima Customer", fake_file)
  end
end
```

produces:

```
Run options: --seed 29322
# Running:

.

Finished in 0.000279s, 3584.2290 runs/s, 3584.2290 assertions/s.

1 runs, 1 assertions, 0 failures, 0 errors, 0 skips
```

The method under test thinks it's writing to a file, but instead, it's just appending to a string. Actually, even that statement is a little strong—the method under test thinks it's sending the message << to an object that will receive it and do something. Even though the method may have been written with a file in mind, any object that responds to << will work. At the end, we can test that the content is correct given what the receiver does with the message <<.

We didn't have to use a string; an array would work just as well for the purposes of the test:

```
ducktyping/test_add_customer_3.rb
require "minitest/autorun"
require_relative "add_customer"

class TestAddCustomer < Minitest::Test
  def test_add
    customer = Customer.new("Ima", "Customer")
    fake_file = []
    customer.append_name_to_file(fake_file)
    assert_equal(["Ima", " ", "Customer"], fake_file)
  end
end
```

produces:

```
Run options: --seed 31340
# Running:

.

Finished in 0.000239s, 4184.1012 runs/s, 4184.1012 assertions/s.

1 runs, 1 assertions, 0 failures, 0 errors, 0 skips
```

Indeed, this form may be more convenient if we wanted to check that the correct individual elements were inserted.

At this point, you could make the argument that the original method append_name_to_file is misnamed and that the method should be just append_name—especially because the argument is also named file. We can see an argument either way on this point. On the one hand, file is only a limited subset of what this method actually works on; on the other hand, putting file in the method name signals to users of the method what's expected. The point here is to make your intent clear so that future changes aren't surprising. Putting file in the message name clearly sends an intent that other file functionality beyond << might be used in the future. (Of course, using other file functionality means that we might have to rewrite the test.)

So, duck typing is convenient for testing, but what about in the body of applications themselves? Well, it turns out that the same feature that made the tests easy in the previous example also makes it easy to write flexible application code.

In fact, Dave once had an interesting experience where duck typing dug him (and a client) out of a hole. He'd written a large Ruby-based web application that (among other things) kept a database table full of details of participants in a competition. The system provided a comma-separated value (CSV) download capability so administrators could import this information into their local spreadsheets.

Just before competition time, the phone starts ringing. The download, which had been working fine up to this point, was now taking so long that requests were timing out. The pressure was intense because the administrators had to use this information to build schedules and send out mailings.

A little experimentation showed that the problem was in the routine that took the results of the database query and generated the CSV download. The code looked something like this:

```ruby
ruby_style/csv_from_row.rb
def csv_from_row(accumulator, row)
  result = ""
  until row.empty?
    entry = row.shift.to_s
    if /[,"]/.match?(entry)
      entry = entry.gsub(/"/, '""')
      result << '"' << entry << '"'
    else
      result << entry
    end
    result << "," unless row.empty?
  end
  accumulator << result << CRLF
end

result = ""
query.each_row { |row| csv_from_row(result, row) }

http.write(result)
```

When this code ran against moderate-size data sets, it performed fine. But at a certain input size, it suddenly slowed right down. The culprit? Garbage collection. The approach was generating thousands of intermediate strings and building one big result string, one line at a time. As the big string grew, it needed more space, and garbage collection was invoked, which necessitated scanning and removing all the intermediate strings.

The answer was simple and surprisingly effective. Rather than build the result string as it went along, the code was changed to store each CSV row as an element in an array. This meant that the intermediate lines were still referenced and hence were no longer garbage. It also meant that we were no longer building an ever-growing string that forced garbage collection. Thanks to duck typing, the change was trivial:

```
def csv_from_row(accumulator, row)
  # as before
end

result = []
query.each_row { |row| csv_from_row(result, row) }

http.write(result.join)
```

All that changed was that we passed an array into the csv_from_row method. Because it (implicitly) used duck typing, and the only message passed to the accumulator was <<, the csv_from_row method itself was not modified. It continued to append the data it generated to its accumulator parameter, not caring what type that parameter was. After the method returned its result, we joined all those individual lines into one big string. This one change reduced the time to run from more than three minutes to a few seconds.

Coding Like a Duck

If you want to write your programs using the duck-typing philosophy, you need to remember only one thing: an object's type is determined by what it can do, not by its class.

What does this mean in practice? At one level, it simply means that there's often little value explicitly checking for the class of an object.

For example, you may be writing a routine to add song information to a string. If you come from a C# or Java background, you may be tempted to write this:

```
def append_song(result, song)
  unless result.kind_of?(String)
    fail TypeError.new("String expected")
  end
  unless song.kind_of?(Song)
    fail TypeError.new("Song expected")
  end

  result << song.title << " (" << song.artist << ")"
end

result = ""
append_song(result, song)
```

Embrace Ruby's duck typing, and you'd write something far simpler:

```
def append_song(result, song)
  result << song.title << " (" << song.artist << ")"
end

result = ""
append_song(result, song)
```

You don't need to check the type of the arguments. If they support << (in the case of result) or title and artist (in the case of song), everything will just work. If they don't, your method will throw an exception anyway (just as it would've done if you'd checked the types). But without the check, your method is suddenly a lot more flexible. You could pass it an array, a string, a file, or any other object that appends using <<, and it would just work.

Now sometimes you may want more than this style of *laissez-faire* programming. You may have good reasons to check that a parameter can do what you need. Will you get thrown out of the duck typing club if you check the parameter against a class? No, you won't. The duck typing club doesn't check to see whether you're a member anyway…. But you may want to consider checking based on the object's capabilities, rather than its class:

```ruby
def append_song(result, song)
  unless result.respond_to?(:<<)
    raise TypeError.new("'result' needs `<<' capability")
  end
  unless song.respond_to?(:artist) && song.respond_to?(:title)
    raise TypeError.new("'song' needs 'artist' and 'title'")
  end
  result << song.title << " (" << song.artist << ")"
end

result = ""
append_song(result, song)
```

But before going down this path, make sure you're getting a real benefit—it's a lot of extra code to write and maintain.

Standard Protocols and Coercions

Although not technically part of the syntax of the language, the Ruby interpreter and standard library use various protocols to handle issues of type conversion that other languages would deal with using the type system. That is to say that the Ruby interpreter looks for certain standard method names and, if those names exist, uses the methods to convert an arbitrary class to a standard type.

Some objects have more than one natural representation. For example, you may be writing a class to represent Roman numbers (I, II, III, IV, V, and so on). This class wouldn't be implemented as a subclass of Integer because its objects are representations of numbers, not numbers in their own right. At the same time, they do have an integer-like quality. It would be nice to be able to use objects of our Roman number class wherever Ruby was expecting to see an integer.

To do this, Ruby has the concept of *conversion protocols*—an object may elect to have itself converted to an object of another class. Ruby has two different ways of looking at this kind of conversion.

An *explicit* conversion is triggered in the code deliberately by calling the conversion method. The intent here is to say that the original type isn't the same as the type being converted to, but that the method gives a reasonable representation of the data in the new type. By convention, explicit conversion methods have short names, like to_s for Strings, to_h for Hash, and to_i for Integer.

These conversion methods aren't particularly strict. If an object has any kind of decent representation as a string, for example, it'll probably have a to_s method. Our RomanNumeral class would probably implement to_s in order to return the string representation of a number ("VII", for instance).

An *implicit* conversion is triggered by the Ruby interpreter as part of using new objects in the same context where standard types are expected. This form of conversion function uses methods with longer names such as to_str and to_int (though there are some cases where shorter names are used for implicit conversions for historical reasons).

The implicit conversions are stricter. You implement them only if your object can naturally be used every place a string or an integer (or whatever the original type) could be used. For example, our Roman number objects have a clear representation as an integer and so should implement to_int. But when it comes to stringiness, we have to think a bit harder.

Roman numbers clearly have a string representation, but are they strings? Should we be able to use them wherever we can use a string itself? No, probably not. Logically, they're a representation of a number. You can represent them as strings, but they aren't plug-and-play-compatible with strings. For this reason, a Roman number won't implement to_str because it isn't really a string. Just to drive this home, Roman numerals can be converted to strings using to_s, but they aren't inherently strings, so they don't implement to_str.

To see how this works in practice, let's look at opening a file. The first parameter to File.new can be either an existing file descriptor (represented by an integer) or a filename to open. But Ruby doesn't simply look at the first parameter and check whether its type is Fixnum or String. Instead, it gives the object passed in the opportunity to represent itself as a number or a string. If it were written in Ruby, it may look something like this:

```ruby
class File
  def self.new(file, *args)
    if file.respond_to?(:to_int)
      IO.new(file.to_int, *args)
    else
      name = file.to_str
      # call operating system to open file 'name'
    end
  end
end
```

So, let's see what happens if we want to pass a file descriptor integer stored as a Roman number into File.new. Because our class implements to_int, the first respond_to? test will succeed. We'll pass an integer representation of our number to IO.new, and the file descriptor will be returned, all wrapped up in a new IO object.

A small number of strict conversion functions are built into the standard library:

to_ary → *Array*

Used when the interpreter needs a parameter to a method to be an array and when expanding parameters and assignments containing the *xyz syntax on the method definition side. In this case, puts does this conversion in its method definition.

```ruby
class OneTwo
  def to_ary
    [1, 2]
  end
end

ot = OneTwo.new
puts ot
```

produces:

```
1
2
```

to_a → *Array*

Used when the interpreter needs to convert an object into an array for parameter passing on the caller side of the method call or during parallel assignment.

```ruby
class OneTwo
  def to_a
    [1, 2]
  end
end

ot = OneTwo.new
a, b = *ot
puts "a = #{a}, b = #{b}"
printf("%d -- %d\n", *ot)
```

produces:

```
a = 1, b = 2
1 -- 2
```

to_enum → *Enumerator*

Converts an object (presumably a collection) to an enumerator. It's never called internally by the interpreter.

to_hash → *Hash*

Used when the interpreter expects to see Hash, as in when converting a ** in a method call.

to_int → *Integer*

Used when the interpreter expects to see an integer value (such as a file descriptor or as a parameter to Integer).

to_io → *IO*

Used when the interpreter is expecting I/O objects (for example, as parameters to the methods IO.reopen or IO.select).

to_open → *IO*

Called (if defined) on the first parameter to IO.open.

to_path → *String*

Called by the interpreter when it's looking for a filename (for example, by File.open).

to_proc → *Proc*

Used to convert an object prefixed with an ampersand in a method call.

```ruby
class OneTwo
  def to_proc
    proc { "one-two" }
  end
end
def silly
  yield
end
```

```
ot = OneTwo.new
silly(&ot) # => "one-two"
```

to_regexp → Regexp

Invoked by Regexp#try_convert to convert its argument to a regular expression.

to_str → String

Used pretty much any place the interpreter is looking for a String value. Except for string interpolation, which uses to_s.

```
class OneTwo
  def to_str
    "one-two"
  end
end
```

```
ot = OneTwo.new
puts("count: " + ot)
File.open(ot) rescue puts $!.message
```

produces:

```
count: one-two
No such file or directory @ rb_sysopen - one-two
```

to_sym → Symbol

Expresses the receiver as a symbol. This is used by the interpreter when compiling instruction sequences. It's rarely necessary in user code because the most common case, String to Symbol, is often handled in syntax as :"a weird symbol".

Note that Integer implements the to_int method, and String implements to_str. That way, you can call the strict conversion functions polymorphically:

```
# it doesn't matter if obj is a Fixnum or a
# Roman number, the conversion still succeeds
num = obj.to_int
```

Separately, the Kernel module defines a handful of methods that are available anywhere and act as general conversion methods, as listed in the table shown on page 366. These methods are distinctive in Ruby because they begin with capital letters. These methods are generally meant to be the definitive conversions to use when you're just using conversions, rather than defining them.

The Symbol#to_proc Trick

Ruby implements the to_proc method for objects of class Symbol. Say you want to convert an array of strings to uppercase. You could write this:

```
names = %w[ant bee cat]
result = names.map { |name| name.upcase }
```

That's fairly concise, right? Return a new array where each element is the corresponding element in the original, converted to uppercase. But you can instead write this:

```
names = %w[ant bee cat]
result = names.map(&:upcase)
```

Now that's concise, apply the upcase method to each element of names.

Method	Description
Array(obj)	Attempts to call to_ary on the argument (this means that if the argument is already an array, it's returned as-is). If the argument doesn't respond to to_ary, it calls to_a. If the argument responds to neither, the argument is returned as the element in a one-element array.
Complex(real, imag, ex: true)	If the argument is a string, it calls to_c on the string. Otherwise, it creates a complex number that is real + imag * i. If either argument is nil and ex is true, it raises a TypeError, if ex is false, then it returns nil.
Float(obj, ex: true)	If the obj is numeric, Ruby's numeric conversion is performed. Otherwise, to_f is called on the object. An invalid string will result in an ArgumentError, while a nil object will generate a TypeError. Again, if ex is false, nil is returned rather than throwing exceptions.
Hash(obj)	Calls obj.to_hash.
Integer(obj, base=0, ex: true)	If obj is numeric, Ruby's numeric conversions are performed. Other objects attempt to_int and then to_i. String behavior is slightly different than String#to_i, in that if base is 0, then base prefixes, like 0x, will be used to determine the base. Exception behavior is the same as Float.
Rational(num, den=1, ex: true)	If there's only a string argument, it calls to_r on the string. Otherwise, it returns num/den as a rational. Exception behavior is the same as Float.
String(obj)	Calls obj.to_str if it exists and then tries obj.to_s.

Table 9—Kernel module conversion methods

How does it work? It relies on Ruby's type coercions. Let's start at the top.

When you say names.map(&xxx), you're telling Ruby to pass the Proc object xxx to the map method as a block. If xxx isn't already a Proc object, Ruby tries to coerce it into one by sending it a to_proc message.

Now :upcase isn't a Proc object—it's a symbol. So when Ruby sees names.map(&:upcase), the first thing it does is try to convert the symbol :upcase into a Proc by calling to_proc. And, by an incredible coincidence, Ruby implements just such a method. If it was written in Ruby, it would look something like this:

```ruby
def to_proc
  proc { |obj, *args| obj.send(self, *args) }
end
```

This method creates a Proc, which, when called on an object, sends that object the symbol itself. So, when names.map(&:upcase) starts to iterate over the strings in names, it'll call the block, passing in the first name and invoking its upcase method.

It's an incredibly elegant use of coercion and of closures.

Numeric Coercion

In addition to implicit and explicit object conversion, Ruby has coercion logic specific to numeric types.

Here's the problem. When you write 1 + 2, Ruby knows to call the + on the object 1 (an Intger), passing it the Integer 2 as a parameter. But when you write 1 + 2.3, the same + method now receives a Float parameter. How can it know what to do (particularly because checking the classes of your parameters is against the spirit of duck typing)?

The answer lies in Ruby's coercion protocol, based on the method coerce. The basic operation of coerce is simple. It takes one argument and returns a two-element array with the argument first and the original receiver of coerce second. The coerce method guarantees that the two numbers in the array will have the same class and that they can be added, multiplied, compared, or whatever.

```
1.coerce(2)       # => [2, 1]
1.coerce(2.3)     # => [2.3, 1.0]
(4.5).coerce(2.3) # => [2.3, 4.5]
(4.5).coerce(2)   # => [2.0, 4.5]
```

The trick is that the coerce call happens in the reverse of the original arithmetic method—the right side of an arithmetic operation receives coerce with the left side of the operation as an argument to generate this array.

In other words, 1 + 2 is equivalent to the method call 1.+(2) and Ruby calls 2.coerce(1) to generate the array [1, 2] and perform the operation. This technique of calling a method on a parameter is called *double dispatch*, and it allows a method to change its behavior based not only on its class but also on the class of its parameter. In this case, we're letting the parameter decide exactly *what* classes of objects should get added, compared, or whatever.

Let's say that we're writing a new class that's intended to take part in arithmetic. To participate in coercion, we need to implement a coerce method. This takes some other kind of number as a parameter and returns an array containing two objects of the same class, whose values are equivalent to its parameter and itself.

For our Roman number class, it's fairly easy. Internally, each Roman number object holds its real value as an Integer in an instance variable, @value. The coerce method checks to see whether the class of its parameter is also an Integer. If so, it returns its parameter and its internal value. If not, it first converts both to floating point.

```
class Roman
  def initialize(value)
    @value = value
  end

  def coerce(other)
    if Integer === other
      [other, @value]
    else
      [Float(other), Float(@value)]
    end
  end

  # .. other Roman stuff
end

iv = Roman.new(4)
xi = Roman.new(11)

3 * iv    # => 12
1.2 * xi  # => 13.2
```

In the last two lines, the numeric left side of the argument calls coerce on the Roman numeral, receives the coerced array of values, and multiplies them.

Class Roman as implemented doesn't know how to do addition. You couldn't have written xi + 3 in the previous example because Roman doesn't have a + method. Let's go wild and implement addition for Roman numbers.

The whole class might look like this:

ducktyping/roman3.rb

```ruby
class Roman
  MAX_ROMAN = 4999

  attr_reader :value
  protected :value

  def initialize(value)
    if value <= 0 || value > MAX_ROMAN
      fail "Roman values must be > 0 and <= #{MAX_ROMAN}"
    end
    @value = value
  end

  def coerce(other)
    if Integer === other
      [other, @value]
    else
      [Float(other), Float(@value)]
    end
  end

  def +(other)
    if Roman === other
      other = other.value
    end
    if Integer === other && (other + @value) < MAX_ROMAN
      Roman.new(@value + other)
    else
      x, y = other.coerce(@value)
      x + y
    end
  end

  FACTORS = [["m", 1000], ["cm", 900], ["d", 500], ["cd", 400],
    ["c", 100], ["xc", 90], ["l", 50], ["xl", 40],
    ["x", 10], ["ix", 9], ["v", 5], ["iv", 4],
    ["i", 1]]

  def to_s
    value = @value
    roman = ""
    FACTORS.each do |code, factor|
      count, value = value.divmod(factor)
      roman << (code * count)
    end
    roman
  end
end
```

```
iv = Roman.new(4)
xi = Roman.new(11)

iv + 3          # => vii
iv + 3 + 4      # => xi
iv + 3.14159    # => 7.14159
xi + 4900       # => mmmmcmxi
xi + 4990       # => 5001
```

Finally, be careful with coerce—always try to coerce something into a more general type, or you may end up generating coercion loops. This is a situation where A tries to coerce something to B and B tries to coerce it back to A.

Walk the Walk, Talk the Talk

Duck typing can generate controversy. Every now and then, a thread flares on social media or someone blogs for or against the concept. Many of the contributors to these discussions have some fairly extreme positions.

Ultimately, though, duck typing isn't a set of rules; it's just a style of programming. Design your programs to balance paranoia and flexibility. If you feel the need to constrain the types of objects that the users of a method pass in, ask yourself why. Try to determine what could go wrong if you were expecting a String and instead get an Array. Sometimes, the difference is crucially important. Often, though, it isn't. Try erring on the more permissive side for a while and see whether bad things happen. If not, perhaps duck typing isn't just for the birds.

What's Next

In this chapter, we talked about Ruby style in terms of the decisions you make both when writing individual lines and also when writing methods and classes.

But we've only talked about part of Ruby's dynamic toolkit. Ruby has a rich set of options that make metaprogramming easier. These are often referred to as "magic," so let's take a look behind the curtain and see how the magic is done.

## CHAPTER 22

The Ruby Object Model and Metaprogramming

The Jacquard loom, invented more than 200 years ago, was the first device controlled by punched cards—rows of holes in each card were used to control the pattern woven into the cloth. But imagine if instead of churning out fabric, the loom could punch more cards, and those cards could be fed back into the mechanism. The machine could be used to create new programming that it could then execute. And that would be metaprogramming—writing code that writes code.

Programming is all about building layers of abstractions. As you solve problems, you're building bridges from the unrelenting and mechanical world of silicon to the more ambiguous and fluid world we inhabit. Some programming languages—such as C—are close to the machine. The distance from C code to the application domain can be large. Other languages—Ruby, perhaps—provide higher-level abstractions and hence let you start coding closer to the target domain. For this reason, most people consider a higher-level language to be a better starting place for application development (although they'll argue about the choice of language).

But when you metaprogram, you are no longer limited to the set of abstractions built into your programming language. Instead, you create new abstractions that are integrated into the host language. In effect, you're creating a new, domain-specific programming language—one that lets you express the concepts you need to solve your particular problem. Metaprogramming can be an excellent way to manage complex problems where the structure of the underlying data drives the structure of the code.

Ruby makes metaprogramming easy. As a result, Ruby programmers will often use metaprogramming techniques to simplify their code. This chapter shows how they do it. It isn't intended to be an exhaustive survey of metaprogramming techniques. Instead, we'll look at the underlying Ruby object model and structures that make metaprogramming possible. From there, you'll be able to invent your own metaprogramming idioms.

Understanding Objects and Classes

Classes and objects are central to Ruby, but at first sight, they can be confusing. It seems like there are a lot of concepts: classes, objects, class objects, instance methods, class methods, singleton classes, and virtual classes. In reality, all these Ruby constructs are part of the same underlying class and object structure.

Internally, a Ruby object has three components: a set of flags, some instance variables, and an associated class. A Ruby class contains all the things an object has plus a set of method definitions and a reference to a superclass (which is itself another class). A Ruby class is itself an instance of the class Class. Let's look at how that structure lends itself to metaprogramming in Ruby.

Method Calling and self

Ruby has a concept of the *current object*. The current object is referenced by the built-in, read-only variable self. The first time that Noel heard Dave Thomas speak in public, the topic was Ruby metaprogramming and he said "understanding *self* is the key to Ruby. Also the key to life." Words to live by.

The value self has two significant roles in a running Ruby program. First, self controls how Ruby finds instance variables. We already said that every object carries around a set of instance variables. When you access an instance variable using the @<varname> syntax, Ruby looks for that variable in the self object, as defined in the current context. In this section and the next, we'll show how the value of self changes when you call methods or define classes and modules.

Second, self plays a vital role in method calling. In Ruby, each method call is a message passed to some object. This object is called the *receiver* of the call. When you make a call such as items.size, the object on the left side of the dot—here referenced by the variable items—is the receiver and size is the method to invoke.

Often, you'll see a method call with no explicit receiver, such as puts "hi". In this case, Ruby uses the current object, self, as the receiver. It goes to self's class and looks up the method (in this case, puts). If it can't find the method in the class, it looks in the class's superclass and then in that class's superclass, stopping when it runs out of superclasses (which will happen after it has looked in BasicObject). If it can't find the method in the object's class hierarchy, Ruby looks for a method called method_missing on the original receiver, starting back at the class of self and then looking up the superclass chain. (In the case of puts, Ruby will find the method defined in the Kernel module that's included in Object.)

When you make a method call with an explicit receiver (for example, invoking items.size), the process is similar. The only change—but a vitally important one—is that the value of self is changed for the duration of the call. Before starting the method lookup process, Ruby sets self to the explicit receiver (the object referenced by items in this case). Then, after the call returns, Ruby restores self to the value it had before the call.

Let's see how this works in practice. Here's a simple program:

```ruby
class Test
  def one
    @var = 99
    two
  end

  def two
    puts @var
  end
end
```

```
t = Test.new
t.one
```

produces:

```
99
```

The call to Test.new on the second-to-last line creates a new object of class Test, assigning that object to the variable t. Then, on the next line, we call the method t.one. To execute this call, Ruby sets self to t and then looks in t's class for the method one. Ruby finds the method defined in the class and calls it.

Inside the method, we set the instance variable @var to 99. This instance variable will be associated with the current object. What is that object? Since the call to t.one sets self to t, within that call of the one method, self will be that particular instance of class Test.

On the next line, the method one calls the method two. Because there's no explicit receiver, self isn't changed. When Ruby looks for the method two, it looks in Test, the class of t.

The method two references an instance variable @var. Again, Ruby looks for this variable in the current object and finds the same variable that was set by the method one.

The call to puts inside the two method works the same way. Again, because there's no explicit receiver, self will be unchanged. Ruby looks for the puts method in the class of the current object but can't find it. It then looks in Test's superclass, class Object. Again, it doesn't find puts. But Object mixes in the module Kernel. We'll talk more about this later. For now, we can say that mixed-in modules act as if they were superclasses. The Kernel module *does* define puts, so the method is found and executed.

After two and one return, Ruby resets self to the value it had before the original call to t.one. The code is at the top level. The top-level self is an object called main, which is placed there by the Ruby runtime.

This explanation may seem labored, but understanding it is an important part of mastering metaprogramming in Ruby.

Class Definitions and self

We've seen that calling a method with an explicit receiver changes self. Perhaps surprisingly, self is also changed inside a class or module definition, but outside all the method definitions. This is a consequence of the fact that class definitions are actually executable code in Ruby—if we can execute code, we need to have a current object. A simple test shows what this object is:

```
puts "Before the class definition, self = #{self}\n"
class Test
  puts "In the definition of class Test, self = #{self}"
  puts "Class of self = #{self.class}\n"
end
puts "After the class definition, self = #{self}"
```

produces:

```
Before the class definition, self = main
In the definition of class Test, self = Test
Class of self = Class
After the class definition, self = main
```

Outside the class definition, self is set to an object called main, which is what Ruby uses as the implicit top-level object. It's also the object that holds on to method definitions that happen outside of a class definition.

Inside a class or module definition, self is set to the object of the class or module being defined. This means that instance variables set inside a class or module definition will be available to class or module methods (because self will be the same when the variables are defined and when the methods execute):

```ruby
class Test
  @var = 99
  def self.value_of_var
    @var
  end
end

Test.value_of_var # => 99
```

The fact that self is set to the class during a class definition turns out to be a dramatically elegant decision, but to see why, we'll first need to have a look at singleton methods.

Defining Singleton Methods

Ruby lets you define methods that are specific to a particular object. These are called *singleton methods*.

Here's a simple string object and a regular, non-singleton method call:

```ruby
animal = "cat"
puts animal.upcase
```

produces:

```
CAT
```

This call results in the object structure shown in the following illustration:

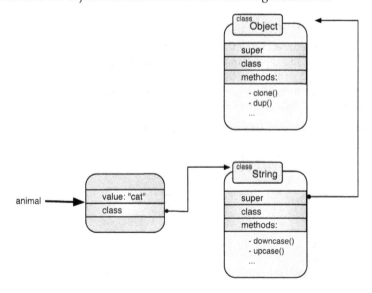

The animal variable points to an object containing (among other things) the value of the string ("cat") and a pointer to the object's class, String.

When we call animal.upcase, Ruby checks the object referenced by the animal variable and then looks up the method upcase in the class object referenced from the animal object. Our animal is a string and so all the methods of class String are available.

Now let's make it more interesting. We'll define a singleton method on the string referenced by animal. We've seen this syntax before, we use a method name that includes a reference to a specific object:

```ruby
animal = "cat"
def animal.speak
  puts "The #{self} says miaow"
end

animal.speak
puts animal.upcase
```

produces:

```
The cat says miaow
CAT
```

The call to animal.speak is handled similar to the way animal.upcase was invoked earlier. Ruby sets self to the string object "cat", which is referenced by animal, and then looks for a method called speak in that object's class. Surprisingly, it finds it. This is initially surprising because the class of "cat" is String, and String doesn't have a speak method. But the specific object called animal has a speak method that we've defined for that object and that object only.

So, does Ruby have some kind of special-case magic for these methods that are defined on individual objects?

Not exactly.

When we defined animal.speak, the singleton method for the "cat" object, Ruby created a new anonymous class and placed the speak method in that class. This anonymous class goes by a couple of different names, but you'll most likely see it called a *singleton class* (it's sometimes called an *eigenclass*). We prefer the former name because it ties in to the idea of singleton methods.

Every object in Ruby has the potential of having its own singleton class. When you define a singleton class, Ruby creates that anonymous class and makes it the singleton class of that object.

You can access that singleton class via the singleton_class method, and you can get a list of methods defined there with singleton_methods.

```ruby
animal = "cat"
def animal.speak
  puts "The #{self} says miaow"
end

animal.speak
puts animal.class
puts animal.singleton_class
puts animal.singleton_methods
```

produces:

```
The cat says miaow
String
#<Class:#<String:0x0000000103209258>>
speak
```

If an object has a singleton class, that's the first place Ruby looks for object lookup. It's as if Ruby makes String (which was the original class of "cat") the superclass of the singleton class. The picture looks like this:

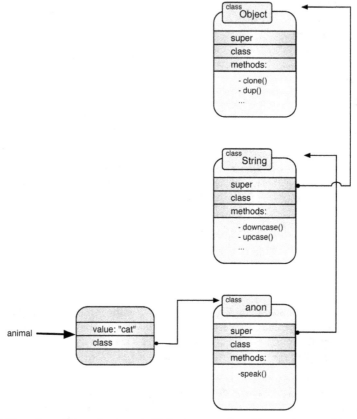

Now let's follow the call to animal.speak. Ruby goes to the object referenced by animal and then looks in its singleton class class for the method speak. The singleton class of the animal object is the newly created singleton class, and it contains the method we need.

What happens if we instead call animal.upcase? The processing starts the same way: Ruby looks for the method upcase in the singleton class but fails to find it there. It then follows the normal processing rules and starts looking up the chain of superclasses. The superclass of the singleton is String, and Ruby finds the upcase method there. Notice that no special-case processing is here—Ruby method calls always work up the object chain in the same way.

Singletons and Classes

Earlier, we said that inside a class definition, self is set to the class object being defined. It turns out that this is the basis for one of the more elegant aspects of Ruby's object model.

Recall that we can define class methods in Ruby using either the def self.xxx or (more rarely) def ClassName.xxx form:

```ruby
class Dave
  def self.class_method_one
    puts "Class method one"
  end
  def Dave.class_method_two
    puts "Class method two"
  end
end

Dave.class_method_one
Dave.class_method_two
```

produces:

```
Class method one
Class method two
```

Now we can explain why the two forms are identical: inside the class definition, self is set to the class object Dave.

But now that we've looked at singleton methods, we also know that, in reality, no such thing as a class method exists in Ruby. Both of the previous definitions define singleton methods on the class object. As with all other singleton methods, we can then call them via the object (in this case, the class Dave).

Before we created the two singleton methods in class Dave, the class pointer in the class object pointed to class Class. (That's a confusing sentence. Another way of saying it is "Dave is a class, so the class of Dave is class Class," but that's pretty confusing, too.) The situation looks like this:

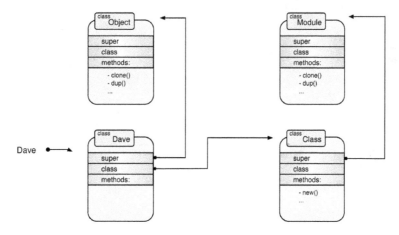

The object diagram for class Dave after the methods are defined looks like this:

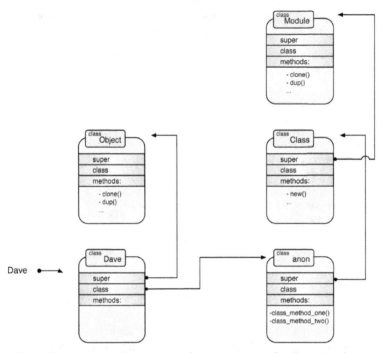

Do you see how the singleton class is created, just as it was for the animal example? The class is inserted as the singleton class of the class Dave, and the original class of Dave is made this new singleton class's parent.

We can now tie together the two uses of self, the current object. We talked about how instance variables are looked up in self, and we talked about how singleton methods defined on self become class methods. Let's use these facts to access instance variables for class objects:

```ruby
class Test
  @var = 99

  def self.var
    @var
  end

  def self.var=(value)
    @var = value
  end
end

puts "Original value = #{Test.var}"
Test.var = "cat"
puts "New value = #{Test.var}"
```

produces:

```
Original value = 99
New value = cat
```

Newcomers to Ruby commonly try to set instance variables inline in the class definition (as we did with @var in the previous code) and then attempt to access these variables from instance methods. As the code illustrates, this won't work because instance variables are associated with self in their current context. In the context of the instance variables defined in the class body, self is the class, and therefore instance variables defined in the class body outside of methods are associated with the class object, not with instances of the class.

Another Way to Access the Singleton Class

We've seen how you can create methods in an object's singleton class by adding the object reference to the method definition using something like def animal.speak.

You can also access the singleton class using Ruby's class << an_object notation:

```ruby
animal = "dog"
class << animal
  def speak
    puts "The #{self} says WOOF!"
  end
end

animal.speak
```

produces:

```
The dog says WOOF!
```

Inside this kind of class definition, self is set to the singleton class for the given object (animal in this case). Because class definitions return the value of the last statement executed in the class body, we can use this fact to get the singleton class object:

```ruby
animal = "dog"
def animal.speak
  puts "The #{self} says WOOF!"
end

singleton = class << animal
  def lie
    puts "The #{self} lies down"
  end
  self     # << return singleton class object
end

animal.speak
animal.lie
puts "Singleton class object is #{singleton}"
puts "It defines methods #{singleton.instance_methods - animal.methods}"
puts "You can also access it as #{animal.singleton_class}"
puts "And the list of methods as #{animal.singleton_methods}"
```

produces:

```
The dog says WOOF!
The dog lies down
Singleton class object is #<Class:#<String:0x0000000100337628>>
It defines methods []
You can also access it as #<Class:#<String:0x0000000100337628>>
And the list of methods as [:lie, :speak]
```

Pay attention to the notation that Ruby uses to denote a singleton class: #<Class:#<String:...>>.

Ruby goes to some trouble to stop you from using singleton classes outside the context of their original object. For example, you can't create a new instance of a singleton class:

```ruby
singleton = class << "cat"; self; end
singleton.new
```

produces:

```
        from prog.rb:2:in `<main>'
prog.rb:2:in `new': can't create instance of singleton class (TypeError)
```

Let's tie together what we know about instance variables, self, and singleton classes. We could write class-level accessor methods to let us get and set the value of an instance variable defined in a class object. Ruby already has attr_accessor, which defines getter and setter methods for instances. Normally, these are defined as instance methods and hence will access values stored in instances of a class. To make them work with class-level instance variables, we have to invoke attr_accessor in the singleton class:

```ruby
class Test
  @var = 99

  class << self
    attr_accessor :var
  end
end

puts "Original value = #{Test.var}"
Test.var = "cat"
puts "New value = #{Test.var}"
```

produces:

```
Original value = 99
New value = cat
```

Inheritance and Visibility

Method definition and class inheritance have a wrinkle, but it's fairly obscure. Within a class definition, you can change the visibility of a method in an ancestor class. For example, you can do something like this:

```ruby
class Base
  def a_method
    puts "Got here"
  end
  private :a_method
end

class MakeItPublic < Base
  public :a_method
end

class KeepItPrivate < Base
end
```

In this example, you could invoke a_method in instances of class MakeItPublic, but not via instances of Base or KeepItPrivate.

So, how does Ruby pull off this feat of having one method with two different visibilities? Simply put, it cheats.

If a subclass changes the visibility of a method in a parent, Ruby effectively inserts a hidden proxy method in the subclass that invokes the original method using super. It then sets the visibility of that proxy to whatever you requested.

For example, you might have this code:

```ruby
class MakeItPublic < Base
  public :a_method
end
```

Which is effectively the same as this:

```ruby
class MakeItPublic < Base
  def a_method(*)
    super
  end
  public :a_method
end
```

The call to super can access the parent's method regardless of its visibility, so the rewrite allows the subclass to override its parent's visibility rules.

Modules and Mixins

As we saw in Mixins, on page 107, when you include a module into a Ruby class, the instance methods in that module become available as instance methods of the class, like this:

```ruby
module Logger
  def log(msg)
    STDERR.puts Time.now.strftime("%H:%M:%S: ") + "#{self} (#{msg})"
  end
end

class Song
  include Logger
end

s = Song.new
s.log("created")
```

produces:

```
17:16:19: #<Song:0x0000000104717708> (created)
```

Ruby implements include very simply. The module you include is added as an ancestor of the class being defined. It's as if the module is the parent of the class that it's mixed into. And that would be the end of the description except for one small wrinkle. Because the module is injected into the chain of superclasses, it must itself hold a link to the original parent class. If it didn't, there'd be no way of traversing the superclass chain to look up methods. But you can mix the same module into many different classes, and those classes could potentially have totally different superclass chains. If there were just one module object that we mixed into all these classes, there'd be no way of keeping track of the different superclasses for each.

To get around this, Ruby uses a clever trick. When you include a module in class Example, Ruby constructs a new class object, makes it the superclass of Example, and then sets the superclass of the new class to be the original superclass of Example. It then references the module's methods from this new class object in such a way that when you look a method up in this class, it actually looks it up in the module, as shown here:

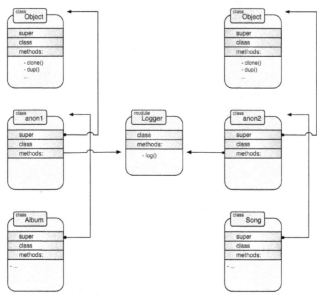

A nice side effect of this arrangement is that if you change a module after including it in a class, those changes are reflected in the class (and the class's objects). In this way, modules behave just like classes:

```ruby
module Mod
  def greeting
    "Hello"
  end
end

class Example
  include Mod
end

ex = Example.new
puts "Before change, greeting is #{ex.greeting}"

module Mod
  def greeting
    "Hi"
  end
end

puts "After change, greeting is #{ex.greeting}"
```

produces:

```
Before change, greeting is Hello
After change, greeting is Hi
```

If a module itself includes other modules, a chain of proxy classes will be added to any class that includes that module—one proxy for each module that's directly or indirectly included.

Finally, Ruby will include a particular module only once in an inheritance chain. Including a module that's already included by one of your superclasses has no effect.

Using prepend

Ruby enables you to place a module at a different point in the method lookup chain using the prepend method. Logically, prepend behaves just like include, but the methods in the prepended module take precedence over those in the host class. Ruby pulls off this magic by inserting a dummy class in place of the original host class. Actually, it inserts the dummy class above the original class, moves the methods from the original to the copy. and then inserts the prepended module between the two.

If a method inside a prepended module has the same name as the one in the original class, it'll be invoked instead of the original. The prepended method can then call the original using super:

```ruby
module VanityPuts
  def puts(*args)
    args.each do |arg|
      super("Dave says: #{arg}")
    end
  end
end

class Object
  prepend VanityPuts
end

puts "Hello and", "goodbye"
```

produces:

```
Dave says: Hello and
Dave says: goodbye
```

But there's a problem—the change we just made to class Object is global. We'll see how to manage that shortly when we look at refinements.

Using extend

The include method effectively adds a module as a superclass of self. This method is used inside a class definition to make the instance methods in the module available to instances of the class.

However, it's sometimes useful to add the instance methods directly to a particular object and not to its class. For example, you'd want to do this to add methods directly to a class object that you want to be treated like class methods. You do this using Module#extend. Here's an example:

```ruby
module Humor
  def tickle
    "#{self} says hee, hee!"
  end
end
```

```
obj = "Grouchy"
obj.extend(Humor)
obj.tickle # => "Grouchy says hee, hee!"
```

Stop for a second to think about how this might be implemented.

When Ruby executes obj.tickle in this code example, it does the usual trick of looking in the class of obj for a method called tickle. For extend to work, it has to add the Humor module's instance methods into the superclass chain for the class of obj. Just as with the singleton method definitions, Ruby creates a singleton class for obj and then includes the module Humor in that class. To prove this is all that happens, here's the C implementation of extend in the current Ruby interpreter:

```
void
rb_extend_object(VALUE obj, VALUE module)
{
    rb_include_module(rb_singleton_class(obj), module);
}
```

There is an interesting trick with extend. If you use it within a class definition, the module's methods become class methods. This is because calling extend is equivalent to self.extend, so the methods are added to self, which in a class definition is the class itself.

Here's an example of adding a module's methods at the class level:

```
module Humor
  def tickle
    "#{self} says hee, hee!"
  end
end

class Grouchy
  extend Humor
end

Grouchy.tickle # => "Grouchy says hee, hee!"
```

Later, in Class Methods and Modules, on page 390, we'll see how to use extend to add macro-style methods to a class.

Using Refinements

We previously looked at applying a change to a built-in class by defining the altered version of a method in a module and then prepending that module in the class. When we subsequently call the method on instances of the class, it finds the version in the module first. We've also seen that Ruby allows you to reopen an existing class or module and add new methods to it. When we subsequently use instances of the class, the new methods exist along with the ones that were previously defined.

These techniques are time-honored, and frameworks such as Ruby on Rails rely on them. But they come with a price. Any changes we make with prepend and monkey patches are global to our running application. They apply not just to the code we wrote for our application but also to the code in all the libraries and gems we use while the application is running, too.

It's possible that a change that made our code easier to write breaks someone else's library code that we rely on. This is clearly a problem in theory. Does it happen in practice? Actually, surprisingly rarely. But you can never be sure that things will quite work as you expect.

Even if you don't override these classes yourself, it's possible you're using two separate libraries whose patches to third-party classes clash.

Ruby has a feature called *refinements*. They allow you to make these changes locally without affecting code outside the file you're writing. The goal of using refinements is to continue to allow you to make changes to existing classes, but to only allow those changes to be in effect when you explicitly say that they are. Not only are the changes no longer global, but when an added method is used in a file, an explicit statement says where the added method is coming from. This means a reader of the code has a better chance of finding the source more easily.

Now, before going any further, here's the mandatory warning. Refinements have been a part of Ruby since 2.0, but their actual uptake has been minor. It's unusual to see refinements in the wild. Even though it seems they solve a problem in theory, not many teams seem to have found them to solve a problem in fact.

A refinement is a way of packaging a set of changes to one or more classes. These refinements are defined within a module. You can then elect to use this module with the refinements within a source file, in which case the change will apply to the source in that module past the point where the refinement is used. However, code outside this file isn't affected. Alternatively, you can elect to use the module with refinements inside a module or class, in which case the refinement applies inside that module or class, but not outside of it.

Let's make this concrete. Here's a vanity version of puts rewritten using refinements:

metaprogramming/vanity_puts.rb
```
module VanityPuts
  refine Object do
    private def puts(*args)
      args.each do |arg|
        Kernel.puts("Dave says: #{arg}")
      end
    end
  end
end
```

The refinement is contained in the module VanityPuts. The line refine Object do starts the definition. What's happening here is we're calling the method Module#refine, and the receiver is the VanityPuts module. The refine method takes an argument, which is a class or module and a block. Within the block, you define the methods that you'd like to update in that class. At this point, no change is made to the underlying class. You have defined a method, but haven't yet told Ruby to use it.

That's what the using method does:

metaprogramming/use_in_class.rb
```
require_relative "vanity_puts"

class DavesStuff
  using VanityPuts

  def greet(msg)
    puts msg
  end
end

DavesStuff.new.greet("in DavesStuff")
```

produces:

```
Dave says: in DavesStuff
```

You give it a module containing one or more refinements, and it marks the refined objects to say "for the rest of the scope of this method, when you make a call to an instance of Object, first check to see if the method can be found in the refinement. If so, invoke it, otherwise invoke the original."

The basic scoping rule is that a refinement is activated in a source file by calling using. If using is called inside a module or class, the refinement is in effect for the duration of that definition.

You can also invoke using at the top level of a file, in which case for the rest of that source file, the methods that are defined in that refinement are active inside any classes or methods yet to be defined in the source file:

metaprogramming/use_in_file.rb
```ruby
require_relative "vanity_puts"
using VanityPuts
puts "Hello", "world"
```

produces:

```
Dave says: Hello
Dave says: world
```

Let's step it up a notch. We'll define three source files.

Here's one that contains a refinement definition:

metaprogramming/ref1/vanity_refinement.rb
```ruby
module VanityPuts
  refine Object do
    private def puts(*args)
      args.each do |arg|
        Kernel.puts("Dave says: #{arg}")
      end
    end
  end
end
```

And here's a file that uses this refinement:

metaprogramming/ref1/file_using_refinement.rb
```ruby
class VanityShouter
  using VanityPuts

  def shout(msg)
    puts(msg.upcase)
  end
end

VanityShouter.new.shout("I'm here!")
```

Finally, let's run them from a third file:

metaprogramming/ref1/main_program.rb
```ruby
require_relative "vanity_refinement"

puts "About to require file using refinement"
require_relative "file_using_refinement"
```

```
puts "Back from require"
```

```
VanityShouter.new.shout("finished")
```

produces:

```
About to require file using refinement
Dave says: I'M HERE!
Back from require
Dave says: FINISHED
```

Notice how the puts calls in the main program are unadorned, but the calls in the file that uses the refinement have the vanity prefix.

Designing with Refinements

In general, refinements can be used any place you'd want to extend or monkey-patch a third-party tool. There are two main use cases.

The first is the case where a developer wants to make changes to a third-party class for the developer's own use. For example, Rake, which issues a lot of calls to run external programs using the system method, might want to modify the built-in version of system so that it logs errors differently. But it doesn't want that logging to apply to other calls to system that aren't part of Rake. In this case, the code could use the refinement locally within its own source files. The refinement would be an implementation detail, hidden from users of the code.

The second use case is where a library writer offers the refinement as part of the external interface. For example, the Rails Active Support gem defines methods such as hours, minutes, and ago on numbers, allowing you to write 3.days.ago. Right now, those changes to numbers are global. But, using refinements, the Rails team could code the new methods, but not add them in to any system classes. Instead, their API would document how to add them for yourself into just those source files that use them. They might tell you to write this in any source file that needs to use them:

```
using Rails::Extensions::Durations
```

There are many more potential use cases. And the two we've mentioned aren't mutually exclusive. The Rails framework, for example, is likely to want to use these duration-related methods itself, as well as making them available via a documented refinement.

Metaprogramming Class-Level Macros

If you've used Ruby for any time at all, you're likely to have used attr_accessor, the method that defines reader and writer methods for instance variables:

```
class Song
  attr_accessor :duration
end
```

If you've written a Ruby on Rails application, you've probably used has_many:

```
class Album < ActiveRecord::Base
  has_many :tracks
end
```

These are both examples of class-level methods that generate code behind the scenes. Because of the way they expand into something bigger, folks sometimes call these kinds of methods *macros*.

Let's create a trivial example and then build it up into something realistic. We'll start by implementing a simple method that adds logging capabilities to instances of a class. We previously did this using a module. This time we'll do it using a class-level method. Here's the first iteration:

metaprogramming/logging_0.rb
```ruby
class Example
  def self.add_logging
    def log(msg)
      $stderr.puts("#{Time.now.strftime("%H:%M:%S: ")} #{self} (#{msg})")
    end
  end

  add_logging
end

ex = Example.new
ex.log("hello")
```

produces:
```
17:16:20:  #<Example:0x0000000104e77610> (hello)
```

This is a silly piece of code because it includes a very general concern—logging—in a very specific class. But bear with us—it'll get better. And we can still learn from it. First, notice that add_logging is a class method—it's defined in the class object's singleton class. That means we can call it later in the class definition without an explicit receiver because self is set to the class object inside a class definition.

Then, notice that the add_logging method contains a nested method definition. This inner definition will get executed only when we call the add_logging method. The result is that log will be defined as an instance method of class Example.

Let's take one more step. We can define the add_logging method in one class and then use it in a subclass. This works because the singleton class hierarchy parallels the regular class hierarchy. As a result, class methods in a parent class are also available in the child class, as the following example shows:

metaprogramming/logging_1.rb
```ruby
class Logger
  def self.add_logging
    def log(msg)
      $stderr.puts("#{Time.now.strftime("%H:%M:%S: ")} #{self} (#{msg})")
    end
  end
end

class Example < Logger
  add_logging
end

ex = Example.new
puts ex.log("hello")
```

produces:

```
17:16:20:  #<Example:0x00000001049b9718> (hello)
```

Think back to the two examples at the beginning of this section. Both work in the same way as our add_logging example. attr_accessor is an instance method defined in class Module and so is available in all module and class definitions. has_many is a class method defined in the Base class within the Rails ActiveRecord module and so is available to all classes that subclass ActiveRecord::Base.

This example is still not particularly compelling. It would still be easier to add the log method directly as an instance method of our Logger class. But what happens if we want to construct a different version of the log method for each class that uses it? For example, let's add the capability to add a short class-specific identifying string to the start of each log message. We want to be able to say something like this:

```ruby
class Song < Logger
  add_logging "Song"
end

class Album < Logger
  add_logging "CD"
end
```

To do this, let's define the log method on the fly. We can no longer use a straightforward def…end-style definition—doing so won't allow us to dynamically determine the method behavior on the fly. Instead, we'll use one of the cornerstones of Ruby metaprogramming, define_method. This takes the name of a method and a block, defining a method with the given name and with the block as the method body. Any arguments in the block definition become parameters to the method being defined:

```ruby
metaprogramming/logging_2.rb
class Logger
  def self.add_logging(id_string)
    define_method(:log) do |msg|
      now = Time.now.strftime("%H:%M:%S")
      $stderr.puts("#{now}-#{id_string}: #{self} (#{msg})")
    end
  end
end

class Song < Logger
  add_logging "Tune"
end

class Album < Logger
  add_logging "CD"
end

song = Song.new
puts song.log("rock on")
```

produces:

```
17:16:20-Tune: #<Song:0x00000001006f8e88> (rock on)
```

There's an important subtlety in this code. The body of the log method contains this line:

```ruby
$stderr.puts("#{now}-#{id_string}: #{self} (#{msg})")
```

The value now is a local variable, and msg is the parameter to the block. But id_string is the parameter to the enclosing add_logging method. It's accessible inside the block because block definitions create closures, allowing the context in which the block is defined to be carried forward and used when the block is used. In this case, we're taking a value from a class-level method and using it in an instance method we're defining. This is a common pattern when creating these kinds of class-level macros.

In addition to passing parameters from the class method into the body of the method being defined, we can also use the parameter to dynamically determine the name of the method or methods to create. Here's an example that creates a new kind of attr_accessor that logs all assignments to a given instance variable:

```
metaprogramming/accessor_1.rb
class AttrLogger
  def self.attr_logger(name)
    attr_reader name

    define_method(:"#{name}=") do |val|
      puts "Assigning #{val.inspect} to #{name}"
      instance_variable_set("@#{name}", val)
    end
  end
end

class Example < AttrLogger
  attr_logger :value
end

ex = Example.new
ex.value = 123
puts "Value is #{ex.value}"
ex.value = "cat"
puts "Value is now #{ex.value}"
```

produces:

```
Assigning 123 to value
Value is 123
Assigning "cat" to value
Value is now cat
```

Again, we use the fact that the block defining the method body is a closure, accessing the name of the attribute in the log message string. Notice we also make use of the fact that attr_reader is simply a class method—we can call it inside our class method to define the reader method for our attribute. There's another bit of metaprogramming—we use instance_variable_set to set the value of an instance variable. The argument to instance_variable_set is possibly unexpected—it's a string starting with @ containing the name of the variable you want to set. There's a corresponding instance_variable_get method that fetches the value of a named instance variable.

Class Methods and Modules

You can define class methods in one class and then use them in subclasses of that class. But it's often inappropriate to use subclassing for the kinds of metaprogramming we have been showing because either we already have to subclass some other class or our design aesthetic rebels against making Song a subclass of Logger.

In these cases, you can use a module to hold your metaprogramming implementation. As we've seen, using extend inside a class definition will add the methods in a module as class methods to the class being defined:

```
metaprogramming/accessor_2.rb
module AttrLogger
  def attr_logger(name)
    attr_reader name

    define_method("#{name}=") do |val|
      puts "Assigning #{val.inspect} to #{name}"
      instance_variable_set("@#{name}", val)
    end
  end
end

class Example
  extend AttrLogger
  attr_logger :value
end

ex = Example.new
ex.value = 123
puts "Value is #{ex.value}"
ex.value = "cat"
puts "Value is now #{ex.value}"
```

produces:

```
Assigning 123 to value
Value is 123
Assigning "cat" to value
Value is now cat
```

Things get a little trickier if you want to add both class methods and instance methods into the class being defined. Here's one technique that's used extensively in the implementation of Rails. This technique makes use of a Ruby hook method, included, which is called automatically by Ruby when you include a module into a class. It is passed the class object of the class being defined:

```
metaprogramming/accessor_3.rb
module GeneralLogger
  # Instance method to be added to any class that includes us
  def log(msg)
    puts Time.now.strftime("%H:%M: ") + msg
  end

  # module containing class methods to be added
  module ClassMethods
    def attr_logger(name)
      attr_reader name

      define_method("#{name}=") do |val|
        log "Assigning #{val.inspect} to #{name}"
        instance_variable_set("@#{name}", val)
      end
    end
  end
```

```ruby
  # extend host class with class methods when we're included
  def self.included(host_class)
    host_class.extend(ClassMethods)
  end
end

class Example
  include GeneralLogger

  attr_logger :value
end

ex = Example.new
ex.log("New example created")
ex.value = 123
puts "Value is #{ex.value}"
ex.value = "cat"
puts "Value is #{ex.value}"
```

produces:

```
17:16: New example created
17:16: Assigning 123 to value
Value is 123
17:16: Assigning "cat" to value
Value is cat
```

Notice how the included callback is used to extend the host class with the methods defined in the inner module ClassMethods. Ruby on Rails uses this pattern, where a module provides both class and instance methods, extensively. The Rails name for this pattern is a *Concern*. The Rails Concern implementation also provides shortcut methods so that you don't need to add the included hook yourself.

Now, as an exercise, try walking through the previous example in your head. For each line of code, work out the value of self. Master this, and you've pretty much mastered this style of metaprogramming in Ruby.

Struct and Subclassing Expressions

In Ruby, we've seen that that you can create a superclass relationship with <:

```ruby
class Parent
  ...
end

class Child < Parent
  ...
end
```

What you might not know is that the thing to the right of the < needn't be just a class name; it can be any expression that returns a class object. In this code example, we have the constant Parent. A constant is a simple form of expression, and in this case, the constant Parent holds the class object of the first class we defined.

Ruby comes with a class called Struct, which allows you to define classes that contain simple data attributes. For example, you could write this:

```ruby
Person = Struct.new(:name, :address, :likes)
```

```
dave = Person.new('Dave', 'TX')
dave.likes = "Programming Languages"
puts dave
```

produces:

```
#<struct Person name="Dave", address="TX", likes="Programming Languages">
```

The return value from Struct.new(...) is a class object. By assigning it to the constant Person, we can thereafter use Person as if it were any other class.

But say we wanted to change the to_s method of our structure. We could do it by opening up the class and writing the following method:

```
Person = Struct.new(:name, :address, :likes)
class Person
  def to_s
    "#{self.name} lives in #{self.address} and likes #{self.likes}"
  end
end
```

We can do this more elegantly (although at the cost of an additional class object) by writing this:

```
class Person < Struct.new(:name, :address, :likes)
  def to_s
    "#{self.name} lives in #{self.address} and likes #{self.likes}"
  end
end

dave = Person.new('Dave', 'Texas')
dave.likes = "Programming Languages"
puts dave
```

produces:

```
Dave lives in Texas and likes Programming Languages
```

This mechanism is useful enough that Struct provides a shortcut by taking a block in which you can define your own methods on the Struct, like this:

```
Person = Struct.new(:name, :address, :likes) do
  def to_s
    "#{self.name} lives in #{self.address} and likes #{self.likes}"
  end
end

dave = Person.new('Dave', 'Texas')
dave.likes = "Programming Languages"
puts dave
```

produces:

```
Dave lives in Texas and likes Programming Languages
```

Using Data for Immutable Structs

Structs are often used to create small classes that represent constrained, encapsulated values with minimal behavior, but where it's useful to be able to treat the value as one thing, like a point with x and y coordinates. It's also sometimes useful to have those values be *immutable*, meaning that their values cannot be changed. Immutable objects can be easier to reason about and manage when sharing objects across threads.

True immutability in Ruby is hard, but you can achieve it with the Data class. You use Data.define to create a new class with a particular set of attributes. Once you've created the new class, you can construct instances using either positional or keyword arguments.

```
LineItem = Data.define(:name, :price_in_cents, :count)
li_1 = LineItem.new("Apple", 105, 3)
li_2 = LineItem.new(name: "Orange", count: 2, price_in_cents: 75)

li_1.name            # => "Apple"
li_2.price_in_cents # => 75
```

Once you have a Data instance, you can convert it to a hash with to_h.

Since the instances are immutable, you can't directly set the attributes, but you can create a new instance using with:

```
LineItem = Data.define(:name, :price_in_cents, :count)
li_1 = LineItem.new("Apple", 105, 3)
li_2 = li_1.with(name: "Orange")
```

The new instance is created using any keyword arguments passed to with and the values of the original instance for the attributes that aren't included. Including a keyword argument that doesn't match an attribute raises an error.

Creating Classes Dynamically

Let's look at some Ruby code:

```
class Example
end

ex = Example.new
```

When we call Example.new, we're invoking the method new on the class object Example. This is a regular method call—Ruby looks for the method new in the class of the object (and the class of Example is Class) and invokes it. So we can also invoke Class#new directly to create a new class dynamically at runtime:

```
some_class = Class.new
puts some_class.class
```

If you pass Class.new a block, that block is used as the body of the class:

metaprogramming/class_new.rb
```
some_class = Class.new do
  def self.class_method
    puts "In class method"
  end

  def instance_method
    puts "In instance method"
  end
end

some_class.class_method
obj = some_class.new
obj.instance_method
```

produces:

```
In class method
In instance method
```

By default, these classes will be direct descendants of Object. You can give them a different parent by passing the parent's class as a parameter:

```
some_class = Class.new(String) do
  def vowel_movement
    tr 'aeiou', '*'
  end
end

obj = some_class.new("now is the time")
puts obj.vowel_movement
```

produces:

```
n*w *s th* t*m*
```

How Classes Get Their Names

You may have noticed that the classes created by Class.new have no name. However, if you assign the class object for a class with no name to a constant, Ruby automatically names the class after the constant:

```
some_class = Class.new
obj = some_class.new
puts "Initial name is #{some_class.name}"
SomeClass = some_class
puts "Then the name is #{some_class.name}"
puts "also works via the object: #{obj.class.name}"
```

produces:

```
Initial name is
Then the name is SomeClass
also works via the object: SomeClass
```

We can use these dynamically constructed classes to extend Ruby in interesting ways. For example, here's a simple reimplementation of the Ruby Struct class:

```
def MyStruct(*keys)
  Class.new do
    attr_accessor *keys

    def initialize(hash)
      hash.each do |key, value|
        instance_variable_set("@#{key}", value)
      end
    end
  end
end

Person = MyStruct :name, :address, :likes
dave = Person.new(name: "dave", address: "TX", likes: "Stilton")
chad = Person.new(name: "chad", likes: "Jazz")
chad.address = "Berlin"

puts "Dave's name is #{dave.name}"
puts "Chad lives in #{chad.address}"
```

produces:

```
Dave's name is dave
Chad lives in Berlin
```

Using instance_eval and class_eval

No matter where you are in a Ruby program, self always has a value determined by your location in the code. Sometimes it's useful to be able to manage that relationship and change the value of self for a while.

The methods Module#instance_eval, Module#class_eval, and Module#module_eval let you set self to be an arbitrary object, evaluate the code in a block with that object as self, and then reset self:

```ruby
"cat".instance_eval do
  puts "Upper case = #{upcase}"
  puts "Length is #{self.length}"
end
```

produces:

```
Upper case = CAT
Length is 3
```

Inside the instance_eval block, the variable self is temporarily given the value of the object that received the instance_eval message.

All the _eval methods take a string instead of a block argument, where the string is evaluated by Ruby with the receiver as self. But the string version is considered dangerous, and you shouldn't use it. First, it's slow—calling eval effectively compiles the code in the string before executing it. But, even worse, eval from a string can be dangerous. If there's any chance that external data—stuff that comes from outside your application—can wind up inside the string argument to eval, then you have a security hole because that external data may end up containing arbitrary code that your application will blindly execute.

class_eval and instance_eval both set self for the duration of the block. But they differ in the way they set up the environment for method definition. This can make a big difference when the receiver is a class. The method class_eval sets things up as if you were in the body of a class definition, so when the receiver is a class, method definitions will define instance methods in that class:

```ruby
class MyClass
end

MyClass.class_eval do
  def instance_method
    puts "In an instance method"
  end
end

obj = MyClass.new
obj.instance_method
```

produces:

```
In an instance method
```

In contrast, calling instance_eval acts as if you were working inside the singleton class of self.

So, if the receiver is a class, any methods you define will become singleton methods of that class, which is to say that they become class methods:

```ruby
class MyClass
end

MyClass.instance_eval do
  def class_method
    puts "In a class method"
  end
end

MyClass.class_method
```

produces:

```
In a class method
```

It might be helpful to remember that class_eval and instance_eval refer to the context in which self is being replaced—and not the kind of method that's defined inside the block. For method definition, class_eval defines instance methods, and instance_eval defines class methods.

Ruby has variants of these methods. instance_exec, class_exec, and module_exec behave identically to their _eval counterparts but only have the block version (that is, they don't take a string). Any arguments given to the methods are passed to the block as block parameters. This is an important feature. Using _eval, it's impossible to pass an instance variable into a block given to one of the _eval methods—because self is changed by the call, these variables go out of scope. With the _exec form, you can pass them in:

```ruby
@animal = "cat"
"dog".instance_exec(@animal) do |other|
  puts "#{other} and #{self}"
end
```

produces:

```
cat and dog
```

instance_eval and Constants

When using instance_eval, constants are looked up in the lexical scope in which they were referenced. This (artificial) example shows the behavior:

```ruby
module One
  CONST = "Defined in One"
  def self.eval_block(&block)
    instance_eval(&block)
  end
end

module Two
  CONST = "Defined in Two"
  def self.call_eval_block
    One.eval_block do
      CONST
    end
  end
end

Two.call_eval_block      # => "Defined in Two"
```

instance_eval and Domain-Specific Languages

It turns out that instance_eval has a pivotal role to play in a certain type of domain-specific language (DSL). For example, we might be writing a simple DSL for turtle graphics. In turtle graphics systems, you imagine you have a turtle you can command to move forward n squares, turn left, and turn right. You can also make the turtle raise and lower a pen. If the pen is lowered, a line will be drawn tracing the turtle's subsequent movements. Few of these turtles exist in the wild, so we tend to simulate them inside computers. To draw a set of three 5x5 squares, we might write the following:

```
3.times do
  forward(8)
  pen_down
  4.times do
    forward(4)
    left
  end
  pen_up
end
```

Yes, the forward(4) is correct in this code. The initial point is always drawn.

Clearly, pen_down, forward, left, and pen_up can be implemented as Ruby methods. But this API has all the methods being called without receivers. For that to work, we have to either be within a class that defines those methods (or is a child of such a class) or have to make the methods global. Neither of those allows for the API to be as simple as we've defined it here.

instance_eval comes to the rescue. We can define a class Turtle that defines the various methods we need as instance methods. We'll also define a walk method, which will execute our turtle DSL, and a draw method to draw the resulting picture:

```
class Turtle
  def left; ... end
  def right; ... end
  def forward(n); ... end
  def pen_up; .. end
  def pen_down; ... end
  def walk(...); end
  def draw; ... end
end
```

If we implement walk correctly, we can then write the code like this:

```
turtle = Turtle.new
turtle.walk do
  3.times do
    forward(8)
    pen_down
    4.times do
      forward(4)
      left
    end
    pen_up
  end
end
```

```
turtle.draw
```

Inside the walk block we want all the methods to have turtle as the receiver, but they have self as the implicit receiver. And as written, self is based on the class or location where this whole block is defined, and that isn't the object named turtle.

So, what is the correct implementation of walk? Well, we clearly have to use instance_eval because we want the DSL commands in the block to call the methods in the turtle object. We also have to arrange to pass the block given to the walk method to be evaluated by that instance_eval call. Our implementation looks like this:

```
def walk(&)
  instance_eval(&)
end
```

Notice how we use Ruby's anonymous block syntax to grab the block passed to walk and pass it as-is as a block to instance_eval.

Is this a good use of instance_eval? It depends on the circumstances. The benefit is that the code inside the block looks simple—you don't have to make the receiver explicit:

```
4.times do
  turtle.forward(4)
  turtle.left
end
```

There's a drawback, though. Inside the block, scope isn't what you might think it is, so this code wouldn't work:

```
@size = 4
turtle.walk do
  4.times do
    turtle.forward(@size)
    turtle.left
  end
end
```

Instance variables are looked up in self, and self in the block isn't the same as self in the code that sets the instance variable @size. Because of this kind of confusion, you may want to move away from using this style of instance_eval blocks.

Using Hook Methods

In Class Methods and Modules, on page 390, we defined a method called included in our GeneralLogger module. When this module was included in a class, Ruby automatically invoked this included method, allowing our module to add class methods to the host class.

included is an example of a *hook method* (sometimes called a *callback*). A hook method is a method that you write but that Ruby calls from within the interpreter when some particular event occurs. The interpreter looks for these methods by name. If you define a method in the right context with an appropriate name, Ruby will call it when the corresponding event happens.

The methods that can be invoked from within the interpreter are:

Method-related hooks
> method_added, method_missing, method_removed, method_undefined, singleton_method_added, singleton_method_removed, singleton_method_undefined

Class and module-related hooks
> append_features, const_missing, extend_object, extended, included, inherited, initialize_clone, initialize_copy, initialize_dup

Object marshaling hooks
> marshal_dump, marshal_load

Coercion hooks
> coerce, induced_from, various to_xxx methods

We won't discuss all of them in this chapter—instead, we'll show just a few examples of use.

The inherited Hook

If a class defines a class method called inherited, Ruby will call that method whenever that class is subclassed (that is, whenever any class inherits from the original).

This hook is often used in situations where a base class needs to keep track of its children. For example, an online store might offer a variety of shipping options. Each might be represented by a separate class, and each of these classes could be a subclass of a single Shipping class. This parent class could keep track of all the various shipping options by recording every class that subclasses it. When it comes time to display the shipping options to the user, the application could call the base class, asking it for a list of its children:

```
metaprogramming/shipping.rb
class Shipping # Base class
  @children = [] # this variable is in the class, not instances

  def self.inherited(child)
    @children << child
  end

  def self.shipping_options(weight, international)
    @children.select { |child| child.can_ship(weight, international) }
  end
end

class MediaMail < Shipping
  def self.can_ship(_weight, international)
    !international
  end
end

class FlatRatePriorityEnvelope < Shipping
  def self.can_ship(weight, international)
    weight < 64 && !international
  end
end

class InternationalFlatRateBox < Shipping
  def self.can_ship(weight, international)
    weight < 9*16 && international
  end
end
```

```
puts "Shipping 16oz domestic"
puts Shipping.shipping_options(16, false)

puts "\nShipping 90oz domestic"
puts Shipping.shipping_options(90, false)

puts "\nShipping 16oz international"
puts Shipping.shipping_options(16, true)
```

produces:

```
Shipping 16oz domestic
MediaMail
FlatRatePriorityEnvelope

Shipping 90oz domestic
MediaMail

Shipping 16oz international
InternationalFlatRateBox
```

Command interpreters often use this pattern: the base class keeps a track of available commands, each of which is implemented in a subclass.

The method_missing Hook

Earlier, we saw how Ruby executes a method call by looking for the method, first in the object's class, then in its superclass, then in that class's superclass, and so on. If the method call has an explicit receiver, then private methods are skipped in this search. If the method isn't found by the time we run out of superclasses (because BasicObject has no superclass), then Ruby tries to invoke the hook method method_missing on the original object. Again, the same process is followed—Ruby first looks in the object's class, then in its superclass, and so on. Ruby predefines its own version of method_missing in class BasicObject, so typically the search stops there. The built-in method_missing basically raises an exception (either a NoMethodError or a NameError depending on the circumstances).

The key here is that method_missing is simply a Ruby method. We can override it in our own classes to handle calls to otherwise undefined methods in an application-specific way.

The method_missing method has a signature that includes the name of the method being sought and the arguments:

```
def method_missing(name, *args, &block)
```

The name argument receives the name of the method that couldn't be found. It's passed as a symbol. The args argument is an array of the arguments that were passed in the original call. And the often forgotten block argument will receive any block passed to the original method.

```
def method_missing(name, *args, &block)
  puts "Called #{name} with #{args.inspect} and #{block}"
end

wibble
wobble 1, 2
wurble(3, 4) { stuff }
```

produces:

```
Called wibble with [] and
Called wobble with [1, 2] and
Called wurble with [3, 4] and #<Proc:0x00000001026f73d8 prog.rb:7>
```

Before we get too deep into the details, we'll offer a tip about etiquette. There are two main ways that people use method_missing. The first intercepts every use of an undefined method and handles it. The second is more subtle; it intercepts all calls but handles only some of them. In the latter case, it's important to forward on the call to a superclass if you decide not to handle it in your method_missing implementation.

In this snippet, imagine there's some method called name_handled_by_method_missing? that determines if the name matches whatever criteria we're using for dynamic methods:

```
class MyClass < OtherClass
  def method_missing(name, *args, &block)
    if name_handled_by_method_missing?(name)
      # handle call
    else
      super    # otherwise pass it on
    end
  end

  def respond_to_missing?(name)
    name_handled_by_method_missing?(name)
  end
end
```

If you fail to pass on calls that you don't handle, your application will silently ignore calls to unknown methods in your class.

It's also important to keep the respond_to_missing? method consistent with method_missing. As we mentioned in Duck Typing, on page 356, respond_to? is used to query what messages an instance expects. Using method_missing changes the list of expected messages, so there's a parallel to respond_to? called respond_to_missing? that's similarly invoked if respond_to? returns false, as a final check on whether the class actually responds to the message.

Using method_missing to Simulate Accessors

The OpenStruct class is distributed with Ruby. It allows you to write objects with attributes that are created dynamically by assignment.

For example, you could write this:

```
require 'ostruct'
obj = OpenStruct.new(name: "Dave")
obj.address = "Texas"
obj.likes   = "Programming"

puts "#{obj.name} lives in #{obj.address} and likes #{obj.likes}"
```

produces:

```
Dave lives in Texas and likes Programming
```

Let's use method_missing to write our own version of OpenStruct:

metaprogramming/open_struct.rb

```ruby
class MyOpenStruct < BasicObject
  def initialize(initial_values = {})
    @values = initial_values
  end

  def _singleton_class
    class << self
      self
    end
  end

  def method_missing(name, *args, &block)
    if name[-1] == "="
      base_name = name[0..-2].intern
      _singleton_class.instance_exec(name) do |name|
        define_method(name) do |value|
          @values[base_name] = value
        end
      end
      @values[base_name] = args[0]
    else
      _singleton_class.instance_exec(name) do |name|
        define_method(name) do
          @values[name]
        end
      end
      @values[name]
    end
  end

  def respond_to_missing?(_)
    true
  end
end

obj = MyOpenStruct.new(name: "Dave")
obj.address = "Texas"
obj.likes = "Programming"

puts "#{obj.name} lives in #{obj.address} and likes #{obj.likes}"
```

produces:

```
Dave lives in Texas and likes Programming
```

Notice how we base our class on BasicObject. BasicObject is the root of Ruby's object hierarchy and contains only a minimal number of methods:

```ruby
p BasicObject.instance_methods
```

produces:

```
[:equal?, :!, :__send__, :==, :!=, :instance_eval, :instance_exec, :__id__]
```

This is good because it means that our MyOpenStruct class will be able to have attributes such as display or class. If instead, we'd based MyOpenStruct on class Object, then these names, along with forty-nine others, would've been predefined and hence wouldn't trigger method_missing.

Notice also another common pattern inside method_missing. The first time we reference or assign a value to an attribute of our object, we access or update the @values hash appropriately. But we also use define_method to define the method that the caller was trying to access. This means that the next time this attribute is used, it'll use the method and not invoke method_missing. In theory, this will make subsequent calls to the same accessor perform faster. This may or may not be worth the trouble, depending on the access patterns to your object.

Also notice how we had to jump through some hoops to define the method. We want to define the method only for the current object. This means we have to put the method into the object's singleton class. Ordinarily, we could do that via a Ruby method called define_singleton_method, but that method is defined in Object, not BasicObject, so it's not available to us here.

So we hack it ourselves. We can do that using instance_exec and define_method. But that means we have to use the class << self trick to get the object's singleton class. Through an interesting implementation subtlety, define_method will always define an instance method, regardless of whether it's invoked via instance_exec or class_exec.

But this code reveals a dark underbelly of using method_missing and BasicObject:

```
metaprogramming/open_struct_flaw.rb
obj = MyOpenStruct.new(name: "Dave")
obj.address = "Texas"

o1 = obj.dup
o1.name = "Mike"
o1.address = "Colorado"
```

produces:

```
code/metaprogramming/open_struct_flaw.rb:41:in `<main>': undefined method `name='
for nil (NoMethodError)

o1.name = "Mike"
   ^^^^^^^
```

The dup method isn't defined by BasicObject; it appears in class Object. So when we called dup, it was picked up by our method_missing handler, and we just returned nil (because we don't have an attribute called dup yet). We could fix this so that it at least reports an error:

```
def method_missing(name, *args, &block)
  if name[-1] == "="
    # as before...
  else
    super unless @values.has_key? name
    # as before...
  end
end
```

This class now reports an error if we call dup (or any other method) on it. But we still can't dup or clone it (or inspect, convert to a string, and so on). Although BasicObject seems like a natural fit for method_missing, you may find it to be more trouble than it's worth.

Using method_missing as a Filter

As the previous example showed, method_missing has some drawbacks if you use it to intercept all calls. It's probably better to use it to recognize certain patterns of call, passing on those it doesn't recognize to its parent class to handle.

An example of this is the dynamic finder facility used to be found in the Ruby on Rails ActiveRecord module. ActiveRecord is the object-relational library in Rails—it allows you to access relational databases as if they were object stores. One particular feature allows you to find rows that match the criteria of having given values in certain columns. For example, if an Active Record class called Book were mapping a relational table called books and the books table included columns called title and author, you used to be able to write this (it's since been deprecated, but we kind of miss it):

```
pickaxe = Book.find_by_title("Programming Ruby")
daves_books = Book.find_all_by_author("Dave Thomas")
```

Active Record didn't predefine all these potential finder methods. Instead, it uses our old friend method_missing. Inside that method, it looks for calls to undefined methods that match the pattern /^find_(all_)?by_(.*)/. It also looks for /^find_or_(initialize|create)_by_(.*)/. If the method being invoked doesn't match this pattern or if the fields in the method name don't correspond to columns in the database table, Active Record calls super so that a genuine method_missing exception will be generated.

A Metaprogramming Example

Let's bring together all the metaprogramming topics we've discussed in a final example by writing a module that allows us to trace the execution of methods in any class that mixes the module in. This would let us write the following:

```
metaprogramming/trace_calls_example.rb
require_relative "trace_calls"

class Example
  def one(arg)
    puts "One called with #{arg}"
  end
end

ex1 = Example.new
ex1.one("Hello") # no tracing from this call

class Example
  include TraceCalls
  def two(arg1, arg2)
    arg1 + arg2
  end
end

ex1.one("Goodbye") # but we see tracing from these two
puts ex1.two(4, 5)
```

produces:

```
One called with Hello
==> calling one with ["Goodbye"]
One called with Goodbye
<== one returned nil
```

```
==> calling two with [4, 5]
<== two returned 9
9
```

We can see immediately that there's a subtlety here. When we mix the TraceCalls module into a class, it has to add tracing to any existing instance methods in that class. It also has to arrange to add tracing to any methods we subsequently add.

Let's start with the full listing of the TraceCalls module:

```
metaprogramming/trace_calls.rb
module TraceCalls
  def self.included(klass)
    klass.instance_methods(false).each do |existing_method|
      wrap(klass, existing_method)
    end

    def klass.method_added(method) # note: nested definition
      unless @trace_calls_internal
        @trace_calls_internal = true
        TraceCalls.wrap(self, method)
        @trace_calls_internal = false
      end
    end
  end

  def self.wrap(klass, method)
    klass.instance_eval do
      method_object = instance_method(method)

      define_method(method) do |*args, &block|
        puts "==> calling #{method} with #{args.inspect}"
        result = method_object.bind_call(self, *args, &block)
        puts "<== #{method} returned #{result.inspect}"
        result
      end
    end
  end
end
```

When we include this module in a class, the included hook method gets invoked. It first uses the instance_methods reflection method to find all the existing instance methods in the host class (the false parameter limits the list to methods in the class itself, and not in its super-classes). For each existing method, the module calls a helper method, wrap, to add some tracing code to it. We'll talk about wrap shortly.

Next, the included method uses another hook, method_added. This is called by Ruby whenever a method is defined in the receiver. Note that we define this method in the class passed to the included method. This means that the method will be called when methods are added to this host class and not to the module. This is what allows us to include TraceCalls at the top of a class and then add methods to that class—all those method definitions will be handled by method_added.

Now look at the code inside the method_added method. We have to deal with a potential problem here. As you'll see when we look at the wrap method, we add tracing to a method by creating a new version of the method that calls the old one. Inside method_added, we call the wrap function to add this tracing. But inside wrap, we'll define a new method to handle this wrapping, and that definition will invoke method_added again, and then we'd call wrap again, and so on, until the stack gets exhausted. To prevent this, we use an instance variable and do the wrapping only if we're not already doing it.

The wrap method takes a class object and the name of a method to wrap. It finds the original definition of that method (using instance_method) and saves it. It then redefines this method. This new method outputs some tracing and then calls the original, passing in the parameters and block from the wrapper. Note how we call the method by binding the method object to the current instance and then invoking that bound method.

The key to understanding this code, and most metaprogramming code, is to follow the principles we worked out at the start of this chapter—how self changes as methods are called and classes are defined and how methods are called by looking for them in the class of the receiver. If you get stuck, do what we do and draw little boxes and arrows. We find it useful to stick with the convention used in this chapter: class links go to the right, and superclass links go up. Given an object, a method call is then a question of finding the receiver object, going right once, and then following the superclass chain up as far as you need to go.

Top-Level Execution Environment

Finally, there's one small detail we have to cover to complete the metaprogramming environment. Many times in this book we've claimed that everything in Ruby is an object. But we've used one thing time and time again that appears to contradict this—the top-level Ruby execution environment:

```
puts "Hello, World"
```

Not an object in sight. We may as well be writing some variant of Fortran or Basic. But dig deeper, and you'll come across objects and classes lurking in even the simplest code.

We know that the literal "Hello, World" generates a Ruby String, so that's one object. We also know that the bare method call to puts is effectively the same as self.puts. But what is self?

```
self      # => main
self.class # => Object
```

At the top level, we're executing code in the context of a predefined object, called main. When we define methods using def method_name at the top level, Ruby defines those as (private) instance methods for class Object. This is why methods defined at the top level are available inside all objects. In the following sample, the top-level be_polite method is visible from inside the introduce method of class Person:

```
metaprogramming/top_level.rb
def be_polite
  "Why, if it isn't #{self.to_s}? So glad to see you."
end

class Person
  attr_accessor :first_name, :last_name

  def initialize(first_name, last_name)
    @first_name = first_name
    @last_name = last_name
  end
```

```ruby
  def to_s = "#{first_name} #{last_name}"

  def introduce
    be_polite
  end
end
clark = Person.new("Clark", "Kent")
p clark.introduce
```

produces:

```
"Why, if it isn't Clark Kent? So glad to see you."
```

This is fairly subtle—since they are defined in class Object, these methods are available everywhere. And because we're in the context of Object, we can use all of Object's methods (including those mixed in from Kernel) in function form. This explains why we can call Kernel methods such as puts at the top level (and indeed throughout Ruby); it's because these methods are part of every object. Top-level instance variables also belong to this main, top-level object.

What's Next

Metaprogramming is one of Ruby's sharpest tools. Don't be afraid to use it to raise up the level at which you program. But, at the same time, use it only when necessary—overly metaprogrammed applications can become pretty obscure pretty quickly.

There's one more piece of the Ruby metaprogramming puzzle: reflection, which is how Ruby knows things about the runtime environment. Let's take a look.

CHAPTER 23

Reflection and Object Space

One of the advantages of dynamic languages such as Ruby is the ability to *introspect*—to examine aspects of a program from within the program itself. This is also called *reflection*.

When people introspect, they think about their thoughts and feelings. This is interesting because we're using thought to analyze thought. It's the same when programs use introspection—a program can discover the following information about itself:

- What objects it contains
- Its class hierarchy
- The attributes and methods of objects
- Information on methods

Armed with this information, we can look at particular objects and decide which of their methods to call at runtime—even if the class of the object didn't exist when we first wrote the code. We can also start doing clever things, perhaps modifying the program while it's running. We're going to look at Ruby's ObjectSpace, which allows us to reflect on Ruby's internals. Later in this chapter, we'll look at distributed Ruby and marshaling, two reflection-based technologies that let us send objects around the world and through time.

Looking at Objects

Have you ever craved the ability to traverse all the living objects in your program? We have! Ruby has a global object called ObjectSpace that lets you do some fun tricks with the set of objects Ruby is tracking (this means all the objects that have been created and not yet destroyed by garbage collection).

What Is Garbage Collection?

Ruby is a dynamic language, and it doesn't require the programmer to manage the memory that the program uses during runtime. Instead, Ruby uses a process called garbage collection. Garbage collection looks for objects that have been allocated into memory but are no longer in scope or are otherwise not accessible. Those objects are released back into the memory heap so that the space can be reused.

We're not going to go into the details of how Ruby handles garbage collecting in this book. For one thing, the details change from version to version as newer and better algorithms for identifying discarded objects are developed.

To traverse live objects, Ruby provides the method ObjectSpace.each_object, which takes a block and applies it to each object that ObjectSpace knows about. The method takes an optional argument, which is a class or module, and filters the result to only the objects that are of that class, module, or subclass.

For example, to iterate over all objects of type Complex, you'd write the following:

```
a = Complex(1, 2)
b = Complex(99, -100)
ObjectSpace.each_object(Complex) { |x| puts x }
```

produces:

```
0+1i
99-100i
1+2i
```

Where did that extra number (0+1i) come from? We didn't define it in our program. Well, the Complex class defines a constant for *I*, which is the square root of -1. Because we're examining all living objects in the system, this object turns up as well.

Let's try the same example with different values. This time, they're objects of type Integer:

```
a = 102
b = 95
ObjectSpace.each_object(Integer) { |x| p x }
```

produces:

```
9223372036854775807
```

Neither of the Integers objects we created showed up, although another integer did. That's because ObjectSpace doesn't know about objects with *immediate* values. Immediate values are cases where the value is small enough to be stored as part of the internal chip instructions rather than being separately stored in memory. In Ruby, Symbol, true, false, and nil are immediate, and Integer and Float values are also immediate if they are close enough to zero (for machine-specific values of "close enough"). (Symbol is weird because if you do this exercise with Symbol, you'll see a lot of symbols with what seems to be internal-facing names, but new ones you create won't show up.)

For what it's worth, $9223372036854775807 = 2 ** 63 - 1$ (we did have to look that up), which suggests it's a memory-specific number being generated internally somewhere, possibly being used as a boundary for integer values.

Looking inside Objects

Once you've found an interesting object, you may be tempted to find out what it can do. Unlike static languages, where a variable's type determines its class, and hence the methods it supports, Ruby supports dynamic objects. You cannot tell exactly what an object can do until you look under its hood (or under its bonnet, for objects created to the east of the Atlantic). We talked about this in Duck Typing, on page 356.

For instance, we can get a list of all the methods to which an object will respond (these include methods in an object's class and that class's ancestors) with this:

```
r = 1..10
list = r.methods
list.length # => 123
list[0..3]  # => [:last, :exclude_end?, :step, :cover?]
```

We can check to see whether an object responds to a particular method:

```
r = 1..10
r.respond_to?("frozen?") # => true
r.respond_to?(:key?)      # => false
"me".respond_to?("==")    # => true
```

We can get the method object for a particular method:

```
r = 1..10
method = r.method(:frozen?)
method.call  # => true
```

And we can ask for an object's class and unique object ID and test its relationship to other classes:

```
num = 1
num.object_id             # => 3
num.class                 # => Integer
num.kind_of? Integer      # => true
num.kind_of? Numeric      # => true
num.instance_of? Integer  # => true
num.instance_of? Numeric  # => false
```

Looking at Classes

Knowing about objects is one aspect of reflection, but to get the whole picture, you also need to be able to look at classes—and the methods and constants that they contain.

Looking at the class hierarchy is easy. You can get the parent of any particular class using Class#superclass and its children using Class#subclasses. For classes *and* modules, the Module#ancestors method lists both superclasses and mixed-in modules:

```
ospace/relatives.rb
klass = Integer
print "Inheritance chain: "
begin
  print klass
  klass = klass.superclass
  print " < " if klass
end while klass
puts
p "Ancestors: #{Integer.ancestors}"
p "Subclasses: #{Integer.subclasses}"
```

produces:

```
Inheritance chain: Integer < Numeric < Object < BasicObject
"Ancestors: [Integer, Numeric, Comparable, Object, Kernel, BasicObject]"
"Subclasses: []"
```

If you want to build a complete class hierarchy, simply run that code for every class in the system. We can use ObjectSpace to iterate over all Class objects like this:

```
ObjectSpace.each_object(Class) do |klass|
  # ...
end
```

Looking inside Classes

We can find out a bit more about the methods and constants in a particular object. We can ask for methods by access level, and we can ask for just singleton methods. We can also take a look at the object's constants, local, and instance variables:

```
class Demo
  @@var = 99
  CONST = 1.23

  private def private_method
  end

  protected def protected_method
  end

  public def public_method
    @inst = 1
    i = 1
    j = 2
    local_variables
  end

  def Demo.class_method
  end
end

Demo.private_instance_methods(false)    # => [:private_method]
Demo.protected_instance_methods(false)  # => [:protected_method]
Demo.public_instance_methods(false)     # => [:public_method]
Demo.singleton_methods(false)           # => [:class_method]
Demo.class_variables                    # => [:@@var]
Demo.constants(false)                   # => [:CONST]

demo = Demo.new
demo.instance_variables                 # => []
# Get 'public_method' to return its local variables
# and set an instance variable
demo.public_method                      # => [:i, :j]
demo.instance_variables                 # => [:@inst]
```

You may be wondering what all the false parameters were in the previous code. These reflection methods will by default continue recursively into parent classes, their parents, and so on, up the ancestor chain. Passing in false stops this kind of prying.

Given a list of method names, we may now be tempted to try calling them. Fortunately, that's easy with Ruby.

Calling Methods Dynamically

The Object#send method lets you tell any object to invoke a method by name. The first argument is a symbol or a string representing the name, and any remaining arguments are passed along to the method of that name. Let's have a look at the following code:

```
"John Coltrane".send(:length)          # => 13
"Miles Davis".send("sub", /iles/, '.') # => "M. Davis"
```

There are two twists to send. First, your class might define its own send method if it wanted to send something somewhere. Ruby provides the _send_ method, defined in BasicObject, which is identical to send and is meant to be used in cases where send might have been overwritten .

Second, the send method doesn't enforce method access, meaning that it'll happily send to a method that is private or protected. You might reasonably think that this undermines the point of having access control in the first place. Ruby provides the related method public_send, which will only send to methods that are public. For most usages, public_send is preferred.

Another way of invoking methods dynamically uses Method objects. A Method object is like a Proc object: it represents a chunk of code and a context in which it executes. In this case, the code is the body of the method, and the context is the object that created the method. Once we have our Method object, we can execute it sometime later by sending it the message call:

```
trane = "John Coltrane".method(:length)
miles = "Miles Davis".method("sub")

trane.call              # => 13
miles.call(/iles/, '.') # => "M. Davis"
```

You can pass the Method object around as you would any other object, and when you invoke Method#call, the method is run as if you had invoked it on the original object. It's like having a C-style function pointer but in a fully object-oriented style.

In languages like JavaScript and Python, mentioning a method without arguments returns the method itself, whereas in Ruby, mentioning the method without arguments calls the method with no arguments, and if you want the method itself, you need to call method.

You can use Method objects wherever you use proc objects. For example, they work with iterators:

```
def double(a)
  2 * a
end

method_object = method(:double)
[ 1, 3, 5, 7 ].map(&method_object) # => [2, 6, 10, 14]
```

Method objects are bound to one particular object, and that object acts as the receiver when the method object is invoked. You can create *unbound* methods (of class UnboundMethod) by calling instance_method on a class with the name of the method. Subsequently, you can bind the method to one or more objects with bind. The binding creates a new Method object, that is bound to the argument of bind. As with aliases, unbound methods are references to the definition of the method at the time they are created and don't reflect later changes:

```ruby
unbound_length = String.instance_method(:length)
  class String
    def length
       99
    end
    end

str = "cat"
str.length          # => 99

bound_length = unbound_length.bind(str)
bound_length.call # => 3
```

The pattern of binding a method and immediately calling it is common enough that Ruby has a shortcut, bind_call. We can replace the last two lines of the previous snippet with the single line unbound_length.bind_call(str). The first argument to bind_call is the object to bind to, and any subsequent arguments are passed to the call.

Because good things come in threes, here's yet another way to invoke methods dynamically. The eval method (and its variations such as class_eval, module_eval, and instance_eval) will parse and execute an arbitrary string of legal Ruby source code:

```ruby
trane = %q{"John Coltrane".length}
miles = %q{"Miles Davis".sub(/iles/, '.')}

eval(trane) # => 13
eval(miles) # => "M. Davis"
```

When using eval, it can be helpful to state explicitly the context in which the expression should be evaluated, rather than using the current context. You obtain a context using Kernel#binding at the desired point:

```ruby
def get_a_binding
  val = 123
  binding
end

val = "cat"

the_binding = get_a_binding
eval("val", the_binding) # => 123
eval("val")              # => "cat"
```

The first eval evaluates val in the context of the binding *as it was* when the method get_a_binding was executing. In this binding, the variable val had a value of 123. The second eval evaluates val in the top-level binding, where it has the value "cat".

Performance Considerations

As we've seen in this section, Ruby gives us several ways to invoke an arbitrary method of some object: Object#send, Method#call, and the various flavors of eval.

You may prefer to use any one of these techniques depending on your needs, but be aware that, as the following benchmark shows, eval is significantly slower than the others (or, for optimistic readers, send and call are significantly faster than eval).

```
require "benchmark"
include Benchmark

test = "Stormy Weather"
m = test.method(:length)
n = 100000

bm(12) do |x|
  x.report("call") { n.times { m.call } }
  x.report("send") { n.times { test.send(:length) } }
  x.report("eval") { n.times { eval "test.length" } }
end
```

produces:

	user	system	total	real
call	0.004716	0.000001	0.004717 (0.004719)
send	0.004930	0.000001	0.004931 (0.004934)
eval	0.203683	0.001516	0.205199 (0.205515)

System Hooks

A *hook* is a technique that lets you trap some Ruby event, such as object creation. Let's take a look at some common Ruby hook techniques.

Intercepting Method Calls

The simplest hook technique in Ruby is to intercept calls to methods in core classes. Perhaps you want to log all the operating system commands your program executes. You could simply use alias_method to rename the system method and replace it with a system method of your own that both logs the command and calls the original Kernel#system method.

For example:

```
class Object
  alias_method :old_system, :system

  def system(*args)
    old_system(*args).tap do |result|
      puts "system(#{args.join(', ')}) returned #{result.inspect}"
    end
  end
end

system("date")
system("kangaroo", "-hop 10", "skippy")
```

produces:

```
Thu Nov  2 17:16:24 CDT 2023
system(date) returned true
system(kangaroo, -hop 10, skippy) returned nil
```

But the problem with this technique is that you're relying on there not being an existing method called old_system.

A better alternative is to make use of method objects, which are effectively anonymous:

```ruby
class Object
  old_system_method = instance_method(:system)

  define_method(:system) do |*args|
    old_system_method.bind_call(self, *args).tap do |result|
      puts "system(#{args.join(', ')}) returned #{result.inspect}"
    end
  end
end

system("date")
system("kangaroo", "-hop 10", "skippy")
```

produces:

```
Thu Nov  2 17:16:24 CDT 2023
system(date) returned true
system(kangaroo, -hop 10, skippy) returned nil
```

You can also achieve a similar behavior by using prepend to insert a module with a method of the same name earlier in the call chain. Within the module's methods, calling super calls the host's method of the same name. This gives us:

```ruby
module SystemHook
  private def system(*args)
    super.tap do |result|
      puts "system(#{args.join(', ')}) returned #{result.inspect}"
    end
  end
end

class Object
  prepend SystemHook
end

system("date")
system("kangaroo", "-hop 10", "skippy")
```

produces:

```
Thu Nov  2 17:16:24 CDT 2023
system(date) returned true
system(kangaroo, -hop 10, skippy) returned nil
```

Object Creation Hooks

Ruby lets you get involved when objects are created. If you can be present when every object is born, you can do all sorts of interesting things with them: you can wrap them, add methods to them, remove methods from them, and add them to containers to implement persistence—you name it. We'll show a simple example here. We'll add a timestamp to every object as it's created. First, we'll add a timestamp attribute to every object in the system. We can do this by hacking the class Object itself:

```ruby
class Object
  attr_accessor :timestamp
end
```

Then, we need to hook object creation to add this timestamp. One way to do this is to do our method-renaming trick on Class#new—the method that's called to allocate space for a new object. The technique isn't perfect—some built-in objects, such as literal strings, are constructed without calling new—but it'll work just fine for objects we write:

```ruby
class Class
  old_new = instance_method(:new)
  define_method(:new) do |*args, **kwargs, &block|
    result = old_new.bind_call(self, *args, **kwargs, &block)
    result.timestamp = Time.now unless result.is_a?(Time)
    result
  end
end
```

Finally, we can run a test. We'll create a couple of objects a few milliseconds apart and check their timestamps:

```ruby
class Test
end

obj1 = Test.new
sleep(0.002)
obj2 = Test.new
obj1.timestamp.to_f # => 1698963384.31296
obj2.timestamp.to_f # => 1698963384.315474
```

Tracing Your Program's Execution

While we're having fun reflecting on all the objects and classes in our programs, let's not forget about the humble expressions that make our code actually do things. It turns out that Ruby lets us look at these expressions, too.

First, you can watch the interpreter as it executes code, using the TracePoint class. TracePoint is used to execute a proc while adding all sorts of juicy debugging information whenever a new source line is executed, methods are called, objects are created, and so on.

Here's a bit of what TracePoint can do (run this in your own irb window, but be aware that it'll produce a *lot* of output):

```ruby
class Test
  def test
    a = 1
  end
end

TracePoint.trace(:line) do |trace_point|
  p trace_point
end

t = Test.new
t.test
```

How Did We Get Here?

That's a fair question...one we ask ourselves regularly. Mental lapses aside, in Ruby you can find out "how you got there" using the method Kernel#caller, which returns an array of strings representing the current call stack:

```
def cat_a
  puts caller[0..2]
end

def cat_b
  cat_a
end

def cat_c
  cat_b
end

cat_c
```

produces:

```
prog.rb:6:in `cat_b'
prog.rb:10:in `cat_c'
prog.rb:13:in `<main>'
```

In this case, we're limiting printing the first three elements of the call stack because beyond that, we get into the depths of irb, which is unlikely to be useful for debugging purposes.

Ruby also provides the method __callee__, which returns the name of the current method.

Source Code

Ruby executes programs from plain old files. You can look at these files to examine the source code that makes up your program using one of a number of techniques.

The special variable __FILE__ contains the name of the current source file. This leads to a fairly short (if cheating) quine—a program that outputs its own source code:

```
print File.read(__FILE__)
```

produces:

```
print File.read(__FILE__)
```

As we saw in the previous section, the method Kernel#caller returns the call stack as a list. Each entry in this list starts off with a filename, a colon, and a line number in that file. You can parse this information to display the source of the method call. In the following example, we have a main program, main.rb, that calls a method in a separate file, sub.rb. That method, in turn, invokes a block, where we traverse the call stack and write out the source lines involved. Notice the use of a hash of file contents, indexed by the filename.

Here's some code that dumps out the call stack, including source information:

```
ospace/caller/stack_dumper.rb
def dump_call_stack
  file_contents = {}
  puts "File            Line  Source Line"
  puts "---------------+----+-----------"
  caller.each do |position|
    match_data = position.match(/\A(.*?):(\d+)/)
    next if match_data.nil?
    file = match_data[1]
    line = Integer(match_data[2])
    file_contents[file] ||= File.readlines(file)
    printf("%-15s:%3d - %s",
```

```
        File.basename(file),
        line,
        file_contents[file][line - 1].lstrip)
  end
end
```

The file sub.rb contains a single method:

ospace/caller/sub.rb
```
def sub_method(v1, v2)
  main_method(v1 * 3, v2 * 6)
end
```

The following is the main program, which invokes the stack dumper after being called back by the submethod:

ospace/caller/main.rb
```
require_relative "sub"
require_relative "stack_dumper"

def main_method(arg1, arg2)
  dump_call_stack
end

sub_method(123, "cat")
```

produces:
```
File             Line  Source Line
---------------+----+------------
main.rb        :  5 - dump_call_stack
sub.rb         :  2 - main_method(v1 * 3, v2 * 6)
main.rb        :  8 - sub_method(123, "cat")
```

The SCRIPT_LINES__ constant is closely related to this technique. If a program initializes a constant called SCRIPT_LINES__ with a hash, that hash will receive a new entry for every file subsequently loaded into the interpreter using require or load. The entry's key is the name of the file, and the value is the source of the file as an array of strings.

Behind the Curtain: The Ruby VM

If you'd like to know what Ruby is doing with all that code you're writing, you can ask the Ruby interpreter to show you the intermediate code that it's executing.

You can ask it to compile the Ruby code in a string or in a file and then disassemble it and even run it. You might wonder if it can dump the opcodes out and later reload them. The answer is no—the interpreter has the code to do this, but it's disabled because there isn't yet an intermediate code verifier for the Ruby interpreter.

Here's a trivial example of disassembly:

```
code = RubyVM::InstructionSequence.compile('a = 1; puts 1 + a')
puts code.disassemble
```

produces:
```
== disasm: #<ISeq:<compiled>@<compiled>:1 (1,0)-(1,17)>
local table (size: 1, argc: 0 [opts: 0, rest: -1, post: 0, block: -1, kw: -1@-1,
kwrest: -1])
[ 1] a@0
```

```
0000 putobject_INT2FIX_1_                                                    (   1)[Li]
0001 setlocal_WC_0                           a@0
0003 putself
0004 putobject_INT2FIX_1_
0005 getlocal_WC_0                           a@0
0007 opt_plus                               <calldata!mid:+, argc:1,
ARGS_SIMPLE>[CcCr]
0009 opt_send_without_block                 <calldata!mid:puts, argc:1,
FCALL|ARGS_SIMPLE>
0011 leave
```

Maybe you want to know how Ruby handles #{...} substitutions in strings. Ask the VM:

```
code = RubyVM::InstructionSequence.compile('a = 1; puts "a = #{a}."')
puts code.disassemble
```

produces:

```
== disasm: #<ISeq:<compiled>@<compiled>:1 (1,0)-(1,23)>
local table (size: 1, argc: 0 [opts: 0, rest: -1, post: 0, block: -1, kw: -1@-1,
kwrest: -1])
[ 1] a@0
0000 putobject_INT2FIX_1_                                                    (   1)[Li]
0001 setlocal_WC_0                           a@0
0003 putself
0004 putobject                              "a = "
0006 getlocal_WC_0                           a@0
0008 dup
0009 objtostring                            <calldata!mid:to_s, argc:0,
FCALL|ARGS_SIMPLE>
0011 anytostring
0012 putobject                              "."
0014 concatstrings                          3
0016 opt_send_without_block                 <calldata!mid:puts, argc:1,
FCALL|ARGS_SIMPLE>
0018 leave
```

For a full list of the opcodes, print out RubyVM::INSTRUCTION_NAMES.

Marshaling and Distributed Ruby

Ruby features the ability to *serialize* objects, letting you store them somewhere and reconstitute them when needed. You can use this facility, for instance, to save a tree of objects that represent some portion of the application state—a document, a CAD drawing, a piece of music, and so on.

Ruby calls this kind of serialization *marshaling* (think of railroad marshaling yards where individual cars are assembled in sequence into a complete train, which is then dispatched somewhere). Saving an object and some or all of its components is done using the method dump. Typically, you'll dump an entire object tree starting with some given object. Later, you can reconstitute the object using load.

Here's a short example. We have a class Chord that holds a collection of musical notes. We'd like to save away a particularly wonderful chord so we can e-mail it to a couple hundred of our closest friends so they can load it into their copy of Ruby and savor it too. Let's start with the classes for Note and Chord:

```
ospace/chord.rb
Note = Struct.new(:value) do
  def to_s
    value.to_s
  end
end

class Chord
  def initialize(arr)
    @arr = arr
  end

  def play
    @arr.join("-")
  end
end
```

Now we'll create our masterpiece and use dump to save a serialized version to disk:

```
ospace/chord.rb
c = Chord.new(
  [
    Note.new("G"),
    Note.new("Bb"),
    Note.new("Db"),
    Note.new("E")
  ]
)

File.open("posterity", "w+") do |f|
  Marshal.dump(c, f)
end
```

Finally, our friends read it in and are transported by our creation's beauty:

```
chord = Marshal.load(File.open("posterity"))
chord.play                    # => "G-Bb-Db-E"
```

Custom Serialization Strategy

Not all objects can be dumped. Bindings, procedure objects, instances of class IO, and singleton objects cannot be saved outside the running Ruby environment (a TypeError will be raised if you try). Even if your object doesn't contain one of these problematic objects, you may want to take control of object serialization yourself.

Marshal provides the hooks you need. In the objects that require custom serialization, simply implement two instance methods: one called marshal_dump, which writes the object out to a string, and the other called marshal_load, which reads a string that you had previously created and uses it to initialize a newly allocated object.

The instance method marshal_dump should return an object representing the state to be dumped. When the object is subsequently reconstituted using load, the method marshal_load will be called with this object and will use it to set the state of its receiver—it'll be run in the context of an allocated but not initialized object of the class being loaded.

For instance, here is a sample class that defines its own serialization. For whatever reasons, Special doesn't want to save one of its internal data members, @volatile. The author has decided to serialize the two other instance variables in an array:

```ruby
ospace/marshal_load.rb
class Special
  def initialize(valuable, volatile, precious)
    @valuable = valuable
    @volatile = volatile
    @precious = precious
  end

  def marshal_dump
    [@valuable, @precious]
  end

  def marshal_load(variables)
    @valuable = variables[0]
    @precious = variables[1]
    @volatile = "unknown"
  end

  def to_s
    "#{@valuable} #{@volatile} #{@precious}"
  end
end

obj = Special.new("Hello", "there", "World")
puts "Before: obj = #{obj}"
data = Marshal.dump(obj)

obj = Marshal.load(data)
puts "After: obj = #{obj}"
```

produces:

```
Before: obj = Hello there World
After: obj = Hello unknown World
```

Using YAML and JSON for Marshaling

The Marshal module is built into the interpreter and uses a binary format to store objects externally. Although fast, this binary format has a couple of disadvantages. If the interpreter changes significantly, the marshal binary format may also change and old dumped files may no longer be loadable. Also, using Marshal assumes that the code on the other end loading the object is also a Ruby program. You might be sending an object across the web on a remote call to another server that might not be in Ruby, and in that case, you'll want a more general conversion format.

An alternative is to use a less fussy external format, preferably one using text rather than binary files. One option, supplied as a standard library, is YAML.[1] YAML stands for YAML Ain't Markup Language, but that hardly seems important. Another common option in the standard library is JavaScript Object Notation, or JSON.[2] In Ruby, the YAML module is an alias for Psych, which is the name of the Ruby YAML parser.

---

1.   http://www.yaml.org
2.   https://www.json.org/json-en.html

We can adapt our previous marshal example to use YAML. Rather than implement specific loading and dumping methods to control the marshal process, we define the method encode_with, which explicitly sets the values to be saved into its parameter:

```
ospace/yaml_load.rb
require "yaml"

class Special
  def initialize(valuable, volatile, precious)
    @valuable = valuable
    @volatile = volatile
    @precious = precious
  end

  def encode_with(properties)
    properties["precious"] = @precious
    properties["valuable"] = @valuable
  end

  def to_s
    "#{@valuable} #{@volatile} #{@precious}"
  end
end

obj = Special.new("Hello", "there", "World")

puts "Before: obj = #{obj}"
data = YAML.dump(obj)
obj = YAML.load(data, permitted_classes: [Special])
puts "After: obj = #{obj}"
```

produces:

```
Before: obj = Hello there World
After: obj = Hello  World
```

For security purposes, YAML.load takes a list of classes that you expect to find in the incoming YAML text. The expectation is that you're willing to create instances of any of these classes based on data included in the YAML text.

We can take a look at what YAML creates as the serialized form of the object—it's pretty simple:

```
obj = Special.new("Hello", "there", "World")
puts YAML.dump(obj)
```

produces:

```
Before: obj = Hello there World
After: obj = Hello  World
--- !ruby/object:Special
precious: World
valuable: Hello
```

JSON is another commonly used interchange format, and Ruby also has a JSON module that provides JSON loading and dumping. But Ruby's JSON module doesn't, by itself, parse Ruby objects into Ruby objects; it converts Ruby objects to hash data. If we want to restrict the attributes or convert to and from actual objects, we need to do this ourselves:

```
ospace/json_load.rb
require "json"

class Special
  def initialize(valuable, volatile, precious)
    @valuable = valuable
    @volatile = volatile
    @precious = precious
  end

  def self.from_json(json_string)
    result = JSON.parse(json_string)
    Special.new(result["valuable"], nil, result["precious"])
  end

  def to_json
    JSON.dump(
      {
        precious: @precious,
        valuable: @valuable
      }
    )
  end

  def to_s
    "#{@valuable} #{@volatile} #{@precious}"
  end
end

obj = Special.new("Hello", "there", "World")

puts "Before: obj = #{obj}"
data = obj.to_json
new_obj = Special.from_json(data)
puts "After: obj = #{new_obj}"
```

produces:

```
Before: obj = Hello there World
After: obj = Hello  World
```

Notice that the new object no longer has the volatile attribute, since that was not marshaled.

Distributed Ruby

Because we can serialize an object or a set of objects into a form suitable for out-of-process storage, we can transmit objects from one process to another. Couple this capability with the power of networking, and *voilà*—you have a distributed object system. To save you the trouble of having to write the code, we suggest using Masatoshi Seki's Distributed Ruby library, often abbreviated drb or dRuby, which is available as a standard Ruby library at https://github.com/ruby/drb.

Using drb, a Ruby process may act as a server, a client, or both. A drb server acts as a source of objects, while a client is a user of those objects. To the client, it appears that the objects are local, but in reality, the code is still being executed remotely.

A server starts a service by associating an object with a given port. Threads are created internally to handle incoming requests on that port:

```
ospace/drb/drb_server.rb
require "drb"

class TestServer
  def add(*args)
    args.inject { |n, v| n + v }
  end
end

server = TestServer.new
DRb.start_service("druby://localhost:9000", server)
```

A simple drb client simply creates a local drb object and associates it with the object on the remote server; the local object is a proxy:

```
ospace/drb/drb_client.rb
require "drb"
DRb.start_service
obj = DRbObject.new(nil, "druby://localhost:9000")

puts "Sum is: #{obj.add(1, 2, 3)}"
```

The client connects to the server and calls the method add, which uses the magic of inject to sum its arguments. It returns the result, which the client prints out. You can see that by writing a script that loads the server and then the client.

```
ospace/drb/drb_integration.rb
require_relative "drb_server"
require_relative "drb_client"
#sleep 1
```

produces:

```
Sum is: 6
```

The initial nil argument to DRbObject indicates that we want to attach to a new distributed object. We could also use an existing object.

Yes, this is a functional distributed object mechanism, but it's written in a few hundred lines of Ruby code—no C, nothing fancy, just plain old Ruby code. Of course, it has no naming service, trader service, or anything like you'd see in a full-fledged distributed system, but it's simple and faster than you might think.

What's Next

The important thing to remember about Ruby is that there's no big difference between "compile time" and "runtime." It's all the same. You can add code to a running process. You can redefine methods on the fly, change their scope from public to private, and so on. You can even alter basic types, such as Class and Object. Once you get used to this flexibility, it's hard to go back to a static language such as C++ or even to a half-static language such as Java.

But then, why would you want to do that?

Now it's time to take a look at Ruby's syntax in a more structured way.

Part IV

Ruby Language Reference

This part looks at the Ruby language from the bottom up. Most of what appears here is the syntax and semantics of the Ruby language. The extensive library of classes and modules will mostly be covered in Part V. However, Ruby's syntax and the library are closely entangled—literal values are part of syntax, but they create objects in the library, so we'll cover parts of the library as needed to explain the syntax.

## CHAPTER 24

Language Reference: Literal Types and Expressions

So far, we've given a narrative look at how Ruby works. In this chapter, we're going to follow more of a reference structure to discuss Ruby's syntax as it concerns literal types and expressions. In the next chapter, we'll cover syntax relating to objects and classes.

Source Layout

Ruby is a line-oriented language. Ruby expressions and statements are terminated at the end of a line unless the parser can determine that the statement is incomplete. Some examples are when the last token on a line is an operator or comma, or when an open delimiter, such as a parenthesis, square bracket, or curly brace has not been closed. A backslash at the end of a line also tells Ruby to continue the expression onto the next line:

```
# no backslash '\' needed -- ends with an operator
d = 4 + 5 +
    6 + 7

# no backslash '\' needed -- has an unclosed parenthesis
e = (4 + 5
    + 6 + 7)

# backslash '\' needed -- ends with a number
f = 8 + 9   \
    + 10
```

A semicolon can be used to separate multiple expressions on a line:

```
a = 1
b = 2; c = 3
```

Comments start with # and run to the end of the physical line. Comments are ignored during syntax analysis.

The first line of a multiline comment starts with =begin, and the last line starts with =end. The lines in-between are ignored by Ruby and may be used to comment out sections of code or to embed documentation. The =begin and =end markers can't be indented; they must start in the first column of a line, like this:

```
=begin
this is
all a
multiline comment
=end
```

Ruby uses comment syntax at the top of a file for directives that affect how a file is parsed. These are often called "magic comments," and they must appear in the file before the first line of uncommented Ruby code. The syntax of these magic comments is # directive: value.

If you have more than one magic comment, you may put them on separate lines, as long as all of them come before the first line of Ruby code:

```
# frozen_string_literal: true
# encoding: big5
```

You may also put them on a single line, delimited by semicolons and surrounded by -*-, like this:

```
-*- frozen_string_literal: true; encoding: big5 -*-
```

This syntax is based on the file configuration syntax used by the Emacs editor.

The following table lists the magic comment directives Ruby supports:

Comment	Definition
coding	Synonym of encoding.
encoding	The default encoding used for string literals in the file, and the encoding of the source code as a whole. The default is utf-8.
frozen_string_literal	If true, when string literals are loaded during parsing, they are automatically frozen to make them immutable. String literals with interpolation are never frozen. The default is false.
sharable_con- stant_value	This directive changes the behavior of immutable constants to allow them to be shared by ractors. The default value is none, in which case constants aren't frozen and can't be shared with ractors. With the value literal, constants that are assigned literal values are frozen and can be shared. With the value experimental_copy, constants are automatically copied when shared with ractors, and with the value experimental_everything, all constant values are sharable. This directive is experimental and likely to change. Unlike the other magic comments, this directive may be used multiple times in a file and is applicable until the next instance of this directive or the end of the scope in which it's declared.
warn_indent	If true, mismatched indentation in the source code triggers a warning when the file is loaded. The default is false, unless Ruby is run with the -w switch, in which case the default is true.

Table 10—Magic comment directives

Ruby source files are assumed by default to be written with a UTF-8 encoding, but this can be changed with the encoding magic comment.

You can pipe programs to the Ruby interpreter's standard input stream:

```
$ echo 'puts "Hello"' | ruby
```

If Ruby comes across a line anywhere in the source containing just __END__, with no leading or trailing whitespace, it treats that line as the end of the program, and any subsequent lines won't be treated as program code. Those subsequent lines are treated as data, and they can be read into the running program using the global IO object DATA. The DATA object only contains the subsequent lines from the main file of the program, and the lines after __END__ in other files will be ignored.

```
DATA.each_line do |line|
  p line
end

__END__
line one
line two
```

produces:

```
"line one\n"
"line two\n"
```

BEGIN and END Blocks

Every Ruby source file can declare blocks of code to be run as the file is being loaded (the BEGIN blocks) and after the program has finished executing (the END blocks):

```
BEGIN {
  begin code
}

END {
  end code
}
```

A program may include multiple BEGIN and END blocks. BEGIN blocks are executed in the order they are encountered. END blocks are executed in reverse order.

These blocks are admittedly a little obscure. They seem mostly to be used on the command line for one-line commands to allow initialization or teardown around the actual one-line command.

```
$ ruby -ne "BEGIN {result = ""}; END {p result}; result += gets.upcase" testfile
```

With the -n acting as a while loop and the blocks, this code is equivalent to the following:

```
result = ""
while gets
  result << gets.upcase
end
p result
```

Because gets is used as the while condition, this code prints every other line of the file.

Unicode in Syntax

Ruby allows you to use Unicode characters as variable and method names, as in the following example:

```
def ∑(*args)
  args.sum
end

puts ∑(1, 3, 5, 9)
```

produces:

```
18
```

This can lead to some pretty obscure and hard-to-use code. (For example, is the summation character in the previous code a real summation, \u2211, or a Greek sigma, \u03a3?) Just because we *can* do something doesn't mean we necessarily *should*.

Ruby Literals

Ruby has special syntax for scalar values that are booleans, numbers, lambdas, ranges, regular expressions, strings, symbols, and array and hash collections. Although all types in Ruby are implemented as classes, these types have special syntax for creating literal values of them. Lambda literals will be covered in Proc Objects, on page 482; we're going to discuss the rest here.

Boolean Literals

Ruby provides the literal values true and false. The true value is the instance of the singleton class TrueClass and represents a true value in logical expressions. The false value is the instance of the singleton class FalseClass and represents a false value in logical expressions. The literal value nil is the only instance of the singleton NilClass and also represents a false value in logical expressions.

The only logically false values in Ruby are false and nil. You'll sometimes see the term "falsey" used to cover both values. All other values, including empty strings and arrays, are logically true. These are sometimes called the "truthy" values. Currently, Ruby doesn't have a way to create a new value that will behave as logically false.

Integer and Floating-Point Numbers

Ruby integers are objects of class Integer. Integer objects hold integers that fit within the native machine word minus 1 bit. The internal storage of integers changes depending on the size of the number, but for nearly every purpose in Ruby, that internal detail is abstracted away from you.

Integers are written using an optional leading sign and an optional base indicator (0 or 0o for octal, 0d for decimal, 0x for hex, or 0b for binary), followed by a string of digits in the appropriate base. Underscore characters are ignored in the digit string.

```
123456         => 123456
0d123456       => 123456
123_456        => 123456    # - underscore ignored
-543           => -543      # - negative number
0xaabb         => 43707     # - hexadecimal
```

```
0377                       => 255      # - octal
0o377                      => 255      # - octal
-0b10_1010                 => -42      # - binary (negated)
123_456_789_123_456_789   => 123456789123456789 # Big number internal storage
```

A numeric literal with a decimal point and/or an exponent is turned into a Float object, corresponding to the native architecture's double data type. You must follow the decimal point with a digit; if you write 1.e3, Ruby tries to invoke the method e3 on the Fixnum 1. You must place at least one digit before the decimal point.

```
12.34     # => 12.34
-0.1234e2 # => -12.34
1234e-2   # => 12.34
```

Rational and Complex Numbers

Classes that support rational numbers (ratios of integers) and complex numbers are built into the Ruby interpreter. Rational numbers have a literal syntax with an expression followed by the letter r:

```
2r       # => (2/1)
3/4r     # => (3/4)
-2/5r    # => (-2/5)
2/-5r    # => (-2/5)
1.4r     # => (7/5)
3/9r     # => (1/3)
```

Complex numbers are integers with an i suffix for the complex part:

```
2i       # => (0+2i)
4 + 3i   # => (4+3i)
```

A number can be rational and imaginary, but the r needs to come before the i in the suffix list.

Strings

Ruby provides a number of mechanisms for creating literal strings. Each generates objects of type String. The different mechanisms vary in terms of how a string is delimited and how much substitution is done on the literal's content. Literal strings are encoded using the source encoding of the file that contains them.

Single-quoted string literals ('_stuff_' and %q/_stuff_/) undergo the least substitution. They convert the sequence \\ into a single backslash, and a backslash can be used to escape the single quote or the string delimiter. All other backslashes appear literally in the string.

```
'hello'                          # => hello
'a backslash \'\\\''             # => a backslash '\'
%q/simple string/                # => simple string
%q(nesting (really) works)       # => nesting (really) works
%q(escape a\) with backslash)    # => escape a) with backslash
%q no_blanks_here ;              # => no_blanks_here
```

Double-quoted strings ("_stuff_", %Q/_stuff_/, and %/_stuff_/) undergo additional substitutions. Refer to the table shown on page 434.

#{code}	Value of *code*	\b	Backspace (0x08)	\t	Tab (0x09)
\nnn	Octal *nnn*	\cx	Ctrl+*x*	\uxxxx	Unicode character
\x	*x*	\e	Escape (0x1b)	\u{xx xx xx}	Unicode characters
\C-x	Ctrl+*x*	\f	Formfeed (0x0c)	\v	Vertical tab (0x0b)
\M-x	Meta+*x*	\n	Newline (0x0a)	\xnn	Hex *nn*
\M-\C-x	Meta+Ctrl+*x*	\r	Return (0x0d)		
\a	Bell/alert (0x07)	\s	Space (0x20)		

Table 11—Substitutions in double-quoted strings

Here are some examples:

```
a   = 123
"\123mile"                  # => Smile
"Greek pi: \u03c0"          # => Greek pi: π
"Greek \u{70 69 3a 20 3c0}" # => Greek pi: π
"Say \"Hello\""             # => Say "Hello"
%Q!"I said 'nuts'\!," I said!  # => "I said 'nuts'!," I said
%Q{Try #{a + 1}, not #{a - 1}} # => Try 124, not 122
%<Try #{a + 1}, not #{a - 1}>  # => Try 124, not 122
"Try #{a + 1}, not #{a - 1}"   # => Try 124, not 122
%{ #{ a = 1; b = 2; a + b } }  # =>  3
```

Last, and probably least (in terms of usage), you can get the string corresponding to an ASCII character by preceding that character with a question mark, where "a" can represent any ASCII character. Refer to the following table:

?a	a	ASCII character
?\n	\n	newline (0x0a)
?\C-a	\u0001	control a (0x65 & 0x9f) == 0x01
?\M-a	\xE1	meta sets bit 7
?\M-\C-a	\x81	meta and control a
?\C-?	\u007F	delete character

Table 12—ASCII character expressions

Inside a double-quoted string, the sequence #{EXPR} will cause the expression inside the curly braces to be evaluated, converted to a string, and interpolated into the string. If you want to interpolate an instance, class, or global variable, you can do so without the braces; just use #@var, #@@var, or #$var. But the braces are recommended for consistency.

Strings can continue across multiple input lines, in which case they will contain newline characters.

You can use *here documents* to express long string literals. When Ruby parses the sequence <<IDENTIFIER or <<QUOTED_STRING, it replaces it with a string literal built from successive logical input lines. It stops building the string when it finds a line that starts with an *identifier* or a *quoted string*. You can put a minus sign immediately after the << characters, in which case the terminator can be indented from the margin. If a quoted string was used to specify the terminator, its quoting rules are applied to the here document; otherwise, double-quoting rules apply.

```
reference/quoting.rb
print <<HERE
Double quoted
here document.
It is #{Time.now}
HERE

print <<-'THERE'
    This is single quoted.
    The above used #{Time.now}
THERE
```

produces:

```
Double quoted
here document.
It is 2023-11-02 17:16:26 -0500
    This is single quoted.
    The above used #{Time.now}
```

Putting a tilde (~) in front of the identifier removes all leading spaces from each line of the here document, allowing the heredoc to be indented for readability:

```
reference/heredoc.rb
print <<~HERE
  This is indented.
  But the result will not have
  the indentation.
HERE
```

produces:

```
This is indented.
But the result will not have
the indentation.
```

A quirk of the heredoc syntax is that if you want to call a method on the resulting string, you chain the method after the opening identifier, as in this example that calls upcase.

```
reference/heredoc_2.rb
print <<~HERE.upcase
  This is indented.
  But the result will not have
  the indentation.
HERE
```

produces:

```
THIS IS INDENTED.
BUT THE RESULT WILL NOT HAVE
THE INDENTATION.
```

Adjacent single- and double-quoted strings are concatenated to form a single String object—in fact, the parser considers them a single string:

```
'Con' "cat" 'en' "ate" # => "Concatenate"
```

A new String object is created every time a string literal is assigned or passed as a parameter.

```
3.times do
  print "hello".object_id, " "
end
```

produces:

```
60 80 100
```

To avoid this behavior, Ruby has the concept of a *frozen* string. A frozen string isn't mutable and is only allocated once. There's one exception, strings with interpolation are never frozen. Future attempts to allocate a frozen string will result in the same object. You can create a frozen string by calling freeze on a string.

```
3.times do
  print "hello".freeze.object_id, " "
end
```

produces:

```
60 60 60
```

You can automatically freeze all non-interpolated literal strings in a file with the frozen_string_literal magic comment.

String literals are always encoded using the encoding of the source file that contains them, regardless of the content of the string:

```
# encoding: utf-8
def show_encoding(str)
  puts "'#{str}' (size #{str.size}) is #{str.encoding.name}"
end

show_encoding "cat"    # latin 'c', 'a', 't'
show_encoding "∂og"    # greek delta, latin 'o', 'g'
```

produces:

```
'cat' (size 3) is UTF-8
'∂og' (size 3) is UTF-8
```

Symbols and regular expression literals that contain only 7-bit characters are encoded using US-ASCII. Otherwise, they will have the encoding of the file that contains them.

```
# encoding: utf-8
def show_encoding(str)
  puts "#{str.inspect} is #{str.encoding.name}"
end
show_encoding :cat
show_encoding :∂og

show_encoding /cat/
show_encoding /∂og/
```

produces:

```
:cat is US-ASCII
:∂og is UTF-8
/cat/ is US-ASCII
/∂og/ is UTF-8
```

You can create arbitrary Unicode characters in strings and regular expressions using the \u escape. This has two forms: \uxxxx lets you encode a character using four hex digits, and the delimited form \u{x... x... x...} lets you specify a variable number of characters, each with a variable number of hex digits:

```
# encoding: utf-8
"Greek pi: \u03c0"          # => "Greek pi: π"
"Greek pi: \u{3c0}"         # => "Greek pi: π"
"Greek \u{70 69 3a 20 3c0}" # => "Greek pi: π"
```

Literals containing \u will always be encoded in UTF-8, regardless of the source file encoding.

The bytes method is a convenient way to inspect the bytes in a string object. Notice that in the following code, the 16-bit codepoint is converted to a two-byte UTF-8 encoding:

```
# encoding: utf-8
"pi: \u03c0".bytes  # => [112, 105, 58, 32, 207, 128]
```

Ranges

expression .. expression

expression ... expression

Outside the context of a conditional expression, EXPR..EXPR and EXPRESSION...EXPRESSION construct Range objects. The two-dot form is an inclusive range; the one with three dots is a range that excludes its last element.

If the range is being used for comparison purposes to identify objects that are inside the range, then the objects defining the range only need to implement the <=> comparison operator. If the range is being used to iterate over the values inside the range, then the elements on either side of the range can be any object that implements a method called succ that returns the next object in the sequence, for example, integers and strings.

A range can be constructed without a start value, as in ..5, or without an end value, 5... In these cases, the range is an infinite sequence on the unbounded end. An unbounded range can be useful in matching a set of values (as in using ...today to indicate days in the past). Unbounded ranges can also be used when taking a subelement of an array or string, where the infinite side is a stand-in for the edge of the array:

```
["a", "b", "c", "d", "e"][..2] # => ["a", "b", "c"]
["a", "b", "c", "d", "e"][2..] # => ["c", "d", "e"]
```

Arrays

[expression, expression, ...]

Literals of class Array are created by placing a comma-separated series of object references between square brackets. The objects can be of any type and don't have to be of the same type as each other. A trailing comma is ignored.

```
arr = [fred, 10, 3.14, "This is a string", barney("pebbles"),]
```

Arrays of strings can be constructed using the shortcut notations %w and %W. The lowercase form extracts space-separated tokens into successive elements of the array. No substitution is performed on the individual strings. The uppercase version also converts the words to an array but performs all the normal double-quoted string substitutions on each individual word. A space between words can be escaped with a backslash. The shortcut notation %i creates an array of symbols, as in %i[a b c]. These are forms of general delimited input, which is described in General Delimited Input, on page 444.

```
arr = %w(fred wilma barney betty great\ gazoo)
arr        # => ["fred", "wilma", "barney", "betty", "great gazoo"]
arr = %w(Hey!\tIt is now -#{Time.now}-)
arr        # => ["Hey!\tIt", "is", "now", "-#{Time.now}-"]
arr = %W(Hey!\tIt is now -#{Time.now}-)
arr        # => ["Hey!   It", "is", "now", "-2023-11-02 17:16:26 -0500-"]
```

Hashes

{key expression => value expression, ...}

{key expression: value expression, ...}

{key and value expression:, ...}

A literal Ruby Hash is created by placing a list of key/value pairs between braces. Keys and values can be separated by the sequence =>. A comma appears between each key/value pair:

```
colors = {"red" => 0xf00, "green" => 0x0f0, "blue" => 0x00f}
```

If the keys are symbols, you can use this alternative notation:

```
colors = {red: 0xf00, green: 0x0f0, blue: 0x00f}
```

The key syntax here exactly matches the symbol-literal syntax, except with the colon at the end instead of the beginning, allowing for symbols with syntactically challenging names like {"do-this": 3, "do that": 4}. The resulting keys will be symbols, not strings.

The keys and/or values in a particular hash need not have the same type. The keys and values will be accessible in sequence in the same order in which they were added to the hash.

Requirements for a Hash Key

Hash keys must be objects that respond to the message hash by returning a hash code, and the hash code for a given key must not change. The keys used in hashes must also be comparable using eql?. If eql? returns true for two keys, then those keys must also have the same hash code. This means that you need to be careful when using certain classes (such as Array and Hash) as keys because their hash values can change based on their contents.

If you keep an external reference to an object that's used as a key and use that reference to alter the object, thus changing its hash code, the hash lookup based on that key may not work. You can force the hash to be reindexed by calling its rehash method.

```
arr = [1, 2, 3]
hash = {arr => "value"}
hash[arr] # => "value"
arr[1] = 99
hash       # => {[1, 99, 3]=>"value"}
hash[arr] # => nil
hash.rehash
hash[arr] # => "value"
```

Because strings are frequently used as hash keys and string contents are often changed, Ruby treats string keys as a special case. If you use a String object as a hash key, the hash will duplicate the string internally and will use that copy as its key. The copy will be frozen. Any changes made to the original string won't affect the hash.

If you write your own classes and use instances of them as hash keys, you need to make sure that either (a) the hashes of the key objects don't change once the objects have been created or (b) you remember to call the rehash method to reindex the hash whenever a key hash is changed.

Hash Shortcuts

Often, a hash key has the same name as a value in the current context, and you want to assign that value to that key as in {red: red, green: green, blue: blue}. If the value already exists in the context where the hash is being created, then you can leave off the value and the existing local value is used instead:

```
red = 0xf00
green = 0x0f0
blue = 0x00f
colors = {red:, green:, blue:}
```

The key can be a local variable or a method that takes no arguments.

Symbols

A Ruby symbol is an identifier similar to a string, but optimized for fast lookup. If the symbol you want is an identifier—with no spaces and no unusual characters–you construct the symbol for a name by preceding the name with a colon. You can construct the symbol for any other arbitrary string by preceding a string literal with a colon. Substitution occurs in double-quoted strings. You can also use the %s delimited notation to create a symbol.

A particular name or string will always generate the same symbol and the same internal object, regardless of how that name is used within the program.

```
:Object
:my_variable
:"Ruby rules"
a = "cat"
:'catsup'                  # => :catsup
:"#{a}sup"                 # => :catsup
:'#{a}sup'                 # => :"\#{a}sup"
%s{"symbol with quotes"} # => :"\"symbol with quotes\""
```

Other languages might use the term *interning* to refer to the process of having a single internal representation for all objects with the same value. Those languages might call symbols *interned strings* or *atoms*.

Regular Expressions

Regular expression literals are objects of type Regexp. They are created explicitly by calling Regexp.new or implicitly by using the literal forms, /_pattern_/ and %r{_pattern_}. The %r construct is a form of general delimited input as described in General Delimited Input, on page 444.

/pattern/

/pattern/*options*

%r{pattern}

%r{pattern}*options*

Regexp.new("pattern" ‹, *options*›)

options is one or more of i (case insensitive), o (substitute once), m (matches newline), and x (allow spaces and comments). You can additionally override the default encoding of the pattern with n (no encoding-ASCII), e (EUC), s (Shift_JIS), or u (UTF-8).

Within a regular expression, each entry in the following table matches the characters described in its description. Most characters match themselves, but several special characters or patterns have defined matches.

characters	All except . | ( ) [\ ^ { + $ * and ? match themselves. To match one of these characters, precede it with a backslash.
\a \cx \e \f \r \t \u*nnnn* \v \x*nn* \n*nn* \C-\M-*x* \C-*x* \M-x	Match the character derived according to Table 11, Substitutions in double-quoted strings, on page 434.
^	Matches the beginning of a line.
$	Matches the end of a line.
\A	Matches the beginning of the entire string.
\z, \Z	Match the end of the entire string. \Z ignores trailing \n.
\d, \h	Match any decimal digit or hexadecimal digit ([0-9a-fA-F]). If Unicode is set, matches a Unicode decimal number.
\s	Matches any whitespace character: tab, newline, vertical tab, formfeed, return, and space. If Unicode is set, also matches [\t\n\r\x{000B}\x{000C}\x{0085}] plus *Line_Separator, Paragraph_Separator, Space_Separator*.
\w	Matches any word character: alphanumerics and underscores. If Unicode is set, matches *Letter, Mark, Number ,Connector_Punctuation*.
\D, \H, \S, \W	The negated forms of \d, \h, \s, and \w, matching characters that aren't digits, hexadecimal digits, whitespace, or word characters, per whatever encoding is specified.
\b, \B	Match word/nonword boundaries.
\G	The position where a previous repetitive search completed.
\K	Discards the portion of the match to the left of the \K.

\R	A generic end-of-line sequence. If Unicode is set, also matches Unicode end-of-line characters.
\X	A Unicode grapheme. Generally only useful in Unicode encodings.
\p{property}, \P{property}, \p{!property}	Match a character that is in/not in the given property.
. (period)	Appearing outside brackets, matches any character except a newline. (With the /m option, it matches newline, too).
[characters]	Matches a single character from the specified set.
re*	Matches zero or more occurrences of *re*.
re+	Matches one or more occurrences of *re*.
re{m,n}	Matches at least *m* and at most *n* occurrences of *re*.
re{m,}	Matches at least *m* occurrences of *re*.
re{,n}	Matches at most *n* occurrences of *re*.
re{m}	Matches exactly *m* occurrences of *re*.
re?	Matches zero or one occurrence of *re*.
	The ?, *, +, and {m,n} modifiers are greedy by default. Append a question mark to make them minimal, and append a plus sign to make them possessive (that is, they are greedy and won't backtrack).
re1 | re2	Matches either *re1* or *re2*.
(...)	Parentheses group regular expressions and introduce extensions.
#{...}	Substitutes expression in the pattern, as with strings. By default, the substitution is performed each time a regular expression literal is evaluated. With the /o option, it's performed just the first time.
\1, \2, ... \n	Match the value matched by the *n*th grouped subexpression.
(?# comment)	Inserts a comment into the pattern.
(?:re)	Makes *re* into a group without generating backreferences.
(?=re), (?!re)	Matches if *re* is/is not at this point but doesn't consume it.
(?<=re), (?<!re)	Matches if *re* is/is not before this point but doesn't consume it.
(?>re)	Matches *re* but inhibits subsequent backtracking.
(?adimux), (?-imx)	Turn on/off the corresponding a, d, i, m, u, or x option. If used inside a group, the effect is limited to that group.
(?adimux:re), (?-imx:re)	Turn on/off the i, m, or x option for *re*.
\n, \k'n', and \k<n>	The nth captured subpattern.
(?<name>...) or (?'name'...)	Name the string captured by the group.
\k<name> or \k'name'	The contents of the named group.
\k<name>+/-n or \k'name'+/-n	The contents of the named group at the given relative nesting level.
\g<name> or \g<number>	Invokes the named or numbered group.

Table 13—Regular expression special characters

Regular Expression Matching Variables

Ruby sets a number of variables after a successful regular expression match. Although these variables start with $, they are scoped to the current thread, rather than being truly global. These variables are set to nil after an unsuccessful regular expression match. Refer to the following table.

$& → String	The string matched (following a successful pattern match). This variable is local to the current scope. [r/o, thread]
$+ → String	The contents of the highest-numbered group matched following a successful pattern match. Thus, in "cat" =~ /(c|a)(t|z)/, $+ will be set to "t." This variable is local to the current scope. [r/o, thread]
$` → String	The string preceding the match in a successful pattern match. This variable is local to the current scope. [r/o, thread]
$' → String	The string following the match in a successful pattern match. This variable is local to the current scope. [r/o, thread]
$1...$n → String	The contents of successive groups matched in a pattern match. In "cat" =~ /(c|a)(t|z)/, $1 will be set to "a" and $2 to "t." This variable is local to the current scope. [r/o, thread]
$~ → MatchData	An object that encapsulates the results of a successful pattern match. The variables $&, $`, $', and $1 to $9 are all derived from $~. Assigning to $~ changes the values of these derived variables. This variable is local to the current scope. [thread]

Table 14—Regular expression match variables

In these descriptions, the notation [r/o] indicates that the variables are read-only; an error will be raised if a program attempts to modify a read-only variable. Entries marked [thread] are thread local.

Character Classes

If you look at the table, you'll see that some of the character classes have different interpretations depending on the character set option defined for the regular expression. These options tell the regexp engine whether (for example) word characters are just the ASCII alphanumerics, or whether they should be extended to include Unicode letters, marks, numbers, and connection punctuation. The options are set using the sequence (?_option_), where the option is d for the default mode, a for ASCII-only support, or u for full Unicode support. If you don't specify an option, it defaults to (?d). There doesn't seem to be much difference between d and a.

```
show_regexp('über.', /\w+/)       # => ü->ber<-.
show_regexp('über.', /(?a)\w+/)   # => ü->ber<-.
show_regexp('über.', /(?d)\w+/)   # => ü->ber<-.
show_regexp('über.', /(?u)\w+/)   # => ->über<-.

show_regexp('über.', /\W+/)       # => ->ü<-ber.
show_regexp('über.', /(?a)\W+/)   # => ->ü<-ber.
show_regexp('über.', /(?d)\W+/)   # => ->ü<-ber.
show_regexp('über.', /(?u)\W+/)   # => über->.<-
```

The POSIX character classes, as shown in Table 15, POSIX character classes, on page 443, correspond to the ctype(3) macros of the same names. They can also be negated by putting an up arrow (or caret) after the first colon:

```
show_regexp('Price $12.', /[aeiou]/)        # => Pr->i<-ce $12.
show_regexp('Price $12.', /[[:digit:]]/)    # => Price $->1<-2.
show_regexp('Price $12.', /[[:space:]]/)    # => Price-> <-$12.
show_regexp('Price $12.', /[[:^alpha:]]/)   # => Price-> <-$12.
show_regexp('Price $12.', /[[:punct:]aeiou]/) # => Pr->i<-ce $12.
```

These versions are much rarer in actual Ruby code, in our experience. But the POSIX classes do match non-ASCII characters.

You can create the intersection of character classes using &&. So, to match all lowercase ASCII letters that aren't vowels, you could use this:

```
str = "now is the time"
str.gsub(/[a-z&&[^aeiou]]/, '*') # => "*o* i* **e *i*e"
```

The \p construct gives you an encoding-aware way of matching a character with a particular Unicode property (shown in Table 16, Unicode character properties, on page 444):

```
 # encoding: utf-8
string = "∂y/∂x = 2πx"
show_regexp(string, /\p{Alnum}/) # => ∂->y<-/∂x = 2πx
show_regexp(string, /\p{Digit}/) # => ∂y/∂x = ->2<-πx
show_regexp(string, /\p{Space}/) # => ∂y/∂x-> <-= 2πx
show_regexp(string, /\p{Greek}/) # => ∂y/∂x = 2->π<-x
show_regexp(string, /\p{Graph}/) # => ->∂<-y/∂x = 2πx
```

POSIX Character Classes (Unicode)	
	Text in parentheses indicates the Unicode classes. These apply if the regular expression's encoding is one of the Unicode encodings.
[:alnum:]	Alphanumeric (*Letter* | *Mark* | *Decimal_Number*)
[:alpha:]	Uppercase or lowercase letter (*Letter* | *Mark*)
[:ascii:]	7-bit character including nonprinting. This is a non-standard class supported by Ruby.
[:blank:]	Blank and tab (+ *Space_Separator*)
[:cntrl:]	Control characters—at least 0x00–0x1f, 0x7f (*Control* | *Format* | *Unassigned* | *Private_Use* | *Surrogate*)
[:digit:]	Digit (*Decimal_Number*)
[:graph:]	Printable character excluding space (Unicode also excludes *Control*, *Unassigned*, and *Surrogate*)
[:lower:]	Lowercase letter (*Lowercase_Letter*)
[:print:]	Any printable character (including space)
[:punct:]	Printable character excluding space and alphanumeric (*Connector_Punctuation* | *Dash_Punctuation* | *Close_Punctuation* | *Final_Punctuation* | *Initial_Punctuation* | *Other_Punctuation* | *Open_Punctuation*)
[:space:]	Whitespace (same as \s)
[:upper:]	Uppercase letter (*Uppercase_Letter*)
[:xdigit:]	Hex digit (0–9, a–f, A–F)
[:word:]	Alphanumeric, underscore, and multibyte (*Letter* | *Mark* | *Decimal_Number* | *Connector_Punctuation*) This is a non-standard class supported by Ruby.

Table 15—POSIX character classes

Character Properties	
\p{name}	Matches character with named property
\p{^name}	Matches any character except named property
\P{name}	Matches any character except named property

Property names.

Spaces, underscores, and case are ignored in property names.

All encodings	Alnum, Alpha, Blank, Cntrl, Digit, Graph, Lower, Print, Punct, Space, Upper, XDigit, Word, ASCII
EUC and SJIS	Hiragana, Katakana
UTF-n	Any, Assigned, C, Cc, Cf, Cn, Co, Cs, L, Ll, Lm, Lo, Lt, Lu, M, Mc, Me, Mn, N, Nd, Nl, No, P, Pc, Pd, Pe, Pf, Pi, Po, Ps, S, Sc, Sk, Sm, So, Z, Zl, Zp, Zs, Arabic, Armenian, Bengali, Bopomofo, Braille, Buginese, Buhid, Canadian _Aboriginal, Cherokee, Common, Coptic, Cypriot, Cyrillic, Deseret, Devanagari, Ethiopic, Georgian, Glagolitic, Gothic, Greek, Gujarati, Gurmukhi, Han, Hangul, Hanunoo, Hebrew, Hiragana, Inherited, Kannada, Katakana, Kharoshthi, Khmer, Lao, Latin, Limbu, Linear_B, Malayalam, Mongolian, Myanmar, New_Tai_Lue, Ogham, Old_Italic, Old_Persian, Oriya, Osmanya, Runic, Shavian, Sinhala, Syloti_Nagri, Syriac, Tagalog, Tagbanwa, Tai_Le, Tamil, Telugu, Thaana, Thai, Tibetan, Tifinagh, Ugaritic, Yi

Table 16—Unicode character properties

General Delimited Input

In addition to the normal quoting mechanism, Ruby supports a generalized delimiter sequence that allows you to write alternative forms of literal strings, arrays of strings and symbols, regular expressions, and shell commands. All these literals start with a percent character followed by a single character that identifies the literal's type. These characters are summarized in the following table (the actual literal values are described later in this chapter):

Type	Meaning	Example
%q	Single-quoted string	%q{\a and #{1+2} are literal}
%Q, %	Double-quoted string	%Q{\a and #{1+2} are expanded}
%w, %W	Array of strings	%w[one two three]
%i, %I	Array of symbols	%i[one two three]
%r	Regular expression pattern	%r{cat|dog}
%s	A symbol	%s!a symbol!
%x	Shell command	%x(df -h)

Table 17—Literal input delimiters

Unlike their lowercase counterparts, %I, %Q, and %W will perform interpolation:

```
%i{one digit#{1+1} three} # => [:one, :"digit\#{1+1}", :three]
%I{one digit#{1+1} three} # => [:one, :digit2, :three]
%q{one digit#{1+1} three} # => "one digit\#{1+1} three"
%Q{one digit#{1+1} three} # => "one digit2 three"
%w{one digit#{1+1} three} # => ["one", "digit\#{1+1}", "three"]
%W{one digit#{1+1} three} # => ["one", "digit2", "three"]
```

Following the type character is a delimiter, which can be any nonalphanumericic or nonmultibyte character. If the delimiter is the (, [, {, or < character, the literal consists of the characters up to the matching closing delimiter, taking account of nested delimiter pairs. For all other delimiters, the literal comprises the characters up to the next occurrence of the delimiter character.

```
%q/this is a string/
%q-string-
%q(a (nested) string)
```

Delimited strings may continue over multiple lines; the line endings and all spaces at the start of continuation lines will be included in the string:

```
meth = %q{def fred(a)
  a.each {|i| puts i }
end}
```

Names

Ruby names are used to refer to constants, variables, methods, classes, and modules. The first character of a name helps Ruby determine its intended use. Certain names, listed in the following table, are keywords and shouldn't be used as variable, method, class, or module names. (Technically, many of these names are legal method or variable names; it's just very confusing to use them in that way.) Method names are described later in Method Definition, on page 465.

__ENCODING__		__FILE__	__LINE__	BEGIN	END	alias	and	begin
break	case	class	def	defined?	do	else	elsif	end
ensure	false	for	if	in	module	next	nil	not
or	redo	rescue	retry	return	self	super	then	true
undef	unless	until	when	while	yield			

Table 18—Reserved words

In these descriptions, an *uppercase letter* is a capital letter from any Unicode alphabet, and a *digit* means 0 through 9. A *lowercase letter* means any non-7-bit character that's valid in the current encoding, specifically including the underscore (_). Names using non-7-bit character names won't be usable from other source files with different encoding.

A *name* is an uppercase letter, a lowercase letter, or an underscore, followed by *name characters*, which are any combination of upper and lowercase letters, underscores, and digits.

A *local variable name* consists of a lowercase letter followed by name characters. It's conventional to use underscores rather than CamelCase to write multiword names, but the interpreter doesn't enforce this.

```
fred  anObject  _x  three_two_one
```

If the source file encoding is UTF-8, ∂elta and été are both valid local variable names.

An *instance variable name* starts with an "at" sign (@) followed by name characters. The general practice is to use a lowercase letter after the @. The @ sign forms part of the instance variable name.

```
@name  @_  @size
```

A *class variable name* starts with two "at" signs (@@) followed by name characters.

```
@@name  @@_  @@Size
```

A *constant name* starts with an uppercase letter followed by name characters. Class names and module names are constants and follow the constant naming conventions.

By convention, constant object references are normally spelled using uppercase letters and underscores throughout, while class and module names are MixedCase:

```ruby
module Math
  ALMOST_PI = 22.0/7.0
end
class BigBlob
end
```

Global variables and some special system values start with a dollar sign ($) followed by name characters. In addition, Ruby defines a set of two-character global variable names in which the second character is a punctuation character. These predefined variables are listed in Predefined Values, on page 450. Finally, a global variable name can be formed using $- followed by a single letter or underscore. These latter variables typically mirror the setting of the corresponding command-line option (see Execution Environment Values, on page 451, for details):

```ruby
$params  $PROGRAM  $!  $_  $-a  $-K
```

Variable/Method Ambiguity

When Ruby sees a name such as a in an expression, it needs to determine whether it's a local variable reference or a call to a method with no parameters. To decide which is the case, Ruby uses a heuristic. As Ruby parses a source file, it keeps track of symbols that have had values assigned to them. Ruby assumes that these symbols are variables. When it subsequently comes across a symbol that could be a variable or a method call, it checks to see whether it has seen a prior assignment to that symbol. If so, it treats the symbol as a variable; otherwise, it treats it as a method call.

As a somewhat pathological case of this, consider the following code fragment, submitted by Clemens Hintze:

```ruby
def a
  puts "Function 'a' called"
  99
end

(1..2).each do |i|
  if i == 2
    puts "i==2, a=#{a}"
  else
    a = 1
    puts "i==1, a=#{a}"
  end
end
```

produces:

```
i==1, a=1
Function 'a' called
i==2, a=99
```

When parsing the file, Ruby sees the use of a in the puts statement in the main branch of the if and, because it hasn't yet seen any assignment to a, assumes that a is a method call. But by the time it gets to the puts statement in the else branch, it *has* seen an assignment and so treats a as a variable.

Note that the assignment doesn't have to be executed—Ruby just has to have seen it. This program doesn't raise an error.

```
a = 1 if false # => nil
a              # => nil
```

Values, Variables, and Constants

Ruby variables and constants hold references to objects. Variables themselves don't have an intrinsic type. Instead, the type of a variable is defined solely by the messages to which the object referenced by the variable responds. (When we say that a variable is not typed, we mean that any given variable can at different times hold references to objects of different types.)

A Ruby *constant* is also a reference to an object. Constants are created when they are first assigned to (normally in a class or module definition). Ruby, unlike other less flexible languages, lets you alter the value of a constant, although this will generate a warning message, which gets sent to $stderr:

```
MY_CONST = 1
puts "First MY_CONST = #{MY_CONST}"

MY_CONST = 2   # generates a warning but sets MY_CONST to 2
puts "Then MY_CONST = #{MY_CONST}"
```

produces:

```
First MY_CONST = 1
Then MY_CONST = 2
```

Note that although constants shouldn't be changed, you can alter the internal states of the objects they reference (you can freeze objects to prevent this). This is because assignment potentially *aliases* objects, creating two references to the same object.

```
MY_CONST = "Tim"
MY_CONST[0] = "J"   # alter string referenced by constant
MY_CONST   # => "Jim"
```

Scope of Constants and Variables

Constants defined within a class or module may be accessed anywhere within the class or module without needing to reference the enclosing class or module. Outside the class or module, the constant can be accessed using the *scope operator* (::) prefixed by an expression that returns the appropriate class or module object.

Constants defined outside any class or module may be accessed unadorned or by using the scope operator with no prefix. Constants may not be defined in methods. Constants may be added to existing classes and modules from the outside by using the class or module name and the scope operator before the constant name.

```
OUTER_CONST = 99
class Const
```

```
  def get_const
    CONST
  end
  CONST = OUTER_CONST + 1
end

Const.new.get_const # => 100
Const::CONST         # => 100
::OUTER_CONST        # => 99
Const::NEW_CONST = 123
```

Global variables are available throughout a program. Every reference to a particular global name returns the same object. Referencing an uninitialized global variable returns nil.

Class variables are available throughout a class or module body. Class variables must be initialized before use. A class variable is shared among all instances of a class and its subclasses and is available within the class itself:

```
class Song
  @@count = 0

  def initialize
    @@count += 1
  end

  def Song.get_count
    @@count
  end
end
```

Class variables belong to the innermost enclosing class or module at the point they are defined. You can't use a class variables at the top level, you'll receive a RuntimeError.

Class variables are inherited by children, but they propagate upward if first defined in a child:

```
class Top
  @@A = "top A"
  @@B = "top B"
  def dump
    puts values
  end
  def values
    "#{self.class.name}: @@A = #@@A, @@B = #@@B"
  end
end

class MiddleOne < Top
  @@B = "One B"
  @@C = "One C"
  def values
    super + ", C = #@@C"
  end
end

class MiddleTwo < Top
  @@B = "Two B"
  @@C = "Two C"
```

```
  def values
    super + ", C = #@@C"
  end
end

class BottomOne < MiddleOne; end

class BottomTwo < MiddleTwo; end

Top.new.dump
MiddleOne.new.dump
MiddleTwo.new.dump
BottomOne.new.dump
BottomTwo.new.dump
```

produces:

```
Top: @@A = top A, @@B = Two B
MiddleOne: @@A = top A, @@B = Two B, C = One C
MiddleTwo: @@A = top A, @@B = Two B, C = Two C
BottomOne: @@A = top A, @@B = Two B, C = One C
BottomTwo: @@A = top A, @@B = Two B, C = Two C
```

Because of this behavior, class variables tend to be confusing, difficult to debug, and hard to reason about, so we recommend avoiding them.

Instance variables are available within instance methods throughout a class body. Referencing an uninitialized instance variable returns nil. Each object (instance of a class) has a unique set of instance variables.

Local variables are unique in that their scopes are statically determined but their existence is established dynamically. A local variable is created dynamically when it's first assigned a value during program execution. But the scope of a local variable is statically determined to be the immediately enclosing block, method definition, class definition, module definition, or top-level program. Local variables with the same name are different variables if they appear in disjoint scopes.

Method parameters are considered to be variables local to that method.

Block parameters are assigned values when the block is invoked. If a local variable is first assigned in a block, it's local to the block. If a block uses a variable that's previously defined in the scope containing the block's definition, the block will share that variable with the scope.

There are two exceptions to this rule. Block parameters are always local to the block. In addition, variables listed after a semicolon at the end of the block parameter list are also always local to the block:

```
a = 1
b = 2
c = 3

some_method do |b; c|
  a = b + 1
  c = a + 1
  d = c + 1
end
```

In this example, the variable a inside the block is shared with the surrounding scope. The variables b and c aren't shared because they are listed in the block's parameter list, and the variable d is not shared because it occurs only inside the block.

A block takes on the set of local variables in existence at the time that it's created. This forms part of its binding. Note that although the binding of the variables is fixed at this point, the block will have access to the *current* values of these variables when it executes. The binding preserves these variables even if the original enclosing scope is destroyed.

The bodies of while, until, and for loops don't act as blocks. They are part of the scope that contains them; previously existing locals can be used in the loop, and any new locals created will be available outside the bodies afterward.

Predefined Values

The following values are predefined in the Ruby interpreter. In these descriptions, the notation [r/o] indicates that the variables are read-only. An error will be raised if a program attempts to modify a read-only variable. After all, you probably don't want to change the meaning of true halfway through your program (except perhaps if you're a politician). Entries marked [thread] are thread local.

Many global variables look like comic book swearing ($_, $!, $&, and so on). This is for "historical" reasons—most of these variable names come from Perl. If you find memorizing all this punctuation difficult, you may want to take a look at the English library, which gives the commonly used global variables more descriptive names.

In the tables of variables and constants that follow, we list the variable name, the type of the referenced object, and a description.

Exception Information

$! → Exception	The exception object passed to raise. [thread]
$@ → Array	The stack backtrace generated by the last exception. [thread]

Input/Output Values

$/ → String	The input record separator (newline by default). This is the value that routines such as Kernel#gets use to determine record boundaries. If set to nil, gets will read the entire file.
$-0 → String	Synonym for $/.
$\ → String	The string appended to the output of every call to methods such as Kernel#print and IO#write. The default value is nil.
$, → String	The separator string output between the parameters to methods such as print and join. Defaults to nil, which adds no text.
$. → Fixnum	The number of the last line read from the current input file.
$; → String	The default separator pattern used by String#split. May be set using the -F command-line option.
$< → ARGF.class	Synonym for ARGF. See ARGF, on page 238.
$> → IO	The destination stream for print and printf. The default value is STD-OUT.

$_ → String	The last line read by gets or readline. Many string-related functions in the Kernel module operate on $_ by default. The variable is local to the current scope. [thread]
$-F → String	Synonym for $;.
$stderr, $stdout, $stdin, → IO	The current standard error, standard output, and standard input streams.

Execution Environment Values

$0 → String	The name of the top-level Ruby program being executed. Typically this will be the program's filename. On some operating systems, assigning to this variable will change the name of the process reported (for example) by the 'ps(1)' command.
$* → Array	An array of strings containing the command-line options from the invocation of the program. Options used by the Ruby interpreter will have been removed. [r/o]
$" → Array	An array containing the filenames of modules loaded by require. [r/o]
$$ → Fixnum	The process number of the program being executed. [r/o]
$? → Process::Status	The exit status of the last child process to terminate. [r/o, thread]
$: → Array	An array of strings, where each string specifies a directory to be searched for Ruby scripts and binary extensions used by the load and require methods. The initial value is the value of the arguments passed via the -I command-line option, followed by an installation-defined standard library location. This variable may be updated from within a program to alter the default search path; typically, programs use $: << dir to append dir to the path. [r/o]
$-a → Object	True if the -a option is specified on the command line. [r/o]
callee → Symbol	The name of the lexically enclosing method.
$-d → Object	Synonym for $DEBUG.
$DEBUG → Object	Set to true if the -d command-line option is specified.
ENCODING → String	The encoding of the current source file. [r/o]
FILE → String	The name of the current source file. [r/o]
$F → Array	The array that receives the split input line if the -a command-line option is used.
$FILENAME → String	The name of the current input file. Equivalent to $<.filename. [r/o]
$-i → String	If in-place edit mode is enabled (perhaps using the -i command-line option), $-i holds the extension used when creating the backup file. If you set a value into $-i, enables in-place edit mode, as described in the options descriptions on page 235.
$-I → Array	Synonym for $:. [r/o]
$-l → Object	Set to true if the -l option (which enables line-end processing) is present on the command line. See the options description on page 234. [r/o]

__LINE__ → String	The current line number in the source file. [r/o]
$LOAD_PATH → Array	A synonym for $:. [r/o]
$LOADED_FEA- TURES → Array	Synonym for $". [r/o]
__method__ → Symbol	The name of the lexically enclosing method.
$PROGRAM_NAME → String	Alias for $0.
$-p → Object	Set to true if the -p option (which puts an implicit while gets...end loop around your program) is present on the command line. See the options description on page 234. [r/o]
$VERBOSE → Object	Set to true if the -v, --version, -W, or -w option is specified on the command line. Set to false if no option, or -W1 is given. Set to nil if -W0 was specified. Setting this option to true causes the interpreter and some library routines to report additional information. Setting to nil suppresses all warnings (including the output of Object#warn).
$-v, $-w → Object	Synonyms for $VERBOSE.
$-W → Object	Return the value set by the -W command-line option.

Standard Objects

ARGF → Object	Provides access to a list of files. Used by command line processing. See ARGF, on page 238.
ARGV → Array	A synonym for $*.
ENV → Object	A hash-like object containing the program's environment variables. An instance of class Object, ENV implements the full set of Hash methods. Used to query and set the value of an environment variable, as in ENV["PATH"] and ENV["term"]="ansi".
false → FalseClass	Singleton instance of class FalseClass. [r/o]
nil → NilClass	The singleton instance of class NilClass. The value of uninitialized instance and global variables. [r/o]
self → Object	The receiver (object) of the current method. [r/o]
true → TrueClass	Singleton instance of class TrueClass. [r/o]

Global Constants

DATA → IO	If the main program file contains the directive __END__, then the constant DATA will be initialized so that reading from it'll return lines following __END__ from the source file.
RUBY_COPYRIGHT → String	The interpreter copyright.
RUBY_DESCRIPTION → String	Version number and architecture of the interpreter.
RUBY_ENGINE → String	The name of the Ruby interpreter. Returns "ruby" for Matz's version. Other active interpreters include jruby, ruby, opal, and truffleruby.
RUBY_PATCHLEVEL → String	The patch level of the interpreter.

RUBY_PLATFORM → String	The identifier of the platform running this program. This string is in the same form as the platform identifier used by the GNU configure utility (which is not a coincidence).
RUBY_RELEASE_DATE → String	The date of this release.
RUBY_REVISION → String	The revision of the interpreter.
RUBY_VERSION → String	The version number of the interpreter.
STDERR → IO	The actual standard error stream for the program. The initial value of $stderr.
STDIN → IO	The actual standard input stream for the program. The initial value of $stdin.
STDOUT → IO	The actual standard output stream for the program. The initial value of $stdout.
SCRIPT_LINES__ → Hash	If a constant SCRIPT_LINES__ is defined and references a Hash, Ruby will store an entry containing the contents of each file it parses, with the file's name as the key and an array of strings as the value.
TOPLEVEL_BINDING → Binding	A Binding object representing the binding at Ruby's top level— the level where programs are initially executed.

The constant __FILE__ and the variable $0 can be used together to run code only if it appears in the file run directly by the user. For example, library writers often use this to include tests in their libraries that will be run if the library source is run directly, but not if the source is loaded into another program using require.

```
# library code ...

if __FILE__ == $0
  # tests...
end
```

Expressions, Conditionals, and Loops

Single terms in an expression may be any of the following:

- *Literal*. Ruby literals are boolean, numbers, strings, arrays, hashes, ranges, symbols, and regular expressions. These are described in Ruby Literals, on page 432.

- *Shell command*. A shell command is a string enclosed in backquotes or in a general delimited string starting with %x. The string is executed using the host operating system's standard shell, and the resulting standard output stream is returned as the value of the expression. The execution also sets the $? variable with the command's exit status:

```
filter = "*.c"
files = `ls #{filter}`
files = %x{ls #{filter}}
```

- *Variable reference* or *constant reference*. A variable is referenced by citing its name. Depending on scope (see Scope of Constants and Variables, on page 447), you reference a constant either by citing its name or by qualifying the name, using the name of the class or module containing the constant and the scope operator (::):

```
barney    # variable reference
APP_NAMR  # constant reference
Math::PI  # qualified constant reference
```

- *Method invocation.* The various ways of invoking a method are described in Invoking a Method, on page 470.

Operator Expressions

Expressions may be combined using operators. The Ruby operators in precedence order are listed in the following table. The operators with a ✓ in the Method column are implemented as methods and may be overridden.

Method	Operator	Description
✓	! ~ + -	Not, complement, unary plus (method name for unary plus is +@)
✓	**	Exponentiation
✓	-	Unary minus (method names is -@)
✓	* / %	Multiply, divide, and modulo
✓	+ -	Plus and minus
✓	>> <<	Right and left shift (<< is also the append operator)
✓	&	"And" (bitwise for integers)
✓	^		Exclusive "or" and regular "or" (bitwise for integers)
✓	<= < > >=	Comparison operators
✓	<=> == === != =~ !~	Equality and pattern match operators
	&&	Logical "and"
	||	Logical "or"
	.. ...	Range (inclusive and exclusive)
	? :	Ternary if-then-else
	rescue	When used as a modifier at the end of a line
	= %= /= -= += |= &= >>= <<= *= &&= ||= **= ^=	Assignment
	defined?	Test for if a value is defined in current binding
	not	Logical negation
	or and	Logical composition
	if unless while until	Expression modifiers at the end-of-line
	{ }	Block expression
	do end	Block expression

Table 19—Ruby operators (high to low precedence)

More on Assignment

The assignment operator assigns one or more *rvalues* (the *r* stands for "right," because rvalues tend to appear on the right side of assignments) to one or more *lvalues* ("left" values). The meaning of assignment depends on each individual lvalue.

As the following shows, if an lvalue is a variable or constant name, that variable or constant receives a reference to the corresponding rvalue. Ruby will handle nested values on the left if they match the values to the right:

```
a = /regexp/
b, c, d = 1, "cat", [3, 4, 5]
e, (f, g), h = [6, [7, 8], 9]
```

If the lvalue is an object attribute, the corresponding attribute-setting method will be called in the receiver, passing as a parameter the rvalue:

```
class A
  attr_writer :value
end

obj = A.new
obj.value = "hello"    # equivalent to obj.value=("hello")
```

If the lvalue is an array or string element reference, Ruby calls the element assignment operator ([]=) in the receiver, passing as parameters any indices that appear between the brackets followed by the rvalue. This is illustrated in the following table.

Element Reference	Actual Method Call
var[] = "one"	var.[ ]=("one")
var[1] = "two"	var.[ ]=(1, "two")
var["a", /^cat/] = "three"	var.[ ]=("a", /^cat/, "three")

Table 20—Element assignment method calls

If you're writing an []= method that accepts a variable number of indices, it might be convenient to define it using this:

```
def []=(*indices, value)
  # ...
end
```

The value of an assignment expression is its rvalue. This is true even if the assignment is to an attribute method that returns something different.

In addition, an assignment expression may have one or more lvalues and one or more rvalues. The following explains how Ruby handles assignment with different combinations of arguments:

- If any rvalue is prefixed with an asterisk and implements to_a, the rvalue is replaced with the elements returned by to_a, with each element forming its own rvalue.

- If the assignment contains one lvalue and multiple rvalues, the rvalues are converted to an array and assigned to that lvalue.

- If the assignment contains multiple lvalues and one rvalue, the rvalue is expanded if possible into an array of rvalues as described in first bullet point.

- Successive rvalues are assigned to the lvalues. This assignment effectively happens in parallel so that (for example) a,b=b,a swaps the values in a and b.

- If there are more lvalues than rvalues, the excess will have nil assigned to them.

- If there are more rvalues than lvalues, the excess will be ignored.

- At most, one lvalue can be prefixed by an asterisk. This lvalue will end up being an array and will contain as many rvalues as possible. If there are lvalues to the right of the starred lvalue, these will be assigned from the trailing rvalues, and whatever rvalues are left will be assigned to the splat lvalue.

- If an lvalue contains a parenthesized list, the list is treated as a nested assignment statement, and then it's assigned from the corresponding rvalue as described by these rules.

See Parallel Assignment, on page 148, for examples of parallel assignment. The value of a parallel assignment is its array of rvalues.

Rightward Assignment, or Single Pattern Matching

expression => pattern

expression in pattern

Ruby's pattern matching allows for a single-line form that effectively works as "rightward" assignment, where the existing value is on the left and the variables to be assigned are on the right. Note that the delimiter around the right-hand side can be omitted:

```
3 => x
puts x

{a: 1, b: 2} in {a:, b:}
puts a
puts b

{a: 1, b: 2} in a:, b:
puts a
puts b
```

produces:

```
3
1
2
1
2
```

The difference between the two forms is what happens if the pattern and the expression don't match.

The => form returns nil on a successful match and throws a NoMatchingPatternKeyError if it can't match the pattern. The in form returns true if the pattern matches and false if the pattern doesn't match. In the non-matching case, the behavior of the variables that would've been matched is undefined—if the match returns false, you can't depend on those values being matched, unmatched, or anything else.

For the exact syntax of patterns, see Case Pattern Matching, on page 460. The definition of a pattern is the same, and we'll talk more about the semantics of patterns there.

Block Expressions

```
begin
  body
end
```

Expressions may be grouped between begin and end. The value of the block expression is the value of the last expression executed.

Block expressions also play a role in exception handling (see Exceptions, on page 484).

Boolean Expressions

Ruby predefines the values false and nil. Both of these values are treated as being false in a boolean context. All other values are treated as being true. The constant true is available for when you need an explicit "true" value.

And, Or, Not

The and and && operators evaluate their first operand. If false, the expression returns the value of the first operand; otherwise, the expression returns the value of the second operand:

```
expr1 && expr2
expr1 and expr2
```

The or and || operators evaluate their first operand. If true, the expression returns the value of their first operand; otherwise, the expression returns the value of the second operand:

```
expr1 || expr2
expr1 or expr2
```

The not and ! operators evaluate their operand. If true, the expression returns false. If false, the expression returns true.

The word forms of these operators (and, or, and not) have a lower precedence than the corresponding symbol forms (&&, ||, and !). For details, see Table 19, Ruby operators (high to low precedence), on page 454. When used, these versions are used for control flow more than logical operations.

defined?

The defined? keyword returns nil if its argument, which can be an arbitrary expression, is not defined. Otherwise, it returns a description of that argument. For examples, check out The defined? Keyword, on page 151.

Comparison Operators

Ruby defines the generic comparison operator, <=>. This operator should return -1 if the left operand is smaller, 1 if the right operand is smaller, and 0 if the two operands are equal. Although the operators have intuitive meaning, it's up to the classes that implement them to produce meaningful comparison semantics. The module Comparable allows a class to use the definition of <=> to implement the operators ==, <, <=, >, and >=, as well as the methods between? and clamp. All these operators are implemented as methods (see Table 3, Common comparison operators, on page 153).

By convention, the language also uses the standard methods eql? and equal? to test for equality and the method =~ to test for a regular expression match. The operator === is used in case expressions, as described in case Expressions, on page 459.

Both == and =~ have negated forms, != and !~. If an object defines these methods, Ruby will call them. Otherwise, a != b is mapped to !(a == b), and a !~ b is mapped to !(a =~ b).

Ranges in Boolean Expressions

if *expr1 .. expr2*
while *expr1 .. expr2*

A range used in a boolean expression acts as a flip-flop: .. (two dots) or ... (three dots). It has two states—set and unset—and is initially unset.

1. For the three-dot form of a range, if the flip-flop is unset and expr1 is true, the flip-flop becomes set and the flip-flop returns true.

2. If the flip-flop is set, it'll return true. But, if expr2 isn't true, the flip-flop becomes unset.

3. If the flip-flop is unset, it returns false.

The first step differs for the two-dot form of a range. If the flip-flop is unset and expr1 is true, then Ruby only sets the flip-flop if expr2 is not also true.

The difference is illustrated by the following code:

```
a = (11..20).collect { |i| (i % 4 == 0)..(i % 3 == 0) ? i : nil }
a          # => [nil, 12, nil, nil, nil, 16, 17, 18, nil, 20]
a = (11..20).collect { |i| (i % 4 == 0)...(i % 3 == 0) ? i : nil }
a          # => [nil, 12, 13, 14, 15, 16, 17, 18, nil, 20]
```

Regular Expressions in Boolean Expressions

If Ruby has been invoked via the -e parameter in the command line, and only in that case, a regular expression by itself without any other operator in a boolean expression matches against the current value of the variable $_, the most recent line input by gets or readline:

```
$ ruby -ne 'print if /one/' testfile
This is line one
```

In regular code, the use of implicit operands and $_ has been largely phased out, so it's better to use an explicit match against a variable.

if and unless Expressions

if *boolean-expression* ‹then›   unless *boolean-expression* ‹then›
   body   *body*
‹elsif *boolean-expression* ‹then› ‹else
   body ›*   *body* ›
‹ else   end
   body ›
end

The then keyword separates the body from the condition and is not required if the body starts on a new line. The value of an if or unless expression is the value of the last expression evaluated in whichever body is executed.

if and unless Modifiers

expression if *boolean-expression*
expression unless *boolean-expression*

This evaluates *expression* only if *boolean-expression* is true (for if) or false (for unless).

Ternary Operator

boolean-expression ? *expr1* : *expr2*

This returns *expr1* if *boolean-expression* is true and *expr2* otherwise.

case Expressions

Ruby has two forms of conditional case expressions (and another pattern-matching case expression). The first allows a series of conditions to be evaluated, executing code corresponding to the first condition that's true:

```
case
when ‹ boolean-expression ›+ ‹ then ›
    body
when ‹ boolean-expression ›+ ‹ then ›
    body
    ...
‹else
    body ›
end
```

The second form of a case expression takes a target expression following the case keyword. It searches for a match starting at the first (top left) comparison, using the triple-equals operator: _comparison_ === _target_ (as a performance optimization, comparisons between literal strings and between numbers don't use ===):

```
case target
when ‹ comparison ›+ ‹ then ›
    body
when ‹ comparison ›+ ‹ then ›
    body
    ...
‹else
    body ›
end
```

A comparison can be an array reference preceded by an asterisk, in which case it's expanded into that array's elements before the tests are performed on each of them. When a comparison returns true, the search stops and the body associated with the comparison is executed (nothing like a break statement is required). The case statement then returns the value of the last expression executed. If no comparison matches and an else clause is present, the body of that clause will be executed; otherwise, the case statement returns nil.

The then keyword separates the when comparisons from the bodies and is not needed if the body starts on a new line.

Case Pattern Matching

```
case expression
in pattern
  body
in pattern
  body
else
  body
end
```

Pattern matching is a powerful construct to extract values from complicated data structures.

The expression is an already existing piece of data, typically featuring nested hashes and arrays. The case statement selects the first branch where the pattern matches the expression, assigns any variables that are part of the pattern, executes the body associated with that branch, and exits the case expression. If no patterns match, the else branch is executed. If no patterns match and no else branch exists, Ruby throws a NoMatchingPatternError.

Defining Patterns

The simplest pattern is a Ruby object. The pattern matches an expression if the two values are ===. This is useful for classes that define === for extended matching, like Class and String, though there are also cases where you might just match against a regular literal value.

Even so, it's probably more useful matched with a data structure:

```
[pattern, pattern, ...]
```

```
[*variable, pattern, pattern, ..., *variable]
```

An array pattern matches if every element of the array expression matches, so [Integer, Integer] matches [1, 2], but not [1]. But you can use the splat character as a wild card to match more than one element at the beginning or end of an array pattern. If you use a splat at both the beginning and the end, that's called a *find pattern*:

```
case [1, 2, 3]
in [Integer, Integer, Integer]
  puts "all integers"
in [*, Integer, *]
  puts "contains an integer"
else
  puts "no integers"
end
```

If the pattern is not a find pattern, the brackets around the array pattern in the in clause can be omitted.

```
{key: pattern, key: pattern, ..., ‹**nil ›⁺}
```

Hash patterns behave differently from array patterns. A hash pattern will match if all the keys in the pattern match the target expression, even if there are additional keys in the target expression. Appending **nil to the end of the pattern will change this behavior; then the pattern will only match if the keys in the pattern are the only keys in the target expression.

```ruby
case {first_name: "Ron", last_name: "Lithgow"}
in {first_name: String}
  puts "this person has a first name"
else
  puts "this data does not have a first name"
end
```

produces:

```
this person has a first name
```

The curly braces around the hash in the pattern can be omitted.

The empty hash is an exception. It only matches other empty hashes.

pattern | pattern

The pipe character (|) can be used to specify multiple alternative patterns that might match. Ruby will bind to the first of the multiples that matches.

Binding Variables in Patterns

pattern => variable

At any point in a pattern, you can bind a subpattern to a local variable by appending => VAR_NAME to the subpattern:

```ruby
case [1, 2, 3]
in [Integer, Integer => middle, Integer]
  puts "all integers, the middle one is #{middle}"
in [*, Integer, *]
  puts "contains an integer"
else
  puts "no integers"
end
```

produces:

```
all integers, the middle one is 2
```

There are a couple of shortcuts. If you don't need to pattern match the part of the pattern with the local variable, you can just use the variable name without the hash rocket:

```ruby
case [1, 2, 3]
in [Integer, middle, Integer]
  puts "The middle one is #{middle}"
in [*, Integer, *]
  puts "contains an integer"
else
  puts "no integers"
end
```

produces:

```
The middle one is 2
```

In a hash, you can bind a variable to the same name as the key of the hash by just including the key:

```
case {first_name: "Ron", last_name: "Lithgow"}
in {first_name:}
  puts "this person's name is #{first_name}"
else
  puts "this data does not have a first name"
end
```

produces:

```
this person's name is Ron
```

The splatted parts of an array or hash can be bound to a local variable by putting the variable name after the splat, as in [Integer, Integer, *rest].

One limitation comes with this. If you use the | character to match multiple patterns, you can't bind variables inside any of the multiple patterns. This is a limitation of the pattern-matching parser.

If you want to reuse an existing variable, local, global, expression, or instance, as part of a pattern, or if you want to set a variable at the beginning of a pattern and use it later in the pattern, a ^ (caret) in front of the variable name or expression means "use the existing value for this variable."

```
count = 2

case [1, 2, 3]
in [Integer, ^count, last]
  puts "The middle one 2, the last one is #{last}"
in [*, Integer, *]
  puts "contains an integer"
else
  puts "no integers"
end
```

produces:

```
The middle one 2, the last one is 3
```

```
case [1, 2, 2]
in [*, value, ^value]
  puts "This has a pair of the same value, #{value}"
else
  puts "no pairs"
end
```

produces:

```
This has a pair of the same value, 2
```

Guard Clauses in Patterns

pattern if *boolean_expression*

You can limit the ability of a pattern to match by putting a guard clause after it. The match only occurs if the pattern matches the target expression and the boolean expression in the guard clause is true. The guard clause may use values bound in the pattern.

Loops

```
while boolean-expression ‹do›
    body
end
```

This executes *body* zero or more times as long as *boolean-expression* is true.

```
until boolean-expression ‹do›
    body
end
```

This executes *body* zero or more times as long as *boolean-expression* is false.

In both forms, the do separates *boolean-expression* from the *body* and can be omitted when the body starts on a new line:

```
for ‹name›⁺ in expression ‹do›
    body
end
```

The for loop is executed as if it were the following each loop, except that local variables defined in the body of the for loop will be available outside the loop, and those defined within an iterator block will not.

```
expression.each do | ‹name›⁺ |
    body
end
```

loop, which iterates its associated block, isn't a language construct—it's a method in module Kernel.

```
loop do
  print "Input: "
  break unless line = gets
  process(line)
end
```

while and until Modifiers

expression while *boolean-expression*
expression until *boolean-expression*

If *expression* is anything other than a begin/end block, then it executes *expression* zero or more times while *boolean-expression* is true (for while) or false (for until).

If *expression* is a begin/end block, the block will always be executed at least one time.

break, redo, and next

break, redo, and next alter the normal flow through a while, until, for, or an iterator-controlled loop.

The break keyword terminates the immediately enclosing loop—control resumes at the statement following the block. redo repeats the loop from the start but without reevaluating the condition or fetching the next element (in an iterator). The next keyword skips to the end of the loop, effectively starting the next iteration.

break and next may optionally take one or more arguments. If used within a block, the given arguments are returned as the value of the yield. If used within a while, until, or for loop, the value given to break is returned as the value of the statement. If break is never called or if it's called with no value, the loop returns nil.

```
match = for line in ARGF.readlines
  next if line =~ /^#/
  break line if line =~ /ruby/
end
```

## CHAPTER 25

Language Reference: Objects and Classes

In this second chapter of language reference, we'll cover the syntax of Ruby objects and classes.

Method Definition

```
def defname ‹(‹, param ›*) ›
    body
end
```

```
def defname ‹(‹, param ›*) › = expression
```

defname ← *methodname* | *expr.methodname*

The *defname* contains the name of the method and optionally an expression defining the context in which the method is valid, the most common expression here is self, as in def self.method_name, but the expression can be any Ruby object.

A *methodname* is either a redefinable operator (see Table 19, Ruby operators (high to low precedence), on page 454) or a name. If *methodname* is a name, it starts with a letter or underscore optionally followed by uppercase and lowercase letters, underscores, and digits. A method can start with an uppercase letter, but that's normally only done for the conversion methods in Kernel. A *methodname* may optionally end with a question mark (?), exclamation point (!), or equal sign (=). The question mark and exclamation point are simply part of the name. The equal sign is also part of the name but additionally signals that this method may be used as an lvalue (see the description of writeable attributes in Writing to Attributes, on page 38).

Most methods are written over multiple lines, in which case the method ends with a matching end keyword.

A single expression method can be written with the method name and optional argument list followed by a space, then by an =, and then by a single-expression body. Note that the space before the equal sign is important to distinguish this from a method name ending in =. Because this method form doesn't need a matching end, it's sometimes referred to as an "endless method."

The statement which creates the method returns the method name as a symbol. This is useful for interacting with Ruby methods that take a symbol expecting it to be a method name (for example, the access control methods, as in private def foo = 1 + 1).

Within a class or module definition, a method definition that doesn't have an expression before the method name creates an instance method. An instance method defined in a class may be invoked only by sending its name to a receiver that's an instance of the class that defined it, or one of that class's subclasses. An instance method defined in a module may be invoked by a receiver that's an instance of a class that has included or prepended the module somewhere in its ancestor list.

Outside a class or module definition, a definition without an expression before the method name is added as a private instance method to class Object. It may be called in any context without an explicit receiver.

A definition that does have an expression before the method name of the form *expr.methodname* creates a method associated with the object that's the value of the expression; the method will be callable only by supplying the object referenced by the expression as a receiver. This style of definition creates per-object or *singleton methods*. You'll find it most often inside class or module definitions, where the *expr* is either self or the name of the class/module. This effectively creates a class or module method (as opposed to an instance method).

```ruby
class MyClass
  def MyClass.method      # definition
  end
end

MyClass.method            # call

obj = Object.new

def obj.method            # definition
end

obj.method                # call

def (1.class).fred        # receiver may be an expression
end

Integer.fred              # call
```

Method definitions may not contain class or module definitions. They may contain nested instance or singleton method definitions. The internal method is defined when the enclosing method is executed. The internal method doesn't act as a closure in the context of the nested method—it's self-contained.

```ruby
def toggle
  def toggle
    "subsequent times"
  end
  "first time"
end

toggle    # => "first time"
toggle    # => "subsequent times"
toggle    # => "subsequent times"
```

The body of a method acts as if it were a begin/end block, in that it may contain exception-handling statements (rescue, else, and ensure).

Method Parameters

A method definition may list zero or more positional parameters, zero or more keyword parameters, an optional splat parameter, an optional double splat parameter, and an optional block parameter. Parameters are separated by commas, and the parameter list may be (and usually is) enclosed in parentheses. As described in Passing Parameters Through, on page 469, the parameter list may be replaced by one or more forwarding markers. The elements of a method are called parameters when discussing the definition of the method, and arguments when discussing calling the method.

A positional parameter is a local variable name, optionally followed by an equals sign and an expression defining a default value. The expression is evaluated at the time the method is called. If there are multiple parameters with default expressions, the expressions are evaluated from left to right. An expression may reference a parameter that precedes it in the argument list.

```ruby
def options(a = 99, b = a + 1)
  [a, b]
end
options        # => [99, 100]
options(1)     # => [1, 2]
options(2, 4) # => [2, 4]
```

Parameters without default values may appear after parameters with defaults. When such a method is called, Ruby will use the default values only if fewer arguments are passed to the method call than the total number of parameters.

```ruby
def mixed(a, b = 50, c = b + 10, d)
  [a, b, c, d]
end
mixed(1, 2)       # => [1, 50, 60, 2]
mixed(1, 2, 3)    # => [1, 2, 12, 3]
mixed(1, 2, 3, 4) # => [1, 2, 3, 4]
```

As with parallel assignment, one of the parameters may start with an asterisk. If the method call specifies any arguments in excess of the regular parameter count, all these extra arguments will be collected into this newly created array.

```ruby
def varargs(a, *b)
  [a, b]
end
varargs(1)       # => [1, []]
varargs(1, 2)    # => [1, [2]]
varargs(1, 2, 3) # => [1, [2, 3]]
```

This parameter need not be the last in the parameter list. See the description of parallel assignment to see how values are assigned to this parameter.

```ruby
def splat(first, *middle, last)
  [first, middle, last]
end
splat(1, 2)       # => [1, [], 2]
```

```
splat(1, 2, 3)    # => [1, [2], 3]
splat(1, 2, 3, 4) # => [1, [2, 3], 4]
```

If an array parameter follows arguments with default values, parameters will first be used to override the defaults. The remainder will then be used to populate the array.

```
def mixed(a, b = 99, *c)
  [a, b, c]
end
mixed(1)          # => [1, 99, []]
mixed(1, 2)       # => [1, 2, []]
mixed(1, 2, 3)    # => [1, 2, [3]]
mixed(1, 2, 3, 4) # => [1, 2, [3, 4]]
```

Keyword Parameters

Ruby methods may declare keyword parameters using the syntax <name>: <default_value> for each. These arguments must follow any positional parameters in the list. The default value is optional, in which case you just type <name>:.

reference/kwargs.rb
```
def header(name, level:, upper: false)
  name = name.upcase if upper
  "<h#{level}>#{name}</h#{level}>"
end

header("Introduction", level: 1)            # => "<h1>Introduction</h1>"
header("Getting started", level:2)          # => "<h2>Getting started</h2>"
header("Conclusion", upper: true, level: 1) # => "<h1>CONCLUSION</h1>"
```

When calling a method with keyword parameters, the keyword arguments don't need to be in the same order in the method call as they are in the method definition. If you call a method that has keyword parameters, you must provide values for each keyword that doesn't have a default value. If you don't provide a value for a keyword with a default, the default will be used.

If you pass keyword arguments that aren't defined as arguments, an error will be raised unless you also define a double splat parameter, **<arg>. The double splat argument will be defined as a hash containing any undeclared keyword arguments passed to the method.

reference/kwargs_2.rb
```
def header(name, level: 1, upper: false, **attrs)
  name = name.upcase if upper
  attr_string = attrs.map { |k, v| %(#{k}="#{v}") }.join(" ")
  "<h#{level} #{attr_string}>#{name}</h#{level}>"
end

puts header("TOC", class: "nav", level: 2, id: 123)
```
produces:
```
<h2 class="nav" id="123">TOC</h2>
```

Block Parameter

The optional block parameter must be the last in the list. Whenever the method is called, Ruby checks for an associated block. If a block is present, it's converted to an object of class Proc and assigned to the block parameter. If no block is present, the argument is set to nil.

```
def example(&block)
  p block
end

example
example { "a block" }
```

produces:

```
nil
#<Proc:0x0000000104ee8180 prog.rb:6>
```

Passing Parameters Through

Often in Ruby, we want to pass all the parameters from one method as arguments to another method. Because a Ruby method can take three different kinds of parameters, simply doing pass-throughs can feel kind of cumbersome:

```
def outer(*args, **kwargs, &block)
  other(*args, **kwargs, &block)
end
```

Ruby has some shortcuts if you aren't actually using the parameters in the method. For all three types, you can pass through the parameters of that particular kind by using the splat, double-splat, or ampersand without a variable name:

```
def outer(*)
  other(*)
end

def outer(**)
  other(**)
end

def outer(&)
  other(&)
end
```

These splats can't be assigned to variables directly, but they can be used in other assignments where you might use a splat. So you can't do x = *, but you can do x = [*].

If you're passing multiple types of variables, you can forward them all with ... (three dots).

```
def outer(...)
  other(...)
end
```

You can even include leading positional parameters before the pass-through shortcuts:

```
def outer(first, ...)
  other(first, ...)
end
```

Undefining a Method

The keyword undef allows you to undefine a method.

undef *name* | *symbol* ...

An undefined method still exists; it's simply marked as being undefined. If you undefine a method in a child class and then call that method on an instance of that child class, Ruby will immediately raise a NoMethodError and it won't look for the method in the child's parents.

Invoking a Method

‹ receiver.›name‹ arguments › ‹ {block} ›
‹ receiver::›name‹ arguments › ‹ {block} ›

arguments ← (‹arg›* ‹, hashlist› ‹*array› ‹&a_proc›)

block ← { blockbody } or do blockbody end

When invoking a method, the parentheses around the arguments may be omitted if the expression is otherwise unambiguous. So, foo 3, 4 as a line by itself is a legal call to foo with two arguments. Usually, the ambiguity happens if there are method calls in the arguments. If you had both foo and bar as methods, then foo 3, bar 4, 5 would trigger an error because the parser would attempt to resolve bar 4 as the second argument to foo. Fully parenthesizing as foo(3, bar(4, 5)) is preferred, but foo 3, (bar 4, 5) would also be legal.

Positional arguments are assigned to the matching parameters of the method. Following these arguments may be a list of _key_: _value_ pairs, which correspond to keyword parameters of the method.

Any argument may be prefixed with an asterisk. If a starred argument responds to the to_a method, that method is called, and the resulting array is expanded inline to provide arguments to the method call. If a starred argument doesn't respond to to_a, the argument is simply passed through unaltered.

```ruby
def regular(a, b, *c)
  "a = #{a}, b = #{b}, c = #{c}"
end
regular 1, 2, 3, 4                     # => a = 1, b = 2, c = [3, 4]
regular(1, 2, 3, 4)                    # => a = 1, b = 2, c = [3, 4]
regular(1, *2, *3, 4)                  # => a = 1, b = 2, c = [3, 4]
regular(1, *[2, 3, 4])                 # => a = 1, b = 2, c = [3, 4]
regular(1, *[2, 3], 4)                 # => a = 1, b = 2, c = [3, 4]
regular(1, *[2, 3], *4)                # => a = 1, b = 2, c = [3, 4]
regular(*[], 1, *[], *[2, 3], *[], 4)  # => a = 1, b = 2, c = [3, 4]
```

When a method defined with keyword parameters is called, Ruby matches the keys in the passed hash with each parameter, assigning values when it finds a match.

```ruby
def keywords(a, b: 2, c: 3)
  "a = #{a}, b = #{b}, c = #{c}"
end

keywords(99)                            # => a = 99, b = 2, c = 3
keywords(99, c: 98)                     # => a = 99, b = 2, c = 98

args = {b: 22, c: 33}
keywords(99, **args)                    # => "a = 99, b = 22, c = 33"
keywords(99, **args, b: "override")     # => "a = 99, b = override, c = 33"
```

If the passed hash contains any keys not defined as parameters, Ruby raises a runtime error unless the method also declares a double splat parameter. In that case, the double splat receives the excess key-value pairs from the passed hash. If the passed hash is missing keys that are defined as required parameters without default values, Ruby raises a runtime error.

```ruby
def keywords1(a, b: 2, c: 3)
  "a = #{a}, b = #{b}, c = #{c}"
end

keywords1(99, d: 22, e: 33)
```

produces:

```
        from prog.rb:5:in `<main>'
prog.rb:1:in `keywords1': unknown keywords: :d, :e (ArgumentError)
```

```ruby
def keywords2(a, b: 2, c: 3, **rest)
  "a = #{a}, b = #{b}, c = #{c}, rest = #{rest}"
end

keywords2(99, d: 22, e: 33)    # => a = 99, b = 2, c = 3, rest = {:d=>22, :e=>33}
```

Any argument may be prefixed with two asterisks (a double splat). Such arguments are treated as hashes, using to_hash to convert if the parameter isn't a hash, and their key-value pairs are added as additional keyword arguments to the method call.

```ruby
def regular(a, b)
  "a = #{a}, b = #{b}"
end
regular(99, a: 1, b: 2)                  # => a = 99, b = {:a=>1, :b=>2}

others = { c: 3, d: 4 }
regular(99, a: 1, b: 2, **others)        # => a = 99, b = {:a=>1, :b=>2,
                                         # ..  :c=>3, :d=>4}
regular(99, **others, a: 1, b: 2)        # => a = 99, b = {:c=>3, :d=>4,
                                         # ..  :a=>1, :b=>2}

rest = {e: 5}
regular(99, **others, a: 1, b: 2)        # => a = 99, b = {:c=>3, :d=>4,
                                         # ..  :a=>1, :b=>2}
regular(99, **others, a: 1, b: 2, **rest) # => a = 99, b = {:c=>3, :d=>4,
                                         # ..  :a=>1, :b=>2, :e=>5}
```

As with hash literals, if an existing local value has the same name as the keyword argument, you can pass the argument without a value and the local value will be found and used:

```ruby
x = 10
y = 5
foo(x:, y:)
```

A block may be associated with a method call using either a literal block (which must start on the same source line as the last line of the method call) or an argument containing a reference to a lambda, Proc, or Method object prefixed with an ampersand character. If the object prefixed by an ampersand responds to to_proc, then to_proc is invoked and the resulting proc passed to the method.

```ruby
def some_method
  yield
end

some_method { }
some_method do
end

a_proc = lambda { 99 }
some_method(&a_proc)
```

Ruby provides the method Kernel#block_given?, which is always available and reflects the availability of a block associated with the call, regardless of the presence of a block parameter. An explicit block parameter will be set to nil if no block is specified on the call to a method.

```ruby
def other_method(&block)
  puts "block_given = #{block_given?}, block = #{block.inspect}"
end
other_method { }
other_method
```

produces:

```
block_given = true, block = #<Proc:0x00000001043d9280 prog.rb:4>
block_given = false, block = nil
```

A method is called by passing its name to a receiver using a reciever.method syntax. If no receiver is specified, self is assumed. The receiver checks for the method definition in its own class and then sequentially in its ancestor classes. The instance methods of included modules act as if they were in anonymous superclasses of the class that includes them. If the method isn't found, Ruby invokes method_missing in the receiver. The default behavior defined in method_missing is to report an error and terminate the program.

When a receiver is explicitly specified in a method invocation, it may be separated from the method name using either a period (.) or, much more rarely, two colons (::). The only difference between these two forms occurs if the method name starts with an uppercase letter. In this case, Ruby will assume that receiver::Thing is an attempt to access a constant called Thing in the receiver *unless* the method invocation has an argument list between parentheses. Using :: to indicate a method call is soft-deprecated because of its potential for confusion with constant access.

```ruby
Foo.Bar()        #  method call
Foo.Bar          #  method call
Foo::Bar()       #  method call
Foo::Bar         #  constant access
```

Safe Navigation

Ruby defines a *safe navigation* operator, &., as in receiver&.method. If the receiver is nil, then the method isn't called and the entire expression returns nil. If the receiver isn't nil, then the expression proceeds normally. So, safe navigation is roughly equivalent to receiver.nil? ? nil : receiver.method or, written more succinctly, receiver.nil? && receiver.method.

The safe navigation operator only works for the one method call, if you want to chain multiple methods safely, they all need the safe navigation operator.

```ruby
post&.writer&.address&.country
```

You may sometimes see this referred to as the "lonely" operator because Matz said that he thought &. looks like "someone sitting on the floor looking at a dot...by themself."

Return Value

The return value of a method is the value of the last expression executed. The method in the following example returns the value of the if statement it contains, and that if statement returns the value of one of its branches:

```ruby
def odd_or_even(val)
  if val.odd?
    "odd"
  else
    "even"
  end
end

odd_or_even(26) # => "even"
odd_or_even(27) # => "odd"
```

A return expression immediately exits a method with the value of the expression passed to return:

return ‹expr›*

The value of a return expression depends on its parameters. If a return is called with no parameters, its value is nil. If it's called with one parameter, its value is the value of that parameter. If it's called with more than one parameter, its value is an array of all the parameters.

A return expression can be used at the top level, outside of a method call, in which case it stops execution of the current file being loaded. If the load was from a require statement, the file which called require will continue to load.

super

super ‹ (‹, param ›* ‹, *array ›) › ‹block›

Within the body of a method, a call to super acts like a call to the original method, except that the search for a method body starts one step after from the original method. In an inheritance hierarchy with no included modules, this means the search will start in the parent class. Using super gives you access to the method of the same name in a parent class.

If modules are mixed in, the search still starts one step after the original method, so a method defined in a module added using include will be found by a call to super. Similarly, if super is called from a method that has been prepended to the original class, then super starts its search one step later, in the original class.

The arguments to super are a little unusual. If super is called with arguments, then those arguments are passed to the next method up the chain. This allows you to specify a different set of arguments if the original method has a different parameter list than the parent method. If no arguments are passed to super, the arguments to the original method will be passed.

This is the only functionality in Ruby where a method call without parentheses behaves differently than a method call with empty parentheses. Calling super() with empty parentheses explicitly passes an empty argument list to the next method up the lookup path, whereas calling super with no arguments or parentheses passes the argument list from the original method.

Operator Methods

expr operator
operator expr
expr1 operator expr2

If the operator in an operator expression is marked as "method" (see Table 19, Ruby operators (high to low precedence), on page 454), then the operator can be treated like a method, and Ruby will execute the operator expression as if it had been written like this:

(expr1).operator() or
(expr1).operator(expr2)

You can use dot syntax for operators in your own code, as in: 1.+(2) is perfectly legal Ruby. Using the dot syntax enables you to use other Ruby features specific to method calls, such as the safe navigation operator 1&.+(2), and the ability to chain method calls. Operators not marked as method cannot be called in this way.

Attribute Assignment

receiver.attrname = rvalue

When the form receiver.attrname appears as an lvalue in an assignment statement, Ruby invokes a method named attrname= in the receiver, passing rvalue as a single parameter. The value returned by this assignment is always rvalue—the return value of the method is discarded. If you want to access the return value (in the unlikely event that it isn't the rvalue), send an explicit message to the method.

```ruby
object_ref/attribute.rb
class Demo
  attr_reader :attr

  def attr=(val)
    @attr = val
    "return value"
  end
end

d = Demo.new

# In all these cases, @attr is set to 99
d.attr = 99          # => 99
d.attr=(99)          # => 99
d.send(:attr=, 99)   # => "return value"
```

Element Reference Operator

receiver[‹ expr ›+]
receiver[‹ expr ›+] = rvalue

When used as an rvalue, an element reference invokes the method [] in the receiver, passing as parameters the expressions between the brackets.

When used as an lvalue, an element reference invokes the method []= in the receiver, passing as parameters the expressions between the brackets, followed by the *rvalue* being assigned. In the most common case, as in an Array, the expression foo[3] = 5 is equivalent to foo.[]=(3, 5). But if the class allows it, comma-separated expressions inside the brackets are passed to the method, so array slice access with foo[3, 2] = 5 is equivalent to foo.[]=(3, 2, 5). It's up to the receiving class what to do with the arguments or even if it accepts them at all (for example, an extra argument to Array, as in foo.[]=(3, 2, 4, 5). is an ArgumentError).

Aliasing

alias *new_name old_name*

This creates a new name that refers to an existing method, operator, global variable, or regular expression backreference ($&, $", $', and $+). Local variables, instance variables, class variables, and constants may not be aliased. The parameters to alias may be names or symbols.

```
object_ref/alias_1.rb
class Integer
  alias plus +
end
1.plus(3)          # => 4

alias $prematch $`
"string" =~ /i/   # => 3
$prematch         # => "str"

alias :cmd :`
cmd "date"        # => "Thu Nov  2 17:16:30 CDT 2023\n"
```

When a method is aliased, the new name refers to a copy of the original method's body. If the original method is subsequently redefined, the aliased name will still invoke the original implementation.

```
object_ref/alias_2.rb
def meth
  "original method"
end

alias original meth

def meth
  "#{original} is now new and improved"
end

original  # => "original method"

meth      # => "original method is now new and improved"
```

Note that the new version can call the old version.

You can also alias inside a module or class with the method Module.alias_method(new_name, old_name), which has the same behavior as alias but acts as a method and not a keyword.

Defining Classes

```
class ‹scope::› classname ‹< superexpr›
   body
end

class << obj
   body
end
```

A Ruby class definition creates or extends an object of class Class by executing the code in body. In the first form, a named class is created or extended. The resulting Class object is assigned to a constant named classname (keep reading for scoping rules). This name should start with an uppercase letter. In the second form, an anonymous (singleton) class is associated with the specific object.

If present, superexpr should be an expression that evaluates to a Class object that will be the superclass of the class being defined. If omitted, the superclass defaults to class Object.

Within body, most Ruby expressions are executed as the definition is read. A few exceptions:

- Method definitions will register the methods in a table in the class object.

- Nested class and module definitions will be stored in constants within the class, not as global constants. These nested classes and modules can be accessed from outside the defining class using :: to qualify their names:

```
module NameSpace
   class Example
      CONST = 123
   end
end
obj = NameSpace::Example.new
a = NameSpace::Example::CONST
```

- Calling the Module#include method with modules as arguments will add those modules as anonymous superclasses of the class being defined.

The classname in a class definition may be prefixed by the names of existing classes or modules using the scope operator (::). This syntax inserts the new definition into the namespace of the prefixing modules and/or classes but doesn't interpret the definition in the scope of these outer classes. A classname with a leading scope operator places that class or module in the top-level scope.

In the following example, class C is inserted into module A's namespace but isn't interpreted in the context of A. As a result, the reference to CONST resolves to the top-level constant of that name, not A's version. We also have to fully qualify the singleton method name because C on its own isn't a known constant in the context of A::C.

```
CONST = "outer"

module A
  CONST = "inner"    # This is A::CONST
end
```

```
module A
  class B
    def self.get_const
      CONST
    end
  end
end

A::B.get_const # => "inner"

class A::C
  def self.get_const
    CONST
  end
end

A::C.get_const # => "outer"
```

Remember that a class definition is executable code. Many of the directives used in class definitions (such as attr and include) are actually private instance methods of class Module. The value of a class definition is the value of the last executed statement.

Chapter 22, The Ruby Object Model and Metaprogramming, on page 371, describes in more detail how Class objects interact with the rest of the environment and how the class << obj syntax works.

Creating Objects from Classes

obj = *classexpr*.new ‹ (‹ , *args* ›*) ›

The class Class defines the instance method new, which creates an instance of the class of its receiver (classexpr). This is done by calling the method classexpr.allocate. You can override the allocate method, but your implementation must return an object of the correct class. The new method then invokes initialize in the newly created object and passes it any arguments originally passed to new.

You can override new in your own classes, though we wouldn't recommend it without a good reason. If you want your override of new to have the same instance-creating behavior, you usually would call super within the new override. If for some reason you need to do this behavior manually, you can explicitly call the method Class.allocate inside your new method and then call initialize on the result.

Like any other method, initialize should call super if it wants to ensure that parent classes have been properly initialized. This isn't necessary when the parent is Object because class Object does no instance-specific initialization.

Class Attribute Declarations

Class attribute declarations aren't part of the Ruby syntax; they are simply methods defined in class Module that create accessor methods automatically.

class *name*
  attr *attribute* ‹ , *writable* ›
  attr_reader ‹ *attribute* ›+
  attr_writer ‹ *attribute* ›+

```
  attr_accessor ‹attribute›+
end
```

All of these methods return an array of the symbols defined, so you can apply access control to them, as in private attr_accessor :attribute, :other_attribute.

Defining Modules

```
module name
  body
end
```

A module is a collection of behaviors that are grouped together. The grouping can be used to include all the behaviors in a different module or class as one unit, or it can be used for name spacing. Like a class, the module body is executed during definition, and the resulting Module object is stored in a constant. A module may contain both class and instance methods and may define constants and class variables. (A module can also reference instance variables, but those are dependent on the module being added to a class; see the next section.)

As with classes, a module's own methods (called *module methods*) are invoked using the Module object as a receiver, and constants are accessed using the :: scope resolution operator. The name in a module definition may optionally be preceded by the names of enclosing classes and/or modules.

```
CONST = "outer"
module Mod
  CONST = 1

  def self.method1     # module method
    CONST + 1
  end
end

module Mod::Inner
  def self.method2
    CONST + " scope"
  end
end

Mod::CONST             # => 1
Mod.method1            # => 2
Mod::Inner::method2 # => "outer scope"
```

Mixins: Including Modules

```
class|module name
  include expr
end
```

A module may be included within the definition of another module or class using the include method. The module or class definition containing the include gains access to the constants, class variables, and instance methods of the module it includes.

If a module is included within a class definition, the module's constants, class variables, and instance methods are made available as if the module was an additional superclass for that class. Objects of the class will respond to messages sent to the module's instance methods.

Calls to methods not defined in the class will be passed to the modules mixed into the class before being passed to any parent class. A module may define an initialize method, which will be called upon the creation of an object of a class that mixes in the module if either the class doesn't define its own initialize method or the class's initialize method invokes super.

A module may also be included at the top level, in which case the module's constants, class variables, and instance methods become available at the top level.

```
class|module name
  prepend expr
end
```

The method prepend behaves like include except that the prepended module's methods are placed in the lookup chain before the methods in the enclosing class or module.

```
class|module name
  extend expr
end
```

The method extend adds the module's methods directly to the singleton class of self. In typical usage, extend is at the top level of a class, and so the new methods act as class or module methods of the enclosing class or module. But foo.extend Module also works and adds the methods of the module to the singleton class of foo.

Module Functions

Instance methods defined in modules can be mixed into a class using include. But what if you want to call the instance methods in a module directly?

```
module Math
  def sin(x)
    #
  end
end
include Math      # The only way to access Math.sin
sin(1)
```

The method module_function solves this problem by taking module instance methods and copying their definitions into corresponding module methods:

```
module Math
  def sin(x)
    #
  end
  module_function :sin
end
Math.sin(1)
include Math
sin(1)
```

The instance method and module method are two different methods: the method definition is copied by module_function, not aliased.

You can also use module_function with no parameters, in which case all subsequent methods will be module methods.

Access Control

private ⟨*symbol*⟩*
protected ⟨*symbol*⟩*
public ⟨*symbol*⟩*

Ruby defines three levels of access protection for module and class constants and methods:

- *Public*—Accessible to anyone.
- *Protected*—Can be invoked only by objects of the defining class and its subclasses.
- *Private*—Can be called only with self as the receiver, including both implicit and explicit uses of self. Private methods therefore can be called in the defining class and by that class's descendants and ancestors, but only within the same object. (See Specifying Access Control, on page 45 for examples.)

These levels are invoked with the methods public, protected, and private, which are defined in class Module. Each access control function can be used in three different ways:

- If used with no arguments, the three functions set the default access control of subsequently defined methods.

- If the method call has arguments, as in private :secret_method, :other_method, the functions set the access control of the methods and constants named in the arguments.

- Since def returns the method name as a symbol, the functions can be used to decorate a method declaration, as in private def foo = 1 + 1.

Access control is enforced when a method is invoked.

Blocks, Closures, and Proc Objects

A code block is a set of Ruby statements and expressions inside braces or a do/end pair. The block may start with an argument list between vertical bars. A code block may appear only immediately after a method invocation. The start of the block (the brace or the do) must be on the same logical source line as the end of the invocation:

```
invocation do | a1, a2, ... |
end

invocation { | a1, a2, ... |
}
```

Braces have a high precedence; do has a low precedence. If the method invocation has parameters that aren't enclosed in parentheses, the brace form of a block will bind to the last parameter, not to the overall invocation. The do form will bind to the entire invocation.

Within the body of the invoked method, the code block may be called using the yield keyword. Parameters passed to yield will be assigned to arguments in the block. The return value of yield is the value of the last expression evaluated in the block or the value passed to a next statement executed in the block.

A block is a *closure*; it remembers the context in which it was defined, and it uses that context whenever it's called. The context includes the value of self, the constants, the class variables, the local variables, and any captured block:

```ruby
class BlockExample
  CONST = 0
  @@a = 3

  def return_closure
    a = 1
    @a = 2
    lambda { [ CONST, a, @a, @@a, yield ] }
  end

  def change_values
    @a += 1
    @@a += 1
  end
end

be = BlockExample.new
block = be.return_closure { "original" }
block.call # => [0, 1, 2, 3, "original"]
be.change_values
block.call # => [0, 1, 3, 4, "original"]
```

Here, the return_closure method returns a lambda that encapsulates access to the local variable a, the instance variable @a, the class variable @@a, and the constant CONST. We call the block outside the scope of the object that contains these values, but they're still available via the closure. If we call the object to change some values, the values accessed via the closure also change.

Block Arguments

Block argument lists are similar to method argument lists:

- You can specify default values.

- You can specify splat (starred) arguments.

- You can specify keyword arguments.

- You can specify a double-splat argument.

- The last argument can be prefixed with an ampersand, in which case it'll collect any block passed when the original block is called.

- Block-local variables are declared after a semicolon in the argument list.

- You can't use these anonymous forwarding syntaxes: *, **, &, or ... (three dots).

Within a block, you can avoid giving positional arguments names and instead refer to them by their numerical position using _1, _2, and so on.

```ruby
[1, 2, 3].map { _1.sqrt }
```

Using both named positional arguments and numerical ones is a syntax error. Naming a local variable using the _1 pattern is also a syntax error.

In Ruby 3.4, the keyword it is expected to be enabled as a synonym for _1. In Ruby 3.3, a use of it that might conflict with this future usage will result in a warning.

Proc Objects

Ruby's blocks are chunks of code attached to a method. Blocks aren't objects, but they can be converted into objects of class Proc. There are many ways to convert a block into a Proc object:

- You can pass a block to a method whose last parameter is prefixed with an ampersand. That parameter will receive the block as a Proc object:

```
def meth1(p1, p2, &block)
  puts block.inspect
end

meth1(1,2) { "a block" }
meth1(3,4)
```

produces:

```
#<Proc:0x0000000105188868 prog.rb:5>
nil
```

- You can call Proc.new, again associating it with a block. There's also a built-in Kernel#proc method, which is the same as Proc.new:

```
block = Proc.new { "a block" }
block       # => #<Proc:0x0000000104418bb0 prog.rb:1>
```

- You can call the method Kernel#lambda and associating a block with the call:

```
block = lambda { "a block" }
block       # => #<Proc:0x00000001024f8c08 prog.rb:1 (lambda)>
```

- You can use the -> syntax:

```
lam = -> (p1, p2) { p1 + p2 }
lam.call(4, 3) # => 7
```

The first two styles of Proc object are identical in use. We'll call these objects *raw procs*. The third and fourth styles, generated by lambda and ->, add some functionality to the Proc object, as we'll see in a minute. We'll call these objects *lambdas*.

Here's the big thing to remember: raw procs are designed to work as the bodies of control structures such as loops. Lambdas are intended to act like methods. So, lambdas are stricter when checking the parameters passed to them, and a return in a lambda exits much as it would from a method.

Calling a Proc

You call a proc by invoking its methods call, yield, or []. The three forms are identical. Each takes arguments that are passed to the proc, just as if it were a regular method. If the proc is a lambda, Ruby will check that the number of supplied arguments match the expected parameters. You can also invoke a proc using the syntax name.(_args..._). This is mapped internally into name.call(args...).

Procs, break, and next

Within both raw procs and lambdas, executing next causes the block to exit back to the caller of the block. The return value is the value (or values) passed to next, or nil if no values are passed.

```ruby
def ten_times
  10.times do |i|
    if yield(i)
      puts "Caller likes #{i}"
    end
  end
end

ten_times do |number|
next(true) if number ==7
end
```

produces:

```
Caller likes 7
```

Within a raw proc, a break terminates the method that invoked the block. The return value of the method is any parameters passed to the break.

Return and Blocks

A return from inside a *raw block* that's inside a scope acts as a return from that scope. A return from a block whose original context is no longer valid raises an exception (LocalJumpError or ThreadError depending on the context). The following example illustrates the first case:

```ruby
def meth1
  (1..10).each do |val|
    return val          # returns from meth1
  end
end

meth1    # => 1
```

The following example shows a return failing because the context of its block no longer exists:

reference/local_jump_error.rb

```ruby
def meth2
  proc { return }
end
res = meth2
res.call
```

produces:

```
code/reference/local_jump_error.rb:2:in `block in meth2': unexpected return
(LocalJumpError)
        from code/reference/local_jump_error.rb:5:in `<main>'
```

And here's a return failing because the block is created in one thread and called in another:

reference/local_jump_error_2.rb
```
def meth3
  yield
end

t = Thread.new do
  meth3 { return }
end

t.join
```

produces:

```
#<Thread:0x00000001047f9bf8 code/reference/local_jump_error_2.rb:5 run>
terminated with exception (report_on_exception is true):
code/reference/local_jump_error_2.rb:6:in `block (2 levels) in <main>':
unexpected return (LocalJumpError)
        from code/reference/local_jump_error_2.rb:2:in `meth3'
        from code/reference/local_jump_error_2.rb:6:in `block in <main>'
code/reference/local_jump_error_2.rb:6:in `block (2 levels) in <main>':
unexpected return (LocalJumpError)
        from code/reference/local_jump_error_2.rb:2:in `meth3'
        from code/reference/local_jump_error_2.rb:6:in `block in <main>'
```

The proc behavior still holds even if you create the raw proc using Proc.new:

reference/proc_new.rb
```
def meth4
  p = Proc.new { return 99 }
  p.call
  puts "Never get here"
end

meth4      # => 99
```

A lambda behaves more like a free-standing method body—a return simply returns from the block to the caller of the block:

reference/lambda.rb
```
def meth5
  p = lambda { return 99 }
  res = p.call
  "The block returned #{res}"
end

meth5      # => "The block returned 99"
```

Because of this, if you use define_method with a pre-existing proc and use an explicit return, you'll probably want to pass it a proc created using lambda, rather than Proc.new. In the lambda version, return will work as expected and return from the method, while the proc version will generate a LocalJumpError on return.

Exceptions

Ruby exceptions are objects of class Exception and its descendants.

Raising Exceptions

The raise method raises an exception:

```
raise
raise string cause: $!
raise thing ‹, string ‹, stack trace›‹, cause: $!››
```

When an exception is raised, Ruby places a reference to the Exception object in the global variable $!. The first form reraises the exception in $! or creates a new RuntimeError if $! is nil. The second form creates a new RuntimeError exception, setting its message to the given string. The third form creates an exception object by invoking the method exception on its first argument, setting this exception's message and backtrace to its second and third arguments. Class Exception and objects of class Exception contain a factory method called exception, so an exception class name or instance can be used as the first parameter to raise.

Handling Exceptions

Exceptions may be handled in the following ways:

- Within the scope of a begin/end block:

```
begin
  code...
  code...
‹rescue ‹, parm›* ‹, => var› ‹, then›
  error handling code... ›*
‹else
  no exception code... ›
‹ensure
  always executed code... ›
end
```

- Within the body of a method or a block:

```
def method name and args
  code...
  code...
‹rescue ‹, parm›* ‹, => var› ‹, then›
    error handling code... ›*
‹else
    no exception code... ›
‹ensure
    always executed code... ›
end
```

- After the execution of a single statement:

```
statement ‹rescue statement›*
```

A block or method may have multiple rescue clauses, and each rescue clause may specify zero or more exception parameters. A rescue clause with no parameter is treated as if it had a parameter of StandardError. Some lower-level exceptions won't be caught by a parameterless rescue class. If you need to rescue those low-level exceptions, use this to explicitly set the target of the rescue to Exception:

```
rescue Exception
```

When an exception is raised, Ruby scans the call stack until it finds an enclosing begin/end block, method body, or statement with a rescue modifier. For each rescue clause in that block, Ruby compares the raised exception against each of the rescue clause's parameters in turn; each parameter is tested using _parameter_ === $!. If the raised exception matches a rescue parameter, Ruby executes the body of the rescue and stops looking. If a matching rescue clause ends with => and a variable name, the variable is set to $!.

Although the parameters to the rescue clause are typically the exception classes (not instances of expression classes), they can be arbitrary expressions (including method calls) that return an appropriate class or module.

If no rescue clause matches the raised exception, Ruby moves up the stack looking for a higher-level begin/end block that matches. If an exception propagates to the top level of the main thread without being rescued, the program terminates with a message.

If an else clause is present, its body is executed if the *code* reaches its end without returning and without raising an exception. Exceptions raised during the execution of the else clause aren't captured by rescue clauses in the same block as the else.

If an ensure clause is present, its body is always executed as the block is exited (even if an uncaught exception is in the process of being propagated). If an ensure clause is present, the return value of the method is still the return value of the main block—the last expression of the ensure block is never the return value of the method.

Within a rescue clause, raise with no parameters will reraise the exception in $!.

Rescue Statement Modifier

A statement may have an optional rescue modifier followed by another statement (and by extension another rescue modifier, and so on). The rescue modifier takes no exception parameter and rescues StandardError and its children.

If an exception is raised to the left of a rescue modifier, the expression on the left is abandoned, and the value of the overall line is the value of the statement on the right:

```
values = ["1", "2.3", /pattern/]
result = values.map { |v| Integer(v) rescue Float(v) rescue String(v) }
result    # => [1, 2.3, "(?-mix:pattern)"]
```

Retrying a Block

The retry statement can be used within a rescue clause to restart the enclosing begin/end block from the beginning.

Catch and Throw

The method catch executes its associated block:

```
catch ( object ) do
   code...
end
```

The method throw interrupts the normal processing of statements:

```
throw( object ‹, obj› )
```

When a throw is executed, Ruby searches up the call stack for the first catch block with a matching object. If it's found, the search stops, and execution resumes past the end of the catch's block. If the throw is passed a second parameter, that value is returned as the value of the catch. Ruby honors the ensure clauses of any block expressions it traverses while looking for a corresponding catch.

If no catch block matches the throw, Ruby raises an ArgumentError exception at the location of the throw.

Typed Ruby

RBS has its own syntax for defining Ruby types. The definitive source for the syntax reference is found at https://github.com/ruby/rbs/blob/master/docs/syntax.md. We'll go over the structure here.

RBS Declarations and File Structure

RBS syntax has a few main parts (we're adopting the naming convention from the official syntax file):

- *Declarations* are class, module, and interface structures that can be used as types in other parts of the file.

- *Members* are things that are inside declarations that might have type information, including instance variables, attributes, and methods.

- *Types* are the things that RBS uses to specify actual type information, including class names, union of class names, or literal types, as well as a few RBS-specific keywords.

An RBS file looks like the skeleton of a Ruby file. It declares classes and methods, but doesn't include the body of methods. You'd typically have more than one class in a single RBS file (one namespace per file is common), and I'd say it's rare for an RBS-using application to have top-level methods included in the RBS file.

RBS Declarations

You can declare a class in RBS:

```
class ‹ namespace:: › classname module_types ‹ < superclass superclass_types ›
    body
end
```

An RBS class definition looks like a Ruby class definition except that both the class name and the superclass name can be augmented with type parameters. Those type parameters are used for *Generics*, and we'll talk about what those do and the syntax for them in RBS Generics, on page 492.

A class definition with the type modifiers looks like this:

```
class LinkedList[I] < List[I]
  # body
end
```

A module definition is similar, but a module has an additional type definition, like this:

```
module ‹namespace::› module_name module_types ‹‹ superclass superclass_types ›‹ : module-self-types ›
  body
end
```

The module self type is type information about the kinds of classes that can include a module. So, you might have a whole class hierarchy underneath a class named AbstractPolicy and a module that you only want included within AbstractPolicy or one of its subclasses:

```
module PolicyPrinter : AbstractPolicy
end
```

Where this gets a little more interesting is with the inclusion of an interface. RBS allows you to specify an interface that has a set of methods, and then any class that has those methods also matches the interface. (We'll cover the method syntax in RBS Members, on page 488.) Here's an example:

```
interface Postish
  def title: () -> String
  def description: () -> String
end

module Htmlable : Postish
end
```

In this case, the Htmlable module can only be included by classes that implement the Postish interface, meaning they have methods called title and description.

An interface declaration is syntactically similar to a module:

```
interface ‹namespace::› module name module_types ‹‹ superclass superclass_types ›
  body
end
```

You can also declare aliases using the keyword type, which allows you to specify shortcuts:

```
type alias type-parameters = type
```

The type parameters are the same generics that modules and classes have, and the type at the end is any RBS type as defined in RBS Types, on page 491.

In the RBS documentation, constants and globals are considered declarations, and they both work the same way with the name followed by a colon and then by the type:

```
constant: type
$global: type
```

As in:

```
class Post
  DEFAULT_TITLE: String
end

$ADMIN_EMAIL: String
```

RBS Members

An RBS member is essentially something that you'd expect to live inside a class, like a method definition or an instance variable. Unlike regular Ruby, RBS expects you to declare the type of instance variables. Instance variables that aren't declared will be type errors as far as RBS tools are concerned:

@instance_variable: type

If you're using `attr_accessor` and its sibling methods, you can declare the type of the internal variable. By default, this also declares an instance variable of the same name, but you can override that by putting a different variable name in parentheses, or you can omit declaring a variable name by including empty parentheses (presumably because the variable name has already been declared).

attr_attribute_type name : type
attr_attribute_type name (ivar) : type
attr_attribute_type name () : type

Any of the `attr` methods can be used here:

```
class Person
  @id_number: String
  attr_accessor name: String
  attr_reader height (@height_in_inches): Integer
  attr_writer id_number (): String
end
```

Most of the body of RBS classes are going to be method names where you're specifying the types of the arguments and the type of the return value. This gets a little tangled because Ruby has a lot of different ways to define method parameters, but the basic idea is that every element of the method definition can have a type decoration.

The simplest version of the syntax is the method name followed by a colon, then by all the parameters, a skinny arrow, and the return type:

def method_name: (params) -> type
def method_name: (params) -> type‹ | (params) -> type ›

If the method name starts with `self`, that indicates a singleton method—in normal usage that would be a class or module method. If the method name starts with `self?`, that makes it both a public singleton method and a private instance method.

If the method has multiple type signatures, you can separate them with a pipe character. Typically you'd do that on multiple lines:

```
def add_money: (Integer) -> Integer
             | (RomanNumeral) -> RomanNumeral
```

You can have an arbitrary amount of overloads.

The parameter list can be empty, in which case you do include the empty parentheses:

```
def price_in_cents: () -> Integer
```

Take a deep breath here while we go through all the ways in which to specify parameters....

A required positional parameter is denoted by the type optionally followed by the name of the parameter:

```
def add(Integer)
```

```
def add(Integer other)
```

An optional positional parameter—meaning a parameter with a default value—is specified with the same syntax, but with a ? prefix to the type:

```
def expand(?String)
```

```
def expand(?String delimeter)
```

A splat parameter is denoted with a splat before the type name, with or without the name of the variable:

```
def join_all(*String)
```

Keyword parameter syntax is a little different. The keyword is followed by a colon and then by the type. Optional keywords—again, meaning keywords with defaults—are prefixed with a ?, and the type double-splats are preceded by ** (we'll show how to specify hash types in the next section):

```
def lots_of_args(arg1: String, ?arg2: Integer, **HashType)
```

A block argument has its own syntax:

{parameters ‹ [self: self_type] › -> return_type}

?{parameters ‹ [self: self_type] › -> return_type}

If the block is optional, the ? prefix is used. The parameters in the block have the same syntax as we just described for method parameters, and the return type can be any type:

```
def each_users_posts { User -> Array[Post] }
```

The optional "self type" is used when you expect the block to be a target of an instance_eval call and limits the type of objects that can call instance_eval on this block:

```
def each_users_posts { (User) [self: Document] -> Array[Post] }
```

Proc objects have essentially the same syntax as blocks, except that they start with ^ rather than having braces:

^parameters ‹ [self: self_type] › ‹ block › -> return_type

There are a couple of other things you can do with inside an RBS class or module definition:

- You can include, extend, or prepend modules just as you can in Ruby, and with the same meaning.

- The private, protected, and public modifiers can be used on methods or attributes and specify the access that the member will have in the actual class. They can either be directly modifying individual methods or used on their own, as they can be in Ruby.

- You can use alias to declare that two methods are the same.

RBS Types

To this point, we've kind of hand-waved what goes into the place where RBS asks for a "type." A type can be several things in RBS.

A type can be a literal value, in which case the object of this type can only have that one literal value. This seems of little practical use, but you can do it.

A type can be a class, model, or interface name (or a declared alias to one of those things), which declares that the member must be an instance of that class or a subclass of that class:

```
def height: () -> Integer
```

If you want to specify that your type is the singleton class, then you use singleton(type), so singleton(User), for example, would mean that your type is the singleton class associated with User.

In some cases, the type is a container of other objects, and you can specify the type of the objects contained using square brackets, as in Array[String] or Hash[Symbol, Integer]. We'll see how to implement this in RBS Generics, on page 492.

You can specify hash objects with fixed keys with key: type syntax, as in {name: String, height: Integer}. You can specify array types with fixed lengths with Array syntax, as in [Integer, String, Integer].

By default, types declared with RBS can't have nil values. To specify that nil is a potential value, you append the type with a ?, as in String?. This is called an *optional type*. Note that if you have an optional parameter that's also an optional type, you can have both leading and trailing question marks, as in ?String?.

You can combine types. The pipe character indicates a *union*, meaning that the value can be a member of one or more of the grouped types. A common use case is for a method to take either a record or the ID of that record, which you could annotate as (id_or_record: User | Integer). Somewhat more rarely, the & indicates an intersection, meaning the value has to match all the types in the group, which you'd most commonly see as a set of interfaces: (admin: Customer & Employee).

RBS defines a handful of keywords that stand in for various kinds of types, often in the context of the class or method being defined:

- bool—An alias of true | false.

- boolish—An alias of top, which means you're expecting an arbitrary value here but treating it as a boolean. It's recommended over bool for method arguments and return values unless you're strictly limiting the values to true and false.

- bot—A subtype of all RBS types.

- class—Equivalent to the singleton class of the class being defined.

- instance—The type of an instance of the class being defined.

- nil—Means nil.

- self—Indicates the type of the receiver of the method.

- top—A supertype of all RBS types, similar to untyped.

- untyped—RBS doesn't care what this variable is. The equivalent of TypeScript's any.

- void—Equivalent to top. Use in cases where the return value of a method won't be used.

RBS Generics

A common problem in a type system is a container that behaves similarly no matter what type of objects are inside it. So, an array of String has a lot of methods that return a String, while an array of Integer has all the same methods, but they return an Integer. The container doesn't care what type the values are, but it does care that the values are consistent for any particular container.

The term for this in typed languages is a *generic*. Typically, the container class or module or interface defines one or more generic types as being part of the container, and then methods within that container use those generics to represent the type as a parameter or return type.

In RBS, a class, interface, or module can define one or more generic types in square brackets at the top of the definition. The type names are capitalized, and by convention, they are usually a single letter.

In this case, the Scheduler class defines a generic, the next method returns an element of that type, and the perform method takes an element of that type as an argument:

```
class Scheduler[T]
  def next: () -> T
  def perform: (T) -> void
end
```

When you use Scheduler in other RBS definitions, you augment it with the type to be used as a generic. So Scheduler[RedisJob] would imply that next will return an object of type RedisJob and that perform will take an object of type RedisJob.

You might want to limit the input type going to the generic. You can specify a limiting parent class to the generic:

```
class Scheduler[T < Job]
  def next: () -> T
  def perform: (T) -> void
end
```

So now, when Scheudler[RedisJob] is declared, RBS ensures that RedisJob is a subclass of Job.

By default, the contained classes must match with their usages. If you declare that something is of type Scheduler[RedisJob] and then try to pass that variable to something that expects Scheduler[Job], RBS will consider that to be a type mismatch, even though Job is a superclass of RedisJob.

To make this work, you can describe the scheduler generic as [out T]. If so described, then Scheduler instances will type match with generics that are superclasses of the generic. The technical term is *covariant*. A declaration can also be [unchecked out T], which means the RBS type system doesn't try to match the types of the generic class.

If you want to go the other way and have classes be type matched with subclasses, then the term is *countervariant*, and you indicate that with [in T].

Part V

Ruby Library Reference

Ruby gets much of its functionality from its extensive library. That library is sometimes described as having two parts: the "core," which is part of Ruby and is included as part of every Ruby program, and the "standard library," which is shipped with Ruby but must be explictly required in code to be used.

In this part, we cover a curated list of the most important classes and their most useful methods in both the core and the standard library. We didn't separate the two. If a class in this list needs to be explicitly required, we note that as part of the description of that class. Note that we tried to keep related functionality together, so when you browse for one method, you might find another one that fits your needs more completely.

## CHAPTER 26

Library Reference: Core Data Types

In this chapter, we'll take a closer look at Ruby's core data types. The goal is to give you more information about what you can do with these classes and also to discuss related functions together so that you can browse and perhaps find a new feature that might help. We're presenting the topics in alphabetical order for easier browsing, and we'll cross-reference between topics as needed.

This isn't intended to be a complete listing of every class, method, or option. For that, please refer to the official Ruby documentation at https://docs.ruby-lang.org.

In this chapter, when a method is mentioned for the first time, we provide its complete name and signature. The notation Foo.bar indicates a class or module method, while Foo#bar indicates an instance method. Optional arguments are indicated with Ruby syntax and their default value, as in Foo#bar(name, size = 0). Dynamically sized arguments are indicated with splat syntax, as in Foo#bar(*files, **options). Block arguments are indicated with brace syntax and an indication of what the arguments to the block will be, as in Foo#bar { |object| block }. An optional block argument will be surrounded by square brackets, Foo#bar [{block}]. Please note that this description syntax is slightly different from the official documentation, and that in some cases, what the official documentation shows as multiple method signatures, we've chosen to show as one signature with default values. Also, parameter names sometimes differ from the official documentation to make the naming clearer.

Dates and Times

Ruby has three separate classes to represent date and time data: Time, Date, and DateTime.

- Time represents a specific moment in time, and you can retrieve both date and time information based on that. The Time class is based on a library that is common to Unix systems and is used by many programming languages.

- Date represents a date only with no time information attached. It's useful for calendar arithmetic that doesn't depend on the time of day. You need require "date" to use the Date class.

- DateTime also represents a specific moment in time but uses a different internal representation than Time. DateTime is now considered deprecated—at one point it had a more complete API than Time, but that is no longer true. Currently, the only recommended use of DateTime is if you're dealing with dates in the distant past. You need require "date-time" to use the DateTime class.

Creating Time Instances

There are a few ways to create a new Time instance. The method you're most likely to see is Time.new(in: nil), with no arguments, which is also aliased as Time.now, and which returns the current time. This example shows when this section was most recently executed when building the book:

```
Time.new  # => 2023-11-02 17:16:31.356058 -0500
```

By default, the resulting time is in the current time zone. To change the time zone, you use an optional keyword argument, in, that takes the time zone, as in Time.now(in: nil).

You'll see a few time methods that allow you to specify a time zone. For those methods, Ruby allows a time zone to be specified in these ways:

- A string representing the offset from UTC in hours and minutes in the form "+HH:MM" or "-HH:MM".

- An integer representing the offset from UTC in seconds.

- A single letter representing military time zones, as specified here.[1]

- A custom object that responds to the methods local_to_utc and utc_to_local with logic that performs the appropriate transition. (Time.new and Time.now can't take an object like this, but other time methods can.)

A different form of Time.new(string, precision: 9, in: nil) takes in a string in a YYYY-MM-DD HH:MM:SS format and returns that exact time. This version takes a keyword argument, precision, which limits the number of decimal places kept for the seconds, and also takes an optional time zone with the in: keyword argument.

A more flexible way to create a new Time instance from a string is Time.parse(time_string, now = Time.now) [{year}]. The parse method isn't available by default. The parse method isn't part of the core library of Time, to use Time.parse you must call require "time" somewhere in your code before use.

The Time.parse method takes a string and converts it to a time object based on Ruby's best guess as to the underlying format. Missing parts of the time are set to 0, and missing parts of the date will be filled in based on the current date. If you want to use a different date as the baseline, you can pass in a date as the optional second positional argument.

You have some leeway in how you pass in the string, and Ruby will try to do the right thing. Here are some examples:

```
require "time"
Time.parse("2023-2-10")                    # => 2023-02-10 00:00:00
                                           # .. -0600
Time.parse("2023-10-2")                    # => 2023-10-02 00:00:00
                                           # .. -0500
Time.parse("2023-2-28")                    # => 2023-02-28 00:00:00
                                           # .. -0600
Time.parse("1:00")                         # => 2023-11-02 01:00:00
                                           # .. -0500
```

---

1.   https://en.wikipedia.org/wiki/List_of_military_time_zones

```
Time.parse("February 26, 2023, 3:00 America/Chicago") # => 2023-02-26 03:00:00
                                                       # .. -0600
```

Time.parse takes an optional block that accepts the year of the parsed time and allows you to return a different year. This functionality is specifically there to allow you to manage two-digit year formats.

If you're using strings for dates as specified by the HTTP protocol, you can use Time.http-date(time) to get the given date and time in the format used by HTTP requests. The output format is day-of-week, DD month-name CCYY hh:mm:ss GMT. As I write this, that corresponds to Sun, 26 Feb 2023 20:26:12 GMT. Similarly, you can use Time.rfc2822(time) to parse the very similar date format specified by that RFC.

If the unspecified nature of Time.parse bothers you, you can use Time.strptime(time, format, now = Time.now), which is short for "string parse time." The first argument to strptime is a string representation of a time. The second argument is a format string, and the third argument is an optional date that fills in any missing date information. Like parse, an optional block can be used to manage two-digit years.

The format string uses the same format characters as strftime, which are shown in Table 21, directives, on page 498. The strptime method uses the format string to interpret the string and convert it to a Time. To use Time.strptime you must call require "time", as the strptime method isn't available by default. These are some examples:

```
require "time"
Time.strptime("2023-2-10", "%Y-%m-%d") # => 2023-02-10 00:00:00 -0600
Time.strptime("2023-2-10", "%Y-%d-%m") # => 2023-10-02 00:00:00 -0500
```

Another way to create a Time instance is using the multi-argument form of Time.new:

Time.new(year, month = 1, day_of_month = 1, hour = 0, minute = 0, second = 0, time_zone = local, in: nil)

All the positional arguments other than the year are optional, and all the values can be of type Integer, Float, Rational, or String instances that can be converted to integers. The arguments accept different valid values:

- The month value range is 1 to 12, or it can be the three-letter English abbreviation of the month (case-insensitive).

- The day of the month ranges from 1 to 31. If the month in question has fewer than 31 days, then Ruby will push forward into the next month, so Time.new(2023, 2, 31) returns 2023-03-03 00:00:00 -0600.

- The hour ranges from 0 to 23, but you can use 24 if and only if the minute and second are zero.

- Minute ranges from 0 to 59.

- Second ranges from 0 to 60, where 60 indicates a leap second. The second can also be a float or rational number.

If any of the values are out of range, Ruby throws an ArgumentError.

The time zone can be specified via the last positional argument or the in: keyword argument using the same timezone specifiers we saw earlier with Time.now.

A couple of variations on Time.new return output based on the time zone:

- Time.gm or Time.utc, which returns the time in UTC.
- Time.local or Time.mktime, which returns the time in the local time zone.

All of these methods take up to seven positional arguments that match the arguments to Time.now but with an additional argument for microseconds. Alternatively, the methods are set up such that if they are called with exactly ten arguments, they assume the arguments are in order as if they were generated by Time#to_a. So x = Time.now; Time.gm(*x.to_a) will work as expected even though the order of the result of to_a doesn't match the order of positional arguments in Time.now.

The method Time.at(time, subseconds = false, unit = :microseconds, in: nil) returns a new time object that gives the number of seconds since the beginning of the Unix Epoch on Jan 1, 1970. It takes an optional in: keyword argument to specify the time zone of the result using the time zone specifiers discussed earlier. An optional second positional argument can specify sub-seconds, and an optional third argument specifies the unit of the subseconds. The unit can be :millisecond, :microsecond, or :nanosecond. The default is :microsecond.

Format	Meaning
	Unless otherwise specified, numerical fields are padded with zeroes if the numbers are too small to fit the width of the field. Prefixing any format code with %0, as in %0Y pads with zeros, prefixing with %_, as in %_Y pads with blanks, and %-, as in %-Y, doesn't pad.
%%	Literal %
%a	The abbreviated weekday name ("Sun")
%A	The full weekday name ("Sunday")
%b	The abbreviated month name ("Jan")
%B	The full month name ("January")
%c	The preferred local date and time representation
%C	The first two digits of a four-digit year (currently 20)
%d	Day of the month (01..31)
%D	Date (%m/%d/%y)
%e	Day of the month, blank padded (␣1..31)
%F	ISO8601 date (%Y-%m-%d)
%g	Last 2 digits of ISO8601 week-based year
%G	ISO8601 week-based year
%h	The abbreviated month name ("Jan")
%H	Hour of the day, 24-hour clock (00..23)
%I	Hour of the day, 12-hour clock (01..12)
%j	Day of the year (001..366)
%k	Hour of the day, 24-hour clock, blank padded (␣0..23)
%l	Hour of the day, 12-hour clock, blank padded (␣1..12)
%L	Milliseconds of the second
%m	Month of the year (01..12)
%M	Minute of the hour (00..59)
%n	Newline
%N	Fractional seconds, 9 digits in width, an optional width specifier changes the width, as in %3N
%p	Meridian indicator, uppercase ("AM" or "PM")
%P	Meridian indicator, lowercase ("am" or "pm")
%r	12-hour time (%I:%M:%S %p)
%R	24-hour time (%H:%M)
%s	Number of seconds since 1970-01-01 00:00:00 UTC

Format	Meaning
%S	Second of the minute (00..60)
%t	Tab
%T	24-hour time (%H:%M:%S)
%u	Day of the week (Monday is 1, 1..7)
%U	Week number of the current year, starting with the first Sunday as the first day of the first week (00..53)
%w	Day of the week (Sunday is 0, 0..6)
%v	VMS date (%e-%^b-%4Y)
%V	ISO8601 week number (01..53)
%W	Week number of the current year, starting with the first Monday as the first day of the first week (00..53)
%x	Preferred representation for the date alone, no time
%X	Preferred representation for the time alone, no date
%y	Year without a century (00..99)
%Y	Year with century, four digits.
%z	Time zone offset (+/-hhmm). Use %:z or %::z to format with colons
%Z	Time zone name
%+	Date and time, not supported by Time class.

Table 21—Time#strftime directives

Using Time Instances

Once you have a Time instance, you can extract all the various attributes. Every attribute that might get passed in as part of a constructor call has an associated getter method: Time#year, Time#month (aliased as Time#mon), Time#day (aliased as Time#mday), Time#hour, Time#min, Time#sec, and Time#subsec. All of these methods return the integer value of that attribute except for subsec, which returns either a Rational or integer zero.

A Time instance includes a few calculated attributes:

- Time#dst? returns true if the time zone is a daylight savings time zone.

- Time#nsec returns the subseconds in nanoseconds.

- Time#usec returns the subseconds in microseconds.

- Time#wday returns the day of the week as an integer with Sunday as 0, Monday as 1, and so on.

- There are also a series of methods called sunday?, Time#monday? and so on that return true if the day of the week matches that day.

- Time#yday returns the integer day of the year, so January 1st is 1, February 12th is 33, and so on.

- Time#zone returns the name of the time zone.

A Time instance can be the left side of an addition operation and have a number added to it. A new time object is returned with the number of seconds added to the time.

```
t = Time.now
t          # => 2023-11-02 17:16:31.572387 -0500
t + 100    # => 2023-11-02 17:18:11.572387 -0500
```

A Time instance can be the left side of a subtraction operation. The right side can be a number, in which case a new instance is returned with the number of seconds subtracted from the time. Alternatively, a second Time instance can be the right operand, in which case the result is the number of seconds between the two times as a float:

```
t = Time.now
t          # => 2023-11-02 17:16:31.643105 -0500
t2 = t - 100
t2         # => 2023-11-02 17:14:51.643105 -0500
t - t2     # => 100.0
```

Time implements the Time#<=> operator and includes the Comparable module, so Time instances can be sorted and compared using all the logical comparison operators.

Converting Time

You can convert a Time instance to a number with the methods Time#to_f, Time#to_i, and Time#to_r. These return the number of seconds that have passed since the Unix Epoch date as a float, integer, or rational, respectively.

A Time instance can be converted to a Time instance in a different time zone with Time#getutc or Time#getlocal, both of which have the corresponding methods Time#utc and Time#localtime, which change the receiver in place. You can convert a Time instance to a Date or DateTime with Time#to_date or Time#to_datetime.

You can convert a Time instance to an array using Time#to_a, which returns a 10-element array made up of the attributes [sec, min, hour, day, month, year, wday, yday, dst?, zone]. This array can be passed back to some of the Time constructors to create a new Time instance. Although you cannot convert a Time to a hash directly, Time does implement Time#decon-struct_keys so you can use a Time instance in pattern matching. Here's an example:

```
require "time"
x = Time.parse("April 12, 2023")
case x
in {month: 3|4|5, day:}
  puts "Spring is here and it's the #{day}th"
else
  puts "It's not winter"
end
```

produces:

```
Spring is here and it's the 12th
```

You can convert a Time instance to a string in several ways. The most general is Time#strf-time(format_string), which takes a format string as an argument. The format string uses the characters shown in Table 21, directives, on page 498, to insert parts of the actual time in the string. Here are examples of the string formatting methods:

- Time#asctime (also ctime) formats as %a %b %e %T %Y, which has a shortcut %c.
- Time#httpdate formats as %a, %d %b %Y %T GMT.
- Time#inspect formats as %Y-%m-%d %H:%M:%S %N %z.
- Time#rfc2822 formats as %a, %-d %b %Y %T %z.
- Time#to_s formats as %Y-%m-%d %H:%M:%S %z, which is the same as inspect except for the subseconds.

Here are the methods in action:

```
require "time"
t = Time.now
t.strftime("%m/%d/%y")                  # => "11/02/23"
t.strftime("%a %b %e %H:%M:%S %Z %Y")   # => "Thu Nov  2 17:16:31 CDT 2023"
t.ctime                                 # => "Thu Nov  2 17:16:31 2023"
t.httpdate                              # => "Thu, 02 Nov 2023 22:16:31 GMT"
t.inspect                               # => "2023-11-02 17:16:31.78857 -0500"
t.rfc2822                               # => "Thu, 02 Nov 2023 17:16:31 -0500"
t.to_s                                  # => "2023-11-02 17:16:31 -0500"
```

Creating Date and DateTime Instances

The date library implements the classes Date and DateTime, which provide a comprehensive set of facilities for storing, manipulating, and converting dates with or without time components. The classes can represent and manipulate civil, ordinal, commercial, Julian, and standard dates, starting January 1, 4713 BCE. The DateTime class extends Date with hours, minutes, seconds, and fractional seconds, and it provides some support for time zones. The classes also provide support for parsing and formatting date and datetime strings. To use them, you need to require "date".

DateTime is a subclass of Date and is generally considered deprecated in favor of plain-old Time unless you specifically need its calendar calculation facilities. In this section, we'll talk about Date mostly, since DateTime is a subclass, so you can assume anything about Date also applies to DateTime.

Many methods of Date that create or compare dates take an optional positional argument at the end, start = Date::ITALY. This is for Gregorian vs. Julian dates, and you're unlikely to need this in regular work, so we've left it off of all the methods that use it.

The main method for creating a Date is with Date.today, which returns the current date as a Date instance. You'll also often see Date.new(year, month day) or Date.parse(string, current_century = true, limit: 128)—the parse method uses similar logic to Time.parse. If the current_centry argument is true, a two-digit year is augmented with the current century, otherwise, it's taken as referring to a two-digit year. There's also a Date.strptime(string, format = "%F") that takes a format string, again, just like Time.strptime. The DateTime class has DateTime.now and also a DateTime.new that takes in arguments similar to the multi-argument format of Time.new

Date can be the left side of an addition operation. The second operand is a number in days to be added to the Date.

```
require "date"
d = Date.new(2023, 2, 12)
d         # => #<Date: 2023-02-12 ((2459988j,0s,0n),+0s,2299161j)>
d + 25    # => #<Date: 2023-03-09 ((2460013j,0s,0n),+0s,2299161j)>
```

Date can be the left side of a subtraction operation. Subtraction either takes a numeric and returns a new Date that many days earlier, or another Date and returns the number of days in between the two of them.

Date also takes Date#<<, which adds a number of months to the date, as in Date.today << 3.

Date also supports <=> and Comparable.

You can get a following day with Date#next, Date#next_day(n = 1), Date#next_month(n = 1), Date#next_year(n = 1). The last three take an optional argument for the number of steps you want to move forward. You also have Date#prev_day(n = 1), Date#prev_month(n = 1), and Date#prev_year(n = 1).

Once you have a Date, the components are accessible as Date#year, Date#month (aliased as Date#mon), and Date#day (aliased as Date#mday). All the weekday predicate methods like Date#sunday? also exist, as do Date#wday (day of week), and Date#yday (day of year). The DateTime class also adds DateTime#hour, DateTime#minute (aliased as DateTime#min), DateTime#second (aliased as DateTime#sec), DateTime#second_fraction (aliased as DateTime#sec_fraction), and DateTime#zone.

Date has most of the same string methods as Time, including Date#ctime and Date#strftime(format = "%F"), and also implements Date#deconstruct_keys for pattern matching. There's also Date#to_datetime and Date#to_time.

Math

The Numeric class and its subclasses handle a lot of the basic arithmetic in Ruby. (For more see Numbers, on page 503.) But sometimes you need to do more advanced math. The Math module provides a couple dozen math functions, largely trigonometry, but it also handles other branches of advanced math. The BigMath model recreates a subset of those methods for BigDecimal arguments and values.

All of these methods are module methods, so they are all called with module syntax, as in Math.cos(value).

The Math module contains multitudes, especially if you like trigonometry. Specifically, it contains:

- The constant values Math::Pi and Math::E.

- Math.sqrt(x) and Math.cbrt(x), which return the square and cube roots of the argument, respectively.

- Logarithm functions, so Math.log(x, base = Math::E) returns the logarithm of the value and has an inverse method Math.exp(x), which returns e raised to that value. The sibling log methods Math.log10(x) and Math.log2(x) are also available and return the log of the argument in the base of the method name.

- A related method, Math.frexp(x), which returns a two-element array with the fraction and exponent base two of that number, so the return value is [y, z], where $x = y * 2**z$. The inverse method Math.ldexp(y, z), returns the x value in that equation.

- A method Math.hypot(x, y), which takes two arguments and returns sqrt(x**2, y**2)—in other words, the hypotenuse of a right triangle with sides x and y.

- Error and gamma functions Math.erf(x), Math.erfc(x), Math.gamma(x), and Math.gammac(x). We're just going to assume that if you know what these are, you'll know what they do.

- Lots of trig functions, including the basic Math.sin(x), Math.cos(x), and Math.tan(x). The input value is in radians, and for sin and cos it must be between -1 and 1. There's also the inverse trig functions Math.acos, Math.asin(x), Math.atan(x), and Math.atan2(x). Finally, the hyperbolic and inverse hyperbolic functions Math.cosh(x), Math.sinh(x), Math.tanh(x),

Math.acosh(x), Math.asinh(x), and Math.atanh(x) are all also there, and all also take arguments in radians. Some of these methods have their own range limits.

Numbers

We talked about numeric literals in Integer and Floating-Point Numbers, on page 432. Here, let's talk about the library methods for numbers.

Numeric Class

All number classes inherit from the class Numeric. If you want to define your own number subclass, it's recommended that you also inherit from Numeric because Numeric does some internal things about storing numbers in memory that are useful to have.

It might go without saying—but it's our job to say it—that Numeric implements Numeric#<=> and includes Comparable. As with other <=>, the return value is -1 if the left side is smaller, 1 if the left side is greater, and 0 if the two are equal. The equality test is also aliased as eql?.

It's also our job to say that the actual arithmetic operators—Numeric#+(other), Numeric#-(other), Numeric#*(other), Numeric#/(other), and Numeric#**(other)—aren't defined by Numeric but are defined by the subclasses individually, presumably for performance reasons. The Numeric class does define unary Numeric#@- for negating a number and unary Numeric#@+, which is a no-op. Numeric also defines Numeric#%(other), which does modular arithmetic, but this is also overridden in most of the subclasses. And Numeric also defines Numeric#abs for the absolute value of the number.

The basic mechanism of converting between number types for the purposes of doing arithmetic is Numeric#coerce(other). The coerce method takes another numeric argument and returns a two-element array with the argument as the first element and the original receiver as the second. The two numbers are in a common type—broadly, an integer and a non-integer argument will both be converted to floats. A float receiver and pretty much any argument will be converted to floats. A rational or complex receiver will convert an integer argument, but will be converted to float by a float argument, see Numeric Coercion, on page 366, for more examples.

Numeric defines Numeric#ceil(digits = 0), Numeric#floor(digits = 0), Numeric#round(digits = 0), and Numeric#truncate(digits = 0) for the common mathematical definitions. All of these take an optional argument that is the number of digits beyond the decimal point to keep; the default is 0. So, ceil returns the smallest number above the receiver at that precision, floor returns the largest number below, round returns whichever of floor or ceil is closer, halfway point rounds up, and truncate cuts off the number.

Somewhat counterintuitively, Numeric does define a couple of division methods. It defines Numeric#div(x) as integer division self / x using the self objects definition of /. If you want a float result, then Numeric#fdiv(x) does the same division but returns a float. The method Numeric#quo(x) does the same division but returns a rational if the argument is an integer or rational, or a float if the argument is a float. The method Numeric#divmod(x) returns a two-element array such that self.divmod(x) = [(self / x).floor, self % x]. The mod value is also available as Numeric#remainder(other).

Any number can be converted to an integer with Numeric#to_int, but the kernel method Integer is preferred, and you can go to a complex number with Numeric#to_c. Although they makes the most sense for rationals, Numeric#numerator and Numeric#denominator are defined in Numeric.

Numeric defines a set of query methods that are valid for all number types. The set Numeric#positive?, Numeric#negative?, Numeric#nonzero?, and Numeric#zero? all return true or false based exactly on the check in the name of the method. It's fairly common to see x.zero? rather than x == 0 as a condition. The Numeric#infinite? method checks against the -Infinity or +Infinity special values; the inverse method is Numeric#finite?. If the number is an Integer, then Numeric#integer? returns true, and similarly Numeric#real?. Note that the check is based on the type of the number, not the value; 1.0.integer? is false.

You can convert any number to a collection with the Numeric#step(to = nil, by = 1) [{ |n| block}] or Numeric#step(to: nil, by: 1) [{ |n| block}] method, which takes a variety of arguments and a block. It can take two positional arguments (to and by), in which case the block is called with self as an argument. The by amount is added to self, and the block is called again until the to argument is crossed. If by is positive, it crosses by going higher; if by is negative, it crosses by going lower. So it's roughly equivalent to this implementation:

```
def step(to = nil, by = 1, &block)
  counter = self
  start_relationship = self <=> to
  while (counter <=> to) == start_relationship
    block.call(counter)
    counter += by
  end
end
```

As you can see, to defaults to nil, meaning an infinite sequence, and by defaults to 1. You can also specify to: and by: as keyword arguments. If no block is given, the real method, unlike our scratch implementation earlier, will return an Enumerator that will successively return the values that would've been passed to the block.

Integer Class

The Integer class inherits from the Numeric class and implements a number of the methods described earlier on its own for memory or speed performance purposes. It also adds some additional functionality of its own.

Integer implements these regular arithmetic operators: Integer#+, Integer#-, Integer#*, Integer#/ (which is integer division and truncates the result), Integer#% (also available as Integer#modulo), and Integer#** (also available as Integer#pow). Integer also implements bitwise arithmetic.

The bitwise AND (Integer#&) operator returns a new number with a 1 in each bit that is 1 in the binary representation of both operands. The bitwise OR (Integer#|) operator returns a new number with a 1 in the binary representation of either operand. The bitwise XOR (Integer#^) operator returns a new number with a 1 in each bit that is 1 in the binary representation of one but not both operands. The Integer#<< shifts the bits of the left operand the number in the right operand, and Integer#~ is the one's complement—it flips all the bits. The Integer#[] operator can be used to read (but not write) the bit at the given offset in the binary representation of the integer.

Ruby also provides Integer#allbits?(mask), which returns true if every bit that's set to 1 in the mask is also set to 1 in the receiver. (In other words, it is equivalent to self & mask == mask).

The method Integer#anybits?(mask) returns true if any bit set to 1 in the mask is also set to 1 in the receiver, so, self & mask != 0. The method Integer#nobits?(mask) returns true if no bit set to 1 in the mask is set to 1 in the receiver, so self & mask == 0.

```
0b0111 & 0b0100          # => 4
0b0111.allbits?(0b0100)  # => true
0b0111.anybits?(0b0100)  # => true
0b0111.nobits?(0b0100)   # => false
0b0111 | 0b0100          # => 7
0b0111 ^ 0b0100          # => 3
~0b0110                  # => -7
1.even?                  # => false
2.odd?                   # => false
```

The method Integer#gcd(other) takes an integer argument and returns the greatest common denominator of the two integers. The Integer#lcm(other) method returns the least common multiple of the two integers. The Integer#gcdlcm(other) method returns a two-element array that returns the greatest common denominator and the least common multiple of the two integers.

```
10.gcd(15)    # => 5
10.lcm(15)    # => 30
10.gcdlcm(15) # => [5, 30]
```

Integers can be used to iterate inside ranges, which means integers implement Integer#next to return the next integer going upward and Integer#pred to return the previous integer going downward.

Integers define the query methods Integer#even? and Integer#odd?, which return true or false based on the value of the integer.

The Integer#chr(encoding = Encoding::UTF_8) method converts the integer to a single character string represented by that integer in a particular encoding. The default is UTF-8, but you can pass any encoding as an optional argument.

The Integer class also defines some base-transitioning methods. The Integer#digits(base = 10) method returns an array of all the individual digits in the integer but reversed (with the "ones" digit being the first digit of the array). An optional base argument puts the digits in whatever base you want as long as the base is greater than two. The default is base ten.

You can use an integer to drive a loop using the Integer#times [{ |n| block }] method, which takes a block and calls the block with every integer value from 0 to the receiving value minus one. If you want to do this starting at the integer rather than ending at it, the Integer#upto [{ |n| block }] method takes a required limit that's higher and calls the block for each integer from the receiver up to the limit, inclusive. To go the other direction, you can use the Integer#downto [{ |n| block }] method, which takes a required limit argument that is lower and calls the block for each integer value from the receiver value down to the value of the limit, inclusive. Without a block, all these methods return an Enumerator.

Integers are convertible to other objects with Integer#to_d for BigDecimal, Integer#to_f for Float, Integer#to_i and Integer#to_int which just return the integer, Integer#to_r for Rational, and Integer#to_s for String.

Float Class

The Float class implements several methods for performance purposes but doesn't add a whole lot to the functionality of Numeric.

Float defines constants, here are some of them:

- Float::DIG—Machine dependent; the number of significant digits in a double-precision floating point. (DIG for digits, not for digging.) Usually 15 on most current Ruby implementations.

- Float::EPSILON—Machine dependent: the smallest difference between two numbers that can be represented. The documentation says it usually defaults to 2.2204460492503131e-16.

- Float::INFINITY—The representation of infinity.

- Float::MAX—The largest possible value in a double-precision floating point.

- Float::MAX_EXP—The largest exponent in a double-precision floating point; should be 1024.

- Float::MIN—The smallest possible value in a double-precision floating point.

- Float::MIN_EXP—The smallest exponent in a double-precision floating point; should be 1021.

- Float::NAN—Represents not a number, usually the result of zero divided by zero.

Floats implement the basic arithmetic operators, Float#+, Float#-, Float#*, Float#/, Float#%, and Float#**, and have a query operator for Float#nan?.

Floats can't be in iterable ranges, but they do have Float#next_float and Float#prev_float methods that return the adjacent representable float values.

Floats can be approximately converted to rationals with the Float#rationalize method, and have Float#to_d, Float#to_f, Float#to_i and Float#to_int (both of which truncate the float to an integer), Float#to_r, and Float#to_s.

Beyond that, the Float class has the same features as a generic Numeric object.

Rational Class

The Rational class is a subclass of Numeric. Rationals can be created with the literal syntax (see Rational and Complex Numbers, on page 433) or with the Kernel method Rational, which takes the numerator and denominator as arguments.

Nearly all the methods of Rational are performance improvements over methods that exist in Numeric. The arithmetic methods Rational#+, Rational#-, Rational#*, Rational#/, and Rational#** are defined. The conversion methods Rational#to_d, Rational#to_f, Rational#to_i, Rational#to_r, and Rational#to_s are defined.

If the JSON add-on library has been included, then Rational#to_json returns a JSON representation of the hash {"json_class" => "Rational", "n" => self.numerator, "d" => self.denominator}. (See JSON, on page 609, for more information.) The JSON string can be deserialized with the class method Rational.json_create(json_string).

Complex Class

The Complex class is a subclass of Numeric. Complex numbers can be created with the literal syntax (see Rational and Complex Numbers, on page 433) or with the Kernel method Complex(real, imaginary = 0), which takes the real and imaginary parts as arguments. The Complex class also defines Complex.polar(magnitude, phase = 0) and Complex.rectangular(real, imaginary = 0) methods that create complex objects in different formats.

The real part has a getter method Complex#real; the imaginary part has a getter method Complex#imaginary, which is aliased as Complex#imag. The method Complex#rectangular or Complex#rect returns a two-element array, [real, imaginary]. For complex numbers, the query method Complex#real? always returns false, no matter the value of the imaginary part.

In polar form, the getters are Complex#magnitude (aliased as Complex#abs) and Complex#phase (aliased as Complex#arg). The getter Complex#polar returns the two polar values as a two-element array, [magnitude, phase].

The Complex#infinite? boolean will return true if either the real or imaginary part of the number is infinite.

Nearly all the methods of Complex are performance improvements over methods that exist in Numeric. The arithmetic methods Complex#+, Complex#-, Complex#*, Complex#/, and Complex#** are defined.

Complex has its own feature of the Complex#<=> operator. A comparison involving a complex number with an imaginary part that isn't zero will return nil. In other cases, it'll compare the real part of the complex number with the other operand. The Complex#== method will compare the equality of complex numbers including their imaginary dimension.

The conversion methods Complex#to_c, Complex#to_d, Complex#to_f, Complex#to_i, Complex#to_json, Complex#to_r, and Complex#to_s are defined. The numeric methods will return a RangeError if the imaginary part isn't integer 0.

If the JSON additions library is included, the Complex#to_json method returns a JSON representation of the hash {"json_class" => "Complex", "r" => self.real, "i" => self.imaginary}. (See JSON, on page 609, for more information.) The JSON string can be deserialized with the class method Complex.json_create(json_string).

BigDecimal

Ruby has a lot of literal numeric types: integers, floating-point numbers, rational numbers, and complex numbers. There's one common need that isn't filled by Ruby's literals and for which you need the standard library: precise representation of decimal values.

What do we mean by precision? Well, here's an example that you can replicate in your own IRB session:

```
1.1 - 0.8 # => 0.30000000000000004
```

That seems...wrong? Your fourth grade math teacher would probably be appalled.

It's important that you're familiar with two important facts:

- Floating-point numbers are inherently imprecise—it's not just a Ruby issue—and shouldn't be used for values like money, where exact precision is necessary. (Floating-point numbers are used because they are smaller in memory and faster in calculation.)

- When you do need a precise number in Ruby, use BigDecimal.

Floating-point numbers are imprecise because they are trying to represent base-10 decimals in a base-2 format, and there just isn't a one-to-one match.

Internally, floating-point numbers are represented as a set of bytes (64 on most of the machines you'll be using) some of which are used for a base number, and the rest are used for an exponent, so 24.68 might be represented as 2468 x 10**-2. Without getting too deep into the exact details of the representation, this also means that, as the floating-point numbers get farther from zero, the worse the floating-point standard gets at matching floats to actual numbers. One implication is that floating-point number errors are worse if the two operands of an operation are of vastly different magnitudes.

When you need precise decimal values, Ruby provides the BigDecimal class. Internally, BigDecimal uses a decimal format that allows you to specify the number of digits used and then represents that value exactly in any future math operations you might perform.

To use BigDecimal, you must use require "bigdecimal" in your application. Once you've done this, creating new instances of BigDecimal is a little odd. The BigDecimal class doesn't have a constructor. Instead, you use a Kernel method, also called BigDecimal(value, number_of_digits = 0, exception: true), which makes it look like you're using one of the conversion methods:

```
require "bigdecimal"
BigDecimal("3.14")  # => 0.314e1
BigDecimal(4.2, 2)  # => 0.42e1
```

The first argument to BigDecimal is the value you're converting, and the second argument is the number of digits of precision you want. Depending on what the first argument is to BigDecimal, you may or may not be required to specify the second argument.

The number of digits of precision is the number of digits used regardless of what side of the decimal point the digit is on. In these examples, you can see that the number of digits of precision changes the value of the BigDecimal as it's converted to a float using BigDecimal#to_f:

```
require "bigdecimal"
BigDecimal(31.419, 5).to_f # => 31.419
BigDecimal(31.419, 4).to_f # => 31.42
BigDecimal(31.419, 3).to_f # => 31.4
BigDecimal(31.419, 2).to_f # => 31.0
BigDecimal(31.419, 1).to_f # => 30.0
```

If the first argument is a Complex, an Integer, a String, or another BigDecimal, the conversion doesn't need to know the digits of precision. If the first argument is a Float or a Rational, then you must include the digits of precision.

Strings are parsed and assumed to use the number of digits equivalent to characters in the string:

```
require "bigdecimal"
BigDecimal("31.419").to_f # => 31.419
```

If you have another type as the first value, Ruby attempts to convert it to a string using to_str and parses that string. (According to the documentation, it doesn't appear that Ruby attempts to convert it to a number.) If the conversion fails, the method returns nil. An optional keyword argument, exception: true, will cause BigDecimal to raise an exception in that case instead.

Once you have a BigDecimal, you can use it like any other numeric. If it's the left side of an operation, the result will also be a BigDecimal:

```
require "bigdecimal"
x = BigDecimal("31.419") + 5.3
x.class    # => BigDecimal
```

BigDecimal defines the full range of numeric operators: BigDecimal#+, BigDecimal#-, BigDecimal#*, BigDecimal#/, BigDecimal#**, BigDecimal#%, BigDecimal#@-, and BigDecimal#@+ as well as BigDecimal#<=> and the Comparable module.

You can convert out of BigDecimal with the usual suspects, BigDecimal#to_i, BigDecimal#to_f, BigDecimal#to_s, and BigDecimal#to_r for Rational. There's also a module called bigdecimal/util—requiring that gives you a to_d method on Integer, Float, Rational, and String that converts to a BigDecimal.

A few special values—Infinity, +Infinity, -Infinity, and NaN—are all valid values, which you normally trigger by dividing by zero:

```
require "bigdecimal"
BigDecimal("1.0") / BigDecimal("0.0") # => Infinity
BigDecimal("0.0") / BigDecimal("0.0") # => NaN
```

BigDecimal also allows you to control how values are rounded to the number of significant digits. If you're like us, you were taught in school to round to the closest digit, and that the value in the middle—5—rounds up. It turns out that this is just a convention, and other conventions are also valuable. You can change the rounding mode globally with BigDecimal.mode(BigDecimal::ROUND_MODE, [value]), where the value may be one of the following:

- BigDecimal:ROUND_CEILING—Always round toward the higher number.

- BigDecimal:ROUND_DOWN—Always round toward zero, so 8.2 rounds to 8.

- BigDecimal:ROUND_FLOOR—Always round toward the lower number.

- BigDecimal::ROUND_HALF_DOWN—Round to the nearest value; the midpoint rounds down. So 8.5 rounds to 8, which is different than the normal default.

- BigDecimal::ROUND_HALF_EVEN—Round to the nearest value; the midpoint rounds to whichever neighbor is an even number. So 8.5 rounds to 8, but 9.5 rounds to 10. This is sometimes called "banker's rounding."

- BigDecimal::ROUND_HALF_UP—Round to the nearest value; the midpoint rounds up. This is the default you were probably taught in school.

- BigDecimal:ROUND_UP—Always round away from zero, so 8.2 rounds to 9.

Why Do Bankers Round Differently?

If you're adding up a very large set of numbers, one thing you want is for the sum to be essentially the same no matter where you round the value. Using traditional rounding, the fact that the midpoint rounds up will tend to result in rounded numbers having a higher sum than the same set of numbers with the values just truncated, making the sum less accurate when rounded. Using banker's rounding, the midpoint number tends to go up or down more or less equally, so the rounded number doesn't have a biased sum relative to the truncated sum.

Random and SecureRandom

Random numbers are an important part of games and cryptographic security, and Ruby has a few different ways to get randomness. The easiest is the method Kernel#rand(max = 0). Because it's available in Kernel, you can call rand anytime. If you call rand with no arguments, you get a pseudo-random float greater than or equal to zero and less than one. If you call rand with an argument and the argument is an integer one or greater, then you get a pseudo-random integer greater than or equal to zero and less than the argument. Note this means that rand(1) will always equal 0.

Non-integer arguments are converted using to_i.abs, meaning that negative arguments will return positive values and floating-point arguments will be truncated. If arg.to_i.abs is equal to zero, then rand reverts to its no-argument behavior.

If the argument is a range, rand returns a value within that range. If both ends of the range are integers, the result will be an integer. If either end is a float, the result will also be a float.

Often you may want to have a repeatable sequence of random numbers. In testing or in debugging it can be useful to know that the random numbers are consistent from run to run. You can do this in Ruby with the Kernel method Kernel#srand(number = Random.new_seed). If you call srand without an argument, it generates a seed based on the operating system's randomizer, but if you call it with an integer argument, it uses that number as the seed, and then it'll provide a replicable stream of random numbers. Using the same seed later on will result in the same set of numbers.

Ruby also provides an object-oriented interface to the random number generator. The Random class provides the same features as rand, but allows you to have multiple streams. The formatter module, which gets mixed in with require "random/formatter", gives you a set of methods on Random to produce structured random output.

You use Random by creating a new instance with Random.new(seed = Random.new_seed), which takes an optional argument that is the seed, exactly as described in srand. You can then get new random numbers with rand (and recover the seed with seed):

```
generator = Random.new(1234)
generator.rand          # => 0.1915194503788923

another_generator = Random.new(generator.seed)
another_generator.rand  # => 0.1915194503788923
```

The Random#rand(max_or_range = 0) method takes exactly the same arguments as Kernel#rand. If the argument is a range then you get a random number whose value is inside the range.

You can also get a string of random bytes with the Random#bytes(size) method, which takes one argument: the length of the string.

With the line require "random/formatter", you get a number of useful methods mixed into Random. All of these methods are available as class methods, as in Random.alphanumeric, or as instance methods, as in x.alphanumeric.

- Random#alphanumeric(length = nil)—Returns a randomly generated string with just the characters A-Z, a-z, and 0-9. The argument is the length, and if left off, it defaults to 16.

- Random#base64(length = nil)—Returns a randomly generated base-64 string using the characters in alphanumeric as well as +, /, and =. The length is the length in bytes, not in characters, so the resulting string will be about ⅓ longer than n, since some characters are less than one byte. A version of this method, called urlsafe_base64, uses - and _ instead of + and /. That method also uses = as padding if a second argument is passed with the value true.

- Random#hex(length = nil)—Returns a random hexadecimal string, so the characters are 0-9 and a-f. The resulting string is twice as long as the argument (because the length is in bytes and each character is half a byte), and the default is still 16 (meaning a 32-character string).

- Random#random_bytes(length = nil)—Returns a random binary string. The length is in bytes, and the default is 16.

- Random#uuid—Generates a UUID, with 122 random bits. It corresponds to version 4 of the UUID specification.

One downside of the main Random class is that it isn't considered powerful enough for true cryptographic uses. The cryptographically secure randomizers are a little slower, so Ruby provides them in a separate class, called SecureRandom, which you must add to your app with require "securerandom". The only default method of SecureRandom is called SecureRandom#bytes(size), but SecureRandom automatically includes the methods in the formatter, so all the methods presented in the previous list are available on a SecureRandom instance. There isn't a way to specify the seed of a SecureRandom instance—presumably, that would be insecure.

Regexp

The Regexp class is the Ruby representation of a regular expression. We discussed the basic syntax of regular expressions at length in Chapter 8, Regular Expressions, on page 129. Here we focus on the API for the Regexp class itself and then cover some advanced regular expression syntax.

You can create a regular expression using the literal syntax, which is two foreword slashes with the regular expression in the middle, such as /.*rb/. (All the escape sequences and whatnot inside the slashes are discussed in Chapter 8, Regular Expressions, on page 129. The alternate delimiter %r{...} will also create regular expressions.

The method, Regexp.new(string, options = 0, timeout: nil) creates a new regular expression with the string argument as the pattern. The options argument is the equivalent of the i, m, n, or x options that go at the end of a regular expression literal, and it can be passed as a string of one or more of those four letters. Alternatively, each of those letters has a constant. In order they are: Regexp::IGNORECASE, Regexp::MULTILINE, Regexp::NOENCODING, and Regexp::EXTENDED.

The constants are encoded as integers, and you can combine them with the bitwise OR operator, which would look like Regexp.new("*.foo", "im") or Regexp.new("*.foo", Regexp::IGNORECASE | Regexp::MULTILINE). In practice, we think this might be one of the few cases in Ruby where the more compact form might also be more legible. The optional timeout: argument allows you to override the class-level timeout. If set, the regular expression engine throws an error if the time is reached before a match resolves. More on that in a bit.

You can copy an existing regular expression with Regexp.new(regexp, timeout: nil). (You can pass an options argument but it'll be ignored.) This creates a new regular expression identical to the old, but it allows you to set a different timeout value. Regexp.new is also aliased as Regexp.compile.

You can combine multiple regular expressions with Regexp.union(*patterns)—the patterns can be an array of patterns or just a list of positional arguments. Each pattern can be an existing Regexp object or a string, in which case the string is converted to a Regexp using Regexp.new. The resulting pattern matches a string if any of the subpatterns matches the string. If the patterns argument is empty, union produces a regular expression that can't match any string (specifically, it returns /?!/). According to the official documentation, the behavior of parenthesized capture groups in a union string is undefined, so you can only use a union string to determine a match or no match, not to capture partial matches.

We mentioned the timeout keyword parameter. The purpose of a timeout is to prevent a regular expression match from stalling your application. This is potentially a vector for a denial-of-service attack to force your application to match a complicated regular expression against long strings. You can get and set a global timeout value in seconds with Regexp.timeout and Regexp.timeout=(seconds). For an individual regex, you can override this value on creation with the timeout: key of Regexp.new. There's no individual setter (at least not yet); if you want to change the timeout for an existing regexp, you need to convert it with the regex form of Regexp.new. The default timeout is nil, meaning no timeout, but if the timeout is set, Ruby will throw an exception if matching the regular expression to a string takes longer than the timeout value.

The Regexp class provides a few different methods that match the regular expression against a string. The most recommended ones are Regexp#match(string, offset = 0) [{|matchdata|}] and Regexp#match?(string, offset = 0). In both cases, the primary argument is the string to be matched against, and the optional offset is the index of the string where the match algorithm should begin. One difference between the two methods is the return value—match? returns boolean true if there is a match or false otherwise, whereas match returns a MatchData object (see MatchData, on page 513) if there is a match or nil otherwise. If a block is passed to match, then the block is invoked with the MatchData object and the result of the block is returned. Note that because match returns nil on a negative result it can be used as a boolean clause, since the nil will evaluate as falsey.

The =~ operator is implemented as Regex#=~(string) and returns the integer index of the beginning of the match if there is a match and nil otherwise. The opposite operator, !~, doesn't have a separate method definition; Ruby just reverses the boolean result of =~. Note that =~ and match both update the set of Ruby global variables that hold the value of the last matched regular expressions, but match? doesn't. You can also get the value of that last matched regular expression with the class method Regexp.last_match.

The Regexp#=== case equality operator essentially behaves like match?. It returns true if the string matches the regular expression and false otherwise. The difference is that match? throws an error if the argument isn't a string and === just returns false in that case.

Regular expressions have an equality operator, Regexp#== or Regexp#eql?, which returns true if both expressions have the same source, optional flags, and encoding.

A few methods of Regexp allow you to read some information about the regular expression. You can recover the source string of the expression with Regexp#source, which returns the string with regular expression escape characters intact, but with typographical escape characters evaluated. The methods Regexp#to_s and Regexp#inspect all return slightly different versions of the source string. The to_s version is specifically designed to be passed back to Regexp.new. The class method Regexp#escape(string), aliased Regexp#quote, returns a string that escapes characters that have meaning in a regular expression:

```
r = /ru+by\x10\//ix
r.source            # => "ru+by\\x10/"
r.inspect           # => "/ru+by\\x10\\//ix"
r.to_s              # => "(?ix-m:ru+by\\x10\\/)"
Regexp.escape("+*?") # => "\\+\\*\\?"
```

If your regular expression uses named captures, Regexp#names returns an array of the names of the captures, which can then be used as the keys of any resulting MatchData objects. The method Regexp#named_captures returns a hash where the key is the name of the named capture and the value is an array of all the integer indexes in the regular expression which map to that name. So, the first named capture in the expression gets the value [1] and so on, with the array getting multiple elements if the named capture repeats in the regular expression. In both of these methods, if there are no named captures, the result is an empty data object.

You can get the option flags from your regular expression with Regexp#options, which returns an integer of the combined bits of the option flag constants. Three constants are the most important here: i, m, and x, with a couple of other ones that match encodings or group behavior. A partial method that converts those three options to a useful string might look like this:

```
built_in_data/options.rb
class Regexp
  OPTION_MAP = {IGNORECASE => "i", EXTENDED => "x", MULTILINE => "m"}

  def option_string
    option_bits = options
    OPTION_MAP.map do |bit, string|
      ((option_bits & bit) > 0) ? string : nil
    end.compact.join
  end
end
```

MatchData

The MatchData class is what's returned by a regular expression using match to compare to a string, and the class contains all the data about the resulting match. The most commonly used method of MatchData is probably square bracket access via MatchData[]. The argument inside the bracket is one of the following:

- An integer. The index 0 corresponds to the entire matched section of the string, the index 1 corresponds to the first captured part of the string, and higher numbers match subsequent captures. If the index is higher than the number of matches, then nil is returned. Negative indexes work from the last capture toward the zero index.

- A string or symbol name. The returned value is a matching named capture in the resulting match, or it is nil if no such named capture exists.

- Two integers separated by a comma. In this case you get the same start index and length behavior that you get for strings and arrays. The starting index can be 0, and the resulting value is no longer than the actual data (it's not padded with nil or anything like that).

- A range of integers. In this case you get the subset of indexes corresponding to the indexes of the integers in the range, again, the result truncates at the length of the actual data.

You can also get the integer or name behavior with MatchData#match(value), but negative indexes, pairs of integers, and ranges don't work with match. The method MatchData#match_length(value) takes an integer, string, or symbol argument and returns the length of the section of the match data corresponding to that argument, or it returns nil if no such match exists.

The method MatchData#values_at(*indexes) is more flexible. It takes an arbitrary number of indexes and returns an array of the matched values at each index. The arguments can be strings, symbols, integers (including negative integers), and ranges. The final result is flattened, meaning a range argument doesn't result in a sub-array in the output.

There are other ways to get at the data. MatchData#matches returns all the positional matches as an array, meaning it's equivalent to match[1..]. This method is aliased MatchData#deconstruct, which means you can use a MatchData object as the pattern in a pattern match expression. The other pattern match API method, MatchData#deconstruct_keys, also exists and returns a hash of all named captures as symbol keys and their matches as the values. The method MatchData#to_a returns all the matches as an array including the entire match that would be in index 0. The method MatchData#size, aliased MatchData#length, gives the length of the capture array. The method MatchData#to_s gives the entire match, which means it's equivalent to match[0]. You can get all the named captures in a hash with MatchData#named_captures — the keys are the symbol names of each capture and the value is the associated part of the match. If you just want the names of the captures, MatchData#names gives that list.

You can recreate the original match with MatchData#regexp, which returns the regular expression used to create the match data, and MatchData#string, which returns the entire original string in the match, including the non-matched parts. These parts of the original string can be retrieved with MatchData#pre_match, which returns the part of the original string before the match, and MatchData#post_match, which returns the part of the string after the match. Both methods return an empty string if match goes to the boundary of the original string. So, for a given match data object, match.string = match.pre_match + match[0] + match.post_match.

The method MatchData#begin(value = 0) returns the integer index of the beginning of the match within the original string. If no argument is passed, it uses the entire match at index 0; otherwise, it uses the submatch corresponding to the argument. The method MatchData#end(value = 0) returns the integer index of the end of the match within the original string.

Match data objects define == and eql? as aliases and return true if the two match datas have the same regular expression and string, and therefore presumably the same set of matches.

Regular Expression Extensions

Ruby uses the Onigmo regular expression library, which is an extension of the Oniguruma regular expression engine.[2,3] Onigmo offers a number of extensions beyond traditional Unix regular expressions. Most of these extensions are written between the opening characters (? and the closing character). The parentheses that bracket these extensions are groups, but they don't necessarily generate backreferences—meaning that they don't necessarily set the values of \1, $1, and so on.

The sequence (?#COMMENT) inserts a comment into the pattern. The content is ignored during pattern matching. Commenting complex regular expressions can be as helpful as commenting other complex code.

The notation (?:EXPRESSION) makes the subexpression inside the parenthesis into a group without generating backreferences. This may be useful when you need to group a set of constructs but don't want the group to set the value of $1 or whatever. In the example that follows, both patterns match a date with either colons or slashes between the month, day, and year. The first form stores the separator character (which can be a slash or a colon) in $2 and $4, but the second pattern uses (?: to avoid storing the separator in an external variable:

```
date = "12/25/2022"

date =~ %r{(\d+)(/|:)(\d+)(/|:)(\d+)}
[$1,$2,$3,$4,$5] # => ["12", "/", "25", "/", "2022"]

date =~ %r{(\d+)(?:/|:)(\d+)(?:/|:)(\d+)}
[$1,$2,$3]        # => ["12", "25", "2022"]
```

Using Dynamic Regular Expressions

You'll sometimes want to match a pattern only if the matched substring is preceded or followed by some other pattern. That is, you want to set some context for your match but don't want to capture that context as part of the match.

For example, you might want to match every word in a string that is followed by a comma, but you don't want the comma to form part of the match. Here you could use the charmingly named *zero-width positive lookahead* extension, which is (?=EXPRESSION). This extension matches EXPRESSION at this point but doesn't consume it—you can look forward for the context of a match without affecting the magic match variables like $&. In this example, we'll use String#scan to pick out the words that are followed by a comma:

```
str = "red, white, and blue"
str.scan(/[a-z]+(?=,)/) # => ["red", "white"]
```

You can also match before the pattern using the *zero-width positive lookbehind*, which is (?<=EXPRESSION). This lets you look for characters that precede the context of a match without affecting $&. The following example matches the letters *dog* but only if they are preceded by the letters *hot*:

---

2.   https://github.com/k-takata/Onigmo
3.   https://github.com/kkos/oniguruma

```
show_regexp("seadog hotdog", /(?<=hot)dog/) # => seadog hot->dog<-
```

It's worth noting that while these complex regular expressions are definitely powerful, they can be hard to read, and you can often get similar effects by combining simpler regular expressions with filtering code.

For the lookbehind extension, EXPRESSION either must be a fixed length or consist of a set of fixed-length alternatives. So (?<=aa) and (?<=aa|bbb) are valid, but (?<=a+b) is not.

Both forms have negated versions, (?!EXPRESSION) and (?<!EXPRESSION), which are true if the context isn't present in the target string.

The \K sequence is related to backtracking. If included in a pattern, it doesn't affect the matching process. But, when Ruby comes to store the entire matched string in $&, it only stores the text to the right of the \K:

```
show_regexp("thx1138", /[a-z]+\K\d+/) # => thx->1138<-
```

Controlling Backtracking

Say you're given the problem of searching a string for a sequence of X characters not immediately followed by an O. You know that a string of Xs can be represented as X+, and you can use a lookahead to check that it isn't followed by an O, so you code up the pattern /(X+)(?!O)/. Let's try it.

This matches:

```
re = /(X+)(?!O)/
re.match("test XXXY")[0] # => "XXX"
```

But, unfortunately, so does this, though with a slightly different match:

```
re = /(X+)(?!O)/
re.match("test XXXO")[0] # => "XX"
```

Why did the second match succeed? Well, the regular expression engine saw the X+ in the pattern and happily gobbled up all the Xs in the string. It then saw the pattern (?!O), saying that it shouldn't now be looking at an O. Unfortunately, it's looking at an O, so the match doesn't succeed. But the engine doesn't give up. No sir! Instead it says, "Maybe I was wrong to consume every single X in the string. Let's try consuming one less and see what happens." This is called *backtracking*—when a match fails, the engine goes back and tries to match a different way. In this case, by backtracking past a single character, it now finds itself looking at the last X in the string (the one before the final O). And that X isn't an O, so the negative lookahead succeeds, and the pattern matches. Look at the output of the previous program: there are three _X_s in the first match but only two in the second.

But this wasn't the intent of our regexp. Once it finds a sequence of Xs, those Xs should be considered as a unit. We don't want the sequence to have a split containing all but one of the Xs, with the last of them then being the terminator of the pattern. We can get that behavior by telling Ruby not to backtrack once it finds a string of Xs. There are a couple of ways of doing this.

The sequence (?>EXPRESSION) nests an independent regular expression within the first regular expression. This expression is anchored at the current match position when the expression is encountered. If it consumes characters, these will no longer be available to the higher-level regular expression. This construct, called *atomic grouping* therefore inhibits backtracking.

Let's try it with our previous code, making the set of Xs an atomic grouping.

This one still works:

```
re = /((?>X+))(?!0)/
re.match("test XXXY")[0] # => "XXX"
```

But now this one doesn't:

```
re = /((?>X+))(?!0)/
re.match?("test XXX0") # => false
```

And this finds the second string of Xs:

```
re = /((?>X+))(?!0)/
re.match("test XXX0 XXXXY")[0] # => "XXXX"
```

You can also control backtracking by using a third form of repetition. We've already seen a greedy repetition, such as EXPRESSION+, and a lazy repetition, such as EXPRESSION+?. The third form is called *possessive*. You code it using a plus sign after the repetition character, as in EXPRESSION++. It behaves just like greedy repetition, consuming as much of the string as it can. But once consumed, that part of the string can never be reexamined by the pattern—the regular expression engine can't backtrack past a possessive qualifier. This means we could also write our code as this:

```
re = /(X++)(?!0)/
re.match("test XXXY")[0]       # => "XXX"
re.match?("test XXX0")         # => false
re.match("test XXX0 XXXXY")[0] # => "XXXX"
```

Backreferences and Named Matches

Within a pattern, the sequences \n (where *n* is a number), \k'n', and \k<n> all refer to the nth captured subpattern. These references can be used later in the pattern. Thus, the expression /(...)\1/ matches six characters with the first three characters captured by (...) being the same as the last three referenced by \1.

Rather than refer to matches by their number, you can give them names and then refer to those names. A subpattern is named using either one of these syntaxes: (?<name>...) or (?'name'...). You then refer to these named captures using either \k<name> or \k'name'.

For example, the following shows different ways of matching a time range (in the form hh:mm-hh:mm) where the hour is the same on both sides of the range:

```
tut_regexp/named_backreference_1.rb
same   = "12:15-12:45"
differ = "12:45-13:15"

 # use numbered backreference
same   =~ /(\d\d):\d\d-\1:\d\d/                  # => 0
differ =~ /(\d\d):\d\d-\1:\d\d/                  # => nil

 # use named backreference
same   =~ /(?<hour>\d\d):\d\d-\k<hour>:\d\d/  # => 0
differ =~ /(?<hour>\d\d):\d\d-\k<hour>:\d\d/  # => nil
```

Negative backreference numbers count backward from the place they're used, so they are relative, not absolute, numbers.

The following pattern matches four-letter palindromes (words that read the same forward and backward):

```
tut_regexp/named_backreference_2.rb
"abab" =~ /(.)(.)\k<-1>\k<-2>/  # => nil
"abba" =~ /(.)(.)\k<-1>\k<-2>/  # => 0
```

You can invoke a named subpattern using \g<name> or \g<number>. Note that this reexecutes the match in the subpattern, in contrast to \k<name>, which matches whatever is matched by the subpattern:

```
tut_regexp/named_backreference_3.rb
re = /(?<color>red|green|blue) \w+ \g<color> \w+/
re =~ "red sun blue moon"   # => 0
re =~ "red sun white moon"  # => nil
```

You can use \g recursively, invoking a pattern within itself. The following code matches a string in which braces are properly nested:

```
re = /
  \A
    (?<brace_expression>
      {
(
   [^{}]                      # anything other than braces
 |                            # ...or...
   \g<brace_expression>       # a nested brace expression
 )*
      }
    )
  \Z
/x
```

We use the x option to allow us to write the expression with lots of space, which makes it easier to understand. We also indent it, just as we would indent Ruby code. And we can also use Ruby-style comments to document the tricky stuff. You can read this regular expression as follows: a brace expression consists of an open brace, a sequence of zero or more characters or brace expressions, and then a closing brace.

Nested Groups

The ability to invoke subpatterns recursively means that backreferences can get tricky. Ruby solves this by letting you refer to a named or numbered group at a particular level of the recursion—add a +n or -n for a capture at the given level relative to the current level.

Here's an example from the Oniguruma cheat sheet that matches palindromes:

```
/\A(?<a>.|.|(?:(?<b>.)\g<a>\k<b+0>))\z/
```

That's pretty hard to read, so let's spread it out:

```
tut_regexp/palindrome_re.rb
palindrome_matcher = /
\A
```

```
(?<palindrome>
                    # nothing, or
      | .           # a single character, or
      | (?:         # x <palindrome> x
          (?<some_letter>.)
          \g<palindrome>
          \k<some_letter+0>
        )
    )
  \z
/x
```

```
palindrome_matcher.match "madam"  # => madam
palindrome_matcher.match "m"      # => m
palindrome_matcher.match "adam"   # =>
```

A palindrome is an empty string, a string containing a single character, or a character followed by a palindrome and then that same character. The notation \k<some_letter+0> means that the letter matched at the end of the inner palindrome will be the same letter that was at the start of it. But inside the nesting, a different letter may wrap the interior palindrome.

Conditional Groups

Say you were validating a list of banquet attendees:

```
"Mr Jones and Sally",
"Mr Bond and Ms Moneypenny",
"Samson and Delilah",
"Dr Jekyll and himself",
"Ms Hinky Smith and Ms Jones",
"Dr Wood and Mrs Wood",
"Thelma and Louise"
```

The rule is that if the first person in the list has a title, then so should the second. This means that the first and fourth lines in this list are invalid.

We can start with a pattern to match a line with an optional title and a name. We know we've reached the end of the name when we find the word *and* with spaces around it. Since we're using the x modifier, the regex engine will ignore whitespace to allow us to change the layout of the regex, we need to explicitly identify the spaces that we're matching.

```
re = %r{ (?:(Mrs | Mr | Ms | Dr )\s)? (.*?) \s and \s }x
"Mr Bond and Ms Monneypenny".match(re).captures # => ["Mr", "Bond"]
"Samson and Delilah".match(re).captures         # => [nil, "Samson"]
```

Let's try again. We've defined the regexp with the x (extended) option so we can include whitespace. We also used the ?: modifier on the group that defines the optional title followed by a space. This stops that group getting captured into $1. We do however use a nested group to capture just the title part.

So now we need to match the second name. We can start with the same code as for the first:

```
re = %r{
  (?:(Mrs | Mr | Ms | Dr )\s)? (.*?)
  \s and \s
  (?:(Mrs | Mr | Ms | Dr )\s)? (.+)
```

```
}x
"Mr Bond and Ms Monneypenny".match(re).captures # => ["Mr", "Bond", "Ms",
                                               # .. "Monneypenny"]
"Samson and Delilah".match(re).captures        # => [nil, "Samson", nil,
                                               # .. "Delilah"]
```

Before we go any further, let's clean up the duplication using a named group:

tut_regexp/attendee_validator_1.rb
```
re = %r{
  (?:(?<title>Mrs | Mr | Ms | Dr )\s)? (.*?)
  \s and \s
  (\g<title>\s)? (.+)
}x
match_data = re.match("Mr Bond and Ms Monneypenny")
match_data[0]          # => "Mr Bond and Ms Monneypenny"
match_data[:title]     # => "Ms"

second_match = re.match("Samson and Delilah")
second_match[0]          # => "Samson and Delilah"
second_match[:title]   # => nil
```

But this code also matches a line where the first name has a title and the second doesn't:

tut_regexp/attendee_validator_2.rb
```
re = %r{
  (?:(?<title>Mrs | Mr | Ms | Dr )\s)? (.*?)
  \s and \s
  (\g<title>\s)? (.+)
}x
match_data = re.match("Mr Smith and Sally")
match_data[0]          # => "Mr Smith and Sally"
match_data[:title]   # => "Mr"
```

We need to make the second test for a title mandatory if the first test matches. That's where the conditional subpatterns come in.

The syntax (?(n)subpattern) will apply the subpattern match only if a previous group number *n* also matched. You can also test named groups using either of these syntaxes: (?(<name>)subpattern) or (?('name')subpattern).

In our case, we want to apply a test for the second title if the first title is present. That first title is matched by the group named title, so the condition group looks like (?(<title>)...):

tut_regexp/attendee_validator_3.rb
```
re = %r{
  (?:(?<title>Mrs | Mr | Ms | Dr )\s)? (.*?)
  \s and \s
  (?(<title>)\g<title>\s) (.+)
}x
match_data = re.match("Mr Smith and Sally")
match_data[0]          # => "Mr Smith and Sally"
match_data[:title]   # => nil
```

This didn't work—the match succeeded when we expected it to fail. That's because the regular expression applied *backtracking*. It matched the optional first name, the *and,* and then it was told to match a second title (because group 1 matched the first). There's no second title, so the match failed. But rather than stopping, the engine went back to explore alternatives.

It noticed that the first title was optional, and so it tried matching the whole pattern again, this time skipping the title. It successfully matched *Mr Smith* using the (.*?) group and matched *Sally* with the second name group. So we want to tell it never to backtrack over the first name—once it has found a title there, it has to use it. (?>...) to the rescue:

```ruby
tut_regexp/attendee_validator_4.rb
re = %r{
  ^(?>
      (?:(?<title>Mrs | Mr | Ms | Dr )\s)? (.*?)
      \s and \s
    )
    (?(<title>)\g<title>\s) (.+)
}x
match_data = re.match("Mr Smith and Sally")
match_data                     # => nil

successful_match = re.match("Mr Smith and Ms Sally")
successful_match[0]        # => "Mr Smith and Ms Sally"
successful_match[:title]  # => "Ms"
```

The match failed, as we expected, but when we add a title to Sally, it succeeds. Note that the title named group only gets the last of the two values, for our purposes here, that's not a big deal, but it might cause an issue in other cases.

Let's try this on our list:

```ruby
tut_regexp/validate_attendees.rb
NAMES = [
  "Mr Jones and Sally",
  "Mr Bond and Ms Moneypenny",
  "Samson and Delilah",
  "Dr Jekyll and himself",
  "Ms Hinky Smith and Ms Jones",
  "Dr Wood and Mrs Wood",
  "Thelma and Louise"
]

NAMES.each do |line|
  re = %r{ ^(?>
             (?:(?<title>Mrs | Mr | Ms | Dr )\s)? (.*?) \s and \s
           )
             (?(<title>)\g<title>\s) (.+)
         }x
  if line.match?(re)
    puts("VALID:    #{line}")
  else
    puts("INVALID: #{line}")
  end
end
```

produces:

```
INVALID: Mr Jones and Sally
VALID:    Mr Bond and Ms Moneypenny
VALID:    Samson and Delilah
```

```
INVALID: Dr Jekyll and himself
VALID:   Ms Hinky Smith and Ms Jones
VALID:   Dr Wood and Mrs Wood
VALID:   Thelma and Louise
```

Alternatives in Conditions

As they say in infomercials, "But wait! There's more!" Conditional subpatterns can also have an *else* clause.

```
(?(group_id) true-pattern | fail-pattern )
```

If the identified group was previously matched, the true pattern is applied. If it failed, the fail pattern is applied.

Here's a regular expression that deals with red and blue balls or buckets. The deal is that the colors of the ball and bucket must be different.

```
re = %r{(?:(red)|blue) ball and (?(1)blue|red) bucket}
```

```
re.match?("red ball and blue bucket")  # => true
re.match?("blue ball and red bucket")  # => true
re.match?("blue ball and blue bucket") # => false
```

If the first group (the red alternative) matches, then the conditional subpattern is blue, otherwise it's red.

Named Subroutines

There's a trick that allows us to write subroutines inside regular expressions. Recall that we can invoke a named group using \g<name>, and we define the group using (?<name>...). Normally, the definition of the group is itself matched as part of executing the pattern. But, if you add the suffix {0} to the group, it means "zero matches of this group," so the group isn't executed when first encountered.

In this example, we use that trick to name all our subgroups up front and then use the named versions to build the final match:

```
tut_regexp/named_subroutines.rb
sentence = %r{
  (?<subject>    cat   | dog   | gerbil    ){0}
  (?<verb>       eats  | drinks| generates ){0}
  (?<object>     water | bones | PDFs      ){0}
  (?<adjective>  big   | small | smelly    ){0}
  (?<opt_adj>    (\g<adjective>\s)?         ){0}

  The\s\g<opt_adj>\g<subject>\s\g<verb>\s\g<opt_adj>\g<object>
}x

md = sentence.match("The cat drinks water")
puts "The subject is #{md[:subject]} and the verb is #{md[:verb]}"

md = sentence.match("The big dog eats smelly bones")
puts "The last adjective in the second sentence is #{md[:adjective]}"

sentence =~ "The gerbil generates big PDFs"
puts "And the object in the last sentence is #{$~[:object]}"
```

produces:

```
The subject is cat and the verb is drinks
The last adjective in the second sentence is smelly
And the object in the last sentence is PDFs
```

Setting Options

We saw earlier that you can control the characters matched by \b, \d, \s, and \w (along with their negations). To do that, we embedded a sequence such as (?u) in our pattern. That sequence sets an option inside the regular expression engine.

We also saw at the beginning of this chapter that you can add one or more of the options i (case insensitive), m (multiline), and x (allow spaces) to the end of a regular expression literal. You can also set these options within the pattern itself. They are set using (?i), (?m), and (?x). You can also put a minus sign in front of these three options to disable them.

Here is the full list of available options:

Option	Description
(?adimux)	Turns on the corresponding option. If used inside a group, the effect is limited to that group.
(?-imx)	Turns off the i, m, or x option.
(?adimux:re)	Turns on the option for _re_.
(?-imx:re)	Turns off the option for *re*.

Strings

Strings are probably the most commonly used data type in Ruby, and they have a powerful and wide-ranging API to prove it. Here are some of the most useful and most interesting String methods.

Finding Information about a String

The length of a string is accessible with the method String#length or String#size, which are aliases of each other. The length is in characters and is determined by the current encoding. You can get the length in bytes with the method String#bytesize. The method String#empty? returns true if the length of the string is zero.

If you want to know how many times a given character is used in a string, you can use String#count(*selectors). This works, as you probably expect, if you pass in a single character, but it gets a little confusing if you pass in a longer string or multiple strings, as you can see in the following example:

```
"Banana bread".count("b")        # => 1
"Banana bread".count("ba")       # => 5
"Banana bread".count("bad", "a") # => 4
```

The argument to count is called a *character selector*. A multi-character string selector matches for any of the characters included. For example, ba as an argument finds the counts for all characters that are b or a. A character selector can use a hyphen to suggest a range of characters, and a caret to invert the selection:

```
"Banana bread".count("a-d") # => 6
"Banana bread".count("^ba") # => 7
```

The count method can take more than one of these selectors as arguments, in which case a character needs to be a part of *all* the selectors in order to be counted. In our "Banana bread".count("bad", "a") example, bad and a only overlap with a, so we get the count of a.

Testing the Content of Strings

The most generic way to determine if a string contains a particular content is with the String#index(substring_or_regex, offset = 0) method. The index method takes an argument that's either a string or a regular expression. It returns the index of the first position in the receiver that matches the argument or returns nil if no match exists:

```
"The pickaxe book".index("ck") # => 6
"The pickaxe book".index(/\s/) # => 3
"The pickaxe book".index("z")  # => nil
```

An optional second argument is an index. If the index is a positive integer, it returns the first match after that index. If the index is a negative integer, index still returns the first match after the index, but it counts the index from the end of the string:

```
"The pickaxe book".index("e")      # => 2
"The pickaxe book".index("e", 4)  # => 10
"The pickaxe book".index("e", -7) # => 10
```

In the last line, the search starts at index -7, which is seven characters from the end of the string, but then it moves to the end of the string and returns the index of the second e.

If you want the index of the last element of the string that matches, use the method String#rindex(substring_or_regex, offset = self.length). The first argument to rindex behaves exactly the same except the return value is based on the last match. In the case of a regular expression, last match means "starts as late in the string as possible" not "ends as late in the string as possible."

```
"The pickaxe book".index("e")    # => 2
"The pickaxe book".rindex("e")   # => 10
"The pickaxe book".rindex(/o.*/) # => 14
```

The index arguments for rindex behave a little differently. They delimit the ending point for the search, which is to say they indicate the maximum index the result can have before returning nil. A positive argument indicates the maximum index directly, while a negative argument implies the maximum index based on adding the negative offset to the length of the string:

```
"The pickaxe book".rindex("e")     # => 10
"The pickaxe book".rindex("e", 2)  # => 2
"The pickaxe book".rindex("e", 4)  # => 2
"The pickaxe book".rindex("e", 8)  # => 2
"The pickaxe book".rindex("e", -7) # => 2
```

If all you want is a boolean yes/no about the substring, you can use String#include?(substring), which only takes a string argument and returns true if the argument is in the string and false otherwise. For regular expressions, you use String#match?(regex) for the same behavior:

```
"The pickaxe book".include?("e") # => true
"The pickaxe book".include?("z") # => false
"The pickaxe book".match?(/o{2}/) # => true
```

If you specifically want to test one end or another of a string, use String#start_with?(*string_or_regex) or String#end_with?(*string). Somewhat weirdly, these methods take different sets of arguments. The start_with? method takes one or more strings or regular expressions and returns true if the start end of the string matches any of the arguments. The end_with? is the same but doesn't take regular expression arguments:

```
"The pickaxe book".start_with?("e")       # => false
"The pickaxe book".start_with?("T")       # => true
"The pickaxe book".start_with?(/[A-Z]/)  # => true
"The pickaxe book".end_with?("k")         # => true
"The pickaxe book".end_with?("k", "q")   # => true
```

Retrieving Substrings

In Ruby's library, a substring of a string is sometimes called a *slice*. The most common way to retrieve a slice from a string is to use square brackets. Five kinds of arguments may be used inside the square brackets:

- A single integer index, as in "abcdefg"[3] or "abcdefg"[-3]. An index of zero will return the first character of the string, and a positive number will return the string at that index from the left, so "abcdefg"[3] is d. A negative number will return the index from the right, with -1 being the last character of the string, so "abcdefg"[-3] is e.

- A range, as in "abcdefg"[1..3]. This returns the substring that starts at the index of the beginning of the range and ends at the index of the end of the range. If both parts of the range are positive, that's the same as the indexes that correspond to the numbers in the range. But negative numbers correspond to indexes from the end of the string, so "abcdefg"[4..-1] returns "efg", since e is the character at index 4, and g is the character at index -1, the last character. Halfway ranges also work, so "abcdefg"[..-2] returns all but the last character, and "abcdefg"[3..] returns everything from index 3 on. If both ends of the range are outside the string, the result is an empty string. If the ends of the range are in the wrong order relative to the string (like 4..2), you also get an empty string.

- Two arguments representing an index and a length, as in "abcdefg"[1, 3]. This gives you the substring starting at the given index, for the given length, in this case bcd. There are a few special cases. If the length goes off the end of the string, you just get the characters up to the end of the string—you don't get a bunch of whitespace padding or anything like that. If the length is zero or the index exactly matches the end of the string, you get an empty string. If the length is negative or if the index is greater than the length of the string, you get nil.

- The argument could be a regular expression, as in "abcdefg"[/d.*/]. In this case, you get the first match, so the bracket syntax is equivalent to "abcedfg".match(/d.*/), but the brackets are way more confusing here. If there's no match, the return value is nil. A second argument is optional and it makes the expression return the capture group associated with the argument, as though you had returned a match object and looked up that value. If the second argument is a number that doesn't have a corresponding capture group, you get nil; if it's a name that doesn't have a corresponding named capture group, you get an IndexError.

- The argument can be a string as in "abcdefg"["def"]. In this case, you get the string in the brackets if that substring exists in the receiving string, or you get nil, which is the equivalent of "abcdefg.include?("def") ? "def" : nil.

If you don't like the bracket syntax, the method is aliased as String#slice() and takes the same arguments, such as slice(1..3) or whatever. There's a destructive version—String#slice!(args)—that returns the substring and modifies the original string by removing that substring:

```
sample = "abcdefg"
sample.slice!(1..3) # => "bcd"
sample              # => "aefg"
```

Other Substring Retrieval Methods

Some additional patterns of extracting substrings are common enough to have dedicated methods. The method String#strip returns a new version of the string with leading and trailing whitespace removed. The variant String#lstrip removes leading whitespace only, and the variant String#rstrip removes trailing whitespace only. All three methods have ! variants that modify the string in place like this: String#strip!, String#lstrip!, and String#rstrip!. The return values of all three modifying methods are the newly modified string if the string changed or nil if the string isn't changed. That's a common Ruby pattern for methods that mutate the original. But, if you're using the ! variants, you normally aren't using the return value; you're just using the receiving object later in the code.

For the purposes of the strip family of methods, Ruby defines whitespace as:

- A space character, Unicode \x20 or " "
- A tab character, escaped as \t or Unicode \x09
- A newline, or line feed, \n, or Unicode \x0a
- A carriage return, \r or Unicode \x0d
- A form feed, \f or Unicode \x0c
- A vertical tab, \v or Unicode \x0b
- Unicode null, x00 or \u0000

Removing the Last Character from a String

When doing text processing, especially from files or command-line input, a common task is to remove the last character of a string if it's the end of a line marker. Ruby adapted a couple of versions of this feature from Perl.

The method String#chop always removes the last character of a string, but if the last two characters of the string are \r\n (the Windows end-of-line marker), chop removes both of them.

The similarly named but more useful in practice method called String#chomp(line_separator = $/) removes the last character if it is a line separator. By default, that means \r, \n, or \r\n, but the documentation makes a point of mentioning, not \n\r.

You can pass an argument to chomp. If that argument is an empty string, chomp will remove a series of \n or \r\n characters at the end of the string. If the string includes any other character, chomp will remove that character if it's the last character of the string.

All these versions with arguments seem likely to be confusing. If you need this functionality, we recommend using chomp without arguments and perhaps writing a more explicit version of anything more complex that you need. Both chop and chomp have modifier versions, String#chop! and String#chomp!. As with other versions we've seen, they return the string if the string changed and return nil otherwise.

Iterating within Strings

If you want to iterate over different parts of the string, you have a few options that allow you to split a string up or to perform the iteration without actually splitting the string.

The method String#chars splits the string up into an array of characters. Ruby doesn't actually have a character class, so chars splits the string up into an array of one-length strings. The method String#each_char [{ |c| block }] takes a block and calls it with each character in succession. As with other enumeration methods, if called without a block, the method returns a Ruby enumerator that can be invoked later or chained to other enumerators.

Similar methods break the string down a little differently. The method String#bytes returns an array of the numerical bytes that make up each character, where some characters might be more than one byte long. The String#codepoints method returns the codepoint for each character in the current encoding. That array produces one entry for each character. The iterators String#each_byte [{ |byte| block }] and String#each_codepoint [{ |codepoint| block }] take blocks or return enumerators and allow you to enumerate over the bytes or code points. And the method String#each_grapheme_cluster [{ |cluster| block}] allows you to loop over Unicode grapheme clusters.

The method String#lines(line_separator = $/, chomp: false) splits the string into an array of strings based on line separators. By default, the separator is $/, the global line separator, but you can pass your own line separator as any character you want. If the argument is an empty string, lines(''), then the method acts as a paragraph splitter and splits when there are two or more line separators in a row. An optional second argument, chomp: true, removes the last instance of the line separator from each element in the array. The related method String#each_line(line_separator = $/, chomp: false) [{ |substring| block }] takes the same argument and returns an enumerator, or takes a block argument and invokes the block once for each separated line.

The String#scan(string_or_regex) method takes a string or a regular expression argument and returns an array of all the times the string matches the regular expression. If the regular expression doesn't have groups, it's an array of the entire matched string. If the regular expression does have groups, it's an array of arrays containing the matches:

```ruby
"The pickaxe book".scan(/w+/)        # => []
"The pickaxe book".scan(/\s.{1}/)    # => [" p", " b"]
"The pickaxe book".scan(/(\s)(.{1})/) # => [[" ", "p"], [" ", "b"]]
```

Most generically, the String#split(separator = $; limit = nil) [{ |substring| block }] method allows you to split a string on an arbitrary value. When called with no arguments, it splits based on spaces. But you can call it with any string or regular expression argument. If the last substrings are empty, they aren't part of the output:

```ruby
"The pickaxe book".split        # => ["The", "pickaxe", "book"]
"The pickaxe book".split("e")   # => ["Th", " pickax", " book"]
"The pickaxe book".split(/\b/)  # => ["The", " ", "pickaxe", " ", "book"]
"The pickaxe book".split("k")   # => ["The pic", "axe boo"]
```

An optional second argument is a limit. If the limit is greater than zero, the number of elements in the resulting array is limited to that number and the rest of the string comes together at the end. If the limit is negative, it has no effect, except that trailing empty substrings are part of the return value:

```ruby
"The pickaxe book".split("e", 2)  # => ["Th", " pickaxe book"]
"The pickaxe book".split("k", -1) # => ["The pic", "axe boo", ""]
```

The split method can take an optional block, in which case the block is called once with each substring as an argument and the return values of the block calls are returned.

A special case of splitting is where you want to split the string exactly once. The String#partition(string_or_regex) method takes a string or regular expression as an argument and returns an array with three elements: the part of the string before the match, the match, and the remainder of the string. If the argument doesn't appear in the string, then the result is [string, "", ""]. The method String#rpartition(string_or_regex) does the same thing, but it finds the last match in the string, rather than the first:

```ruby
"The pickaxe book".partition("e")  # => ["Th", "e", " pickaxe book"]
"The pickaxe book".rpartition("e") # => ["The pickax", "e", " book"]
```

Replacing Text in Strings

Ruby strings are mutable, meaning that the value of the string can change over time.

Partial String Assignment

The most general way to replace an arbitrary part of the string is by using square bracket syntax, []=. If a string is being accessed with square brackets on the left side of an assignment statement, the right side of the statement replaces the referenced part of the string, even if the new part of the string is a different length than the substring. The return value of the assignment is the right side of the assignment, but the string itself changes:

```ruby
x = "the pickaxe book"
x[12..] = "podcast"
x           # => "the pickaxe podcast"
```

This assignment works no matter which form you use inside the square brackets.

String Insertion

Several other methods change the text in strings, either in place or by returning a new string. The String#insert(index, other_string) method takes an index and another string and inserts the new string at that index. This both returns the original string and mutates it:

```ruby
x = "the pickaxe book"
x.insert(4, "new ") # => "the new pickaxe book"
x                   # => "the new pickaxe book"
```

String Deletion

If you just want to delete a known string from within a larger string, use the String#delete(*selectors) method. The base method takes one or more character selectors, as shown in Finding Information about a String, on page 523, and returns a copy of the string with matching characters removed. The method String#delete!(*selectors) does the same thing, but mutates the receiving string and returns the mutated string. Like other mutation string methods, it returns nil if the string is unchanged:

```ruby
"The pickaxe book".delete("k")   # => "The picaxe boo"
```

You're also able to delete the prefixes and suffixes in strings with String#delete_prefix(prefix) and String#delete_suffix(suffix). These methods take actual substrings (not selectors) and remove them from the requested end of the string if that end of the string matches. They return a copy of the string with the change:

```
"The pickaxe book".delete_prefix("The")      # => " pickaxe book"
"The pickaxe book".delete_prefix("Banana")   # => "The pickaxe book"
"The pickaxe book".delete_suffix("book")     # => "The pickaxe "
"The pickaxe book".delete_suffix("podcast")  # => "The pickaxe book"
```

Mutator versions of these methods, String#delete_suffix!(suffix) and String#delete_prefix!(prefix) return either the mutated original string or nil.

String Replacement

It's quite common to want to change a string by changing a specific character or pattern to a different character or pattern. Ruby has a couple of different methods for this.

One family of methods consists of String#sub(pattern, replacement), String#sub!(pattern, replacement), String#gsub(pattern, replacement), and String#gsub!(pattern, replacement). The gsub method is the most general and takes two arguments: a pattern and a replacement. The pattern is a String or a regular expression; the replacement is a String, a Hash, or a block, in which case the method signature looks like String#sub(pattern) { |substring| block } for all four methods.

The gsub method returns a copy of the receiving string with *all* occurrences of pattern replaced using the replacement value.

The pattern will typically be a Regexp. If it's a String, then no regular expression metacharacters will be interpreted (that is, /\d/ will match a digit, but "\d" will match a backslash followed by a d).

How the replacement value is created depends on the other arguments. If the replacement is a string, the string is put in place of the pattern:

```
"The pickaxe book".gsub("e", "!")       # => "Th! pickax! book"
"The pickaxe book".gsub(/[aeiou]/, "y") # => "Thy pyckyxy byyk"
```

If a string is used as the replacement, special variables from the match (such as $& and $1) cannot be substituted into it because substitution into the string occurs before the pattern match starts. But the sequences \1, \2, and so on, may be used to interpolate successive numbered groups in the match, and \k<_name_> will substitute the corresponding named captures. There are a couple of other regular expression bits that can be included in the replacement string (see the full Ruby documentation for details).

If the replacement is a block, the block is called with the matched part of the string and the value of the block is the replacement:

```
"The pickaxe book".gsub(/[aeiou]/) { |str| str.upcase }   # => "ThE pIckAxE bOOk"
```

If the replacement is a Hash, the keys should be strings, and each matched text is either replaced by the value associated with that key in the hash or is removed if no matching key. Note that the keys have to be strings, so we need hash rocket syntax here.

```
"The pickaxe book".gsub(/[aeiou]/, {"a" => "b", "e" => "f"})   # => "Thf pckbxf
                                                              # .. bk"
```

The gsub! method has the same behavior as gsub except that it mutates its receiver.

The sub method is like gsub except that it only replaces the first match in the string—the "g" in gsub is for "global." The sub! method is like sub except that it mutates its receiver.

When you want to replace a specific character with a specific other character, Ruby provides the String#tr(selector, replacements) method, which should be faster than gsub for the cases in which it applies. The tr method is probably most commonly used with two one-character strings as arguments, and it converts all instances of the first string into the second.

But the method is actually more powerful. The first argument can be any character selector (as in Finding Information about a String, on page 523) and the second argument is a string of replacements. It returns a copy of the receiving string with the characters in the first argument replaced by the corresponding characters in the second argument. If the second argument is shorter than the first argument, it is padded with its last character. Both strings may use the entire character selector syntax. Here are some examples:

```
"hello".tr("l", "$")      # => "he$$o"
"hello".tr("aeiou", "*")  # => "h*ll*"
"hello".tr("^aeiou", "*") # => "*e**o"
"hello".tr("el", "ip")    # => "hippo"
"hello".tr("a-y", "b-z")  # => "ifmmp"
```

The related String#tr!(selector, replacements) method has the same behavior but changes the receiving string in place.

The String#squeeze(*selectors) method takes a list of character selectors (as in Finding Information about a String, on page 523) and replaces any case where more than one of the characters happens in a row with a single instance. It's most commonly used as squeeze(" ") to clean up extra spaces. The String#squeeze!(*selectors) method changes the receiver in place.

Formatting Strings

A trio of methods pad a string inside a larger string: String#ljust(size, padding_string = " "), which left justifies the string; String#rjust(size, padding_string = " "), which right justifies it; and String#center(size, padding_string = " "), which places the receiving string inside a larger string. All three take two arguments: the size of the larger string and an optional string to pad the space. A space character is the default.

```
"book".center(15)      # => "     book      "
"book".ljust(15)       # => "book           "
"book".rjust(15)       # => "           book"
"book".center(15, "0") # => "00000book000000"
```

If you want to change the case of a string, Ruby provides these methods:

- String#upcase(*options), which makes all the characters uppercase.
- String#downcase(*options), which makes them all lowercase.
- String#capitalize(*options), which capitalizes the first letter of every word.
- String#swapcase(*options), which swaps the case of every character in the string.

By default, these methods all use Unicode case mapping, but all three take optional arguments for :ascii (which limits case behavior to only ASCII a-z characters) or :turkic (which adapts to the unique case mapping of Turkic languages). downcase, and downcase alone, takes :fold (which uses Unix case folding instead of case mapping).

Using Strings and Binary Operators

Strings do respond to some other binary operators. A string plus a string is a new string concatenating the two strings. Ruby will also concatenate strings with String#<<. Ruby will even concatenate strings if you put two strings next to each other with no operator between them:

```
"ab" + "cd"  # => "abcd"
"ab" << "cd" # => "abcd"
"ab" "cd"    # => "abcd"
```

The inverse of concatenation is prepending. If for some reason you need to use prepending, Ruby provides String#prepend(other), as in "ab".prepend("cd").

A string can be multiplied by a non-negative integer to produce a new string that repeats the original string that many times:

```
"ab" * 10 # => "abababababababababab"
```

Strings respond to the String#<=> and use Comparable, so all your comparison operators work. The <=> comparison is case-sensitive. A case-insensitive version is String#casecmp(other). The expression a.casecmp(b) is equivalent to a.downcase <=> b.downcase. The method casecmp? returns true if the downcased versions of each string are equal. Strings also define String#=== as an alias for ==.

We've seen String#=~ for regular expression match and String#!~ for non-regular expression match.

Finally, you can reverse a string with String#reverse, which returns a new string, or with String#reverse!, which changes the receiving string in place.

Strings also define unary + and unary -. Unary + as in +"foo" returns the string itself if the string isn't frozen, or it returns an unfrozen duplicate of the string if the string is frozen. Unary -, as in -"foo" does the inverse. If the string is frozen, it returns the string itself; if not, it returns a frozen duplicate of the string. In the - case, the string will also be "deduped" (also known as "interned"), meaning that if the string is created multiple times, all instances will point to the same memory location, potentially saving memory. Unary - is also aliased as String#dedup.

Unpacking Data

The method String#unpack(template, offset: 0) is the inverse of Array#pack (see Packing Data, on page 567). The method takes a template string and decodes the string (which may contain binary data) according to the format string, and it returns an array of the extracted values. The directives are the same for the template and can be found in Table 26, Template characters for packed data, on page 568.

```
"abc \0\0abc \0\0".unpack('A6Z6')     # => ["abc", "abc "]
"abc \0\0".unpack('a3a3')             # => ["abc", " \x00\x00"]
"aa".unpack('b8B8')                   # => ["10000110", "01100001"]
"aaa".unpack('h2H2c')                 # => ["16", "61", 97]
"\xfe\xff\xfe\xff".unpack('sS')       # => [-2, 65534]
"now=20is".unpack('M*')               # => ["now is"]
"whole".unpack('xax2aX2aX1aX2a')      # => ["h", "e", "l", "l", "o"]
```

Encoding

The encoding determines how Ruby converts the bytes making up a string into individual characters. We can verify that Ruby correctly interprets π as a single character:

```
# encoding: utf-8
pi = "π"
puts "The size of a string containing π is #{pi.size}"
```

produces:

```
The size of a string containing π is 1
```

Now, let's get perverse. The two-byte sequence \xcf\x80 represents π in UTF-8, but it's not a valid byte sequence in SJIS encoding. Let's see what happens if we tell Ruby that this same source file is SJIS encoded. (Remember, when we do this, we're not changing the actual bytes in the string—we're just telling Ruby to interpret them with a different set of encoding rules.)

```
# encoding: sjis
PI = "π"
puts "The size of a string containing π is #{PI.size}"
```

produces:

```
prog.rb:
prog.rb:2: invalid multibyte char (Windows-31J) (SyntaxError)
prog.rb:3: invalid multibyte char (Windows-31J)
```

This time, Ruby complains because the file contains byte sequences that are illegal in the given encoding.

Ruby supports an encoding called ASCII-8BIT. Despite the *ASCII* in the name, this is intended to be used on data streams that contain binary data. It's the default encoding that Ruby uses for reading binary streams. (It also has an alias of BINARY}.) But you can also use this as an encoding for source files. If you do, Ruby interprets all characters with codes below 128 as regular ASCII and all other characters as valid constituents of variable names. This is a neat hack because it allows you to compile a file written in an encoding you don't know—the characters with the high-order bit set will be assumed to be printable.

```
# encoding: ascii-8bit
π = 3.14159
puts "π = #{π}"
puts "Size of 'π' = #{'π'.size}"
```

produces:

```
π = 3.14159
Size of 'π' = 2
```

The last line of output illustrates why ASCII-8BIT is a dangerous encoding for source files. Because it doesn't know to use UTF-8 encoding, the π character looks to Ruby like two separate characters.

Converting Encodings

Strings, symbols, and regular expressions are labeled with their encoding. You can convert a string from one encoding to another using the encode method. For example, we can convert the word *olé* from UTF-8 to ISO-8859-1:

```
ole_in_utf = "olé"
ole_in_utf.encoding      # => #<Encoding:UTF-8>
ole_in_utf.bytes.to_a    # => [111, 108, 195, 169]

ole_in_8859 = ole_in_utf.encode("iso-8859-1")
ole_in_8859.encoding     # => #<Encoding:ISO-8859-1>
ole_in_8859.bytes.to_a   # => [111, 108, 233]
```

You have to be careful when using encode—if the target encoding doesn't contain characters that appear in your source string, Ruby will throw an exception. For example, the π character is available in UTF-8 but not in ISO-8859-1:

```
pi = "pi = π"
pi.encode("iso-8859-1")
```

produces:

```
        from prog.rb:2:in `<main>'
prog.rb:2:in `encode': U+03C0 from UTF-8 to ISO-8859-1
(Encoding::UndefinedConversionError)
```

You can override the exceptional behavior, for example supplying a placeholder character to use when no direct translation is possible.

```
pi = "pi = π"
puts pi.encode("iso-8859-1", undef: :replace, replace: "??")
```

produces:

```
pi = ??
```

The String#encode(destination_encoding, source_encoding = nil, **encoding_options) method takes a set of keyword options to specify encoding behavior (see the following table). These options are also available when opening a file or I/O stream.

Option	Meaning
cr_newline: true	If true, converts lf to cr. Only one of cr_newline, crlf_newline, and universal_newline can be true.
crlf_newline: true	If true, converts lf to crlf. Only one of cr_newline, crlf_newline, and universal_newline can be true.
fallback: nil | *hash* | *method* | proc	A fallback value if the replacement value is not set. This allows a dynamic value to be set based on the missing value. If the missing value is foo then the replacement value is hash[foo] or method(foo) or proc.call(foo).
invalid: nil | :replace	Replaces invalid characters in the source string with the replacement string. If :invalid is not specified or is set to nil, raises an exception. The default value is nil.
undef: nil | :replace	Replaces characters that are not available in the destination encoding with the replacement string. If :undef is not specified or nil, raises an exception. The default value is nil.
replace: nil | *string*	Specifies the string to use if :invalid or :undef options are present. If not specified or set to nil, uFFFD is used for Unicode encodings and ? for others. The default value is nil.

Option	Meaning
universal_newline: true	If true, converts crlf and cr line endings to lf. Only one of cr_newline, crlf_newline, and universal_newline can be true.
xml: nil | :text | :attr	If the value is nil, which is the default, then no special processing takes place. Otherwise, after encoding, escape any characters that would have special meaning in XML PCDATA or attributes. In both cases, converts & to &, < to <, > to >, and undefined characters to a hexadecimal entity (&#xhh;). For :attr, it also converts " to " and puts double-quotes around the entire string.

Table 22—Options to encode and encode!

Sometimes you'll have a string containing binary data and you want that data to be interpreted as if it had a particular encoding. You can't use the encode method for this because you don't want to change the byte contents of the string—you're just changing the encoding associated with those bytes. Use the String#force_encoding(encoding) method to do this:

```
# encoding: ascii-8bit
str = "\xc3\xa9"      # e-acute in UTF-8
str.encoding    # => #<Encoding:ASCII-8BIT>
str.force_encoding("utf-8")
str.bytes.to_a # => [195, 169]
str.encoding    # => #<Encoding:UTF-8>
```

Finally, you can use encode (with two parameters) to convert between two encodings if your source string is ASCII-8BIT. This might happen if, for example, you're reading data in binary mode from a file and choose not to encode it at the time you read it. Here we fake that by creating an ASCII-8BIT string that contains an ISO-8859-1 sequence (our old friend *olé*). We then convert the string to UTF-8. To do this, we have to tell encode the actual encoding of the bytes by passing it a second parameter:

```
# encoding: ascii-8bit
original = "ol\xe9"      # e-acute in ISO-8859-1
original.bytes.to_a # => [111, 108, 233]
original.encoding    # => #<Encoding:ASCII-8BIT>
new = original.encode("utf-8", "iso-8859-1")
new.bytes.to_a      # => [111, 108, 195, 169]
new.encoding        # => #<Encoding:UTF-8>
```

Symbols

Symbols don't have a lot of methods in Ruby. We've seen Symbol#to_proc as a shortcut for creating a block. The to_proc method creates a block that is effectively equivalent to { |receiver, ...| receiver.send(symbol, ...)}. You usually see it used implicitly with &, but it can be used explicitly, too:

```
proc = :split.to_proc
proc.call("The pickaxe book")        # => ["The", "pickaxe", "book"]
proc.call("The pickaxe book", "e")   # => ["Th", " pickax", " book"]
```

You can also use Symbol#to_s to convert a symbol to a string; the Symbol#name and Symbol#inspect methods perform basically the same conversion.

Symbols respond to the following string-like methods, which are effectively shortcuts for calling to_s so that you don't have to explicitly convert them to a string and then back to a symbol.

- Symbol#<=>, and all Comparable methods
- Symbol#[]
- Symbol#=== and Symbol#==
- Symbol#=~
- Symbol#casecmp and Symbol#casecmp?
- Symbol#empty?
- Symbol#encoding
- Symbol#end_with?
- Symbol#length and Symbol#size
- Symbol#match and Symbol#match?
- Symbol#start_with?

The following string-like methods are shortcuts for converting to a string and then back to a symbol, as in :foo.to_s.METHOD.to_sym.

- Symbol#capitalize
- Symbol#downcase
- Symbol#swapcase
- Symbol#upcase

Ruby also gives you Symbol::all_symbols, which returns an array of all Symbols Ruby knows about at the time of the call.

## CHAPTER 27

Library Reference: Ruby's Object Model

In this chapter, we'll take a closer look at the classes that make up Ruby's object model. The goal is to give you more information about what you can do with these classes and also to discuss related functions together so that you can browse and perhaps find a new feature that might help.

This isn't intended to be a complete listing of every class, method, or option. For that, please refer to the official Ruby documentation at https://docs.ruby-lang.org.

In this chapter, when a method is mentioned for the first time, we provide its complete name and signature. The notation Foo.bar indicates a class or module method, while Foo#bar indicates an instance method. Optional arguments are indicated with Ruby syntax and their default value, as in Foo#bar(name, size = 0). Dynamically sized arguments are indicated with splat syntax, as in Foo#bar(*files, **options). Block arguments are indicated with brace syntax and an indication of what the arguments to the block will be, as in Foo#bar { |object| block }. An optional block argument will be surrounded by square brackets, Foo#bar [{block}]. Please note that this description syntax is slightly different than the official documentation, and that in some cases, what the official documentation shows as multiple method signatures, we've chosen to show as one signature with default values. Also, parameter names sometimes differ from the official documentation to make the naming clearer.

BasicObject

For most purposes in Ruby, you can consider the Object class to be the root of Ruby's class hierarchy, and the Kernel module to be mixed into all objects. But in some specialized classes, you might want a Ruby object that doesn't have the basic functionality contained in Object and Kernel. For example, you might want a very minimal data object, or you might want to experiment with your own metaprogramming tools or object semantics.

For those cases, you want the class BasicObject which is the *real* root of Ruby's class hierarchy. BasicObject deliberately has just a few methods, allowing it to be conveniently used as the basis for a number of metaprogramming techniques.

If you write code in a direct descendent of BasicObject, you won't have unqualified access to the methods in Kernel, which normally get mixed into Object. This example illustrates how to invoke Kernel methods explicitly as module-level methods:

```
ref_meta_ruby/basic_object.rb
class SimpleBuilder < BasicObject
  def initialize
    @indent = 0
  end

  def __indented_puts__(string)
    ::Kernel.puts "#{" " * @indent} #{string}"
  end

  def respond_to_missing?
    true
  end

  def method_missing(name, *args)
    __indented_puts__("<#{name}>")
    @indent += 2
    __indented_puts__(args.join) unless args.empty?
    yield if ::Kernel.block_given?
    @indent -= 2
    __indented_puts__("</#{name}>")
  end
end

r = SimpleBuilder.new
r.person do
  r.name("Dave")
  r.address do
    r.street("123 Main")
    r.city("Pleasantville")
  end
end
```

produces:

```
<person>
  <name>
    Dave
  </name>
  <address>
    <street>
      123 Main
    </street>
    <city>
      Pleasantville
    </city>
  </address>
</person>
```

Because this class uses BasicObject, the method_missing method can respond to all the methods that would be defined in Object, allowing them to be used as data in this case.

Here is a complete list of the methods defined by BasicObject, suitable for placing on a notecard:

- BasicObject::new returns a new BasicObject. Note that if you type BasicObject.new into irb, you'll get a message that the BasicObject doesn't support inspect.

- BasicObject#! is boolean negation, returns false unless obj is false. Because it's in BasicObject, ! is defined for all objects in Ruby.

- BasicObject#!=(other) is the inverse of equality.

- BasicObject#==(other) is equality. At the BasicObject level, == returns true only if obj and other_obj are the same object. Typically, this method is overridden in descendent classes to provide class-specific meaning.

- BasicObject#_id_ returns an integer ID specific to each individual object.

- BasicObject#_send_(method_name[, args]) sends the instance the method name and args as a message.

- BasicObject#equal?(other) for BasicObject is equivalent to ==.

- BasicObject#instance_eval {block} executes block with self set to the object receiving instance_eval. It has a rarer form where the argument is a string of Ruby code instead of a block.

- BasicObject#instance_exec(args) {block} is similar to instance_eval except that the arguments to the method are passed through as arguments to the block.

- BasicObject#method_missing(method_name[, args]) is called when a method isn't found. It allows for additional processing based on the method name.

- BasicObject#singleton_method_added(method_name),   BasicObject#singleton_method_removed(method_name), and BasicObject#singleton_method_undefined(method_name) are all callback methods invoked when methods are added, removed, or undefined in the receiver's singleton object.

Some of these methods reflect very commonly used functionality.

The method BasicObject#instance_eval(string, filename = nil, line_number = nil) or BasicObject#instance_eval { |object| block } evaluates either a string containing Ruby source code, or the given block, within the context of the receiver. To set the context, the variable self is set to the receiver object while the code is executing, giving the code access to the receiver object's instance variables. In the version of instance_eval that takes a String, the optional second and third parameters supply a filename and a starting line number that are used when reporting compilation errors:

```
ref_meta_ruby/instance_eval.rb
class Klass
  def initialize
    @secret = 99
  end
end
k = Klass.new
k.instance_eval { @secret }   # => 99
```

The BasicObject#instance_exec(...) method has the same feature of evaluating the block in the receiver's context, but it takes arbitrary arguments and passes them to the block.

BasicObject#method_missing(name, *args) is invoked by Ruby when obj is sent a message it cannot handle. The name is the symbol for the unhandled method that was called, and args are any arguments that were passed to it. method_missing can be used to implement proxies, delegators, and forwarders. It can also be used to simulate the existence of methods in the receiver, as the example at the beginning of this section shows. When invoked by a class that is a subclass of Object, the method respond_to_missing? should also be defined (see Object, on page 557).

Class

Classes in Ruby are first-class objects—each is an instance of class Class. Since Class is a subclass of Module, most of the behavior of Class is actually defined in the class Module (see Module, on page 552). The Class class itself adds a small number of new methods.

You can create an anonymous class with Class.new and assign it to a variable and use it like a regularly defined class. If you assign it to a variable whose name starts with a capital letter, it's treated as a constant and behaves exactly like a regularly defined class.

When a new class is defined (typically using class SomeName ... end), an object of type Class is created and assigned to a constant (SomeName, in this case). When SomeName.new is called to create a new object, the new instance method in Class is run by default, which in turn invokes Class.allocate to allocate memory for the object before finally calling the new object's initialize method.

The class Class has a private instance method called Class#inherited(subclass) that you can override in your own classes. If defined, the method is automatically invoked by Ruby when a subclass of the class is created. The new subclass is passed as a parameter. Here's an example:

```ruby
class Top
  def self.inherited(sub)
    puts "New subclass: #{sub}"
  end
end

class Middle < Top
end

class Bottom < Middle
end
```

produces:

```
New subclass: Middle
New subclass: Bottom
```

The class Class also defines a method called Class#subclasses, which returns a list of the known subclass objects in an arbitrary order, and a method called Class#superclass, which returns the superclass of the given Class or, if you happen to try this with BasicObject.superclass, it returns nil.

Comparable

If you want to be able to compare two objects of the same class in general, all you need to do is implement the <=> operator and include the Comparable module:

```ruby
built_in_data/team.rb
class Team
  include Comparable
  attr_accessor :wins, :losses, :name

  def initialize(name, wins, losses)
    @name = name
    @wins = wins
    @losses = losses
  end
```

```
  def percentage = (wins * 1.0) / (wins + losses)

  def <=>(other)
    raise ArgumentError unless other.is_a?(Team)
    percentage <=> other.percentage
  end

  def to_s = name
end
brewers = Team.new("Brewers", 73, 89)
cardinals = Team.new("Cardinals", 86, 76)
cubs = Team.new("Cubs", 103, 58)
pirates = Team.new("Pirates", 78, 83)
reds = Team.new("Reds", 68, 94)

puts cubs > cardinals
puts "\n"
puts cardinals.between?(cubs, reds)
puts "\n"
puts [brewers, cardinals, cubs, pirates, reds].sort
```

produces:

```
true

false

Reds
Brewers
Pirates
Cardinals
Cubs
```

In this case, we're using the <=> operator to order teams based on their winning percentage, so using sort on an array of teams gives you the standings, lowest to highest.

The comparable module defines <, <=, >, >=, and == as methods that can be used as operators. It also defines Comprable#between?(low, high) as a boolean and a method called Comparable#clamp(low, high) or Comparable#clamp(range). The call obj.clamp(low, high) takes two values or a range and returns the object if it's between the low and high values, but returns the border value if the clamp isn't between the two values. The range version does the same thing for the endpoints of the range, but also allows for infinite ranges.

```
7.clamp(5..10)  # => 7
3.clamp(5..10)  # => 5
3.clamp(5..)    # => 5
12.clamp(..10)  # => 10
7.clamp(5, 10)  # => 7
3.clamp(5, 10)  # => 5
12.clamp(5, 10) # => 10
```

Kernel

The Kernel module is included by class Object, so its methods are available in every Ruby object. One of the reasons for the Kernel module is to allow methods like puts and gets to be available everywhere and even to look like global commands. Kernel methods allow Ruby to still maintain an "everything is an object" semantics. Kernel methods actually use the implicit receivers and could be written as self.puts and self.gets. As a result, Kernel methods are both available everywhere and resolve like any other method.

Since Kernel is mixed into Object, there is no practical difference between a method defined in Kernel and a method defined in Object. Logically, the distinction is that the methods in Object manage the object-oriented semantics of Ruby, while the methods in Kernel are a general functionality that Ruby wants to be available anywhere in the code. You can find more about this distinction in Object, on page 557.

In most cases, your code will be inside an object that includes Kernel and these methods can be invoked like any other instance method. Kernel methods are typically invoked without an explicit receiver, which makes them look like commands, as in require, not self.require.

Methods of Kernel that don't refer to the self object are also made module methods by calling module_method (see Module, on page 552). This is to support calling Kernel methods by using the syntax Kernel.puts, and it's there to support calling Kernel methods inside BasicObject instances that don't include Kernel. You can see an example of the module method usage in BasicObject, on page 537.

Here's a guide to the most useful or interesting methods of Kernel.

Conversion

In Standard Protocols and Coercions, on page 362, we listed the conversion methods defined by Kernel for converting values to basic Ruby types—meaning types that have literal syntax. Kernel also defines a few other conversions as outlined in the following table:

Method	Description
BigDecimal(value, digits = 0, exception: true)	Available after require "bigdecimal" is executed. If value is a numerical object, it's converted to a BigDecimal. If value is a string, it's parsed to an integer or float and then converted. Other objects that implement to_str call that method, and convert the resulting string. Any other object raises an exception if the exception argument is true, otherwise, nil is returned. If the digits argument isn't 0 and is less than the number of significant digits in the value, then the resulting BigDecimal is rounded to that number of significant digits.
JSON(object, *args)	If the object is a string or responds to to_str, then this assumes that you want to convert a JSON string to Ruby, and it calls JSON.parse and returns the resulting object. Otherwise, it assumes you have a Ruby object and want JSON, so it calls JSON.generate with the object. In either case, the args is passed to the called method.
Pathname(path)	Available after you call require "pathname". It creates a new Pathname object from the given pathname.
URI(uri)	Creates a URI object from the argument, which is a string or an existing URI

Table 23—More kernel module conversion methods

Control Flow

The Kernel module has many methods that affect the control flow of a Ruby program.

Exiting a Program

One way to affect the control flow of a program is to end it. The method Kernel#abort(message = nil) terminates execution immediately with an exit code of 1. The optional message argument, if it exists, is written to the standard error stream before the program terminates.

The method Kernel#at_exit {block} takes the block object, converts it to a Proc object and holds on to the object. The block is executed when the program ends. If multiple at_exit blocks are declared, they are executed in reverse order—last declared, first executed.

You can also terminate a Ruby process with the methods exit and exit!. Kernel#exit(status = true) ends a Ruby program and raises a SystemExit exception, which you can catch in your code and handle. If the exception isn't handled, the program runs any at_exit handlers and then terminates. A true status is reported as successful to the operating system (typically meaning 0), a false status is reported as unsuccessful (typically meaning 1), and any integer status is just returned to be interpreted by the underlying operating system. Kernel#exit!(status = false) behaves similarly except the at_exit handlers are *not* called, and the default status is failure.

The difference here is that abort allows you to send a text message out, but always sends an exit code of 1, while exit allows you to change the exit code, but doesn't allow you to send out a message.

If you don't want to end the program permanently but just want it to rest a while, Kernel#sleep(seconds = nil) suspends the current thread for the given number of seconds. The argument can be any numeric object, including a float or rational with partial seconds. It returns the actual number of seconds slept, which may be less than that asked for if the thread was interrupted by a SIGALRM or if another thread calls Thread#run. An argument of zero causes sleep to return immediately. An argument of nil causes the thread to sleep forever unless interrupted by another thread.

Exception Handling

A few methods of Kernel control exceptional behavior. The main way of raising an exception is the method Kernel#raise(*args), which is aliased as Kernel#fail. There are a couple of different argument patterns that can be passed to raise. With no arguments, raise raises the exception in $! or, if $! is nil, raises a RuntimeError. If the argument is a String (or an object that responds to to_str), raise raises a RuntimeError with the string as a message.

If the argument isn't a string, the first parameter should be the name of an Exception class (or an object that returns an Exception when its exception method is called). The optional second parameter is the message associated with the exception, the third parameter is an array of callback information, and the default is the result of the method Exception#backtrace. An optional keyword argument, cause:, is the cause of the exception; it defaults to $! but you can set it to an arbitrary Exception object or to nil. See Chapter 10, Exceptions, on page 171, for more details on how exceptions are managed in Ruby.

Control Flow

The Kernel#loop {block} method takes a block and invokes that block repeatedly, with no argument, until the block is exited with break, return, or by raising a StopIteration error. If loop is called without a block argument, then an Enumerator is returned.

The Kernel#tap { |x| block} method takes a block and just yields self to the block and returns self. It took us a little while to see where this is useful. The tap method allows you to "tap into" a chain of method calls without interfering.

For example, if you had dog.reverse.capitalize but wanted to see the intermediate object for debugging purposes, you could use tap right in the middle:

```ruby
puts "dog"
  .reverse
  .tap { |o| puts "Reversed: #{o}" }
  .capitalize
```

produces:

```
Reversed: god
God
```

The similar method, Kernel#then { |x| block }, aliased as yield_self, also passes the receiver to the block but returns the result of the block, rather than the original receiver. This allows for pipelining an object in a method chain. Here's a slightly contrived example:

```ruby
result = "testfile"
  .then { |filename| File.readlines(filename) }
  .then { |lines| lines.count }
puts result
```

produces:

```
4
```

The pair of methods Kernel#catch(tag) { |tag| block } and Kernel#throw(throw_tag, value) also allow you to manipulate control flow.

The catch method executes its block immediately, passing the tag argument as a parameter. If a throw method is encountered, Ruby searches up its stack for a catch block with a tag argument identical to the throw method's tag argument. If found, that block is terminated and catch returns the value given as the second parameter to throw. If there is no matching catch block, then Ruby raises a NameError.

If throw isn't called, the block terminates normally, and the value of catch is the value of the last expression evaluated. catch expressions may be nested, and the throw call doesn't need to be in lexical scope.

```ruby
ref_meta_ruby/catch_throw.rb
def routine(n)
  print n, " "
  throw :done if n <= 0
  routine(n - 1)
end
catch(:done) { routine(4) }
```

produces:

```
4 3 2 1 0
```

If you want to send a warning, rather than raise an exception, the method Kernel#warn(*messages, uplevel: nil, category: nil) will send each message in its first argument to Warning.warn. This does nothing if warnings have been disabled, but if warnings are enabled, it'll behave like a deprecation warning. If the uplevel argument isn't nil, the warning string will have the file and line location prepended to it. The category is either :deprecated or :experimental and, if included, allows the warning system to treat the warning as that type when choosing if the warning should be displayed.

Evaluation and Loading Code

The method Kernel#eval(string, binding = nil, filename = nil, line_number = nil) takes a Ruby expression as its first argument and evaluates it. By default, the expression is evaluated in the current context, but if a Binding object is passed as the second argument, the expression is evaluated in that context. If the filename and line_number arguments are passed, they'll be used to identify the code when reporting errors.

Local variables assigned within an eval are available after the eval only if they were defined at the outer scope before the eval executed. In this way, eval has the same scoping rules as blocks.

```
a = 1
eval("a = 98; b = 99")
puts a
puts b
```

produces:

```
puts b
      ^
98
prog.rb:4:in `<main>': undefined local variable or method `b' for main
(NameError)
```

The method Kernel#require(path), which we've seen many times in this book, loads in a Ruby file at the given path.

Ruby tries to load the file at path, returning true if successful. If the path isn't an absolute path, it'll be searched for in the directories listed in $:. If the file has the extension rb, it's loaded as a source file. If the extension is so, .o, .dll, or whatever the default shared library extension is on the current platform, Ruby loads the shared library as a Ruby extension. Otherwise, Ruby tries adding rb, .so, and so on, to the name until found. The name of the loaded file is added to the array in $". A file won't be loaded if its name already appears in $".'.

If RubyGems is required, which will be true of most Ruby programs, if the file isn't found in the absolute path, the installed gems are also searched for a file that matches, and the gem that matches the file is added to the load path.

The method Kernel#require_relative(path) works similarly, except that the path is resolved relative to the file it's included in, rather than the root of the program. This also means that gems can't be installed via require_relative.

Ruby also provides Kernel#load(path, wrap = false), which loads and executes the Ruby program in the file path. If the filename doesn't resolve to an absolute path, the file is searched for in the library directories listed in $:. If the optional wrap parameter is true, the loaded script will be executed under an anonymous module, protecting the calling program's global namespace. In no circumstance will any local variables in the loaded file be propagated to the loading environment. The load method differs from require in that if the same file is referenced again, load will load it again, whereas require will note that it has already been loaded and not reload the file.

Shortcuts

Several Kernel methods are shortcuts for full methods that exist in other classes. Here's a roundup:

- Kernel#chomp(string) is equivalent to String#chomp. If no argument is given, it uses $_ (the result of the most recent line that was received as input). This is only available when Ruby is invoked with -n or -p looping command-line flags.

- Kernel#chop takes no argument and is equivalent to $_.dup.chop(), except that if chop performs no action, $_ is unchanged and nil isn't returned. This is only available when Ruby is invoked with -n or -p looping command-line flags.

- Kernel#gsub(pattern, replacement) or Kernel#gsub(pattern) { |...| block } is only available when Ruby is invoked with -n or -p looping command-line flags. This is equivalent to $_.gsub.

- Kernel#j(*objects) and Kernel#jj(*objects) are both shortcuts to puts JSON.generate and are used to output objects to the console. The j version prints on a single line, and is equivalent to calling JSON::generate(obj, :allow_nan => true, :max_nesting => false) on each object argument. The jj version prints on multilines and is equivalent to calling JSON::pretty_generate(obj, :allow_nan => true, :max_nesting => false).

- Kernel#lambda { block } converts its block into a Proc object with lambda semantics as described in Using Blocks as Objects, on page 73.

- Kernel#p(*objects) is a shortcut for $stdout.write(object.inspect, "\n") for each object passed as an argument.

- Kernel.pretty_inspect is equivalent to PP.pp(self, "".dup) and only works if require "pp" has been called.

- Kernel#print(*objects) is a shortcut for $stdout.print(*objects).

- Kernel#proc { block } converts its block into a Proc object with proc semantics as described in Using Blocks as Objects, on page 73.

- Kernel#pp(*objects) is shortcut for PP.pp(obj) and returns the pretty-printed form of the object.

- Kernel#puts(*objects) is a shortcut for $stdout.puts(*objects).

- Kernel#rand(max = 0) is a shortcut for Random.rand(max).

- Kernel#srand(number = Random.new_seed) seeds the random number generator for future rand usages.

- Kernel#sub(pattern, replacement) or Kernel#sub(pattern) { |...| block } is only available when Ruby is invoked with -n or -p looping command-line flags. This is equivalent to $_.sub.

- Kernel#y(*objects) is equivalent to YAML.dump_stream(*objects) and is used for formatted output, often in irb.

Formatting

The method Kernel#printf(format_string, *objects), which is aliased as sprintf and the methods IO#printf and ARGF.printf, all return the string resulting from applying format_string to any additional arguments. Within the format string, any characters other than format sequences are copied to the result.

A format sequence consists of a percent sign; followed by optional flags, width, precision indicators, an optional name, and then terminated with a field type character. The field type controls how the corresponding sprintf argument is to be interpreted, and the flags modify that interpretation.

The flag characters are listed in the following table:

Flag	Applies To	Meaning
␣ (space)	bdEefGgiouXx	Leaves a space at the start of positive numbers.
digit$	all	Specifies the absolute argument number for this field. Absolute and relative argument numbers cannot be mixed in a sprintf string.
#	beEfgGoxX	Uses an alternative format. For the conversions b, o, X, and x, prefixes the result with b, 0, 0X, 0x, respectively. For E, e, f, G, and g, forces a decimal point to be added, even if no digits follow. For G and g, does not remove trailing zeros.
+	bdEefGgiouXx	Adds a leading plus sign to positive numbers.
-	all	Left-justifies the result of this conversion.
0 (zero)	bdEefGgiouXx	Pads with zeros, not spaces.
*	all	Uses the next argument as the field width. If negative, left-justifies the result. If the asterisk is followed by a number and a dollar sign, uses the indicated argument as the width.

Table 24—Format string flag characters

The field width is an optional integer, followed optionally by a period and a precision. The width specifies the minimum number of characters that will be written to the result for this field. For numeric fields, the precision controls the number of decimal places displayed. The number zero is converted to a zero-length string if a precision of 0 is given. For string fields, the precision determines the maximum number of characters to be copied from the string. Thus, the format sequence %10.10s will always contribute exactly ten characters to the result.

The field type characters are listed in the following table:

Field	Conversion
A	Same as %a, but uses uppercase X and P.
a	Converts a float into hexadecimal representation 0x*significand*p*decimal-exp*.
B	Converts argument as a binary number (0B0101 if # modifier used).
b	Converts argument as a binary number (0b0101 if # modifier used).
c	Argument is the numeric code for a single character.
d	Converts argument as a decimal number.
E	Equivalent to e but uses an uppercase E to indicate the exponent.
e	Converts floating-point argument into exponential notation with one digit before the decimal point. The precision determines the number of fractional digits (default six).

Field	Conversion
f	Converts floating-point argument as [|-]ddd.ddd, where the precision determines the number of digits after the decimal point.
G	Equivalent to g but uses an uppercase E in exponent form.
g	Converts a floating-point number using exponential form if the exponent is less than -4 or greater than or equal to the precision, or in d.dddd form otherwise.
i	Identical to d.
o	Converts argument as an octal number.
p	The value of argument.inspect.
s	Argument is a string to be substituted. If the format sequence contains a precision, at most that many characters will be copied.
u	Treats argument as an unsigned decimal number.
X	Converts argument to hexadecimal with uppercase letters. Negative numbers will be displayed with two leading periods (representing an infinite string of leading FFs).
x	Converts argument to hexadecimal. Negative numbers will be displayed with two leading periods (representing an infinite string of leading FFs).

Table 25—Format string field characters

Here are some examples of sprintf in action:

```
ref_meta_ruby/sprintf_1.rb
sprintf("%d %04x", 123, 123)              # => "123_007b"
sprintf("%08b '%4s'", 123, 123)          # => "01111011_'_123'"
sprintf("%1$*2$s %2$d %1$s", "hello", 8) # => "___hello_8_hello"
sprintf("%1$*2$s %2$d", "hello", -8)     # => "hello_____-8"
sprintf("%+g:% g:%-g", 1.23, 1.23, 1.23) # => "+1.23:_1.23:1.23"
```

You can pass a hash as the second argument and insert values from this hash into the string. The notation <name> can be used between a percent sign and a field-type character, in which case the name will be used to look up a value in the hash, and that value will be formatted according to the field specification. The notation {name} is equivalent to <name>s, substituting the corresponding value as a string. You can use width and other flag characters between the opening percent sign and the {. Here's an example:

```
ref_meta_ruby/sprintf_2.rb
sprintf("%<number>d %04<number>x", number: 123)    # => "123_007b"
sprintf("%08<number>b '%5{number}'", number: 123)  # => "01111011_'_123'"
sprintf("%6<k>s: %<v>s", k: "Dave", v: "Ruby")     # => "__Dave:_Ruby"
sprintf("%6{k}: %{v}", k: "Dave", v: "Ruby")       # => "__Dave:_Ruby"
```

Ruby Runtime Information

The Kernel module includes a bunch of methods that return various parts of internal Ruby information. A few methods in Kernel can tell you where you're in the system and what's available.

A commonly used method is Kernel#block_given?, which returns true if the current method was passed a block and therefore would execute that block if yield was invoked.

The method class, when called with an explicit receiver, returns the Class object of the class of that object.

Kernel#_dir_ returns the path of the directory of the file from which it's called. It's related to _FILE_, which is a globally available value and not a method of Kernel. The value of _dir_ is equivalent to File.dirname(File.realpath(_FILE_)).

Kernel#_callee_ returns the name of the current method or nil outside the context of a method. If a method is called by an aliased name, that alias is returned, not the original name. The Kernel#_method_ returns the current method and calls the original name if the method is called by an alias.

The flip side of _callee_ is Kernel#caller(start = 1, length = nil) also callable as Kernel#caller(range). The caller method returns the current execution stack or a backtrace. It returns strings formatted as file:line: in method (the related method Kernel#caller_location takes the same arguments but returns an array of Ruby objects). If it takes start and length arguments, the start parameter is the index at which the returned array starts (you can think of this as the number of entries at the top of the stack that are discarded). The length argument limits the number of entries returned; otherwise, the entire call stack is returned. A range argument indicates the subset of the call stack that should be returned.

You can get an entire binding with the Kernel#binding method. The binding returns an object of class Binding that contains all the local variable information at a current point.

Objects of class Binding encapsulate the execution context at some particular place in the code and retain this context for future use. Access to the variables, methods, value of self, and possibly an iterator block accessible in this context are all retained. The binding object responds to the method local_variables and returns a list of symbols of defined local variables in the binding. The method local_variable_get(symbol) returns the value of the local variable in the binding along with local_variable_set(symbol, obj), which sets the value of the local variable in the binding. The list of local variables is available directly as Kernel#local_variables as is a list of global variables as Kernel#global_variables.

System Info

Several methods in Kernel allow you to interact with the underlying operating system.

Executing System Commands

Several methods allow you to execute operating system commands.

The use of backticks to send a system command, as seen in Command Expressions, on page 146, is defined as the method Kernel#`, which executes the command and returns a string containing any output that would've gone to $stdout. It also sets the global variable $? to the return status of the command.

The method Kernel#exec(command, *options) replaces the current process by running the given external command, ending the current process. The behavior of the command depends on the arguments. There are a few possibilities:

- The only argument is a single command string, which doesn't contain a new line or any of the meta characters ?*?{}[]<>()~&|$;'". In this case, Ruby invokes the command without loading an operating system shell.

- If the single command string does contain a newline or meta-character, it's executed in the default shell, and is subject to shell expansion before being executed. On Unix system,

Ruby does this by prepending sh -c. Under Windows, it uses the name of a shell in either RUBYSHELL or COMSPEC.

- If multiple arguments are given, the first argument is the command, and the second and subsequent arguments are passed as parameters to command with no shell expansion.

- If the first argument is a two-element array rather than a string, the first element is the command to be executed, and the second argument is used as the argv[0] value, which may show up in process listings.

Any of these versions can have a prepended argument that is a hash (so the signature is Kernel#exec(hash, command, *options)) and adds to the environment variables in the subshell. The keys must be strings. An entry with a nil value clears the corresponding environment variable. Any version can have a final argument options, if present. It's a hash that controls the setup of the subshell.

The method Kernel#fork [{ block }] takes an optional block. If the block is given, it forks a subprocess, executing the block in that subprocess. If a block isn't given, fork is run in the operating system twice, the parent process gets a return value of nil, and the child process gets a process ID. See Blocks and Subprocesses, on page 199, for more uses.

The method Kernel#spawn(command, options = "") or Kernel#spawn(environment, command, options = "") executes the given command and returns its process ID. The spawn method doesn't block the Ruby program. If you use it, you should call Process.wait(pid) if you need to wait for the command to complete. The environment argument, if given, sets environment variables. There are a lot of somewhat edge-case options that can affect the execution, please check the official documentation.

The similar method Kernel#system with the same argument patterns executes the command in a subshell and waits for the command to complete, returning true if the command executes successfully, false if it reports a non-successful exit status, and nil if the command fails without reporting status.

I/O

The method Kernel#gets(sep = $/, limit = nil) or Kernel#gets(limit), when called without an argument, returns the next line of text from standard input, meaning all the text until it hits an end-of-line character. In a program that has command line files specified and placed in ARGV (or otherwise assigns values to ARGV, gets will read the next line from ARGV instead. An optional argument specifies a nonstandard line separator. Like other I/O methods, if the argument is nil it'll read the entire content of the stream (or, the entire content of the current ARGV file), and an empty string argument reads until it gets two consecutive line separators. If the argument is an integer, it limits the number of bytes read. The method Kernel#readline with the same argument signature is identical except that it raises an exception if the stream has already ended, and it takes a keyword argument chomp: that determines if the separator character is removed. The method Kernel#readlines (again, same argument signature) returns an array of lines, reading until the end of the input stream is reached. It has the same arguments as readline plus it takes the same encoding options as other methods described in Chapter 29, Library Reference: Input, Output, Files, and Formats, on page 587.

The flip side of gets is Kernel#puts(*objects), which prints its objects to standard out. It's the same as calling $stdout.puts(objects), which is equivalent to $stdout.print(*objects). The difference between print and puts is covered in Printing Things, on page 289.

```
ARGV << "testfile"
print while gets
```

produces:

```
This is line one
This is line two
This is line three
And so on...
```

The method Kernel.open(path, mode = "r", permissions = 0666, **options) [{ |io| ...}], does a lot of stuff. It has three modes:

- If the path is a normal string, that string is assumed to be a file path, and the behavior is essentially as if you called File.open(path, mode, permissions, options).

- If the path argument is a pipe character followed by a shell command, then the shell command is run in a new subprocess and a stream is returned connected to that subprocess. If there's a block argument, then the stream is passed to the block and the stream is closed at the end of the block.

- If the path argument is exactly |-, the process forks, the return value to the parent is a stream connected to the child, and the return value to the child is nil, so you can tell the two apart. Again, a block argument is passed the stream, and the stream is automatically closed at the end of the block.

The Kernel module does a lot, and some less commonly used methods have been omitted. In particular, if you're doing Unix-specific operating system interactions, you should check out the official documentation.

Method

A Ruby Method object represents a method that is attached (the technical term is "bound") to a specific receiver. You create Method objects via Object#method(name), which returns the method object for a given name.

Once you have a method object, you can call the method with call(*, **, &), which forwards the arguments to the method and invokes it with the method object's receiver. The call method is aliased as [] and also as ===.

You can compose Ruby methods in a functional programming style with Method#<<(other_proc), which takes a proc or callable object as the right-hand side and returns a new proc. The new proc takes arguments, calls other_proc, and then calls the given method with the result of the call to other_proc. The flip side of Method#<<(other_proc) is Method#>>(other_proc), which returns a new proc that calls this method and then passes the result to other_proc. Here's an example:

```
ref_meta_ruby/compose_methods.rb
class Foo
  def triple(x)
    x + x + x
  end
end

squarer = proc { |x| x * x }
foo_instance = Foo.new
method = foo_instance.method(:triple)
```

```
pointing_left = (method << squarer)
pointing_right = (method >> squarer)

pointing_left.call(5)    # => 75
pointing_right.call(5)   # => 225
```

The number of arguments that a method takes is called the *arity* of the method, and Method#arity returns that value for the method. If the method has a variable number of arguments, arity returns the number of required arguments * -1 - 1, so a method with a signature of (a, b, *c) returns an arity of -3. All keyword arguments are collectively treated as one argument, which is a required argument if any of the individual keyword arguments is required. Internal methods written in C that take variable arguments return -1.

Another functional programming thing you can do with a method is use Method#curry(arity = nil). *Currying* is the term for creating a new method with a lower arity. The curry method returns a new proc. Calling that proc with fewer than the required number of arguments for the original method returns a new proc that holds on to those arguments. You can call the new proc again with more arguments until you finally have enough arguments to match the original method, at which time the original method is called. If the original method takes a variable number of arguments, the arity argument is used to say how many arguments you want the whole deal to take before the original method is invoked:

ref_meta_ruby/curry.rb
```
class Currier
  def add_four_things(a, b, c, d)
    a + b + c + d
  end
end

currier = Currier.new
add_two_things = currier.method(:add_four_things).curry.call(1, 2)
add_two_things.call(3, 4)   # => 10

add_one_thing = add_two_things.call(5)
add_one_thing.call(7)       # => 15
```

The Method class is useful in debugging or investigating code. In irb or in code you can acquire a Method object and learn about where it's defined and how to call it. You can get the name of the method with Method#name and the original name of an aliased method with Method#original_name. Method#receiver returns the object the method is bound to, and Method#owner is the class or module where the method is defined. Method#source_location returns an array of the filename and line number where the method is defined. Method#inspect shows a lot of these details in one string.

You can unbind the method with Method#unbind, which returns an UnboundMethod, see Unbound Method, on page 634.

Module

The Module class is the class of any module you declare with the module keyword. Each module is an instance of the class Module. The class Class is a subclass of the class Module, and so it inherits all the functionality described here.

You can create an anonymous module with Module.new [{block}], the block body is the body of the module. You can assign the module to a variable. If that variable name starts with a capital letter, then it's a constant and you can treat it exactly like a module that's created in the more common way.

Information about Modules

The Module class has a number of methods that allow you to dynamically access information about a module or class.

Module (and Class) Hierarchy

You can compare two modules to determine the relationship between them. Modules define the spaceship operator via inclusion, so module <=> other_module returns -1 if module includes other_module, 0 if module is the same module as other_module, +1 if module is included by other_module or, nil if module has no relationship with other_module.

As for the other comparison operators, <, <=, ==, >, and >=, they behave similarly as a hierarchy query. One module is considered greater than another if it's included in (or is a parent class of) the other module. The other operators are defined accordingly. If there is no relationship between the modules, all operators return nil.

```
ref_meta_ruby/module_comp.rb
module Mixin
end

module Parent
  include Mixin
end

module Unrelated
end

Parent > Mixin        # => false
Parent < Mixin        # => true
Parent <= Parent      # => true
Parent < Unrelated    # => nil
Parent > Unrelated    # => nil

Parent <=> Mixin      # => -1
Parent <=> Parent     # => 0
Parent <=> Unrelated  # => nil
```

The triple-equal case equality operator, ===, as in User === u, returns true if the object on the right is an instance of the module or one of the module's descendants. This is also useful when the left side is a Class rather than a Module.

The method ancestors returns an array of all the modules included or prepended in this module. For classes, ancestors also includes superclasses, so the result is the method lookup sequence when this module or class is called.

Module (and Class) Attributes

Many Module methods give you access to components of the module. The name, for example, is accessible with Module#name. The method Module#singleton_class? returns true if the module is a singleton class, and false if it's a regular module.

Class variables are defined with @@, and you can get the list of all known class variables with the Module#class_variables method. The return value is a list of the names as symbols, with the @@ prefix attached. You can get the value of a specific class variable with Module#class_variable_get(name), which takes the name of the variable as a symbol or string, with the @@ prefix, and returns the current value. The method Module#class_variable_set(name, value) takes the same name argument and sets its value to the value argument. The method Module#class_variable_defined?(name) takes the same name argument and returns true if the variable is defined, while the method Module#remove_class_variable(name) takes the same name argument and undefines the variable at that name.

There's a similar pattern with constants defined in the module or class. The method Module#constants(inherit = true) returns an array of the names of all constants defined in the module as symbols. Constants also have getters and setters. The Module#const_get(name, inherit=true) method takes the name of the constant as a symbol or string and returns its current value or raises a NameError if the constant isn't defined. In both these methods, if the inherit argument is true, the search for constants also includes constants defined in modules that have been included in the current module.

The method Module#const_set(name, value) takes the name of a constant as a string or symbol and sets its value to the new value. If the constant doesn't exist, then it's created; if the name doesn't start with a capital letter or is otherwise not valid, a NameError is raised. If the constant already has a value, the value will be changed but a warning will be raised.

Constants have two other interesting methods. The method Module#const_source_location(name, inherit=true) takes a constant name and returns a two-element array [filename, line_number] of the location in the source where the constant is defined. If the constant doesn't exist, it returns nil, but if the constant exists but doesn't have a source location, it returns an empty array. This might happen if the constant is defined in Ruby's internal C libraries rather than in Ruby code. The inherit argument has the same meaning as described earlier.

The method Module#const_missing(name) is similar to method_missing. It's a hook invoked when a constant is looked for and not found. The name of the constant is passed to const_missing as a symbol, and the return value of the method is returned as the value of the constant.

You can also track down methods with, well, methods. Module#instance_methods(include_super = true) returns an array of the names of all the non-private instance methods as symbols. If include_super is false, then methods from superclasses or other included modules aren't included. Module#instance_method(method_name) takes a method name as a symbol and returns the method as an UnboundMethod object or raises a NameError if the method doesn't exist. Module#method_defined?(method_name, inherit=true) returns true if the method exists in the module as a public or protected method. If inherit is false then it only looks in the module itself.

There are similar methods that explicitly only return methods of a particular security level:

- private_instance_methods, protected_instance_methods, and public_instance_methods all take an optional argument include_super=true and behave the same as instance_method except they only return methods at that given security level.

- private_method_defined?, protected_method_defined?, and public_method_defined? all take (method_name, inherit=true) and behave the same as method_defined except they only return true if the method is part of that security level.

Modifying Modules

Many methods of Module actually change the behavior of the module as it's being loaded. We've seen a lot of these before. They tend to look like commands but are actually methods of Module that are generally called inside a module's definition with an implicit receiver.

The method Module#alias_method(new_name, old_name) makes the new name a copy of the method referenced by the old name. The new name points to the existing method even if the method at the old name is redefined.

We've seen the attr family of methods in Chapter 3, Classes, Objects, and Variables, on page 33. Module#attr_reader(*names) takes a list of names as symbols or strings and creates a getter method for each name (aliased as just attr), while Module#attr_writer(*names) takes the list of names and creates a setter method for each name, and Module#attr_accessor(*names) creates both getter and setter methods for each name.

We've also seen include and prepend before in Chapter 6, Sharing Functionality: Inheritance, Modules, and Mixins, on page 101. They are implemented as methods of the Module class that take one or more modules as arguments. Internally, include calls a method named Module#append_feautres(module) that actually adds the elements of the Module to the call chain. Similarly, prepend calls a method named Module#prepend_features(module). There is also Module#included_modules, which returns an array of all the modules included or prepended in the receiving module or one of its ancestor modules, and Module#included?(module), which returns true if the argument module has been included or prepended in the receiving module or one of its ancestor modules. The method Module#extend_object(obj) is used internally by Object#extend to handle extensions.

The refinement methods refine and using, as seen and more fully described in Using Refinements, on page 384, are also defined as Module methods. Module#refine(module) {block} takes a class or module as an argument and a block in which new methods are defined for that class or module. Module#using(module) takes as an argument a module that does such a refinement and applies the refinement in the current context.

We've also covered method access control, you can see the definitions of the various levels in Specifying Access Control, on page 45. Those control features are implemented as methods of Module: Module#private(*method_names), Module#protected(*method_names), and Module#public(*method_names). All three of these methods work the same way. When called with no arguments, they change the default access level for methods that are defined after the method call. When called with one or more symbols, or an array of symbols, the symbols are treated as the names of methods in the module and those methods' access levels are changed to match. Since def returns a symbol, you can do this access setting inline with something like private def foo or protected def bar.

Several additional methods of Module take one or more method or constant names and do something to that method or constant. The names can be strings or symbols:

- Module#module_function(*names) makes an existing method that is defined as an instance method into a module method, meaning it can be called with Module.method syntax. The module method is a copy, so the original can change without affecting it. The instance version becomes private. As with access control methods, if module_function is called with no arguments, it becomes the default for any methods defined later in the code.

- Module#private_class_method(*names) makes existing class methods private.

- Module#private_constant(*symbols) makes existing constants private.

- Module#public_class_method(*names) makes existing class methods public.

- Module#public_constant(*symbols) makes existing constants public.

- Module#remove_method(symbol) removes the method from the module or class (one argument only).

- Module#remove_const(symbol) removes the constant from the module or class (one argument only).

- Module#ruby2_keywords(*names) has the given methods manage positional and keyword arguments using Ruby 2 semantics, rather than Ruby 3. This is sometimes useful for compatibility with older code.

- Module#undef_method(name) removes the method from the module or class, but unlike remove_method, subsequent calls to the method won't look for the method in superclasses or included modules.

Executing Dynamic Code

Several methods of Module allow you to execute arbitrary code at runtime in the module's context.

The method Module#class_eval, aliased as module_eval has two different forms. The first form is Module#class_eval(string, filename = nil, line_number = nil). This form evaluates the string in the module's context. If the filename and line number are given, those are used if any error is raised while evaluating the text and are also used as the source location of any method defined in the string. You can use a heredoc as the string:

```
ref_meta_ruby/class_eval.rb
class EmptyClass
end
EmptyClass.module_eval <<-STRING, __FILE__, __LINE__ + 1
  def greeting()
    "Hi There!"
  end
STRING

puts EmptyClass.new.greeting
```

produces:

```
Hi There!
```

The second form takes a block argument Module#class_eval {|module|} and evaluates the block in the context of the string, passing the module as an argument to the block. In both cases, the return value of the executed code is the return value of the executed method.

The similar method Module#class_exec(...), aliased as module_exec, takes a block. Unlike class_eval, arguments passed to class_exec will be passed to the block. The block will then be executed in the class context and, as with class_eval, can be used to add class or module methods.

To add instance methods, you use Module#define_method(symbol) {block}. This method dynamically creates an instance method in the receiving class or module. The block is the body of the method, and any parameters that the block takes are expected to be arguments to the new method when called. Instead of a block, a second argument that is Proc, Method, or UnboundMethod can be passed.

Event Hooks

Ruby has several callback methods in Module that, if defined, are automatically called when an event happens, typically but not necessarily, when the code is loaded:

- Module#const_added(constant_name) is called after a new constant is added to the module. The argument is the name of the new constant.

- Module#extended(other_module) is called with the extending module as the argument after a module is used to extend another module or class with extend. So, given module Foo; extend Bar; end, the method Bar#extended is called with Foo as an argument.

- Module#included(other_module) is called after the module is included in another module with the including module as the argument. So, given module Foo; include Bar; end, the method Bar#included is called with Foo as an argument.

- Module#method_added(method_name) is called after a method is added to the module or class, with the name of the new method as an argument.

- Module#method_removed(method_name) is called after a method is removed from the module or class, with the name of the method to be removed as an argument.

- Module#method_undefined(method_name) is called after a method is undefined from the module or class, with the name of the method to be undefined as an argument.

- Module#prepended(other_module) is called after the module is prepended in another module with the prepending module as the argument. So, given module Foo; prepend Bar; end, the method Bar#prepended is called with Foo as an argument.

Object

Object is the parent class of (almost) all classes in Ruby unless a class explicitly inherits from BasicObject. So, its methods are available to all objects unless explicitly overridden.

Object mixes in the Kernel module, making the built-in kernel functions globally accessible (see Kernel, on page 541). The methods discussed here for the Object class mostly pertain to Ruby's object-oriented semantics.

An interesting fact about Ruby's actual implementation is that even these methods that are documented here (and in Ruby's official documentation) as being part of Object are actually all internally defined in Kernel. You can prove this by calling owner on any Method object in Object, as in Object.instance_method(:itself).owner. The official documentation has a special case in which the documentation for some methods is put in the Object documentation rather than the Kernel, and we've maintained that distinction here. But by the time you read this, the documentation may have been changed.

Comparison

The Object class doesn't, by default, include Comparable, but it does define the <=> operator, which returns 0 if the two objects are the same and returns nil if they aren't. This isn't useful for sorting or comparing, so your subclass should redefine <=> and include Comparable if you want that behavior.

There are four different equality methods in Object: ==, ===, eql?, and equal?. They all behave slightly differently.

- ==, for Object, returns true if the two things being compared are the same object in memory. This method is often overridden by subclasses to have behavior more similar to eql?.

- === is defined to be identical to == for Object, but it's expected that it'll be overridden by subclasses to provide matching behavior in case statements.

- eql? is equivalent to == for instances of Object. Subclasses that override eql? should also override hash with the same value semantics.

- equal? returns true of the two things being compared are the same object in memory. This shouldn't be overridden by subclasses.

Ruby provides an Object#object_id or Object#__id__ that is used to determine if two objects are the same in memory.

Methods and Variables

The Object class allows you access to instance variables and instance methods.

You can retrieve the value of any instance variable with Object#instance_variable_get(name) the name is a symbol or string, and it does have to begin with the @ sign. If the variable hasn't been defined, it returns nil, if the name isn't a valid name, it'll raise a NameError. Otherwise, it'll return the current value of that instance variable. You can set the value with Object#instance_variable_set(name, object), the name is as in the getter method, and the instance variable will be created if it doesn't already exist. You can get an array of all the currently defined instance variables with Object#instance_variables and you can get a boolean true/false of whether a value is defined with Object#instance_variable_defined?(name), again, the name must start with the @ sign. Notice that this means that even though instance variable methods are technically private, they are accessible to external objects if the external object wants it badly enough.

For method, you can get a list of the public and protected instance methods available to an object with Object#methods(regular = true). If the regular parameter is false, you get a list of the singleton methods instead of the, I guess you'd say, regular methods. You can search for a specific method with Object#method(name) which returns the method as a Method object, the argument can be a string or a symbol.

You can limit methods by access type with Object#public_methods(all = true), Object#protected_methods(all = true), Object#private_methods(all = true), and Object#singleton_methods(all = true). In each case, if the all parameter is false, then only methods in the receiving object itself are returned as opposed to the receiving object and all its superclasses. The singleton_methods list will exclude private singleton methods if, for some reason, you had one.

You can search for individual methods using Object#public_method(name), Object#protected_method(name), and Object#singleton_method(name). There doesn't seem to be an analogous method that only returns private methods.

While we're talking about singletons, there is also Object#singleton_class which returns the singleton class of the object as an instance of type Class. And you can programmatically add a method to the singleton class with Object#define_singleton_method(symbol) {block} or Object#define_singleton_method(symbol, proc), the semantics are similar to Module#define_method, the proc or block is the body of the method and the symbol is the name, and the method is added to the object's singleton class.

You can programmatically send a message to an object with Object#send(name, ...). The name can be a symbol or string, and the method corresponding to that name is called with any remaining arguments to send being passed through. The send method is aliased as __send__, which is safer because some objects may have their own method named send. The send method can be used to call private methods, if you want to limit the feature to public methods, then you can use Object#public_send(name, ...).

You can prevent the object from being modified by calling Object.freeze. Subsequent attempts to modify the object will raise a FrozenError. You can tell if an object is frozen with Object.frozen?.

You can create a shallow copy of an object with Object#dup – a shallow copy means that a new object is created, but any referenced objects aren't copied.

Query

Some methods allow you to query the object in various ways. For example, Object#hash returns the integer value that is used for hash comparisons. Actual Hash objects use this to determine if two objects are identical for the purpose of being keys in the hash.

You need to override this method in your subclass such that two objects that are eql? also have the same result when calling hash. Often, this is needed if your subclass has a definition of equality that is different from "all the instance values of each object are the same". (For instance, you might have an instance value that isn't relevant for equality). It's recommended that if you override the method, you use hash on the class itself and all the values that you're combining rather than roll your own function, which would look like [self.class, first_name, last_name, birth_date].hash.

You can get the internal string representation of an object with Object#inspect and the external string representation of an object with Object#to_s.

There are several slightly different mechanisms for a boolean test of whether an object is related to a class:

- Object#instance_of?(class) returns true if the object is exactly an instance of the class.

- Object#is_a?(other_class), aliased as Object#kind_of?(other_class) returns true if the object is an instance other_class, an instance of a subclass of other_class, or if other_class is a module included in the class—in other words, if other_class is in the ancestors list of the object.

- Object#respond_to?(name, include_all = false) the name is a string or symbol representing a method, and respond_to? returns true if the object will actually respond to the method. Only public methods will be included unless the include_all parameter is set to true. Before a false result is returned, Ruby will call a respond_to_missing?(name, include_all = false) if it exists. This method is supposed to match the behavior of method_missing for an object such that an object with method_missing will have respond_to? behavior consistent with how the object actually behaves.

Ruby also offers Object#nil?, which returns true if the object is nil, and Object#itself, which returns the receiver. The itself method can be useful as part of method chains or inside blocks.

Duplication

You can create a shallow copy of an object with Object#dup or Kernel#clone(freeze: nil). By "shallow copy," we mean that a new object is created. The instance variables of the new object are new copies of the instance variables in the original object. But any object that those instance variables reference won't be duplicated; the new copy will continue to point to the existing object. For example, if your object has an array of instances, the array will be copied, but the instances in the array won't. Ruby doesn't have a deep copy mechanism, though Ruby on Rails does add one.

The two methods behave slightly differently. The dup method copies the instance variables representing the state of the object, while clone copies the instance variables plus the singleton class of the object, plus the frozen state of the original object (though the freeze argument will set the frozen state of the clone if the argument is set). One effect of this difference is that a new object created using dup won't get any modules that were added to the original object using extend because those would be in the singleton class. If the new object is created using clone, those module extensions would also be copied.

Library Reference: Enumerators and Containers

In this chapter, we'll take a closer look at Ruby's collection classes, especially those features that are based on the Enumerable module, which is the basis for the functionality of all container classes in Ruby. The goal is to give you more information about what you can do with these classes and also to discuss related functions together so that you can browse and perhaps find a new feature that might help.

This isn't intended to be a complete listing of every class, method, or option. For that, please refer to the official Ruby documentation at https://docs.ruby-lang.org.

In this chapter, when a method is mentioned for the first time, we provide its complete name and signature. The notation Foo.bar indicates a class or module method, while Foo#bar indicates an instance method. Optional arguments are indicated with Ruby syntax and their default value, as in Foo#bar(name, size = 0). Dynamically sized arguments are indicated with splat syntax, as in Foo#bar(*files, **options). Block arguments are indicated with brace syntax and an indication of what the arguments to the block will be, as in Foo#bar { |object| block }. An optional block argument will be surrounded by square brackets, Foo#bar [{block}]. Please note that this description syntax is slightly different than the official documentation, and that in some cases, what the official documentation shows as multiple method signatures, we've chosen to show as one signature with default values. Also, parameter names sometimes differ from the official documentation to make the naming clearer.

Array

Arrays are ordered, integer-indexed collections that may contain any Ruby object. The objects in the array do not need to be of the same type. They can be created using the literal square bracket syntax discussed in Chapter 4, Collections, Blocks, and Iterators, on page 53. The %w delimiter with a space-delimited list can create an array of strings, and %i can similarly create an array of symbols. The Array.new(size, default = nil) method creates a new array with the given size and populated with the default object. The Kernel#Array(object) method converts its argument into an array if the argument isn't already an array.

Arrays implement Array#each [{ |element| block}] and mix in the Enumerable module, so all methods of Enumerable described in Enumerable, on page 568, can be applied to arrays. In this section, we'll focus on the things Array does above and beyond what it includes from Enumerable.

Accessing Array Values

Arrays use square brackets for access, and the square brackets can contain one of four things:

- A single integer, as in array[3]. Zero returns the first element of the array and a positive integer counts forward, so array[1] is the second element. A negative index counts from the end, with -1 being the last element, -2 the next to last, and so on. If the index is outside the actual array, it returns nil.

- Two integers separated by a comma, as in array[2, 3]. In this case, you get the subarray starting at the index represented by the first integer and the length indicated by the second integer. The first integer is interpreted the way it would be if it were passed by itself, meaning that negative numbers count from the end of the array. If the length goes past the end of the array, you just get the end of the array and don't get blank elements or anything like that. If the length is negative, you get nil, and if the first element is exactly the length of the array, you get an empty array.

- A range. In this case, you get the subarray starting at the index represented by the first element of the range and ending at the index represented by the last element of the range. Again, negative numbers are counted from the end of the array, meaning you can get weird things like [0, 1, 2, 3][-3..2], which returns [1, 2] because -3 is the third element from the end, and 2 is farther in the array than that. If the start of the range is outside the array, you get nil. If the end of the range is outside the array, you get elements up until the end of the array. Endless ranges work too, so [...-1] will give you everything but the last element of the array.

- An arithmetic sequence, as returned by Range#step and Numeric#step. In this case, the return value is based on the entries in the sequence.

All the square bracket behavior is aliased as the method Array#slice. The single argument behavior also works as the method Array#at(index). The behavior of both of these methods is to return nil if you completely go outside the bounds of the array.

If you want different behavior, the Array#fetch(index, default_value = nil) or Array#fetch(index) { |index| block } method behaves like at, taking a single index argument, but fetch takes an optional second argument that can either be a positional argument or a block. If the index is out of range, the behavior of fetch depends on which argument is used: either the positional argument is returned or the block is called with the index argument and the block's value is returned.

Common use cases have shortcuts: Array#first(n = 1) and Array#last(n = 1) return the first or last element of the array, respectively. An optional argument allows you to specify more than one return value. If the optional argument is 0, you get an empty array in response. The method Array#values_at(*indexes) takes an arbitrary number of index arguments and returns a new array of the values at those indexes.

The method Array#dig(index, *more_indexes) takes an arbitrary number of arguments, takes the value of the array at the first index, then sends to that result the message dig with the remainder of the arguments, and so on until we run out of arguments. Here's an example:

```
array = [1, 2, 3, 4, [5, 6], 7]
array[2]                                    # => 3
array[-3]                                   # => 4
array[1, 3]                                 # => [2, 3, 4]
array[2..4]                                 # => [3, 4, [5, 6]]
array.fetch(10, 100)                        # => 100
array.fetch(10) { |i| "No value at #{i}" } # => "No value at 10"
array.first                                 # => 1
array.first(3)                              # => [1, 2, 3]
array.last                                  # => 7
array.last(2)                               # => [[5, 6], 7]
array.values_at(2, 4, 6)                    # => [3, [5, 6], nil]
array.dig(-2, 1)                            # => 6
```

Ruby also allows you to search an array by value. The Array#index(object) or Array#index { |element| block } method takes an argument or a block. With an argument, it returns the index of the first element that's equal to the argument or nil if there's no element. With a block, index returns the index of the first element that causes the block to return a truthy value. If you want the last element, the method Array#rindex does the same thing but starts from the end of the array.

Changing Arrays

The Ruby array has lots of options for assigning new values or changing the array. As with strings, the Array#[]= method replaces whatever subarray would be returned by the square bracket lookup with the right side of the assignment, even if the two parts are different lengths. The Array#[]= method has three forms: Array#[]=(index), Array#[]=(range), and Array#[]=(start, length).

Ruby provides multiple methods for adding and removing elements from an array that are specialized based on where in the array the change will be made:

- The beginning of the array—Items can be added to the beginning of the array using the Array#prepend(*objects) method (aliased as unshift), which takes multiple arguments and adds them to the front of the array. The method Array#shift(n = 1) returns the first element of the array and removes it from the array. An optional argument allows you to return and remove an arbitrary number of elements.

- The end of the array—Items can be added to the end of the array with the Array#<<(object) operator, which takes one argument, or the Array#append(*objects) method (aliased as push), which takes multiple arguments and adds them one by one to the end of the array. To retrieve the last element of the array, the method Array#pop(n = 1) returns the last element and removes it from the array. An optional argument allows you to return and remove an arbitrary number of elements.

- An arbitrary location in the array—Items can be added at an arbitrary location with Array#insert(index, *objects). The first argument to insert is the index, and then any additional arguments are added to the array one by one at that position. To remove an element at a specific index, Array#delete_at(index) takes the index, returns the element at that index, and removes it from the array. The method Array#delete(object) [{ |object| block }] takes an object argument and removes that object from the array any time it appears. The optional block argument is the return value if the object isn't found in the array; without a block, it'll return nil.

The combination of push and pop allows you to treat an array as a last-in-first-out stack, whereas the combination of push and shift gives you a first-in-first-out queue.

The Array#rotate(count = 1) method, called with no arguments, returns a new array where the first element of the original array is now the last element of the new array. With a positive integer argument, it performs that amount of rotations. If the argument is greater than the size of the array, the effective final number of elements rotated is argument % array.size. If the argument is negative, the rotation reverses—the end moves to the beginning:

```
x = [1, 2, 3, 4, 5]
x.rotate     # => [2, 3, 4, 5, 1]
x.rotate(2)  # => [3, 4, 5, 1, 2]
x.rotate(-1) # => [5, 1, 2, 3, 4]
x.rotate(-2) # => [4, 5, 1, 2, 3]
```

The Array#flatten(level = nil) method returns a new array that converts the original array to a one-dimensional array. That is, any subarray is replaced by inserting its original elements. The optional level argument determines how many levels are flattened. If the argument is nil or negative, all levels are flattened:

```
[1, [2, 3], 4, [5, 6, [7, 8]]].flatten    # => [1, 2, 3, 4, 5, 6, 7, 8]
[1, [2, 3], 4, [5, 6, [7, 8]]].flatten(1) # => [1, 2, 3, 4, 5, 6, [7, 8]]
```

A convenient way to convert an array to a string is Array#join(delimiter = $,), which takes a string delimiter and returns a string by converting each element of the array using to_s (recursively flattening if the element is itself an array). If no argument is given for the delimiter, the default is an empty string (well, the default is technically the global field separator value in $,):

```
[1, [2, 3], 4, [5, 6, [7, 8]]].join("|") # => "1|2|3|4|5|6|7|8"
```

Ruby offers two ways to access random elements of an array: the Array#sample(n = 1, random: Random) method and the Array#shuffle(random: Random) method. The sample method returns a random member of the array, with an optional argument of how many elements to return. No matter how big the optional argument is, sample won't return the same element twice, so the effective limit on the argument is the size of the array. The duplicate restriction is by index, not value, which means that if the array contains duplicate values, so will the sample and in the same proportion.

The shuffle method returns a new array with the elements in a random order; x.shuffle is effectively equivalent to x.sample(x.size). Both methods take an optional keyword argument random:, which is expected to contain a Random instance or something that responds to rand that's used as the generator for the random ordering.

Unlike Enumerable but like String, Array implements versions of many of its methods that add the ! suffix. In these cases, the original method returns a new array, and the ! version has the same logic but modifies the original array in place. In most of these cases, the return value is the original array if it has been modified or nil if it hasn't.

In general, the ! versions are used for performance reasons. They don't create a new array and so might be faster or use less memory. They tend to be more confusing, so we recommend you use them only when needed.

The following ! methods related to the methods we've discussed in this section or in Enumerable, on page 568, are all defined:

- Array#compact!
- Array#filter! (and also Array#select!)
- Array#flatten!
- Array#map! (and also Array#collect!)
- Array#reject!
- Array#reverse!
- Array#rotate!
- Array#shuffle!
- Array#slice!
- Array#sort!
- Array#sort_by!
- Array#uniq!

Array Math

In addition to the count method, arrays define Array#length and Array#size, which are aliases of each other, take no argument, and just return the raw element count. The Array#empty? method returns true if the size of the array is zero.

Arrays are Comparable and define the Array#<=> operator. Array comparisons in Ruby are managed element by element. So, if a[0] <=> b[0] isn't 0, return that value, otherwise test a[1] <=> b[1] and so on until one array ends or there is a non-equal pair. The first non-equal pair is the result of the comparison. If all the pairs are equal, the shorter array is "less than" the larger array. So, equality for two arrays means that the arrays are the same size and all their elements are equal. Here are some examples:

```
[1, 2, 3] <=> [2, 2, 3]    # => -1
[1, 2, 3] <=> [1, 1, 3]    # => 1
[1, 2, 3] <=> [1, 2, 3, 4] # => -1
[1, 2, 3, 4] <=> [1, 2, 3] # => 1
[1, 2, 3] <=> [1, 2, 3]    # => 0
```

Some mathematical operators are defined for arrays. Adding two arrays returns a new array concatenating the two operands:

```
[1, 2, 3] + [4, 5, 6] # => [1, 2, 3, 4, 5, 6]
```

Subtracting two arrays returns a new array with every element in the first array that isn't in the second array. This is aliased as Array#difference(*other_arrays):

```
[1, 2, 3, 4, 5, 4, 3, 2] - [2, 4] # => [1, 3, 5, 3]
```

You can multiply an array with an integer or string. The integer version returns that many copies of the array concatenated together. The string version returns each element of the array separated by the string—it's the same as join. Multiplying two arrays together to get the cross-product of all combinations of their elements is done with the Array#product(*other_arrays) method:

```
[2, 4, 6] * 3              # => [2, 4, 6, 2, 4, 6, 2, 4, 6]
[2, 4, 6] * ", "           # => "2, 4, 6"
```

```
[2, 4, 6].product(["a", "b"]) # => [[2, "a"], [2, "b"], [4, "a"], [4, "b"], [6,
                              # .. "a"], [6, "b"]]
```

Arrays can also do set operations. The Array#intersection(*other_arrays) method takes an arbitrary number of other arrays as arguments and returns a new array of all the elements that are in the original array and all the arguments. The resulting array will contain no duplicates and will preserve the order of the elements. If there is only one other array being compared, you can use the Array#& operator as a shortcut:

```
[1, 2, 3, 4, 5].intersection([1, 2, 3, 6], [-2, 2, 4]) # => [2]
[1, 2, 3, 4, 5] & [1, 2, 3, 6]                          # => [1, 2, 3]
```

Similarly, the Array#union(*other_arrays) method takes an arbitrary number of array arguments and returns all elements that are in any of the arrays. Duplicates are removed, and the order of the elements remains the same. If there is only one other array, you can use Array#| as a shortcut:

```
[1, 2].union([3, 5, 1], [12, -3, 2]) # => [1, 2, 3, 5, 12, -3]
[1, 2] | [3, 5, 1]                   # => [1, 2, 3, 5]
```

Ruby does combinatorics, too! The Array#combination(n) [{ |element| block }] method takes an integer argument and returns an enumerator that will return every combination of elements in the array that's the size of the argument. If passed a block, it'll yield the block to each combination. The Array#permutation(n) [{ |element| block }] method does the same thing for every permutation—the difference being that the order is significant in each permutation, but not in each combination:

```
[1, 2, 3].combination(2).to_a # => [[1, 2], [1, 3], [2, 3]]
[1, 2, 3].permutation(2).to_a # => [[1, 2], [1, 3], [2, 1], [2, 3], [3, 1], [3,
                              # .. 2]]
```

Both methods have a form—Array#repeated_combination(n) [{ |element| block }] and Array#repeated_permutation(n) [{ |element| block }]—that allows the elements of an array to be repeated as the values in the resulting array.

```
[1, 2, 3].repeated_combination(2).to_a # => [[1, 1], [1, 2], [1, 3], [2, 2], [2,
                                       # .. 3], [3, 3]]
[1, 2, 3].repeated_permutation(2).to_a # => [[1, 1], [1, 2], [1, 3], [2, 1], [2,
                                       # .. 2], [2, 3], [3, 1], [3, 2], [3, 3]]
```

Arrays and Binary Search

Ruby has a binary search feature built into arrays. It isn't quite math, but it's algorithmic, and one day it'll likely save you a great deal of time. The great thing about Ruby's binary search feature is that it's fast and it handles the edge cases that make coding a binary search hard. The tricky thing is that the setup might not be what you expect.

In order for this feature to work, the array has to be sorted, but exactly what Ruby means by that is a little different from a simple numerical sort.

The Array#bsearch { |element| block } method takes a block. The block takes an element and returns a value. One of these two cases must be true of the block and the array:

- The block returns true or false. All elements of the array for which the block returns false must come before any element of the array for which the block returns true. In this case, bsearch returns the first element of the array for which the block returns true, or nil if there aren't any such elements.

- The block returns a numeric value. The numeric values don't have to be in order, but all the elements for which the block returns positive must come first, followed by all the elements for which the block returns zero and then all the elements for which the block returns negative. In this case, bsearch will return an element for which the block returns zero, but it isn't guaranteed to be the first such element. Again, it returns nil if there are no elements for which the block returns zero.

Note that for speed purposes, bsearch doesn't check that the ordering matches the constraints presented (because the time to do so would defeat the purpose of the bsearch method). It's on you to guarantee the precondition.

The related method Array#bsearch_index { |element| block } does the same logic but returns the index of the result rather than the value:

```
sample = (1 .. 10000).to_a
sample.bsearch { |i| i  >= 512 }  # => 512
sample.bsearch { |i| 512 <=> i }  # => 512
```

The first search is an example of the first condition; the second search is an example of the second condition.

Packing Data

Ruby has a mechanism for converting arrays into binary strings and back again, which can be useful for compact custom encoding of data or for decoding known binary data.

On the array side, the Array#pack(template, buffer: nil) method takes a template string as an argument and packs the contents of the receiver into a binary sequence according to the directives in template (see Table 26, Template characters for packed data, on page 568). Directives A, a, and Z may be followed by a count, which gives the width of the resulting field. The remaining directives also may take a count, indicating the number of array elements to convert. If the count is an asterisk (*), all remaining array elements will be converted. The integer directives i, I, l, L, q, Q, s, and S, may be followed by an underscore (_) or bang (!) to use the underlying platform's native size for the specified type; otherwise, they use a platform-independent size. The integer directives i, I, l, L, q, Q, s, and S may be followed by a less than sign to signify little endian or greater than sign for big endian. Spaces are ignored in the template string. Comments starting with # to the next newline or end of string are also ignored.

```
a = [ "a", "b", "c" ]
n = [ 65, 66, 67 ]
a.pack("A3A3A3") # => "a␣␣b␣␣c␣␣"
a.pack("a3a3a3") # => "a\x00\x00b\x00\x00c\x00\x00"
n.pack("ccc")    # => "ABC"
```

See Unpacking Data, on page 531 for the inverse operation, String#unpack.

Directive	Meaning
@	Move to absolute position
A	Sequence of bytes, equivalent to a binary string (space padded, count is width), nil indicates an empty string
a	Sequence of bytes, equivalent to a binary string (null padded, count is width)
B	Bit string (most significant first)
b	Bit string (least significant first)
C	Unsigned byte integer
c	Signed byte integer
D, d	Double-precision float, native format
E	Double-precision float, little-endian byte order
e	Single-precision float, little-endian byte order
F, f	Single-precision float, native format
G	Double-precision float, network (big-endian) byte order
g	Single-precision float, network (big-endian) byte order
H	Hex string (high nibble, or two bytes, first)
h	Hex string (low nibble, or two bytes, first)
I	Platform default sized unsigned integer, native endian°
i	Platform default sized signed integer, native endian°
J	64-bit pointer-width unsigned integer, native endian°
j	64-bit pointer-width signed integer, native endian°
L	32-bit unsigned long integer, native-endian°
l	32-bit signed integer, native-endian°
M	Quoted printable, MIME encoding (see RFC2045)
m	Base64-encoded string; count specifies bytes between newlines, to nearest multiple of three; "m0" suppresses linefeeds
N	32-bit long integer, network (big-endian) byte order
n	16-bit short integer network, (big-endian) byte order
P	Pointer to a structure (fixed-length string)
p	Pointer to a null-terminated string
Q	64-bit unsigned integer, native endian°
q	64-bit signed integer, native-endian°
S	Unsigned 16-bit short integer
s	Signed 16-bit short integer°
U	UTF-8 character
u	UU-encoded string
V	32 bit long integer, little-endian byte order
v	16 bit short integer little-endian byte order
w	BER-compressed integer. The octets of a BER-compressed integer represent an unsigned integer in base 128, most significant digit first, with as few digits as possible. Bit eight (the high bit) is set on each byte except the last (*Self-Describing Binary Data Representation*, MacLeod).
X	Back up a byte
x	Null byte

Directive	Meaning
Z	Same as "a," except a null byte is appended if the * modifier is given
	° *Directive can be modified by appending _ or ! to the directive to use the platform's native integer size, or with > to indicate a big-endian integer or < to indicate a little endian integer.*

Table 26—Template characters for packed data

Enumerable

Ruby's Enumerable module is the basis for the functionality of all container classes in Ruby. The most common container classes in use are Array, Hash, and sometimes Set, but this functionality applies to any other class that defines an each method and includes the Enumerable module.

In this section, we'll be talking about features common to all Enumerables. Other sections in this chapter will talk about how the core implementations of Array, Hash, and Set add their own features.

Iterating

The Enumerable module looks for a method called each as the building block for basically all of its functionality. The Enumerable module doesn't define each; instead, it depends on any class that includes Enumerable to define each. The basic contract of each is that it accepts a block and yields each element of the container in turn to that block. For most Enumerable clients that's straightforward—an Array or Set yields each element in the container in order. Hash#each is slightly different—it yields each key/value pair as a two-element array in order.

Unless otherwise specified, every method in this section that takes a block has an alternate form that doesn't take a block and returns an Enumerator. (We'll talk about that form in Enumerator, on page 577.)

There are a handful of methods that are just slightly different structures of each, starting with Enumerable#reverse_each [{ |element| block }], where foo.reverse_each is equivalent to foo.to_a.reverse.each, but the single-method version is a little faster because it only creates one intermediate structure, not two.

If you want to call each element through the array more than once, you can use Enumerable#cycle(n = nil) [{ |element| block }], which takes one argument and executes that argument's amount of successive calls to each:

```
result = []
arr = ["a", "b", "c"]
arr.cycle(3) { |x| result << x } # => nil
result                           # => ["a", "b", "c", "a", "b", "c", "a", "b",
                                 # .. "c"]
```

If you want to call a block with multiple successive elements of the data structure, you can do that with Enumerable#each_slice(n) [{ |slice| block }] or Enumerable#each_cons(n) [{ |cons| block }]. Both of these methods take an argument that's the number of elements that each block call gets. The methods differ in how they generate the list of successive elements.

The each_slice method yields non-overlapping lists. The second call starts with the element after the end of the first call. The each_cons method yields overlapping lists. The second call starts with the second element of the list, and so on:

```
elements = [1, 2, 3, 4, 5, 6, 7, 8, 9, 10]
puts "each_slice"
elements.each_slice(3) { |x, y, z| puts "#{x} #{y} #{z}" }

puts
puts "each_cons"
elements.each_cons(3) { |x, y, z| puts "#{x} #{y} #{z}" }
```

produces:

```
each_slice
1 2 3
4 5 6
7 8 9
10

each_cons
1 2 3
2 3 4
3 4 5
4 5 6
5 6 7
6 7 8
7 8 9
8 9 10
```

It's quite common to need to hold on to what the index of each successive element is in the block. You can do this using Enumerable#each_with_index [{ |element, index| block }], which takes a two-element block, the second element of which is the index, starting at zero:

```
elements = ["a", "b", "c", "d"]
elements.each_with_index { |x, i| puts "#{x} is at index #{i}" }
```

produces:

```
a is at index 0
b is at index 1
c is at index 2
d is at index 3
```

Accessing

In general, the Enumerable interface isn't used for arbitrary access—subclasses like Array and Hash typically override the square bracket operator to enable this. But a couple of Enumerable methods do allow for access. The simplest is Enumerable#to_a (aliased to Enumerable#entries), which returns an array of the successive elements in the container that you can then treat like any other array.

You can get the first elements of an Enumerable with Enumerable#take(n), which takes one argument and returns that many elements from the start of the array. There's also Enumerable#first(n = 1), which behaves the same except you can call first with no arguments to get the single first element.

On the other side, the Enumerable#drop(n) method takes an argument and returns all the elements after that many arguments from the start of the array:

```
ex = ["a", "b", "c", "d", "e", "f", "g"]
ex.first    # => "a"
```

```
ex.take(2)  # => ["a", "b"]
ex.drop(2)  # => ["c", "d", "e", "f", "g"]
```

Enumerable#drop_while [{ |element| block }]. Each method takes a block and applies the block to successive elements of the array until the block returns a falsey value. At that point, take_while returns all the previously processed elements, while drop_while returns the failing element and all subsequent elements. Here's an example:

```
ex = [2, 4, 8, 16, 32, 64]
ex.take_while { |x| x < 10 } # => [2, 4, 8]
ex.drop_while { |x| x < 10 } # => [16, 32, 64]
```

Map and Reduce

A common pattern when dealing with data in containers is to process the data in two steps: a *map* step, where each element of the container is transformed, and a *reduce* step, where the entire container is combined to a single value. At large scale, the map-reduce pattern is a way to structure big data manipulations such that they can be easily parallelized. At a smaller scale, map-reduce is a clean, manageable way to structure data management. The Ruby Enumerable module provides support for both parts of the pattern.

The Enumerable#map [{ |element| block }] method (which is aliased to collect for historical reasons, namely that Smalltalk calls this function collect) takes a block and applies it to each element in turn, returning a new array with the block's return value for each element:

```
x = [1, 2, 3, 4]
x.map { |element| element * 11 }  # => [11, 22, 33, 44]
```

The Enumerable#reduce(initial = nil, symbol = nil) [{ |accumulator, element| block }] method (which is aliased to inject, again for Smalltalk-related historical reasons) is a way to convert a collection of values into a single value. The reduce method works in a couple of different ways. The most general way takes an optional initial value as an argument and a block.

The block takes two arguments: the first is the accumulator and the second is each element in the list in turn. If the reduce method passed the initial value as an argument, then that value is used as the value of the accumulator on the first call to the block. If not, the first call to the block uses the first element of the list as the accumulator, and the second element of the list as the element argument.

Inside the block, the idea is to do something to update the accumulator with the new value and return the new accumulated value, which is then passed forward to the next iteration of the block:

```
x = [2, 5, 9, 12]
x.reduce { |sum, element| sum + element }                        # => 28

words = %w(major league baseball)
words.reduce("") { |acronym, element| acronym << element[0].upcase } # => "MLB"
```

In the first example, there's no starter value, so the block is called with arguments 2 and 5 from the array, resulting in 7. The block is then called with that 7 as the first argument and the third element of the list—9—as the next argument. The result is 16, and the next call to the block is 16 and 12, so the final result is 28.

In the second example, there is a starter value so the first block is called with "" and "major". The result of that block is "M", so the next call is "M" and league and so on until the final result is "MLB".

The reduce method also has a form that's somewhat unusual in the Ruby libraries. It takes a second argument that's a symbol, where the symbol is a method that takes two arguments. It then uses that method as if it were the body of the block. In other words, the following lines are equivalent:

```
x = [2, 5, 9, 12]
x.reduce { |sum, element| sum + element } # => 28
x.reduce(0, :+)                            # => 28
x.sum                                      # => 28
```

Here, + is a method that takes two arguments, and so the reduce method treats it as the body of a block. So, reduce(0, :+) is an older and reduce-specific way of writing reduce(0, &:+)—the newer version that uses the to_proc trick is more common in current code.

In fact, the sum pattern is so common that Ruby eventually added a Enumerable#sum(initial_value = 0) [{ |element| block }] method, as you can see in the final line. The sum method takes its own optional block, in which case it sums the return values of the block. In other words, the following lines are equivalent:

```
x = %w[these are all words]
x.sum { |word| word.length }        # => 16
x.map { |word| word.length }.sum  # => 16
```

Another common pattern for the reduce behavior is to build up a new container from the data in an existing one, for example, a hash based on the data in an array. Ruby provides Enumerable#each_with_object(object) [{ |*args, accumulator| block }] as a shortcut for this pattern:

```
x = %w[bananas are the funniest fruit]
result = x.each_with_object({}) do |word, result|
  initial = word[0]
  result[initial] ||= []
  result[initial] << word
end
puts result
```

produces:

```
{"b"=>["bananas"], "a"=>["are"], "t"=>["the"], "f"=>["funniest", "fruit"]}
```

The basic idea of each_with_object is the same as reduce but there are two differences: the order of the block arguments is [element, accumulator] rather than [accumulator, element], and what is passed from iteration to iteration is the accumulator itself, rather than the return value of the block. In this case, the two are different, since the return value of the block is the return value of result[initial] << word.

A few kinds of object-creation techniques are common enough to get their own methods. The Enumerable#group_by [{ |element| block }] method is a generalization of what we just did: converting a list to a hash based on the value of some block. So we could write our initializer like so:

```
x = %w[bananas are the funniest fruit]
result = x.group_by { |word| word[0] }
puts result
```

produces:
```
{"b"=>["bananas"], "a"=>["are"], "t"=>["the"], "f"=>["funniest", "fruit"]}
```

In this case, the existence of the resulting hash and the accumulation of the values is handled by group_by.

The Enumerable#partition [{ |element| block }] method takes a block and returns a two-element array of arrays. The first element of the result is an array of all entries in the initial list for which the block returns a truthy value. The second is the entries for which this isn't so:

```
x = [1, 2, 3, 4, 5]
x.partition { |z| z.even? } # => [[2, 4], [1, 3, 5]]
```

The Enumerable#zip(*other_enums) [{ |element| block }] method combines a list with one or more other lists to create a new array of arrays, where each element in the result is made up of the corresponding element of the original list and all the arguments, like this:

```
foo = [1, 2, 3, 4, 5]
bar = ["a", "b", "c", "d", "e"]
foo.zip(bar)  # => [[1, "a"], [2, "b"], [3, "c"], [4, "d"], [5, "e"]]
```

Filtering

Ruby provides a wide variety of ways to find a particular object or objects in a collection along with the related task of filtering a collection based on some arbitrary criteria.

The most basic method is Enumerable#find(proc = nil) [{ |element| block }], aliased as detect. The find method takes a block and returns either the first object for which the block returns a truthy value or nil if there is no such object. The find method takes as an optional argument a proc that's called and its value returned in lieu of returning nil if no matching object is found.

If you'd rather have the index of the object, you can call Enumerable#find_index(object = nil) which can also be Enumerable#find_index() { |element| block } with the same behavior. The object version returns the index of the first object in the list that's == to the argument. The block version returns the index of the first object for which the block returns a truthy value. In both cases, the method returns nil if there's no such object.

Often you may want to return all objects in a list that match a given block, and Enumerator provides that behavior under three different aliases: Enumerator#select [{ |element| block }], aliased as filter and find_all. These are all names for the same behavior, which is to take a block and return every element of the list for which that block returns a truthy value. The inverse is Enumerator#reject [{ |element| block }], which returns every element of the block for which the block returns a falsey value.

The similar method Enumerable#grep(pattern) [{ |element| block }] takes a pattern argument, not a block, and returns every element of the array that is === to the argument. It's inverse, Enumerable#grep_v(pattern) [{ |element| block }] returns every element of the array that's *not* === to the argument. If there's a block, then each matching element that would be returned by the method is passed to the block and the return value of the block is used instead.

```
list = [1, 1, 2, 3, 5, 8, 13, 21]
list.find { |i| i.even? }                 # => 2
list.find(proc { "nope" }) { |i| i.zero? } # => "nope"

list.find_index { |i| i.even? }           # => 2
list.find_index(5)                        # => 4
```

```
list.select { |i| i.even? }                 # => [2, 8]
list.reject { |i| i.even? }                 # => [1, 1, 3, 5, 13, 21]

list.grep(4..10)                            # => [5, 8]
list.grep_v(4..10)                          # => [1, 1, 2, 3, 13, 21]

list.grep(4..10) { |x| 10 ** x }            # => [100000, 100000000]
```

Two common filter patterns have their own methods: Enumerable#compact and Enumerable#uniq. The compact method removes all nil elements from an array and is particularly useful for cleaning up arrays before passing them forward to map or sum or something else that might break if passed a nil.

The uniq method removes duplicate elements (based on eql?). Normally uniq is based on the actual elements of a collection, but with a block, it'll compare values based on the return value of the block for each element:

```
[1, 2, nil, 3, nil, 4, 5].compact # => [1, 2, 3, 4, 5]
[1, 2, 3, 2, 3, 1].uniq           # => [1, 2, 3]
```

You might want to split an enumerable into sub-lists based on some criteria, similar to the way split works for strings. For Enumerable, you can do this with Enumerable#slice_after(pattern = nil) [{ |element| block }], Enumerable#slice_before(pattern = nil) [{ |element| block }], and Enumerable#slice_when(pattern = nil) [{ |element| block }]. All three of these methods return Enumerator instances rather than arrays.

The slice_after method takes a pattern or a block. It tests each element of the collection in turn. If the element is either === to the argument or causes the block to return a truthy value, then that element is the end of a slice and a new slice begins with the next element.

The slice_before method performs the same test but if an element matches, then it ends the slice before that element and the element is the first element of the next slice.

If those aren't flexible enough, the slice_when method takes a block with two arguments, applies it to overlapping pairs of the list in turn, and splits the slice between the two elements if the block returns true. For example:

```
list = [1, 1, 2, 3, 5, 8, 13, 21]
list.slice_after { |i| i.even? }.to_a  # => [[1, 1, 2], [3, 5, 8], [13, 21]]
list.slice_before { |i| i.even? }.to_a # => [[1, 1], [2, 3, 5], [8, 13, 21]]

list = [18, 17, 3, 11, 3, 10]
list.slice_when { |a, b| a > b }.to_a  # => [[18], [17], [3, 11], [3, 10]]
```

Querying

The most basic query about a collection is "how big is it?" The Ruby method here is Enumerable#count [{ |element| block }], which without a block returns the size of the collection. With a block argument, it returns the number of elements in the collection for which the block returns a truthy value. With a positional argument, it returns the count of elements that are equal to that argument.

The Enumerable#tally(hash = nil) method is a generalization of count. It returns a Hash whose keys are elements in the list and whose values are the count of how many times the element appears in the list. If the optional argument is passed in, that's the starting point of the tally, and new items are added to that.

```
sample = [1, 2, 3, 2, 3, 1, 3, 5]
sample.count                 # => 8
sample.count(2)              # => 2
sample.count { |x| x.even? } # => 2
sample.tally                 # => {1=>2, 2=>2, 3=>3, 5=>1}
```

The Enumerable#include?(object) method (aliased as member?) takes an argument and returns true if there is an element in the collection that's equal to that argument.

A series of methods returns true or false based on how many times a block or pattern is matched by the collection. All of these methods behave the same way: they take a block or a positional argument. With a positional argument, the method counts how many elements of the list are === to that argument. With a block, the method counts how many elements of the list cause the block to return true. Given that count, these are the results:

- Enumerable#none? returns true if and only if the count is zero.
- Enumerable#one? returns true if and only if the count is one.
- Enumerable#any? returns true if the count is one or more.
- Enumerable#all? returns true if the count is the size of the list (all elements of the list match).

Sorting and Comparing

When you create a new object, you often want to be able to sort a list of those objects or compare two objects along some default criteria.

The most general feature in Ruby for sorting is the Enumerable#sort [{ |x, y| block }] method. The receiver of sort is the item to be sorted, which can be any object that includes the Enumerable module. For our purposes, the most important class that can respond to sort is Array.

If sort is called without a block, it calls <=> on each element, which means the following two lines are identical:

```
list_of_users.sort { |a, b| a <=> b }
list_of_users.sort
```

The sort method can also take a block. The block takes two elements and returns the following:

- A positive integer if the first argument is, for the purposes of the sort, greater than the second argument.

- A negative integer if the first argument is less than the second argument.

- Zero if the two elements are tied.

Assuming the objects have a numeric height element, both of these lines will return identical sorts:

```
list_of_users.sort { |a, b| a.height <=> b.height }
list_of_users.sort { |a, b| a.height - b.height }
```

The first line takes advantage of the <=> operator's behavior, matching the expected behavior of the block, while the second line takes advantage of just plain subtraction having the same result. (We'd consider the first line to be clearer in most contexts.)

Sorting elements in an array based on an attribute of each element is common enough that Ruby provides Enumerable#sort_by [{ |element| block }] as a shortcut. The sort_by method takes a block with a single argument and uses that argument to sort the list.

Given all the ways in Ruby to write a one-expression block, the following are all equivalent:

```
list_of_users.sort { |a, b| a.height <=> b.height }
list_of_users.sort_by { |x| x.height }
list_of_users.sort_by { _1.height }
list_of_users.sort_by(&:height)
```

You'll likely see the last form most frequently for simple cases like this, but we kind of hope the next to last form catches on.

If you're just interested in the upper or lowermost elements rather than the entire sorted list, Ruby has you covered with Enumerable#min(n = 1) [{ |a, b| block }] and Enumerable#max(n = 1) [{ |a, b| block }] and their related methods Enumerable#min_by(n = 1) [{ |element| block }] and Enumerable#max_by(n = 1) [{ |element| block }].

When called without an argument, these methods treat the array exactly like sort and sort_by, which is to say that min and max use <=> or take a two-argument block, while min_by and max_by take a one-argument block. The difference is the return value. The min methods return the lowest element of the list, and the max methods return the highest element of the list.

If you want more than one element returned, you can pass the number of elements you want to the method and you'll receive an array of results rather than a single scalar result. The method Enumerable#minmax [{ |a, b| block }] returns a two-element array with the lowest and highest elements of the list using the same logic as sort. The related Enumerable#minmax_by [{ |element| block }] uses the same logic as sort_by. Here are some examples:

```
[4, 11, 2, 7]          # => [4, 11, 2, 7]
[4, 11, 2, 7].min      # => 2
[4, 11, 2, 7].max      # => 11
[4, 11, 2, 7].min(2)   # => [2, 4]
[4, 11, 2, 7].max(2)   # => [11, 7]
[4, 11, 2, 7].minmax   # => [2, 11]

["one", "three", "eleven", "four"].min_by(&:length)     # => "one"
["one", "three", "eleven", "four"].max_by(&:length)     # => "eleven"
["one", "three", "eleven", "four"].min_by(2, &:length)  # => ["one", "four"]
["one", "three", "eleven", "four"].max_by(2, &:length)  # => ["eleven", "three"]
["one", "three", "eleven", "four"].minmax_by(&:length)  # => ["one", "eleven"]
```

Other Enumerables

Several other classes in Ruby core or the Ruby standard library respond to each and include Enumerable in a useful way. Here's a quick tour:

- ARGF is the combination of all files passed to a command-line tool. ARGF#each iterates over each line in the concatenated set of files—not each file, but each line in the files one by one.

- CSV implements each to iterate over each parsed row in the CSV file.

- Dir implements each for the files in the directory, passing each filename to the block one by one.

- ENV, the repository for environment variables at runtime, behaves like a hash, and each will pass each successive environment variable name and value as a pair.

- IO, the generic input/output class implements each to go line by line through the item being read. Its subclasses, including File and StringIO behave similarly.

- Net::HTTPHeader contains the values in the header of an HTTP request, and each takes a block for each entry in the headers as a key/value pair.

- Range responds to each as an array would, calling it once for every element inside the range.

- Struct responds to each as a hash would, calling the block once for each attribute in the struct as a key/value pair.

Enumerator

Nearly every Enumerable method that takes a block argument can also be called without a block, in which case the method returns an Enumerator. (There are a few subclasses of Enumerator that you wouldn't create by hand but which implement some specialized logic.) In addition to those Enumerable methods, you can create an enumerator in a few other ways.

Creating Enumerators

Any object can be converted into an Enumerator with the Object#to_enum(method = :each, *args) method (aliased as enum_for). The first argument to to_enum is a symbol that's the name of a method that converts the object to something enumerable. Any further arguments to to_enum are passed to the method named in the first argument. You can then treat that enumerator like any other enumerator. Here's an example:

```
x = "a string with lots of words"
enum = x.to_enum(:split)
enum.with_index.map { |word, index| [word.upcase, index] }   # => [["A", 0],
                                                              # .. ["STRING", 1],
                                                              # .. ["WITH", 2],
                                                              # .. ["LOTS", 3],
                                                              # .. ["OF", 4],
                                                              # .. ["WORDS", 5]]
```

You can create an infinite enumerator using the Enumerator#produce(initial_value = nil) [{ |previous_value| block}] method, which takes an optional initial value as an argument and a block. The block takes an argument, and each time the enumerator is invoked, the previous block return value is passed to the block and a new value is returned. This is most useful when combined with Enumerable#lazy or with some kind of find method. This uses map, select, and take to return the first five even triangular numbers:

```
triangular_numbers = Enumerator.produce([1, 2]) do |number, count|
  [number + count, count + 1]
end

triangular_numbers.lazy.map { _1.first }.select(&:even?).take(5).to_a # => [6,
                                                                      # .. 10,
                                                                      # .. 28,
                                                                      # .. 36,
                                                                      # .. 66]
```

An enumerator can be created for a series of enumerables with the Enumerator#product(*enumerables) method, which takes one or more enumerable objects as arguments and returns a new Enumerator that's made up of the Cartesian product of all the arguments:

```
product = Enumerator.product("a".."c", -1..1, [:x, :y])
product.to_a # => [["a", -1, :x], ["a", -1, :y], ["a", 0, :x], ["a", 0, :y],
             # .. ["a", 1, :x], ["a", 1, :y], ["b", -1, :x], ["b", -1, :y], ["b",
             # .. 0, :x], ["b", 0, :y], ["b", 1, :x], ["b", 1, :y], ["c", -1,
             # .. :x], ["c", -1, :y], ["c", 0, :x], ["c", 0, :y], ["c", 1, :x],
             # .. ["c", 1, :y]]
```

Using Enumerators

There are a few things you can do with an enumerator. You can cause it to move through its values externally by calling Enumerator#next. This will move through any chained logic but isn't associated with a block, so it won't invoke a block. The Enumerator#rewind method puts the enumerator back to the beginning of the sequence.

You can also use Enumerator#peek to look at the next value in the enumerator without moving the iterator forward—successive calls to peek will return the same object:

```
x = [1, 2, 3].to_enum.with_index
x.next    # => [1, 0]
x.next    # => [2, 1]
x.peek    # => [3, 2]
x.peek    # => [3, 2]
x.rewind  # => #<Enumerator: #<Enumerator: [1, 2, 3]:each>:with_index>
x.next    # => [1, 0]
```

As shown in this example, enumerators can be chained together. The Enumerator#with_index(offset = 0) [{ |*arguments, index| block}] method chains the iterator to a new iterator that includes the index of each object as a second argument to the block. The related method Enumerator#with_object(object) [{ |*arguments| block}] takes an object (usually a container like an array or a hash) and creates a new enumerator that passes that object as a second argument.

You can also use Enumerator#+ to add another enumerable to the end of the current enumerator, appending those values to the end of what's already there.

Using Enumerator#each(*appending_args) [{ |element| block}] with a block causes the entire enumerator to be invoked. The each method also takes arguments that might have needed to be passed to earlier parts of the enumerator. In this case, the string is converted to an enumerator based on the split method, but the each call passes the argument that determines what the string is split on:

```
x = "a string of words".to_enum(:split)
x.each("o").to_a  # => ["a string ", "f w", "rds"]
```

Lazy Enumerators

A lazy enumerator is formed by calling the method Enumerable#lazy. Usually, it's the beginning of a chain of enumerator methods, as shown in the produce example earlier. Once lazy is part of the method chain, it changes the behavior of the entire chain so that values are passed through the chain one at a time, rather than all at once.

For example, if you have a chain of calls like x.map(&:foo).select(&:bar).map(&:baz).take(5), the entire array is mapped, then filtered, and then mapped again, and then the first five elements are retrieved. If the original object x is long or if it's infinite, this chain can be quite slow, especially because we only want five elements. By making it lazy, as in x.lazy.map(&:foo).select(&:bar).map(&:baz).take(5), the behavior changes. The first element of x is mapped, then filtered through select, and, if it passes, mapped through baz and added to the list for take. This continues one by one only until the take(5) is completed, meaning that if x is long, far fewer elements have been processed.

You can un-lazy an enumerator chain by calling eager, which allows you to convert the lazy enumerator to something that can be returned from a method or used as an argument to a method that expects an enumerator.

Hash

The Hash, which associates arbitrary indexes to arbitrary values, is the most flexible basic class in Ruby. Although Hash does implement each and Enumerable, hashes behave slightly differently than arrays and sets.

Creating Hashes

Hashes have a literal syntax that uses curly braces to associate keys with values. The original form of separating keys from values uses the => symbol, often called a *hash rocket*:

```
hash = {"a" => 1, "b" => 2, "c" => 3}
```

In general, you want the hash keys to be immutable values, and symbols are commonly used. If the key is a symbol, then you can use a colon to separate the key from a value. The colon will also convert strings to symbols. The keys in this literal are :a, :b, and :c, all symbols:

```
hash = {a: 1, "b": 2, c: 3}
```

You can use both styles in a single hash literal, but if you use the colon style, the key must be a string or a bare word. Anything else will result in a syntax error.

If the key is a symbol, and the symbol has a meaning in the current context, then you can use just the key and the value will be assumed to be the local value. So, the following two hashes are equivalent:

```
a = 1
b = 2
c = 3
{a: a, b: b, c: c}
{a:, b:, c:}
```

The class Hash also responds to [] to create new hashes, which is a less frequently used alternative to the literal syntax, Hash[a: 1, b: 2]. The argument can be key/value pairs, another hash, a list of two-element arrays, or just a list of arguments, in which case Ruby assumes that the keys and values alternate.

The method Hash.new(default_value = nil) [{ |hash, key| block}] will create an empty hash. This method takes an optional argument that acts as the default value for keys that aren't in the hash. In this usage, the default value isn't duplicated each time it's used, so you should use an immutable value, like a scalar, and not a mutable value, like an empty array. So, this won't do what you want:

```
sample = Hash.new([])
sample[:a] << "alpha" # => ["alpha"]
sample[:b] << "beta"  # => ["alpha", "beta"]
sample[:a]            # => ["alpha", "beta"]
sample[:b]            # => ["alpha", "beta"]
```

The idea here is to bypass having to create an array for each new key and just use a default, but in this version, only one array is used for the default, so adding values to it in different keys only updates the single default value.

Alternatively, you can pass a block, which is invoked when a key that's not in the hash is requested. The block takes two arguments—the hash and the new key—and returns a default value for the key. This enables you to create a new default object for each key:

```
sample = Hash.new { |hash, key| hash[key] = [] }
sample[:a] << "alpha" # => ["alpha"]
sample[:b] << "beta"  # => ["beta"]
sample[:a]            # => ["alpha"]
sample[:b]            # => ["beta"]
```

Hash Values

Hash values are accessed using the Hash#[] method:

```
hash = {a: 1, "b": 2, c: 3}
hash[:a]  # => 1
```

The value associated with the key is returned. Ruby uses eql? (or ==) to determine the key. Symbol keys aren't matched by string values (although you may see this in Ruby on Rails, which has a popular extension to allow string and symbol keys to overlap).

If there's no matching key and the hash has a default value, Ruby will return the default. If there's no matching key and the hash has a default block, Ruby will invoke the block and return the resulting value. If the hash has no defaults, Ruby will return nil.

Ruby does have a way to retrieve values with different semantics. The Hash#fetch(key, default_value = nil) [{ |key| block }] method takes a key and an optional default. The default is either a second positional argument or a block that takes a single argument, the key. If fetch is called with a key that isn't in the hash, it returns the default. If there's no default, fetch raises a KeyError.

So, we could write our earlier example using fetch like this:

```
sample = {}
sample[:a] = sample.fetch(:a, []) << "alpha"
sample[:b] = sample.fetch(:b, []) << "beta"
sample[:a] # => ["alpha"]
sample[:b] # => ["beta"]
```

You can change the default value with the setter method Hash#default=(value), which takes any arbitrary value on the right side and makes it the new default for missing keys. Similarly, the Hash#default_proc=(proc) method takes a proc and makes it the new default. As with

Hash.new the proc takes two arguments, the receiving hash, and the key being sought. There are getters, Hash#default and Hash#default_proc that return the current value of the defaults.

If you want to retrieve values from multiple keys at the same time, the Hash#values_at(*keys) method takes multiple keys and returns an array of the values at those keys, in order, returning nil or the default value for keys that don't exist. The Hash#fetch_values(*keys) [{ |key| block }] method does the same thing, except it takes a block that's invoked for missing keys, and if there's no block, it raises a KeyError:

```
hash = {a: 1, b: 2, c: 3, d: 4}
hash.values_at(:b, :g, :d)                    # => [2, nil, 4]
hash.fetch_values(:b, :g, :d) { |key| key.to_s } # => [2, "g", 4]
```

Hashes also respond to Hash#dig(key, *identifiers) by looking up the first argument in the hash and then sending to that result the message dig with the remainder of the arguments, and so on until we run out of arguments.

If for some reason you want the key value pair, the Hash#assoc(key) method takes a key and returns the matching key/value pair as a two-element array.

If you have the value and want the matching key, the Hash#key(value) method returns the first key in the hash that has that value. The Hash#rassoc(value) method gives you the entire key/value pair as an array (we'll cover hash ordering in Iterating Hashes, on page 582, and some boolean queries for hashes in Querying a Hash, on page 582):

```
hash = {a: 1, b: 2, c: 3, d: 4}
hash.assoc(:b) # => [:b, 2]
hash.key(2)    # => :b
hash.rassoc(2) # => [:b, 2]
```

Setting Values

You set a value in a hash using the Hash#[]= method, which is aliased as the method Hash#store(key, value). When you call []=, if the key in the brackets exists in the hash, the value associated with that key is updated. If the key doesn't exist in the hash, it's added with the value, and it's appended to the end of the hash for ordering purposes.

To completely remove a key from the hash, the Hash#delete(key) [{ |key| block }] method takes the key. If the key is in the hash, it removes the key and returns the associated value, otherwise it returns nil. An optional block is called with the key if the key isn't in the hash, and that value is returned:

```
hash = {a: 1, b: 2, c: 3, d: 4}
hash[:b] = 700
hash[:e] = 5
hash.delete(:c) # => 3
hash            # => {:a=>1, :b=>700, :d=>4, :e=>5}
```

A related method, Hash#delete_if [{ |key, value| block }], takes a block with a key and a value and removes every element from the hash for which the block returns true:

```
hash = {a: 1, b: 2, c: 3, d: 4}
hash.delete_if { |key, value| value.even? } # => {:a=>1, :c=>3}
hash                                          # => {:a=>1, :c=>3}
```

If you want to combine two or more hashes, the Hash#merge(*other_hashes) [{key, old_value, new_value}] method is likely what you want. merge takes one or more hashes as arguments and an optional block. It returns a new hash, starting with the original receiving hash, and adds each key value pair from the arguments one by one. If it encounters a key that already exists in the hash and there's no block argument, the new value overwrites the old. If there's a block argument, then the block takes three arguments—the key, the existing value, and the new value—and the result of the block is added to the hash.

The Hash#merge!(*other_hashes) [{key, old_value, new_value}] (also aliased as update) behaves the same except that it changes the receiving hash in place, and also returns that hash:

```
hash_1 = {a: 1, b: 2, c: 3}
hash_2 = {c: 5, d: 4, e: 6}
hash_1.merge(hash_2)                          # => {:a=>1, :b=>2, :c=>5,
                                              # .. :d=>4, :e=>6}
hash_1.merge(hash_2) { |key, old, new| old + new } # => {:a=>1, :b=>2, :c=>8,
                                              # .. :d=>4, :e=>6}
```

Querying a Hash

There are several ways to query a hash for information. The Hash#length method, aliased as size, returns the number of key/value pairs in the hash. The Hash#empty? method returns true if there are no key/value pairs in the hash.

If you want to find out if a particular key is in the hash, you'd use Hash#key?(key), which is aliased as has_key?, include?, or member?, but key? is the most common. It takes one argument and returns true if that argument is in the list of keys.

Going the other way, if you want to know whether a hash has a particular value no matter what the key, you'd use the Hash#value?(value) method, aliased as has_value?.

Hashes also have a separate version of Hash#any?(key_value-array) [{ |key, value| block }]. The version that doesn't take a block, takes a two-element array (that is, a key and a value) and returns true if that key value pair is in the hash.

Iterating Hashes

When iterating over hashes in Ruby, it's important to remember that the order of the hash is consistent and based on the order in which the key/value pairs were added to the hash. So, the first element to be added will be first any time you iterate over the hash using any of the hash iteration methods, the second element added will be second, and so on.

Hashes implement Hash#each [{ |key, value| block }] slightly differently than arrays in that the block argument to each takes as an argument a two-element array: the key and the value. As the method signature shows, you can dereference the array to have it look like two arguments are being passed to the block. Then the block is called on each key/value pair in turn. This method is also aliased as Hash#each_pair.

You can iterate with one-argument blocks using Hash#each_key [{ |key| block }], which iterates over all the keys in order, or Hash#each_value [{ |value| block}], which iterates over all the values in order. Or you can just get an array of all the keys in order with Hash#keys or all the values in order with Hash#values.

Hashes respond to the same select and reject methods as other classes that include Enumerable, but as with each, the block takes an array with two elements: the key and the value. Also, the Hash version returns a new Hash. Hashes also define select! and reject!, which modify the original argument in place rather than returning a new hash.

Comparing Hashes

Two hashes are equal (Hash#==) if they have the same keys and the value at each key is equal. The order of the keys doesn't matter; it only matters that the value matches.

Comparing two hashes is somewhat similar to comparing sets. The Hash class defines Hash#< as true if the left side is a proper subset of the right, meaning that every key/value pair on the left side must be on the right side, and the right side has more pairs. The Hash#<= method is a regular subset method, so the two hashes can be equal. The Hash#> and Hash#>= methods work for proper superset and superset.

Hashes don't implement their own implementation of <=>. Instead, they take the parent class (Object) implementation. This appears to return true if the hashes are equal and nil otherwise, which is to say that it's probably not a useful way to compare hashes.

Modifying Hashes

There are several methods that work to modify hashes. The Hash#clear method removes all key/value pairs from the hash. The Hash#compact method returns a new hash removing all pairs where the value is nil. The Hash#compact! method has the same behavior but changes the original argument in place.

Hashes also respond to Hash#shift, which removes and returns the first key/value pair.

If you want a subset of a hash, you can use the Hash#slice(*keys) method, which takes an arbitrary number of arguments and returns a new hash containing only key/value pairs whose keys are in the list of arguments. The inverse is Hash#except(*keys), which returns a new hash for all the key/value pairs whose keys aren't in the list of arguments.

Converting Hashes

Hashes can be converted or transformed in a variety of ways. The Hash#to_a method converts a hash to an array of two-element [key, value] arrays. If you want a single-dimensional array, you can use Hash#flatten(level = 1), which is equivalent to hash.to_a.flatten(level). By default, Hash#flatten doesn't recursively flatten values that happen to be arrays—you can do that with an optional argument that specifies how many levels of sub-array values are flattened. The default is 1 level of array flattening, and a negative argument flattens all values no matter how deeply nested they are.

The Hash#to_s method converts to a string, and the only reason to mention it here is that the string uses key => value syntax no matter which syntax was used to create the hash.

The Hash#invert method creates a new hash where all values are keys and all keys are values. If values are shared across multiple keys, the keys that are later in the hash sequence will replace the earlier keys.

A fun conversion is to_proc. The Hash#to_proc method returns a Proc that takes arguments and uses those arguments as though they were keys to the hash, returning the associated value.

A side effect of the existence of to_proc means that the same & trick that we often use for symbols can also be used for hashes:

```
hash = {a: 1, b: 2, c: 3}
hash.to_a                   # => [[:a, 1], [:b, 2], [:c, 3]]
hash.flatten                # => [:a, 1, :b, 2, :c, 3]
hash.to_s                   # => "{:a=>1, :b=>2, :c=>3}"
hash.invert                 # => {1=>:a, 2=>:b, 3=>:c}
hash_proc = hash.to_proc
hash_proc.call(:a)          # => 1
[:a, :b, :c].map(&hash) # => [1, 2, 3]
```

The Hash#transform_keys(hash = nil) [{ |key| block}] and Hash#transform_values [{ |value| block }] methods are good alternatives to map if you only want to change part of the hash. Each takes a block, and transform_keys returns a new hash where each key/value pair has the same value as the original, but the key is the result of the block. If the optional hash argument is passed, keys are looked up there before trying the block. The transform_values method is similar, but each resulting pair has the same key, and the value is the result of the block. Both methods have ! forms, transform_keys! and transform_values!, which modify the original hash in place rather than return a new hash:

```
hash = {a: 1, b: 2, c: 3}
hash.transform_keys { |key| key.upcase }      # => {:A=>1, :B=>2, :C=>3}
hash.transform_values { |value| value ** 3 } # => {:a=>1, :b=>8, :c=>27}
```

Set

A Ruby Set is somewhere between an Array and a Hash—it's a collection of unique items. The Set class is a subclass of Object, and it defines each and includes Enumerable, so all Enumerable methods described in this chapter apply to sets. The elements of a Set are ordered the way that Hash keys are ordered—they preserve the sequence in which the elements were added to the Set. In other words, iterating over a set multiple times will always result in the same ordering, but you can't access arbitrary elements of the set via an index.

To use Set in versions of Ruby before 3.2, you need to explicitly call require "set".

Creating Sets

There are several ways to create a Set. The Enumerable class defines Enumerable#to_set, which converts the collection into a set, removing duplicates along the way. The Set class has a unique API, where Set.new(enumerable = nil) [{ |element| block }] takes an Enumerable and converts it to a set. If you have just a bunch of objects and you want to make a set out of them, well the Set class implements []:

```
Set.new([1, 2, 3]) # => #<Set: {1, 2, 3}>
Set[1, 2, 3]        # => #<Set: {1, 2, 3}>
```

If you pass a value to Set.new that isn't an Enumerable, you'll get an ArgumentError. To be honest, it takes a little getting used to the second form.

Set elements are unique, and the unique value is based on Object#hash, which under normal circumstances is the same as eql?. (It's the same logic that Hash uses for unique keys.) You can change that behavior for an individual set with the compare_by_identity method, which changes the set to compare elements based on their internal object ID.

Modifying Sets

You can add a single object to a Set with the Set#add(object) method, which is also aliased as <<. If you want to add more than one item, you use Set#merge(*enumerables), which takes one or more Enumerable objects as arguments and adds their elements one by one to the Set. The Set#add?(object) method takes one argument. If that argument isn't in the set, the argument is added and the set is returned. If the argument is already in the set, nothing happens and the method returns nil. This is a deviation from the idiomatic Ruby practice of returning literal true or false from a question mark method.

To remove an object from a set, the Set#delete(object) method removes the object from the set and returns the updated set. The similar method Set#delete?(object) removes the object and returns the set if the object is in the set, otherwise it does nothing and returns nil. If you want to remove every element in an enumerable from the set, you use the subtract method. This method is different from the arithmetic methods we'll see in a bit because it changes the set in place. The clear method empties the set entirely.

For conditional deletion, sets define Set#delete_if { |object| block }, which takes a block and deletes the items for which the block returns a truthy value, and the inverse Set#keep_if { |object| block }, which takes a block and deletes the items for which the block returns a falsey value. (Sets also define Set#select! { |object| block }, which is equivalent to keep_if, and Set#reject! { |object| block }, which is equivalent to delete_if, except that the bang methods return nil if the set doesn't change.)

Comparing Sets

Set comparison is a little bit different than comparisons of other enumerable types. Two sets are Set#eql?(other) or Set#==(other) if they contain the same elements and order doesn't matter. A set is Set#===(other) to an object if the object is in the set, making sets useful in case statements. The === operator is aliased as both member? and include?. Sets also define Set#length as the number of elements in the set, and Set#empty? as true if the set has 0 elements.

Sets implement Comparable and the Set#<=> operator, but the implementation may not be quite what you'd expect. The <=> operator mimics the behavior of eql?, meaning that it returns 0 if the two sets have the same elements. The greater then/less than behavior is based only on the logical relationship between the two sets, not the values of the elements. If the left set is a proper subset of the right set, then <=> returns -1. If the right set is a proper subset of the left set, then <=> returns 1. If the two sets don't have a subset/superset relationship, meaning that each set has elements that aren't in the other set, then <=> returns nil.

Basically, < is aliased as proper_subset? and <= is aliased as subset?, > is proper_superset?, and >= is superset?. Sets also define Set#disjoint?(other_set), which is true if the sets have no common element, and Set#intersect?(other), which is true if the sets have at least one common element.

```
a = Set[1, 2, 3]
b = Set[3, 2, 1]
c = Set[2, 1]
d = Set[1, 2, 3, 4]
e = Set[2, 3, 4, 5]

a == b          # => true
b === 3         # => true
b === "3"       # => false
c <=> b         # => -1
```

```
d <=> c              # => 1
d < c                # => false
d > c                # => true
d <=> e              # => nil
d.disjoint?(e)       # => false
d.intersect?(e)      # => true
```

Set Operations

Sets respond to arithmetic operators similar to the way arrays do:

- Set union returns a new set containing all elements from either operand, with no duplicates. The method is Set#union(other), and it's aliased as + and | .

- Set intersection returns a new set containing all elements that are in both operands. The method is Set#intersection(other), and it's aliased as & .

- Set difference returns a new set with elements in the left operand that aren't in the right operand. The method is Set#difference(other), and it's aliased as - .

- Set xor returns a new set containing all the elements that are in exactly one of the two operands, and the operator is Set#^ .

- You can split a set into subsets based on various criteria with the Set#classify { |element| block } method, which takes a block and returns a hash. The keys of the hash are unique values of the block and the value of the hash is every element of the set that returns the same value.

```
require "set"
d = Set[1, 2, 3, 4]
e = Set[2, 3, 4, 5]
d | e                    # => #<Set: {1, 2, 3, 4, 5}>
d.union(e)               # => #<Set: {1, 2, 3, 4, 5}>
d & e                    # => #<Set: {2, 3, 4}>
d.intersection(e)        # => #<Set: {2, 3, 4}>
d.difference(e)          # => #<Set: {1}>
d - e                    # => #<Set: {1}>
d ^ e                    # => #<Set: {5, 1}>
d.classify { |x| x.even? } # => {false=>#<Set: {1, 3}>, true=>#<Set: {2, 4}>}
```

## CHAPTER 29

Library Reference: Input, Output, Files, and Formats

In this chapter, we'll take a closer look at Ruby's input and output (I/O) classes, including reading and writing from files, manipulating files, and managing file formats. We'll investigate their API and functionality in somewhat more detail than we did in Part I of this book. The goal of this chapter is to give you more information about what you can do with these classes and also to discuss related functions together so that you can browse and perhaps find a new feature that might help.

This isn't intended to be a complete listing of every class, method, or option. For that, please refer to the official Ruby documentation at https://docs.ruby-lang.org.

In this chapter, when a method is mentioned for the first time, we provide its complete name and signature. The notation Foo.bar indicates a class or module method, while Foo#bar indicates an instance method. Optional arguments are indicated with Ruby syntax and their default value, as in Foo#bar(name, size = 0). Dynamically sized arguments are indicated with splat syntax, as in Foo#bar(*files, **options). Block arguments are indicated with brace syntax and an indication of what the arguments to the block will be, as in Foo#bar { |object| block }. An optional block argument will be surrounded by square brackets, Foo#bar [{block}]. Please note that this description syntax is slightly different than the official documentation, and that in some cases, what the official documentation shows as multiple method signatures, we've chosen to show as one signature with default values. Also, parameter names sometimes differ from the official documentation to make the naming clearer.

CSV

Comma-separated data files are often used to transfer tabular information, especially for importing and exporting spreadsheet and database information. Ruby's current CSV library is based on James Edward Gray II's FasterCSV gem. The CSV object has possibly the best official documentation in the entire Ruby library, and it goes beyond what's discussed here.

Ruby's CSV library deals with arrays (corresponding to the rows in the CSV file) and strings (corresponding to the elements in a row). If an element in a row is missing, it'll be represented as nil in Ruby.

The generic CSV parsing method is CSV.parse(string_or_io, headers: nil, **options) [{|row|}] and takes an optional block. The main argument is either a string or an IO object and potentially a File, but not a filename. A string object is converted to StringIO (see StringIO, on page 612).

If there is no block and no headers option, the CSV file is converted to an array of arrays and returned. If there is a block and no headers option, the block is called once with the data from each row parsed into an array.

If the headers option is set to an array of strings and there is no block, then the method returns the data as a CSV::Table, which is a data structure that you can treat as an array of arrays or an array of hashes. So, you can reference an item by its header name or its position in the row. If the headers option is set to true, then the header names will be inferred from the first row of the CSV data. With a block, each row is converted to a CSV::Row object and passed to the block.

The remaining options allow you to control the parsing, including row_sep, col_sep, and quote_char.

Often you'll have a filename for your object and won't need to create a File object. The method CSV.read(source, headers: nil, **options) opens the source argument to create an IO object and passes it to CSV.parse in one step returning an array of arrays or a CSV::Table. The method CSV.foreach(source, mode = "r", **options) {block} takes a block and returns each row to the block as an array or CSV::Row depending on whether the headers: option is set.

The files used in these examples are as follows:

```
sl_csv/csvfile.csv
12,eggs,2.89,
2,"shirt, blue",21.45,special
1,"""Hello Kitty"" bag",13.99
```

```
sl_csv/csvfile_with_header.csv
Count,Description,Price
12,eggs,2.89,
2,"shirt, blue",21.45,special
1,"""Hello Kitty"" bag",13.99
```

This example reads a file containing CSV data and processes it line by line:

```
sl_csv/sample_0.rb
require "csv"
CSV.foreach("#{__dir__}/csvfile.csv") do |row|
  qty = row[0].to_i
  price = row[2].to_f
  printf "%20s: $%5.2f %s\n", row[1], qty * price, row[3] || " ---"
end
```

produces:

```
             eggs: $34.68    ---
     shirt, blue: $42.90 special
"Hello Kitty" bag: $13.99    ---
```

In this case, we process a CSV file that contains a header line. Notice that CSV automatically converts fields that look like numbers:

```
sl_csv/sample_1.rb
require "csv"
total_cost = 0
CSV.foreach(
  "#{__dir__}/csvfile_with_header.csv",
  headers: true, converters: :numeric
) do |data|
  total_cost += data["Count"] * data["Price"]
end
puts "Total cost is #{total_cost}"
```

produces:

```
Total cost is 91.57
```

You can write to a CSV file by creating a new CSV with CSV.new(string_or_io, **options) or CSV.open(path, mode = "rb", options) [{ |csv| block }]. The open method passes the new CSV object to a block. You can then add rows to the file by passing an array to the CSV object with the << operator (aliased as the method add_row).

This example writes CSV data to an existing open stream, standard out, using | as the column separator:

```
sl_csv/sample_2.rb
require "csv"
csv = CSV.new($stdout, col_sep: "|")
csv << [1, "line 1", 27]
csv << [2, nil, 123]
csv << [3, "|bar|", 32.5]
csv.close
```

produces:

```
1|line 1|27
2||123
3|"|bar|"|32.5
```

This example reads and writes from a CSV file being treated as a two-dimensional table:

```
sl_csv/sample_3.rb
require "csv"

table = CSV.read(
  "#{__dir__}/csvfile_with_header.csv",
  headers: true, header_converters: :symbol
)
puts "Row count = #{table.count}"
puts "First row = #{table[0].fields}"
puts "Count of eggs = #{table[0][:count]}"
table << [99, "red balloons", 1.23]
table[:in_stock] = [10, 5, 10, 10]
puts "\nAfter adding a row and a column, the new table is:"
puts table
```

produces:

```
Row count = 3
First row = ["12", "eggs", "2.89", nil]
Count of eggs = 12
```

After adding a row and a column, the new table is:

```
count,description,price,,in_stock
12,eggs,2.89,,10
2,"shirt, blue",21.45,special,5
1,"""Hello Kitty"" bag",13.99,10
99,red balloons,1.23,,10
```

Dir

The Dir class is used to interact with directories in the file system. Like many of Ruby's file manipulation classes, it has both a lot of class methods and instance methods, in some cases duplicating functionality.

You create a Dir instance with Dir.new(path), where the path is a string or something that can be implicitly converted to a string because it implements to_str (so Pathname objects can be used here). The path is relative to the current system working directory. There's an optional keyword argument, encoding:, which specifies the encoding of the directory as you look at it.

Directories can technically be opened and closed in Ruby; when open, they stream a list of their children files. The class method Dir.open(path) {|dir|} takes a path and a block. It passes the new directory as an argument to the block and closes the directory when the block has completed.

Directory instances implement each, yielding once for each file in the directory (including the special files . and ..). They also include Enumerable, so all the methods discussed in Enumerable, on page 568, can be used on Dir instances.

Dealing with Files

Most of what you want to do with directory objects in Ruby is search their files. The most flexible and probably most common method for doing so in Ruby is Dir.glob(pattern, *flags, base: nil, sort: true) [{block}]. The glob method takes one required parameter: a pattern for matching files. It returns an array of files in the current directory that match the pattern. The pattern can be a string or an array of strings. If it's an array, a file is returned if it matches any of the elements of the array.

Optionally, glob can take a block argument, in which case, each matching filename is passed to the block and the method returns nil.

There are three optional parameters to glob. The flags are a positional argument that can affect the matching (see Table 30, File pattern match flags, on page 597, for a list). An optional keyword argument, base:, allows you to change the directory to be searched and pass it a string relative to the current directory. An optional sort: keyword argument defaults to true; if false, the resulting matches aren't sorted.

The pattern matching is what you normally use glob for. It's not a regular expression pattern, it's closer to (but not identical to) the glob pattern used by a Unix shell. Like a file glob, normal characters match themselves, and special characters match specific patterns. The table shown on page 591 describes the special characters.

The glob method is also sort of aliased as []. The main difference is that the square bracket method can take multiple partners, so Dir["*.x", "*.y"] is equivalent to passing an array to glob: Dir.glob(["*.x", "*.y"]).

Pattern	Meaning
*	Any sequence of characters in a filename: * will match all files, c* will match all files beginning with *c*, *c will match all files ending with *c*, and *c* will match all files that have *c* in their name.
**	Matches zero or more directories (so **/fred matches a file named *fred* in or below the current directory).
?	Matches any one character in a filename.
[chars]	Matches any one of the *chars*. If the first character in *chars* is ^, it matches any character that's not in the remaining set.
{patt,...}	Matches one of the patterns specified between braces. These patterns may contain other metacharacters.
\	Removes any special significance in the next character.

Table 27—Glob patterns

The directory used in the following examples contains two regular files (config.json and pick-axe.rb), the parent directory (..), and the directory itself (.):

```
ref_io/dir.rb
Dir.chdir("testdir")                      # => 0

Dir.glob("config.?")                      # => []
Dir.glob("*.[a-z][a-z]")                  # => ["pickaxe.rb"]
Dir.glob("*.[^r]*")                       # => ["config.json"]
Dir.glob("*.{rb,json}")                   # => ["pickaxe.rb", "config.json"]
Dir.glob("*")                             # => ["config.json", "pickaxe.rb"]
Dir.glob(%w[*.rb *.json])                 # => ["pickaxe.rb", "config.json"]
Dir.glob("*", File::FNM_DOTMATCH)         # => [".", "config.json", "pickaxe.rb"]

Dir.chdir("..")                           # => 0
Dir.glob("code/**/fib*.rb")               # => ["code/irb/fibonacci_sequence.rb",
                                          # ..    "code/rdoc/fib_example.rb",
                                          # ..    "code/tut_containers/fibonacci_up_to.rb",
                                          # ..    "code/tut_threads/fiber_word_count.rb"]
Dir.glob("**/rdoc/fib*.rb")               # => ["code/rdoc/fib_example.rb"]

Dir["config.?"]                           # => []
Dir["*.json"]                             # => ["data.json"]
Dir["*.rb"]                               # => []
Dir["*.rb", "*.json"]                     # => ["data.json"]
```

There is no instance method equivalent for Dir.glob, but you could mostly manage with Dir#filter.

If you just want a list of all the files in a directory, the class method Dir.children(path) takes a path and returns an array of all the files in that directory, excluding the . and .. special file markers. The Dir.entries(path) method does the same thing, but includes the special file markers. The children method is available on instances, but entries is not.

To iterate over a directory, the class method Dir.each_child(path) {block} takes a block and executes the block once for each entry in the directory as returned by children, so it's effectively equivalent to Dir.children("foo").each. The iteration method Dir.foreach(path) {block} does the same, but for the result of entries, so it's effectively Dir.entries("foo").each. Instances of dir also have Dir#each_child {block}, which skips the special dot file descriptors, and Dir#each {block}, which doesn't. Here's an example:

```
ref_io/dir_2.rb
Dir.children("testdir")                             # => ["pickaxe.rb",
                                                    # .. "config.json"]

Dir.entries("testdir")                              # => [".", "..",
                                                    # .. "pickaxe.rb",
                                                    # .. "config.json"]

result = []
Dir.each_child("testdir") { |name| result << name } # => nil
result                                              # => ["pickaxe.rb",
                                                    # .. "config.json"]

instance = Dir.new("testdir")
instance.children                               .   # => ["pickaxe.rb",
                                                    # .. "config.json"]

instance_result = []
instance.each { |name| instance_result << name }    # => #<Dir:testdir>
instance_result                                     # => [".", "..",
                                                    # .. "pickaxe.rb",
                                                    # .. "config.json"]
```

If the directory has no children, the class method Dir.empty? returns true; if the directory has children, the method returns false.

You can also externally iterate over a directory with Dir#read. Here's an example:

```
ref_io/dir_3.rb
instance = Dir.new("testdir")
instance.read  # => "."
instance.read  # => ".."
```

Managing the File System with Dir

You can use the Ruby Dir class to manipulate the external environment.

The method Dir.exist?(pathname) returns true if the path already exists in the file system, relative to where the Ruby code is executing.

The class method Dir.chdir(path) [{block}] takes a string and an optional block. The no-block version of the method changes the current directory of the process running the Ruby code. The block version changes the current directory, runs the block, and then changes the directory back to its original setting. The instance method chdir changes the directory of the process to the directory represented by the instance. It only has a no-block form.

The directory can be deleted from the current system's file structure with the class method Dir.delete(path), which is also aliased as Dir.rmdir(path) and Dir.unlink(path). (We'll also see a FileUtils version.) The directory can be created with the class method Dir.mkdir(path). There's an optional second option, which is an integer that sets the Unix permissions of the new directory. The method raises SystemCallError if the directory can't be created for some reason.

The method Dir.tmpdir returns the system's temporary file path, and you can create a temporary directory inside with Dir.mktmpdir(prefix_suffix = nil, *rest, **options) [{ |dir| }]. This takes no required arguments and returns the path of the temp directory. If it's passed a block, the new directory is the argument to the block, the block is executed, and the temporary directory is removed at the end of the block.

The class methods Dir.pwd and Dir.getwd return the current process working directory, and Dir.home(username = nil) returns the current home directory of the given user (or the current user if no argument is given). Instances will return their path with path—this will return the path as it was given to the constructor; it won't normalize the pathname in any way.

File

The File class in Ruby does two things. First, it's a subclass of IO, meaning it handles reading data from and writing data to files. Second, it adds a number of methods for manipulating files as objects, similar to the Dir class. Since the reading and writing behavior is mostly managed by methods defined in IO, we'll discuss it when we look at IO in IO, on page 600. Here, we'll look at file-specific manipulations.

Most File manipulation methods are class methods, while most of the read/write methods are instance methods.

Opening a File

You create a File instance with File.new(filename, mode = "r", permissions = 0666, *options) or File.open(filename, mode = "r", permissions = 0666, *options) [{block}]. (Note that this doesn't necessarily create the file in the underlying system.)

Both File.new and File.open take the same arguments: a filename, an optional mode (which defaults to r), an optional Unix permission (which defaults to 0666), and some keyword options.

Both methods open the file named by filename according to mode (the default is "r") and return a new File object. The mode string contains information about the way the file is to be opened and optionally on the encodings to be associated with the file data. Mode strings have the form "file-mode[:external-encoding[:internal-encoding]]". The file-mode portion is one of the options listed in the following table. The two encodings are the names (or aliases) of encodings supported by your interpreter. See Encoding, on page 532, for more information about encodings.

String	Description
r	Read-only, starts at beginning of file (default mode).
r+	Read/write, starts at beginning of file.
w	Write-only, truncates an existing file to zero length or creates a new file for writing.
w+	Read/write, truncates an existing file to zero length or creates a new file for reading and writing.
a	Write-only, starts at end of file if file exists; otherwise, creates a new file for writing.
a+	Read/write, starts at end of file if file exists; otherwise, creates a new file for reading and writing.
b	Binary file mode (may appear with any of the key letters listed earlier). As of Ruby 1.9, this modifier should be supplied on all ports opened in binary mode (on Unix as well as on DOS/Windows). To read a file in binary mode and receive the data as a stream of bytes, use the modestring "rb:ascii-8bit".

Table 28—Mode values

The new method returns a File instance that you can then read or write from. The file remains open until close is called on the instance.

The open method takes a block and passes the new file instance to the block. Inside the block, you can read, write, or manage the file however you want. The file is automatically closed at the end of the block.

The read and write methods that you would use with a File are methods of the parent class IO, and are discussed in IO, on page 600.

The options argument takes any of the following keyword options listed in the following table:

Option	Description
autoclose:	If false, the underlying file will not be closed when this I/O object is finalized.
binmode:	Opens the I/O object in binary mode if true (same as mode: "b").
encoding:	Specifies both external and internal encodings as "external:internal" (same format used in mode parameter.
external_encoding:	Specifies the external encoding.
flags	Specifies file open flags. If mode: is also used, the two values are combined using bitwise OR.
internal_encoding:	Specifies the internal encoding.
mode:	Specifies what would have been the *mode* parameter. For example, File.open("xx", "r:utf-8") is the same as File.open("xx", mode: "r:utf-8").
path:	A string value is used in inspect and as a getter method called path.
textmode:	Opens the file in text mode (the default).

Table 29—File and I/O open options

In addition, the options parameter can use these key/value pairs to control encoding. The encoding pairs are also the same as used in String#encode. See Table 22, Options to encode and encode!, on page 533.

If you want to change the operating system mode of the file, you can use either a class method or an instance method to do so, called File.chmod(mode_integer, *filenames) or File#chmod(mode_integer). The class version takes the new mode as an integer (usually an octal integer, such as 0644) and one or more filenames (relative to where the Ruby program started) as the remaining arguments. The instance method just takes the mode integer as an argument. In both cases, the underlying system is invoked to change the file's execution mode.

Similarly, you can change the owner of a file with the class method File.chown(owner_int, group_int, *file_names) or the instance method File#chown(owner_int, group_int). The arguments to the class method chown are the integer ID of the new owner, the integer ID of the new group, and a list of filenames. The instance method, because it's already attached to a file, takes just the owner and group IDs.

You can delete one or more files with File.delete(*filenames) (aliased as unlink), which takes a series of filenames and deletes them from the underlying file system.

You can create a symlink in the underlying operating system with File.symlink(old_name, new_name). If the underlying operating system doesn't have symbolic links, you get a NotImplementedError.

Filenames

The File class has methods that allow you to separate a filename into component parts. These are all class methods of File. But, if you're doing more complicated name logic on a file, you should check out the Pathname class, which provides a lot more functionality. (See Pathname, on page 611, for more.)

The File.basename(file_name, suffix = nil) method returns what you would casually call the "filename." It's the last component of the entire path plus the extension. An optional second argument is a suffix. If the argument is used and it matches the end of the filename, the suffix is removed from the result—the suffix doesn't need to be the same length as the extension, only to match the end of the string. The special value .* matches any extension.

The File.dirname(file_name, level = 1) method returns everything in the filename that isn't the basename—that's the directory names in the path. An optional second argument is a level, signifying the number of subdirectory names from the end of the file to be left off. The default is 1, which causes the filename to be left off. Using 0 returns the entire path name.

In both cases, the separators between components are the constants File::SEPARATOR and File::ALT_SEPARATOR, which are operating system–dependent. (Not all systems will have an alternate separator.)

The File.extname(file_name) method returns just the extension part of the filename, dot included. If there are multiple extensions (like .rb.old), only the last one is returned. If the filename starts with a dot (like .gitignore), the filename isn't considered an extension; you need to have another dot (like .my.zsh). If the filename ends with just a dot for some reason, you get a dot on Windows platforms and an empty string on non-Windows platforms.

All these filenames are just doing string manipulation. They aren't dependent on the filename being manipulated actually existing in the file system:

```
ref_io/filenames.rb
File.basename("/usr/pickaxe/ruby/code.rb")          # => "code.rb"
File.basename("/usr/pickaxe/ruby/code.rb", ".rb")   # => "code"
File.basename("/usr/pickaxe/ruby/code.rb", "e.rb")  # => "cod"
File.basename("/usr/pickaxe/ruby/code.rb", ".*")    # => "code"

File.dirname("/usr/pickaxe/ruby/code.rb")           # => "/usr/pickaxe/ruby"
File.dirname("/usr/pickaxe/ruby/code.rb", 2)        # => "/usr/pickaxe"
File.dirname("/usr/pickaxe/ruby/code.rb", 3)        # => "/usr"

File.extname("/usr/pickaxe/ruby/code.rb")           # => ".rb"
```

To go the other way, if you have a series of path names and you want an entire string, the File.join(*partial_path) method connects the path names using /. Note that join will use the forward slash no matter what operating system you're on and this will work just fine even on Windows systems. Some people find join more readable than string interpolation when you're building a filename dynamically:

```
File.join("usr", "pickaxe", "ruby", "code.rb") # => "usr/pickaxe/ruby/code.rb"
```

Paths

The File class can also do some manipulation based on the entire path name of the file.

The class method File.absolute_path(file_name, directory_string = nil) method takes a presumably partial filename and returns the absolute path. By default, the filename is assumed to be relative to the current working directory, but an optional second argument can be used as the base point. The related method File.absolute_path?(file_name) returns true if the argument is an absolute path.

The method File.expand_path(file_name, directory_string = nil) does the same as absoulute_path except when the filename argument starts with a tilde ~, such as ~noel, which would indicate a home directory in a Unix system. In the tilde case, expand_path expands the ~ using the Unix HOME environment variable, whereas absolute_path just treats that as a regular directory that happens to start with a tilde.

The File.path(path) method will return the argument converted to a string, which is only interesting if the argument isn't a string (for example, it's a Pathname or something).

The File.realpath(pathname, directory_string = nil) and File.realdirpath(pathname, directory_string = nil) will return the absolute pathname—realpath will throw an error if the file doesn't exist, while realdirpath will allow the last component of the path to not exist, but any other component of the path name must exist.

In other words, given a fictional filename nope.rb, the absolute_path and expand_path methods will happily give you a full path to the nonexistent file, but realpath will throw an error. The realdirpath will work fine, but if the argument adds a fictional subdirectory, like File.realdirpath("fake/nope.rb") then that method will also throw an error.

The method File.identical?(file_one, file_two) takes two different path names or I/O objects and returns true if they point to the same file.

Times

Files have a lot of time-based stats associated with them. All of these methods are available as class methods or instance methods:

- File.atime(file_name), File#atime: The time the file was last accessed.

- File.birthtime(file_name), File#birthtime: The time the file was created.

- File.ctime(file_name), File#ctime: The time the file or the directory was last changed (on Windows this returns the creation time).

- File.mtime(file_name), File#mtime: The time the file was last modified.

The class method File.stat(file_name) or instance method File#stat returns an instance of a class called File::Stat. The File::Stat instance also has instance methods for all those time attributes, as well as several other attributes such as size. It's also worth mentioning that File::Stat defines <=> based on the modification time of the file, so it can be used to sort files based on most recently changed.

Booleans

The File class has a lot of boolean predicate methods. These are all class methods:

- File.exist?(file_name) returns true if the filename argument is or resolves to a path that actually exists in the underlying file system.

- File.directory?(file_name) returns true if the argument is or resolves to the path of a directory or a symbolic link to a directory. If the path isn't a directory or doesn't exist, it returns false.

- File.file?(file_name) returns true if the argument is or resolves to the path of a file or symbolic link to an existing file. If the path doesn't exist or isn't a file, it returns false.

- File.symlink?(file_name) returns true if the file path points to an existing symbolic link in the underlying operating system.

- File.executable?(file_name) returns true if the effective user has permission to execute the file named in the argument. File.executable_real?(file_name) is the same, but for the real user. Note that Windows systems don't use permissions to determine whether a file is executable.

- Similarly, File.readable?(file_name), File.readable_real?(file_name), File.world_readable?(file_name), File.writeable?(file_name), File.writeable_real?(file_name), and File.world_writable?(file_name) all return true if the file exists and the permission described by the name of the method is available. The method File.owned?(file_name) returns true if the file exists and is owned by the user ID of the calling process.

The size of a file is available via the class method File.size and the instance method size. The boolean class method File.empty? aliased as zero? returns true if the file exists and has zero size.

The class method File.fnmatch?(pattner, path, *flags) (aliased as fnmatch) takes a pattern, a path, and optional flags. The pattern is a glob pattern using the rules we've seen in Table 27, Glob patterns, on page 591. The path is the filename being matched, and the optional flags control the pattern matching and are listed in the following table.

File::FNM_EXTGLOB	Expand braces in the pattern.
File::FNM_NOESCAPE	A backslash doesn't escape special characters in globs, and a backslash in the pattern must match a backslash in the filename.
File::FNM_PATHNAME	Forward slashes in the filename are treated as separating parts of a path and so must be explicitly matched in the pattern.
File::FNM_DOTMATCH	If this option isn't specified, filenames containing leading periods must be matched by an explicit period in the pattern. A leading period is one at the start of the filename or (if FNM_PATHNAME is specified) following a slash.
File::FNM_CASEFOLD	Filename matches are case insensitive.

Table 30—File pattern match flags

FileUtils

In addition to the functionality in File, Ruby has an entire module called FileUtils that defines many module level methods that are basically wrappers around operating system features or Dir and File features.

To use these methods, you need to use require "fileutils". All the methods here are defined as module methods and as instance methods, though you would typically use them as module methods, as in FileUtils.mkdir.

Methods in FileUtils that take paths expect either a string, an object with a to_path method, or an object with a to_str method. Methods in FileUtils that are described as working recursively can take directories as arguments and act on all files in the directory.

Let's take a quick tour of the FileUtils.

Common Arguments

Several methods in FileUtils have arguments that mean the same thing. Rather than describe what the arguments mean in each method that uses them, we're just defining them here. These descriptions are valid for any method that has an argument matching any of these names:

- dereference_root, if true, allows the source argument to be a symbolic link.

- force controls how the method behaves if it has to override existing file system behavior. If force is true, then the method's change carries. If force isn't true, then typically an exception is raised.

- noop, if true, causes the method to actually not do anything, which is useful in testing. For example, you can test with verbose: true, noop: true and see what the command is doing without modifying the file system.

- preserve, if true, preserves the timestamp of a file when moving or changing it.

- remove_destination, if true, removes the destination argument before executing a move or copy.

- secure for file removal, if true, securely removes a file by ensuring that permissions don't change during the removal process (see the official Ruby documentation for more information).

- verbose, if true, outputs more information to standard out.

Directory Management

- FileUtils.mkdir(list, mode: nil, noop: nil, verbose: nil) creates a new entry for every path in list. If mode isn't nil, it sets permissions on each new directory. If multiple subdirectories need to be created or if the directory already exists, it raises an error.

- FileUtils.mkdir_p(list, mode: nil, noop: nil, verbose: nil) is the same, but if elements in the list require multiple subdirectories to be created, it'll create all the subdirectories. It's aliased as FileUtils.makedirs and FileUtils.mkpath.

- FileUtils.remove_dir(path, force = false) removes the directory entry at path recursively.

- FileUtils.rmdir(list, parents: nil, noop: nil, verbose: nil) removes all directories in list. If parents is true, it'll remove parent directories that are made empty by the removal.

File Management

- FileUtils.copy(source, destination, preserve: nil, noop: nil, verbose: nil) copies the file at source to destination if both the source and the destination are files. If the source is a file and the destination is a directory, it copies the source to destination/source. If destination is a directory, source can be a list of files, in which case all are copied to the destination. It throws an exception if source is a directory. Aliased as FileUtils.cp. The related method FileUtils.copy_file(source, destination, preserve = false, dereference = false) allows the source to be a symbolic link if dereference is true.

- FileUtils.cp_r(source, destination, preserve: nil, noop: nil, verbose: nil, dereference_root: nil, remove_destination: nil) is the recursive version of copy, meaning that source can be a directory, in which case the entries in source are recursively copied to destination. FileUtils.copy_entry(source, destination, preserve = false, dereference_root.= false, remove_destination = false) behaves similarly but with a slightly different argument pattern. FileUtils.cp_lr behaves similarly but creates a Unix hard link rather than a copy using FileUtils.link_entry.

- FileUtils.install(source, destination, mode: nil, owner: nil, group: nil, preserve: nil, noop: nil, verbose: nil) behaves like copy but allows you to set the permissions and ownership on the destination file. It overwrites the destination if it already exists.

- FileUtils.copy_stream(source, destination) copies the source stream to the destination.

- FileUtils.mv(source, destination, force: nil, noop: nil, verbose: nil, secure: nil) moves the file at the source path to the destination path if both paths are files. If the destination is a directory, the source is one or more paths and they are all moved to destination/source. Aliased as FileUtils.move.

- FileUtils.rm(list, force: nil, noop: nil, verbose: nil) removes all the files in the list. Aliased as FileUtils.remove. Also FileUtils.remove_file(path, force = false) and remove_entry_secure(path, force = false), which is used by mv when secure is true. FileUtils.rm_f(list, noop: nil, verbose: nil) is like rm but with force: true.

- FileUtils.rm_r(list, force: nil, noop: nil, verbose: nil, secure: nil) is the recursive version of rm, meaning that elements in the list can be directories. FileUtils.rm_rf(list, noop: nil, verbose: nil) is the same but with force: true.

- FileUtils.touch(list, noop: nil, verbose: nil, mtime: nil, nocreate: nil) touches each file in the list, updating its modification time. If mtime is nil, it uses the current time; otherwise, it uses the value of mtime. If nocreate is true, it raises an exception if the path doesn't exist.

- FileUtils.uptodate?(new, old) returns true if the element at new is newer than all the files in the list of paths in old.

Symbolic Links

- FileUtils.ln(source, destination, force: nil, noop: nil, verbose: nil) creates a Unix hard link at destination pointing to source if both source and destination are files. If destination is a directory, it creates the link at destination/source. If source is a list of paths, it creates links for all of them in destination. Aliased as FileUtils.link.

- FileUtils.link_entry(source, destination, dereference_root = false, remove_destination = false) behaves as FileUtils.ln, but with different arguments.

- FileUtils.ln_s(source, destination, force: nil, relative: false, target_directory: true, noop: nil, verbose: nil) creates a Unix symbolic link. As with other copy methods, if both the source and destination are files, it creates the link at destination pointing to source. If destination is a directory, it creates the link at destination.source, and if source is a list, it creates links for all the entries inside destination. If relative is true, the links are relative to the destination. The target_directory argument appears to be unused. Aliased as FileUtils.symlink. FileUtils.ln_sf is the same method but with force: true, and FileUtils.ln_sr is the same method but with relative: true.

Changing Settings

- FileUtils.cd(dir, verbose: nil) changes the current directory to dir. Aliased as FileUtils.chdir.

- FileUtils.chmod(permissions, list, noop: nil, verbose: nil) changes the permissions of all paths to the new permissions. The permissions is an integer Unix permission number or a string Unix permission string, and the list is one or more paths. The method FileUtils.chmod_R does the same thing but works recursively and has a force: argument.

- FileUtils.chown(user, group, list, noop: nil, verbose: nil) changes the owner of each path in list to the given user and group. If user or group is nil, the path isn't changed. FileUtils.chown_R is the recursive version, and also takes a force: argument.

Queries

- FileUtils.compare_file(a, b) returns true if the contents of the two files at a and b are identical. Aliased as FileUtils.identical? and FileUtils.cmp. The related method FileUtils.compare_streams(a, b) works on streams.

- FileUtils.pwd or FileUtils.getwd return the current working directory.

IO

Class IO is the basis for all input and output in Ruby. An I/O stream may be *duplexed* (that is, bidirectional) and so may use more than one native operating system stream. Many of the examples in this section use class File, which is the only standard subclass of IO. The two classes are closely associated.

As used in this section, *portname* may take any of the following forms:

- A plain string represents a filename suitable for the underlying operating system.

- A string starting with | indicates a subprocess. The remainder of the string following | is invoked as a process with appropriate input/output channels connected to it.

- A string equal to |- will create another Ruby instance as a subprocess.

The IO class uses the Unix abstraction of *file descriptors* (fds), which are small integers that represent open files. Conventionally, standard input has an fd of 0, standard output has an fd of 1, and standard error has an fd of 2.

Ruby will convert path names between different operating system conventions if possible. For instance, on Windows (non-WSDL) the filename /gumby/ruby/test.rb will be opened as \gumby\ruby\test.rb. When specifying a Windows-style filename in a double-quoted Ruby string, remember to escape the backslashes, as in "c:\\gumby\\ruby\\test.rb".

Note that our examples here use the Unix-style forward slashes; to get the platform-specific separator character, use File::SEPARATOR.

I/O ports may be opened in any one of several different modes, which are shown in this section as *mode*. This mode string must be one of the values listed in Table 28, Mode values, on page 593. The mode may also contain information on the external and internal encoding of the data associated with the port. If an external encoding is specified, Ruby assumes the data it received from the operating system uses that encoding. If no internal encoding is given, strings read from the port will have this encoding. If an internal encoding is given, data will be transcoded from the external to the internal encoding, and strings will have that encoding. The reverse happens on output.

Creating, Opening, and Closing Streams

You can create I/O streams with new or open. Unlike File objects, the first argument to IO.new(fd, mode="r", **opts) or IO.open(fd, mode="r", **opts) is an integer file descriptor, not the name of a file. Like the File methods, the second argument is a mode string, defined in Table 28, Mode values, on page 593, followed by the options defined in Table 29, File and I/O open options, on page 594 and Table 22, Options to encode and encode!, on page 533. Like File, the open method takes a block, passes the new IO object to the block, and opens the stream for the duration of the block. The new method requires you to explicitly close the string with the close method.

You can convert a filename or path to a file descriptor with File.sysopen(path, mode = "r", permissions = 0666), which takes a filename, an optional mode string, and an optional Unix permissions, and then opens the file and returns the integer file descriptor. If the file doesn't exist, it's created if the mode is for writing, or an error is thrown if the mode is for reading.

The method IO.pipe(external_encoding = nil, internal_encoding = nil, **options) [{ |read_io, write_io} block] creates a pair of pipe endpoints that are connected to each other and returns them as a two-element array of IO objects as in [read_io, write_io]. The write_io endpoint is automatically placed into sync mode. It's not available on all platforms.

Encodings for the pipes can be specified as a string ("external" or "external:internal") or as two arguments specifying the external and internal encoding names (or encoding objects). If both external and internal encodings are present, keyword arguments specify conversion options (see Table 22, Options to encode and encode!, on page 533).

The method takes an optional block, in which case the two I/O streams are opened and sent to the block. The two streams are then closed at the end of the block, and the method returns the return value of the block.

The IO class also allows you to run arbitrary command-line commands and manage I/O via the method IO.popen(environment = {}, command, mode = "r", **opts) with an optional block argument.

The popen method runs the specified command string as a subprocess. In the non-block version of the method, the subprocess's standard input and output will be connected to the returned IO object.

The parameter command may be a string or an array of strings. In the latter case, the array is used as the argv parameter for the new process, and no special shell processing is performed on the strings. In addition, if the array starts with a hash, it'll be used to set environment variables in the subprocess. If it ends with a hash, the hash will be used to set execution options for the subprocess.

See Kernel#spawn for more options. If command is a string, it'll be subject to shell expansion. If the command string starts with a minus sign (-) and the operating system supports fork, then the current Ruby process is forked. The default mode for the new file object is r, but mode may be set to any of the modes listed in Table 28, Mode values, on page 593.

If a block is given, Ruby will run the command as a child connected to Ruby with a pipe. Ruby's end of the pipe will be passed as a parameter to the block. In this case, popen returns the value of the block.

If a block is given with a command of just "-", the block will be run in two separate processes: once in the parent and once in a child. The parent process will be passed the pipe object as a parameter to the block, the child version of the block will be passed nil, and the child's standard in and standard out will be connected to the parent through the pipe. It's not available on all platforms. Here's an example:

```
ref_io/io_popen.rb
pipe = IO.popen("uname")
p(pipe.readlines)
puts "Parent is #{Process.pid}"
IO.popen("date") { |pipe| puts pipe.gets }
IO.popen("-") { |pipe| $stderr.puts("#{Process.pid} is here, pipe=#{pipe}") }
Process.waitall
```

produces:

```
["Darwin\n"]
Parent is 43752
Thu Nov  2 17:16:42 CDT 2023
43752 is here, pipe=#<IO:0x0000000100528f40>
43767 is here, pipe=
```

Here's a different example that merges standard error and standard output into a single stream (note that buffering means that the error output comes back ahead of the standard output):

```
ref_io/io_popen_2.rb
pipe = IO.popen(["bc", {$stderr => $stdout}], "r+")
pipe.puts "1 + 3; bad_function()"
pipe.close_write
puts pipe.readlines
```

produces:

```
Runtime error: undefined function: bad_function()
    Function: (main)
```

4

Reading and Writing Streams

The IO class has read and write methods at both the class level and the instance level.

Class Method Reading and Writing

You can read an entire I/O stream with the class method IO.read(command_or_path, length = nil, offset = 0, **opts). If the first argument is a path string, it reads the file at the path and returns the entire file as a string. If the first argument starts with a pipe character (|), the argument is interpreted as a command. In that case, the command is executed in a subprocess and anything the command sends to standard output is returned as a single string. If the length argument is set, then only that number of bytes are read starting at the beginning of the string, unless offset is also set, in which case the reading starts that many bytes into the string. The keyword options are the same file opening and encoding options available for File.open (see Opening a File, on page 593).

The method IO.binread takes the same options but treats the result as a binary string encoded with Ruby's ASCII-8BIT binary encoding.

The method IO.readlines(command_or_path, separator = $/, limit = nil, **opts) takes similar arguments plus an optional line separator and returns the string split into lines. The default line separator is \n—the global Ruby line separator. In this method, the limit argument is the maximum number of lines returned. The keyword options are the same as those used in File.open. If the separator is nil, no separation is performed. If the separator is an empty string, the separator is a paragraph spacer, meaning two consecutive line separators.

You can write from a class method with IO.write, which has two forms: IO.write(path, data, offset = 0, **opts) and IO.write(command, data, **opts). As with the read method, a command is denoted because it starts with a pipe character (|). The optional arguments are the same as for File.new.

By default, the path version replaces the contents of the file at path with the data. If the offset argument isn't zero, it starts writing the data an offset number of bytes from the beginning, which results in the latter part of the file being overwritten. If the offset is bigger than the file, Unicode null characters are used as padding.

The command version executes the command in a shell and writes the data argument to standard input. In both cases, the return value is the length of the data string in bytes.

The binwrite command has the same arguments but opens the stream in binary mode using Ruby's ASCII-8BIT encoding.

Instance Method Reading and Writing

Once you have an instance (either by using IO.new or inside the block argument to IO.open), you can read or write to that instance. These methods also work on files.

To read from an I/O stream or file, the file must have been opened in a read mode (see Table 28, Mode values, on page 593).

The most general method is IO#read(max_length = nil, out_string = nil). If the max_length argument is nil, it reads all the remaining data in the stream. Otherwise, you get the next max_length bytes of the stream, and the stream remembers the position for the next read. If the out_string argument is specified, that variable is also set to the same value that's returned by the read method.

The following read methods just return the next available thing in the stream. These methods all raise EOFError if the stream is at the end:

- IO#readbyte returns the integer of the next byte in the stream. The IO#getbyte method is similar but returns nil at the end of the stream rather than raise an error.

- IO#readchar returns the next character in a text stream as a one-character string. The IO#getc method is similar but returns nil at the end of the stream rather than raise an error.

- IO#readline(separator = $/, limit = 1, chomp: false), aliased as IO#gets, returns the next line. If separator is specified, it uses that value as the separator (including the special values of nil and empty string). If limit is specified, that number is the maximum number of bytes returned in the line (not the number of lines), and if chomp is true, the line separator is removed from the return value. IO#readlines with the same arguments returns an array of all remaining lines in the stream.

- IO#readpartial(max_length, out_string = nil) returns the next max_length bytes both as a return value and as the value of the variable passed in as out_string. The encoding is binary ASCII-8BIT if out_string isn't specified, or the encoding of out_string if it's. This method blocks only when the stream is currently empty but not at the end of the stream. The related method IO#read_nonblock takes the same options but is non-blocking.

- IO#pread(max_length, offset = 0, out_string = nil) has similar behavior to IO#readpartial but doesn't move the read position of the stream. It reads max_length bytes starting at the offset position of the string. This method is thread-safe because it doesn't change the read position of the stream. The main instance method for writing to a stream that has been opened in writing mode is IO#write(*objects), which takes an array of items that are then converted to strings via the to_s method and written one by one to the stream.

If you just want to write a single string, you can use the push operator << as in stream << "write this!". This will also convert the argument using to_s.

The related method IO#print(*objects) also writes each object to the string but separates the objects with the global field separator, which is in the global variable $, or $OUTPUT_FIELD_SEP-ARATOR. After the last object, the method adds the value of the global record separator, which is the global variable $/ or $OUTPUT_RECORD_SEPARATOR. If there is no argument, it writes the value of the global variable $_, which is the last variable assigned, as in the following example:

```
File.open("foo.txt", "w+") do |f|
  gets
  f.print
end
```

When you're done reading or writing an instance, you call close to close the stream. If you have been writing to the file, closing the file may be required to flush the operating system's I/O buffer and send any remaining data over the stream.

The IO class also has a printf method that behaves the same as the Kernel#printf method.

Iteration

I/O streams implement each and import Enumerable. The each method reads one line at a time and passes it to the block argument. If no arguments are passed, lines are delimited by the global line separator $/, which is usually \n. The each method takes arguments similar to other line-based methods. You can pass a separator as an argument to be used instead of $/. An integer argument limits the number of bytes returned in each line, and a keyword argument chomp: removes the line delimiter if it's true. This method is aliased as each_line.

You can get similar behavior from the class method IO.foreach(command, separator = $/, limit = nil, **options) [{ |line| block}], which takes an initial string argument that's either a path name or a command starting with the pipe character. The remaining arguments are the same as for IO#each. The class method, if called with a path, reads from that path and sends each line to the block argument in turn. If called with a command, it executes that command and passes each line of the resulting output to the block.

You can iterate over a stream at a different level with the instance methods File#each_byte [{byte}], File#each_char [{char}], and File#each_codepoint [{codepoint}], all of which pass one element at a time to their associated block.

External File Encodings

Playing around with encodings within a program is all very well, but in most code, we'll want to read data from and write data to external files. And often that data will be in a particular encoding.

Ruby's I/O objects support both encoding and transcoding of data. What does this mean?

Every I/O object has an associated external encoding. This is the encoding of the data being read from or written to the outside world. With a little bit of magic that we'll describe in Default External Encoding, on page 607, all Ruby programs run with the concept of a default external encoding. This is the external encoding that will be used by I/O objects unless you override it when you create the object (for example, by opening a file).

Now, your program may want to operate internally in a different encoding. For example, some of my files may be encoded with ISO-8859-1, but we want our Ruby program to work internally using UTF-8. Ruby I/O objects manage this by having an optional associated *internal encoding*. If set, then input will be transcoded from the external to the internal encoding on read operations, and output will be transcoded from internal to external encoding on write operations.

Let's start with the simple cases. On our MacOS box, the default external encoding is UTF-8. If we don't override it, all our file I/O will therefore also be in UTF-8. We can query the external encoding of an I/O object using the external_encoding method:

ref_io/encoding_simple.rb
```
f = File.open("/etc/passwd")
puts "File encoding is #{f.external_encoding}"
line = f.gets
puts "Data encoding is #{line.encoding}"
```

produces:
```
File encoding is UTF-8
Data encoding is UTF-8
```

Notice that the data is tagged with a UTF-8 encoding even though it (presumably) contains just 7-bit ASCII characters. Only literals in your Ruby source files have the "change encoding if they contain 8-bit data" rule.

You can force the external encoding associated with an I/O object when you open it—simply add the name of the encoding, preceded by a colon, to the mode string. Note that this in no way changes the data that's read; it simply tags it with the encoding you specify:

ref_io/encoding_external.rb
```
f = File.open("/etc/passwd", "r:ascii")
puts "File encoding is #{f.external_encoding}"
line = f.gets
puts "Data encoding is #{line.encoding}"
```

produces:
```
File encoding is US-ASCII
Data encoding is US-ASCII
```

You can force Ruby to transcode—change the encoding—of data it reads and writes by putting two encoding names in the mode string, again with a colon before each. For example, the file iso-8859-1.txt contains the word *olé* in ISO-8859-1 encoding, so the e-acute (é) character is encoded by the single byte \xe9. I can view this file's contents in hex using the od command-line tool. (Windows users can use the d command in debug to do the same.)

```
0000000    6f  6c  e9  0a
0000004
```

If we try to read it with our default external encoding of UTF-8, we'll encounter a problem:

```
ref_io/encoding_transcode_problem.rb
f = File.open("#{__dir__}/iso-8859-1.txt")
puts f.external_encoding.name
line = f.gets
puts line.encoding
puts line
```

produces:

```
UTF-8
UTF-8
ol?
```

The problem is that the binary sequence for the e-acute isn't the same in ISO-8859-1 and UTF-8. Ruby just assumed the file contained UTF-8 characters, tagging the string it read accordingly.

We can tell the program that the file contains ISO-8859-1:

```
ref_io/encoding_transcode_problem_2.rb
f = File.open("#{__dir__}/iso-8859-1.txt", "r:iso-8859-1")
puts f.external_encoding.name
line = f.gets
puts line.encoding
puts line
```

produces:

```
ISO-8859-1
ISO-8859-1
ol?
```

This doesn't help us much. The string is now tagged with the correct encoding, but our operating system is still expecting UTF-8 output.

The solution is to map the ISO-8859-1 to UTF-8 on input:

```
ref_io/encoding_transcode.rb
f = File.open("#{__dir__}/iso-8859-1.txt", "r:iso-8859-1:utf-8")
puts f.external_encoding.name
line = f.gets
puts line.encoding
puts line
```

produces:

```
ISO-8859-1
UTF-8
olé
```

If you specify two encoding names when opening an I/O object, the first is the external encoding, and the second is the internal encoding. Data is transcoded from the former to the latter on reading and the opposite way on writing.

Binary Files

If you want to open a file containing binary data in Ruby, you must now specify the binary flag, which will automatically select the 8-bit clean ASCII-8BIT encoding. To make things explicit, you can use "binary" as an alias for the encoding:

```
ref_io/encoding_binary.rb
f = File.open("#{__dir__}/iso-8859-1.txt", "rb")
puts "Implicit encoding is #{f.external_encoding.name}"
f = File.open("#{__dir__}/iso-8859-1.txt", "rb:binary")
puts "Explicit encoding is #{f.external_encoding.name}"
line = f.gets
puts "String encoding is #{line.encoding.name}"
```

produces:

```
Implicit encoding is ASCII-8BIT
Explicit encoding is ASCII-8BIT
String encoding is ASCII-8BIT
```

Default External Encoding

If you look at the text files on your computer, chances are they all use the same encoding, probably UTF-8. But whatever encoding you use, chances are good that you'll stick with it for the majority of your work. In fact, you probably don't think about it much.

On Unix-like boxes, including MacOS, you may find you have the LANG environment variable set. These days MacOS has the value en_US.UTF-8 by default, which says that we're using the English language in the U.S. territory and the default code set is UTF-8. On startup, Ruby looks for this environment variable and, if present, sets the default external encoding from the last part of this value.

If instead we were in Japan and the LANG variable were set to ja_JP.sjis, the encoding would be set to Shift JIS. We can look at the default external encoding by querying the Encoding class. While we're at it, we'll experiment with different values in the LANG environment variable:

```
$ echo $LANG
en_US.UTF-8
$ ruby -e 'p Encoding.default_external.name'
"UTF-8"
$ LANG=ja_JP.sjis ruby -e 'p Encoding.default_external.name'
"Windows-31J"
$ LANG= ruby -e 'p Encoding.default_external.name'
"US-ASCII"
```

The encoding set from the environment *doesn't* affect the encoding that Ruby uses for source files—it affects only the encoding of data read and written by your programs.

Finally, you can use the -E command-line option (or the long-form --encoding) to set the default external encoding of your I/O objects, as shown in the following commands:

```
$ ruby -E utf-8 -e 'p Encoding.default_external.name'
"UTF-8"
```

```
$ ruby -E sjis -e 'p Encoding.default_external.name'
"Windows-31J"
$ ruby -E sjis:iso-8859-1 -e 'p Encoding.default_internal.name'
"ISO-8859-1"
```

Encoding Compatibility

Before Ruby performs operations involving strings or regular expressions, it first has to check that the operation makes sense. For example, it's valid to perform an equality test between two strings with different encodings, but it isn't valid to append one to the other. The basic steps in this checking are as follows:

1. If the two objects have the same encoding, the operation is valid.

2. If the two objects each contain only 7-bit characters, the operation is permitted regardless of the encodings.

3. If the encodings in the two objects are compatible (which we'll discuss next), the operation is permitted.

4. Otherwise, an exception is raised.

Let's say you have a set of text files containing markup. In some of the files, authors used the sequence … to represent an ellipsis. In other files, which have UTF-8 encoding, authors used an actual ellipsis character (\u2026). We want to convert both forms to three periods.

We can start off with a simplistic solution:

```
while (line = gets)
  result = line.gsub(/&hellip;/, "...")
               .gsub(/\u2026/, "...") # unicode ellipsis
  puts result
end
```

In my environment, the content of files is by default assumed to be UTF-8. Feed our code ASCII files and UTF-encoded files, and it works just fine. But what happens when we feed it a file that contains ISO-8859-1 characters?

```
dots.rb:4:in `gsub': broken UTF-8 string (ArgumentError)
```

Ruby tried to interpret the input text, which is ISO-8859-1 encoded, as UTF-8. Because the byte sequences in the file aren't valid UTF, it failed.

There are three solutions to this problem. The first is to say that it makes no sense to feed files with both ISO-8859 and UTF-8 encoding to the same program without somehow differentiating them. That's perfectly true. This approach means we'll need some command-line options, liberal use of force_encoding, and code to delegate the pattern matching to different sets of patterns depending on the encoding of each file.

A second hack is to simply treat both the data and the program as ASCII-8BIT and perform all the comparisons based on the underlying bytes. This isn't particularly reliable, but it might work in some circumstances.

The third solution is to choose a master encoding and transcode strings into it before doing the matches. Ruby provides built-in support for this with the default_internal encoding mechanism.

Default Internal Encoding

By default, Ruby performs no automatic transcoding when reading and writing data. But two command-line options allow you to change this.

We've already seen the -E option, which sets the default encoding applied to the content of external files. When you say -E _xxx_, the default external encoding is set to _xxx_. But -E takes a second option. In the same way that you can give open both external and internal encodings, you can also set a default internal encoding using the option -E _external:internal_.

Thus, if all your files are written with ISO-8859-1 encoding, but you want your program to have to deal with their content as if it were UTF-8, you can use this:

```
$ ruby -E iso-8859-1:utf-8
```

You can specify just an internal encoding by omitting the external option but leaving the colon:

```
$ ruby -E :utf-8
```

Because UTF-8 is probably the best of the available transcoding targets, Ruby has the -U command-line option, which sets the internal encoding to UTF-8.

You can query the default internal encoding in your code with the default_internal method. This returns nil if no default internal encoding has been set.

One last note before we leave this section: if you compare two strings with different encodings, Ruby doesn't normalize them. Thus, "é" tagged with a UTF-8 encoding will not compare equal to "é" tagged with ISO-8859-1 because the underlying bytes are different.

JSON

JSON[1] is a language-independent data interchange format based on key/value pairs (hashes in Ruby) and sequences of values (arrays in Ruby). JSON is frequently used to exchange data between JavaScript running in browsers and server-based applications. JSON isn't a general-purpose, object marshaling format.

Ruby makes JSON methods available with require "json".

Parsing JSON

The general Ruby method for parsing JSON is JSON.parse(source, options = {}). The source is a JSON string. The output is a Ruby object. If the JSON is an object, you get a Ruby hash. If the JSON string is an array, you get a Ruby array. If the JSON is a scalar, you get a Ruby object of the matching type, and that's true recursively of sub-objects as well. The commonly used option symbolize_names: true ensures that the keys in the returned hash are symbols rather than strings; other options are less commonly used.

---

1.   https://www.json.org

If you have a filename, then JSON.load_file(path, options={}) is a shortcut for JSON.parse(File.read(path), options). More generally, if you have a file or other source for the JSON rather than the JSON data, you can save yourself a step with JSON.load(source, proc = nil, options = {}). A value based on the source argument is passed to parse. If source responds to to_str, then that value is parsed. If source responds to to_io, then source.to_io.read is parsed. If the source responds to open—meaning a file or a URI—then source.read is parsed.

Generating JSON

If you have a Ruby object and want to turn it into JSON, you can use the default Ruby libraries. We note that there are many third-party alternatives here that may provide you with more flexibility or an easier API.

The method JSON.generate(object, options = nil) converts the object into JSON. The related method fast_generate does the same thing but doesn't check for circular references. The method pretty_generate returns a string that's formatted to be more human readable. Most objects in Ruby will have a to_json method that does the same thing.

In all these cases, the resulting JSON string depends on the object:

- If the object is a Hash, it creates a JSON object, recursively generating JSON for all the keys and values.

- If the object is an array, it creates a JSON array, again recursively generating JSON for all the values.

- A Ruby string is converted to a JSON string.

- An integer or float results in a string representing the number.

- Boolean or nil results in the corresponding JSON token: true, false, or null.

- Any other object can have a custom representation by defining the method to_json.

Note that many classes in Ruby have JSON extensions that must be explicitly required. The file pattern is json/add/bigdecimal, and the available extensions are for "bigdecimal", "complex", "date", "date_time", "exception", "ostruct", "range", "rational", "regexp", "set", "struct", "symbol", and "time".

This sample writes JSON data to a file:

```
ref_io/write_json.rb
require "json"
data = {name: "dave", address: %w[tx usa], age: 17}
serialized = data.to_json
serialized   # => {"name":"dave","address":["tx","usa"],"age":17}
File.open("data.json", "w") { |f| f.puts serialized }
```

This sample reads the serialized data from the file and reconstitutes it:

```
ref_io/read_json.rb
require "json"
data = JSON.load_file("data.json")
data      # => {"name"=>"dave", "address"=>["tx", "usa"], "age"=>17}
```

Pathname

A Pathname represents the absolute or relative name of a file. It has two distinct uses. First, it allows manipulation of the parts of a file path (extracting components, building new paths, and so on). Second, it acts as a facade for some methods in the Dir and File classes and the FileTest module, forwarding on calls for the file named by the Pathname object.

The class Pathname is part of the Ruby Standard Library, meaning it ships with Ruby but is only available to code that explicitly requires it using require "pathname".

You create a pathname with Pathname.new(path), which takes a string argument. The method Pathname.pwd returns the current working directory as a path, and the method Pathname.glob is essentially a wrapper around Dir.glob.

Path instances have a limited ability to be treated like strings, files, I/O streams, or directories. You can append to a pathname with + (the right argument is converted to a Pathname before it's added). The addition argument is aliased as /, which might seem odd but lets you write something like this (which looks a little like file manipulation):

```
ref_io/pathname_concat.rb
require "pathname"
dir_name = Pathname.new("/usr/bin")
dir_name / "ruby"   # => #<Pathname:/usr/bin/ruby>
```

Most of the methods in Pathname are just wrappers around File, Dir, or IO. (Check out the Ruby documentation for a complete list.) Here's a sample:

```
ref_io/pathname_1.rb
require "pathname"

p1 = Pathname.new("/usr/bin")
p2 = Pathname.new("ruby")
p3 = p1 + p2
p4 = p2 + p1
p3.parent          # => #<Pathname:/usr/bin>
p3.parent.parent   # => #<Pathname:/usr>
p1.absolute?       # => true
p2.absolute?       # => false
p3.split           # => [#<Pathname:/usr/bin>, #<Pathname:ruby>]
```

```
ref_io/pathname_2.rb
require "pathname"
p5 = Pathname.new("testdir")
puts p5.realpath
puts p5.children
```

produces:

```
/Users/noel/projects/pragmatic/ruby5/Book/testdir
testdir/pickaxe.rb
testdir/config.json
```

```
ref_io/pathname_3.rb
require "pathname"

p1 = Pathname.new("/usr/bin/ruby")
p1.file?                    # => true
p1.directory?               # => false
```

```
p1.executable?              # => true
p1.size                     # => 167952

p2 = Pathname.new("testfile")   # => #<Pathname:testfile>

p2.read                     # => "This is line one\nThis is line two\nThis is
                            # .. line three\nAnd so on...\n"
p2.readlines                # => ["This is line one\n", "This is line two\n",
                            # .. "This is line three\n", "And so on...\n"]
```

StringIO

In some ways, the distinction between strings and file contents is artificial: the contents of a file are basically a string that happens to live on disk, not in memory. The StringIO class, available by using require "stringio", aims to unify the two concepts, making strings act as if they were opened IO objects. Once a string is wrapped in a StringIO object, it can be read from and written to as if it were an open file. This can make unit testing a lot easier.

The StringIO class isn't a subclass of IO, it just implements many of the same read/write methods. Using StringIO lets you pass strings into classes and methods that were originally written to work with files. StringIO objects take their encoding from the string you pass in—if no string is passed, the default external encoding is used.

You create a StringIO with either the method StringIO.new(string = "", mode = "r+") or the method StringIO.open(string = "", mode = "r+"). In both cases, the string argument is the initial value of the StringIO and the mode still controls whether you can read or write to the value the same way it does for files (see Table 28, Mode values, on page 593). The open method takes a block and passes the new StringIO to the block. The new method returns the new StringIO. You can then do most of your file or I/O processing on the new object. Here's an example:

ref_io/string_io.rb
```ruby
require "stringio"

sio = StringIO.new("time flies like an arrow")
sio.read(5)              # => "time "
sio.read(5)              # => "flies"
sio.pos = 19
sio.read(5)              # => "arrow"
sio.rewind               # => 0
sio.write("fruit")       # => 5
sio.pos = 16
sio.write("a banana")    # => 8
sio.rewind               # => 0
sio.read                 # => "fruitflies like a banana"
```

And here's an example of testing using a StringIO to test CSV processing:

ref_io/string_io_test.rb
```ruby
require "stringio"
require "csv"
require "minitest/autorun"

class TestCSV < Minitest::Test
  def test_simple
    StringIO.open do |op|
      CSV(op) do |csv|
```

```
        csv << [1, "line 1", 27]
        csv << [2, nil, 123]
      end
      assert_equal("1,line 1,27\n2,,123\n", op.string)
    end
  end
end
```

produces:

```
Run options: --seed 40457
# Running:

.

Finished in 0.000287s, 3484.3209 runs/s, 3484.3209 assertions/s.

1 runs, 1 assertions, 0 failures, 0 errors, 0 skips
```

Tempfile

Class Tempfile creates managed temporary files. Although they behave the same as any other IO objects, temporary files are automatically deleted when the Ruby program terminates. Once a Tempfile object has been created, the underlying file may be opened and closed a number of times in succession.

Tempfile doesn't directly inherit from IO. Instead, it delegates calls to a File object. From the programmer's perspective, apart from the unusual new, open, and close semantics, a Tempfile object behaves as if it were an IO object.

If you don't specify a directory to hold temporary files when you create them, the Dir.tmpdir location will be used to find a system-dependent location. Here's an example:

```
ref_io/tempfile.rb
require "tempfile"
tf = Tempfile.new("afile")
tf.path     # => "/var/folders/lw/ybl1dt397hn5t38r2f70_bv00000gn/T/afile20231102-4
            # .. 3981-pxovuj"
tf.puts("Cosi Fan Tutte")
tf.close
tf.open
tf.gets     # => "Cosi Fan Tutte\n"
tf.close(true)
tf.unlink  # => nil
```

If you create a Tempfile, it's deleted when the application ends. But it's useful to explicitly close it with close and delete it with unlink, especially if you're creating a lot of Tempfile objects, so as not to take up extra space.

The method Tempfile.create takes a block, passes the tempfile to the block, and closes and removes the file at the end of the block.

```
ref_io/tempfile_block.rb
require "tempfile"
Tempfile.create("afile") do |tf|
  tf.path
  tf.puts("Cosi Fan Tutte")
  tf.gets
end
```

URI

URI encapsulates the concept of a Uniform Resource Identifier (URI), a way of specifying some kind of (potentially networked) resource. URIs are a superset of URLs. URLs (such as the addresses of web pages) allow specification of addresses by location, and URIs also allow specification by name. The URI classes are available with require "uri".

The URI class can be used to do the following:

- Parse URIs into component parts.
- Open a stream to the network location referred to by the URI.
- Manage encoding and decoding of strings to be safe for use in URLs.

URIs consist of a scheme (such as http, mailto, ftp, and so on), followed by structured data identifying the resource within the scheme.

Parsing is managed with the method URI.parse(string), which takes in a string URI and returns a parsed object in a subclass of a URI specific to the scheme. The library explicitly supports the file, ftp, http, https, ldap, mailto, ws, and wss schemes; others will be treated as generic URIs.

The class Net::HTTP accepts URI objects where a URL parameter is expected.

```
ref_io/uri.rb
require "uri"

uri = URI.parse("http://pragprog.com:1234/mypage.cgi?q=ruby")
uri.class      # => URI::HTTP
uri.scheme     # => "http"
uri.host       # => "pragprog.com"
uri.port       # => 1234
uri.path       # => "/mypage.cgi"
uri.query      # => "q=ruby"

uri = URI.parse("mailto:ruby@pragprog.com?Subject=help&body=info")
uri.class      # => URI::MailTo
uri.scheme     # => "mailto"
uri.to         # => "ruby@pragprog.com"
uri.headers    # => [["Subject", "help"], ["body", "info"]]

uri = URI.parse("ftp://dave@anon.com:/pub/ruby;type=i")
uri.class      # => URI::FTP
uri.scheme     # => "ftp"
uri.host       # => "anon.com"
uri.port       # => 21
uri.path       # => "pub/ruby"
uri.typecode   # => "i"
```

The module also has convenience methods to escape and unescape URIs.

The method URI.open(uri, *args, &block) opens a generic URI. The first argument is either an object that responds to open or a string that can be parsed by URI.parse and converts to an object that responds to open—all URI subclasses do. That object is sent an open message with any remaining args. The resulting I/O stream is sent to the block and can be treated like any I/O stream. The stream is then closed at the end of the block.

The module also has convenience methods to escape and unescape URIs. There are three pairs of methods and they are similar. URI.encode_www_form_component(string, encoding = nil) and

URI.decode_www_form_component(string, encoding = nil) convert a string to URL formatting. Characters in the ranges "a".."z", "A".."Z", "0".."9" are preserved as-is, along with the characters "*", ".", "-", and "_". Spaces are converted to +. All other characters are converted to the format "%" followed by the ord value of the character as a hexadecimal number. The resulting string is in UTF-8 encoding unless an encoding is specified. The decode_www_form_component does the reverse: It takes an encoded string, puts the spaces back, and converts the % back to regular characters.

The pair URI.encode_uri_component(string, encoding = nil) and URI.decode_uri_component(string, encoding = nil) are exactly the same except that spaces are converted to "%20".

The method URI.encode_www_form(enumerable, encoding = nil) converts a list of items to a format that can be used as HTTP form data in a query string. In the normal case, the enumerable is a hash, and each element is converted to a string key=value. If the value is an array with multiple elements, each element is matched to the key separately. The individual elements are joined by an ampersand (&). Here's an example:

```
ref_io/uri_encode_1.rb
require "uri"
URI.encode_www_form({first: "not", homes: ["earth", "other earth"]})  # => "first
                                                                      # .. =not&h
                                                                      # .. omes=e
                                                                      # .. arth&h
                                                                      # .. omes=o
                                                                      # .. ther+e
                                                                      # .. arth"
```

Alternatively, each element of the argument can be a two-element array[name, value] and that element is converted into a string name=value:

```
ref_io/uri_encode_2.rb
require "uri"
URI.encode_www_form([%w[first jennifer], %w[last weaver]])  # => "first=jennifer&
                                                            # .. last=weaver"
```

If the individual element is a one-element array or just a single element, that name is used directly:

```
ref_io/uri_encode_3.rb
require "uri"
URI.encode_www_form([%w[first jennifer], ["admin"]])  # => "first=jennifer&admin"
```

The associated method URI.decode_www_form(string, encoding = UTF-8, separator: "&", use__charset_: false, isindex: false) takes a string and converts it back to the set of key/value pairs:

```
ref_io/uri_decode.rb
require "uri"
URI.decode_www_form("first=not&homes=earth&homes=other+earth")  # => [["first",
                                                                # .. "not"],
                                                                # .. ["homes",
                                                                # .. "earth"],
                                                                # .. ["homes",
                                                                # .. "other
                                                                # .. earth"]]
```

Similar encoding and decoding is provided by the CGI module. CGI.escape(string) and CGI.escapeURIComponent(sting) encodes an arbitrary string using the same rules as URI.encode_www_form_component and URI.encode_uri_component, while CGI.escapeHTML(string) escapes the special HTML characters &, <, and >. The encodings can be reversed with CGI.unescape, CGI.unescapeURIComponent, and CGI.unescapeHTML.

YAML

The YAML library, available with require "yaml", serializes and deserializes Ruby object trees to and from an external, readable, plain-text format. YAML can be used as a portable object marshaling scheme, allowing objects to be passed in plain text between separate Ruby processes. In some cases, objects may also be exchanged between Ruby programs and programs in other languages that also have YAML support.

The YAML module in Ruby is an alias to Psych, which is the name of the YAML parser being used. We mention this because it may be easier to find further documentation searching for Psych rather than YAML.

Writing YAML

YAML can be used to store an object tree in a string. The API call is YAML.dump(object, io = nil, options = {}). The object is the object being converted to YAML. The io parameter is an optional IO argument, potentially a File or StringIO. The options argument is a hash with the following keys:

- :cannonical, default false. If true, prints a more verbose and formal YAML structure.

- :header, default false. If true, adds %YAML <version> at the top of the document.

- :indentation, default 2. The number of spaces used for line indentation. Only values between 0 and 9 can be used.

- :line_width, default 0. Maximum line width. If exceeded, the library will split lines. The default of 0 is equivalent to 80.

If no io argument is provided, the resulting YAML is returned as a string. If an io argument is provided, the IO object is returned. This code uses the io form to write the YAML directly to an open file.

```
ref_io/yaml_store.rb
require "yaml"
tree = {
  name: "ruby",
  uses: %w[scripting web testing etc]
}
File.open("tree.yml", "w") { |f| YAML.dump(tree, f) }
```

The class Object defines Object#to_yaml(options = {}), which is a shortcut to YAML.dump(self, options).

The similar method YAML.safe_dump(object, io = nil, options = {}) behaves almost identically but limits the set of classes that can be dumped.

By default, the safe set of classes are: Array, Integer, FalseClass, Float, Hash, NilClass, String, and TrueClass. You can add other classes to the safe list with the option permitted_classes:. Any classes in that list will be added to the list of safe classes, as in permitted_classes: [Symbol, Time]. If the data to be dumped contains an instance of a class that isn't in the safe list, a Psych::DisallowedClass exception is thrown.

Reading YAML

The YAML module provides methods to read from a string or a file, and also for safe and unsafe reading.

Loading involves two steps: parsing the YAML file and then converting YAML data structures to Ruby objects. The most generic method is load, which has a long method signature with keyword options: YAML.load(yaml, permitted_classes: [Symbol], permitted_symbols: [], aliases: false, filename: false, fallback: nil, symbolize_names: false, freeze: false, strict_integer: false). The return value is a Ruby object loaded from the YAML data.

The yaml is a string of YAML or an I/O object containing YAML. The various keyword arguments, in alphabetical order, are the following:

- aliases: If true, then YAML alias syntax is allowed. If false, and the YAML contains aliases, a Psych::AliasesNotEnabled error is raised.

- fallback: If the source yaml is empty, then the fallback value is returned.

- filename: Not the source of the string, just used as a filename to report errors if there is a parsing error.

- freeze: If true, then freeze is called on the resulting Ruby object before it's returned.

- permitted_classes: As with this option for dump, a list of classes that are allowed to be loaded. The default list is the same as for dump plus load adds Symbol to that list.

- permitted_symbols: If this list isn't empty, then any symbol that's loaded is compared against this list. If the symbol isn't on the list, then a Psych::DisallowedClass exception is thrown.

- strict_integer: If true, the YAML parser uses a stricter definition of integer when parsing.

- symbolize_names: If true, any hash object in the YAML resolves to have symbols as keys instead of strings.

If there's a syntax error in the YAML, a Psych::SyntaxError exception is raised.

```
ref_io/yaml_read.rb
require "yaml"
tree = YAML.load_file("tree.yml")
tree[:uses][1]              # => "web"
```

There are a few variants of this method. YAML.load_file(filename, **kwargs) is a convenience method that opens the file at filename, then calls YAML.load with the open file as the yaml argument (the filename as the filename: argument), and passes along any of the other keyword arguments. The method YAML.safe_load has the exact arguments as YAML.load except that it doesn't include Symbol as a permitted class.

If you don't want the safety of limiting classes (which, to be clear, is a protection against malicious YAML documents), you can use YAML.unsafe_load(yaml, filename: nil, fallback: false, symbolize_names: false, freeze: false, strict_integer: false), where all the arguments have the same meaning as in load and safe_load, but there are no type checks. There's also YAML.unsafe_load_file(filename, **kwargs), which has the same behavior as load_file except for the lack of type checks.

Using YAML

The YAML format is also a convenient way to store configuration information for programs. Because it's readable, it can be maintained by hand using a normal editor and then read as objects by programs. For example, a configuration file may contain the following:

```
ref_io/config.yml
---
username: dave
prefs:
  background: dark
  foreground: cyan
  timeout: 30
```

We can use this in a program:

```
ref_io/yaml_config.rb
require "yaml"

config = YAML.load_file("#{__dir__}/config.yml")
puts config["username"]
puts config["prefs"]["timeout"] * 10
```

produces:

```
dave
300
```

## CHAPTER 30

Library Reference: Ruby on Ruby

In this chapter, we'll take a closer look at some useful classes in Ruby that you might use for metaprogramming or observation. We'll investigate their API and functionality in somewhat more detail than we did in Part I of this book. The goal of this chapter is to give you more information about what you can do with these classes and also to discuss related functions together so that you can browse and perhaps find a new feature that might help.

This isn't intended to be a complete listing of every class, method, or option. For that, please refer to the official Ruby documentation at https://docs.ruby-lang.org.

In this chapter, when a method is mentioned for the first time, we provide its complete name and signature. The notation Foo.bar indicates a class or module method, while Foo#bar indicates an instance method. Optional arguments are indicated with Ruby syntax and their default value, as in Foo#bar(name, size = 0). Dynamically sized arguments are indicated with splat syntax, as in Foo#bar(*files, **options). Block arguments are indicated with brace syntax and an indication of what the arguments to the block will be, as in Foo#bar { |object| block }. An optional block argument will be surrounded by square brackets, Foo#bar [{block}]. Please note that this description syntax is slightly different than the official documentation, and that in some cases, what the official documentation shows as multiple method signatures, we've chosen to show as one signature with default values. Also, parameter names sometimes differ from the official documentation to make the naming clearer.

Benchmark

The Benchmark module allows code execution to be timed and the results tabulated. Benchmark is easier to use if you include it in your top-level environment.

The most useful method of Benchmark is Benchmark.bm(label_width = 0, *labels) { |report| ...}. The bm method passes a report object to the block. Inside the block, you call report(caption) on that object one or more times, passing a block each time. Ruby will execute each block and emit a table with an entry for each block listing the time spent by the CPU executing code (user time), the CPU time spent by the system during the block (system time), the total of those two (total), and the amount of clock time that passed during the block.

This example compares the costs of four kinds of method dispatch:

```
ref_meta_ruby/benchmark_1.rb
require "benchmark"
string = "Stormy Weather"
m = string.method(:length)
Benchmark.bm(6) do |x|
  x.report("direct") { 100_000.times { string.length } }
  x.report("call") { 100_000.times { m.call } }
  x.report("send") { 100_000.times { string.send(:length) } }
  x.report("eval") { 100_000.times { eval("string.length") } }
end
```

produces:

```
              user      system      total            real
direct     0.002317    0.000000    0.002317 (    0.002337)
call       0.004806    0.000000    0.004806 (    0.004806)
send       0.005009    0.000000    0.005009 (    0.005008)
eval       0.205992    0.002032    0.208024 (    0.210398)
```

The Benchmark module offers the Benchmark#bmbm(width = 0) method, which does a test run of all the blocks being benchmarked before doing the actual benchmark. This is an attempt to ensure that the memory garbage collector is stable before the benchmark, which can make the results more consistent and accurate.

Which is better: reading all of a dictionary and splitting it or splitting it line by line? This example uses bmbm to run a rehearsal before doing the timing:

```
ref_meta_ruby/benchmark_2.rb
require "benchmark"
Benchmark.bmbm(6) do |x|
  x.report("all") do
    str = File.read("/usr/share/dict/words")
    words = str.scan(/[-\w']+/)
  end
  x.report("lines") do
    words = []
    File.foreach("/usr/share/dict/words") do |line|
      words << line.chomp
    end
  end
end
```

produces:

```
Rehearsal ------------------------------------------------
all        0.076054    0.006898    0.082952 (    0.083685)
lines      0.048711    0.003024    0.051735 (    0.068264)
--------------------------------- total: 0.134687sec

              user      system      total            real
all        0.067480    0.003470    0.070950 (    0.071092)
lines      0.040801    0.001468    0.042269 (    0.042386)
```

Data

Ruby provides the Data class to be used as an immutable data object. The intent of Data is to create an object similar to a Struct, but whose attributes cannot be changed (see Struct, on page 632).

You create new Data classes with the define method. As with Struct, you can then create new instances with either positional or keyword arguments, and you can read those arguments:

```
ref_meta_ruby/data_1.rb
Classroom = Data.define(:name, :capacity)
auditorium = Classroom.new("auditorium", 1000)
math = Classroom.new(name: "X 206", capacity: 30)

auditorium.capacity  # => 1000
```

Unlike Struct, you can't write the attributes of a Data object, but you can create new instances using with. The with method takes keyword arguments and returns a new data object. That data object is a copy of the original, but any attributes passed as arguments to with are set to those new values. The original instance continues to exist unchanged.

```
ref_meta_ruby/data_2.rb
LightBulb = Data.define(:brightness, :watts, :color)
cool_bulb = LightBulb.new(1600, 15, 4000)
warmer_bulb = cool_bulb.with(color: 2700)

cool_bulb.to_h    # => {:brightness=>1600, :watts=>15, :color=>4000}
warmer_bulb.to_h  # => {:brightness=>1600, :watts=>15, :color=>2700}
```

Objects created via Data respond to a minimal set of other methods, including == for equality, and to_h to convert to a hash. Notably, Data objects don't respond to each or dig but they do respond to deconstruct and deconstruct_keys, so they can be used in pattern matching:

```
ref_meta_ruby/data_3.rb
LightBulb = Data.define(:brightness, :watts, :color)
bulb = LightBulb.new(1600, 15, 5000)

case bulb
in {brightness:, color: 5000}
  puts "a daylight bulb with #{brightness} lumens"
in {brightness:, color: 2700}
  puts "a warm bulb with #{brightness} lumens"
else
  puts "a different bulb"
end
```

produces:

```
a daylight bulb with 1600 lumens
```

Data objects can be created with a block, which allows for instance methods to be defined for the data object:

```
ref_meta_ruby/data_4.rb
LightBulb = Data.define(:brightness, :watts, :color) do
  def warmth
    (color < 4500) ? "cool" : "warm"
  end
end
```

```
bulb = LightBulb.new(1600, 15, 5000)
puts bulb.warmth
```

produces:

```
warm
```

Delegator and SimpleDelegator

Object delegation is a way of *composing* objects—extending an object with the capabilities of another—at runtime. The Ruby Delegator class implements a simple but powerful delegation scheme, where requests are automatically forwarded from a master class to delegates or their ancestors and where the delegate can be changed at runtime with a single method call. The class SimpleDelegator is an implementation of Delegator that's good enough for most purposes.

The typical use of SimpleDelegator is as a decorator. You create a class as a subclass of SimpleDelegator. You create new instances of the simple delegator class by passing it an existing instance of another class. When you call a method on the delegator, it'll automatically pass methods that the delegator doesn't define over to the original object. Here's an example:

ref_meta_ruby/simple_delegator.rb
```
require 'delegate'

class User
  attr_accessor :first_name, :last_name

  def initialize(first_name, last_name)
    @first_name = first_name
    @last_name = last_name
  end
end

class SortableUser < SimpleDelegator
  def sort_name
    "#{last_name}, #{first_name}"
  end
end

fozzie = User.new("Fozzie", "Bear")
sortable_user = SortableUser.new(fozzie)

p sortable_user.first_name
p sortable_user.sort_name
```

produces:

```
"Fozzie"
"Bear, Fozzie"
```

In this case, the SortableUser defines sort_name but any other method called on a SortableUser instance will be delegated to the original object.

You can get the underlying object from a SimpleDelegator with SimpleDelegator#__getobj__ and change it with SimpleDelegator#__setobj__(new_object).

For simple cases where the class of the delegate is fixed, make the new class a subclass of DelegateClass, passing the name of the class to be delegated as an argument in the class declaration. In the new class's initialize method, call super with the object that's being delegated, which must be of the type passed in the class definition. Here's an example:

```
ref_meta_ruby/delegate_class.rb
require "delegate"

class Words < DelegateClass(Array)
  def initialize(list = "/usr/share/dict/words")
    words = File.read(list).split
    super(words)
  end
end

words = Words.new
words[9999]       # => "anticonscience"
words.size        # => 235976
words.grep(/matz/) # => ["matzo", "matzoon", "matzos", "matzoth"]
```

In this case, the Words class will delegate any instance variables that it doesn't know to Array. This is extremely close to just subclassing from Array.

The Delegator class gives you more control over the delegation (SimpleDelegator and DelegateClass are defined in terms of Delegator). To use Delegator you would create a class that inherits from it and implements __getobj__ and __setobj__ to determine the object to delegate to.

Logger

Ruby has a Logger class that's accessible with require "logger". It writes log messages to a file or stream and supports automatic time- or size-based rolling of log files. Messages can be assigned severities, and only those messages at or above the logger's current reporting level will be logged.

A new logger is created with Logger.new(location, shift_age = 0, shift_size = 1048576, **options).

The location is one of the following:

- A string, which is interpreted as a filename; log entries are appended to the file.

- An IO stream, in which case log entries are written to the stream. The stream can be an open File object or any of Ruby's global streams, like $stdout, but any stream will work.

- nil (or File::NULL), in which case log entries are ignored.

Valid keyword arguments for the options hash include level to set the log's severity level and progname to set the default program name. Entries that are less severe than the level are ignored. The default is Logger::DEBUG, which is the lowest level.

Levels can be defined using the provided constants or by corresponding strings. In order, from the least severe to the most severe, the defined logger severities are:

- Logger::DEBUG, aka debug
- Logger::INFO, aka info
- Logger::WARN, aka warn
- Logger::ERROR, aka error
- Logger::FATAL, aka fatal
- Logger::UNKNOWN, aka unknown

You add new entries to the log with Logger#add(severity, message = nil, progname = nil), aliased as log. The severity is one of the seven constants or strings listed above, the message is what is sent to the logger, and the program name is an optional prefix. The message is a string, which is used as-is, an Exception, in which case the .message attribute of the exception is used, or anything else, in which case inspect is called to convert it to a string.

For each severity level, there are three convenience functions:

- The level name (debug, info, warn, and so on), which takes a message argument and adds a log entry at that severity.

- A predicate method (debug?, info?, and so on), which returns true if the level of the logger matches the method name. You can also get the level with Logger#level.

- A bang method (debug!, info!, and so on), which sets the level of the log going forward based on the method name. You can also set the level with Logger#level=.

You can see the default message pattern in this code:

```
ref_meta_ruby/logger.rb
require "logger"

log = Logger.new($stdout, level: Logger::DEBUG)
log.info("Application starting")
3.times do |i|
  log.debug("Executing loop, i = #{i}")
  temperature = some_calculation(i)  # defined externally
  if temperature > 50
    log.warn("Possible overheat. i = #{i}")
  end
end

log.info("Application terminating")
```

produces:

```
I, [2023-11-02T17:16:45.716996 #44233]  INFO -- : Application starting
D, [2023-11-02T17:16:45.717020 #44233] DEBUG -- : Executing loop, i = 0
D, [2023-11-02T17:16:45.717025 #44233] DEBUG -- : Executing loop, i = 1
D, [2023-11-02T17:16:45.717028 #44233] DEBUG -- : Executing loop, i = 2
W, [2023-11-02T17:16:45.717030 #44233]  WARN -- : Possible overheat. i = 2
I, [2023-11-02T17:16:45.717033 #44233]  INFO -- : Application terminating
```

Ruby will automatically rotate the log files based on the shift_size and shift_age parameters. If both parameters are positive integers, then the rotation is based on file size. When the log first reaches the shift_size, the file is closed and renamed with a .0 extension and a new log file is opened. If there is an existing log with the .0 extension, it's moved to .1 and so on. The shift_age parameter is the maximum number of files to keep; files over that number are removed. If the shift_age is a string, then the rotation is based on time, and the parameter can have the value daily, weekly, monthly, everytime, or now. When the time period ends, the existing file is renamed based on the timestamp and a new file is opened. If the parameter is everytime or now, a new file is created on each new log entry.

ObjectSpace

The ObjectSpace module contains a number of routines that interact with the garbage collection facility and allow you to traverse all living objects with an iterator.

ObjectSpace also provides support for object finalizers. These are procs that will be called when a specific object is about to be destroyed by garbage collection. Typically, you either call ObjectSpace methods as module methods as in ObjectSpace.count_objects or you include ObjectSpace as a module in another class and call the methods directly.

This is just a glance at what ObjectSpace can do; there's more in the official documentation.

The method ObjectSpace.define_finalizer(object, proc = proc()) adds proc as a finalizer, called automatically when object is about to be destroyed. If you use lambda to create the proc object, you must remember to include a parameter with the block. If you don't, the invocation of the lambda will silently fail when the finalizer is called because of a mismatch in the expected and actual parameter count. Finalization of an object is never guaranteed and may not happen until program exit.

The method ObjectSpace.each_object(module = nil) [{block}] calls the block once for each living object in this Ruby process that's not an "immediate" object. An immediate object is an object that's stored directly as its value, rather than as a pointer in memory to its value. In Ruby, small enough Integer objects, symbols, true, false, and nil are considered immediate objects, though the exact definition is implementation-dependent. If module is specified, each_object calls the block for only those classes or modules that match (or are a subclass of) module. The return value is the number of objects found. In the following example, each_object returns the large integer we defined and several numeric constants defined elsewhere in Ruby. If you don't provide a block, an Enumerator is returned. Here's an example:

```
a = 98.6
b = "banana"
c = 12345678987654321672312341241234124124
d = 12
count = ObjectSpace.each_object(Numeric) {|x| p x }
puts "Total count: #{count}"
```

produces:

```
NaN
Infinity
1.7976931348623157e+308
2.2250738585072014e-308
(0+1i)
9223372036854775807
12345678987654321672312341241234124124
Total count: 7
```

Observable

The Observer pattern, also known as Publish/Subscribe, provides a simple mechanism for one object (the source) to inform a set of interested third-party objects when its state changes. In the Ruby implementation, the notifying class mixes in the module Observable, which provides the methods for managing the associated observer objects. The observers must implement the update method to receive notifications.

The way this works is that the class that's sending the notifications adds include Observable. To add subscribers to the notifications, you call Observable#add_observer(observer, method = :update). The observer is an object that receives a notification, and method is the method that's automatically called when a notification is triggered.

To send a notification, the publishing object calls Observable#changed(state=true) to mark that the object has changed and then calls Observable#notify_observers(*args), which goes through each subscriber and calls the method registered when add_observer was invoked. You need to call changed again before you call notify_observers again. You can see the status of that with Observable#changed?. Any arguments passed to notify_observers are passed through to the update method. Here's an example:

ref_meta_ruby/observable.rb
```ruby
class Temperature
  @p = [83, 75, 90, 134, 134, 112, 79]
  def self.fetch
    exit if @p.empty?
    @p.shift
  end
end
require "observer"

class CheckWaterTemperature # Periodically check the water
  include Observable

  def run
    last_temp = nil
    loop do
      temp = Temperature.fetch # external class...
      puts "Current temperature: #{temp}"
      if temp != last_temp
        changed # notify observers
        notify_observers(Time.now, temp)
        last_temp = temp
      end
    end
  end
end

class Warner
  def initialize(&limit)
    @limit = limit
  end

  def update(time, temp) # callback for observer
    if @limit.call(temp)
      puts "--- #{time}: Temperature outside range: #{temp}"
    end
  end
end

checker = CheckWaterTemperature.new
checker.add_observer(Warner.new { |t| t < 80 })
checker.add_observer(Warner.new { |t| t > 120 })
checker.run
```

produces:
```
Current temperature: 83
Current temperature: 75
--- 2023-11-02 17:16:45 -0500: Temperature outside range: 75
Current temperature: 90
Current temperature: 134
```

```
--- 2023-11-02 17:16:45 -0500: Temperature outside range: 134
Current temperature: 134
Current temperature: 112
Current temperature: 79
--- 2023-11-02 17:16:45 -0500: Temperature outside range: 79
```

The publishing object has access to Observable#count_observers, which returns the number of current observers, and Observable.delete_observer(object), which removes a specific observer. You can remove all observers with Observable.delete_observers.

OpenStruct

If Data is the most immutable way to get a small object, OpenStruct is the most flexible. An OpenStruct isn't a class generator, rather, it's more a way to allow you to have hash-like data with attribute-like syntax.

You create an OpenStruct with new method, taking either a hash argument or an arbitrary set of keyword arguments. After that, you can read, write, and create attributes just by using them, and you can also use hash syntax:

```ruby
require "ostruct"

bulb = OpenStruct.new(brightness: 1600, watts: 15, color: 2500)
bulb.color     # => 2500
bulb[:watts]   # => 15
bulb.shape = "A19"
bulb.to_h      # => {:brightness=>1600, :watts=>15, :color=>2500, :shape=>"A19"}
```

Internally OpenStruct uses method_missing, which means it's very flexible, but also quite slow. We'd recommend trying Struct or Data for production code, though OpenStruct is nice for test data. It's possible that you might overwrite existing Object or Kernel methods with your attribute, in which case you can access the underlying method by appending it with a !.

The OpenStruct class defines == for equality tests and each_pair for use in loops, and it also implements dig but doesn't implement the pattern-matching methods.

PP

PP uses the PrettyPrint library to format the results of inspecting Ruby objects. In addition to the methods in the class, it defines a global function, pp, which works like the existing p method but formats its output.

PP has a default layout for all Ruby objects. But you can override the way it handles a class by defining the method pretty_print, which takes a PP object as a parameter. It should use that PP object's methods (text, breakable, nest, group, and pp) to format its output:

ref_meta_ruby/pretty_print.rb
```ruby
require 'pp'

Customer = Struct.new(:first_name, :last_name, :dob, :country)
cust = Customer.new("Walter", "Wall", "12/25/1960", "Niue")

puts "Regular print"
p cust

puts "\nPretty print"
pp cust
```

produces:

```
Regular print
#<struct Customer first_name="Walter", last_name="Wall", dob="12/25/1960",
country="Niue">

Pretty print
#<struct Customer
 first_name="Walter",
 last_name="Wall",
 dob="12/25/1960",
 country="Niue">
```

Prism

Prism is a new parsing gem in Ruby 3.3 that's likely to be the future parsing library for Ruby and Ruby tooling. Prism can be used as a stand-alone gem; it is also included with the Ruby standard library. You can use it with require "prism".

Prism is designed to be a common parser across Ruby implementations, and as of this writing, it's also integrated into Ruby and TruffleRuby, among others. It's also used by the ruby-lsp language server.

Prism is designed to be tolerant to errors. For example, if you're typing a file in your editor, Prism tries not to let syntax errors in one part of the file affect the parsing of the rest of the file, making for a much better development experience while typing.

Prism includes an API that you can use directly:

```
ref_meta_ruby/prism_1.rb
require "prism"

content = "a=1;b=2;puts a+b"

puts
p "Lexical analysis"
pp Prism.lex(content)
puts
p "Parsing"
pp Prism.parse(content)
```

produces:

```
"Lexical analysis"
#<Prism::ParseResult:0x00000001031c8d98
 @comments=[],
 @errors=[],
 @magic_comments=[],
 @source=
  #<Prism::Source:0x00000001030cbaf8 @offsets=[0], @source="a=1;b=2;puts a+b">,
 @value=
  [[IDENTIFIER(1,0)-(1,1)("a"), 32],
   [EQUAL(1,1)-(1,2)("="), 1],
   [INTEGER(1,2)-(1,3)("1"), 2],
   [SEMICOLON(1,3)-(1,4)(";"), 1],
   [IDENTIFIER(1,4)-(1,5)("b"), 32],
   [EQUAL(1,5)-(1,6)("="), 1],
   [INTEGER(1,6)-(1,7)("2"), 2],
```

```
    [SEMICOLON(1,7)-(1,8)(";"), 1],
    [IDENTIFIER(1,8)-(1,12)("puts"), 32],
    [IDENTIFIER(1,13)-(1,14)("a"), 1026],
    [PLUS(1,14)-(1,15)("+"), 1],
    [IDENTIFIER(1,15)-(1,16)("b"), 1026],
    [EOF(1,16)-(1,16)(""), 1026]],
 @warnings=[]>

"Parsing"
#<Prism::ParseResult:0x0000000103165568
 @comments=[],
 @errors=[],
 @magic_comments=[],
 @source=
  #<Prism::Source:0x00000001034a18f8 @offsets=[0], @source="a=1;b=2;puts a+b">,
 @value=
  @ ProgramNode (location: (1,0)-(1,16))
  ├── locals: [:a, :b]
  └── statements:
      @ StatementsNode (location: (1,0)-(1,16))
      └── body: (length: 3)
          ├── @ LocalVariableWriteNode (location: (1,0)-(1,3))
          │   ├── name: :a
          │   ├── depth: 0
          │   ├── name_loc: (1,0)-(1,1) = "a"
          │   ├── value:
          │   │   @ IntegerNode (location: (1,2)-(1,3))
          │   │   └── flags: decimal
          │   └── operator_loc: (1,1)-(1,2) = "="
          ├── @ LocalVariableWriteNode (location: (1,4)-(1,7))
          │   ├── name: :b
          │   ├── depth: 0
          │   ├── name_loc: (1,4)-(1,5) = "b"
          │   ├── value:
          │   │   @ IntegerNode (location: (1,6)-(1,7))
          │   │   └── flags: decimal
          │   └── operator_loc: (1,5)-(1,6) = "="
          └── @ CallNode (location: (1,8)-(1,16))
              ├── receiver: ∅
              ├── call_operator_loc: ∅
              ├── message_loc: (1,8)-(1,12) = "puts"
              ├── opening_loc: ∅
              ├── arguments:
              │   @ ArgumentsNode (location: (1,13)-(1,16))
              │   └── arguments: (length: 1)
              │       └── @ CallNode (location: (1,13)-(1,16))
              │           ├── receiver:
              │           │   @ LocalVariableReadNode (location: (1,13)-(1,14))
              │           │   ├── name: :a
              │           │   └── depth: 0
              │           ├── call_operator_loc: ∅
              │           ├── message_loc: (1,14)-(1,15) = "+"
              │           ├── opening_loc: ∅
              │           ├── arguments:
              │           │   @ ArgumentsNode (location: (1,15)-(1,16))
```

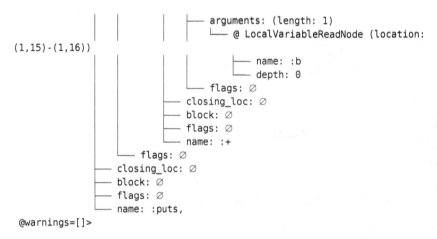

```
                              ├── arguments: (length: 1)
                              │   └── @ LocalVariableReadNode (location:
(1,15)-(1,16))
                                      ├── name: :b
                                      └── depth: 0
                              └── flags: ∅
                      ├── closing_loc: ∅
                      ├── block: ∅
                      ├── flags: ∅
                      └── name: :+
              └── flags: ∅
      ├── closing_loc: ∅
      ├── block: ∅
      ├── flags: ∅
      └── name: :puts,

@warnings=[]>
```

In addition to Prism.lex(source, filepath=nil), which takes a source string, there is also Prism.lex_file(filepath), which takes the file directly. Similarly, Prism.parse(source, filepath=nil) includes a related Prism.parse_file(filepath). There are also other more specialized methods, including compatibility with Ripper.

Ripper

The ripper library, available with require "ripper", gives you access to Ruby's parser. It can tokenize input, meaning it can convert a string of Ruby code into a series of semantic elements called tokens. It can return a lexical analysis of those tokens and what they mean to Ruby. And it can return a nested S-expression, which is a tree-like structure that represents the relationship between the tokens in the code. Ripper also supports event-based parsing.

Here's an example that shows the possibilities on a single string of Ruby code:

```
ref_meta_ruby/ripper_1.rb
require "ripper"

content = "a=1;b=2;puts a+b"

p "Tokens"
p Ripper.tokenize(content)
puts
p "Lexical analysis"
pp Ripper.lex(content)[0,5]
puts
p "S-Expressions"
pp Ripper.sexp(content)
```

produces:

```
"Tokens"
["a", "=", "1", ";", "b", "=", "2", ";", "puts", " ", "a", "+", "b"]

"Lexical analysis"
[[[1, 0], :on_ident, "a", CMDARG],
 [[1, 1], :on_op, "=", BEG],
 [[1, 2], :on_int, "1", END],
 [[1, 3], :on_semicolon, ";", BEG],
 [[1, 4], :on_ident, "b", CMDARG]]
```

```
"S-Expressions"
[:program,
 [[:assign, [:var_field, [:@ident, "a", [1, 0]]], [:@int, "1", [1, 2]]],
  [:assign, [:var_field, [:@ident, "b", [1, 4]]], [:@int, "2", [1, 6]]],
  [:command,
   [:@ident, "puts", [1, 8]],
   [:args_add_block,
    [[:binary,
      [:var_ref, [:@ident, "a", [1, 13]]],
      :+,
      [:var_ref, [:@ident, "b", [1, 15]]]]],
    false]]]]
```

The method signatures for tokenize, lex, and, sexp are all the same (source, filename = "-", line_number = "1", **kwargs). They all basically ignore filename, but the line_number is used in the output, and sexp has a keyword argument called raise_errors: false which, if true, raises a SyntaxError if the source has an error.

As an example of event-based lexical analysis, here's a program that finds class definitions and their associated comment blocks. For each, it outputs the class name and the comment. It might be considered the zeroth iteration of an RDoc-like program.

The parameter to parse is an accumulator—it's passed between event handlers and can be used to construct the result:

ref_meta_ruby/rdoc.rb
```ruby
require "ripper"

# This class handles parser events, extracting
# comments and attaching them to class definitions
class BabyRDoc < Ripper::Filter
  def initialize(*)
    super
    reset_state
  end

  def on_default(event, token, output)
    reset_state
    output
  end

  def on_sp(_token, output)
    output
  end
  alias_method :on_nil, :on_sp

  def on_comment(comment, output)
    @comment << comment.sub(/^\s*#\s*/, "    ")
    output
  end

  def on_kw(name, output)
    @expecting_class_name = (name == "class")
    output
  end

  def on_const(name, output)
    if @expecting_class_name
```

```
      output << "#{name}:\n"
      output << @comment
    end
    reset_state
    output
  end

  private

  def reset_state
    @comment = ""
    @expecting_class_name = false
  end
end

BabyRDoc.new(File.read(__FILE__)).parse($stdout)
```

produces:

```
BabyRDoc:
    This class handles parser events, extracting
    comments and attaching them to class definitions
```

Singleton

The Singleton design pattern ensures that only one instance of a particular class may be created for the lifetime of a program.

The Singleton module makes this simple to implement. Mix the Singleton module into each class that's to be a singleton, and that class's new method will be made private. In its place, users of the class call the method instance, which returns a singleton instance of that class.

Ruby overrides a few other methods of the class when Singleton is mixed in: inherited, clone, _load, and dup, all of which are changed to prevent multiple instances of the class from existing.

In this example, the two instances of MyClass are the same object:

```
ref_meta_ruby/singleton.rb
require "singleton"

class MyClass
  attr_accessor :data
  include Singleton
end

a = MyClass.instance    # => #<MyClass:0x00000001011e0300>
b = MyClass.instance    # => #<MyClass:0x00000001011e0300>
a.data = 123            # => 123
b.data                  # => 123
a.object_id             # => 60
b.object_id             # => 60
```

Struct

Sometimes you want to create a small object to hold data that has little to no behavior of its own, and a Ruby class seems like too much structure to bother with.

Ruby has a few lightweight ways to create classes that have little to no behavior.

The most commonly used is probably Struct. You can use Struct to create instance-like objects that have attributes and can respond to messages that you define.

Using Struct creates a class that you then create instances of. Let's say you want to represent a classroom that has a name and a capacity. You use Struct.new to create a Classroom class, with the desired attribute names as arguments. You can then use Classroom.new to create new classrooms. The positional arguments in new match the order of the arguments to the original Struct call, or you can use keyword arguments. If you pass the original Struct call the argument keyword_init: true, then the resulting class must use keyword arguments in its constructor.

Once the struct instance has been built, you can access the attributes to read and write, both as attributes and as hashes:

```
Classroom = Struct.new(:name, :capacity)
small = Classroom.new("Room 203", 25)
small.name        # => "Room 203"
small.name = "Room 205"

large = Classroom.new(name: "Auditorium", capacity: 1000)
large[:capacity] # => 1000
```

In other words, the Struct single line is more or less equivalent to this, except that the resulting Struct version can take either positional or keyword arguments:

```
class Classroom
  attr_accessor :name, :capacity
  def initialize(name:, capacity:)
    @name = name
    @capacity = capacity
  end
end
```

A Struct can even get instance methods. Passing a block to Struct.new gives you a chance to define methods that can be called on the created instances of the struct. Technically, the new struct class is passed to the block as an argument, so methods defined inside it are added as instance methods:

```
Classroom = Struct.new(:name, :capacity) do
  def full_name
    "Classroom: #{name}, capacity: #{capacity}"
  end
end
small = Classroom.new("Room 203", 25)
small.full_name # => "Classroom: Room 203, capacity: 25"
```

The main thing you can't do is have an inheritance hierarchy of Structs or include other modules inside the block. The Struct class also gives the structs you create some default behavior for free. These are some of the most useful behaviors:

- == returns true if all the attributes are equal.

- to_a, to_h, and to_s.

- deconstruct and deconstruct_keys so that you can use pattern matching against a Struct as though it were a Hash.

- each_pair, which takes a block with the name and value of each attribute and applies the block in turn. Also each, which just passes the block each value.

Also, Struct objects respond to dig, so you can treat them like hashes or arrays in a dig call.

If all you have is some data and a couple of methods on that data, a Struct can be a succinct way of defining that data.

One potential downside of a Struct is that the data inside a struct can be changed. In some situations, you want to be clear that an object's value won't change. This can be particularly important for applications sharing data across multiple threads.

Unbound Method

UnboundMethod is a method that's not currently attached to an instance, which means it can't yet be called. UnboundMethod instances are created by Module methods such as instance_method and can also be created by calling unbind on a Method object.

To use an UnboundMethod, you must bind it to an object using UnboundMethod#bind(object), which returns a Method that can be called. The object must be a member of the class that the unbound method came from or a subclass of that class. You can get that class with UnboundMethod#owner. It's pretty common to call the method immediately so the shortcut method Unbound-Method#bind_call(object, ...) is equivalent to bind(object).call(...) but with a performance improvement because it doesn't create an intermediate Method object.

Otherwise, UnboundMethod has much the same attributes as Method (see Method, on page 551), including arity, name, original_name, and parameters.

Part VI

Appendixes

Included in the appendixes is information on troubleshooting misbehaving Ruby code, a collection of Ruby symbols and their meanings that might be hard to look up, a more detailed introduction to using a command line, information about Ruby runtimes, and a list of significant changes made to Ruby in each version since 2.0.

Troubleshooting Ruby

You've read through this entire book, you start to write your very own Ruby program, and…it doesn't work. Here's a list of common gotchas and other tips to help get you back up and running.

Common Issues

- In Ruby, unlike in JavaScript and Python, a method name with no parentheses calls the method with no arguments. It doesn't return the method as an object to be used later. To get the method object, use the method named method.

- In Ruby, calling a class as if it were a method, as in Classname(), is an error. To create a new instance, you need to call Classname.new().

- If you happen to forget a comma (,) in an argument list—especially to print—you can produce some very odd error messages.

- Ruby allows you to have a trailing comma at the end of an array or hash literal, method call, or block method list, but not at the end of the parameter list of a method definition.

- If Ruby is telling you that the number of arguments being passed to a method is incorrect, this is often due to a mismatch in which arguments are meant to be keyword arguments and to be positional.

- If an attribute setter is not being called, it may be because within a class definition, Ruby will parse setter = as an assignment to a local variable, not as a method call. Use the form self.setter= to indicate the method call. Here's an example:

```ruby
class Incorrect
  attr_accessor :one, :two
  def initialize
    one = 1          # incorrect - sets local variable
    self.two = 2
  end
end

obj = Incorrect.new
obj.one    # => nil
obj.two    # => 2
```

- Objects that don't appear to be properly set up may have been victims of an incorrectly spelled initialize method:

```ruby
class Incorrect
  attr_reader :answer
  def initialise        # <-- spelling error
    @answer = 42
  end
end

ultimate = Incorrect.new
ultimate.answer # => nil
```

- If you misspell an instance variable name, you don't get a runtime error; instead, the uninitialized variable has a nil value:

```ruby
class Incorrect
  attr_reader :answer
  def initialize
    @anwser = 42         #<-- spelling error
  end
end

ultimate = Incorrect.new
ultimate.answer # => nil
```

- A parse error at the last line of the source often indicates a missing end keyword, and sometimes that missing keyword is quite a bit earlier. The Ruby interpreter will try to make a good guess about where the actual issue is.

- This message—syntax error, unexpected $end, expecting keyword_end—means you have an end missing somewhere in your code. (The $end in the message means end-of-file, so the message means that Ruby hit the end of your code before finding all the end keywords it was expecting.) Try running the file with the -w option, which will warn you when it finds ends that aren't aligned with their opening if/while/class.

- Watch out for precedence issues, especially when using {...} instead of do...end. Use parentheses to remove potential parser ambiguity.

```ruby
def one(arg)
  if block_given?
    "block given to 'one' returns #{yield}"
  else
    arg
  end
end

def two
  if block_given?
    "block given to 'two' returns #{yield}"
  end
end

result1 = one two {
  "three"
}
```

```
result2 = one two do
  "three"
end

result3 = one(two) { "three" }

result4 = one(two) do "three" end

puts "With braces, result = #{result1}"
puts "With do/end, result = #{result2}"
puts "With braces and parens, result = #{result3}"
puts "With do/end and parens, result = #{result4}"
```

produces:

```
With braces, result = block given to 'two' returns three
With do/end, result = block given to 'one' returns three
With braces and parens, result = block given to 'one' returns three
With do/end and parens, result = block given to 'one' returns three
```

The difference here is which method gets called if there are no parentheses. In the result1 line, the braces bind tightly and are considered an argument to the method two. In the do/end line, the braces bind after a method call, so the parser interprets it as a call to the method one with two and the block as arguments.

- If numbers don't come out right, perhaps they're strings. Text read from a file will be a String and will not be automatically converted to a number by Ruby. A call to Integer will work wonders (and will throw an exception if the input isn't a well-formed integer). The following is an example of the issue:

```
while line = gets
  num1, num2 = line.split(/,/)
  # ...
end
```

num1 and num2 are strings. You can rewrite this using map:

```
while line = gets
  num1, num2 = line.split(/,/).map { |val| Integer(val) }
  # ...
end
```

- Unintended aliasing can be a concern. If you're using an object as the key of a hash, make sure it doesn't change its hash value (or arrange to call rehash if it does):

```
arr = [1, 2]
hash = {arr => "value"}
hash[arr]   # => "value"
arr[0] = 99
hash[arr]   # => nil
hash.rehash # => {[99, 2]=>"value"}
hash[arr]   # => "value"
```

- Make sure your method names start with a lowercase letter and class and constant names start with an uppercase letter.

- Make sure the opening parenthesis of a method's parameter list butts up against the end of the method name with no intervening spaces. Otherwise, the parser will not interpret the parenthesized list as the parameters to the method.

Debugging Tips

- Read the error message! Ruby error messages have a lot of information, including the type of error, the location of the error, and the entire sequence of method calls that lead to the error. If the error is because a method name wasn't found, Ruby will suggest similarly named methods that actually exist. If the error is potentially at several points along a line, Ruby will attempt to show you where along the line the error happened.

- Running your scripts with warnings enabled (the -w command-line option) can give you insight into potential problems.

- If you cannot figure out where a method is defined, you can access the source location with obj.method(:method_name).source_location. This will return a two-element array with the filename and line number where the method was defined. This works even if the method was defined dynamically with define_method or implicitly with method_missing.

- Output written to a terminal may be buffered. This means you may not see a message you write immediately. In addition, if you write messages to both STDOUT and STDERR, the output may not appear in the order you were expecting. Always use nonbuffered I/O (set sync=true) for debug messages.

- Make sure the class of the object you're using is what you think it is. If in doubt, check with puts my_obj.class.

- Use irb and the debugger.

- Use freeze. If you suspect that some unknown portion of code is setting a variable to a bogus value, try freezing the variable. The culprit will then be caught by raising an exception during the attempt to modify the variable.

- Modern editors have increasingly powerful tools to identify Ruby errors in the editor. Using YARD or RBS can increase the ability of these editors to infer issues from your code.

- One major technique makes writing Ruby code both easier and more fun. *Develop your applications incrementally.* Write a few lines of code, and then write tests. Write a few more lines of code, and then exercise them. One of the major benefits of a dynamically typed language is that things don't have to be complete before you use them.

I Can't Look It Up!

Ruby has a lot of notation and typography that is called by a name that isn't necessarily obvious, making it hard to search for the meaning of a particular line of code. Here are a few particularly important symbols:

Symbol	Name	Functionality
||=	Or-equals	Is like other Ruby operate and assign operators. x ||= y is equivalent to x = x || y. Because of Ruby's short circuit of boolean operators, the expression means that if x is nil, the new value is y, and if x isn't nil, then x's value remains the same. Is often used as a shortcut to set a default value.
=~ !~	Match operators	With a string on one side of the operator and a regular expression on the other, =~ returns true if the string matches the regular expression, and !~ returns true if the string doesn't match the regular expression.
%i()	Symbol delimiter, symbol percent literals	Takes a set of barewords and converts them to an array of symbols. For example, %i[a b c] becomes [:a, :b, :c]. The delimiter after the %i is arbitrary, and the array continues until the matching delimiter is encountered at the end of the expression.
%w()	Array delimiter, array percent literals	Takes a set of barewords and converts them to an array of strings. For example, %w[a b c] becomes ["a", "b", "c"]. The delimiter after the %w is arbitrary, the array continues until the matching delimiter is encountered at the end of the expression.
%q() or %Q()	String delimiter, string percent literals	Acts as a literal string delimiter. Lowercase q acts as a single quote string, uppercase Q acts as a double quote string. Usually used to avoid escaping if the quote mark is part of the string. The delimiter is arbitrary, the string continues until the matching delimiter is encountered.
%r()	Regular expression delimiter, regular expression percent literals	Acts as a literal regular expression delimiter. Usually used to avoid escaping if the / is part of the regular expression. The delimiter after the r is arbitrary, and the string continues until the matching delimiter is encountered.

Symbol	Name	Functionality
Array(), Integer()	Conversion methods or conversion wrappers	Converts the argument to the stated type.
<<	Shovel	Used by a lot of different classes, including 'String', 'Array', and 'File', to append a value to the end of the existing value.
class << foo	Singleton operator	Allows access to the singleton class of object foo. Most often it used with a class name to define class methods.
&.	Safe navigation or lonely operator	In a method call such as foo&.bar, if the left side of the safe navigation operator is nil, allows the method call to proceed and return nil rather than throw an error.
<=>	Spaceship operator	In x <=> y, if x is less than y, returns -1, if x is greater than y, returns 1, and if they are equal, returns 0.
#{EXPRESSION}	String interpolation	Inside a double-quoted string, evaluates the expression, converts it to a string, and inserts it in the string.
x ? y : z	Ternary operator	If x is true, returns y and otherwise (else) returns z
(ARGS) -> { EXPR }	Stabby lambda	Creates a lambda equivalent to lambda { |ARGS| EXPR }.
::	Scope resolution	Looks up a constant value inside a module or class, as in Foo::Bar. If nothing exists on the left of the operator, like ::Foo, forces a lookup in the top-level global scope, which can be useful if you're doing a lookup from inside a nested set of modules.
*	Splat	In a method call, as in thing(*[1, 2, 3]), converts an array to a series of positional arguments in the method. In a method definition, converts an arbitrary number of optional arguments to an array.
**	Double splat	In a method call, converts a hash to a set of keyword arguments in the method. In a method definition, converts an arbitrary number of keyword arguments to a hash.
&, specifically &:foo	Proc operator	In a method call, converts a proc or lambda passed as an explicit argument to the implicit block argument of the method. If the parameter decorated with the & isn't a Proc, Ruby will try to convert it to one by calling the method to_proc. For example, thing(&:foo) will call to_proc on the symbol :foo. In a method definition, captures the implicit block argument and converts it to a Proc that can be referred to in the method.
...	Argument Forwarding	Passes all the arguments of a given method to a new method, whether they are positional arguments, keyword arguments, or block arguments. The outer method needs to define the arguments as something like def outer(...), and the inner call has to also use the three dots: user.inner(...).

Symbol	Name	Functionality
{x:, y:}	Hash shortcut syntax, shorthand hash syntax, or "punning"	Adds a key/value pair to a hash literal by only referencing the key. The value will come from a value in the current binding with the same name as the key. Also works for keyword arguments in method calls.
_1, _2	Numbered block parameter	In a block, _1 through _9 reference the positional arguments passed to that block, with the first argument being _1, the second being _2, and so on.
\1, \2	Numbered match captures	In a regular expression, can be used to refer to text captured by a parenthesized group elsewhere in the expression, with \1 being the first group, \2 being the second, and so on.

Command-Line Basics

Although great support exists for Ruby in IDEs, you'll probably still end up spending a lot of time at your system's command prompt, also known as a *shell prompt* or just plain *prompt*. The most popular IDEs also provide their own shell prompts in another window right next to your code.

The Command Prompt

If you're a Linux user, you're probably already familiar with the command prompt. If you don't already have a desktop icon for it, hunt around for an application called Terminal or xterm.

On macOS, run Applications → Utilities → Terminal.app. (We also recommend the excellent iTerm2[1] on macOS.)

On Windows, you can install Windows Subsystem for Linux[2] and have a shell that behaves like the Linux or MacOS shells, or you can use the default Windows Power Shell, which, as we'll see, behaves a little differently. On Windows, we recommend installing Windows Terminal (https://docs.microsoft.com/en-us/windows/terminal/install), which makes it easier to use other shell type.

When you run the application, a fairly empty window pops up that contains a banner and a prompt. Try typing echo hello at the prompt and hitting Enter (or Return, depending on your keyboard). You should see hello echoed back, and another prompt should appear.

Folders, Directories, and Navigation

If you're used to a GUI tool such as Explorer on Windows or Finder on MacOS for navigating to your files, then you'll be familiar with the idea of *folders*—locations on your hard drive that can hold files and other folders.

When you're at the command prompt, you have access to these same folders. But at the prompt, these folders are usually called *directories* (because they contain lists of other directories and files). These directories are organized into a strict hierarchy. On Unix-based systems (including macOS and WSL), there's one top-level directory, called / (a forward slash). On

---

1. https://iterm2.com
2. https://learn.microsoft.com/en-us/windows/wsl/about

plain Windows, there is a top-level directory for each drive on your system, so you'll find the top level for your C: drive at C:\ (that's the drive letter C, a colon, and a backslash).

The path to a file or directory is the set of directories that you have to traverse to get to it from the top-level directory, followed by the name of the file or directory itself. Each component in this name is separated by a forward slash (on Unix) or a backslash (on Windows). For example, if you organized your projects in a directory called projects under the top-level directory, and if the projects directory had a subdirectory for your time_planner project, the full path to the README file would be /projects/time_planner/readme.txt on Unix and C:\projects\time_planner\readme.txt on Windows.

Spaces in Directory Names and Filenames

Operating systems allow you to create folders with spaces in their names. This is great when you're working at the GUI level. But, from the command prompt, spaces can be a headache because the shell that interprets what you type will treat the spaces in file and folder names as being parameter separators and not as part of the name. You can get around this (typically by putting the entire filename in quotation marks), but it generally isn't worth the hassle. If you're creating new folders and files, it's easiest to avoid spaces in their names.

To navigate to a directory, use the cd command. (Because the Unix prompt varies from system to system, we'll just use a single dollar sign to represent it here.)

```
$ cd /projects/time_planner     (on Unix)
C:\> cd \projects\time_planner     (on Windows)
```

On Unix systems, the parent directory is represented as .. (two dots) and the current directory is . (a single dot). So, cd .. takes you up one level, and cd ..\.. takes you up two levels. (Some Unix shell programs have more shortcuts available. For example, in ZShell, cd - takes you back to the previous directory.)

On Unix systems, you usually don't want to be creating top-level directories. Instead, Unix gives each user their own *home directory*. So, if your username is dave, your home directory might be located in /usr/dave, /home/dave, or /Users/dave. At the shell prompt, the special character ~ (a single tilde) stands for the path to your home directory. You can always change directories to your home directory using cd ~.

To find out the directory you're currently in, you can type pwd (on Unix) or cd on Windows. For example, on Unix you could type this:

```
$ cd /projects/time_planner
$ pwd
/projects/time_planner
$ cd
$ pwd
/Users/dave
```

On Windows, the commands are similar:

```
C:\> cd \projects\time_planner
C:\projects\time_planner> cd \projects
C:\projects> cd %userprofile%
```

In Unix, you can create a new directory under the current directory using the mkdir command:

```
$ cd /projects
$ mkdir expense_tracker
$ cd expense_tracker
$ pwd
/projects/expense_tracker
```

Notice that to change to the new directory, you can just give its name relative to the current directory. You don't have to enter the full path.

We suggest you create a directory called pickaxe to hold the code you write while reading this book:

```
$ mkdir ~/pickaxe        (on Unix)
C:\> mkdir \pickaxe      (on Windows)
```

It's helpful to get into the habit of changing into that directory before you start your work:

```
$ cd ~/pickaxe           (on Unix)
C:\> cd \pickaxe         (on Windows)
```

Ruby Runtimes

Ruby code is converted to executable code using an interpreter. The current default interpreter is called YARV (Yet Another Ruby VM) and has been the standard since Ruby 1.9, replacing the original interpreter, which was known as CRuby or MRI (Matz's Ruby Interpreter). You'll actually still see the names CRuby and MRI used interchangeably with YARV for the current version of the interpreter.

The interpreter makes dozens of choices about how to convert Ruby code to machine code, such as how to store objects, associate objects with their methods, and so on. Each of these choices has implications for the runtime performance of Ruby.

Not all uses of Ruby are equal. A one-off script could be optimized for a quick startup even if that might cause performance issues later—a short script might not have a "later." Conversely, a long-running web server may be willing to trade a longer start-up time for better performance later.

Several options for Ruby interpreters are available. Some, like the just-in-time compilers, are options that ship with core Ruby. Others, like TruffleRuby, are third-party solutions with different speed characteristics. And yet others, like JRuby, also give Ruby access to other runtime libraries.

Let's go on a tour of the various available interpreters.

Just-in-Time Compilers

Historically, computer languages are translated in one of two different ways. A language might use a *compiler* to convert the program code directly to machine language. This compilation happens in a separate step before the code is executed and produces machine-language artifacts. When it's time to run the code, the machine-language version is run, and the original source code isn't used.

Ruby typically uses a different tool called an *interpreter*. An interpreter converts the source code to machine language at runtime, generally without creating an intermediate machine-language artifact. In an interpreted language, you typically use the original source code at runtime.

That said, the line between compilers and interpreters is blurry. A common technique, used by Java among languages, is to compile to a machine-independent byte code and then use a machine-specific runtime interpreter to execute the code. An advantage of this technique is that the machine-specific part of the translation is minimized, making it easier to port the languages to different operating systems. (In fact, YARV internally compiles to a byte code at runtime before interpreting it, but this byte code version is typically for internal use only.)

Another way of blurring the distinction is by using a just-in-time compiler (JIT). A JIT compiler operates at runtime and starts as an interpreter but can then compile frequently used code as it executes from Ruby's byte code to machine code. Typically, this increases initial startup cost because of the extra compilation step, but if parts of the code are executed repeatedly in a long-lived process, the machine-compiled versions will eventually be faster.

Ruby ships with two different JIT implementations: RJIT and YJIT.

RJIT

RJIT—the "r" stands for "ruby"—is a Ruby implementation of a JIT compiler that was added in Ruby 3.3. Older versions of Ruby had a different JIT implementation called MJIT. You can enable RJIT on your Ruby execution by using --rjit when you call Ruby:

```
$ ruby options.foo --rjit
```

RJIT is meant to be experimental and is not for use in production code.

RJIT will watch for methods that are called frequently in your code and compile methods that it sees as being highly used. RJIT is written in Pure Ruby.

From your perspective as a Ruby developer, RJIT should run just like YARV, but with some kind of performance boost. Exactly how much of a boost depends on your application parameters (and there aren't a lot of solid Ruby 3.3 benchmarks to choose from at this point).

A handful of command-line options change how RJIT works; but most of these are for testing purposes if you were actually working on RJIT, rather than just writing Ruby:

--rjit-call-threshold=num	Notes the number of calls to a method needed to trigger RJIT compilation. The default is 10.
--rjit-exec-mem-size=num	The size of an executable memory block in RJIT, the default is 64.
--rjit-stats	Allows for collection of RJIT statistics.

YJIT

A second JIT compiler ships with Ruby that takes a significantly different approach to compilation. YJIT (yet another Yet Another acronym) is a complete compiler on its own, and as of Ruby 3.2, it's also implemented in Rust. YJIT uses a mechanism called "lazy basic block versioning" for compilation, which means it compiles sections of code based on chunks of code that are smaller than methods, such as loops.

YJIT also takes advantage of runtime type information to optimize compilation for known types. If it sees that a chunk of code is called with integer values, it will optimize the compiled steps for integer values. If the chunk is called often enough with a different type of value, then different compiled code is generated. That's the "versioning" part of basic block versioning—YJIT creates different compiled versions of blocks based on input values. The "lazy" part is that YJIT only generates versions for blocks that it sees on the fly during runtime. The combination means that YJIT can generate fast-compiled code without compromising on Ruby's flexibility.

YJIT is installed along with Ruby, provided that you have the Rust language version 1.58 or higher installed on your computer when Ruby is installed. Rust installation instructions can be found at https://www.rust-lang.org/tools/install.

YJIT can be executed as part of the ruby runtime by adding --yjit to the call:

```
ruby options.foo --yjit
```

YJIT can also be enabled by setting the environment variable RUBY_YJIT_ENABLE to true.

Using YJIT can provide a significant performance boost for long-running processes. Because YJIT only compiles methods after they have been repeated several times—the default is 30—you likely won't see a benefit in shorter scripts or in unit tests. The current Rust version of YJIT is brand-new in the wild, so there aren't a lot of use cases to check, but one early test suggests that performance on benchmarks can double using YJIT.[1]

YJIT has some additional command-line options that tweak the behavior and allow for more debugging information if you're actually working on YJIT itself. Note that some of the debugging information depends on having a version of Ruby compiled to produce YJIT stats.

--yjit-call-threshold=num	The number of times a method is called before YJIT optimizes it by compiling. The default is 30.
--yjit-exec-mem-size=num	The size, in MiB, of the memory dedicated to executable code. The default is 128.
--yjit-greedy-versioning	If set, enables greedy versioning mode, which may increase the size of the compiled code.
--yjit-max-versions=N	The maximum number of versions of a compiled block YJIT will generate for different type information. The default is 4.
--yjit-stats	If enabled, stats about YJIT usage are displayed at the end of the program.
--yjit-trace-exits	Produces a stack trace when YJIT exits compile mode. Also enables --yjit-stats.

TruffleRuby

Now we move away from runtime engines that ship with the Ruby virtual machine and toward Ruby implementations that run in various other environments. In general, these implementations offer performance improvements at the cost of lagging behind new features in Ruby and also limiting access to the Ruby ecosystem, since not all gems can run in the other environments.

GraalVM[2] is a virtual machine environment implemented in Java and designed to be a high-performance, cross-language, virtual environment. TruffleRuby,[3] created by Chris Seaton, is a Ruby implementation built on top of GraalVM. TruffleRuby provides very high performance relative to the standard Ruby implementations, but it's not completely compatible with standard Ruby.

---

1.   https://www.solnic.dev/p/benchmarking-ruby-32-with-yjit
2.   https://www.graalvm.org
3.   https://www.graalvm.org/ruby

If you use a Ruby version manager to install Ruby, it likely includes TruffleRuby as one of its downloadable options. This is true of rbenv, which is the recommended setup in this book, as well as the other commonly used version managers such as RVM, asdf, and chruby. The current version is 23.1.1, but new versions come out on a regular schedule.

In rbenv, you can install TruffleRuby just as you would any other Ruby implementation (rbenv install truffleruby-23.1.1 or rbenv install truffle ruby+graalvm-23.1.1). In the default version, TruffleRuby has already been compiled to a native executable. The +graalvm version runs inside the Graal Java virtual machine at runtime, just like any other Java application. The GraalVM version gives you better compatibility with other language tools at the cost of some short-term performance degradation. The TruffleRuby team recommends the native configuration for shorter-running programs, smaller memory use, or any situation where startup time is important. The GraalVM version is recommended for better performance in a long-lived process.

Once you have TruffleRuby installed, it runs just like regular Ruby. All the CLI commands for normal Ruby apply, except for ones that cover things like JIT compilers that don't exist in TruffleRuby.

A great feature of TruffleRuby is that it tries to re-implement the core library in Ruby. (Most of the core library in the main runtime is written in C.) The idea is that TruffleRuby is better off having the core in Ruby where the same optimizations can be used as opposed to having them outsourced to a nominally faster language. You can find those definitions at https://github.com/oracle/truffleruby/tree/master/src/main/ruby/truffleruby/core, and they can be helpful in understanding how some of Ruby's core methods work.

One downside of using a third-party Ruby runtime is that it's not guaranteed to be compatible with the current versions of CRuby. TruffleRuby 22.3.0 is based on Ruby 3.2.2, and according to one comparison of Ruby runtimes,[4] it passes 97% of the ruby-spec test suite, with most of the failures being related to the CLI or edge cases in the language. If you're going to try to use TruffleRuby in your application, you should have good test coverage and make sure that TruffleRuby passes your tests.

TruffleRuby can offer a substantial performance improvement. One set of benchmarks[5] suggests a six times improvement over Ruby 3.1, and while Ruby 3.2 is somewhat faster, TruffleRuby seems worth considering for long-running processes that are particularly performance intensive and which aren't dependent on those parts of Ruby that TruffleRuby doesn't handle.

JRuby

JRuby is the older and more established Java runtime version of Ruby. After several years of falling behind core Ruby, the November 2022 release (JRuby 9.4) brought JRuby to parity with Ruby 3.1, with Ruby 3.2 support expected in the near future. There are some substantial limitations in JRuby's support as of this writing.

- Ruby's threading constructs aren't completely supported, specifically Ractors and the thread scheduler aren't supported yet. But you can interoperate with Java thread-safe data.

---

4. https://eregon.me/rubyspec-stats
5. https://eregon.me/blog/2022/01/06/benchmarking-cruby-mjit-yjit-jruby-truffleruby.html

- The readme for this version says "Nearly all features from CRuby's NEWS file have been implemented." Again, we recommend making sure your tests continue to run if you're considering switching to JRuby.

- Rails support for most databases is incomplete.

Improvement on all these fronts is in progress, and by the time you read this, it's possible the situation has improved.

JRuby is also available via most Ruby version managers, and rbenv install jruby-9.4.4.0 will do it if you've been following along with this book's defaults. You can also get standalone download installers at https://www.jruby.org/download. You need to have a Java Standard Edition runtime installed for the standalone versions[6], but there's a decent chance your computer already has one installed.

You can use the installed standalone JRuby to run a file with jruby <filename>, and you can run irb with jirb. If you install it using rbenv, then the regular ruby and irb commands work. In the standalone mode, if you're running a Ruby-based command-line tool like rake, the recommendation is to use jruby -S <COMMAND> to ensure that JRuby is actually executing the command.

Ruby gems that compile to C won't work with JRuby.

When using JRuby, you can import any Java library in your Java class path. If you add require "java" to your file, you can access Java classes via their fully qualified class names. JRuby will convert method names from Ruby-style underlines to Java-style CamelCase, so calling JavaClass.do_a_thing will reference the Java method doAThing. Similarly, Java getters and setters will be converted to Ruby getter and setter methods, so a JavaClass.getFoo() and JavaClass.setFoo() will be accessible as instance.foo and instance.foo = value. JRuby will convert Ruby strings, booleans, and numbers to the appropriate Java types and vice versa. Arrays need to call the method to_java in order to be passed back and forth. See the JRuby[7] documentation for full details.

If you're able to use JRuby, meaning that your code is compliant with Ruby 3.1 and doesn't use gems that use native C code (like Nokogiri), you can get a significant (two to three times) performance boost. If you're working in an environment that already has a Java backend, access to the Java libraries and resources can be a big win. (Be careful, though: one of us once worked on a JRuby project that had two User classes that both backed to the same database table, one using Ruby and ActiveRecord, the other using Java and Hibernate. This wasn't helpful.)

mRuby

mRuby (Minimalist Ruby) is an offshoot of official Ruby and is led by many of the same developers. It implements a subset of Ruby that's designed for a minimal memory footprint and for use embedded inside C programs where memory might be tight, such as inside devices. The idea is to allow hardware developers access to Ruby as a scripting language.

---

6. https://www.oracle.com/java/technologies/downloads
7. https://github.com/jruby/jruby/wiki/CallingJavaFromJRuby

You can install mRuby via your ruby version manager (rbenv install mruby-3.1.0), or you can install it standalone from the download site.[8] If you install it via a version manager, you can run it using ruby; if you install it standalone, the command is mruby.

Other Runtimes

Other attempts to create Ruby runtimes that are in progress, aren't used much, or have been abandoned.

Artichoke Ruby

Artichoke Ruby is an attempt to build a CRuby-compliant Ruby runtime in Rust. It's currently in pre-production.

Opal

Opal is a Ruby-to-JavaScript compiler.

MagLev

MagLev is a Ruby runtime built on top of the GemStone Smalltalk runtime. It appears to have had very little development since 2016.

Rubinius

Rubinius is an attempt to build a Ruby runtime in Ruby, partially for use as a reference implementation. It appears to have had little development since 2020.

Iron Ruby

Iron Ruby was a .NET implementation of Ruby that appears to have had little development since 2011.

---

8.   https://mruby.org/downloads

Ruby Changes

For most of this book, we assume you're using the most current Ruby version, which is version 3.3. With a couple of exceptions, we don't specify when particular features were added to Ruby, as we find that makes the main text more confusing.

This appendix covers changes to Ruby that involve features that are mentioned in this book. There are many more changes in each version, many having to do with core library and gem methods that aren't covered here. Ruby's documentation[1] contains a listing of what was added to each version since 1.8.7. The Ruby Evolution site,[2] maintained by Victor Shepelev, contains more details about the changes. This appendix is only here to tell you when major changes first appeared, starting with version 2.0. (Older versions are covered by previous versions of this book and were on a different numbering scheme.)

Version 2.0

- Module#prepend is introduced.

- Default source encoding changes to UTF-8.

- Refinements are added.

- Keyword arguments are added, but a default value is always required, and the internal implementation still overlaps with positional arguments.

- %i is added as a delimiter for a list of symbols.

- Lazy enumerators are added.

- to_h and Kernel#Hash are added as the convention to convert to Hash objects.

- TracePoint is added.

- Numeric values are frozen.

Version 2.1

- Keyword arguments without a default are now allowed.
- def now returns the symbol name of the method.

---

1.   https://docs.ruby-lang.org/en
2.   https://rubyreferences.github.io/rubychanges/evolution.html

- Literal syntax for rational and complex numbers is added.
- Array and Enumerable get a default to_h.

Version 2.2

- The method Object#itself is added, returning the receiving object.
- Unusual symbols are allowed as Hash keys as a string with a trailing colon, as in {"unusual symbol": 1}.

Version 2.3

- The safe navigation operator, &., is added.

- dig is added to Array, Hash, and Struct.

- Heredoc with ~ that removes leading spaces, allowing for indented text, is added.

- Hash#to_proc is added.

Version 2.4

- Using return at the top level exits the program.

- All integers are now of class Integer. Previously, smaller integers were Fixnum and bigger ones were Bignum.

- Boolean methods for regular expression matches, match? are added.

- Refinements can be used in send and Symbol#to_proc.

Version 2.5

- Structs can be initialized with keywords.
- Exception rescue is allowed inside a block.

Version 2.6

- Object#then is added to allow chained functions.
- Ranges without ending values are allowed.

Version 2.7

- Experimental support for pattern matching is added.

- Blocks now support numbered parameters to match positional arguments, as in [1, 2, 3].map { _1 * _1}.

- Safety concepts are deprecated. They aren't covered in this book, but they were covered in the previous edition.

- Private methods are now accessible with self as the receiver. Previously, this had been an error.

- Keyword and positional arguments are differentiated internally, but old semantics aren't removed.

- The ability to forward arguments with ... is added.

- The Enumerator#produce method is added.

- Ranges without beginning values are allowed.

Version 3.0

- Class variables can no longer be overridden in subclasses or including modules.

- One-line "endless" syntax for method definition is added.

- Keyword and positional arguments are now completely separated. Previously, def foo(*arg) would capture keyword arguments in arg.

- RBS is added for type definitions.

- Rightward assignment => is added via pattern matching. The in operator for pattern matching becomes a boolean check.

- The pattern matching find pattern, [*start, pattern, *rest], is added.

- Argument forwarding with ... now allows specific arguments before the ....

- Non-blocking Fibers and the Fiber scheduling API are added.

Version 3.1

- The pattern-matching pin operator ^ allows expressions and variables that have a sigil.

- Values in keywords and hashes where the key is already a name in the local binding can be omitted. {x:} if x has a value.

- Block arguments can be received anonymously with &.

- Ractors are added.

- Major updates are made to IRB.

- Major updates are made to the internal debugging tool.

Version 3.2

- Set is added to the core library.
- Anonymous positional and keyword arguments can be passed through with * and **.
- Data object is added to the core library.
- Struct no longer requires keyword_init: true to be used with keyword arguments.
- The Rust implementation of YJIT is considered production-ready.

Version 3.3

- The Prism parser is added as a way to work with parsing Ruby code.
- MJIT is replaced with RJIT.
- YJIT gets substantial performance improvements.
- In Ruby 3.4, the keyword it is expected to be enabled as a synonym for _1. In Ruby 3.3, a use of it that might conflict with this future usage will result in a warning.

Index

SYMBOLS

! (exclamation point)
    array methods suffix, 564
    bang methods syntax, 86
    logical not conditional expression, 151, 457
    in method names, 131
    methods style conventions, 346
    negation operator style conventions, 345
!!, implicit conversion to boolean, 151
!!!, debugging with Pry, 294
!=
    comparison operator, 152, 458
    specifying gem versions, 259
!~
    comparison operator, 152, 458
    negative match operator, 512
    regular expressions, 131, 133
    strings, 531
" (double quotes)
    heredocs, 434
    replacing double/single quotes in RuboCop, 351, 353
    string literals, 20, 120, 348, 354, 433
#
    for comments, 19, 31, 430
    string interpolation for variables, 120
#! (shebang notation)
    making code executable, 237
    program files, 13
#++, start of comment processing in RDocs, 316
#--, end of comment processing in RDocs, 316
#{...}
    string interpolation, 21, 120
    string substitution, 21

$ (dollar sign)
    global variables prefix, 22, 446
    regular expressions anchor, 135
$! variable, exceptions, 173, 485
$$ variable, processes, 199
$& variable, regular expressions, 134
$' variable, regular expressions, 134
$_ variable
    regular expressions in boolean expressions, 458
    running files from command line, 232
$: variable, loaded files, 244
$? variable
    command expressions, 146, 453, 549
    processes, 196, 199
$' variable, regular expressions, 134
$~ variable, regular expressions, 134, 139
% (percent sign)
    ERB templates, 330, 332
    literals and irb prompt configuration, 288
%% irb configuration, 288
& (ampersand)
    bitwise AND, 504
    block arguments, 481
    intersection operator in RBS, 306, 491
    invoking methods with blocks, 471
    parameters and, 92, 469
    proc objects conversion, 97, 482, 584
    set operations with arrays, 566, 586
    using blocks as objects, 73–76, 92

&&
    character classes intersection, 443
    logical and conditional expression, 150, 457
    safe navigation shortcut (&.), 156
&. safe navigation operator, 156, 345, 472
' (single quotes)
    replacing double/single quotes in RuboCop, 351, 353
    string literals, 20, 120, 348, 433
() (parentheses)
    blocks, 480
    calling super without, 473
    conditional expressions, 151, 348
    methods syntax, 20, 86, 88, 95, 467, 470
    nested assignment, 149
    order of execution and, 151
    regular expressions, 27, 138
    RSpec, 221
    stabby lambda operator (->), 76
    style conventions, 346, 348
    troubleshooting, 637, 640
* (asterisk)
    assignment, 149, 455
    block arguments, 481
    case expressions wildcard, 460
    expanding collections, 96, 470
    lists and RDoc documentation, 317
    multiplication, 503–504, 506–507, 509, 565
    parameter lists, variable-length, 89–91
    parameter syntax, 90, 467, 469
    in pattern matching, 164
    regular expressions, 27, 137
    for super, 89

typing with RBS, 490
typing with Sorbet, 309
variable binding, 462
wildcard in glob, 590
wildcard in Sinatra, 339

** (double-splat)
anonymous parameters, 91
block arguments, 481
converting and passing hashes
as arguments, 97, 471
glob pattern matching, 590
hash keys and invoking methods, 471
hash parameters, 91, 468
passing parameters, 469
typing with RBS, 490
typing with Sorbet, 309

**nil
for methods that don't accept
keyword arguments, 91
pattern matching, 164

+ (plus sign)
addition, 503–504, 506–507,
509, 565, 586
enumerators, adding, 578
operator plus assignment, 149
overriding as method, 87
regular expressions, 27, 137

+=, operator assignment, 150

, (comma), troubleshooting tips, 637

- (hyphen), lists and RDoc documentation, 317

- (minus sign)
forking when spawning processes, 197–199
subtraction, 503–504, 506–507,
509, 565, 586

---, rule lines in RDoc documentation, 318

-=, operator assignment, 150

-> (stabby lambda operator)
name, 76
Rack and, 334
using blocks as proc objects,
74–78, 482

. (dot character)
methods syntax, 18, 87, 472,
474
regular expressions, 27, 136

.. syntax
arrays with ranges, 54
range operator, 125

... syntax
arrays with ranges, 54
command delimiter, 146
parameter lists, 93, 469
range operator, 125

.? variable, glob pattern matching,
590

/ (slash)
escaping and CGI encoding,
327
regular expressions, 26

/.../ (regular expression literal), 26,
129, 132, 511

: (colon)
hash key creation, 24
keyword parameters, 91
scope resolution operator (::),
107, 447, 476, 478
symbol literals, 24, 439
typing with RBS, 302, 488

::
labeled lists and RDoc documentation, 318
methods syntax, 472
namespace resolution operator, 265
scope resolution, 107, 447, 476,
478

; (semicolon)
block variables, 66
exception syntax, 172
expression separator for methods, 86, 429
listing block-local variables,
162

<
comparison operator, 108, 153,
457, 541, 553, 583, 585
specifying gem versions, 259
subclass creation, 102

<<
appending to arrays, 43, 563
bitwise shift, 504
CSV files, 589
heredocs, 121, 434
IO with streams, 184
Method objects, 551
sets, 585
string concatenation, 531

<<-, heredocs, 121, 434

<<~, heredocs, 121, 435

<=
comparison operator, 108, 153,
457, 541, 553, 583, 585
specifying gem versions, 259

<=> (spaceship operator)
about, 108, 540
arrays, 565
complex numbers, 507
enumerators, 575
hashes, 583
mixins, 110
modules, 553
Numeric class, 503
Object class, 152, 557
ranges, 126, 437
sets, 585
strings, 531

syntax reference, 437, 457
time and data methods, 500–
501

<>, ERB templates, 332

= (equals sign)
calling methods as left side of
assignment, 94
default parameters, 89
endless methods, 86
headings in RDoc documentation, 318
methods syntax, 87
specifying gem versions, 259
writing to attributes, 38

==
comparison operator, 108, 152,
457, 541, 553, 583, 585
complex numbers, 507
OpenStruct, 627
regular expressions, 513
strings, 531

===
case statements, 152, 155, 163,
458–459
comparison operator, 152, 155,
348, 458, 553
exceptions, 173
pattern matching, 163
procs, 156
ranges, 126, 156, 163
regular expressions, 156, 513
sets, 156, 585

=>
assignment order, 148
binding variables in pattern
matching, 461
comparison operator, 108, 153,
583, 585
hash key creation, 23, 57, 438,
461, 579
pattern matching and variable
binding, 164–166
pattern matching with rightward assignment, 456

=~
comparison operator, 152
match operator, 27, 130, 133,
512
strings, 531

>
comparison operator, 108, 153,
457, 541, 553, 583, 585
ERB templates, 332
specifying gem versions, 259

>=
comparison operator, 457, 541,
553
specifying gem versions, 259

? (question mark)
ASCII character expression
syntax, 434

optional parameters in Sinatra, 339

predicate methods, 86, 226, 346

regular expressions, 137

RSpec booleans, 226

ternary operator conditional expressions, 154

typing with RBS, 302, 490–491

?<...>, regular expressions, 139

@, instance variables prefix, 22, 445

@@, class variables prefix, 22, 445, 553

[..] character class, 136

[] (square brackets)

arrays, 22, 53, 348, 437, 561

case expressions, 460

command-line arguments, passing with Rake, 248

command-line options, specifying with OptionParser, 241

element reference operator, 474

exceptions and documentation with YARD, 323

glob pattern matching, 590

hashes, 23, 57, 579

labeled lists and RDoc documentation, 317

MatchData class, 513

operators, 145

procs, calling, 482

regular expression character classes, 136

regular expression matches, 134

retrieving substrings, 525

style conventions, 348

threads, 190

typing with RBS, 302, 491–492

[]=

arrays, 55, 563

hashes, 581

operators, 145, 455, 474

string replacement, 528

threads, 190

\ (backslash)

escape sequence with, 120, 130, 134, 136, 141, 433

glob pattern matching, 590

regular expressions, 27, 130, 134, 136, 141

substitution in string literals, 20, 433

^ (caret)

bitwise XOR, 504

pinning values, 167

regular expressions anchor, 135

regular expressions, negating character classes, 136

reusing variables in pattern matching, 462

set xor, 586

_ (underscore)

in names, 22, 273, 306, 346

number separator, 117

` (backtick)

command expressions syntax basics, 146, 453, 549

spawning processes, 196

{...} block literal, 28, 65

{} (braces)

blocks, Standard syntax, 354

blocks, style conventions, 345

blocks, syntax basics, 28, 65, 480

hash literals, 23, 57, 345, 348, 354, 438, 579

hashes in case expressions, 461

hyperlinks and RDoc documentation, 317

regular expressions, 130

string interpolation, 345, 434

style conventions, 345, 348

syntax reference, 434

| (pipe)

array unions, 566

bitwise OR, 504

case expressions, 461–462

pattern matching and variable binding, 166

programs, 431

regular expressions, 27, 138

separating types with RBS, 489

set unions, 586

spawning processes, 198

union types with RBS, 306, 491

writing to CSV files, 589

|...| block parameters, 29, 65

||, logical or conditional expression, 151, 457

||=, assigning values to variables, 151

~ (tilde), bitwise flip, 504

~>, specifying gem versions, 259

DIGITS

0 as octal indicator, 117, 432

-0 command-line option, 234

$0 variable, ARGV, 238

0b as binary indicator, 117, 432

0d as decimal indicator, 117, 432

0o as octal indicator, 432

0x as hex indicator, 117, 432

\1, regular expressions, 139, 141

$1 variable, regular expressions, 134, 139

\2, regular expressions, 139, 141

$2 variable, regular expressions, 139

A

\A, regular expressions anchor, 135

-a

command-line option, 233–234

RuboCop command-line option, 351

-A RuboCop command-line option, 353

abort method, programs, 543

abort_on_exception, threads, 191–193

abs for absolute value of numbers, 118, 503, 510

absolute_path method, File class, 596

absolute_path? method, File class, 596

access control

classes and methods, 45–48

default, 45

send and public_send, 413

syntax reference, 480

typing with RBS, 490

accessor methods

simulating with method_missing, 402–404

using, 37–42

ActiveRecord module, finder methods, 405

add

loggers, 624

sets, 585

add?, sets, 585

add_observer method, 625

addition

about, 71

arrays, 565

BigDecimal class, 509

complex numbers, 507

floating-point numbers, 506

integers, 504

Numeric class, 503

sets, 586

strings, 531

alias keyword, 144, 475

alias_method, 475, 555

aliasing

assignment and, 49, 447

classes, 144

methods, 144, 475, 555

RSpec matchers, 226

syntax reference, 475

troubleshooting, 639

typing with RBS, 488, 490

YAML and, 617

alive? method, Thread class, 190

--all, updating gems with Bundler, 258

allocate, 477, 540

allow, 227

alternation, regular expressions, 138

ampersand (&)
    bitwise AND, 504
    block arguments, 481
    intersection operator in RBS,
        306, 491
    invoking methods with blocks,
        471
    parameters and, 92, 469
    proc objects conversion, 97,
        482, 584
    set operations with arrays,
        566, 586
    using blocks as objects, 73–76,
        92
anagram example
    gem packaging, 262–275
    RuboCop, 349–353
    typing with RBS, 301–305
    typing with Sorbet, 307–311
ancestors method
    modules, 114, 411, 553
    RBS, 303
anchors, regular expressions, 135
and, conditional expressions, 150,
    457
any, union types with Sorbet, 310
any?, hashes, 582
ap method, 290
append, arrays, 563
append_features method, modules,
    555
appending
    arrays, 43, 563
    pathnames, 611
Application class, Sinatra, 340
apt-get, 9
ARGF
    command-line arguments syn-
        tax, 31, 238
    in-place editing, 239
    iteration and, 576
*args, blocks as transactions, 72
ArgumentError, 91, 366, 487
arguments
    assignment in variable-length
        parameter lists, 89
    block arguments, passing, 97–
        99
    block syntax, 481
    command line, syntax basics,
        30, 233
    command-line options, specify-
        ing with OptionParser, 241
    converting and passing collec-
        tions as arguments, 96, 470
    keyword, 95, 468, 481
    methods as, 95
    passing command-line to Rake,
        247
    passing to methods, 95

procs, 482
    retrieving substrings, 525
    super and, 473
    troubleshooting, 637
    typing with RBS, 302, 305, 490
    typing with Sorbet, 309
ARGV
    cautions, 238
    command-line options, 235
    command-line syntax, 30, 238
    gets and, 550
    loading files, 44
    option parsing, 239–242
    Rake tasks and, 248
arity, methods, 552
Array class
    conversion with Kernel module,
        366
    library reference, 561–569
    syntax basics, 22, 53–56
    syntax reference, 437
Array method, 561
arrays
    adding/removing elements,
        56, 563
    appending, 43, 563
    assignment and, 455
    binary data and, 567
    binary search, 566
    breaking strings into arrays of
        characters, 263, 531
    case expressions, 460
    comparison operators, 565
    conversion protocols, 363, 366
    converting hashes to, 583
    converting ranges to, 125
    converting strings to, 437, 564
    creating, 22, 53, 437, 561
    creating arrays of arrays, 573
    creating empty, 53
    cross-product of, 72
    defined, 22, 53, 561
    digging, 58, 562
    empty, 562
    indices, 22, 53, 563, 567
    iterators, syntax basics, 159
    library reference, 561–569
    math methods, 565
    modifying methods, 563
    pattern matching, 164, 170
    prepending, 563
    replacement in, 55, 563
    shifting elements, 56
    shortcuts, 562
    style conventions, 348
    symbols, 437
    syntax basics, 22, 53–56
    syntax reference, 437
    syntax in RuboCop, 353
    time and data methods, 500
    typing with RBS, 306
    typing with Sorbet, 310

word frequency example, 58–
    65
    writing to files, 183
Artichoke Ruby, 654
ASCII
    about, 122
    character classes, 442
    character expression syntax,
        434
    reading files with iterators, 181
    regular expressions, 133, 436
ASCII-8BIT encoding, 532, 534
asdf, 4
assert_equal method
    minitest, 209
    word frequency example, 60–
        62
assertions, minitest, 209–212
assignment
    aliasing and, 49, 447
    calling methods, 94
    chaining, 146–148
    conversion protocols, 364
    eval methods in Kernel module,
        545
    expressions, syntax basics,
        145–150
    methods syntax, 87, 474
    modules, 552
    nested, 149, 455–456
    operators, 145, 149
    parallel, 68, 148, 347, 364
    parameter lists, variable-
        length, 89
    rightward, 148, 456
    style conventions, 347–348
    syntax reference, 454–457
assoc, hashes, 581
associative arrays, see hashes
asterisk (*)
    assignment, 149, 455
    block arguments, 481
    case expressions wildcard, 460
    expanding collections, 96, 470
    lists and RDoc documentation,
        317
    multiplication, 503–504, 506–
        507, 509, 565
    parameter lists, variable-
        length, 89–91
    parameters syntax, 90, 467, 469
    in pattern matching, 164
    regular expressions, 27, 137
    for super, 89
    typing with RBS, 490
    typing with Sorbet, 309
    variable binding, 462
    wildcard in glob, 590
    wildcard in Sinatra, 339
at_exit method, 242, 543

atomic grouping and backtracking, 516

atoms, 439

--attach debugging option, 291

attr_accessor
about, 39, 555
as macro, 387, 390
singleton classes, 380
style conventions, 347
syntax reference, 477
typing with RBS, 489
typing with Sorbet, 310

attr_reader
about, 37, 555
instance variables and mixins, 112
style conventions, 347
syntax reference, 477
typing with RBS, 302, 489
typing with Sorbet, 310

attr_writer
about, 39, 555
style conventions, 347
syntax reference, 477
typing with RBS, 302, 489
typing with Sorbet, 310

attributes
accessor methods, 37–42, 555
assignment syntax basics, 147
basics of, 36–42
defined, 37
as methods without arguments, 40–42
troubleshooting, 637
typing with RBS, 302, 305

@author documentation tag, 322

--auto-gen-config RuboCop option, 351

auto-split mode command-line option, 233–234

:AUTO_INDENT, irb configuration option, 285

auto_indent_mode, irb configuration option, 285

--autocomplete irb command-line option, 278

--autocorrect option, Sorbet, 310

autocorrection
RuboCop, 350, 353
Standard, 354
typing with Sorbet, 310

autorun method, minitest, 212, 219

awesome-print, 283, 290

B

\B, regular expressions anchor, 135

b, debugging breakpoints, 292

\b regular expressions anchor, 135

--back-trace-limit n irb command-line option, 278

:BACK_TRACE_LIMIT, irb configuration option, 285

back_trace_limit, irb configuration option, 285

backreferences, 515, 517–522

backslash (\)
escape sequence with, 120, 130, 134, 136, 141, 433
glob pattern matching, 590
regular expressions, 27, 130, 134, 136, 141
substitution in string literals, 20, 433

backtick (`)
command expressions syntax basics, 146, 453, 549
spawning processes, 196

backtrace
command-line option, 234
debugging and, 293
exception handling, 485–487
irb command-line options, 278
irb configuration options, 285

backtrace method, debug gem, 293

--backtrace-limit command-line option, 234

backtracking and regular expressions, 516–517, 520

bang methods, syntax, 86

banner method, OptionParser, 240

Base class, Sinatra, 340

base class, hooks, 400

base indicators, integers, 117, 432

base module, Sinatra, 340

base-transitioning methods, 505

basename method, File class, 595

BasicObject class
about, 403
library reference, 537–539
methods list, 538
as root class, 102
__send__ and, 413
uses, 537

BasicSocket class, syntax basics, 179

Batsov, Bozhidar, 344

before method, RSpec, 223

=begin ... =end for comments, 31, 430

begin method, MatchData class, 514

Benchmark module
calling methods dynamically, 414
debugging performance issues, 296
extending irb, 284
library reference, 619

benchmarking
calling methods dynamically, 414
debugging performance issues, 296
irb, 284
library reference, 619

between?, comparison operator, 108, 457, 541

BigDecimal class
conversion methods, 505
library reference, 502, 507–510
syntax basics, 117

BigDecimal method, 40, 117, 508, 542

bin directory, gems, 267

binary data
arrays and, 567
binary file mode, 593
encodings, 607
passing as strings, 183

binary operators, syntax basics, 144

bind method, calling methods dynamically, 414

bind_call method
calling methods dynamically, 414
UnboundMethod, 634

Binding class, getting bindings, 549

binding method
calling methods dynamically, 414
Kernel module, 549
Pry, 294

binding.break, debugging with, 290, 292

bindings
blocks, 450
defined, 67
ERB templates, 331
eval methods in Kernel module, 545
getting, 549
irb, 282, 286
late binding and dynamic typing, 300
listing, 286
Method objects, 413
pattern matching and, 164–166, 461
popping, 287
printing, 287
Pry, 294
pushing, 287
scope, 450
UnboundMethod, 634

bindings command, irb, 286

binread method, IO class, 603

binstubs, 257

binwrite method, IO class, 603

BitBucket, 260

bitwise operators, Integer class, 504

block argument, method_missing hook, 401

block_given?, 73, 472, 548–549

blocks
  about, 53
  argument syntax, 481
  arrays and, 60–65
  block-comments and RDoc documentation, 316
  checking for, 472
  class-level macros, 389
  as closures, 75, 77, 480
  context, 483
  converting to proc objects, 482
  creating, 534
  creating classes dynamically, 394
  defined, 28, 65, 480
  enumeration and, 62–65
  exception handling, 172–175, 177, 485
  indentation and, 344
  index method, 563
  invoking methods, 471
  iteration basics, 67–72
  loops with Kernel module, 543
  loops with keywords, 161
  methods and block parameters, 92
  opening files, 180
  order, 431
  parameters, 65, 77
  partitioning, 573
  passing block arguments, 97–99
  precedence, 28
  RSpec matchers, 226
  runtime information with Kernel methods, 548
  scope, 66, 75, 161–163, 450, 481, 483
  structs and, 393
  style conventions, 345, 354–355
  subprocesses and, 199
  syntax basics, 28–30, 65–67
  syntax reference, 431, 457, 480–484
  terminating programs and, 543
  transactions, 72
  typing with RBS, 490
  uses, 29
  using as objects, 73–78
  warning messages, 66
  word frequency example, 60–65

bm method, Benchmark module, 296, 619

bmbm method, Benchmark module, 296, 620

body, defining classes, 476

booleans
  conditional expressions, 150
  guard clauses, 168
  implicit conversion to with !!, 151
  loops with ranges, 158
  ranges, 153, 158, 458
  regular expressions, 458
  RSpec matchers, 226
  style conventions, 347, 355
  syntax reference, 432, 457–459, 463
  typing with RBS, 306, 491
  typing with Sorbet, 310

boolish type, RBS, 306, 491

braces ({})
  blocks, Standard syntax, 354
  blocks, style conventions, 345
  blocks, syntax basics, 28, 65, 480
  hash literals, 23, 57, 345, 348, 354, 438, 579
  hashes in case expressions, 461
  hyperlinks and RDoc documentation, 317
  regular expressions, 130
  string interpolation, 345, 434
  style conventions, 345, 348
  syntax reference, 434

branch conditions, ranges, 127

branch: option, accessing unreleased gems, 260

break
  debugging with, 292
  loops, 161, 463
  procs, 483

breakpoints
  debugging, 290, 292
  deleting, 293
  listing, 293

browsers, running Ruby in with Wasm, 327, 340–342

bsearch, arrays, 566

bsearch_index, arrays, 567

bt method, debug gem, 293

build, packaging gems for distribution, 274

BUNDLE_WITH environment variable, 261

BUNDLE_WITHOUT environment variable, 261

Bundler
  about, 251
  binstubs, 257
  gem templates, 261
  Gemfile groups, enabling, 261
  installing, 254
  installing gems, 255, 258
  managing groups of gems, 254–261

multiple versions of gems and, 253

Sinatra and, 338

updating gems, 258

bytes, 437

C

C
  parsing by RDoc, 320
  RuboCop severity level, 350

-C command-line option, 235

-c command-line option, 234

c method, debugging navigation, 292

call method
  Method objects, 413, 551
  procs, 482
  Rack, 334, 336
  using blocks as objects, 74

:call-seq: documentation modifier, 319

callbacks, see hook methods

__callee__ method, 418, 549

caller method
  debugging and, 290
  exceptions, 176
  tracing stack, 417–420

capitalize, 21

caret (^)
  bitwise XOR, 504
  pinning values, 167
  regular expressions anchor, 135
  regular expressions, negating character classes, 136
  reusing variables in pattern matching, 462
  set xor, 586

case
  regular expression options, 132, 440
  string formatting methods, 530

case statements
  === comparison operator, 152, 155, 163, 458–459
  indentation and, 344, 347
  pattern matching in, 166
  ranges, 126
  style conventions, 344, 347
  syntax basics, 143, 154–156
  syntax reference, 459–462

catch method
  control flow, 544
  debugger gem, 293
  exceptions, 177, 486

cb, irb, 286

cd method
  command-line basics, 646
  FileUtils class, 600

cd~ command, 646

CGI class
  about, 327
  cookies, 328
  encodings, 327, 616
  escaping characters, 327
  generating HTML, 329
changed method, observers, 626
character classes
  abbreviations table, 136
  defined, 136
  regular expressions, 27, 136
  syntax reference, 442–444
character selectors, 523
characters
  regular expressions matching, 27
  splitting strings into, 527
chars, 527
chdir method
  Dir class, 592
  FileUtils class, 600
child classes, see subclasses
children method, Dir class, 591
chmod, 237, 272, 594, 600
chomp, 123, 197, 526
chomp!, 526
chop, 526
chop!, 526
chown, 594, 600
chown_R, 600
chr method, Integer class, 181
chruby, 4
clamp, comparison operator, 457, 541
class << an_object notation for single-ton classes, 379
Class class, library reference, 540
class keyword, 34
class method, 548
class methods
  adding module methods as, 109
  blocks as transactions and, 72
  extending modules with self, 384, 404
  instance methods and, 87
  lookup and mixins, 114
  metaprogramming and, 390–392
  notation conventions, xiv
  style conventions, 346
  syntax basics, 87
  syntax reference, 466
class variables
  listing, 553
  Module methods, 553
  names, 22, 445
  safely using, 22

scope, 448
  syntax reference, 448
class_double method, RSpec, 228
class_eval
  calling methods dynamically, 414, 556
  metaprogramming and self, 396
class_exec, 397, 556
class_variable_defined?, 553
class_variable_get, 553
class_variable_set, 553
class_variables, 553
classes
  access control, 45–48
  adding methods or variables to existing, 49–51
  aliasing, 144
  aliasing methods in, 475
  attribute declarations, 477
  basics of, 33–36
  class definitions and self, 373, 388
  coupling and, 45
  creating, 34, 477, 540
  debugging breakpoints, 292
  debugging, with Pry, 294
  debugging tips, 640
  defined, 18
  defining, 33–36, 476
  defining in RBS, 487
  documentation disabling in RDoc, 319–320
  documentation with YARD, 322
  dynamic typing, 357–362
  exceptions as, 173
  generic types in RBS, 492
  as hash keys, 439
  hierarchy of and calling methods, 372
  hierarchy of and class-level macros, 388
  hierarchy of and reflection, 411
  inheritance, 101–105, 380, 388, 540, 553
  intercepting method calls with hooks, 415
  library reference, 540
  main object, 374
  metaprogramming and class-level macros, 387–399
  metaprogramming and creating classes dynamically, 394
  method lookup and mixins, 113–116
  names, 22, 34, 265, 346, 395, 476
  nested, 266, 476
  notation conventions, xiv
  object model and metapro-gramming, 371–380
  operator expressions, 144

refinements, 384–387
  reflection, 411
  reopening, 49–51
  root class, 102
  safe classes and YAML, 616
  singleton classes, 375
  singleton methods and class objects, 377–380
  style conventions, 355
  syntax reference, 465–492
  troubleshooting, 637
  using one file per class, 44
  working with other classes, 42–45
classify, sets, 586
clean task, Rake, 248
CLEAN variable, Rake, 248
clear
  hashes, 583
  sets, 585
clobber task, Rake, 248
CLOBBER variable, Rake, 248
clone, 560
close method
  File class, 180
  IO class, 604
close_incoming method, Ractor class, 206
close_outgoing method, Ractor class, 206
closures
  blocks as, 75, 77, 480
  class-level macros, 390
  conversion protocols, 366
  defined, 75
  syntax reference, 480
cloud-based development, avoiding installation with, 4
CLU, 67
cmp method, FileUtils class, 600
code, see also style
  disassembly, 419
  notation conventions, xiv
  organizing source code for gems, 261, 266–272
coerce method, 367–369, 503
coercions, 362–369, 503
collect method, 70, 571
collections
  arrays, library reference, 561–569
  converting, 96
  converting numbers to, 504
  enumeration, library reference, 569–579
  expanding, 96, 470
  hashes, library reference, 579–584
  sets, library reference, 584–586

colon (:)
  hash key creation, 24
  keyword parameters, 91
  scope resolution operator (::),
    107, 447, 476, 478
  symbol literals, 24, 439
  typing with RBS, 302, 488
--colorize irb command-line option,
  278
combination, arrays, 566
comma (,), troubleshooting tips, 637
command line, *see also* irb
  arguments, processing, 237–
    242
  arguments, syntax basics, 30
  basics, 645–647
  Bundler command-line pro-
    gram, 254
  documentation tool, 14
  environment variables, access-
    ing, 242–244
  ERB, 330
  gem command-line application,
    251
  making code into executable
    programs, 237
  option parsing, 239–242
  options, 232–237, 239–242
  Rake tool, using, 231, 245–249
  RBS, 303
  RuboCop, 351
  running Ruby from, 11, 231
  running tests from, 217
  syntax basics, 231–237
  terminating programs, 242
commands
  debugging breakpoints, 292
  debugging with Pry, 294
  method calls with parentheses
    as, 95
  syntax basics, 146, 453, 549
comments, *see also* magic comments
  documentation with, 313–324
  Gemfile, 259
  multiline, 31, 430
  regular expressions, 133, 348,
    515, 518
  syntax basics, 19, 31
  syntax reference, 430
compact, 574, 583
compact!, 583
Comparable module
  library reference, 540
  as mixin, 108
compare_by_identity, sets, 584
compare_file method, FileUtils class,
  600
comparison operators
  arrays, 565
  Comparable module, 108
  complex numbers, 507

enumerators, 575
hashes, 583
library reference, 540, 557
modules, 553
Numeric class, 503
RSpec, 225
sets, 585
strings, 531
style conventions, 348
syntax reference, 457
time and data methods, 500–
  501
compile method, Regexp class, 512
compilers, defined, 649, *see also* just-
  in-time compilers
Complex class
  conversion with Kernel module,
    366
  library reference, 507
  syntax basics, 118
Complex method, 118, 507
complex numbers
  conversion methods, 503, 508
  conversion protocols, 366
  converting strings to, 118
  library reference, 507
  style conventions, 345
  syntax basics, 117
  syntax reference, 433
concerns, Ruby on Rails, 392
conditional expressions
  conditional execution, 150–157
  modifiers, 154–156
  style conventions, 348
  syntax reference, 459–462
conditional groups, regular expressions, 519–522
conf, 286
config, Bundler, 267
configuration
  gem source code, 267
  irb, 283–288
  rbconfig.rb file, 249
  RuboCop, 352
--conservative, updating gems with
  Bundler, 258
const_get method, 554
const_missing method, 554
const_set method, 554
const_source method, 554
constants
  creating, 540
  instance_eval and, 397
  Module methods, 554
  names, 22, 346, 446, 639
  namespacing and, 265
  reflection, 412
  scope, 397, 447, 453
  syntax reference, 447

typing with RBS, 302, 488
  typing with Sorbet, 310
construct_keys, 500
constructors, defined, 18
containers, Docker, 3, 13
context
  blocks, 483
  calling methods dynamically,
    414
  finding, 414
  irb, 278, 286
  singleton classes, 380
context command, 286
--context-mode irb command-line
  option, 278
continue method, debugging navigation, 292
control flow
  debugging and, 292
  iteration and, 70
  Kernel methods, 542–546
  style conventions, 347
  syntax reference, 463
control structures
  raw procs, 482
  statement modifiers, 26
  syntax basics, 25
controllers, inheritance in, 104
conversion protocols, 362–369
cookie parameter, 328
cookies, handling with CGI class, 328
cookies method, 328
copy method, FileUtils class, 599
copy_entry method, FileUtils class, 599
copy_file method, FileUtils class, 599
copy_stream method, FileUtils class,
  599
--copyright command-line option, 234
corouting, *see* fibers
count
  about, 574
  arrays, 565
  infinite sequences, 81
  strings, 523
count_observers method, 627
countervariant generics, 492
coupling
  classes, 45
  inheritance and, 116
covariant generics, 492
cover? method, ranges, 126
cp method, FileUtils class, 599
cp_lr method, FileUtils class, 599
cp_r method, FileUtils class, 599
create method, Tempfile class, 613
CRuby, 5, 649

CSV
    iteration and, 576
    library reference, 587–590
    parsing files, 42
CSV class, 576
Ctrl+C, terminating irb, 285
Ctrl+D
    end-of-file character, 12
    quitting debugging, 292
curl, 4
current method, Thread class, 190
curry, 552
currying, 552
cycle, 569

D
\D, character class abbreviation, 136
\d
    character class abbreviation,
        136
    regular expressions, 27
-d
    debugging command-line op-
        tion, 192, 235
    ERB command line option, 330
    irb command-line option, 278
    search option for gems, 252
dRuby, see distributed Ruby
data
    binary data and arrays, 567
    style conventions, 348
    template characters for packed
        data, 567
DATA class
    __END__ and, 431
    immutable structs, 393
    library reference, 621
data objects, library reference, 621
data types library reference
    dates and times, 495–502
    math, 502–511
    regular expressions, 511–523
    strings, 523–534
    symbols, 534
Date class
    converting time methods, 500
    library reference, 495, 501
dates, library reference, 495–502
DateTime class
    converting time methods, 500
    library reference, 496, 501
Davis, Ryan, 208
$DEBUG
    command-line options, 235
    ERB command line option, 330
    irb command-line option, 278
    threads and exceptions, 191
--debug command-line option, 235

debug gem, 290–293
debugger gem, 290
debugging
    control flow and, 292
    -d debug flag for, 192, 235
    with debug gem, 290–293
    debug mode, 290
    ERB command line option, 330
    gems, 253
    with inspect, 36
    irb command-line option, 278
    method chains, 64
    navigation while, 292
    performance issues with
        Benchmark, 296
    printing for, 289, 293
    with Pry, 293–296
    remotely, 290, 292
    resources on, 290, 292–293
    threads, 191
    tips, 640
    with TracePoint class, 417
    with Visual Studio Code de-
        bugger plugin, 290
decimals
    character class abbreviation,
        136
    converting to rational num-
        bers, 118
    syntax reference, 433
declarations, RBS, 487
decode_uri_component method, 615
decode_www_form_component method,
    614
decoding
    binary data and arrays, 567
    URI class, 614–616
deconstruct, 170, 514
deconstruct_keys, 169, 500, 514
def
    access control, 46, 480
    metaprogramming and, 407
    syntax basics, 20, 85–93
    typing with RBS, 302
default Rake task, 248
default=, 580
default_ignores: key, 354
default_internal method, 609
default_proc, 580
define method
    Data class, 394, 621
    hook methods, 404
define_finalizer method, 625
define_method
    metaprogramming and, 389
    Module class, 556
define_singleton_method, 559
defined?, conditional expressions,
    151, 457

defname, 465
del NUM, 293
delegation, library reference, 622
Delegator class, library reference, 622
delete
    arrays, 563
    directories, 592
    files, 594
    hash keys, 581
    sets, 585
    strings, 528
delete!, strings, 528
delete?, sets, 585
delete_at, arrays, 563
delete_if
    hashes, 581
    sets, 585
delete_observer method, 627
delete_observers method, 627
delimiters, syntax reference, 444
@deprecated documentation tag, 322
dereference_root FileUtils argument,
    598
desc method, Rake, 246
describe method, RSpec, 221
description lists, see labeled lists
design
    duplication, removing, 101
    identifying domain concepts,
        33
    inheritance and mixins, 115
    internal state and, 41
    with refinements, 387
    RSpec and, 219
    singleton design pattern, 632
dictionaries, see hashes
did_you_mean command-line option,
    236
difference, sets, 586
dig, 58, 562, 581
digits, regular expressions, 27
Dir class
    file system management, 592
    iteration and, 576
    library reference, 590–593
__dir__ method, 184, 549
directories
    changing, 600, 646
    command-line basics, 645
    command-line options, 235–
        236, 244
    creating, 592, 647
    deleting, 592, 598
    Dir class library reference, 590–
        593
    documentation, 321
    environment variables, 242,
        244

FileUtils class methods, 598, 600
getting path of, 549
irb command-line options, 278
libraries, 244
opening and closing, 590
temporary, 592
temporary files, 613
directory? method, File class, 597
dirname method, File class, 595
--disable command-line option, 235–236
disjoint?, sets, 585
distributed Ruby and reflection, 420, 424
Distributed Ruby library, 424
division
BigDecimal class, 509
complex numbers, 507
floating-point numbers, 119, 506
integers, 504
Numeric class, 503
DLN_LIBRARY_PATH environment variable, 242
do
blocks, style conventions, 345
blocks, syntax basics, 28, 65, 480
debugging suffix, 293
doc command, YARD, 324
doc directory
RDoc, 313
YARD, 322
--doc-dir documentation option, 321
:doc: documentation modifier, 319
Docker, 3, 13
.document file, 320
documentation
command-line options, 278
with comments, 313–324
disabling, 319–320
forcing, 319
gems, 252
importance of, 313
including non-source files, 320
in irb, 14
with RDoc, 313–321
ri core documentation tool, 14
showing with Pry, 296
with YARD, 313, 321–324
dollar sign ($)
global variables prefix, 446
regular expressions anchor, 135
DOM elements, Wasm and, 342
domain concepts, identifying, 33
domain-specific language, see DSL (domain-specific language)

dot character (.)
methods syntax, 18, 87, 472, 474
regular expressions, 27, 136
double data type, 433
double dispatch, coercion and, 367
double method, RSpec, 227
double-splat (**)
anonymous parameters, 91
block arguments, 481
converting and passing hashes as arguments, 97, 471
glob pattern matching, 590
hash keys and invoking methods, 471
hash parameters, 91, 468
passing parameters, 469
typing with RBS, 490
typing with Sorbet, 309
downcase, strings, 59
downto method, Integer class, 119, 159
drb, see distributed Ruby
drop, 570
drop_while, 571
DSL (domain-specific language)
defined, 221
instance_eval and, 398–399
RSpec as, 221
duck typing, see dynamic typing
--dump command-line option, 236
dump method
marshaling, 420
strings, 181
writing to YAML, 616
dup method, 49, 404, 559–560
duplication, design and, 101
dynamic typing
debugging and, 640
defined, 300
standard protocols and coercions, 362–369
vs. static typing, 300, 311, 356
style and, 343, 356–369

E
E, RuboCop severity level, 350
-e
execute command-line option, 232, 234
search option for gems, 252
e (regular expressions encoding option), 133
-E, command-line option for encoding, 607, 609
-E
ERB command line option, 330
irb command-line option, 278
each method
about, 63, 69

Array class, 60, 159, 561
Dir class, 590
Enumerable module, 63, 69, 110
Enumerator class, 78, 578
File class, 159
hashes, 582
IO class, 70
iterators, syntax basics, 159
library reference, 569
mixins and, 110
Rack, 335
ranges, 30
streams, 604
using instead of for, 347
each_byte method, 181
each_char method, 79, 527
each_child method, 591
each_cons, 569
each_key, 582
each_line method
IO class, 181
streams, 604
each_object
ObjectSpace, 410, 625
reflection, 410
each_pair, 582, 627
each_slice, 569
each_value, 582
each_with_index, 79, 570
each_with_object, 572
eager, 579
--echo irb command-line option, 278
--echo-on-assignment irb command-line option, 278
editors
about, 12
debugging and, 640
RuboCop and, 350
static typing and, 300
-Eex, command-line option, 235
eigenclasses, see singleton classes
else
case statements, 155
exceptions, 174, 486
regular expressions, 522
style conventions, 347
elsif
conditional expressions, 154
control structures, 25
empty?
arrays, 565
directories, 592
files, 597
hashes, 582
sets, 585
--enable command-line option, 236
encode method, 532
encode_uri_component method, 615

encode_www_form_component method, 614

--encoding command-line option, 235, 607

ENCODING constant, 123

encoding magic comment, 31, 123, 430

encodings
binary data and arrays, 567
binary files, 607
CGI and, 327, 616
command-line options, 235
compatibility, 608
converting, 532–534
default, 605, 607, 609
defined, 122, 605
ERB and, 330
external, 605–609
forcing, 534, 605, 608
internal, 605, 609
IO library reference, 605–609
irb command-line option, 278
magic comment for, 430
mode string and, 600
opening streams, 601
options table, 533
querying, 605, 607, 609
regular expressions options, 133
string syntax reference, 433
StringIO class, 612
strings, 532–534
symbol and regular expressions literals, 436
URIs, 614–616
using custom, 123

END, end of program with, 431

=end for comments, 31, 430

end keyword
blocks, style conventions, 345
blocks, syntax basics, 28, 65, 480
control structures, syntax basics, 25
MatchData class, 514
methods, syntax basics, 20, 86

end-of-file character, 12, 279, 285

:enddoc: documentation modifier, 320

endless (one-line) methods, syntax, 86, 88, 465

endpoints, 601

English library, 450

ensure
exceptions, 174, 486
Mutex class, 196

entries, 570, 591

enum_for method, 78

Enumerable module
vs. Enumerator class, 78

filter methods, 573
library reference, 569–577
map, 70, 81, 571
mixins and, 110
sets, 584

enumeration, see also iteration
blocks and, 62–65
chaining, 578
comparison operators, 575
conversion protocols, 364
converting ranges to enumerators, 125
creating enumerators, 78, 80, 577
defined, 29
enumerators, as objects, 79
enumerators, defined, 63, 67
filter methods, 573
generators and filters with enumerators, 80–83
infinite sequences, 80–83, 577
iteration methods, 569
library reference, 569–579
map and reduce, 571
mixins and, 110
sorting and comparing methods, 575
syntax basics, 78–83
uses, 578
word frequency example, 62–65

Enumerator class
vs. Enumerable module, 78
generators and filters with, 80–83
lazy, 81–83
library reference, 577–579
syntax basics, 78–83

env, Rack, 334, 336

ENV variable, 242, 577

environment
Bundler and, 256, 261
file system management with Dir class, 592
metaprogramming and, 407
Rack and, 334, 336

environment variables
Bundler and, 261
command-line access and, 242–244
iteration and, 577
PATH, 7
standard, 242
writing to, 243

eq method, RSpec, 222, 225

eql?
booleans, 458
library reference, 558
regular expressions, 152, 513
sets, 584–585

equal?, 152, 458, 558

equality
arrays, 565
comparison operators, 152
complex numbers, 507
enumerators, 575
hashes, 583
library reference, 558
OpenStruct, 627
regular expressions, 513
sets, 584–585
strings, 531
style conventions, 348
syntax reference, 458

equals sign (=)
calling methods as left side of assignment, 94
default parameters, 89
endless methods, 86
headings in RDoc documentation, 318
methods syntax, 87
specifying gem versions, 259
writing to attributes, 38

ERB
about, 327
resources on, 332
running from the command line, 330
Sinatra and, 338
using, 329–332

erb method, Sinatra, 338

_erbout string, 331

error_highlight command-line option, 236

errors
access control, 45
catching with debugger, 293
command-line options, 236
Data instances, 394
debugging tips, 640
fibers, 201
file syntax, 231
flushing of text and, 198
hashes, 58
keyword parameters, 91, 468
missing methods, 114, 472
parsing CSV, 43
pattern matching and case statements, 166
pattern matching and variable binding, 165
Rack, 334
raising exceptions, 175
RSpec doubles, 228
RSpec matchers, 226
RuboCop severity level, 350

escape method
CGI class, 328
URIs, 616

escapeElement method, 328

escapeHTML method, 328

escapeURIComponent method, 616

escapeURIHTML method, 616

eval EXPRESSION, debugging gem, 293

eval method, Kernel module, 545

_eval methods, calling methods dynamically, 414, 556

:EVAL_HISTORY, irb configuration option, 285

Example class, 394

@example documentation tag, 323

except, hashes, 583

Exception class
about, 171
creating custom classes, 172
handling basics, 171–178
syntax reference, 484–487

exception method, 485

exceptions
adding information to, 176
with catch and throw, 177, 486, 544
as classes, 173
creating Exception classes, 172
documentation with YARD, 323
filtering trace calls in debug gem, 293
frozen objects, 49
handling basics, 171–178
handling reference, 485–487
hierarchy of, 171
iteration, 79
Kernel module, 543
mutexes, 194
ractors, 206
raising, 175–178, 485, 543
with retry, 175–177, 486
spawning processes, 196
syntax reference, 484–487
threads, 191–193

exclamation point (!)
array methods suffix, 564
bang methods syntax, 86
logical not conditional expression, 151, 457
in method names, 131
methods style conventions, 346
negation operator style conventions, 345

Exclude setting, RuboCop, 353

exe directory, gems, 271, 274

exec method
Bundler, 256, 261
Kernel module, 549
replacing current process, 549
spawning processes, 198

executable? method, File class, 597

execution, tracing, 417–420

exist? method
Dir class, 592
File class, 596

exit method
conditional expressions, 151
debugging with Pry, 294
irb, 279, 287
programs, 242, 543
threads, 190

exit! method, programs, 543

expand_path method, File class, 596

expect method
minitest, 215
RSpec, 221–227

explicit conversion, defined, 362

exponent operators, style conventions, 345

exponential numbers, syntax reference, 433

EXPR, syntax reference, 437

EXPRESSION
conditional expressions, 151
syntax reference, 437

expressions
assignment, syntax basics, 145–150
command, 146
comparison operators, 152
conditional execution, 150–157
escape sequences in, 146
evaluating when debugging, 293
expansion, 146
iterators, 158–163
loops, 157–163
operators, 143
pattern matching, syntax basics, 163–170
pinning, 168
reflection, 417
structs and subclasses in metaprogramming, 392–394
syntax basics, 143–170
syntax reference, 429, 453–464

extend method, modules, 109, 383, 391, 479, 490

extend_config: key, Standard, 354

extend_object method, Module class, 555

extended mode, regular expressions, 132, 440

--external-encoding command-line option, 235

external_encoding method, 605

extname method, File class, 595

--extra-doc-dir irb command-line option, 278

F

F, RuboCop severity level, 350

-f, irb command-line option, 278

-F command-line option, 233–234

$F variable, splitting lines, 233–234

fail method, exceptions, 175, 543

Falcon, 332

false
conditional expressions, 150
as immediate value, 410
iteration and, 69
syntax reference, 432, 457

fast_generate method, JSON, 610

FasterCSV gem, 587

fdiv method, Numeric class, 119

features
appending, 555
command-line options, 235–236
prepending, 555

fetch, 562, 580

fetch_values, 581

fg, activating irb subsessions, 282, 287

FiberError, 201

fibers
about, 188
creating, 200–202
environment variables and, 243
non-blocking, 201
transferring control explicitly, 201

Fibonacci series
defined, 68
irb subsessions example, 282
iteration example, 68

FIFO (first-in-first-out) queues, arrays, 56

file associations, 13

File class
library reference, 593–597
syntax basics, 179

file descriptors, 600

file method, ARGF class, 238

FILE special variable, 184, 418, 453, 549

file? method, File class, 597

filename method, ARGF class, 238

filenames, converting to file descriptor, 601

files
binary file mode, 593
closing, 180
command-line options, 232
copying, 599
creating file objects, 179

CSV parsing, 588
debugging breakpoints, 292
deleting, 594, 599
deleting with Rake, 248
Dir class library reference, 590–593
File class library reference, 593–597
file system management with Dir class, 592
filename methods, 595
FileUtils module library reference, 597–600
finding, 184
gem specifications, 274
ignoring while type checking with Sorbet, 310
loading, 43, 545
loading and irb, 280, 285, 287
loading, stopping with return, 473
making executable, 237
mode string, 179, 593
mode, changing, 237
opening, 179, 593
path methods, 595
permissions, 179
predicate methods, 596
reading, 180–182, 238, 593, 597
removing filenames from ARGV, 238
running as programs, 13
running programs from, 13
searching, 590
sharing and Windows, 10
temporary files with Tempfile class, 613
time methods, 596
using one file per class, 44
writing, 180, 183–185, 593, 597
FileUtils module
library reference, 597–600
Rake and, 245
filter, 573, 591
filtering
directories, 591
with enumerators, 80–83, 573
with method_missing, 405–407
find method, 69, 573
find patterns, 460
find-method, Pry, 295
find_all, 573
find_all?, 110
find_index, 573
first
Array class, 56, 562
Enumerable module, 570
Enumerator class, 81
first-in-first-out (FIFO) queues, arrays, 56
--fix Standard option, 354

fix: key, Standard, 354
flat_map, style conventions, 348
flatten
arrays, 564
hashes, 583
Float class
conversion with Kernel module, 366
immediate values, 410
library reference, 506
syntax basics, 117
floating-point numbers
conversion methods, 503, 505–506, 508
conversion protocols, 366
converting integers to, 119
converting to integers, 40
converting validation, 34
as immediate values, 410
library reference, 506
precision and, 507
syntax basics, 117
syntax reference, 432
time and data methods, 500
fnmatch? method, File class, 597
folders, command-line basics, 645
fonts, documentation with RDoc, 316
for keyword
disadvantages of, 65
iterators syntax basics, 159–160
loop syntax, 463
scope, 450
using each instead, 347
for_each method, Dir class, 591
force FileUtils argument, 598
force_encoding, 534, 608
foreach method
CSV files, 42, 588
File class, 182
IO class, 182
streams, 604
fork method, spawning processes, 198–199, 550
forking, spawning processes, 197–199, 550
--format offenses RuboCop option, 350
format: key, Standard, 354
formatting
field type characters table, 547
Kernel methods, 547–548
string flags table, 547
Fowler, Martin, 249
fractions, syntax basics, 118
frameworks, see also Sinatra
about, 332
ERB and, 331
Rack and, 327, 332–338, 340

freeze
debugging with, 640
Object class, 559
strings, 436
freezing
command-line options, 236
objects, 49, 559
string literals, 31, 236, 430, 436
Friedl, Jeffrey, 26
frozen-string-literal, 236
frozen? method, 559
frozen_string_literal, 31, 430, 436

G

garbage collection
Benchmark module and, 297, 620
defined, 409
environment variables and, 243
ObjectSpace module library reference, 624
strings and, 360
gem command-line application, 251
Gemfile
comments, 259
creating, 254
gem specifications, 274
groups, 260
options, 258–261
organizing source code for gems, 267
specifying versions, 258–260
gemfile method, 263
Gemfile.lock file, 255
gems
accessing unreleased, 260
command-line options, 235–236
defined, 14, 251
documentation, 252
editing files, 253
finding on repositories, 251
Gemfile options, 258–261
groups, 260
installing, 251–253, 255, 258, 274
installing multiple versions, 253
listing, 252
making executable, 272
managing, 251–261
names, 251, 273
names, source files, 268
namespaces, 264
opening directories, 253
organizing code for, 261, 266–272
packaging for distribution, 274
removing, 253
resources on, 14, 252

sharing in repositories, 251, 275

single-file projects, 262–272

specifications and distribution, 273–274

templates for, 261

updating, 258–259

version numbers, 253

versions, configuring with Bundler, 268

versions, installing with Bundler and, 255

versions, specifications, 273

versions, specifying with Gemfile, 258–260

versions, updating, 258–259

writing and packaging, 261–272

gems command-line option, 236

.gemspec file, 267, 269

gemspec method, 274

generate method, JSON, 610

--generate-todo Standard option, 354

generators, with enumerators, 80–83

generic types, typing with RBS, 302, 307, 487, 492

getElementById, Wasm and, 342

getbyte method, 603

getc method, 603

gets method

  ARGF class, 238

  conditional expressions and, 150

  control structures syntax basics, 25

  loops with, 30

  reading with, 30, 180, 232, 550

getters, style conventions, 346

getwd method

  Dir class, 593

  FileUtils class, 600

Git, repository for gems, 267

git:, accessing unreleased gems, 260

GitHub, accessing unreleased gems, 260

glob method, Dir class, 590

global (rbenv), 7

Global Interpreter Lock (GIL), 187

global variables

  names, 22, 446

  resources on, 450

  safely using, 22

  scope, 448

  syntax reference, 448

  table of predefined, 450–453

  threads, 189

  typing with RBS, 488

global_variables method, 549

GraalVM, 651

graph command, YARD, 324

GraphViz, 324

Gray, James Edward, II, 587

greediness

  assignment and, 149

  regular expressions, 138

grep, 159, 573

grep_v, 573

group method, gems, 261

group: option, gems, 260

group_by, 572

grouping

  with Enumerable methods, 572

  regular expressions, 138–141

gsub method, 28, 131, 140–142, 529

gsub! method, 131, 529

guard clauses

  pattern matching, 168, 462

  statement modifiers as, 26

  style conventions, 347, 355

Guilds, see ractors

H

\H, character class abbreviation, 136

\h, character class abbreviation, 136

-h

  help command-line option, 234, 240, 278

  irb command-line option, 278

Hanami, 332

has_key?, hashes, 582

has_many, as macro, 387, 389

has_value?, hashes, 582

Hash class

  conversion with Kernel module, 366

  library reference, 579–584

  syntax basics, 22, 56–58

hash method, 559, 584

hashes

  case expressions, 460

  combining, 582

  comparing, 583

  conversion methods, 583

  conversion protocols, 364, 366

  converting Data instances to, 394

  converting to ENV, 242

  creating, 59, 579

  custom pattern matching, 169

  default values, 23, 580

  defined, 22, 53

  deleting in, 581

  digging, 58, 581

  empty hashes, 579

  empty hashes, pattern matching, 164, 461

  expanding, 97, 471

formatting and Kernel methods, 548

indices, 23, 56, 438

invoking methods, 470

iteration, 582

JSON parsing and, 609

library reference, 579–584

modifying methods, 583

module-level hashes to avoid instance variables in mixins, 112

parameters, 91

pattern matching, 164–165

querying, 559

Rack and, 334

setting values, 581

sorting, 60

style conventions, 345, 348, 354

syntax basics, 22, 56–58

syntax reference, 438

as term, 57

typing with RBS, 306, 490–491

typing with Sorbet, 310

word frequency example, 58–65

headers, parsing CSV files, 42, 588

headings, RDoc documentation, 318

help command, irb, 287

--help

  command line option, 234, 240, 278

  RDoc, 320

heredocs

  style convention, 348

  syntax basics, 121

  syntax reference, 434

hexadecimals, character class abbreviation, 136

Hintze, Clemens, 446

HOME environment variable, 242, 596

home method, Dir class, 593

hooks

  defined, 399, 415

  defining, 404

  event hooks in Module class, 557

  list of methods, 399

  marshaling, 421

  method hooks and metaprogramming, 391, 399–405

  object creation, 416

  reflection, 415–417

HTML

  documentation with RDoc, 313–315, 320

  documentation with YARD, 322, 324

  escaping and CGI encoding, 328

  escaping in URI encodings, 616

  generating, 329

Rack and, 336
Wasm, 340
HTTP
  iteration and, 577
  Rack and, 332–337
  routes and Sinatra, 338–340
  time and date methods, 497
HTTPS, Rack and, 334
hyperlinks, RDoc documentation, 315, 317
hyphen (-), lists and RDoc documentation, 317

I

I, RuboCop severity level, 350
i (case insensitive regular expressions option), 132, 440
i (complex numbers suffix), 118, 433
i debugging command, 293
i i debugging command, 293
i I debugging command, 293
-I, command-line option, 235, 244
-i
  ARGF command-line option, 239
  ARGV command-line option, 235
%i, symbols in arrays, 55, 348, 437, 444, 561
%I, symbols in arrays, 444
__id__ method, 558
identical? method
  File class, 596
  FileUtils class, 600
IDEs
  RuboCop and, 350
  static typing and, 300
idiomatic, defined, 21, 343
if
  debugging breakpoints, 292
  debugging suffix, 293
  guard clauses, 169
  indentation, 347
  modifiers, 459
  regular expressions, 27, 130
  style conventions, 347, 355
  syntax basics, 25, 143, 153–156
  syntax reference, 459
--ignore=PATTERN flag, Sorbet, 310
ignore: key, Standard, 354
IGNORE_EOF, irb configuration option, 279, 285
ignore_eof, irb configuration option, 285
:IGNORE_SIGINT, irb configuration option, 285
ignore_sigint, irb configuration option, 285
immediate values, 410

immutable structs with Data class, 393
implicit conversion, defined, 363
include method
  implementation of, 381
  modules, 108–109, 113, 381, 476, 478, 490, 555
--include option, documentation with RDoc, 319
:include: documentation modifier, 319–320
include? method
  Enumerable module, 575
  hashes, 582
  mixins and, 110
  ranges, 125
  sets, 585
  strings, 524
included method
  class-level macros, 391
  metaprogramming with hook methods, 399, 406
included? method, 555
included_modules, 555
indentation
  case statements, 344, 347
  comments, 19, 31
  documentation with YARD, 323
  heredocs, 121, 434
  irb, 280, 285, 288
  methods, 86
  RDoc, 316–319
  Standard, 354
  style conventions, 344–346, 354
  warnings, magic comment for, 31, 430
index method
  arrays, 563
  regular expressions, 524
  strings, 524
indices
  arrays, 22, 53, 563, 567
  enumerating with, 570, 573
  hashes, 23, 56, 438
  operators, 145
  regular expression matches, 134
  retrieving substrings, 525
  strings, 524
--inf-ruby-mode irb command-line option, 278
infinite sequences
  enumerators, 80–83, 577
  exceptions with retry, 175
  fibers, 201
  ranges, 125, 437
inheritance
  class variables, 448

class-level, 101–105, 380, 388, 540, 553
  coupling and, 116
  hook methods, 400
  mixins, 381
  modules, 105–107, 381, 553
  multiple, 109
  structs, 633
  super and, 473
  Tempfile class, 613
  visibility and, 380
  when to use, 115
  writing to environment variables and, 243
inherited method
  Class class, 540
  hooks, 400
init (rbenv), 5, 7
initialize method
  classes, 34, 477, 479
  in construction pattern, 43
  documentation and, 319
  memory and, 34
  as private method, 45
initializing
  classes, 34, 477, 479
  in construction pattern, 43
  irb initialization file, 283
  memory and, 34
  Ruby, 5, 7
  Sorbet, 308
inject method, 71
inline, Bundler, 263
in keyword
  case pattern matching, 166
  single-line pattern matching, 163
inplace_mode for ARGF, 239
input, Rack, 334, see also IO
insert
  arrays, 563
  strings, 528
insns and --dump command-line option, 236
insns_without_opt and --dump command-line option, 236
inspect method
  debugging with, 36, 289
  irb command-line options, 278
  Object class, 559
  p method and, 36
  regular expressions, 513
  symbols, 534
--inspect irb command-line option, 278
:INSPECT_MODE, irb configuration option, 285
inspect_mode, irb configuration option, 285

install
 Bundler, 255, 258
 FileUtils class, 599
 gems, 252
installing
 Bundler, 254
 debug gem, 290
 gems, 251–253, 255, 258, 274
 Pry, 294
 RSpec, 220
 RuboCop, 349
 Ruby, 3–11
 Ruby for Windows, 3, 7–11
 Ruby with rbenv, 4–7
 Sorbet, 307
 Standard, 354
 WSL (Windows Subsystem for
  Linux), 8
 YARD, 322
instance methods
 adding directly to class objects,
  383
 class methods and, 87
 creating, 556
 defined, 18
 metaprogramming and, 391
 notation conventions, xiv
 Object methods, 558
 structs, 633
 syntax basics, 87
 syntax reference, 466, 479
instance values, debugging options,
 293
instance variables
 accessor methods, 38–42
 defined, 18
 metaprogramming and, 390
 mixins and, 112
 names, 112, 445
 Object methods, 558
 for object state, 34, 36, 41
 pattern matching and variable
  binding, 165
 reflection, 412
 scope, 449
 self and, 372, 374, 378
 syntax reference, 449
 threads, 189
 troubleshooting, 638
 typing with RBS, 302
instance_double method, RSpec, 228
instance_eval
 BasicObject class, 539
 calling methods dynamically,
  414
 DSLs and, 398–399
 metaprogramming and self,
  396–399
 RSpec and, 222
instance_exec, 397, 404, 539
instance_method, 413
instance_methods, 406, 554

instance_variable_defined?, 558
instance_variable_get, 390, 558
instance_variable_set, 390, 558
instance_variables method, 558
instances, defined, 18
Integer class
 conversion with Kernel module,
  366
 immediate values, 410
 library reference, 504
 syntax basics, 117
Integer method, 40, 119
integers
 base indicator, 117, 432
 conversion methods, 503, 505,
  508, 510
 conversion protocols, 364, 366
 converting floats to, 40
 converting strings to, 118
 converting to floats, 119
 as immediate values, 410
 integer directives for packing
  binary data, 567
 small, 205
 syntax basics, 117
 syntax reference, 432
 time and data methods, 500
interactive Ruby, see irb
interfaces
 defined, 306
 dynamic typing and, 357
 generic types in RBS, 492
 names, 306
 typing with RBS, 306, 488
--internal-encoding command-line option, 235
interned strings, 439
interning, 439
interpreters
 default, 649
 defined, 649
 editing gems and, 253
 execution tracing, 417–420
 forking when spawning processes, 197–199
 invoking from command line,
  231
 metaprogramming with hook
  methods, 399
 overview of, 649–654
 parallelism with ractors, 202–
  206
 Ruby VM and, 419
 standard protocols and coercions, 362–369
 syntax errors and, 231
intersect?, 585
intersection
 arrays, 566
 sets, 586

into:, OptionParser, 242
introspection, see reflection
invert, hashes, 583
IO
 conversion protocols, 364
 debugging tips, 640
 iteration and, 70
 Kernel methods, 550
 network communication, 185
 reading/writing streams methods, 602–604
 spawning processes and, 197–
  199
 streams as duplexed, 600
 syntax basics, 30, 179–186
IO class
 iteration and, 577
 library reference, 600–605
 open options, 594
 popen, 197–199
 syntax basics, 179–186
IO library reference
 Dir class, 590–593
 encodings, 605–609
 File class, 593–597
 FileUtils module, 597–600
 IO class, 600–605
 JSON, 609
 pathnames, 611
 StringIO class, 612
 Tempfile class, 613
 URI class, 614–616
 YAML, 616–618
irb
 about, 12, 277
 autocompletion in, 12, 277,
  281, 285
 color coding in, 277, 285
 command-line options, 278
 configuring, 283–288
 configuring prompt, 287
 Docker and, 13
 documentation in, 14
 ending sessions, 279, 287
 exiting, 12
 extending, 284
 JRuby and, 653
 launching, 277
 listing sessions, 282, 287
 multilines, command-line options, 278
 multilines, configuration options, 285
 multilines, navigation with,
  280
 navigation in, 280–282
 string substitutions, 288
 subsessions, 282, 287
 syntax basics, 278–280
 terminating, 285
 working with regular expressions, 132

irb command, subsessions, 282
irb_change_binding, 286
irb_context, 286
irb_cwws, 287
irb_exit, 287
irb_jobs, 287
irb_kill, 287
:IRB_NAME, irb configuration option, 285
irb_name, irb configuration option, 285
irb_quit, 287
:IRB_RC, irb configuration option, 285
irbtools, 283
Iron Ruby, 654
isolation, ractors, 203, 205
it, RSpec, 220
iteration, *see also* enumeration
    about, 53
    blocks, 63–65
    defined, 29
    hashes, 582
    with integers, 119, 159
    iterators, defined, 63, 67
    iterators, uses, 70
    library reference, 569
    mixins and, 110
    ranges, 125
    reading files, 181
    reduce and, 71
    reversing, 60, 63
    with streams, 604
    string methods, 527
    style conventions, 348
    syntax basics, 67–72, 78–83, 158–163
    tracking with with_index, 70
itself method, Object class, 560

J

Java, JRuby and, 652
--jil command-line option, 235
jj, pretty printing JSON, 290
jobs, listing irb subsessions, 282, 287
Johnson, Stephen C., 348
join method
    arrays, 564
    File class, 595
    filenames, 595
    Thread class, 189, 191, 193
JRuby, 5, 652
JSON
    complex numbers and, 507
    converting, 542
    generating, 610
    library reference, 609
    marshaling and, 422–423

pretty printing, 290
rational numbers and, 506
sending, 332
jump-to n, Pry, 295
just-in-time compilers
    command-line options, 235, 650–651
    overview of, 649–651

K

\k<...>, regular expressions, 139
keep_if, sets, 585
Kernel module
    about, 108
    backtick syntax, 549
    control flow methods, 542–546
    conversion methods, 365, 542
    exception handling, 543
    field type characters table, 547
    formatting methods, 547–548
    formatting string flags, 547
    invoking explicitly, 537
    IO methods, 179, 550
    library reference, 541–551
    list of shortcut methods, 546
    method name conventions, 465
    methods, invoking, 542
    mixins and, 108
    name conventions, 86
    Object class and, 541
    runtime information, 548
    style conventions, 346
    system info methods, 549
    top-level execution environment and, 408
key method, hashes, 581
key/value stores, *see* hashes; keys
key? method, hashes, 582
keys
    deleting, 581, 583
    hash syntax basics, 23, 56, 579
    hash syntax reference, 438, 461
    querying, 582
    Rack and, 334
    typing with RBS, 306, 491
keyword arguments
    blocks, 481
    syntax basics, 95
    typing with Sorbet, 309
keyword parameters
    history of, 92
    syntax basics, 91
    syntax reference, 468
    typing with RBS, 490
kill method
    irb subsessions, 287
    quitting debugging, 292
    threads, 190
kill! method, quitting debugging, 292

L

-I
    command-line option, 234
    irb command-line option, 278
%l irb configuration, 288
label, hyperlinks and RDoc documentation, 317
labeled lists, RDoc documentation, 317
lambda method
    stabby lambda shortcut (->), 74, 77
    syntax reference, 482
lambdas
    defined, 482
    finalizers, 625
    invoking methods with blocks, 471
    stabby lambda shortcut (->), 74, 77
    syntax reference, 482
LANG environment variable, 607
last, Array class, 56, 60, 562
last_match, 134
last_status, 146
late binding, defined, 300
Latin-1, 122
lazy evaluation
    infinite sequences, 81–83, 577–578
    regular expressions, 138
lazy method, Enumerator class, 577–578
length
    arrays, 565
    hashes, 582
    sets, 585
    strings, 523
let method
    RSpec, 224
    Sorbet, 310
lib directory, gems, 267
libraries, *see also* gems
    command-line options, 235
    directories, 244
    environment variables, 242
    loading, 44, 244
    loading, and ERB, 330
line numbers, irb prompt configuration, 288
line-ending processing, command-line option, 234
linebreaks, character class abbreviation, 136
lineno method, ARGF class, 238
link method, FileUtils class, 599
link_entry method, FileUtils class, 599

links, methods with FileUtils class, 599

lint, 348

linters, *see also* RuboCop; Standard
    defined, 348
    gems, 268
    using, 343

Liskov Substitution Principle, 115

Liskov, Barbara, 67

list
    gems, 252
    RBS, 303
    threads, 190

lists, RDoc documentation, 317

literals, syntax reference, 432–439

ln method, FileUtils class, 599

ln_s method, FileUtils class, 600

ln_sf method, FileUtils class, 600

load
    files, 545
    irb and, 280, 285
    JSON parsing, 610
    marshaling, 420
    YAML, 617

load_file method
    JSON parsing, 610
    YAML, 617

local (rbenv), 6

local values, debugging options, 293

local variables
    blocks, 66
    ERB templates, 331
    exceptions, 173
    getting information on, 549
    iteration with for vs. each, 160
    vs. left assignment in calling methods, 95
    names, 21, 34, 346, 445
    pattern matching and variable binding, 165
    pinning, 167
    reflection, 412
    scope, 449
    Sinatra and, 338
    syntax reference, 449
    threads, 189
    typing with Sorbet, 310

local_variables method, 549

local_variables_get method, 549

local_variables_set method, 549

LocalJumpError, 483

location, loggers, 623

locks, mutexes, 194–196

LOGDIR environment variable, 242

Logger class, library reference, 623

logging
    levels, 623

Logger class library reference, 623
    logging statements, gems, 253

logical flow, style conventions, 347

lonely operator (&.), 156, 473

lookup table of symbols, 641–643

loop method
    about, 79
    Kernel module, 79, 543
    syntax basics, 157
    syntax reference, 463

loops
    avoiding in tests, 210
    coercion, 369
    command-line options, 233–234
    with gets, 30
    with integers, 119, 159
    Kernel module, 79, 543
    scope, 161–163, 450
    style conventions, 347
    syntax basics, 157–163
    syntax reference, 463
    terminating, 161

ls method, Pry, 295

lvalue
    assignment, 474
    expressions and assignment, 146–150
    syntax reference, 454–456

M

m
    multiline regular expressions option, 132, 440
    regular expressions and repetition, 137

%M irb configuration, 288

%m irb configuration, 288

mRuby, 5, 653

macros, metaprogramming and class-level, 387–399

magic comments
    directives table, 430
    disabling RuboCop, 353
    encoding changes, 123
    static typing with Sorbet, 309
    syntax basics, 31
    syntax reference, 430

MagLev, 654

--main parameter, documentation with RDoc and, 319

main method, Ractor class, 202

main object
    class definitions and, 374
    metaprogramming and, 374, 407

:main: documentation modifier, 319

Make, 245, 248

make_sharable method, Ractor class, 206

makedirs, FileUtils class, 598

map method
    about, 70, 571
    converting files into strings, 124
    Enumerable module, 63, 70, 80–81, 110
    infinite sequences, 81
    iteration and, 63, 81
    mixins and, 110
    passing block arguments, 97
    using enumerators as objects, 80

maps, *see* hashes

Markdown, parsing by RDoc, 320

Marshal module, 420–424

marshal_dump, 421

marshal_load, 421

marshaling
    with JSON, 422–423
    reflection, 420–424
    with YAML, 422, 616

Mastering Regular Expressions, 26

match method, regular expressions, 133, 512, 514

match? method, regular expressions, 27, 130, 133, 512

match_length method, 514

MatchData class
    library reference, 513
    regular expressions, 134, 139

matchers, RSpec, 222, 225–227

matches method, MatchData class, 514

math
    array methods, 565
    library reference, 502–511
    set methods, 586

max, 110, 125, 576

max_by, 576

measure method, Benchmark module, 284

member?
    enumerators, 575
    hashes, 582
    sets, 585

members, RBS, 487–488

memory
    allocation for objects, 540
    initializing and, 34
    ranges and, 125

merge
    hashes, 582
    sets, 585

merge!, hashes, 582

metadata, adding to comments with YARD, 321

metaprogramming
  class-level macros, 387–399
  classes, creating dynamically, 394
  defined, 371
  _eval methods, 396–399
  execution environment, 407
  with hook methods, 391, 399–405
  library reference, 619–634
  modules, understanding, 381–387
  object model, understanding, 371–380
  structs and subclasses, 392–394
  tracing execution example, 405–407
  TypeProf and, 305
method method
  Object class, 99
  RBS, 303
Method objects
  calling methods, 551
  calling methods dynamically, 413
  creating, 551
  invoking methods with blocks, 471
  library reference, 551
method special variable, 549
method_added hook, 406
method_missing
  BasicObject class, 539
  filtering with, 405–407
  metaprogramming with, 372, 401–405
  method lookup and, 114, 401
  method syntax reference, 472
  OpenStruct, 627
methodname, 465
methods
  access control, 45–48, 480
  access control, typing with RBS, 490
  adding to existing classes, 49–51
  aliasing, 144, 475
  ambiguity in parsing, 446
  arity, 552
  attributes as, 40–42
  block parameters and, 92
  calling, 93–95
  calling and metaprogramming, 372–374
  calling as arguments, 95
  calling dynamically, 413, 556
  chaining, 145, 544
  chaining in RSpec, 226
  chaining, debugging, 64
  class-level inheritance and, 101–105

converting and passing collections as arguments, 96, 470
  dangerous, 346
  debugging breakpoints, 292
  debugging, with Pry, 294
  debugging tips, 640
  defined, 12, 18
  defining, 20, 85–93, 465–467
  documentation with YARD, 322
  double dispatch, 367
  dynamic typing, 356–362
  exception handling, 485
  expanding collections, 96, 470
  getting name of, 418, 549
  information on in Pry, 295
  intercepting with hooks, 415
  invoking in Kernel module, 542
  invoking, syntax reference, 470–472
  listing, 558
  lookup and method_missing hook, 401
  lookup and mixins, 113–116
  messages and, 19
  module methods, adding as class methods, 109
  module methods, calling, 107
  module methods, defining, 106
  module methods, invoking, 478
  names, 21, 34, 86, 131, 360, 375, 432, 465, 639
  nesting, 466
  notation conventions, xiv
  one-line (endless), 86, 88, 465
  operator syntax, 474
  operators as, 87
  parameters, syntax, 88–93
  passing arguments to, 95
  passing block arguments, 97–99
  RDoc documentation, 318
  redefining, 85
  refinements, 384–387
  reflection, 410–416
  registering in class object, 476
  renaming, 416
  return values, 96
  singleton methods, metaprogramming and, 374–380
  singleton methods and Object class methods, 559
  singleton methods, syntax reference, 466
  source locations, 284, 295, 640
  stubbing in tests, 216
  style conventions, 346–347, 355
  syntax basics, 18, 85–99
  syntax reference, 465–475
  troubleshooting, 637–640
  typing with RBS, 302, 305, 489
  typing with Sorbet, 309
  unbound, 413

undefining, 469
  visibility and inheritance, 380
methods method, Object class, 558
methods tool, RBS, 303
Meyer, Bertrand, 41
middleware, Rack and, 333, 335–337
min, 110, 576
min_by, 576
minitest
  about, 60, 207–208
  assertions, 209–212
  mock objects, 212, 215–217
  vs. RSpec, 228
  structure and organization, 212–215
  stubs, 216
  using, 208–219
  word frequency example, 60–62
minmax, 576
minus sign (-)
  forking when spawning processes, 197–199
  subtraction, 503–504, 506–507, 509, 565, 586
mixins
  defined, 105
  inheritance, 381
  instance variables and, 112
  metaprogramming and, 381–387
  method lookup, 113–116
  multiple inheritance and, 109
  super and, 473
  as superclasses, 373
  syntax reference, 478
  using, 107–116
  when to use, 115
mkdir
  Dir class, 592
  FileUtils class, 598
  Unix command-line basics, 647
mkdir_p, FileUtils class, 598
mkpath, FileUtils class, 598
mnt directory, 10
Mocha, 217
mock objects
  calling multiple times, 216
  creating, 215
  defined, 215
  minitest, 212, 215–217
  RSpec, 227
  verifying, 215, 227
MockExpectationError, 216
mode string, 179, 593, 600
Module class
  access control, 45, 480
  dynamic code methods, 556

event hooks, 557
library reference, 552–557
metaprogramming and _eval
methods, 396–399

module keyword, 552

module_eval
calling methods dynamically,
414, 556
metaprogramming and self,
396

module_exec, 397

module_function, 479

modules
advantages, 105
aliasing methods in, 475
comparing, 553
composing, 110
creating, 552
defined, 478
defining, 478
defining in RBS, 487
documentation disabling in
RDoc, 319–320
documentation with YARD,
322
environment variables, 242
extending, 109, 383, 391, 479,
490
generic types in RBS, 492
hierarchy, 553
information methods, 553
inheritance, 105–107, 381, 553
irb command-line option, 278
loading, 106, 108
metaprogramming and, 381–
387, 390–392
methods, adding as class
methods, 109
methods, calling, 107
methods, defining, 106
methods, lookup and mixins,
113–116
mixins, 105, 107–116
module methods, invoking,
478
module methods, syntax reference, 466
names, 22, 106, 265, 346, 478
namespaces and, 105–107, 476,
478
nesting, 266, 476
prepending, 110, 113, 383, 416,
479, 490, 555
refinements, 384–387
reflection, 411
scope resolution operator, 107,
447, 476, 478
understanding, 105–107

monkey-patching, 50, 384

more words, documentation with
RDoc, 316

mount point, 10

MRI, 5, 649

multi_route, Sinatra, 339

--multiline irb command-line option,
278

multilines
irb, 278, 280, 285
regular expressions, 132, 440

multiple inheritance, 109

multiple words, documentation with
RDoc, 316

multiplication
about, 71
arrays, 565
BigDecimal class, 509
complex numbers, 507
floating-point numbers, 506
integers, 504
Numeric class, 503
strings, 531

Mutex class, synchronizing threads
with, 193–196

mv method, FileUtils class, 599

N

-n
command-line option for
loops, 233–234
debugging breakpoints, 292
debugging navigation, 292
ERB command line option, 330
regular expressions and repetition, 137

n (regular expressions encoding
option), 133

%N irb configuration, 288

\n
newline character in string literals, 20, 120
reading files, 182

_n numbered block parameter, 30,
67

name method, symbols, 534

named captures, regular expressions, 513–514, 517–522

named groups, regular expressions,
139

named subroutines, regular expressions, 522

named_captures method, regular expressions, 513–514

NameError, 114, 236, 401

names
aliasing, 144
ambiguity in parsing, 446
avoiding name collisions with
namespaces, 105–107
avoiding spaces in, 646
class variables, 22, 445

classes, 22, 34, 265, 346, 395,
476
constants, 22, 346, 446, 639
custom exception classes, 172
gem source files, 268
gems, 251, 273
global variables, 22, 446
instance variables, 112, 445
interfaces, 306
irb sessions, 285
local variables, 21, 34, 346, 445
methods, 21, 34, 86, 131, 360,
375, 432, 465, 639
modules, 22, 106, 265, 346, 478
naming conventions, 21, 86,
346, 465
packages, 273
parameters, 21
ractors, 202
reserved words, 445
singleton methods, 375
symbols, 24, 346, 439
syntax basics, 21
syntax reference, 445
test methods, 213
tests, 217, 219
troubleshooting, 639
Unicode and, 432
variables, 21, 34, 346, 432, 445

names method, regular expressions,
513–514

namespaces
defined, 106
gems, 264
modules, 105–107, 476, 478

navigation
command-line basics, 645
safe navigation operator (&.),
156, 345, 472

nested assignment, 149

nested groups, regular expressions,
518

nesting
classes, 266
modules, 266
pattern matching, 164

Net class, iteration and, 577

networks, IO communication, 185

new method
about, 18
Array class, 53, 561
CGI class, 329
Class class, 394, 416, 477, 540
class instances, creating, 34
classes, creating dynamically,
394
CSV files, 589
Date class, 501
Dir class, 590
Enumerator class, 80
Fiber class, 200
File class, 179, 593

hashes, 59, 579
IO class, 601
loggers, 623
Module class, 552
objects, 18
OpenStruct, 627
OptionParser, 240
Pathname class, 611
Proc class, 75, 482
Ractor class, 202
Regexp class, 132, 511
renaming classes, 416
sets, 584
StringIO class, 612
Struct class, 393, 633
Thread class, 188
Time class, 496

newlines
command expressions, 146
ERB templates and, 331
making visible in reading files, 181
removing from strings, 123
string literals, 20, 120
writing to files, 183

next
debugging navigation, 292
enumerators, 78, 578
loops, 161, 463
procs, 483

nil
assignment and, 455
checking for, 156
conditional expressions, 150
control structures syntax basics, 25
defined, 22
environment variables and, 244
as immediate value, 410
iteration and, 69
minitest and, 212
Object class, 560
safe navigation operator (&.), 156, 472
syntax basics, methods, 86
syntax reference, 432, 457
syntax reference, methods, 473
typing with RBS, 302, 491
typing with Sorbet, 310
writing to files, 183

nilable, typing with Sorbet, 310
%NNi irb configuration, 288
%NNn irb configuration, 288
--noautocomplete irb command-line option, 278
--nocolorize irb command-line option, 278
:nodoc: documentation modifier, 319
--noecho irb command-line option, 278

--noecho-on-assignment irb command-line option, 278
--nofix Standard option, 354
--noinspect irb command-line option, 278
NoMatchingPatternError, 165–166, 460
NoMatchingPatternKeyError, 456
NoMethodError, 401, 470
--nomultiline irb command-line option, 278
noop FileUtils argument, 598
--noprompt irb command-line option, 278
--nosingeline irb command-line option, 278
not, conditional expressions, 151, 457
not_to method, RSpec, 222
notation, conventions, xiv
@note documentation tag, 323
notify_observers method, 626
:notnew: documentation modifier, 319
--noverbose irb command-line option, 278
now method
    Date class, 501
    Time class, 496
numbers, see also complex numbers; decimals; floating-point numbers; integers; rational numbers
    absolute value of, 118, 503, 510
    coercion protocols, 366–369
    conversion methods, 503, 508
    operations, 119
    rounding, 40, 509
    syntax basics, 117–120
    syntax reference, 432
    time and data methods, 500
    troubleshooting, 639
Numeric class, library reference, 502–504
numeric coercions, 366–369

O

o (substitution regular expressions option), 132, 440
Object class
    comparison operators, 152
    as default parent class, 102
    diagnostic methods in, 284
    Kernel module and, 541
    library reference, 557–560
    mixins and, 108
object model library reference
    BasicObject class, 537–539
    Class class, 540
    Comparable module, 540

Kernel module, 541–551
    Module class, 552–557
    Object class, 557–560
object-oriented languages, Ruby as, 17–19, 33
Object-Oriented Software Construction, 41
object_id, 18, 558
objects
    accessor methods, 37–42
    aliasing with assignment, 49
    attaching methods to, 88
    basics of, 36–42
    bindings and irb, 282, 286
    blocks as, 73–78
    comparison operators, 557
    converting and passing as arguments, 96, 470
    creating from classes, 477
    creating with Enumerable methods, 572
    distributed Ruby, 424
    duplicating, 559–560
    dynamic typing, 357–362
    enumerators as, 79
    finalizers, 625
    freezing, 49, 559
    memory allocation, 540
    object model and metaprogramming, 371–380
    Observer pattern, 625
    querying methods, 559
    ractors and sharable objects, 205
    ranges as, 126
    reflection, 409–411
    rendering as strings, 36
    scope and Pry, 294
    singleton methods and, 374–380
    syntax reference, 465–492
    threads as, 189
    troubleshooting, 638
    typing with RBS, 305
    variables as references to, 48
ObjectSpace
    each_object, 410
    library reference, 624
    reflection with, 409–411
Observable module, library reference, 625
Observer pattern, 625
on method, OptionParser, 240
one-line (endless) methods, syntax, 86, 88, 465
Onigmo, 515
Oniguruma, 518
--op documentation option, 321
Opal, 654
opcodes, Ruby VM, 419

--open debugging option, 291
open method
    CSV files, 589
    debugging, 291
    Dir class, 590
    File class, 72, 180, 593
    gems, 253
    IO class, 594, 601
    Kernel module, 198, 551
    modes, 551
    spawning processes, 198
    StringIO class, 612
    URIs, 186, 614
open-uri library, 186
--open_nonstop debugging option,
    291
OpenSSL, environment variable,
    242
OPENSSL_CONF environment variable,
    242
OpenStruct class
    library reference, 627
    simulating accessors with
        method_missing, 402
operator plus assignment, 149
operators
    assignment, 145, 149
    binary, 144
    comparison operators and ex-
        pressions, 152
    defining as methods, 87
    indices, 145
    syntax basics, 143
    syntax reference, 454
option parsers
    gems, 266, 268
    OptionParser, 239–242
OptionParser, 239–242
options, regular expressions, 513
or, conditional expressions, 151, 457
order
    assignment, 148
    blocks, 431
    command line options, 240
    hash keys, 23, 438, 582
    hashes, 58, 582
    passing arguments to methods,
        95
    Rake tasks, 246
    sets, 584
    time and data methods, 498
other_proc, Method objects, 551
outdent, irb, 280
output, see IO
owner method, UnboundMethod, 634

P
-P, ERB command line option, 330
\p, character classes, 443

-p command-line option, 233–234
p method
    object state and, 35
    printing for debugging, 289,
        293
    vs. puts, 35
    syntax basics, 30
    writing with, 35
pack, arrays, 183, 567
packages, names, 273
parallel assignment
    conversion protocols, 364
    expression syntax, 148
    style conventions, 347
    yield and, 68
parallel: key, Standard, 354
parallelism, with ractors, 202–206
@param documentation tag, 323
parameters
    anonymous, 90–91, 93
    blocks, 65, 77, 468
    documentation with YARD,
        323
    double dispatch, 367
    hashes, 91
    keyword, 91
    methods and block parame-
        ters, 92, 449
    methods, default, 89
    methods, scope, 449
    methods, syntax basics, 88–93
    methods, syntax reference,
        449, 467–469
    methods, variable-length lists,
        89–91
    names, 21
    passing through to other
        methods, 469
    RDoc documentation, 318
    Sinatra, 339
    typing with RBS, 489
    typing with Sorbet, 309
params
    Sinatra, 339
    Sorbet, 309
parent classes, see superclasses
parentheses (())
    blocks, 480
    calling super without, 473
    conditional expressions, 151,
        348
    methods syntax, 20, 86, 88, 95,
        467, 470
    nested assignment, 149
    order of execution and, 151
    regular expressions, 27, 138
    RSpec, 221
    stabby lambda operator (->),
        76
    style conventions, 346, 348
    troubleshooting, 637, 640

parse method
    CSV files, 588
    JSON, 609
    ripper library, 631
    time and date methods, 496,
        501
    URIs, 614
parse! method, OptionParser, 240–242,
    248
parsetree and --dump command-line
    option, 236
parsetree_with_comment and --dump
    command-line option, 236
parsing
    command-line option parsing,
        239–242
    CSV, 42, 588
    JSON, 609
    prism gem and, 628
    RDoc and, 320
    ripper library and, 630
    time and date methods, 496,
        501
    troubleshooting, 638
    URIs, 614
    YAML, 617
partition, 528, 573
pass method, Thread class, 193
passed method, minitest, 215
PATH environment variable, 7, 235,
    242, 257
path method, File class, 596
$PATH variable, Bundler, 257
path: option, gems, 260
PATH_INFO key, 334
Pathname class, library reference, 611
pathnames
    converting, 542, 600
    creating, 611
    finding files, 184
    library reference, 611
paths
    absolute pathname, 596
    conversion protocols, 364
    converting to file descriptor,
        601
    Dir class instances, 590
    File class methods, 595
    irb command-line option, 278
    loading files, 545
    temporary file path, returning,
        592
    type checking with Sorbet and,
        310
pattern matching
    case expressions, 460–462
    custom, 169
    defining patterns, 460
    Enumerable methods, 573, 575
    exception handling, 173

File class, 597
glob, 590
guard clauses, 168
with multiple patterns, 164
pinning values, 167
with rightward assignment, 456
single-line, 163
syntax basics, 163–170
variable binding and, 164–166
Patterson, Aaron, 290
peek, 578
percent sign (%)
ERB templates, 330, 332
literals and irb prompt configuration, 288
permutation, arrays, 566
pinning
expressions, 168
values, 167
pipe (|)
array unions, 566
bitwise OR, 504
case expressions, 461–462
pattern matching and variable binding, 166
programs, 431
regular expressions, 27, 138
separating types with RBS, 489
set unions, 586
spawning processes, 198
union types with RBS, 306, 491
writing to CSV files, 589
pipe method
IO class, 601
spawning processes, 198
platforms, gem installation with Bundler, 256
plus sign (+)
addition, 503–504, 506–507, 509, 565, 586
enumerators, adding, 578
operator plus assignment, 149
overriding as method, 87
regular expressions, 27, 137
pop, 56, 563
popb, 287
popen, 197–199, 601
portname, defined, 600
ports
distributed Ruby, 424
modes strings and, 600
web servers and Rack, 334
POSIX character classes, 442
post_match method, 134, 514
pow, Integer class, 504
PP library reference, 627

pp method
PP library reference, 627
printing for debugging, 289, 293
pre, debugging suffix, 293
pre_match method, 134, 514
pread method, IO class, 604
precedence
blocks, 28, 480
boolean operators, 150, 457
method parameters, 467
regular expressions and repetition, 138
troubleshooting, 638
precision
BigDecimal class, 507–510
formatting flags, 547
time methods, 496
predicate methods
File class, 596
syntax, 86, 346
prepend method
arrays, 563
modules, 110, 113, 383, 416, 479, 490, 555
strings, 531
prepend_features method, modules, 555
preserve FileUtils argument, 598
pretty_generate method, JSON, 610
pretty_print method, PP library reference, 627
PrettyPrint library, 627
print method
IO class, 604
printing for debugging, 289
vs. put, 183
threads, 189
writing files, 183
printf, 547, 604
printing
for debugging, 289, 293
files, 183
IO class, 604
with PP, 627
with puts, 550
threads, 189
priority, Thread class, 190
prism library, 628
pristine, gems, 253
private, 45, 345
private methods, 45, 94, 466, 480, 490, 554, 558
Proc class, conversion protocols, 364–365
proc method, 74, 482
proc objects
=== comparison operator, 156

blocks as objects, 73–78, 92
calling, 482
converting blocks to, 482
converting hashes to, 583
currying, 552
default hash value and, 580
finalizers, 625
invoking methods with blocks, 471
irb configuration, 283, 285
Method objects for, 413, 551
passing block arguments, 97–99
Rack and, 334–335
raw procs, 482
syntax reference, 480, 482
typing with RBS, 305, 490
processes
blocks and, 199
child notifications, 199
independent children, 198
IO and, 197–199
replacing current process, 549
running multiple external, 196–199
spawning, 196–198, 550
waiting for child, 198
produce, 80, 577
product, 72, 578
$PROGRAM_NAME, ARGV and, 238
programs
creating, 12
ending with __END__, 431
exiting, 543
loading with Bundler, 256, 261
making code into executable, 237
making gems executable, 272
piping, 431
sleeping, 543
terminating, 242
terminating and threads, 189
:PROMPT, irb configuration, 285
--prompt, irb command-line option, 278, 287
:PROMPT_C, irb configuration, 288
prompt_c, irb configuration, 285
:PROMPT_I, irb configuration, 288
prompt_i, irb configuration, 285
:PROMPT_MODE, irb configuration, 285
prompt_mode, irb configuration, 285
:PROMPT_N, irb configuration, 288
:PROMPT_S, irb configuration, 288
prompt_s, irb configuration, 285
prompts
command-line basics, 645
irb command-line options, 278
irb configuration, 283, 285, 287

proper_subset?, 585
proper_superset?, 585
protected, 45
protected methods, 45–48, 480, 490
provides:, Sinatra, 340
Pry
    exiting, 294
    installing, 294
    method source locations, 284, 295
    using, 293–296
pry-byebug gem, 294
Psych, 422, 616
public, 45
public methods, 45–48, 480, 490, 554, 558
public_send, 413
Publish/Subscribe, 625
Puma, 332, 337, 340
push
    arrays, 56, 563
    sharing gems in repositories, 275
pushb, 287
puts
    about, 12
    conversion protocols, 363
    inheritance and, 101, 103
    methods syntax, 20, 30
    vs. print, 183
    printing for debugging, 289
    vs. p method, 35
    with refinements example, 385–387
    writing with, 30, 35, 183, 550
pwd method
    command-line basics, 646
    Dir class, 593
    FileUtils class, 600
    Pathname class, 611

Q
q method, quitting debugging, 292
%Q string delimiter, 121, 348, 444
%q string delimiter, 121, 348, 444
q! method, quitting debugging, 292
queries
    Enumerable methods, 574
    FileUtils methods, 600
    hashes, 582
    Object class methods, 559
    strings, 524
QUERY_STRING key, 334
question mark (?)
    ASCII character expression syntax, 434
    optional parameters in Sinatra, 339

predicate methods, 86, 226, 346
regular expressions, 137
RSpec booleans, 226
ternary operator conditional expressions, 154
typing with RBS, 302, 490–491
quines, 418
quit method, irb, 279, 287
quotes
    for heredocs, 434
    replacing double/single quotes in RuboCop, 351, 353
    for string literals, 20, 120, 348, 354, 433

R
R, RuboCop severity level, 350
-r
    command-line option, 235, 282
    irb command-line option, 278
    search option for gems, 252
r (rational numbers suffix), 433
-r library, ERB command line option, 330
%r regular expression delimiter, 130, 132, 348, 440, 444
\R, character class abbreviation, 136
race conditions, 187, 191, 193
Rack
    frameworks and, 327, 332–338, 340
    middleware and, 333, 335–337
    Sinatra and, 338, 340
    versions, 334, 340
Rack Specification, 334
rack_url key, 334
rackup file, 333
ractors
    about, 187
    closing, 206
    creating, 202
    isolation, 203, 205
    names, 202
    passing variables, 205
    sharing values, magic comment for, 31, 430
    using, 202–206
    using multiple, 206
Rails
    rails command and Rake, 246
    resources on, 329
    RuboCop and, 354
Rails Active Support gem, 387
rails command, 246
@raise documentation tag, 323
raise method, 175, 485, 543
Rake
    about, 231
    debug gem and, 290

resources on, 249
    using, 245–249
Rakefile, 245
rand method, 510
Random class, library reference, 510–511
random numbers, 510
Range class, syntax basics, 125–127
ranges
    === comparison operator, 156, 163
    arrays, 54, 562
    blocks, 30
    boolean expressions, 153, 458
    clamp comparison operator, 457, 541
    converting to arrays, 125
    converting to enumerators, 125
    creating, 437
    -e command-line option, 234
    exclusive, 125, 127
    inclusive, 125
    infinite sequences, 125, 437
    as intervals, 126
    iteration and, 125, 159, 577
    loops with, 158
    memory and, 125
    as objects, 126
    retrieving substrings, 525
    as sequences, 125
    style conventions, 345
    syntax basics, 30, 125–127
    syntax reference, 437, 458
    unbound, 437
rassoc, hashes, 581
Rational class
    conversion with Kernel module, 366
    library reference, 506
    syntax basics, 118
Rational method, 118, 506
rational numbers
    conversion methods, 503, 505–506, 508
    conversion protocols, 366
    converting decimals to, 118
    converting strings to, 118
    divison and, 503
    library reference, 506
    style conventions, 345
    syntax basics, 117
    syntax reference, 433
    time and data methods, 500
RbConfig, about, 249
rbconfig.rb file, 249
rbenv
    installing Ruby, 4–7
    JRuby and, 653
    mRuby and, 654
    switching versions of Ruby, 6
    TruffleRuby and, 652

.rbi file, 308
RBS
    command-line tools, 303
    keywords list, 491
    resources on, 302, 305, 487
    static typing with, 299, 301–307
    syntax, 302, 305–307, 487–492
    uses, 303
.rbs file, 302
rdbg, debugging with, 290
RDoc
    documentation modifiers, 318
    documentation with, 313–321
    formatting options, 316
    running from command line,
        320
    syntax, 316–320
read method
    ARGF class, 238
    CSV class, 588
    Dir class, 592
    IO class, 182, 602
readable? method, File class, 597
readable_real? method, File class, 597
readbyte method, 603
readchar method, 603
reading
    attributes, 37
    blocks and subprocesses, 199
    creating file objects, 179
    CSV files, 588
    file mode values, 593
    files, 180–182, 238, 593, 597
    iterators, 181
    spawning processes, 197–199
    streams, 602–604
    StringIO class, 612
    strings, 184
    syntax basics, 30
readline method
    ARGF class, 238
    IO class, 604
    using, 550
readlines method
    converting files into strings,
        124
    IO class, 182, 603
README file, RDoc, 320
readnonblock method, 604
readpartial method, 604
realdirpath method, 596
realpath method, 184, 596
receive method, Ractor class, 203–206
receive_if method, Ractor class, 206
receive_messages method, RSpec, 227
receivers
    appending to, 144
    assignment and, 474

calling methods and under-
    standing metaprogramming,
    372
defined, 18
_eval methods and, 396
explicit, 372
Method objects, 413
method syntax reference, 472,
    474
specifying, 472
redefining, methods, 85
redo, loops, 161, 463
reduce method
    collections, 71
    implementation of, 571
    modules, 110
    ranges, 125
ref: option, accessing unreleased
    gems, 260
refine, 385–387, 555
refinements
    Module methods, 555
    reopening classes and, 51
    using, 384–387
reflection
    classes, 411
    defined, 409
    distributed Ruby, 420, 424
    execution tracing, 417–420
    hooks, 415–417
    marshaling, 420–424
    methods, 410–416
    objects, 409–411
    Ruby VM, 419
refute_equal method, minitest, 212
refute_nil method, minitest, 212
Regexp class
    library reference, 511–523
    syntax reference, 440–444
regexp method, MatchData class, 514
regular expressions
    === comparison operator, 156
    alternation, 138
    anchors, 135
    backreferences, 515, 517–522
    backtracking and, 516–517, 520
    in boolean expressions, 458
    character classes syntax, 442–
        444
    comparison operators, 152
    conditional groups, 519–522
    conversion protocols, 365
    creating, 129, 132, 440, 511
    defined, 26, 129
    dynamic, 515
    -e command-line option, 234
    encoding, magic comment for,
        31, 430
    extensions, 515
    grouping, 138–141
    library reference, 511–523

matching variables table, 442
named captures, 513–514, 517–
    522
named subroutines, 522
nested groups, 518
options, 132, 440, 513, 523
repetition and, 27, 137
resources on, 26, 132
retrieving substrings, 525
Sinatra and, 339
special characters table, 440
splitting, 123
style conventions, 348
subexpressions, 515
substitutions, 28
syntax basics, 26–28, 129–142
syntax reference, 436, 440–444,
    458
uses, 129
rehash, 6, 438
reject
    enumeration, 573
    hashes, 583
    ranges, 125
reject!
    hashes, 583
    sets, 585
remove_class_variable method, 553
remove_destination FileUtils argument,
    598
remove_dir, FileUtils class, 598
repeated_combination, arrays, 566
repeated_permutation, arrays, 566
repetition, regular expressions, 27,
    137
REPL, see irb
Replit, 3
REQUEST_METHOD key, 334
require
    Bundler, 257
    loading files, 43, 244, 280, 285,
        545
    loading modules, 106, 108
require_relative
    CSV files, 43
    loading files, 245
    loading modules, 106, 108
    source files and refinements,
        387
required_ruby_version, 273
rescue
    exception handling with, 172–
        175, 485
    modifiers, 486
reserved words, 445
resources and mutexes, 194–196
resources for this book
    debugging, 290, 292–293
    ERB, 332

gems, 14, 252
global variables, 450
Rails, 329
Rake, 249
RBS, 302, 305, 487
regular expressions, 26, 132
RSpec, 227
RuboCop, 353
Ruby, xiii, xv–xvi, 14, 21
schedulers, 202
Sinatra, 338
Sorbet, 307, 310
style, 344
YARD, 323
respond_to_missing?, 402, 539
result method, ERB templates, 331
result_with_hash method, ERB templates, 331
resume method, Fiber class, 200
retry, exceptions, 175–177, 486
return
  blocks, 483
  iteration and control flow, 70
  methods, syntax basics, 85
  with multiple parameters, 96
  omitting, 21, 96
  style conventions, 347
  syntax, 96, 473
Return key, autocompletion in irb, 281
returns method, Sorbet, 310
reverse method, strings, 531
reverse_each method
  arrays, 60
  Enumerable module, 63
  style conventions, 348
  syntax, 569
rewind, 578
--ri RDoc option, 321
ri command, YARD, 324
ri documentation tool
  about, 14
  gems, 252
  RDoc and, 313, 315, 321
  YARD and, 324
--ri-site documentation option, 321
--ri-system documentation option, 321
rightward assignment, 148, 456
rindex method, 524
ripper library, 630
RJIT, 235–236, 650
rjit command-line option, 236
--rjit command-line option, 235
rm method, 245, 599
rm_r method, FileUtils class, 599
rm_rf method, FileUtils class, 599
rmdir, 592, 598

Roda, 332
rotate, arrays, 564
round method, 40
rounding numbers, 40, 509
routes, Sinatra and, 338–340
rpartition, 528
RSpec
  about, 207, 219
  gem testing, 267–271
  installing, 220
  matchers, 222, 225–227
  vs. minitest, 228
  mock objects, 227
  resources on, 227
  RuboCop and, 354
  running specs, 220
  stubs, 227
  style conventions and, 346
  test doubles, 227
  using, 219–228
rspec command, 220
Rubinius, 654
RuboCop
  about, 343, 348
  configuring, 352
  disabling cops, 353
  exclusion list for, 351
  installing, 349
  resources on, 353
  severity levels, 350
  using, 348–353
.rubocop.yml file, 351
Rubular, 132
Ruby, see also style; syntax
  advantages, xiii
  installing, 3–11
  as object-oriented language, 17–19, 33
  programs, creating, 12
  resources on, xiii, xv–xvi, 14, 21
  running from command line, 11, 231
  running from file, 13
  running from Windows, 10–11, 13
  versions, xiii, 3
  versions, listing, 5
  versions, specifying in Gemfile, 255
  versions, Standard and, 354
  versions, switching between, 4, 6
  versions, verifying, 6
ruby command, 231
Ruby Evolution, xiii
Ruby on Rails
  about, 327, 332, 337
  ActiveRecord module, 405
  class inheritance in, 104

  concerns, 392
  has_many as macro, 387
  rails command and Rake, 246
Ruby Signature, see RBS
Ruby VM, reflection and, 419
ruby-build, 4
.ruby-version file, 7
ruby_version: key, Standard, 354
RUBY_YJIT_ENABLE environment variable, 242, 651
RubyDoc, 14
RubyGems
  about, 14, 251
  environment manipulation by bundle exec and, 256
  gem info, 252
  gem specifications, 273–274
  loading files and, 545
  packaging gems for distribution, 274
  writing and packaging code into gems, 261–272
RubyGems.org, 275
RubyInstaller, 7, 10
RUBYLIB environment variable, 242
RUBYLIB_PREFIX environment variable, 242
RubyMine, 10, 303
rubyopt command-line option, 236
RUBYOPT environment variable, 236–237, 242
RUBYPATH environment variable, 235, 242
RUBYSHELL environment variable, 242
rule lines, RDoc documentation, 318
run method
  Rack, 333, 336
  Thread class, 193
runtime type checking, Sorbet, 310
RuntimeError, 49, 175, 485
runtimes
  information with Kernel methods, 548
  overview of interpreters, 649–654
Rust, 651
rvalue
  assignment, 474
  expressions, 146–150
  syntax reference, 454–456
RVM, 4

S

s
    debugging navigation, 292
    regular expressions encoding option, 133
\S character class abbreviation, 136
-S level, ERB command line option, 330
-S, command-line option, 235
-s, command-line option, 235
\s
    character class abbreviation, 136
    regular expressions, 27
%s for symbols, 439, 444
safe level, ERB command line option, 330
safe navigation operator (&.), 156, 345, 472
safe_dump method, writing to YAML, 616
safe_load method, YAML, 617
sample, arrays, 564
--sample-book-mode irb command-line option, 278
:SAVE_HISTORY, irb configuration, 285
save_history, irb configuration option, 285
scan, 59, 124, 527
scheduling
    fibers, 202
    resources on, 202
    threads, 189, 193–196
scope
    blocks, 66, 75, 161–163, 481, 483
    constants, 397, 453
    eval methods in Kernel module, 545
    instance_eval, 397, 399
    loops, 161–163
    Pry and, 294
    refinements, 386
    regular expressions, 442
    syntax reference, 447
    variables, 447–450, 453
scope resolution operator, modules, 107, 447, 476, 478
script tags, Wasm, 341
SCRIPT_LINES_ constant, 419
SCRIPT_NAME key, 334
scripts
    CGI, 327
    ERB command line option, 330
    gem specifications, 274
search, gems, 252
searching
    arrays and binary search, 566

files, 590
gems, 252
Searls, Justin, 353
Seaton, Chris, 651
Seattle Style, 346
secure, FileUtils argument, 598
SecureRandom class, 511
Seki, Masatoshi, 424
select method
    Enumerable module, 573
    Enumerator class, 81
    hashes, 583
    infinite sequences, 81
    Ractor class, 206
select!
    hashes, 583
    sets, 585
self
    << and, 145
    calling methods, 93, 472
    class definitions and, 373, 388
    closures, 480
    extending modules, 384, 404
    instance variables and, 112, 372, 374, 378
    instance_eval, 539
    irb subsessions, 282, 286
    metaprogramming, _eval methods, 396–399
    metaprogramming, singleton methods, 377–380
    metaprogramming, understanding, 372–374, 407
    methods syntax basics, 88
    private methods and, 45, 94, 480
    RSpec and, 221
    style conventions, 347
    typing with RBS, 489
self?, typing with RBS, 489
semicolon (;)
    block variables, 66
    exception syntax, 172
    expression separator for methods, 86, 429
    listing block-local variables, 162
send
    calling methods dynamically, 413, 559
    Ractor class, 202–206
send, calling methods dynamically, 413, 559
serialization
    custom, 421
    marshaling, 420–424
SERVER_NAME key, 334
SERVER_PORT key, 334
servers
    about, 332

distributed Ruby, 424
serving Ruby code to web, 332–342
Set class
    === comparison operator, 156
    library reference, 584–586
set_schedule method, fibers, 202
sets
    comparison methods, 585
    creating, 584
    library reference, 584–586
    math methods, 586
    modifying methods, 585
    operations with arrays, 566
setter functions, attributes, 38–40
setters, style conventions, 346
setup method
    Bundler, 261
    minitest, 214, 216
sharable_constant_value magic comment, 31, 430
shebang notation (#!)
    making code executable, 237
    program files, 13
shell
    command-line basics, 645–647
    environment variables, 242
    exec and, 549
    syntax reference, 453
shell (rbenv), 6
Shepelev, Victor, xiii
shift
    arrays, 56, 563
    hashes, 583
shims, 7
Shopify, 344
short circuit evaluation, 150
show-doc, Pry, 296
show-source, Pry, 295
shuffle, arrays, 564
sig directory
    gems, 267
    type info, 301
sig method, Sorbet, 309
SIGCLD, 199
SimpleDelegator class, library reference, 622
Sinatra
    about, 327, 332
    resources on, 338
    using, 337–340
@since documentation tag, 323
singleton classes
    defined, 375
    extending modules, 384
    hierarchy of and class-level macro, 388

library reference, 632
typing with RBS, 305, 491
singleton methods
defined, 374
metaprogramming and, 374–
380
names, 375
Object class methods, 559
syntax reference, 466
Singleton module, library reference,
632
singleton_class, 375, 559
singleton_methods, 375
site directory, documentation and,
321
site_ruby directories, 244
size
arrays, 565
File class, 597
hashes, 582
strings, 523
typing with TypeProf, 305
slash (/)
escaping and CGI encoding,
327
regular expressions, 26
sleep method
Mutex class, 196
programs, 543
slice
arrays, 562
enumerables, 574
hashes, 583
strings, 526
slice!, 526
slice_after, 574
slice_before, 574
slice_when, 574
slices, retrieving, 525–526
small integers, 205
socket library, 185
Sorbet
installing, 307
resources on, 307, 310
runtime type checking, 310
static typing with, 299, 307–311
syntax, 308–310
sorbet folder, 308
sorbet gem, 308
sorbet-runtime gem, 308
sort, 110, 575
sort_by, 97, 576
source, Gemfile, 254
source control repositories, gems,
267
source filename, irb, 287

source information
debugging tips, 640
reflection, 418
stack trace, 418
space delimiter, setting in command-line options, 233–234
spaces, style conventions, 344–346,
348, 354
spaceship operator (<=>)
about, 108, 540
arrays, 565
complex numbers, 507
enumerators, 575
hashes, 583
mixins, 110
modules, 553
Numeric class, 503
Object class, 152, 557
ranges, 126, 437
sets, 585
strings, 531
syntax reference, 437, 457
time and data methods, 500–
501
spawn method, 198, 550, 601
spec directory, gems, 267
spec.executables, 274
spec.files, 274
spec_helper.rb, 270
Specification.new, 273
split
auto-split mode command-line
option, 233–234
strings, 123, 527
typing with TypeProf, 305
sprintf, 547–548
square brackets ([])
arrays, 22, 53, 348, 437, 561
case expressions, 460
command-line arguments,
passing with Rake, 248
command-line options, specifying with OptionParser, 241
element reference operator, 474
exceptions and documentation
with YARD, 323
glob pattern matching, 590
hashes, 23, 57, 579
labeled lists and RDoc documentation, 317
MatchData class, 513
operators, 145
procs, calling, 482
regular expression character
classes, 136
regular expression matches,
134
retrieving substrings, 525
style conventions, 348
threads, 190
typing with RBS, 302, 491–492

squeeze, 124, 530
squish method (Ruby on Rails), 50
srb command, Sorbet, 308
stabby lambda operator (->)
name, 76
Rack and, 334
using blocks as proc objects,
74–78, 482
stack trace
debugging and, 290, 293
raising exceptions, 176
reflection, 417–420
Standard gem, 268, 343, 353
.standard.yml file, 354
StandardError, 171–173, 485
standardrb, 354
start_with? method
regular expressions, 525
strings, 525
:startdoc: documentation modifier,
320
state
--dump command-line option,
236
instance variables for object,
34, 36, 41
statement modifiers, control structures, 26
static typing
defined, 300
vs. dynamic typing, 300, 311,
356
with RBS, 299, 301–307, 487–
492
with Sorbet, 299, 307–311
status method, Thread class, 190
step method
debugging navigation, 292
Numeric class, 119, 159, 504
stop method, Thread class, 193
:stopcoc: documentation modifier,
320
StopIteration, 79
store, hashes, 581
streams
closing, 604
creating, 601
as duplexed, 600
IO with, 184
iteration, 604
opening, 601
opening and URIs, 614
reading, 602–604
writing, 602–604
strftime method, Time class, 497, 500
String class
about, 123
conversion with Kernel module,
366

idioms, 123
library reference, 523–534
syntax basics, 120–125
string interpolation
  conversion protocols, 365
  defined, 120
  style conventions, 345, 348, 434
string literals
  concatenation, 121
  creating, 120
  defined, 20, 120
  encoding and, 122
  escaping in, 120, 130, 134, 433
  freezing, 31, 236, 430, 436
  syntax basics, 20, 348
  syntax reference, 433
string method, MatchData class, 514
StringIO class, 184, 612
strings, *see also* regular expressions
  arrays shortcut (%W), 437
  arrays shortcut (%w), 55, 348, 437, 444, 561
  binary operators and, 531
  breaking into arrays of characters, 263, 531
  capitalizing, 21
  case and, 59
  concatenation, 121, 531
  conversion methods, 534
  conversion protocols, 363, 365–366
  converting hashes to, 583
  converting to complex numbers, 118
  converting to integers, 118
  converting to rational numbers, 118
  converting to regular expressions, 512
  creating, 120
  defined, 12, 120
  delete methods, 528
  deleting prefixes and suffixes, 529
  duplicating, 49
  encoding, 31, 122, 430, 532–534
  escaping HTML elements and CGI encoding, 328
  escaping in, 120, 130, 134, 433
  _eval methods and, 396
  formatting and Kernel methods, 547–548
  formatting flags table, 547
  formatting methods, 530
  garbage collection and, 360
  gem management with Bundler, 258
  hash keys, 57, 439
  idioms, 123
  incrementing, 70
  inserting into, 528
  inspecting bytes, 437

IO with, 184
iteration methods, 527
library reference, 523–534
multiline strings with heredocs, 121, 434
number conversion methods, 505
prepending, 531
querying, 524
reading, 181
regular expressions, 27
removing characters, 526
removing leading spaces from, 122, 435
removing newlines, 123
removing whitespaces, 124, 526, 530
rendering objects as, 36
replacing double/single quotes in RuboCop, 351, 353
representing objects as, 559
retrieving substrings, 525–526
splitting, 58, 123, 233–234, 527
string interpolation, 21
string substitutions in irb, 288
style conventions, 348, 354
substitutions, 433, 528–530
syntax basics, 120–125
syntax reference, 433–437
time and data methods, 500
troubleshooting, 639
writing files to, 183
strip method, strings, 526
Stripe, 307
strptime method
  Date class, 501
  Time class, 497
Struct class
  about, 123
  iteration and, 577
  library reference, 632
  structs and subclasses in metaprogramming, 392–394
structs
  default behavior, 633
  defined, 123
  digging, 58
  immutable structs with Data class, 393
  iteration and, 577
  library reference, 632
  metaprogramming and, 392–394
stub method, 216
stubs
  minitest, 216
  RSpec, 227
style, *see also* syntax
  coercions, 362–369
  conventions, 343–348
  dynamic typing and, 343, 356–369

idiomatic Ruby, defined, 343
resources on, 344
RuboCop and, 343, 348–353
Seattle Style, 346
Standard and, 343, 353
style guides, 344
team considerations, 343
sub method, 28, 131, 140–142, 529
sub! method, 131, 529
subclasses
  creating, 102
  defined, 101
  library reference, 540
  metaprogramming and, 392
  reflection, 411
  when to use, 115
subclasses method, 411
subset?, 585
substitutions
  arrays, 55, 563
  converting strings into arrays, 437
  Liskov Substitution Principle, 115
  regular expressions, 28, 131–132, 140–142, 440, 528–530
  string literals, 20, 433
  symbols, 439
subtract, sets, 585
subtraction
  arrays, 565
  BigDecimal class, 509
  complex numbers, 507
  floating-point numbers, 506
  integers, 504
  Numeric class, 503
  sets, 586
subtypes, subclasses and, 115
succ method
  ranges, 126, 437
  strings, 70
sum, 72, 572
super
  ActiveRecord module, 405
  asterisk (*) for, 89
  inheritance and visibility, 381
  method lookup and mixins, 114
  mixins, 114, 473
  prepending modules, 110, 113, 383, 416, 479
  style conventions and, 346
  syntax reference, 473
superclass method, 102, 411, 540
superclasses
  default parents in, 102
  defined, 101
  library reference, 540
  method lookup and mixins, 113–116

mixins as, 107, 373
module implementation and, 381
reflection, 411
syntax reference, 476
superexpr, 476
superset?, 585
Sutic, Bruno, 202
switches, command-line options, 235
Symbol class
immediate values, 410
library reference, 534
to_proc and, 97
symbols
accessor methods and, 38
arrays shortcut (%i), 55, 348, 437, 561
conversion methods, 534
conversion protocols, 365
defined, 12
hash keys, 57, 348, 354, 438, 579
as immediate values, 410
JSON parsing and, 609
library reference, 534
lookup table, 641–643
method names, 466
names, 24, 346, 439
reduce and, 572
style conventions, 348, 354
syntax basics, 24
syntax reference, 436, 439
symlink method
File class, 594
FileUtils class, 600
symlink? method, File class, 597
synchronize method, 194
syntax, see also style
basics, 19–31
checking with -c command-line option, 234
expressions, 143–170
idiomatic, defined, 21, 343
language reference, literal types and expressions, 429–464
language reference, objects and classes, 465–492
lookup table of symbols, 641–643
statement modifiers, 26
style conventions, 343–348
troubleshooting, 637
syntax_suggest, command-line options, 236
syntax_suggest command-line option, 236
sysopen, 601
sysread, 183

system directory, documentation and, 321
system method
Kernel module, 550
spawning processes, 196
SystemExit exception, 242
syswrite, 183

T
-T mode, ERB command line option, 330
T module (Sorbet), 310
tables, labeled lists and RDoc documentation, 318
tabs, autocompletion in irb, 281
tag: option, accessing unreleased gems, 260
take, 203–205, 570
take_while, 571
tally method, 62, 574
tap method, 64, 544
tapioca directory, 308
tapioca gem, 308
targets
case statements, 155, 166
pattern matching, syntax basics, 163
task command, 245
tasks, Rake, 245–249
teardown method, minitest, 214, 216
Tempfile class, library reference, 613
template characters for packed data, 567
templates
ERB, 327, 329–332
gems, 261
terminate method, Thread class, 190
ternary operator, 459
test directory, 218
test doubles, RSpec, 227
testing, see also minitest; unit testing
about, 207
default Rake tasks and, 248
ERB templates and, 330
gems, 262, 267–271
with mock objects, 212, 215–217, 227
names of test methods, 213
organizing tests, 217–219
with RSpec, 219–228, 267–271
running tests, 217
running tests by name, 219
with stubs, 216, 227
test names, 217, 219
test suites, 219
word frequency example, 60–62

then
case statements, syntax basics, 155
conditional expressions syntax reference, 460
conditional expressions, syntax basics, 153, 155
conditional expressions, syntax reference, 459
Kernel module, 544
Thin, 332, 338
Thor, 242
Thread class, using, 188–199
thread safety
defined, 187
Global Interpreter Lock (GIL) and, 187
ractors, 203
thread_variable_get method, 190
thread_variable_set method, 190
ThreadError, 483
threads, see also fibers; ractors
block errors, 484
creating, 188
debugging, 191
defined, 187
environment variables and, 243
exceptions, 191–193
multiple CPUs and, 187
as objects, 189
race condition, 187, 191, 193
running, 193
running multiple external processes, 196–199
scheduling and, 189, 193–196
synchronizing with mutexes, 193–196
terminating, 189, 193
thread-local variables, 190
using, 188–199
throw method
control flow, 544
exceptions, 177, 486
tilde (~), bitwise flip, 504
time
File class methods, 596
library reference, 495–502
Time class, library reference, 495–501
time zone methods, 496, 500–501
timeouts
regular expressions, 512
threads, 190
times method, Integer class, 119, 159
timestamps, reflection with hooks, 416
--title parameter, documentation with RDoc and, 319

:title: documentation modifier, 319

tmpdir method, Dir class, 592

to be method, RSpec, 225

to be_an_instance_of method, RSpec, 225

to be_between method, RSpec, 225

to be_falsey method, RSpec, 225

to be_truthy method, RSpec, 225

to contain method, RSpec, 225

to end_with method, RSpec, 225

to have_attributes method, RSpec, 225

to include method, RSpec, 225

to match method, RSpec, 225

to method, RSpec, 222

to raise_error method, RSpec, 226

to start_with method, RSpec, 225

to_a
    conversion protocols, 364
    converting and passing collections as arguments, 96, 470
    converting ranges to arrays, 125
    creating arrays with, 570
    creating enumerators explicitly, 80
    hashes, 583
    time and data methods, 500

to_ary, conversion protocols, 363, 366

to_c
    conversion protocols, 366
    number conversion methods, 503
    strings, 118

to_d, number conversion methods, 505–506, 509

to_enum
    about, 78
    conversion protocols, 364
    converting ranges to arrays, 125
    implementation of, 577

to_f
    conversion protocols, 366
    Integer class, 119
    number conversion methods, 505–506, 509
    time and data methods, 500

to_h
    converting Data, 394
    converting and passing hashes as arguments, 97, 471
    environment variables, 242

to_hash
    arguments, 471
    conversion protocols, 364, 366

to_i
    conversion protocols, 366

number conversion methods, 505–506, 509

Random class, 510

time and data methods, 500

to_int
    conversion protocols, 364, 366
    number conversion methods, 503, 505–506, 509

to_io, conversion protocols, 364

to_json, 332, 506–507, 610

to_open, conversion protocols, 364

to_path, conversion protocols, 364

to_proc
    block creation, 534
    conversion protocols, 364–365
    hashes, 583
    invoking methods with blocks, 471
    passing block arguments, 97–99

to_r
    conversion protocols, 366
    number conversion methods, 505–506, 509
    strings, 118
    time and data methods, 500

to_regexp, conversion protocols, 365

to_s
    class-level inheritance and, 101–103
    conversion protocols, 362, 365–366
    converting arrays, 564
    converting hashes, 583
    converting symbols, 534
    IO with streams, 184
    irb configuration option, 285
    metaprogramming and structs, 393
    number conversion methods, 505–506, 509
    Object class, 289, 559
    printing for debugging and, 289
    puts and, 36, 101, 103
    regular expressions, 513–514
    time and data methods, 500
    writing files, 183

to_set, 584

to_str
    BigDecimal class, 509
    conversion protocols, 363, 365–366

to_sym, conversion protocols, 365

to_yaml, 616

today method, Date class, 501

top, RBS, 306

touch method, FileUtils class, 599

tr method, replacing characters, 530

tr! method, replacing characters, 530

trace call, debug gem, 293

trace exception, debug gem, 293

trace line, debug gem, 293

TracePoint class, 417

--tracer irb command-line option, 278

transactions, blocks, 72

transcoding
    defined, 605
    encodings compatibility and, 609
    forcing, 606

transfer method, Fiber class, 201

transform_keys, 584

transform_keys!, 584

transform_values, 584

transform_values!, 584

trap method, 199

trim mode, ERB, 330–331

trim_mode keyword, ERB, 331

troubleshooting, 637–640

true
    conditional expressions, 150
    as immediate value, 410
    iteration and, 69
    syntax reference, 432, 457

TruffleRuby, 5, 651

--truncate-echo-on-assignment irb command-line option, 278

truth, conditional execution, 150

try_convert, conversion protocols, 365

try_lock method, Mutex class, 195

turtle graphics example of instance_eval and DSLs, 398–399

type conversion, method names, 86

type inference
    defined, 300
    Sorbet, 309

type keyword, 488

type safety, dynamic typing and, 357

TypeError, conversion with Kernel module, 366

TypeProf, 304

types, see also dynamic typing; numbers; ranges; static typing; strings
    defined, 299, 491
    explicit typing, 300
    generic types, 302, 307, 487, 492
    strong typing, 300
    subtypes and subclasses, 115
    understanding, 299–301
    union types, with RBS, 306, 491

union types, with Sorbet, 310
weak typing, 300

U

-U
command-line option for encoding, 609
ERB command line option, 330
irb command-line option, 278
\u, escape sequence in strings and regular expressions, 436
u (regular expressions encoding option), 133
unbind method, 634
UnboundMethod, 413, 634
undef, 469
underscore (_)
in names, 22, 273, 306, 346
number separator, 117
unescape method, CGI class, 328
Unicode
about, 122
character classes, 442
character properties, 443
grapheme character class abbreviation, 136
syntax reference, 432, 436, 443
Unicorn, 332
Uniform Access Principle, 41
uninstall, gems, 253
union
arrays, 566
Regexp class, 512
sets, 586
union types
RBS, 306, 491
Sorbet, 310
uniq, 574
unit testing
advantages, 207
defined, 207
gems, 269–271
with minitest, 207–219
organizing tests, 217–219
with RSpec, 207
structure and organization, 212–215
test cases, 213
unless
guard clauses, 169
modifiers, 459
style conventions, 347
syntax basics, 153–156
syntax reference, 459
unlink method
Dir class, 592
File class, 594
unpack, strings, 263, 531
unsafe_load method, YAML, 617

unshift, arrays, 56, 563
until
loop syntax, 157, 463
scope, 450
untyped, RBS, 306
update
Bundler, 258
hashes, 582
upto method, Integer class, 119, 159
uptodate? method, FileUtils class, 599
URI class, library reference, 614–616
URIs
converting, 542
defined, 614
encoding and decoding methods, 614–616
library reference, 614–616
URLs, URIs and, 186, 614
use method, Rack, 336
:USE_AUTOCOMPLETE, irb configuration, 285
:USE_COLORIZE, irb configuration, 285
:USE_LOADER, irb configuration, 285
use_loader, irb configuration, 285
:USE_MULTILINE, irb configuration, 285
:USE_SINGLELINE, irb configuration, 285
:USE_TRACER, irb configuration, 285
use_tracer, irb configuration, 285
user directory, documentation and, 321
using method, refinements, 386, 555
UTF-8
default encoding, 122, 430, 607
ERB command line option, 330
irb command-line option, 278
literals escapes with \u, 437
regular expressions, 133
-U command-line option for, 609

V

-v
command-line option, 235
command-line option for gems, 253
ERB command line option, 330
validation, converting arguments to floating-point numbers, 34
value method, Thread class, 190, 193
value?, hashes, 582
values
assigning to variables in conditional expressions, 151
debugging options, 293
hash syntax basics, 23, 56, 579
hash syntax reference, 438

immediate values, 410
passing to break or next in loops, 161
pinning in pattern matching, 167
sharing between threads, 189
sharing in ractors, 31, 430
syntax reference, 447
values_at
arrays, 562
hashes, 581
regular expressions, 514
variables
adding to existing classes, 49–51
ambiguity in parsing, 446
assigning values to in conditional expressions, 151
binding in patterns, 461
block-local, 162, 481
names, 21, 34, 346, 432, 445
passing with ractors, 205
pattern matching and variable binding, 164–166
pinning values in pattern matching, 167
scope, 66, 447–450, 453
syntax reference, 445–453
table of predefined global, 450–453
thread-local, 190
typing with RBS, 306, 488
typing with Sorbet, 310
understanding, 48
uses, 48
$VERBOSE
command-line options, 235
irb command-line option, 278
verbose, FileUtils argument, 598
verbose mode, ERB, 330
--verbose
command-line option, 235
irb command-line option, 278
verify method, minitest, 215
VERSION constant, gem source code, 268
version managers
defined, 4
installing Ruby with, 4–7
installing gems, 253
@version documentation tag, 323
--version command-line option, 253
command-line option, 234
irb command-line option, 278
switching versions>, 6
versions
documentation with YARD, 323
gems, configuring with Bundler, 268

gems, installing with Bundler, 255
gems, prerelease, 259
gems, specifications, 273
gems, updating, 258–259
gems, version numbers, 253
irb, 278
Rack, 334, 340
rbenv, 6
Ruby, xiii, 3
Ruby, in Gemfile, 255
Ruby, listing, 5
Ruby, specifying, 7
Ruby, Standard and, 354
Ruby, switching between, 4, 6
Ruby, verifying, 6
RubyInstaller, 10
views subdirectory, Sinatra, 338
Visual Studio Code
    debugger plugin, 290
    TypeProf plugin, 305
    WSL extension, 10
void
    RBS, 306
    Sorbet, 310

W

W, RuboCop severity level, 350
-W
    command-line option, 236
    irb command-line option, 278
-w
    irb command-line option, 278
    warnings command-line option, 233, 236
    warnings command-line options, 66
\W, character class abbreviation, 136
\w
    character class abbreviation, 136
    regular expressions, 27
%w, strings in arrays, 55, 348, 437, 444, 561
%W, strings in arrays, 437, 444
wait method, Process class, 198
warn method, Kernel module, 544
warn_indent magic comment, 31, 430
warnings
    block-local variables, 163
    blocks, 66
    command-line options, 235
    debugging tips, 640
    irb command-line options, 278
    Kernel module, 544
    levels of, setting, 236
    redefining methods, 85
    RuboCop, 350
    -w command-line option, 66, 233, 236

Wasm, about, 327, 340–342
watch, debugger gem, 293
Web Assembly, see WASM
web utilities, about, 327
Weirich, Jim, 245, 346
when
    case statements and indentation, 344
    case statements, syntax basics, 155
    conditional expressions syntax reference, 460
    style conventions, 347
while
    blocks, 77
    loop syntax basics, 157
    loop syntax reference, 463
    reading files, 232
    reading with gets, 30
    regular expressions, 27, 130
    scope, 450
    style conventions, 347
    syntax basics, 25
whitespace
    character class abbreviation, 136
    clearing extra, 50
    defined, 526
    regular expressions, 27, 133
    removing from strings, 124, 526, 530
wildcards
    case expressions, 460
    Sinatra, 339
Windows
    command-line basics, 645–647
    file associations, 13
    installing Ruby, 3, 7–11
    invoking Ruby, 10–11
    RUBYLIB_PREFIX environment variable, 242
    running Ruby programs, 13
    Terminal, downloading, 8, 645
Windows Subsystem for Linux, see WSL (Windows Subsystem for Linux)
Windows Terminal, 8, 645
.with method, RSpec, 227
with_index method, 70, 79, 578
with method, Data class, 394, 621
word boundaries, regular expressions anchor, 135
word characters, character class abbreviation, 136
word, documentation with RDoc, 316
+word+, documentation with RDoc, 316

word, documentation with RDoc, 316
words
    arrays shortcut (%W), 437
    arrays shortcut (%w), 55, 348, 437
    reserved, 445
    splitting strings into, 58
wrap, metaprogramming with hook methods, 406
write method
    File class, 183
    IO class, 603–604
writeable? method, File class, 597
writeable_real? method, File class, 597
writing
    to attributes, 38–40
    blocks and subprocesses, 199
    creating file objects, 179
    CSV files, 589
    to environment variables, 243
    file mode values, 593
    files, 180, 183–185, 593, 597
    spawning processes, 197–199
    streams, 602–604
    StringIO class, 612
    strings, 184
    syntax basics, 30
    YAML, 616–617
WSL (Windows Subsystem for Linux)
    installing, 8
    installing Ruby, 3, 7–10
    using, 645

X

\X, character class abbreviation, 136
-x
    command-line option, 236
    ERB command line option, 330
x (extended mode regular expressions option), 132, 348, 440
%x shell command delimiter, 444
%x{...}, command delimiter, 146

Y

y method, YAML printing, 290
Yacc, 321
YAML
    library reference, 616–618
    marshaling and, 422, 616
    names, 321
    printing, 290
YAML module, library reference, 616–618
YARD
    documentation with, 313, 321–324
    installing, 322
    name, 321

resources on, 323
tags, 322
yardoc command, 324
.yardoc directory, 322
YARV, 649–650
yet more words, documentation with
    RDoc, 316
yield
    and defined in conditional ex-
        pressions, 151
    blocks, invoking, 28, 480
    blocks, iteration, 67–70
    blocks, as transactions, 72
    fibers, 200
    methods and block parame-
        ters, 92

procs, 482
ractors, 203–206
as term, 67
@yield documentation tag, 323
yield_self, Kernel module, 544
yield_value method, ractors, 206
:yields: documentation modifier, 318
YJIT
    command-line options, 235,
        237, 651
    environment variable, 242
    overview of, 650
--yjit command-line option, 651
yjit command-line option, 237
--yjit command-line option, 235

yri command, 324
yydebug and --dump command-line
    option, 236

Z

\Z, regular expressions anchor, 135
\z, regular expressions anchor, 135
Z shell, Rake and, 248
Zeitwerk, 266
zero-width positive lookahead ex-
    tension, 515
zero-width positive lookbehind ex-
    tension, 515
zero? method, File class, 597
zip, 573

Thank you!

We hope you enjoyed this book and that you're already thinking about what you want to learn next. To help make that decision easier, we're offering you this gift.

Head on over to https://pragprog.com right now, and use the coupon code BUYANOTHER2024 to save 30% on your next ebook. Offer is void where prohibited or restricted. This offer does not apply to any edition of the *The Pragmatic Programmer* ebook.

And if you'd like to share your own expertise with the world, why not propose a writing idea to us? After all, many of our best authors started off as our readers, just like you. With up to a 50% royalty, world-class editorial services, and a name you trust, there's nothing to lose. Visit https://pragprog.com/become-an-author/ today to learn more and to get started.

We thank you for your continued support, and we hope to hear from you again soon!

The Pragmatic Bookshelf

Pragmatic Bookshelf

SAVE 30%!
Use coupon code
BUYANOTHER2024

Agile Web Development with Rails 7

Rails 7 completely redefines what it means to produce fantastic user experiences and provides a way to achieve all the benefits of single-page applications – at a fraction of the complexity. Rails 7 integrates the Hotwire frameworks of Stimulus and Turbo directly as the new defaults, together with that hot newness of import maps. The result is a toolkit so powerful that it allows a single individual to create modern applications upon which they can build a competitive business. The way it used to be.

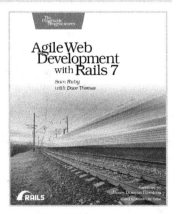

Sam Ruby
(474 pages) ISBN: 9781680509298. $59.95
https://pragprog.com/book/rails7

Ruby Performance Optimization

You don't have to accept slow Ruby or Rails performance. In this comprehensive guide to Ruby optimization, you'll learn how to write faster Ruby code—but that's just the beginning. See exactly what makes Ruby and Rails code slow, and how to fix it. Alex Dymo will guide you through perils of memory and CPU optimization, profiling, measuring, performance testing, garbage collection, and tuning. You'll find that all those "hard" things aren't so difficult after all, and your code will run orders of magnitude faster.

Alexander Dymo
(200 pages) ISBN: 9781680500691. $36
https://pragprog.com/book/adrpo

Metaprogramming Ruby 2

Write powerful Ruby code that is easy to maintain and change. With metaprogramming, you can produce elegant, clean, and beautiful programs. Once the domain of expert Rubyists, metaprogramming is now accessible to programmers of all levels. This thoroughly revised and updated second edition of the bestselling *Metaprogramming Ruby* explains metaprogramming in a down-to-earth style and arms you with a practical toolbox that will help you write your best Ruby code ever.

Paolo Perrotta
(276 pages) ISBN: 9781941222126. $38
https://pragprog.com/book/ppmetr2

Programming Ruby 1.9 & 2.0 (4th edition)

Ruby is the fastest growing and most exciting dynamic language out there. If you need to get working programs delivered fast, you should add Ruby to your toolbox.

This book is the only complete reference for both Ruby 1.9 and Ruby 2.0, the very latest version of Ruby.

Dave Thomas, with Chad Fowler and Andy Hunt
(886 pages) ISBN: 9781937785499. $50
https://pragprog.com/book/ruby4

A Common-Sense Guide to Data Structures and Algorithms in Python, Volume 1

If you thought data structures and algorithms were all just theory, you're missing out on what they can do for your Python code. Learn to use Big O notation to make your code run faster by orders of magnitude. Choose from data structures such as hash tables, trees, and graphs to increase your code's efficiency exponentially. With simple language and clear diagrams, this book makes this complex topic accessible, no matter your background. Every chapter features practice exercises to give you the hands-on information you need to master data structures and algorithms for your day-to-day work.

Jay Wengrow
(502 pages) ISBN: 9798888650356. $57.95
https://pragprog.com/book/jwpython

Text Processing with JavaScript

You might think of regular expressions as the holy grail of text processing, but are you sure you aren't just shoehorning them in where standard built-in solutions already exist and would work better? JavaScript itself provides programmers with excellent methods for text manipulation, and knowing how and when to use them will help you write more efficient and performant code. From extracting data from APIs to calculating word counts and everything in between, discover how to pick the right tool for the job and make the absolute most of it every single time.

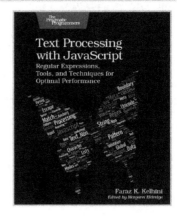

Faraz K. Kelhini
(240 pages) ISBN: 9798888650332. $51.95
https://pragprog.com/book/fkjavascript

From Objects to Functions

Build applications quicker and with less effort using functional programming and Kotlin. Learn by building a complete application, from gathering requirements to delivering a microservice architecture following functional programming principles. Learn how to implement CQRS and EventSourcing in a functional way to map the domain into code better and to keep the cost of change low for the whole application life cycle.

If you're curious about functional programming or you are struggling with how to put it into practice, this guide will help you increase your productivity composing small functions together instead of creating fat objects.

Uberto Barbini
(468 pages) ISBN: 9781680508451. $47.95
https://pragprog.com/book/uboop

Functional Programming in Java, Second Edition

Imagine writing Java code that reads like the problem statement, code that's highly expressive, concise, easy to read and modify, and has reduced complexity. With the functional programming capabilities in Java, that's not a fantasy. This book will guide you from the familiar imperative style through the practical aspects of functional programming, using plenty of examples. Apply the techniques you learn to turn highly complex imperative code into elegant and easy-to-understand functional-style code. Updated to the latest version of Java, this edition has four new chapters on error handling, refactoring to functional style, transforming data, and idioms of functional programming.

Venkat Subramaniam
(274 pages) ISBN: 9781680509793. $53.95
https://pragprog.com/book/vsjava2e

The Pragmatic Bookshelf

The Pragmatic Bookshelf features books written by developers for developers. The titles continue the well-known Pragmatic Programmer style and continue to garner awards and rave reviews. As development gets more and more difficult, the Pragmatic Programmers will be there with more titles and products to help you stay on top of your game.

Visit Us Online

This Book's Home Page
http://pragprog.com/book/ruby5
Source code from this book, errata, and other resources. Come give us feedback, too!

Register for Updates
http://pragprog.com/updates
Be notified when updates and new books become available.

Join the Community
http://pragprog.com/community
Read our weblogs, join our online discussions, participate in our mailing list, interact with our wiki, and benefit from the experience of other Pragmatic Programmers.

New and Noteworthy
http://pragprog.com/news
Check out the latest pragmatic developments, new titles and other offerings.

Save on the ebook

Save on the ebook versions of this title. Owning the paper version of this book entitles you to purchase the electronic versions at a terrific discount.

PDFs are great for carrying around on your laptop—they are hyperlinked, have color, and are fully searchable. Most titles are also available for the iPhone and iPod touch, Amazon Kindle, and other popular e-book readers.

Send a copy of your receipt to support@pragprog.com and we'll provide you with a discount coupon.

Contact Us

Online Orders:	*http://pragprog.com/catalog*
Customer Service:	*support@pragprog.com*
International Rights:	*translations@pragprog.com*
Academic Use:	*academic@pragprog.com*
Write for Us:	*http://pragprog.com/write-for-us*
Or Call:	+1 800-699-7764

Printed in the USA
CPSIA information can be obtained
at www.ICGtesting.com
JSHW050933100124
55102JS00001B/1